Cultural Heritage and Contemporary Change
Series I, Culture and Values, Volume 39
General Editor
George F. McLean

D1825845

The Dialogue
of Cultural Traditions:
A Global Perspective

Edited by
William Sweet
George F. McLean
Tomonobu Imamichi
Safak Ural
O. Faruk Akyol

The Council for Research in Values and Philosophy

Library of Congress Cataloging-in-Publication

The dialogue of cultural traditions : a global perspective / edited by William Sweet ... [et al.].

    p. cm. -- (Cultural heritage and contemporary change. Series I, Culture and values ; v. 39)
    Includes index and bibliography.
    1. Community life--Case studies. 2. Social structure--Case studies. 3. Communities--Case studies. 4. Culture. 5. Globalization. I. Sweet, William. II. Title. III. Series.
HM761.D53 2008   2008024411
307--dc22   CIP

ISBN 978-1-56518-258-5 (pbk.)

TABLE OF CONTENTS

AN AGENDA FOR PHILOSOPHY

JOHN P. HOGAN AND *GEORGE F. MCLEAN*

The new millennium calls philosophers to go beyond the abstract rationalist dichotomies of modernity; they are to look with new insight into their lived cultural heritages for resources with which to humanize modern technological and social progress, and to enable these to promote rather than supplant the riches of their cultural identities and traditions. This search is enlivened, but also made more complex by the economic, political and informational effects of globalisation. If these effects are to be liberating rather than coercive, philosophy is needed as a dialogical partner to help define a key issue of the 21st century, namely, the interface between the plurality of cultures and civilizations in the ongoing process of globalisation. The philosopher's historic search for unity in diversity, recast in today's language, can contribute much to this burning issue. Its task is to deepen the search in each tradition for the prospects of dialogue in which each cultural identity is respected, protected and promoted, while being called to respond with its resources to urgent shared needs.

Unfortunately, while all the world can now see satellite images of the global whole, increasingly this seems to be dominated by more sophisticated forms of economic, political and cultural manipulation, verging on coercion. Yet, if infused with interdependence and solidarity, the process of globalization could be the dawn of new opportunities. For these to be realized, there is need for dramatically new ways of thinking in terms both of the whole in which all are related and of the responsive subjectivity by which values are shaped, freedom is exercised, and hope is generated. Dialogue that is global – open and circular – is needed in the present intercultural context; such conversation, not clash, is the philosopher's trade.

Through such thinking what is personal can become more social, and what is global more humane. Ethics can thereby be enriched by the cumulative cultural experience of the many peoples, and civilizations can be more dialogical in an aesthetic context marked by harmony and beauty. This is the real challenge to philosophers in our day. Such a conversation is most urgent, practical, and filled with promise. The papers in this volume were presented just prior to the XXth World Congress of Philosophy in Istanbul at a pre-Congress conference coordinated by The Council for Research in Values and Philosophy. The issues to which they responded constituted a veritable agenda for the Congress and indeed for philosophy in these times.

A. Ways of Thinking (Epistemology) and of Interpreting (Hermeneutics)

I. *Ways of Thinking (Epistemology)*: Modern philosophy was initiated in a rupture from earlier thought, e.g., Bacon's smashing of the idols, Locke's imagining the mind as a blank tablet, and Descartes' systematic doubt. This created an empty space reserved exclusively for clear and distinct ideas joined in the rigorously deductive process of objective thinking essential to science. More recently questions have been raised regarding, not the fruitfulness, but the adequacy of this mode of thinking. Great effort is now being made to broaden this field of knowledge to include human subjectivity and hence such other modes of awareness as meditative thinking, creative imagination and phenomenological investigation.

II. *Ways of Interpreting (Hermeneutics)*: Hence, philosophy is expanding to include the hermeneutic recognition, interpretation and relation between the multiple values, cultures and civilizations of the many peoples of the world and their varied modes of understanding. Philosophers now are challenged to unveil at a deeper level the cumulative freedom by which we shape ourselves in the subjective terms of values and virtues, which in turn constitute cultures and their traditions. These constitute the hermeneutic vantage points or horizons in terms of which we understand, interpret and respond in the many dimensions of our life.

B. Person and Community; Rights and Duties; Cultural Foundations for Civil Society and Cooperation between Peoples

I. *Rights and Duties*: Family and community have come under strong disaggregating pressures of urban and industrial society. Individualist models see all adscriptive duties and obligations as antithetic to human freedom. There emerges then the issue of whether the individual and the social nature of the human person are mutually antithetic or complementary. In most cultures social concerns have been articulated in terms of duties to family and society, rather than in terms of rights. There is then much work to do on the foundations of human rights in order to relate these to duties and responsibilities and thereby extend and adapt their applicability.

II. *Cultural Foundations and Civil Society*: Conversely in response to excessive centralization personal initiative is needed in cooperation with others to respond to the needs of the community. This inverts the previous social sense in which all was seen as originating at a center and flowing down to the people. In contrast, the importance and richness of the person has emerged along with appreciation of the special dignity of the person whose freedom and responsibility must be respected and protected. Thus civil society sees cohesive social action to flow upward as people take responsibility for the quality of their life and constitute an active civil society. There is need for work in philosophy to be able to conceive humanity not as a set of individuals or as a matter of social exchanges, but as a web of cooperation, justice and love.

C. Global Horizons for Contemporary Life: Pluralism and Tolerance; Hegemony vs Dialogue

Globalization is not only a matter of economic profit or political power, nor is it only matter of the flow of information. Rather the new awareness of human subjectivity and hermeneutics manifest and even constitute new dimensions of relatedness of peoples and the need for new ways of understanding them. Where previously the issue was one of a contrived or instrumental cooperation between people for external purposes, now in terms of a global whole the many can be seen to be inherently related: the welfare of one must now be the concern of all, and vice versa. This is the new cultural universe in which we are destined to live. It is the task proper to philosophers beyond any others to understand and explain this so that truly humane, peaceful and cooperative decisions can be made in and for the future. This entails two lines of problematic:

I. *Pluralism and tolerance*: The various forms of human community raise questions of their interrelation. What can the philosophical experience and creativity of the many peoples contribute to the political philosophy of how peoples large and small can live together? Writ small, this is the ability to bring together in harmony multiple minorities within the one nation; it is also the classical central European issue of pluralism and tolerance in terms of large and small nations.

II. *Dialogue vs Hegemony: Cooperation vs Conflict.* Writ large in these global time it is the issue of the freedom of peoples vs a hegemony which subjects all peoples and nations, politically or culturally. Further, if Huntington is correct in seeing civilizations as religiously based, the possibility of the dialogue of religions is also key to clash or cooperation between civilizations. What then is the role of philosophy in enabling such inter-religious and inter-civilizational dialogue?

D. Ethics: The Bases of Values in Multiple Cultures and Their Implications for Issues of Environment and Public Service

I. *Ethics and Aesthetics*: As the global age brings new possibilities and challenges we need now to think in much broader terms than ever before. Where in the past ethics could be grounded in relatively restricted calculi of good and evil according to the specific character of the persons, substances or natures involved, now we find that actions have global effects and that these are filtered through a massive array of cultures. What should be said about this base? Is the global whole a compilation of individuals, or is it much more? What does this mean for the modes of ethical reasoning?

Moreover, there is an inherent dilemma in ethics. To the degree that ethics strives for normative and directive value it tends to impose upon, rather than to evoke, human freedom, and thus to reduce the inherently unique response of persons and peoples. Hence, to ethics there needs to be added an aesthetic dimension in order that persons and societies be truly mobilized to bring together their distinctive gifts in order to work toward a global world marked by equity and balance, harmony and peace.

II. *Ecology and Public Service*: More concretely, the redevelopment of social life in our times expands the agenda of ethics which Aristotle situated within politics. From within it points to the importance of personal probity and commitment to the values of justice and equality. It is true that perverted structures can impede and frustrate good efforts, but conversely even good structures can be made to serve exploitive purposes by personal corruption. Hence, a major challenge for ethics in public life today is to change the image of public administration from the horizon of personal enrichment to that of public service. This requires reconceiving the relation of the person to society; at base it is the fundamental ethical issue of transcending egoism.

The power of technology enables agriculture and industry seriously to damage the environment, its productivity and healthfulness, and for future as well as present generations. Ecology -- a term which emerged within the last 40 years -- now challenges philosophy to develop this new dimension of ethics.

This indeed is a philosophical agenda for our times.

The Council for Research in Values and Philosophy

A DIALOGUE OF CULTURAL TRADITIONS

ROBERT MAGLIOLA and *WILLIAM SWEET*

The new millennium calls on philosophers to go beyond the rationalistic abstractions and dichotomous thinking characteristic of modernity. It also invites them to look, for example, for insights from within their own cultural traditions. It is here – by drawing on, rather than marginalizing, the riches of their own cultures and heritage – that philosophers may find resources to help to address some of the challenges of modern technological and social change.

Such a (re)turn to cultural traditions is enhanced, but is also made more complex by the economic, political, and social effects of globalisation – particularly those that involve information technology.

People are increasingly able to see the world as part of a global whole – indeed, literally, through satellite images. Yet, at the same time, they are also increasingly subject to sophisticated forms of economic, political and cultural manipulation on a worldwide basis. Globalization certainly brings with it many challenges.

If infused with ideals of cooperation, respect, and solidarity, the process of globalization could be the dawn of new opportunities. And if the effects of globalization are to be liberating rather than coercive, philosophers will have a role here, as well – to help to rethink not only globalization, but the prospect of an interface between the plurality of cultures and civilizations under globalization. (This is perhaps just the present step in the philosopher's historic search for unity in diversity.) More specifically, this task will be to encourage the search within each tradition for the principles of dialogue in which cultural traditions are respected, protected and promoted, to suggest how those traditions might be able to respond to novelty and to other cultures, and to reflect on – and even challenge – some of the values that one finds in the contemporary world.

For this task to be carried out, however, there is need for dramatically new ways of thinking in terms both of the whole in which all are related, and of the responsive subjectivity by which values are shaped, freedom is exercised, and hope is generated. In the present intercultural context, this involves dialogue that is global, open, and respectful. Through such dialogue, what is personal can become more social, and what is global more humane. Ethics can thereby be enriched by the cumulative cultural experience of the many peoples, and civilizations can be more dialogical in a context inspired by harmony and beauty.

The philosopher's trade is conversation, not clash. The challenge to philosophers in our day, then, is to help to facilitate such a dialogue of cultural traditions. Such a conversation is urgent, practical, and filled with promise; the papers in this volume, and the conference from which they have been drawn, are concerned to shape and refine that conversation.

CULTURE, PHILOSOPHY AND A GLOBAL PERSPECTIVE

In a sometimes radically diverse world, what are the prospects for the encounter and dialogue of cultural traditions on matters that are central to life together – i.e., on ways of meaning (e.g., self-understanding, ontologies, ideologies, but also religions), ways of living (e.g., principles and values in ethics and politics), and ways of knowing (e.g., how we understand the world and one another)?

These 'ways' are all central to and constitutive of cultural traditions. They are certainly practical issues; they concern doing, acting, and developing ourselves and our communities. But they also raise theoretical issues, and involve uncovering and understanding the presuppositions and assumptions that underlie – and which may serve to correct – our practice.

Philosophy has a distinctive role here. Philosophy is, of course, a product of cultural traditions. But it can help to discern and define the issues, as well as engage the plurality of cultures and civilizations which we encounter in the ongoing process of globalization.

The authors in this volume address the project of the dialogue of cultural traditions and the role of philosophy by focusing on the above-mentioned constitutive aspects of culture, drawing on their own cultural traditions, but also employing the tools provided by philosophical analysis. Indeed, philosophy is preeminently and has been throughout its history, consistently dialogical. In the West, we may think of Plato's dialogues and the so-called process of Socratic dialectic, and in the East we have the dialogue hymns of the *Rigveda* and the Indian epic *Mahabharata*. Throughout the history of philosophy, key texts have been written in the form of a dialogue: through Augustine and Boethius, the Arabic philosophers, up to Berkeley, Hume, and the present day. Dialogue has been used to seek foundations, achieve consensus, reach a state of wide reflective equilibrium, or attain a 'fusion of horizons'; clearly, philosophy has much to contribute to a dialogue of cultural traditions.

What particularly distinguishes this volume is that the interlocutors provide a genuinely global perspective. Coming from Asia (e.g., Kazakhstan, Kyrgyzstan, India, Iran, Pakistan), the Pacific Rim (e.g., Australia, Taiwan, the Philippines, China, Vietnam, Indonesia), the Middle East (e.g., Georgia, Turkey, Iran), Europe (e.g., Austria, Bulgaria, Greece, Serbia, Spain, the Ukraine, Poland, Russia, Turkey), Africa, (e.g., Nigeria, Ethiopia, Somaliland, South Africa), and the Americas (e.g., Canada and the United States), the authors not only provide insight into their own cultures and traditions, but show some of the successes, failures, and challenges of philosophy in promoting a genuine dialogue among cultural traditions, as well as outlining some of the prospects for the future.

To speak of a global perspective, however, is not to seek a single perspective that is "above" all "local" perspectives. Nor is it simply a sum of the ways in which dialogue occurs around the world. Nevertheless, as we examine and reflect on the various insights provided by the authors, we will come to see what such a perspective involves, and how dialogue can be carried out at a global level.

PERSONS AND COMMUNITY

Before one can go very far into the theme of the dialogue among cultural traditions, or even into the conditions for it, one needs to be conscious of the assumptions made about the participants in the dialogue – about individuals, but also about communities. What are individuals and communities? On what do the 'participants' in dialogue depend, and what is the place of cultural traditions in this? What is the relation between cultural traditions and the promotion of life together?

The prologue, "Person as Essentially Cultural: From Indidivual Self-interest to Cultural Traditions," by George F. McLean proposes that the human person is by nature essentially cultural.

In Part I, "Persons and Community," the authors seek to clarify how we are to understand individuals, cultures, and communities – but also how these work best together.

It is generally recognized that individuals are social beings, embedded in cultures and traditions, and scarcely possible outside of them. Cultures and communities are essential. Indeed, cultures and communities themselves not only have value, but require respect, obedience, and (it is often believed) even rights. Nevertheless, at the same time, it is also generally acknowledged that individuals are persons – beings with dignity, rights and freedoms – who ought never to be used merely as a means to any social or common good, or even to the good of all.

Thus, there is a 'tension' between individuals and the community. This tension is a real one – and it requires us to consider the nature of the person and the community, and also to enquire into the obligations that follow thereon.

The first six chapters in this Part deal broadly with the issue of 'persons, rights, and duties.'

Chapter 1, "The Person as Individual and Social Being," by Rolando M. Gripaldo, seeks to clarify the concept of 'person' *qua* individual but also *qua* social entity. Gripaldo invokes, among others, Strawson, Ryle, Marcel, Heidegger, Buber, Jacinto, Locke, and McLean to construct the background to his thesis. He argues that the person is a unity of body and spirit, that the person is inescapably 'social,' and that 'Personness' and not 'Humanity' is the essence of human being.

In Chapter II, "On the Meaning of Being Human in the World: The Social Dimension," Kazhimurat Abishev surveys a number of definitions of freedom in the Western tradition, analyzing and weighing each in a grand *tour de force.* The author focuses on those that consider freedom in its socio-historical development as humanity learns to increasingly control matter. The Greeks, Spinoza, Hegel, Marx, and many other thinkers are represented and, along the way, the relations to activity and alienation are treated.

Chapter III, "Human Rights: An Islamic Approach," by Mustafa Koylu, explains that the Qur'anic view of life is divided into *haqooqullah* (obligations to Allah) and *haqooqunnas* (obligations to human beings and society). In Islam, bio-psychological rights include the rights to life, to the basic necessities of life, to the protection of honor, and to the sanctity and security of private life. Religious rights – contrary to popular Western opinion – include the right of each person to believe or not, and the right of believers to their own beliefs. Political rights include the right to participate in the affairs of state, to equality, to justice, to protest against tyranny, and to freedom of expression. Economic rights aim at socio-economic justice in society-at-large. Koylu closes with a very interesting treatment of "the situation of women," "the status and rights of non-Muslims," and the "law of apostasy." He is also careful to represent, regarding these issues, contemporary reformist and dissenting views in the Muslim world.

In Chapter IV, "'Person and Community: Rights and Duties': From an Islamic Perspective," M.S. Sujimon proposes some definitions, a description of the meaning of 'dialogue,' and a brief summary of Islamic teaching concerning the relationship between Tradition and Reason. According to Sujimon, Islam makes it a duty for all persons to defend their rights, but also to participate in the life of the community. The controlling idea here is that to be a free citizen is not only a right, but a duty.

In Chapter V, "Human Dignity and Human Rights: An Appraisal from the Viewpoint of Present-Day Indian Islam," Sirajul Islam addresses several of the same issues as Koylu. The paper begins with a review of the philosophical influences on the *Universal Declaration of Human Rights* (1948), and then describes in detail the *Universal Islamic Declaration of Human Rights* (1981), which contains both universal rights and rights specific to Muslims. Supplying pertinent references in the Koran and Hadith, the author explains the following rights: the rights to (1) life, (2) freedom, (3) equality, (4) justice, (5) fraternity, (6) love, (7) education and shelter, and (8) democracy. He concludes with a treatment of the protective rights of women in Islam.

In Chapter VI, "Group-Specific Rights: A Non-Essentialist Approach," Plamen Makariev discusses rights that are neither collective for a society nor appropriate for an individual, but specific to a community within a society. Makariev demonstrates the inadequacy of essentialist definitions of community and turns instead to a novel version of cultural identity – namely, "cultural integrity," which he says allows for the change and growth of cultures. He also proposes Habermasian "rational discourse" ("public deliberation") as the social mechanism whereby each minority can define itself and also be accommodated within the society-at-large.

The nine remaining chapters in Part I build on the preceding discussion of persons, rights, and duties, but focus on a broader issue – that of the place of individuals within communities and the role of civil society.

In Chapter VII, "Cultural Foundation for Person and Community: A View from the Center," Oliva Blanchette forcefully argues that globalization is wreaking havoc "upon the very institutions, political and cultural, it is alleged to be promoting." The author maintains that capitalism raises the cult of the individual to the level of macro-structure, where rich multi-national corporations take on the role of the "individual" or "center," and developing countries and their cultures play the role of the subjected "periphery."

Chapter VIII, "Pluralistic Culture and the Open Society," by Tran Van Doan, proposes that openness – an ability to fuse what is useful into one's own culture – is the recipe for a happy and successful society. The author agrees with Karl Popper that ideologues (such as Plato, Hegel, Marx, etc.) are dangerous because they have absolute confidence in a future-oriented ideal, but he disagrees with Popper's insistence on "science-doing" alone. "Society-making" is broader than "science-doing," and requires the kind of cultural openness suggested by Gadamer's 'fusion of horizons.'

Chapter IX, "Ethnicity and Globalization," by Francis G. Wokabi and Stephen O. Owino, advances what the authors call "cultural synergism." Cultural synergism is designed to avoid the pitfalls of "pluralism," "monadism," and "monism," all of which the authors consider inadequate ways of defending toleration and the celebration of ethnicity. Pluralism is understood to be a kind of postmodern relativism, which is flawed by excessive heterogeneity. Monadism is understood to mean cultural chauvinism, which is exclusive and ultimately self-defeating. Monism refers to totalitarian systems and, in the contemporary world, represents totalitarian capitalism.

In Chapter X, "Between Freedom and Partnalism as Discursive Ethical Practicses: The Ukraine on the Road to Civil Society," Anatolij Karas diagnoses the desperate situation in the Ukraine at the time of its writing, when the former Communist *nomenklatur* had effectively neutralized the democratic features of the new republic and established 'free market fundamentalism' as the only functioning rule of law. Karas shows how the former Communist Party elite controlled power and wealth even after the collapse of communism, having changed only their formal ideological allegiances.

In Chapter XI, "On the Intimate Relation Between Social Fact and Three Types of Values," Gong Qun proposes the notion of 'social fact' to demonstrate that 'fact' and 'value' need not be separated. Defining 'social fact' as "the type of fact which humans can recognize and experience" (as opposed to 'natural facts,' many of which cannot be directly experienced), the author describes three types of value: that implied by "social spiritual affairs," that related to "oughtness," and that "embodied in social material affairs."

In Chapter XII, "Human Studies in Vietnam at the Beginning of the 21st Century," Ho Si Quy describes the discipline of Human Studies in Vietnam, where the author is Deputy Director of the Institute of Human Studies. The author dismisses stereotypes such as the superiority of Asia in terms of 'unity,' and of the West in terms of 'individualism,' arguing that there are regional and cultural identities, but that these are subtle and demand much further study. The 'human development index' established by the United Nations shows that, when compared to progress in the physical sciences, the "social ethical" dimension of humanity remains thus far sorely under-developed.

Chapter XIII, "Ethnic Diversity and Cultural Clash in the Saint Petersburg Press," by S. Vinogradova and T. Shaldenkova, inventories three wide-circulation newspapers in St. Petersburg, Russia, in order to describe the increasing ethnic tension between ethnic minorities and ethnic Russians in the city. The authors find that Russian journalism often indulges in stereotypes and stokes the fires of ethnic hatred. The Russian press is now working with the International Federation of Journalists (Brussels) and others, to inculcate a proper journalistic ethic.

In Chapter XIV, "The Mysticism of Asia in the Philosophical Mirror," Ho Si Quy examines what has been characterized – or, rather, mischaracterized – as Asia's 'mystical philosophy.' What is really involved here, writes the author, are 'Asian particularity' and 'Asian philosophy.' While Buddhism, Confucianism, and similar traditions, reflect strong themes in Asia, indigenous religions of a less systematic type must also be appreciated for their 'philosophical thoughts' and influence. Non-Asian philosophers have a role to play in this research, since they can provide an outsider's point of view on the data.

Chapter XV, "Persons and Communities," by William Sweet, reviews the theme of Part I, and identifies some of the principal issues. The notions of right and duty, for example, rest on prior conceptions of the person; in order for us to make sense of the nature and limits of rights and duties, we need to focus on the human person both as an individual and also as a social being. Yet, as social beings, persons have obligations to the community, and so we also have to consider how rights and duties are to be balanced, and what institutions would be able to support this. Thus, it is argued, we need to turn to the notion of civil society – a society that goes beyond the particularities of any specific culture, and yet which has foundations within each culture.

WAYS OF MEANING AND WAYS OF LIVING: ETHICS, VALUES, AND DIALOGUE

A second key issue for the dialogue of cultural traditions – and for the traditions themselves – is "How is one to live?" What are the values or principles on which cultural traditions depend, and how far are these shared with other traditions?

In Part II, "Ethics, Values, and Dialogue," the authors are interested in the values and ethical ideals that should govern our relations to one another; the ways in which dialogue contributes to ethics, values, and just relations among cultural traditions; the ethical character of dialogue; and the implications for public service, sustainable development, and peace. Specifically, the authors are concerned with what models and traditions of ethics are open to us, how far we can learn from other ethical and religious traditions, and what ethics and values concretely require of us.

One challenge that may be raised here – one which affects interaction and collaboration with other cultures – is that values vary among traditions; there seem to be significant differences on a wide range of issues: the value of life, of the community, of authority, of individual autonomy, of law and the rule of law, and so on.

But are these differences substantive? And what does the fact of difference imply or entail? Does it establish a discontinuity or incommensurability within or among traditions? Is diversity consistent with the existence of shared or common ground? To respond to these questions, we need to consider what values are central to life together, whether the fact that they have a particular source affects the possibility of sharing them, and what implications these values have for our "ways of living."

Chapter XVI, "Dialogue and Justice," by Tadeusz Buksinski, distinguishes among the 'microethics of personal virtues' (in ancient and medieval times), 'bourgeois ethics and constitutional ethics' (in modern times), and 'globalized ethics' (characterizing the contemporary period and the future). Buksinski posits that global ethics and global justice must have dialogue as their precondition. The aims of global justice should include not just humanitarian aid, but the elimination of oppressive economic and political structures. The latter project, to be successful, must be accomplished not by physical force but by "rational argumentation, persuasion, and the setting of examples."

In Chapter XVII, "Evolution as a Foundation of Ethics and Morality," Jerzy A. Wojciechowski advances the thesis that social evolution has outpaced biological evolution, and that the momentum of knowledge-acquisition threatens to get out of hand: thus, there is an urgent need for an authentic morality, one that establishes global justice and peace. Quantitative (technical) advance must be accompanied by qualitative (moral) advance, or humanity will destroy itself.

Chapter XVIII, "Gandhi's Social-Political Philosophy: The Efficacy of Non-Violent Resistance," by Purabi Ghosh Roy, proposes Gandhi's *satyagraha* (what is commonly called "non-violent resistance," but which literally means "insistence on truth") as the only viable solution in a world that is becoming increasingly acrimonious. The author discusses in particular Gandhi's notions of passive resistance, self-purification, and self-reliance (which she calls "experimental existentialism"). She emphasizes in particular Gandhi's feminism – his support of co-education and related social reforms.

In Chapter XIX, "Organismic Ethics: An Indian Spiritual Perspective," S. R. Bhatt proposes to ground ethics upon the organic nature of Reality, viz., that Reality is a totality of occurrences, not just things, and that these occurrences are interdependent and reciprocal. Drawing on the insights of Indian philosophy, Bhatt posits that (1) ethics is duty-based, not rights-based; (2) knowledge and conduct are mutually dependent; (3) perspectivalism is necessary for a democratic ethics; and (4) 'Quality of Life' for everyone is the *summum bonum* of an authentic globalization.

In Chapter XX, "In Defense of Religious Pluralism," Vibha Chaturvedi proposes that pluralism is the only workable model for religious dialogue. Chaturvedi employs Wittgenstein to defend religion against scientific positivists such as R. Carnap and A. Flew. He then faces head-on the philosophical problem with pluralism, viz., that the major faith-traditions are often contradictory. Rejecting the 'inclusivism' of Ramakrishna, Radhakrishnan, and Vivekananda, Chaturvedi suggests that those who engage in dialogue across traditions distinguish between interpretations and Reality, and put their emphasis on explaining their interpretations.

Chapter XXI, "The Ethical Meaning of 'Tian' (Heaven) and Contemporary Ethics Worship," by Dongni Li, presents the view that there is no arch-god or supreme god in traditional Chinese culture. Rather than there being a transcendent realm separate and apart from the human, in Chinese thought there is a unity between heaven and man just as there is between the mind and reason. The author emphasizes that within Chinese cultural traditions, religion is a product of material conditions – pointing out that the switch from more personal gods to an impersonal Heaven began early in Chinese history, when the victorious Zhou Kingdom replaced Di (the more anthropomorphic god of the defeated Yin Kingdom) with their own impersonal Tian. Interestingly, Tian represents both Ethics and Fatality in Chinese thought.

In Chapter XXII, "Appropriating the Other and Transforming Consciousness into Wisdom: Some Philosophical Reflections on Chinese Buddhism," Vincent Shen demonstrates how Chinese Buddhism exemplifies 'strangification' (i.e., an approach that is able to bridge to and learn from the 'other,' but also to apply its insights to the other). Shen argues that the Weishi Buddhist school, a school usually marginalized by Chinese scholars because it is "too Indian," was actually one of the most open and brave, in that it dared to learn from the Indian 'other.' Shen shows how the Weishi progressively developed an understanding of equality that can provide a foundation for dialogue and authentic globalism. Among Shen's many other points, one of the most interesting is that he shows how Chan Buddhism, usually celebrated by Chinese scholars for its

"Chineseness," suffers from an extreme 'immanentism' which discourages both altruism and social change.

Chapter XXIII, "Daoism and Sustainable Development: An Integrative Perspective," by Xia Chen and Yong Chen, demonstrates how Chinese Daoism can provide philosophical and spiritual resources relevant to the "new" concept of 'sustainable development' – i.e., the designing and pacing of technological development in such a way as to ensure that quality of life, natural resources, and ecological systems, can be 'sustained' into the distant future. The authors argue that the "integration of Daoism and sustainable development can transcend the weaknesses of both conceptual models, providing a spiritual basis to sustainable development, and a scientific and socially constructive basis to Daoism."

In Chapter XXIV, "Javanese-Islamic Value Consensus: A Note on the Liberal Commitment to Pluralistic Value," Donny Gahral Adian cites Koranic texts to argue that Islam is properly pluralistic with regard to values, and that its highly monistic form is due to cultural chauvinism more than to doctrine per se. Adian describes how elements of Javanese non-Islamic religion (specifically, *kejawen*, a synthesis of Hinduism and Buddhism) exist collateral to Javanese Islam, sharing with it the 'overlapping values' of solidarity over individualism and 'being' over 'having.'

Chapter XXV, "Humanist Values in Local Manuscripts: Between the Past and the Future," by Irmayanti Meliono, discusses ancient local manuscripts produced by Javanese, Sundanese, Balinese, and other Indonesian cultures. The author examines in particular the *serat Wehatama* and *serat Cabolek* manuscripts, with an eye towards the contribution they can bring to the ethics of contemporary Indonesia. The manuscripts are shown to impart valuable lessons in "coherence-truth," "goodness," and "esthetics."

In Chapter XXVI, "Christian Ethics in Modern Europe," Alfred Rammer describes several "ethics in religious surroundings": Divine Command ethics, Natural Law ethics, Virtue ethics, and Narrative ethics. Rammer argues that what is needed nowadays in the 'post-Eurocentric,' 'post-capitalist,' 'post-socialist,' and 'post-patriarchal' world is not a "decay of ethics but a change of values." He proposes two paths which would permit a Christian ethics to "regain plausibility": (1) a contemporary version of Natural Law theory, and (2) Narrative theology.

Chapter XXVII, "The Dialogue of Cultural Traditions, Ethics and Public Service," by Workineh Kelbessa, calls for a "cultural revolution," arguing that "the present social and economic system promotes organised greed, commodification of all life, monoculture, monopolies and centralised global control...." Kelbessa argues for the restoration of older values such as 'communality' and 'reciprocity.'

In short, then, in Part II the authors show how cultural traditions can provide insight into the kinds of ethical principles and values that can serve to provide a shared ground for, and dialogue among, cultural traditions regarding "ways of living." And, in particular, their work points to the conclusion that the diversity among traditions – and among the values on which they depend – is not so great as to render irrelevant or insignificant efforts at promoting cultural dialogue. The fact that values and ethics are rooted in cultural traditions does not prevent the possibility of bringing them to bear on cultures and traditions other than those of their origin.

WAYS OF THINKING AND WAYS OF INTERPRETING

A third issue that is central to the dialogue of cultural traditions concerns the ways of knowing and understanding that are presupposed in engaging in dialogue, particularly when the interlocutors "cross" cultural traditions. By this, we are interested in not only the various accounts of reason, argument, and logic found in different traditions, but also the ways in which we can recognise the limits of our knowledge and make sense of the views of others outside our culture, while still pursuing goals of knowledge and understanding – e.g., wisdom, justice, and peace.

In Part III, "Ways of Thinking and Ways of Interpreting," the authors focus on questions related to how we know and understand our own cultural traditions as well as those of other cultures. The authors also provide us with a sense of the range of options open to us, beyond that of the rationalism characteristic of modernity. Here, we deal with questions of meaning but also questions of understanding, through translation, the use of hermeneutics and interpretation theory, communication theory, argument, analysis and the like. For many of the authors, the hermeneutical approach seems to be particularly promising.

The possibilities of communication and dialogue among and across cultural traditions, then, are real, though they may not be straightforward. They may require us to be ready to revise our current ways of understanding our cultures, histories and the world itself. But the challenges that this poses – the authors believe – can be met, and met in a way that does not require all interlocutors to opt for a single model of dialogue.

Chapter XXVIII, "Who Are We, and Where Are We Heading?" by Jerzy A. Wojciechowski, develops the author's intriguing re-interpretation of evolution, whereby the 'Knowledge Construct' is such that knowledge tends to develop independently of individual human will; and that the 'Ecology of Knowledge,' under the pressure of humanity's survival instinct, will generate pacifism as a feed-back mechanism checking the drive towards destruction.

Chapter XXIX, "The Present Moment," by Jerzy A. Wojciechowski, supplements the author's remarks in the Chapter above, by supplying a more political framework, arguing that the 'Ecology of Knowledge' leads us towards a more 'moral' globalism, and provides the basis for a genuine "Global Village."

Chapter XXX, "Naturalism, Supernaturalism, and Denaturalism," by Pablo Lopez Lopez, argues that there are three distinctive world-views present in the contemporary world. Naturalism identifies Reality with the natural world, its laws and cycles. Supernaturalism focuses on a Supreme Being separate from nature, though this transcendent Being in the Christian tradition becomes a part of that nature by way of Incarnation. Denaturalism denies both supernaturalism and naturalism: it denies supernaturalism outright; and it denies naturalism as well, reducing the Greek theoretical Logos (a form of naturalism) to a pragmatic and instrumentalist rationality. Sociologically, denaturalism functions as a pseudo-religion.

Chapter XXXI, "On Einstein's Imaginary Dialogue Between Poincaré and Reichenbach," by Samet Bagce, aims to defend the views of Henri Poincaré (1854-1912), the non-positivist mathematician and philosopher of space and time. Bagce argues against the misreadings of Poincaré by Hans Reichenbach (1891-1953), a logical empiricist closely aligned with the Vienna School (though he dissented from the latter in particulars), but also against the misportrayals of Poincaré which appear in Einstein's famous "Imaginary Dialogue." Poincaré, Bagce argues, was in fact not a 'geometrical conventionalist,' nor did he oppose the 'combination of geometry and physical theory.'

Chapter XXXII, "Epistemological Dualism and the Primal Other: Tracing the Contours of the Encounter, Again," by A.O. Balcomb, shows how the 'new remythologizing' characterizes both contemporary theoretical sciences and the *sciences humaines,* thus constituting an epistemic break with modernity's 'rationalism.' Balcomb in particular draws upon John Macmurray's 'relational ontology,' Jeffrey Hopper's studies in the 'non-rationalist tradition,' and V. Y. Mudimbe's traditional African gnosis.

Chapter XXXIII, "Knowledge, Wisdom and a 'Sophialogical Epistemology'," by Cafer S. Yaran, proposes a neo-Socratic philosophy of wisdom, and a restoration of the Greek principle of 'know thyself.' Yaran draws from a range of thinkers, including John Polkinghorne and two Turkish philosophers, H. Arslan and B. Akarsu.

In Chapter XXXIV, "Witold Gombrowicz and Harold Garfinkel: or, About an Attempt to Expose Some Mystification," Dariusz Dobrzanski proposes that in sociology, as in creative literature, the realization of what occurs the work depends upon the author only after the fact. Dobrzanski describes how the sociologist Harold Garfinkel came to this conclusion, and how Witold Gombrowicz argued that real-life ambiguity is often rectified *post-hoc* by 'orthodox' authors in order to satisfy the unrealistic expectations – indeed, demands – that conclusions be unambiguous.

Chapter XXXV, "Avicenna's Method for Translating Greek Philosophical Terms into Persian," by Mostafa Younesie, shows that Avicenna had a brilliantly nuanced method for translating, one that occupied a subtle 'interworld' between meaning and connotation, so that – for example – he sometimes used two Persian renderings for one Greek term. Younesie supplies many practical examples showing Avicenna's hermeneutic at work.

In Chapter XXXVI, "In Quest of Quality of Life: Creativity and Culture," Debika Saha emphasizes the dialectical nature of culture, so that East and West emerge as ethnic and intercultural at the same time. As an example, Saha discusses the influence of Vittoria De Sica's film, "Bicycle Thief," on Satyajit Ray's film "Pather Panchali," showing how the Italian influence actually made Ray's appropriation more 'Indian' rather than less. Saha also discusses the vastly important Indian handicraft industry, which is now reconfiguring itself in terms of 'new prototypes' adapted from foreign craft models.

Chapter XXXVII, "Mahatma Gandhi's *Weltanschauung* and Future Generations," by Geeta Mehta, presents Gandhi's principle of *sarvodaya* – "the welfare and all-round development of all" – as the ideal worldview capable of transforming the unfortunate conditions produced by globalisation. *Sarvodaya* is characterized at the individual level by an orientation towards the reform of one's personality, at the cultural level by an orientation towards non-violence, and at the social level by an orientation towards altruism.

In Chapter XXXVIII, "Phenomenology in Science and Literature," Mamuka G. Dolidze draws analogies between Husserl's phenomenology and Bohr's interpretation of quantum theory in order to develop a "phenomenological conception of quantum theory." The author goes on to extend Bohr's interpretation, via the 'complementarity principle,' so that orthodox quantum theory can be linked with both 'stream of consciousness' writing and 'polyphony' in contemporary fiction.

Chapter XXXIX, "On H.-G. Gadamer's *Truth and Method:* The Hermeneutics of Interpersonal Communication," by Irina Boldonova, examines the light Gadamerian theory sheds on contemporary social structures and, particularly, communication and dialogue. The author explains such key hermeneutical ideas as "historically effected consciousness," false and true "prejudice," the "fusion of horizons," and language as ontological ground.

In Chapter XL, "Contemporary Hermeneutics and Ingarden's Aesthetics as Methodological Supports for Dialogue and Communication," Zbigniew Wendland describes how motifs of Gadamerian hermeneutics, such as the 'linguicity' of knowing and the 'fusion of horizons,' abet our understanding of dialogue; and likewise how motifs of Ingarden's phenomenology, such as 'derivative intentionality' and 'schematic gaps,' also support dialogue.

Throughout Part III, then, the authors discuss issues bearing on the different ways in which one can speak of understanding and knowing beyond those characteristic of a modern, 'rationalistic,' approach. Hermeneutics appears to be a particularly useful means of allowing us to have more insight into our own presuppositions and cultural traditions, but also makes possible a genuine appreciation of the views of others. This, together with a more careful reflection on the options or 'ways of thinking' open to us, promises to provide a means of addressing or avoiding the challenges of bridging the distinctions that may appear to impede a dialogue of traditions.

GLOBAL HORIZONS

In Part IV, "Global Horizons," the authors provide helpful and practical reflections on the concern that, if we pursue a dialogue of cultural traditions and wish to respect different ways of meaning, ways of living, and ways of knowing, how we can enable individuals and national cultures to recognise the importance of adopting a global perspective, and yet resist those cultures of economic, social, political and linguistic domination that are alleged to be characteristic of globalization.

There is no doubt that such a concern is serious, and that the effects of global hegemonic economic systems are especially troubling in developing countries. Yet it is also interesting how some nations and regions of the world have come to acknowledge the advantages of globalism, and have been able to avoid national chauvinisms, economic domination, and a rigid entrenchment of ethnic or cultural difference. The dialogue of cultural traditions seems to be helpful here, and we have several successes: in the European community, Scandinavia, Kazakhstan, Kyrgyzstan, and Vietnam.

Still, a number of questions may be raised: How can we ensure a recognition of the distinctiveness of cultural identity, a respect of values, and a guarantee of a level playing field for all interlocutors – particularly for those from those parts of the world that are in the process of development? These concerns are central to the very project of a dialogue of cultural traditions.

In Chapter XLI, "National and Ethnic Cultures in a Globalizing World," Leon Dyczewski argues that any legitimate globalization must allow for individual national and cultural identities to retain their uniqueness. The author proposes principles which sustain inter-state relations, such as the rejection of division into superior and inferior, rich and poor, developed and undeveloped; the denunciation of national 'megalomania'; and the promotion of dialogue instead of hegemony. Indeed, principles which sustain intra-state relations should include the preservation of cultural diversity, as is the official policy of Sweden and Denmark.

In Chapter XLII, "The *Weicheng* (Fortress Besieged) of Modernization and its Overcoming: On the Values of Constructive Postmodernism," Ouyang Kang explains the special situation of China in the face of postmodernism. The place of postmodernism in countries long ensconced in the Western model of capitalism and democracy must necessarily differ from its place in China, which is currently in the process of modernization. The author argues that a 'deconstructive postmodernism' is too destructive for China, and that a Whiteheadian approach – what has been called 'constructive postmodernism' – is more suitable. The author draws from the work of John Cobb, who provides an account of the constructive postmodern aspects of Whiteheadian thought.

Chapter XLIII, "The Fallacy of Global Peace without Conflict," by Miloslav Bednar, sets forth the views of the Czech philosopher Jan Patočka, one of the founding fathers of the famous "Charter 77." Patočka founds his political philosophy on natural law, and proposes it as a global approach which can ground universal human and civil rights. Patočka's natural-law theory has been opposed in Europe and elsewhere by contemporary neo-Marxisms and by 'relativistic' philosophies. Nevertheless, Bednar sees it as providing principles to address the almost inevitable conflict characteristic of today's world.

In Chapter XLIV, "In Search of Identity: The Fluid Boundaries Between the 'Right to Difference' and 'Entrenchment in Difference'," Panagiotis Noutsos distinguishes between the 'right to difference,' which should be cultivated, and 'entrenchment in difference,' which – especially in the European Union nowadays – is often used as a pretext for racism and fanatical behavior. Noutsos rejects difference as it is understood in 'postmodernism,' 'microsociology,' and 'neo-liberalism,' favoring instead a model wherein "the part does not suffer from the whole, but from the inadequate diffusion of the latter to its individual parts."

Chapter XLV, "The National Idea of Kazakhstan," by Abdumalik Nysanbayev, discusses how the newly sovereign and prosperous Kazakhstan can present a national self-identity despite its 130 ethnic groups, many of which are in diaspora from their native countries. Nysanbayev proposes that the 'national idea' rest on *Atameken*, the "native earth," of Kazakhstan. The author rallies behind Abai Kunanbaev (Abay Ibrahim Qunanbayuli), the greatest poet, prophet, and thinker of the Kazakh land, who said the spirit of the land, unlike that of the "rational" West, is the "substantial unity of mind and heart."

In Chapter XLVI, "Global Horizon: Dialogue versus Hegemony, Co-operation Against Conflict," Rashid Hassan traces the characteristics of the 'new globalization': the internationalizing of production, an international division of labor, new migratory movements from South to North, the appearance of global 'agencies,' and a new competitive economic environment accelerating these processes. Despite arguments that the world is becoming "one place," Hassan writes that the "inhabitants of parts of this so-called global village still face hunger, acute health problems and insecurity," while "other parts of the global village are tremendously rich with advanced facilities for every aspect of life." This situation, Hassan remonstrates, puts the lie to many optimistic readings of globalization.

In Chapter XLVII, "Counter-Hegemony and Sage Philosophy," Daniel Smith argues that the 'Sage Philosophy Project' as advanced by the great Kenyan philosopher Henry Odera Oruka, should be expanded and globalized, as the only effective means to counter Euro-American capitalist hegemony. Among others, Smith draws from sources such as Ernest Wamba-dia-Wamba, Antonio Gramsci, Kwame Gyeke, and the Jesuit 'liberation' theologian and martyr Ignacio Ellacuria, S.J.

In Chapter XLVIII, "Globalization or the 'Englishization' of the World," O. Faruk Akyol argues that globalization has brought with it the imposition of the English language on the whole world. He insists that native languages must resist this, both by retrenching and also by re-tooling vocabularies when needed (e.g., by way of adding advanced scientific vocabulary if such is lacking). In particular, Akyol decries the hypocrisy whereby some English-speaking scholars demand, in the name of academic precision and 'fidelity to sources,' that their own literature be read 'in the original,' while they themselves often cite foreign sources only in English translation.

Chapter XLIX, "The Problem of Dehumanization of Cultural Meaning in the Age of Globalism," by Burhanettin Tatar, challenges the notion that 'globalism' has as its aim a truly global village composed of diverse regional cultures. The author warns that the ideal of a 'global village' may be a pretext for the imposition of a politico-economic hegemony. Tatar finds an affinity between globalism, the identification of meaning with expression, and the identification of expression with the 'reification of instruments,' denounced by Ortega Y Gasset, Horkheimer, Adorno, and others. He concludes by weighing interpretations by 'intentionalists,' 'critical philosophers' (e.g., the Frankfurt school), and phenomenologists/hermeneuts, finding weaknesses and strengths in each approach.

In Chapter L, "Diminishing Tradition, Continuing Transition: The State of Serbia," Jelena Djuric studies the current plight of the Balkans, providing historical background and explaining how this region of the world suffered, first, from the Ottoman occupation and, more recently, Communism – and how it is now too poor and powerless to adapt to the so-called global free-market. Analyzing contemporary Serbia, the author finds that whatever authentic tradition survives is present only in those few Serbian "great-grandmothers" who are left, and not in everyday society.

Chapter LI, "Human Development and Human Resources Development: The People's Attitude towards Democracy and the Market according to the World Value Survey," by Pham Minh Hac and Pham Thanh Nghi, reports the results concerning Vietnam in the World Value Survey (WVS) of 2001. The statistics show a strong improvement in quality of life in Vietnam since the beginning of Vietnam's Renovation (*Doi Moi*) policy (1986). The authors report on the answers to questions such as: Is economy poorly managed under a democratic system? Do democratic systems lack determination? Should differences in income be wide or narrow? An interesting result to one set of questions is that a higher percentage of Vietnamese believe their human rights are respected than the percentage of Americans and Canadians who believe the same about their own rights.

Chapter LII, "Assessment of Democracy and Human Rights in Vietnam: A Value Survy," by Pham Minh Hac and Pham Thanh Nghi, supplements the Vietnamese and comparative data reported in Chapter LI above. It also supplies more historical background, explaining programme KX-07 of the Vietnamese government, a state-level scientific and technological agency that sees the "human" as the "objective and motive force for socio-economic development." The Renovation policy promotes a "socialist oriented market economy," aiming at equality of opportunity. More statistics are provided, in relation to freedom of religion: almost 100 percent of the population practice the traditions of ancestor-worship, though only 25 percent of the population considers itself "religious."

Chapter LIII, "Democracy and the Role of Philosophy in the Process of Democratization in Contemporary Vietnam," by Pham Van Duc, explains what a socialist oriented market is, in terms of Vietnam's Renovation policy. "Democracy should be understood as social equality," and philosophy has a special role to play in this context. Philosophy contributes its special form of *cognition*: this cognition plays a "methodological role in the orientation of human activity," and helps society correctly orient activity. Philosophy also supplies *evaluation*: it helps democracy integrate the objective (founded on material production and corresponding "value-related relation") and the subjective (the reflection of human needs and emotions).

In Part IV, then, the authors identify the concern for identity as a key issue in engaging not only 'global horizons' but also 'globalization.' A dialogue of cultural traditions must respect the different ways of meaning, ways of living, and ways of knowing, of other cultures, and cannot yield to those cultures of domination that are too often characteristic of globalization.

Globalism – the culmination of globalization, at least in a broad sense – seems to be a *fait accompli*, not only in modern industrial societies, but in virtually every corner of the planet. The challenges for identity that this poses are serious, both for those who embrace it, and for those who profess to seek to resist it. The results here, according to the authors in Part IV, are ambiguous; there are successes, but there also seem to be failures. Nevertheless, at the core of any solution to the challenges of globalization and globalism is the prospect of the possibility of a dialogue of cultural traditions.

CONCLUSION

The essays in this volume seek to provide a global perspective on the challenges of living in a world that is home to a multiplicity of cultural traditions. In speaking of culture and cultural traditions, one is obliged to be attentive to the various ways of meaning, ways of living, and ways of knowing that characterise human life. What constitutes a tradition; how far one can legitimately draw on one's traditions for insights; whether traditions themselves can change or develop; and in what circumstances a tradition may properly be abandoned – these are all questions that need to be addressed.

The authors of these essays are drawn from a wide range of cultural, national, and ethnic traditions – and from some 30 different countries – and their work provides a response to many of the questions that the preceding challenges raise.

By providing a global perspective, however, the authors do not claim to have or to be interested in a perspective 'above' all 'local' perspectives. Nor do they seek to provide a single model of how dialogue among these traditions can occur. There can, indeed, be many models of dialogue.

A dialogue of cultural traditions, then, does not dictate a particular way of engaging in dialogue, does not propose a model of the end or purpose of dialogue, does not exclude particular goods or practices in advance, recognizes that different situations give rise to different understandings of the good, is open to metaphysics and religion (though does not require them), is open to new experience, and has a focus on practice and on life in common.

For there to a dialogue of cultural traditions, however, we need to hold that there can be a common or shared space among the interlocutors, and that they are capable of sharing a discourse or language and 'practices' with others that allows them to pursue the discussion. As noted above, philosophy has a central role in this – to encourage the interlocutors to draw on their own traditions for insight, to help to show how traditions can respond to change and to other cultures, and to aid in defining an interface between the plurality of cultures and civilizations at a time where the ongoing process of globalisation poses significant challenges.

Assumption University
Bangkok, Thailand
and
St Thomas University
Fredericton, Canada

PERSON AS ESSENTIALLY CULTURAL: FROM INDIVIDUAL SELF-INTEREST TO CULTURAL TRADITIONS

GEORGE F. McLEAN

The drama of free self-determination, and hence the development of persons and of the dialogue of cultural traditions, is most fundamentally a matter of being as the affirmation or definitive stance against non-being. This was elaborated at the very beginning of Western philosophy in the work of Parmenides, the first Greek metaphysician. This is identically the relation to the good in search of which we live, survive and thrive. The good is manifest in experience as the object of desire, namely, as that which is sought when absent. Basically, it is what completes life; it is the "per--fect", understood in its etymological sense as that which is completed or realized through and through. Hence, once achieved, it is no longer desired or sought, but enjoyed.

This is reflected in the manner in which each thing, even a stone, retains the being or reality it has and resists reduction to non-being or nothing. The most that we can do is to change or transform a thing into something else; we cannot annihilate it. Similarly, a plant or tree, given the right conditions, grows to full stature and fruition. Finally, an animal protects its life – fiercely, if necessary – and seeks out the food needed for its strength. Food, in turn, as capable of contributing to an animal's sustenance and perfection, is for the animal an auxiliary good or means.

In this manner, things as good, that is, as actually realizing some degree of perfection and able to contribute to the well-being of others, are the bases for an interlocking set of relations. As these relations are based upon both the actual perfection things possess and the potential perfection to which they are thereby directed, the good is perfection both as attracting when it has not yet been attained and as constituting one's fulfillment upon its achievement. Hence, goods are not arbitrary or simply a matter of wishful thinking; they are rather the full development of things and all that contributes thereto. In this ontological or objective sense, all beings are good to the extent that they exist and can contribute to the perfection of others. [1]

---

[1] Ivor Leclerc, "The Metaphysics of the Good," *Review of Metaphysics*, 35 (1981), 3-5.

VALUES

The moral good is a more narrow field, for it concerns only one's free and responsible actions. This has the objective reality of the ontological good noted above, for it concerns real actions which stand in distinctive relation to one's own perfection and to that of others – and, indeed, to the physical universe and to God as well. Hence, many possible patterns of actions could be objectively right because they promote the good of those involved, while others, precisely as inconsistent with the real good of persons or things, are objectively disordered or misordered. This constitutes the objective basis for what is ethically good or bad.

Nevertheless, because the realm of objective relations is almost numberless, whereas our actions are single, it is necessary not only to choose in general between the good and the bad, but in each case to choose which of the often innumerable possibilities one will render concrete.

However broad or limited the options, as responsible and moral an act is essentially dependent upon its being willed by a subject. Therefore, in order to follow the emergence of the field of concrete moral action, it is not sufficient to examine only the objective aspect, namely, the nature of the things involved. In addition, one must consider the action in relation to the subject, namely, to the person who, in the context of his/her society, appreciates and values the good of this action, chooses it over its alternatives, and eventually wills its actualization.

The term 'value' here is of special note. It was derived from the economic sphere where it meant the amount of a commodity sufficient to attain a certain worth. This is reflected also in the term 'axiology' whose root means "weighing as much" or "worth as much." It requires an objective content – the good must truly "weigh in" and make a real difference; but the term 'value' expresses this good especially as related to wills which actually acknowledge it as a good and as desirable.[2] Thus, different individuals or groups of persons and at different periods have distinct sets of values. A people or community is sensitive to, and prizes, a distinct set of goods or, more likely, it establishes a distinctive ranking in the degree to which it prizes various goods. By so doing, it delineates among limitless objective goods a certain pattern of values which in a more stable fashion mirrors the corporate free choices of that people.

This constitutes the basic topology of a culture; as repeatedly reaffirmed through time, it builds a tradition or heritage about which we shall speak below. It constitutes, as well, the prime pattern and gradation of goods or values which persons experience from their earliest years and in terms of which they interpret their developing relations. Young persons peer out at the world through lenses formed, as it were, by their family and culture and configured according to the pattern of choices made by that community throughout its history – often in its most trying circumstanc-

---

[2] *Ibid.*

es. Like a pair of glasses values do not create the object; but focus attention upon certain goods rather than upon others. This becomes the basic orienting factor for the affective and emotional life described by the Scotts, Adam Ferguson and Adam Smith, as the heart of civil society. In time, it encourages and reinforces certain patterns of action which, in turn, reinforce the pattern of values.

Through this process a group constitutes the concerns in terms of which it struggles to advance or at least to perdure, mourns its failures, and celebrates its successes. This is a person's or people's world of hopes and fears in terms of which, as Plato wrote in the *Laches*, their lives have moral meaning.[3] It is varied according to the many concerns and the groups which coalesce around them. As these are interlocking and interdependent a pattern of social goals and concerns develops which guides action. In turn, corresponding capacities for action or virtues are developed.

Aristotle takes this up at the very beginning of his ethics. In order to make sense of the practical dimension of our life it is necessary to identify the good or value toward which one directs one's life or which one finds satisfying. This he terms happiness and then proceeds systematically to see which goal can be truly satisfying. His test is not passed by physical goods or honors, but by that which corresponds to, and fulfills, our highest capacity, that is, contemplation of the highest being or divine life.[4]

VIRTUES

Martin Heidegger describes a process by which the self emerges as a person in the field of moral action. It consists in transcending oneself or breaking beyond mere self-concern and projecting outward as a being whose very nature is to share with others for whom one cares and about whom one is concerned. In this process, one identifies new purposes or goals for the sake of which action is to be undertaken. In relation to these goals, certain combinations of possibilities, with their natures and norms, take on particular importance and begin thereby to enter into the makeup of one's world of meaning.[5] Freedom then becomes more than mere spontaneity, more than choice, and more even than self-determination in the sense of determining oneself to act as described above. It shapes – the phenomenologist would say even that it constitutes – one's world of meaning as the ambit of human decisions and dynamic action. This is the making of the complex social ordering of social groups which constitutes civil society.

---

[3] *Laches*, 198-201.

[4] Metaphysics XII, 7.

[5] Gerald F. Stanley, "Contemplation as Fulfillment of the Human Person," in *Personalist Ethics and Human Subjectivity*, vol. II of *Ethics at the Crossroads*, George F. McLean, ed. (Washington, D.C.: The Council for Research in Values and Philosophy, 1996), pp. 365-420.

This process of deliberate choice and decision transcends the somatic and psychic dynamisms. Whereas the somatic dimension is extensively reactive, the psychic dynamisms of affectivity or appetite are fundamentally oriented to the good and positively attracted by a set of values. These, in turn, evoke an active response from the emotions in the context of responsible freedom. But it is in the dimension of responsibility that one encounters the properly moral and social dimension of life. For, in order to live with others, one must be able to know, to choose and finally to realize what is truly conducive to one's good and to that of others. Thus, persons and groups must be able to judge the true value of what is to be chosen, that is, its objective worth, both in itself and in relation to others. This is moral truth: the judgment regarding whether the act makes the person and society good in the sense of bringing authentic individual and social fulfillment, or the contrary.

As will be seen below this capacity is not unrelated to space and time and to their specific conditions. The good can be achieved only in the concrete. Hence creativity, deliberation and voluntary choice are required in order to exercise proper self-awareness and self-governance. By determining to follow this judgment one is able to overcome determination by stimuli and even by culturally ingrained values and to turn these, instead, into openings for free action in concert with others in order to shape one's community as well as one's physical surroundings. This can be for good or for ill, depending on the character of my actions. By definition, only morally good actions contribute to personal and social fulfillment, that is, to the development and perfection of persons with others in community.

It is the function of conscience, as one's moral judgment, to identify this character of moral good in action. Hence, moral freedom consists in the ability to follow one's conscience. However, this work of conscience is not a merely theoretical judgment, but the exercise of self-possession and self-determination in one's actions. Here, reference to moral truth constitutes one's sense of duty, for the action that is judged to be truly good is experienced also as that which I ought to do.

When this is exercised or lived, patterns of action develop which are habitual in the sense of being repeated. These are the modes of activity with which one is familiar; in their exercise, along with the coordinated natural dynamisms they require, one is practiced; and with practice comes facility and spontaneity. Such patterns constitute the basic, continuing and pervasive shaping influence of one's life. For this reason, they have been considered classically to be the basic indicators of what one's life as a whole will add up to, or, as is often said, "amount to". Since Socrates, the technical term for these especially developed capabilities has been 'virtues' or special strengths.

But, if the ability to exercise one's creativity and, hence, to develop one's set of virtues must be established through the interior dynamisms of the person, it must be protected and promoted by the related physical and social realities. This is a basic right of the person–perhaps *the* basic human and social right–because only thus can one transcend one's conditions and strive for fulfillment. Its protection and promotion must be a basic concern of any order which would be democratic and directed to the good of its people.

CULTURE

Synchronic

Together, these values and virtues of a people set the pattern of social life through which freedom is developed and exercised. This is called a "culture". On the one hand, the term is derived from the Latin word for tilling or cultivating the land. Cicero and other Latin authors used it for the cultivation of the soul or mind (*cultura animi*), for just as good land when left without cultivation will produce only disordered vegetation of little value, so the human spirit will not achieve its proper results unless trained or educated.[6] This sense of culture corresponds most closely to the Greek term for education (*paideia*) as the development of character, taste and judgment, and to the German term "formation" (*Bildung*).[7]

Here, the focus is upon the creative capacity of the spirit of a people and their ability to work as artists, not only in the restricted sense of producing purely aesthetic objects, but in the more involved sense of shaping all dimensions of life, material and spiritual, economic and political into a fulfilling pattern. The result is a whole life, characterized by unity and truth, goodness and beauty, and, thereby, sharing deeply in meaning and value. The capacity for this cannot be taught, although it may be enhanced by education; more recent phenomenological and hermeneutic inquiries suggest that, at its base, culture is a renewal, a reliving of origins in an attitude of profound appreciation.[8] This leads us beyond self and other, beyond identity and diversity, in order to comprehend both.

On the other hand, "culture" can be traced to the term *civis* (citizen, civil society and civilization).[9] This reflects the need of a person to belong to a social group or community in order for the human spirit to produce its proper results. By bringing to the person the resources of the tradition, the

---

[6] V. Mathieu, "Cultura" in *Enciclopedia Filosofica* (Firenze: Sansoni, 1967), II, 207-210; and Raymond Williams, "Culture and Civilization," *Encyclopedia of Philosophy* (New York: Macmillan, 1967), II, 273-276, and *Culture and Society* (London: 1958).

[7] Tonnelat, "Kultur" in *Civilisation, le mot et l'idée* (Paris: Centre International de Synthese), II.

[8] V. Mathieu, "Cultura" in *Enciclopedia Filosofica* (Firenze: Sansoni, 1967), II, 207-210; and Raymond Williams, "Culture and Civilization", *Encyclopedia of Philosophy* (New York: Macmillan, 1967), II, 273-276, and *Culture and Society* (London, 1958).

[9] V. Mathieu, "Civilta," *ibid.*, I, 1437-1439.

tradita or past wisdom produced by the human spirit, the community facilitates comprehension. By enriching the mind with examples of values which have been identified in the past, it teaches and inspires one to produce something analogous. For G.F. Klemm, this more objective sense of culture is composite in character.[10] E.B. Tylor defined this classically for the social sciences as "that complex whole which includes knowledge, belief, art, morals, law, customs and any other capabilities and habits required by man as a member of society."[11]

In contrast, Clifford Geertz has focused on the meaning of all this for a people and on how a people's intentional action went about shaping its world. Thus to an experimental science in search of laws he contrasts the analysis of culture as an interpretative science in search of meaning.[12] What is sought is the import of artifacts and actions, that is, whether "it is, ridicule or challenge, irony or anger, snobbery or pride, that, in their occurrence and through their agency, is getting said."[13] Thus there is need to attend to "the imaginative universe within which their acts are signs."[14] In this light, Geertz defines culture rather as "an historically transmitted pattern of meanings embodied in symbols, a system of intended conceptions expressed in symbolic forms by means of which men communicate, perpetuate and develop their knowledge about and attitudes toward life."[15] This is culture taken synchronically or as constituting a particular nature.

Each particular complex whole or culture is specific to a particular people; a person who shares in this is a *civis* or citizen and belongs to a civilization. For the more restricted Greek world in which this term was developed others (aliens) were those who did not speak the Greek tongue; they were "barbaroi", for their speech sounded like mere babel. Though at first this meant simply non-Greek, its negative manner of expression easily lent itself to, perhaps reflected, and certainly favored, a negative axiological connotation, which soon became the primary meaning of the word 'barbarian'. By reverse implication, it attached to the term 'civilization' an exclusivist connotation, such that the cultural identity of peoples began to imply not only the pattern of gracious symbols by which one encounters and engages in shared projects with other persons and peoples, but cultural alienation between peoples. Today, as communication increases and as more widely differentiated peoples enter into ever greater interaction and mutual dependence, we reap a bitter harvest of this negative connotation.

---

[10] G.F. Klemm, *Allgemeine Kulturgeschichte der Menschheit* (Leipzig, 1843-1852).

[11] E.B. Tylor, *Primitive Culture* (London, 1871), VII, p. 7.

[12] Clifford Geertz, *The Interpretation of Cultures* (London: Hutchinson, 1973), p. 5.

[13] *Ibid.*, p. 10.

[14] *Ibid.*, p. 13.

[15] *Ibid.*, p. 85.

The development of a less exclusivist sense of culture and civilization must be a priority task.

Moreover, autogenesis is no more characteristic of the birth of knowledge than it is of persons. One's consciousness emerges, not with self, but in relation to others. In the womb, the first awareness is that of the heart beat of one's mother. Upon birth, one enters a family in whose familiar relations one is at peace and able to grow. It is from one's family and in one's earliest weeks and months that one does or does not develop the basic attitudes of trust and confidence which undergird or undermine one's capacities for subsequent social relations. There one encounters care and concern for others independently of what they do for us and acquires the language and symbol system in terms of which to conceptualize, communicate and understand.[16] Just as a person is born into a family on which he or she depends absolutely for life, sustenance, protection and promotion, so one's understanding develops in community. As persons we emerge by birth into a family and neighborhood from which we learn and in harmony with which we thrive.

Similarly, through the various steps of one's development, as one's circle of community expands through neighborhood, school, work and recreation, one comes to learn and to share personally and passionately an interpretation of reality and a pattern of value responses. The phenomenologist sees this life in the varied civil society as the new source for wisdom. Hence, rather than turning away from daily life in order to contemplate abstract and disembodied ideas, the place to discover meaning is in life as lived in the family and in the progressively wider social circles of civil society into which one enters.

Diachronic: Tradition

The development of values and virtues and their integration as a culture of any depth or richness takes time, and hence depends upon the experience and creativity of many generations. The culture which is handed on, or *tradita,* comes to be called a cultural tradition; as such it reflects the cumulative achievement of a people in discovering, mirroring and transmitting the deepest meanings of life. This is tradition in its synchronic sense as a body of wisdom.

This sense of tradition is vivid in premodern and village communities, but would appear to be much less so in modern urban centers. Undoubtedly this is due in part to the difficulty in forming active community life in large urban centers. However, the cumulative process of

---

[16] John Caputo, "A Phenomenology of Moral Sensibility: Moral Emotion," in George F. McLean, Frederick Ellrod, eds., *Philosophical Foundations for Moral Education and Character Development: Act and Agent* (Washington, D.C.: The Council for Research in Values and Philosophy, 1992), pp. 199-222.

transmitting, adjusting and applying the values of a culture through time is not only heritage or what is received, but new creation as this is passed on in new ways and in response to emerging challenges. Attending to tradition, taken in this active sense, allows us not only to uncover the permanent and universal truths which Socrates sought, but to perceive the importance of values we receive from the tradition and to mobilize our own life project actively toward the future. This diachronic sense of culture will be treated more below under the heading "Cultural Tradition".

But because tradition has sometimes been interpreted as a threat to the personal and to the social freedom essential to a democracy, it is important here to note that a cultural tradition is generated by the free and responsible life of the members of a concerned community or civil society and enables succeeding generations to realize their life with freedom and creativity.

In fact, the process of trial and error, of continual correction and addition in relation to a people's evolving sense of human dignity and purpose, constitutes a type of learning and testing laboratory for successive generations. In this laboratory of history, the strengths of various insights and behavior patterns can be identified and reinforced, while deficiencies are progressively corrected or eliminated. Horizontally, we learn from experience what promotes and what destroys life and, accordingly, make pragmatic adjustments.

But even this language remains too abstract, too limited to method or technique, too unidimensional. While tradition can be described in general and at a distance in terms of feed-back mechanisms and might seem merely to concern how to cope in daily life, what is being spoken about are free acts that are expressive of passionate human commitment and personal sacrifice in responding to concrete danger, building and rebuilding family alliances and constructing and defending one's nation. Moreover, this wisdom is not a matter of mere tactical adjustments to temporary concerns; it concerns rather the meaning we are able to envision for life and which we desire to achieve through all such adjustments over a period of generations, i.e., what is truly worth striving for and the pattern of social interaction in which this can be lived richly. The result of this extended process of learning and commitment constitutes our awareness of the bases for the decisions of which history is constituted.

This points us beyond the horizontal plane of the various ages of history; it directs our attention vertically to its ground and, hence, to the bases of the values which humankind in its varied circumstances seeks to realize.[17] It is here that one searches for the absolute ground of meaning and value of which Iqbal wrote. Without that all is ultimately relative to only an interlocking network of consumption, then of dissatisfaction, and finally of anomie and ennui.

---

[17] H.-G. Gadamer, *Truth and Method* (New York: Crossroads, 1975), pp. 245-253.

The impact of the convergence of cumulative experience and reflection is heightened by its gradual elaboration in ritual and music, and its imaginative configuration in such great epics as the *Iliad* or *Odyssey*. All conspire to constitute a culture which, like a giant telecommunications dish, shapes, intensifies and extends the range and penetration of our personal sensitivity, free decisions and mutual concern.

Tradition, then, is not, as is history, simply everything that ever happened, whether good or bad. It is rather what appears significant for human life: it is what has been seen through time and human experience to be deeply true and necessary for human life. It contains the values to which our forebears first freely gave their passionate commitment in specific historical circumstances and then constantly reviewed, rectified and progressively passed on, generation after generation. The content of a tradition, expressed in works of literature and the many facets of a culture, emerges progressively as something upon which personal character and society can be built. It constitutes a rich source from which multiple themes can be drawn, provided it be accepted and embraced, affirmed and cultivated.

Hence, it is not because of personal inertia on our part or arbitrary will on the part of our forbears that our culture provides a model and exemplar. On the contrary, the importance of tradition derives from both the cooperative character of the learning by which wisdom is drawn from experience and the cumulative free acts of commitment and sacrifice which have defined, defended and passed on through time the corporate life of the community as civil society.[18]

Ultimately, tradition bridges from ancient philosophy to civil society today. It bears the divine gifts of life, meaning and love uncovered in facing the challenges of civil life through the ages. It provides both the way back to their origin in the *arché* as the personal, free and responsible exercise of existence and even of its divine source, and the way forward to their goal; it is the way to both the *Alpha* and the *Omega*.

CULTURAL TRADITIONS

Today, while moving from a centralized to a more open economy, the nations are engaged not only in balancing all the great forces of the world, but in integrating them into a new and viable whole; the future of civilization is in play. Truly humane progress will be possible only to the

---

[18] *Ibid.* Gadamer emphasized knowledge as the basis of tradition in contrast to those who would see it pejoratively as the result of arbitrary will. It is important to add to knowledge the free acts which, e.g., give birth to a nation and shape the attitudes and values of successive generations. As an example, one might cite the continuing impact had by the Magna Carta through the Declaration of Independence upon life in North America, or of the Declaration of the Rights of Man in the national life of many countries.

degree that peoples are able to find ways of inspiring their disparate elements with values in a way that promotes both the dignity of the human person and the social cohesion and cooperation of its peoples.

Prof. S. Shermukhamedov of Uzbekistan describes spiritual culture as

> the system in which the values of human society and humankind are reflected, impressed and incarnated with their needs, wishes, interests, hopes, beliefs, persuasions. This is the world of emotions, sensations, aspirations, views, wills, impulses and actions, as impressed upon the internal world of man and realized through the interaction between society and nature in which man is the subject of national and common values. Man is the highest value and his life, goodness, interests, harmony, happiness are the goals of society.[19]

These words reflect an important shift taking place in contemporary culture.

From the time of the great trio of Greek philosophers, Socrates, Plato and Aristotle, thought has shifted in an objectivist direction. Concern was centered upon the way things were, rather than upon the human person who knows and engages them. This orientation was radicalized at the beginning of modern times which came thereby to be characterized by rationalism.

It is then of epic moment that in our day we should become aware not only of the achievement of this orientation, but also of its limitations and of the way in which it has held us captive. Now new concerns come to the fore reflected not least in the new hopes and aspirations of its peoples. This provides orientation for our search further into the nature of civilizations, their foundations and ways in which they can live together and cooperate in a global age.

One of the most important characteristics of human persons and societies is their capability for development and growth. One is born with open and unlimited powers for knowledge and for love. Life consists in developing, deploying and exercising these capabilities. Given the communitary character of human growth and learning, dependence upon others is not unnatural – quite the contrary. Within, as well as beyond, our social group we depend upon other persons according as they possess abilities which we, as individuals and communities, need for our growth, self-realization and fulfillment.

---

[19] "Issues Regarding the Interaction of Spiritual Culture and Social Progress," in *Spiritual Values and Social Progress: Uzbekistan Philosophical Studies I*, eds. S. Shermukhamedov and V. Levinskaya (Washington, D.C.: The Council for Research in Values and Philosophy, 2000), p. 10.

This dependence is not primarily one of obedience to the will of others, but is based upon their comparative excellence in some dimension – whether this be the doctor's professional skill in healing or the wise person's insight and judgment in matters where profound understanding is required. The preeminence of wise persons in the community is not something they usurp or with which they are arbitrarily endowed; it is based rather upon their abilities as these are reasonably and freely acknowledged by others.

Further, this is not a matter of universal law imposed from above and uniformly repeated in univocal terms. Rather it is a matter of corporate learning developed by the components of a civil society each with its own special concerns and each related to the other in a pattern of subsidiarity.

All of these – the role of the community in learning, the contribution of extended historical experience regarding the horizontal and vertical axes of life and meaning, and the grounding of dependence in competency – combine to endow tradition with authority for subsequent ages. This is varied according to the different components of tradition and their interrelation.

There are reasons to believe, moreover, that tradition is not a passive storehouse of materials simply waiting upon the inquirer, but that its content of authentic wisdom plays a normative role for life in subsequent ages. On the one hand, without such a normative referent, prudence would be as relativistic and ineffectual as muscular action without a skeletal substructure. Life would be merely a matter of compromise and accommodation on any terms, with no sense of the value either of what was being compromised or of that for which it was compromised. On the other hand, where the normative factor is seen to reside simply in a transcendental or abstract vision the result would be devoid of existential content.

The fact that humans, no matter how different in culture, do not remain indifferent before the flow of events, but dispute – even bitterly – the direction of change appropriate for their community reflects that every humanism is committed actively to the realization of some common – if general – sense of perfection. Without this, even conflict would be impossible for there would be no intersection of the divergent positions and, hence, no debate or conflict.

Through history, communities discover vision which both transcends time and directs life in all times, past, present and future. The content of that vision is a set of values which, by their fullness and harmony of measure, point the way to mature and perfect human formation and, thereby, orient life.[20] Such a vision is historical because it arises in the life of a people in time. It is also normative, because it provides a basis upon which past historical ages, present options and future possibilities are judged; it presents an appropriate way of preserving that life through time. What begins to emerge is Heidegger's insight regarding Being. Its char-

---

[20] Gadamer, pp. 245-253.

acteristics of unity, truth and justice, goodness and love are not simply empty ideals, but the ground, hidden or veiled as it were, and erupting into time
through the conscious personal and group life of free human beings in
history. Seen in this light, the process of human search, discussion and
decision – today called democracy – becomes more than a method for
managing human affairs; more substantively, it is the mode of the emergence of being in time, the very reality of the life of persons and societies.

One's cultural heritage or tradition constitutes a specification of the
general sense of being or perfection, but not as if this were chronologically
distant in the past and, therefore, in need of being drawn forward by some
artificial contrivance. Rather, being and its values live and act in the lives of
all whom they inspire and judge. In its synchronic form, through time,
tradition is the timeless dimension of history. Rather than reconstructing it,
we belong to it – just as it belongs to us. Traditions then are, in effect, the
ultimate communities of human striving, for human life and understanding
are implemented, not by isolated individual acts of subjectivity – which
Gadamer describes as flickerings in the closed circuits of personal
consciousness[21] – but by our situatedness in a tradition. By fusing both past
and present, tradition enables the component groupings of civil society to
determine the specific direction of their lives and to mobilize the consensus
and mutual commitments of which true and progressive community life is
built.[22]

Conversely, this sense of the good or of value emerges through the
concrete, lived experience of a people throughout its history and constitutes
its cultural heritage. It enables society, in turn, to evaluate its life in order to
pursue its true good and to avoid what is socially destructive. In the absence
of tradition, present events would be simply facts to be succeeded by
counter-facts. The succeeding waves of such disjointed happenings would
constitute a history written in terms of violence. This, in turn, could be re-
strained only by some utopian abstraction built upon the reductivist
limitations of modern rationalism. Such elimination of all expressions of
democratic freedoms is the archetypal modern nightmare, 1984.

All of that stands in stark contrast to one's heritage or tradition as
the rich cumulative expression of meaning evolved by a people through the
ages to a point of normative and classical perfection. Exemplified architec-
turally in a Parthenon or a Taj Mahal, it is embodied personally in a
Confucius or Gandhi, a Bolivar or Lincoln, a Martin Luther King or a
Mother Theresa. Variously termed "charismatic personalities" (Shils),[23]
"paradigmatic individuals" (Cua)[24] or characters who meld role and per-

---

[21] *Ibid.*, p. 245.

[22] *Ibid.*, p. 258.

[23] Edward Shils, *Tradition* (Chicago: University of Chicago Press, 1981),
12-13.

[24] *Dimensions of Moral Creativity: Paradigms, Principles and Ideals*
(University Park: Pennsylvania State University Press, 1978).

sonality in providing a cultural or moral ideal (MacIntyre),[25] they supersede mere historical facts. As concrete universals, they express in the varied patterns of civil society that harmony and fullness of perfection which is at once classical and historical, ideal and personal, uplifting and dynamizing – in a word, liberating.

Nor is it accidental that as examples the founders of the great religious traditions come most spontaneously to mind. It is not, of course, that people cannot or do not form the component groups of civil society on the basis of their concrete concerns for education, ecology or life. But their motivation in this as fully human goes beyond pragmatic, external goals to the internal social commitment which in most cultures is religiously based.

CIVILIZATIONS

On proceeding into the new millennium we were at a point not only of a change of systems as with a substitution of political parties, but of revision of the very nature of world order itself. Earlier the issue was one of the possession of territory under the leadership of great Emperors or of physical resources and the military-industrial power that entailed. More recently we have seen the world divided by ideologies into great spheres. Since the end of the Cold War, however, it is suggested famously in the work of Samuel Huntington, *The Clash of Civilizations and the Remaking of World Order*,[26] that the world order is being remade on the basis of the pattern of civilizations. The tragic events of Oct. 11, 2001, show how violent this remaking can be.

This reflects a deep transformation in interests and epistemology. Before, attention was oriented objectively, that is, to things as standing over against (*ob*-against; *ject*-thrown) the knowing subject. In this perspective their quantitative characteristics, according to the classical definition of quantity as parts divided against parts, were particularly salient and were given major importance.

In this new century the subject and its intentional life – or subjectivity and values – come to the fore as phenomenological methods are developed for their identification and interpretation. It can be disputed whether it was philosophers who brought this realm of subjectivity into central awareness or whether it was attention to subjectivity which evoked the development of the corresponding philosophical methodologies. Probably the philosophical methods provided the reflective dimension and control over the new self-awareness of human consciousness. In any case, it is suggested that the new world order will be based not on the resources we have, but on the civilizations we are: not on having, but on being.

---

[25] *After Virtue* (Notre Dame: University of Natre Dame Press, 1981), pp. 29-30.
[26] (New York: Simon & Schuster, 1996).

According to Huntington the notion of civilization seems to have developed in the 18th century as a term to distinguish cultivated peoples from the barbarian or native populations being encountered in the process of colonization. In this sense it was a universal term used in the singular. It implied a single elite standard of urbanization, literacy and the like for the admission of a people into the world order. When the standard was met the people was "civilized"; all the rest were simply "uncivilized".

In the 19th century a distinction was made between civilization as characterized by its material and technological capabilities and culture as characterized by development in terms of the values and moral qualities of a people. The two terms tend to merge in expressing an overall way of life, with civilization being the broader term. Where culture focuses on one's understanding of perfection and fulfillment; civilization is more the total working out of life in these terms. Hence civilization is culture, as it were, writ large.

This appears in a number of descriptions of civilization where culture is always a central element: for F. Braudel civilization is "a cultural arena",[27] a collection of cultural characteristics and phenomena; for C. Dawson: it is the product of "a particular original process of cultural activity which is the work of a particular people";[28] for J. Wallerstein it is "a particular concatenation of worldview, customs, structures, and culture (both material culture and high cultures) which form some kind of historical whole."[29]

Taken as a matter of identity it can be said that a civilization is the largest and most perduring unit or whole – the largest "we".[30] The elements included are blood, language, religion and way of life. Among these religion is "the central defining characteristic of civilizations",[31] as it is the point of a person's or people's deepest and most intensive commitment, the foundation on which the great civilizations rest.[32] Hence the major religions (Christianity, Islam, Hinduism and Confucianism) are each associated with a civilization, the exception being Buddhism which came as a reform movement, was uprooted from its native India, and lives now in diaspora among other nations.

---

[27] *On History* (Chicago: Chicago University Press, 1980), pp. 177, 202.
[28] *Dynamics of World History* (La Sulle, Il: Sheed and Ward, 1959), pp. 51, 402.
[29] *Geopolitics and Geoculture: Essays on the Changing World System* (Cambridge: Cambridge University Press, 1992).
[30] Samuel Huntington, *The Clash of Civilizations and the Remaking of the World Order*, p. 43.
[31] *Ibid.*, p. 47.
[32] C. Dawson, p. 128.

Civilizations perdure over long periods of time. While empires come and go, civilizations "survive political, social, economic even ideological upheavals."[33]

> International history rightly documents the thesis that political systems are transient expedients on the surface of civilization, and that the destiny of each linguistically and morally unified community depends ultimately upon the survival of certain primary structuring ideas around which successive generations have coalesced and which then symbolize the society's continuity.[34]

But this does not mean that they are static. On the contrary it is characteristic of a civilization to evolve and the theories of such evolution are attempts to achieve some understanding of the process, not only of the sequence of human events but more deeply of the transformation of human self understanding itself. Famously, Toynbee theorizes that civilizations are responses to human challenges; that they evolve in terms of establishing increasing control over the related factors, especially by creative minorities; and that in the face of troubles there emerges a strong effort at integration followed by disintegration. Such theories vary somewhat in the order of stages, but generally they move from a preparatory period, to the major development of the strengths of a culture or civilization, and then toward atrophy. In any case, these imply cycles extending over very long periods.

It is significant that in the end, however, Huntington is not able to give any clear definition or civilizations or rigorous distinction between them. Whereas Descartes would require just such characteristics for scientific knowledge, Huntington notes that civilizations generally somewhat overlap, and that while no clear concept can be delineated civilization are nonetheless important.

> Civilizations have no clear cut boundaries and no precise beginnings and endings. People can and do redefine their identities and, as a result, the composition and shapes of civilizations change over time. The cultures of peoples interact and overlap. The extent to which the cultures or civilizations resemble or differ from each other also varies considerably. Civilizations are nonetheless meaningful entities, and while the lines between them are seldom sharp, they are real.[35]

---

[33] F. Braudel, *History of Civilizations* (New York: Penguin, 1994), p. 35.

[34] A. Bozeman, *Strategic Intelligence and Statecraft* (Washington: Brassey's, 1992), p. 62.

[35] Huntington, p. 43.

In this light it can be seen that a shift of world order to a pattern not of empires or commercial blocks, but of civilizations bespeaks a great development in human consciousness, beyond the external, objective and physical, to the internal and subjective, the spiritual and indeed the religious. In contrast to Descartes it appears that what is most significant in the relations between peoples, indeed what defines them as peoples, is a matter not accessible by scientific definition, but a matter of far more inclusive aesthetic appreciation. It is in these terms that personal life commitments and interactions between peoples are realized.

But if culture is a matter of values and virtues, that is, of subjectivity, it should be possible to gain rich insight into the reality of, and the relations between, cultures through an approach calculated to examine the dimension of subjectivity from within and in its own proper terms. This will be the special task of the following chapters which will search out this insight in and for the relations between cultures and peoples which have emerged as the central issue of our global times.

The Council for Research in Values and Philosophy

PART I

PERSONS AND COMMUNITY

A. PERSONS, RIGHTS, AND DUTIES

CHAPTER I

THE PERSON AS INDIVIDUAL AND SOCIAL BEING

ROLANDO M. GRIPALDO

INTRODUCTION

The purpose of this brief paper is to elucidate the concept of the person as a member of a communal or civil society. It will try to answer the question as to what makes a person a person, and the corollary question as to how the person should be related to communal society.

CONCEPT OF THE PERSON

The concept of the person is more primitive than the Cartesian concepts of mind and body. As a substance, the person has both material and psychical predicates.[1] Properly speaking, it is a category mistake to assert that the mind thinks or the body walks (see Ryle).[2] It is the person who thinks and the person who walks. It could be argued, I think within reason, that the person is a body incarnate or an embodied spirit.[3] What is

---

[1] See P. F. Strawson, *Individuals: An essay in descriptive metaphysics* (London: Methuen. 1959). Cartesian dualism considers the "I," or "self," or "man" as a unity of two substances, mind or soul and body. (See Rene Descartes, *A Discourse on Method and other works.* Abridged, edited, and with an introduction by Joseph Epstein. Translated by E. S. Haldane and G. R. T. Ross [New York: Washington Square Press, 1965], pp. 48, 61, 63, 65-66, 69, 152, 154, 172, 178, and 188.) Strawson's concept of the person is a unity of one substance, which has both psychical and material predicates (see pp. 81-113)..

[2] See Gilbert Ryle, *The Concept of Mind* (Harmondsworth: Penguin Books, 1979). I interpret the notion of category mistake broadly to mean mistaking a category (logical type) to represent another category without qualification, and vice versa. In this regard, the individual category mind or body, logically speaking, cannot represent the category person as a whole, or vice versa, without qualification. Ryle talks about a foreign guest who is introduced to the university by showing or presenting the colleges, museums, libraries, and so on. The guest however persists, "But where is the university?" as if the category university is one building or some such – that is, the guest mistakes the collective for a single object. (See Ryle, pp. 17-23)

[3] See Gabriel Marcel, *The Mystery of Being*, tr. G. S. Fraser (Chicago: Henry Regnery, 1960), Vol. 1. There is a recent view which argues that the soul or mind partakes of the nature of Cosmic Mind. This view is similar to the Indian notion of the Brahman-Atman relationship. For a discussion on this

important is to view the person as a unity, that is, as one substance, not two substances. Moreover, we are talking about a live natural person. Someone who dies is still a person, but we call him a dead person.[4] A zombie is not a person, but may appear as one. A sleepwalker is a person who walks during his sleep, and is not a zombie though he may appear to be one. A cyborg is not a person in the natural ordinary sense though he may appear as one.[5]

The person is not an island unto himself. For a person's survival and belonging, she or he is not simply a member of a socio-cultural group –

---

matter, see Keith A. Chandler (*The Mind Paradigm: a unified model of mental and physical reality* [New York: Authors Choice Press, 2001]) and Rolando M. Gripaldo (Review of *The Mind Paradigm*, by Keith Chandler, *International Journal of Philosophy*, vol. 31(2) (2002: 211-16). On this view, matter is simply condensed mind, that is to say, mind (human consciousness) and matter (human body) are of the same kind, but are different modes or manifestations of Cosmic Mind. This is a metaphysical expression of the first law of thermodynamics, the conservation of energy (and matter). Chandler's view is different from Russell's neutral monism which says that the substratum is neither mind nor matter but that out of which springs both mind and matter (see Rolando Gripaldo, "The Soul and Bertrand Russell," *Philippines Free Press*, 10 April 1971, pp. 11, 36).

[4] According to the Cartesian concept of man as basically consisting of the substances 'mind' and 'body,' a dead man is logically speaking no longer a man, or an I, or a self – that is, a selfless human body is not a man but simply a corpse (lifeless body). Properly speaking, it is not to be called a "dead man" or a "dead person" since it appears self-contradictory. If "man" is a live object consisting of two substances, body and soul, then a "dead man" is a lifeless object which is alive – that is to say, it is a contradiction in terms. Or putting it differently, if a man consists of two substances while a dead man is only one substance, then a dead man is not a man. In the Strawsonian concept of the person, it still makes sense to speak of a dead person or a dead man, although in a pragmatic sense, it is also called a corpse. If a person is one substance having both material and psychical predicates, then a dead man or person is still one substance with its psychical predicates basically gone. When both material and psychical predicates are gone, then we have a memory of a person who is dead or gone.

[5] A genuine cyborg is half machine and half human. The percentages can go as high as seventy-five percent human and twenty-five percent machine, or vice versa. The aim of developing cyborgs "is to add to or enhance the abilities of the organism using artificial technology." In general, the main consideration is the incapability of a human to survive "without the mechanical part" (see http://www.wikipedia.org/wiki/Cyborg). Currently, however, the use of the term is such that even people with minor surgeries where a mechanical or a synthetic replacement is made – like inserting a synthetic lens in a cataract operation or a piece of metal to strengthen a broken leg – have been labeled as cyborgs. Anyway, these people appear to me more as natural persons rather than as cyborgs or nonnatural persons.

a mere individual – but *cooperates* with the members of that group. In short, the person is also a social being.

The person is a historical being in that each person develops a personality as she or he grows up and circulates within the members of his or her family, peer group, neighborhood, school, church, and eventually the society-at-large.[6] The person lives in a spatio-temporal setting. In the process, each person develops patterns of feeling, of thinking, and of doing things. Persons develop habits.

The person is also a cultural being. "Culture" is rather a broad term as it includes anything in a given society. A broad definition of it is that culture is the sum-total of what mankind did in the past, is currently doing, and will be doing in the future. Culture includes religion, philosophy, science, technology, art, education, politics, and so on. The person develops socio-cultural relations within society.

THE PERSON AS "THROWN"

The person is "thrown" into a socio-cultural world which is not of his or her own making.[7] As a child grows up, it uncritically imbibes or absorbs what is there. Rarely does the child doubt (e.g., the wisdom of the rules in society). Construed broadly, rules can be political, ethical, religious, legal, professional – and more. There are also localized rules that the child may encounter later, such as those of one's school and one's peer group. In the process of growing up, the child simply tacitly follows these rules. In this sense, the child is passive. When children become critical at some point in their lives, they start rejecting some of these rules and select those which seem more useful. Those that children have explicitly accepted they follow.[8] In this sense, children are active. Some of the rules a child discards are harmless, but others – such as legal rules – can be harmful. If caught, a child can be imprisoned or even executed. These rules will generate or carry duties and responsibilities. They are meant to protect human rights, though some of these rules are thought to be infringements of human rights.

Most national cultures are mixed cultures, although there are dominant traits within each culture. As such, the person accepts many of the native cultural traits while accepting likewise some of the foreign cultural influences that enter into society. The person, in other words, is generally a cultural hybrid in contemporary society.[9] Basically, the person is a

---

[6] See Albert Dondeyne, *Faith and the World* (Dublin: Gill and Son, 1964).

[7] See Martin Heidegger, *Being and Time*, tr. Joan Stambaugh (Albany: State University of New York Press, 1996).

[8] See John Locke, *Two Treatises of Civil Government* (Cambridge: Cambridge University Press, 1960).

[9] Cultural hybridization is not necessarily uniform in every individual, and this will explain the ethnic cultural differences – depending upon the exposure

microcosmic culture that reflects, in some meaningful respects, the culture-at-large (i.e., the macrocosmic culture). In a manner of speaking, the individual person is culture writ large.

THE PERSON AS INDIVIDUAL

The person is an individual, not a crowd. A crowd, of course, is composed of individuals, but each of them loses its individuality in the crowd. It is easier to attribute responsibility for an action to a person than to a crowd. Kierkegaard, for example, has argued that the crowd renders the individual completely impenitent and irresponsible.[10] In ordinary language, there is a sense in which the individual and the person are used synonymously. But there is also a sense in which the term individual is used to denote a selfish person. In this extreme usage, an individual is said not to be a person in the real sense because the real person cares for others as she or he cares for himself or herself.[11]

THE PERSON AS A SOCIAL BEING

Since persons are not islands unto themselves, they have to relate themselves to society. It is contended that society is prior to the establishment of government. As Locke writes, even if government is dissolved, society remains and can establish another government.[12] If society is prior to government, then the person exists as a social being – since a society is composed of persons. There is cooperation in society, and competition arises only when private property is introduced. Coupled with competition is individual self-interest. The desire to acquire more property, and therefore more wealth, is the tendency of those who have more. Rugged bourgeois individualism becomes the impetus towards acquiring more wealth. Moreover, bourgeois exploitation of workers can result from such bourgeois individualism. The capitalist government or state can be coercive in that it exists basically to protect private property. If the workers can hardly bear the economic exploitation, then a revolution may erupt to topple the government. On Marx's view, the workers will then set up a

---

to society-at-large – of some members of the same cultural community. However, there are certainly dominant cultural traits that generally define each individual in a cultural community or in society-at-large that will justify – to a large extent – his or her being identified as an Italian, Iranian, Filipino, American, and the like.

[10] Soren Kierkegaard, "That Individual," in *Existentialism from Dostoevsky to Sartre*, ed. Walter Kaufmann (Cleveland: World Publishing Company, 1964).

[11] See Heidegger, *Being and Time*.

[12] See Locke, *Two Treatises of Civil Government*.

dictatorship that will protect their interests in a totalizing manner.[13] When this happens, the collective will then become primary, and the individual may become secondary. Although, theoretically speaking, the collective is set up to protect the interests of the individual, it may turn out in practice that the interests of the individual are sacrificed for the interests of the collective. In this regard, the individual may cease to be a real person or its quality as a real person may be diminished.

THE PERSON AS PERSON

When is a person a real person?[14] A distinction is sometimes made between the person as object and the person as subject. It is also claimed that the person as object is the subject matter of science, while the person as subject is the subject matter of philosophy. As Jaspers notes, when science

---

[13] See Karl Marx and Friedrich Engels, *Communist Manifesto*, in *Marx and Engels: Basic writings in politics and philosophy*, edited by Lewis S. Feuer (Garden City, NY: Anchor Books, 1959).

[14] Many Christians and Muslims believe that "human life begins at the moment of conception, when a sperm penetrates an ovum." A few others believe that a fetus becomes a live entity only three or so months after the fertilization of the egg, when the heart starts beating since, by this time, the fetus is infused with the soul or mind (See Kees Bertens, MSC, "Recent discussions in Indonesia about abortion," in *Impact of High Technology on Health Care* [Forum in Bioethics 6] [Manila: University of Santo Tomas, 1999], p. 137). At this stage – either at the moment of conception or after three months – the fetus has the right to be born. This right, legally construed, means it is essentially illegal to abort the fetus. It is interesting to note that, at this stage, the right of the fetus has no corresponding duties, obligations, or responsibilities. Some parents tell their child, "We decided to let you be born into this world and to care for you because we expected you, or you are obliged, to do good for yourself, your family, and the society-at-large." "Doing good," of course, can be more specific – like studying one's lessons well, being a responsible person, etc. – depending on the situation or circumstances of the parents. If this is the duty or obligation attached to the fetus's right to be born, it certainly unfolds only after the fetus is born and becomes conscious of the world. Of course, the child may reject this obligation by saying, "You never asked me if I wanted to be born or not." Is the human fetus a person? It seems not. From the existential point of view, for the fetus to be a person, it must first exist (or be born) or be thrown into the world. From the Strawsonian point of view, it may not be proper to attribute to the fetus the requisite psychical predicates of the person, and it is also debatable to say that, when the fetus's heart beats, it has already a mind or soul of its own. At the most, the human fetus may be considered a potential human person. And perhaps, it is in this potentiality that we can speak of the fetus's right to be born.

objectifies the person and makes it definable and classifiable, then it ceases to be a real person.[15]

The person as subject is free and self-creating. Each person also transcends its finitude. The person is forward-moving and not a finished project. It is also argued that the person tries to fill the nothingness between what he is at present and what he wants himself to be in the future. Persons may even create their own values in order to make their lives meaningful.[16]

Meaning in life, I contend, holds only in the relation between a subject and another subject. For as long as the subject is somehow related to the Other in some significant way, then meaning exists between both subjects. As Buber writes, there is no authentic meaning in life in an isolated subject.[17] In this regard, the fundamental structure of the person is care, which is a concern for what s/he is to be, for being "thrown," and for being entangled with current preoccupations.[18]

Is subjectivity or human freedom the essence of the person? It would seem so. But there is another view which puts an emphasis on loving one's fellowmen as one loves oneself.[19] In this view, if one loves his or her fellow human beings, then one can and will care for them. Loving one's neighbor as oneself is more primary. In our ordinary experience, care presupposes love. But why should one love his neighbor? Because, according to this view, one's neighbor is like oneself – a human being (in the Strawsonian sense). Being human, or humanity, is therefore the essence of a human person. When the person forgets his or her humanity, she or he becomes tyrannical, authoritarian, exploitative, mean, enslaves others, degrades others, and so on. When a person does not forget his or her humanity, that person as a human being is free and can love and care.

THE PERSON IN COMMUNAL OR CIVIL SOCIETY

A civil society is a communal group or a tribal society. It lies between the family and the state. It is prior to the state but it is the focus of contemporary discussion because it serves to answer the requirements of a contented life of the person as subject, in terms of freedom and participation in communal living. In other words, it avoids the excesses of extreme

---

[15] See Karl Jaspers, "Existenzphilosophie," in *Existentialism from Dostoevsky to Sartre*, ed. Walter Kaufmann (Cleveland: World Publishing Company, 1964).

[16] See Jean-Paul Sartre, *Being and Nothingness*, tr. Hazel E. Barnes (New York. Washington Square Press, Inc., 1956).

[17] See Martin Buber, *I and Thou* (New York: Charles Scribner's Sons, 1958).

[18] See Heidegger, *Being and Time*.

[19] This is the view of Emilio Jacinto. See my *Liberty and Love: The political and ethical philosophy of Emilio Jacinto* (Manila: De La Salle University Press, 2001).

individualism, on the one hand, and the coercive power of the state, on the other. The person works in solidarity with other members of the community and participates in governance in order to achieve the various communal goals for the common good (subsidiarity). The end is for the entire society to flourish.[20]

CONCLUDING REMARKS

My purpose in this paper was the clarification of the concept of the person *qua* individual and social being. There has been no discussion of other aspects of the person – as in personal identity, which appears to me as mainly epistemological or religious or legal in nature – and these can be taken for granted in the meantime. However, there are two more things which I want to comment on.

First, I tend to replace Humanity with Personness as the essence of the human being. If God is likewise a being, then Personness can both apply to man and God. The Being[21] of being (man or God) is therefore Personness. Personness takes the form of Humanity in the case of man, and the form of Divine Spirituality in the case of God.

Second, while I am in full agreement with the view that the person as subject is a subject of philosophy, I am not happy with the view that man as object is a matter only of science. The person as a unity has both psychical and material predicates, that is, both consciousness and body. A philosophical reflection on consciousness or subjectivity and freedom (man as subject) can likewise be made of the body (man as object). The position taken by Marcel and Merleau-Ponty on this matter is, I think, tenable.

------

[20] See George F. McLean, OMI, "Philosophy and civil society: Its nature, its past, and its future (Parts I-IV)," *International Journal of Philosophy*, vol. 30 (2001).

[21] Although Personness is the Being or essence of the human being, it is always in the process of becoming. Biologically speaking, a human being is immediately human, but from an existential point of view, she or he is not immediately necessarily a person. His or her humanity (Being) will still be in the temporal process of becoming, because his or her preoccupations with certain situational contingencies or conditions will oftentimes occasion a lapse into inhumanity. In this regard, insofar as the human person is concerned, Being has both the components of essence and temporal process, or it is Being in Time. What about the Divine Spirituality (Personness or Being) of God? Is it also in Time? If God is eternal, then God's Being is not in Time. We have, however, to think in terms of Whitehead's idea of process and creativity (see his *Process and Reality: An essay in cosmology* [New York: The Free Press, 1969], or Chandler's idea of evolutionary process that goes with the perfection of equations of probabilities in actualizing possibilities in the world. In other words, God's Divine Spirituality is a never-ending or an eternal process of creativity (see his *The Mind Paradigm*).

Department of Philosophy
De La Salle University
Manila, Philippines

CHAPTER II

ON THE MEANING OF BEING HUMAN IN THE WORLD: THE SOCIAL DIMENSION

KAZHIMURAT ABISHEV

INTRODUCTION: LIFE, SOCIETY, AND VALUE

It is not enough – in fact, it is impossible – for Man to lead only an organic life (e.g. to focus simply on organic needs). It has been said that only if life has meaning could there be any justification of human existence. Of course, some may say that it is not rare to meet people for whom the meaning of life is just the sustaining of physical existence, for all their efforts and thoughts aim at just this. But if we start from this idea – that the satisfaction of certain organic needs is the only justification for all human actions and deeds – then many features specific to man would be impossible to explain. First of all, for the satisfaction of purely physical needs, Man does not need to unite with other people into society. And if it is said that such a unity would exist because it makes physical existence easier, we would reply that all we need is to live in a herd, not a society.

The whole specificity of Man and his way of being in the world can be summed up by saying that he is a social creature. Such a definition has existed in philosophy since Aristotle's time. This definition will not change, whether you explain the origin of human beings through biological evolution or through divine creation or in any other way. Moreover, we assume that every individual who is a part of society does not genetically acquire or organically inherit all her or his rights and responsibilities, but learns of them in process of his or her social formation. Consequently, while people naturally establish relations with one another, and while these relations are useful, they are not given from birth. Social relations are, in principle, chosen. And that is why people have been able to change these relations throughout history, although in their biological nature they have remained almost the same.

The organization (or union) of people into society is essential to the establishment of values and not just for survival needs (even if the satisfaction of physical needs are primary values). Of course, there is a difference between simply satisfying one's physical needs and consumption, where the latter is a value. But, in general, relations between people that create and make it possible for society to function also require the mutual penetration of a logic of unity. It also means understanding and living through one another's lives. (Living through each other's lives is possible not only where people are penetrated by some common value, but also when they are opposed in values.) In the end, a common social life involves not just going beyond individual self-sufficiency, but also the establishment of more universal aims.

According to the logic of common social life, Man does not exist only to satisfy his physical needs, but also for higher values. Where there are communal organizations, kin and tribe are higher and more valuable than the life of the individual kin member, and may demand unconditional sacrifice of individual life in the name of the preservation of the community. The individual unconditionally accepts this aim (e.g. makes it his personal aim). At the same time, we cannot say that individual life does not have any value for the entire community. Every life is valuable because value starts from it. But the preservation of the life of the whole is more valuable than preservation of individual life. Consequently, the social organization of people is possible only where the behavior of the individuals in this organization is not always pre-determined by genetic and biological structures. Man connects his being with the being of the rest of the world, and tries to identify his place in it, to find the meaning of the surrounding world, and to find his meaning in this world. While the organization of individuals into society happens a priori, unconsciously, and semi-automatically, it is still a decision, and requires mutual recognition. On the issue of man's self-identification in the world, there is a need to define the value of nature and of all organic life, as well as one's independence from others. All these imply not only an acceptance of the world's existence beyond man as a fact, but a number of other attitudes towards the world and towards people's being in the world. The fact that human society is often substantially different, not only in different regions but in relatively similar geographical conditions, can perhaps be explained by the difference in the ways of their relation to the world. In particular, we see that the East and West are not simply descriptions of geographic parts of the world but cultural paradigms that reflect differences in the way of one's relations to the world and to oneself.

Due to the fact that Man does not directly belong to the world as an internal part, but exists independently of the world, he is able to have a special position as a witness and observer of both himself and of everything that happens. That is why it is possible to talk about the relation of man to the world, and why he can establish new relations with the world or change himself. Without this position of "beyondness," Man could not relate to himself as an external reality or see himself as a stranger.

This explains why values are not given to Man but are chosen by him. Consequently, human communities have some identical values as well as different ones. Values have changed for people, communities, and the whole of mankind throughout history. Values are the essence (core) in which individuals see the meaning of their existence; this is what people consciously – and more often unconsciously – aim at. Values are things that determine the general trend of one's actions and deeds, and what indirectly make one's affairs clearer – thus giving every individual his own special "light." Therefore, in the end, people create values themselves, even if these values existed before and a priori. This is because the establishment of man's relation to this something is valuable by its very content. Man cannot be absolutely neutral to world because, if he were, the world simply would not exist for him. He would be inside the world as, for instance, animals are. But the fact that people create their values does not mean that values are unreal or non-objective. This is seen from the increasing positive and especially negative impact of people on nature. Mutual cooperation and social commonality are objective because this commonality, in its most general form, is the same for everybody. Such values exist independently of their recognition by one or another individual.

In everyday life, we see that people have different values and aims. This is especially obvious in complex societies. Even when it seems that there are common values, they may, in fact, be different and even opposed. This is a result of the autonomy of each individual as a subject. Man consequently is subject of his values.

Even individuals who think that they can live just by satisfying primary vital needs in view of organic survival can, however, find motives beyond the interests of survival. To be alive and to make efforts for this is only a means and not the final goal. In this case, men have demands that go farther than organic needs. They may also consider some actions as just or unjust, and good or evil, independently of their relation to organic needs. This can be seen, for instance, when the deep-rooted egoist tries to hide actions done for his own benefit under some pseudo-noble cover. As a result of this, individuals may often choose as values and as the meaning of their existence, very questionable and even anti-human, destructive aims, targeted against human commonality and harmony. Such values are found not only in individuals but also in ethnic groups and peoples.

Aspirations for unlimited wealth, power, violence and expansion are examples of such values and aims. In the history of humanity, there are many examples of this. History is full of violence and stories of the destruction of peoples or ethnic groups by other peoples merely because of the clash of their values and worldviews. For something to serve as a meaning of existence it is not required that it is an objectively positive fact, but that it is *perceived* as something high or noble. That is why it is possible to speak of true or false values. As in the cognitive sphere, the truth or falsity of a value is not seen directly; sometimes many centuries pass before certain values are revealed as false.

A value that is accepted as a foundation by one or another commonality serves as part of the core meaning of that specific culture. Many facts support this. For instance, for a long time researchers could not understand the "logic" of the thinking of American, Australian and other tribes (which preserved the most archaic forms of organization and culture). It was thought that this thinking was still pre-logical (see Lucien Levy-Bruhl) because the judgments and ideas found often did not fit into the framework of norms and rules of cause-effect logic of thinking of modern Western man. But later it was found that the thinking of earlier man followed a logic that was essentially different from the thinking of contemporary European man. Levy-Bruhl later admitted his mistake. Individuals from earlier cultures usually do not look at nature from the point of view of simple usefulness or utility, and they do not see nature as a tool for the satisfaction of their needs. For them, nature is full of its own meaning, and so they usually tried to merge with it, to copy it and to personify it.

The activity of man in transforming nature has had two main purposes: first, the establishment and strengthening of harmonious relations between man and nature (e.g., for mutual flourishing) and, secondly, the so-called need-use motive. The latter relation started in late antiquity in Europe and then took on momentum in the modern era. Based on this foundation, the culture and spiritual atmosphere changed, so that man came to see everything as useful or useless – something that can or cannot bring benefit, etc. From this position, both nature and man gradually started to lose self-sufficiency and independence. And so, preoccupied by only this desire, man does not want to preserve nature for its own sake; man would revive it where it is necessary only because it is useful for him. The same relation came to be established with people themselves, and so to social aims and norms and institutes, etc. Thus, there is a characteristic of the need-use relation in the most general type, and in its so to say unadulterated 'purity' that happens in life quite rarely. Unfortunately, such a relation received its most crude and naked form of development in the world where we live, e.g. in the former Soviet Union and especially in Kazakhstan. The many environmental catastrophes in our country in the past are results of this relation.

Of course, this does not mean that, in a world where such values and relations are to be found, other relations and values do not exist. We speak here just about the dominance of such aims. Some time ago, they may have seemed even noble and, consequently, had their heroes. But if such an aim becomes unrestrained, then it would become (and has already become) destructive, leading only to catastrophe. There is no doubt about this. The twentieth century was very significant in this respect: two world wars, fascism and totalitarianism, many regional wars, the arms race, economic and environmental catastrophes, etc.

Relations aimed at preserving harmony with nature, although sometimes one-sided, were established in the past in the East. These relations have various forms in different eastern cultures. But currently, we witness an expansion of the Western way of relating to the world in the East too. If the specific feature of human being in the world is the aspiration for a meaning that he chooses and formulates for himself, then the primary objective basis for this is freedom.

FREEDOM

Why do we say that freedom serves as a primary objective ground for some definite meaning or sense? There are many definitions of freedom. Throughout the history of philosophy, many thinkers have made an attempt to study and discuss it, as it is a key to all other issues about the being of man. The old-time philosophers, placid and serene when arguing about most major issues, became peculiarly agitated when the issue of freedom was touched upon. A mere listing of the different definitions of freedom would make up quite a book. Therefore it is necessary to split them into two major groups, according to the following pattern:

1. Views that essentially disclaim freedom – even the mere possibility of it. (These thinkers differ among themselves as well.) The proponents of mechanistic materialism brought it to its logical end. They (for example, Thomas Hobbes, Baruch Spinoza, Julien Offray de La Mettrie, and others) tried to explain man and society as a whole, as made either by a creator's will or through natural necessity. Generally, these views hold that, as inexorable laws or a creator's will rule the world, then all our action and thought is fully determined by them. This is why our ideas about free will are nothing more than illusions. Hobbes writes:

> Liberty and Necessity are consistent [...] so likewise in the actions which men voluntarily do: which, because they proceed from their will, proceed from liberty, and yet, because every act of man's will, and every desire, and inclination proceed from some cause, and that from another cause, in a continual chain (whose first link is in the hand of God the first of all causes) they proceed from necessity. So that to him that could see the connection of those causes, the necessity of all men's voluntary actions, would appear manifest. And therefore God, that sees and disposes all things, sees also that the liberty of man in doing what he will is accompanied with the necessity of doing that which God will, & no more, nor less. For though men may do many things, [...] yet they can have no passion, nor appetite to any thing, of which appetite God's will is not the cause. And did not his will assure the necessity of man's will, and consequently of all that on mans will dependeth, the liberty of men would be a contradiction, and an impediment to the omnipotence and liberty of God. And this shall suffice (as to the matter in hand) of that natural liberty, which only is properly called liberty."[1]

Beginning with Spinoza (1632-1677), the idea of God as some force dwelling in nature came to be ousted from science and philosophy.

---

[1] Hobbes' *Leviathan* (1651), Chapter 21: "Of the Liberty of Subjects."

According to Spinoza, nature itself is a primary force that causes everything; God and nature are a single whole, one substance. Substance is something that exists only through itself, is grounded in itself, is manifested through itself, and is something that can be comprehended and explained only through itself. This entails the unity of God and nature. Every thing and every phenomenon is caused by them. God is the cause of every thing. He is an internal cause, not an external one. According to Spinoza, there is no free will. Not knowing the causes of their own will, people think that they are free. People's thoughts, emotions and actions result from natural (divine) necessity. If we do not know about and are unaware of their true causes, then we are not free; and if are aware of and know about them, then our actions, thoughts, etc., will be free. Freedom is the comprehension (realization) of necessity.

These ideas emerged and began to spread at the time when the Church was at the height of its power and there was some kind of reconciliation between science and religion. Man is regarded as a thing among nature's things, since thought is perceived as an attribute of substance alongside its other attribute – extension. These two attributes of substance are inherent essential qualities (unlike modes). This view though acknowledging freedom in words, in essence is the rejection of it since it is just an unhindered course of natural necessity.

This understanding of freedom was further developed in G.W.F. Hegel's philosophy. According to Hegel, substance is not Nature; it is the "Absolute Spirit" that exists prior to Nature and Man. It is the force that causes Nature and Man via history. Nature and Man (society) are outward forms of its own development and alienation – different stages of its formation and, at the same time, of its self-cognition. Thus, the development of "Absolute Spirit" is an external necessity for Man. Man is free as he cognizes and is aware of necessity. Hence Hegel's definition of freedom, though on a different conceptual basis, is approximately that of Spinoza's – freedom is necessity cognized by Man. Man regards unperceived necessity as a blind, destructive force. The founders of Marxism, Karl Marx and Friedrich Engels, on the whole shared this understanding of freedom, although they rejected Hegel's "Absolute Spirit." According to them, necessity independent of Man constitutes the laws of Nature and human society that Man cognizes and uses in having dominion over natural and communal forces.

There is some truth in such an understanding of freedom. Man is surely able to feel and act freely in his interactions with already cognized forces of nature and society. It is a process that, historically, has expanded the boundaries of cultural and historical space. But this view covers only the external and transient side of Man's being. Man might or might not have this kind of freedom. This freedom cannot, however, be his primary inalienable essence, something without which Man is not Man. Moreover, such an understanding expresses the essence of just one type of Man's relation to the world, i.e., the European or, to be more exact, the Western one. In another way, Man is characterized by the connection between freedom and domination – that is, this freedom is not aimed at the harmonious relations with Nature, etc. Yes, this is the freedom that is widely and soundly established in the human world. It is really so, but what is most familiar to us is the close and plainly seen side of freedom showing Man's expansion in his attitude towards the world and his self-centredness.

2. However if we consider freedom as an ontological basis of Man's being in the world, its other, hidden side is revealed. To serve as a basis, it should be a primary, specifically human way of being in the world. Hence it cannot be an attribute that has not existed until then but, rather, one which is gradually built up, and appears step by step, as Man and human society develop. This is what can be inferred from the first understanding of freedom. According to the Hegelian interpretation, history is a progress in the awareness of freedom. On this second group of views, freedom is a precursor, rather than a result, of human history.

What is freedom? Freedom is primarily the non-determination of Man by external causes, conditions, and outer forces and environment, etc. In other words, it concerns who and what will become of Man, what place he will have in life, what meaning of life he will find for himself, what he will consider valuable and what not, what is only for him and for no other forces to determine, and so on. Furthermore, these faculties and properties that are inherent only in Man and that distinguish him from other living creatures are not given to him together with the body – that is, they are not born with him in their final form. It is obvious that the human body is adapted to the human way of life, but his thought, his capacities, and so on is, on the whole, developed after his birth. This is not predetermined. If a child grows up in the animal world, then he perceives and adopts the animal way of life. (Science records several such cases.)

The above definition (i.e., of non-determination) speaks about what freedom is not. But it has some positive content. The positive dimension lies in the fact that Man initially found himself under conditions in which he had to determine for himself his being in the world. How it happened – whether it resulted from biological evolution or is an *a priori* position, etc. – are issues beyond philosophy.

Thus, Man being Man and not an animal *a priori* raises the problem of self-determination. This is characteristic of both human society and of every single individual. The question "Will I be a man?" is not yet determined for a newborn child. This very openness toward every possible way of formation and development – and not the determination of who and what this creature will turn into – is a situation preserved in the grown man. The situation for the human community will be clearer if we compare it with one that is observed in the animal world. All animal species have, on the whole, their mode of life activities determined. It is given to each species at birth, in the form of genetic and biological structures. The ability to choose is absent in animal species. Man alone possesses this potential.

He is the one to choose a mode of life, to change it, to determine which one is to his liking, etc. The being of Man – what he is to be – is his choice, or more precisely, reflects the possibility of choice. Non-determination also supposes that the act of choice is not vital. Yet Man acts in a certain way, chooses a certain road in life, a profession, and so on. What kind of freedom would it be if choice were inevitable, dictated by necessity? Therefore freedom, as a specific way of Man's being in the world, lies in the possibility of choice – when he can either make a choice or turn it down – rather than in its inevitability. Man creates himself or does not do it. He turns something into the meaning of his existence or renounces it. He aspires to the lofty ideals of humanness or prefers to live a beastly life, is eager to determine himself or entrusts himself to the volition of others, and so on.

One should not, however, understand that, having made his choice once, Man is free from this necessity in the future. Every new act, deed, and situation again brings it to him. Man often seems to choose something that is not external: citizenship, a profession, etc. He chooses himself in many acts of choice (e.g., what he would rather be, what he is attracted by). In particular, choice refers to deeds when Man faces the necessity to take a certain position. The necessity to choose oneself comes up every time when a deed touches upon mental and ethical norms and rules; but, even having coped with them, Man will have to handle them again in a new situation. An individual's way of behavior formulated in the past does not automatically work in every future action. In each new situation, he either verifies himself or not. That is the reason why Man faces this problem time and again. It results from the fact that, as long as he can act, Man has the possibility to be different.

From all said above, however, one should not get the idea that to be free and to make a choice is a simple matter. The most difficult thing for Man is to be free and to long for freedom. This kind of purpose and the relevant actions impose a burden of responsibility on Man; there is the temptation to let oneself drift or bend to the will of other people. Slavery relieves Man from the responsibility of solving worldly problems and of the difficulties of independent being. That is why individuals so often prefer to give in to the force of circumstances, the power of other individuals and states, etc. relying just on their will. The whole paradox of the problem lies in this fact: that the initial condition of freedom and possibilities of choice are also a source of human slavery.

All this said about freedom may tend to confuse the reader. How is this so? It contradicts everything we see around us or have gained – one may say – through our individual experience! Nowadays, just as in the past, we observe Man's dependence on many things: nature, society, etc. What mostly grabs one's attention is that Man's activities are conditioned by different circumstances, etc. But the definition of freedom given earlier did not state that Man is dependent on *nothing*. It just conveyed the idea that, to accept this dependence – to meet the requirements of the circumstances that we are subjected to or to be opposed to them, to bow down or fight against them – is an issue that is non-determined; there is no ready answer prepared in advance. Moreover, whether he is to solve this issue or not, and in what way – this is the destiny of Man. All living creatures, besides Man, have it solved beforehand without their participation.

Consequently, a human individual never entirely loses the opportunity to change or transform both his line of life, profession, activity, socio-political position, and his "self," i.e., to alter the deep-rooted values that determine his actions and infuse them with meaning. It means that he can renounce or lose faith in some value and, in this case, live a meaningless life. In case the "self" that Man has built up in accordance with a certain value remains unchanged in the course of his life, it is his destiny that he has chosen for himself. If this is the case, then his human and spiritual images become recognizable and constant in their specificity and those around him would always expect from him some definite characteristic deeds. Jean Paul Sartre asserts quite a similar idea in a somewhat different way. Every individual for Sartre is the project of himself – i.e., he projects himself the way he is, the way he chooses himself to be and comprehends it. According to Sartre, the choice of oneself is inevitable for Man. He is doomed to make a choice. He does it even when he makes no choice at all (e.g., when he shuns the choice, is idle, or drifts along a new course of circumstances). However, on Sartre's interpretation, freedom itself turns out to be a necessity that Man cannot dismiss; it is a kind of a new perdition for him. Other proponents of this school share this understanding.

Freedom is the universal mode of Man's being since it contains necessity. Man is free to turn something into the necessity of his social reality, establishing these or those relations, enacting the laws of these relations (for example, market relations), setting norms, traditions, etc. Even the "inexorable laws of social development," which ensue from the established relations within society, were first introduced by people.

Yet freedom that cannot be shunned and that acts as necessity and inevitability is no longer freedom, since in this case it is an act independent-from-Man. Man is not a subject in this situation. It is some other force's freedom but not Man's. Freedom extends to the limit of Man's abilities. Freedom, as mentioned already, is found in opportunities or choice – not in necessity. Beyond it lies the world of needs that have nothing to do with Man's solution of the issue of what he should be and do. Man is free to determine his own being. He is not omnipotent, and cannot and need not solve all the problems of the world. Of course, a given individual, or communities, or ethnic groups and peoples, as was mentioned, can be deluded when solving the issues of their own being in the world, choosing the grounds for their attitude towards the world, etc. The debate about values – about a true way and a real value, and so on – is a continuous and incessant one among philosophical doctrines, schools, and systems.

We may say, however, that the meaning which embraces all other meanings of human existence – i.e., the one that imparts reason to all other meanings, the so-called meaning of the meanings – is freedom itself. It is and must be the highest value for Man. It is the value that Man should live for, if he is Man. It is his essence, the only way of his being in the world, the thing that distinguishes him from other living creatures on the earth, and owing to which the so-called world of Man – his community, culture, spirituality, etc. – comes into existence. The striving for freedom, erroneous as it might be, is concealed not infrequently behind the immediate reality of all the actions and doings of people. People who have yielded to necessity and force and found themselves in slavery, still yearn for freedom. It naturally appeals to peoples and individuals who have become dependent and who still have a glimmer of hope for independence. Man's renouncement of freedom, as was said above, is the expropriation of his natural right and destination.

One more thing should be mentioned. Some clarity should be introduced about the notion of choice. We said already that choice, deviation from it, striving for values, etc., are processes that sometimes and partially proceed unconsciously. Moreover, an overwhelming majority of people function at an unconscious level. Hence, a great number of people do not know that some choice is taking place, that they in some way show an inclination to some decisions or a type of behavior, and so on. This is usually observed in routine situations where acts and actions have become stereotyped semi-automatic reactions. In such cases, the directing and regulating function of these values, which an individual is unconsciously drawn to, occur at the sensual level: by way of showing more inclination or preference towards something. Only under some peculiar conditions, when the issue is obvious and urgent, does the individual have to consciously strive for, or thoroughly comprehend, his deep-rooted motivations or his attitude towards life, people, and the meaning of his existence. This mostly depends on the level of a subject's development and his wish to act or to hide in the darkness of the unconscious. At present, however, regarding the issue of the unconscious act of choice, we will confine ourselves to what was said above.

Thus, all the peculiarities of Man result from his main way of being. Freedom makes Man universal. This universality is not a regularity of Man's being; indeed, it reflects the lack of a specific law. The world created by Man is open to all the laws of the universe that Man can comprehend and turn into laws for his own actions and mental operations. Basically he is able to grasp the laws of the whole reality of the world he has access to, and understand them, feel them, and (to some extent) live their life. The spiritual world of an advanced man can equal that of the rest of the world. It is one's freedom that allows a man to be that way, since the specific content of any reality comprehended by him, allows him to turn it into a reference point that, when necessary, will give him a picture of the world as a whole.

The social world does not have laws, like the laws of Nature, that Man basically cannot change – i.e., ones that can only be cognized and used, but not repealed since they represent the laws of people's own activity. Such a lack of freedom would render impossible such a *sine qua non* of human communal life as morals, rights with their notions about the law, good and evil, justice and injustice, virtue, violence, duty and conscience, guilt and punishment, and so on. It is a fact of life that concrete content and relevant requirements differ in different historic epochs and cultures, and they convey the idea that they have a social contract nature and, consequently, are in essence human values. The fact that they are the result of conscious or unconscious human accord does in no way belittle their objective force or their verity.

These characteristics of people towards each other, which are aimed at sustaining their life in the community, testify to the fact that they themselves consciously or unconsciously treat each other as the sole subjects and authors of their actions and doings. That is the gist of these characteristics. Would it be possible to demand from Man something that he has no power over and something that is beyond his possibilities? Would it stand to reason to punish Man for avoiding his duties if they did not depend on him? We are not speaking about the concrete content of these duties – e.g., whether they are just or not; we are speaking about the possibility of punishment. The idea is that the man who is punished could have acted differently, and even was obliged to have acted differently, since he is free *a priori* and is a human, not an animal. A wolf can be exterminated for its mode of life; Man must be punished and prosecuted for his doings, and thus he is treated as a subject. A wolf can be no different from what it is; Man *can* be so, for he has chosen this way himself.

Freedom – the opportunity of self-determination – alone gives meaning to human dignity, one's self-respect and respect for the dignity of others; it is the only objective foundation for equal and free cooperation among humans, peoples, ethnic groups, etc. The lack of such freedom and dignity will turn Man into a mere thing amongst other things, an object that can be treated in any way whatsoever. If correctly perceived, freedom can be a basis for a respectful attitude not only towards humans, peoples, nations, and other cultures, etc., but also towards the world of Nature or the Cosmos since, in the latter case, the world of Nature has primary independence, originality and self-value, and Man is somehow tied to it with co-generic bonds. In this sense, the striving for superiority and domination is both false and immoral, not only in relations with other people, but also with Nature.

Why don't we consider activity as the basis of Man's being in the world? It is through his activity that Man transforms both the outer world of things and himself. If we perceive freedom just as the necessity cognized and realized by Man, this statement would be quite to the point. But even then we would have to have in mind that the provision for and the meeting of his organic and non-organic needs were primary to human existence, since activity is carried out for this purpose alone and not for its own sake. Consequently, in this sense as well, activity is not a value in itself. Beyond any activity there is always something more substantial and guiding, imparting meaning to it. It is obvious that one and the same type of activity can bear different meanings for subjects in various situations and at different periods of time. The functioning of an individual can have one meaning for himself and quite a different one for others and for society as a whole.

Studying, for example, besides its direct goal of learning as much as possible, can mean various things for people: to become a specialist, to use the knowledge in order to outdo others, to rank high in society, and so on. Some individuals and communities may aim to exterminate other individuals and communities or dominate over them using the knowledge they have acquired and the scientific achievements they have made. That is why psychology differentiates between the direct purposes of this or that activity and deep underlying motivations. The examples are numerous. We can mention, in particular, Garin, a character from A.N. Tolstoy's "The Hyperboloid of Engineer Garin," who dared to establish a dictatorship over mankind with the help of a technical invention.[2]

In case a given value underlying this or that system of activities disappears, so do the activities themselves, or they turn into the means of realization of other values. The choice of values or the lack of values determines the direction or the absence of Man's activities. If organic existence becomes the value and the meaning for Man, then any activities aimed at meeting them are suitable for him.

Thus we may say that freedom, as a primary condition, precedes and causes Man's activity, and not vice versa, where freedom as cognized and realized necessity is caused by Man's activity. This primary freedom as a given possibility cannot be lost by Man as long as he is Man, a subject of different possible ways in the world. However, freedom is just the beginning (or primary condition) of Man's being. It is merely a possibility of choice. The realization of one's choices can be carried out only through actions, doings, and activities. Even when Man has not tended to a particular way or mode of action, he still cares to provide for his existence. Consequently the switch to action is inevitable.

There can exist a multitude – if not an infinite number – of types, kinds, and ways of activities that outwardly express the value of Man's being. These types are surely dependent on concrete situations and possibilities that Man is continuously accumulating while creating and causing them. Nevertheless, the world of human meaning and value aspiration is considerably richer, more diversified, more sophisticated and subtler than the forms in which they are expressed and realized. The

---

[2] Aleksey Nikolayevich Tolstoy, *The Garin Death Ray* [also known as *The Death Box* and *The Hyperboloid of Engineer Garin*] (1927), English tr., Bernard Guilbert Guerney, 1st ed. (London: Methuen, 1936).

universality of Man's world does not merely consist in the fact that not all of its variations and hues are represented and testified to outwardly. Actions and doings are just a part of their expression. Moreover, Man creates new levels of faculties, and thus expands his mental space.

ACTIVITY

Activity, actions and doings are an essential form of the manifestation, discovery and being of Man, and of his attitude towards the world. Sometimes these activities are called "practices" (*Practicos*), though their contents differ considerably. Man's activity is a process of cognizing outer forces, transforming them and, through this, transforming and creating himself – making his own being in the world. It should be noted that the outer forces are not only the forces of Nature but also institutions and cultures established in earlier history, etc., and, hence, common cumulative riches which individuals may not yet have become familiar with.

One's attitude to the world, and the relations of individuals towards one another, inevitably exist in acts, actions, deeds and doings – in a word, in their activity. As already said above, the main type of people's attitudes towards the world and each other can remain the same but can be expressed in various forms. Furthermore, these actions and their types can undergo drastic changes. This means that the main content, character and essence of human relations transform, first of all, the spiritual field – i.e., this essence itself is spiritual. This can result in the transformation of activity structures, operations and means, etc., or it can have no such effect.

Though the outward acts in which human value aspirations are diversely expressed are not crucial, they differ fundamentally from animal behavior. Without these acts, Man cannot accomplish his value aspirations or meet their needs, and he himself as their subject will not be realized. If the choice of values (which is the final meaning of life activity) is a deep-rooted choice, then the realization of these values demands a number of daily choices concerning the means, actions, and doings. Moreover, all these private acts of choice either verify or falsify these values.

Since Man makes choices, and since he can make them each time in different ways, they are also acts of freedom and of its manifestation. The structure of Man's activity can be examined from various aspects: social, technical, technological, professional, etc. From a philosophical perspective – i.e. the relations between Man and the world – it needs to be divided into the processes of materialization and dematerialization, or objectiveness and subjectiveness of human values. As the mastering of natural forces, their content is eventually carried out in order to establish these values and expand Man's space of meaning and his real abilities. While mastering objects and forces, Man approaches them according to the historically-developed way of their transformation – i.e., even if his actions are caused by personal motivation, Man's attitude towards an object is not only influenced by his individual direct perception; in his interactions with the environment he acts as a social creature, as a possessor of a socially-developed need.

While transforming the substances and forces of Nature, Man moulds them into a social form of being, imprints his plans on them, and gives them (as Marx put it) social content. Nature obtains through this its subject and sensual being. This is the materialization of Man's social essence: in his activity, Man asserts himself in the environment, transforms Nature into the mastered human world and, finally, "contemplates himself in the world that he has created." Materialization is one of the essential and universal parts of human activity; this fact also distinguishes human activity from all forms of instinctive animal life activity. This crucial difference lies in the achievements made by the human community, not only regarding the bodily transformations of Man as a biological species (i.e., in the form of inherited traits), but also in the shapes and attributes of objects outside his body.

As it gets a social form and a social functioning, Nature transferred into Man's activity is somehow reborn. This "new Nature," having become the means for the comprehension of new content and gaining new strength, now somewhat opposes itself – i.e., as it was prior to the involvement of human activity. The essence of this new functioning can be called a "substance" that acts in the system of human relations as a means to express social (i.e., essential) content. This, however, is just one side of the issue. A more profound understanding of materialization must be (and eventually is) the fact that Nature, reappearing in the form of the human and the social, is gradually, directly or inadvertently, transformed into something personified – into an area of one's life, so that Man should not just use it but regenerate it at a new qualitative level.

All that which has been said above does not refer simply to the productive activity of Man. The outcome of spiritual, cognitive and other activities are not in the least fixed in the content of their objective form. The issue of the materialization of spiritual content was raised by Hegel who made several serious remarks regarding the issue. Hegel perceived activity as a process of Man's self-generation, at the same time understanding materialization as dematerialization and Man as an outcome of his own labor. Hegel envisioned the process in the following way: for him, materialization is the realization in the material of an absolute idea which exists eternally in the world and prior to it. According to Hegel, the essence of Nature is the idea; we can judge the perfection of these or those natural phenomena through the identification of the object with the idea. Materialization is a stage of the idea's self-development and its realization in nature, but it is simultaneously its "self-alienation"; hence, materialization is carried out prior to, outside of, and apart from human activity. Reciprocally, dematerialization is realized in the activity of human spirit, in its understanding that the gist of human history is nothing else than the awakening of an absolute idea, its release from the material, and its birth from nature in the form of spirit. While revealing the ideal essence of

Nature in the process of cognition, Spirit withdraws its materiality (i.e., the materiality passes back into ideal existence). We may say that Hegel imparted to the forms of human activity an extra-human or pre-human universal character, the character of the activity of some extra-world creative force.

In the process of materialization, Man imparts to objective forms his own definite content that has, by its very nature, only social meaning or functioning. If, as the result of materialization, activity takes on the shape of some particular form, then this new activity dismisses the established form. As the social functioning is eventually set, then it is the only thing that can be revealed. Along with the 'content-complication' of activity and its object, the accumulation of experience and knowledge, the complications of the transfer process, and the evolution of aesthetic and other social values, there occurs the transformation of means and forms of their objectiveness. One of the primary universal and dynamic means of communication of socially organized creatures – language – is a means of generalization and of the transfer of achievements from one generation to another. We find various character systems used in the history of writing, which serve as a social way of giving objectiveness to human experience. Art also historically developed its peculiar means to express human feelings, moods, tastes, aesthetic ideals, etc. The very opportunity to create artistic images became possible only through making them external in objective forms.

It is not always in this way, of course, that the materialization and objectiveness of social content are materially expressed: they can exist both in the form of established and constant forms of behavior and action (e.g., customs, traditions, cults and so on). The attitude of every human individual as well as any new generation towards Nature is mediated. Materialized social forces and relations get in between them and Nature. This is what distinguishes Man from an animal. The animal "produces" only its own body; the way of its life activity is given in its bodily organization and, basically, is born together with it; it is what it inherits biologically. Man can grasp the various ways of human life activity only after his birth. Indeed, adult individuals also find themselves in a continuous process of exchanging experience, knowledge, and functions which undergo change continuously. This experience cannot be inherited through the genetic code. This is what freedom is. Only under these conditions can people pass on their experience, functions, and contents to each other and to later generations, fixing them in objective forms external to their bodies: in things, processes, sounds, signs, colors, etc. Human communication is impossible without this. Every individual addressing to another his desires, feelings, knowledge, and meanings, can bring them to the notice of this other only in some definite objective form – i.e., materialized somehow or other. Time and again, actions serve this purpose. If individuals' attitudes towards Nature are mediated by the relations between them, then this "personified nature" (i.e., materialized forms) in their turn mediates their relations. This also explains communication between generations very far apart in time. In the things that are made by people for other people, there is always a meaning and content that is included.

It is obvious that contents and meanings (e.g., thoughts, relations, feelings, and motivations) are not essential to materialized, objective forms. The fact that people express themselves in materialized forms does not mean that their thoughts are converted into objects. Even artists, when painting pictures, do not do this. The ideal made outward, materialized, and converted into an object still remains in Man; the meanings are symbolized by the external forms; they somewhat remind, excite and stimulate respective thoughts, feelings, images of people, things, etc. in others during the process of communication. When making things or performing actions and deeds, Man creates signs and symbols, common and familiar to all – or at least to some other individuals. These signs or symbols may indicate content and meaning, and only a mature individual who has experience of the world of human relations can penetrate into and perceive them.

As the meanings and contents created by people are multilevel and multi-layered, material and objective forms also express diversity. One and the same human object – and this is further extended to the objects of Nature unaffected by Man – can symbolize and be associated with a host of relations, images and meanings. The axe and sickle, for example, express and symbolize at least two layers of Man's relations: they can symbolize certain actions with a certain object (i.e., chop with an axe and reap with a sickle), but they also can indicate some definite relations among people in a given epoch. And this is just a small part of what they can symbolize. If made skillfully, they can express an aesthetic view of Man, his freedom, and values. The levels and meanings of objective forms may vary: from being a basic sign with some definite meaning, to the systems of signs and symbols able to fix and express the movements of thought tinted by Man's attitude towards these thoughts.

It should be noted at the same time that, in every human soul or in every individual's sovereign space, there remain many things that are not expressed outwardly, made objective, or addressed to another, not only because they are insignificant or have no reference towards others, but for various concrete reasons. Still, there is still one common ground: a certain self-sufficiency of an autonomous subject alongside its unity with the world. That is what makes possible communication, social relations, and joint activity. The objective forms, including both social institutions and organizations in general, act as forms of people's activity and communication. In the process, there occurs a dematerialization, since only in active functioning is the human content of these organs revealed. If the formation of a social object involves materialization followed by dematerialization, its somewhat reverse process, is liberation – i.e., the release of the activity from this objective condition. Thus, in activity, human objects (but not natural things) are dematerialized.

The difference between the given processes lies in the fact that in the relations of new forces of Nature entering the human world, there always occurs a *materialization*, and in the relations of the forces previously mastered by Man that have been turned into his means, there always occurs a *dematerialization*. Materialization and dematerialization constitute, on the whole, the integrity of human activity aiming at transforming Nature and Man himself – but there are two sides to this integrity. In other words, what is dematerialization for previously mastered social objects is materialization in respect of newly mastered things and forces. The mastering of each historically-developed form of activity is, for an individual, a kind of transformation of the objective logic of a definite culture into a form of his subjective activity. The processes of materialization and dematerialization constitute a part of human activity, but show the distinctions within it.

ALIENATION

What was said earlier about Man's activities describes their most general characteristics. In a developed human society, the activities of people and their relations, including production, form a diverse and complex process. This includes various opposing processes, directions and spheres of action. The very production of objects is divided into production itself, distribution, exchange, and consummation – which, in industrialized countries, are isolated from each other, and thus constitute independent areas of social life. According to the Marxist interpretation, as is well-known, the production of material welfare is the eventual determinant basis of social life. All other forms of people's life activity originate from here – i.e., from the primary form of Man's being.

However, this view has given rise to several strong objections in contemporary philosophy. Both accumulated historical facts and observations of everyday reality fail to confirm it. Undoubtedly economic life and activity is one of the most important areas of social reality. Nevertheless, it cannot determine the form, character and content of all the areas of Man's activity; it does not reveal the very essence of Man either. As with other areas of social life, it serves to express this essence rather than be one of the most important forms in which this essence is manifested. Economic activity – if we take it in its primary purpose and not in its transformed form caused by later development – is aimed at meeting the bodily and organic needs of man. The "purely" organic vital needs of Man essentially differ from an animal's as well. It is obvious that it is impossible to live without meeting these needs. Many people sincerely believe that life is just organic existence. But if we have a closer look, even such people often see, especially at crucial moments, that deeper, often unconscious, motivations lie behind their strivings. In a more or less developed society, a majority of its members have exceeded what they needed for life a long time ago, and even its criteria vary in different cultures and are historically flexible. Hence the criteria and limits of existence are essentially cultural, as the needs of Man's body have been transformed by culture and social life. For Man, the process of eating became in history not so much an organic act but an aesthetic and social one. (Indeed, Man's body can no longer assimilate food in its primeval natural form.) Ancient Man already carried out eating as a social act; it meant communication between individuals, it acted as a sign of respect, unity, etc. and, consequently, its primary purpose as supporting the life of an organism became less important and was of an auxiliary character.

The craving for the accumulation and increase of property, money, etc., may seem, at first, to be the mere continuation of life. In fact, the motivations here are very far from the original ones. The yearning for unlimited accumulation – which, apart from the desire for life, knows no bounds – has different motivations: wealth is a symbol of an individual's social importance, is a symbol of power over others, is a means of subordination of others, etc. They are all values caused by the social development of Man. Thus, economic values – crucial and primary as they are – do not constitute the main and determining value for the majority of individuals. They gain this status under certain conditions. These conditions in the history of philosophy and social thought were called alienation.

In the most general sense, alienation means that the social world created by people (i.e., the world they most feel at ease in) becomes alien, hostile, and oppressive for them. As was said above, in the long run the essential thing is that people themselves build up their relations, societies, and forms of communication, depending on the way they are, what values they choose, and what they consider to be the meaning of their existence. But alienation means that these relations are turned over – i.e., in them, Man does not determine what kind of values he is striving for; rather, people are united in a given way by some force called "society" *against* their will and desires, and by some external need. This society makes people act according to the way *it* is, and individuals act as the products of circumstances but not as creators of these circumstances.

In the history of philosophy, the separation of people's activity from themselves was noticed a long time ago. The founders of social contract theory (e.g., Hobbes, Rousseau, and others), were the first to touch upon the subject. Rousseau claimed that government was created by people who decided to unite in a state in order to defend their common interests, but it consequently changed its purpose and instead set out to rule over people. This is what he understood as alienation of state agencies from the people. According to Hegel, as mentioned already, alienation is a transfer of World Spirit into Nature, and into its next stage in the process of self-development. Subjecting Hegel's scheme to criticism, Marx claimed that materialization and alienation were congruent, since for him any transformation of an idea into a subject is a transfer into something alien. Ludwig Feuerbach, one of Hegel's followers, linked this alienation with Christianity – specifically, with the idea of God. The idea of God is, for him, just a concentrated form of the essence of Man alienated from and opposed to himself. In alienation, Man worships only his own essence.

Consequently, it is enough to expose the root of this idea, and religion will start to fade away.

The concept of alienation was further elaborated and developed in Marxism. According to Marx, alienation is not just a product of a delusion or a false perception of reality. Alienation is a real phenomenon: a form that is found in the social relations of people and in the material outcomes of their activities, traditions and norms, social ideals, etc. According to Marx, alienation is caused by the division of labour and the presence of many functions, operations and forms of organization that, being isolated, separate aspects of the integral social process. Inasmuch as any particular function performed by an individual in such a system cannot be self-sufficient and must be extended into other functions carried out by other individuals, the link which unites them into a single whole acts in relation towards each of them as some outward coercive power. It is putatively a nonhuman force. As Marx held, it happens first of all in the economic life of people where their relations turn into the relations of things – i.e., into material relations. For example, in a market setting, competition goes on between stores of capital – not between people, the owners of the market. People act as the representatives of wealth; the wealth that determines the motivation of their actions and the character of their activities is the subject of these relations and not the people themselves. The owners of capital are just personified capital. Hence, this means that Man serves wealth and not vice versa.

The relations between individuals, then, are determined by things involved in these relations. This constitutes one of those ever-valuable provisions elaborated by Marx – that every man, when performing some sort of action and expressing himself in some "thingness" (even in the form of services, or delivering a speech), addresses it to another man. The result – a thing, a sound, an action, and so on – bears some content intended for some other individual or individuals. Thus individuals are tied together through social bonds and relations. The socially meaningful result of the actions and doings of individuals becomes the mirror through which their author (or authors) is presented to other individuals.

On this understanding, the social world is the human world – man's world, the world of his activity and its outcome. The social world is nothing more than the form of Man's real and ideal existence. That is why all things created by Man – and in this world everything is created by him – are means, forms and ways of his being, existence, self-activity and development. Everything created by him constitutes his organs; society as a form of men's integration is their organ. Certainly individuals are dependent on their social relations, established conditions, and forms. But these relations are *his* relations, *his* conditions and forms of being, and *his* forces. No other forces that have been turned into substances, things, or objects can be, as such, in isolation from Man and outside Man. Hence, the so-called dependence of individuals on social factors and social relations, is a real objective vision that springs up under alienation and is not an essential dependence. Basically, such dependence is the dependence of people on themselves, their own historically-ensured levels of development, but not an external necessity. The level of people's own historical development that they have realized in outward factors and in themselves, in a given historical period, limits themselves, and is not an external border. This border is not absolute, as they can and do overcome this dependence.

Thus Man is not the product of these or other circumstances or conditions, but these conditions are an internal aspect of human activity. This is the primary relation. Marx considered that alienation had its classical forms under capitalism, where Man alienates wealth – the expression of value – from himself. Thus, classical commodity production manufactures commodities, not for the direct consumption by the manufacturer himself, but for exchange and sale. Varied as the concrete types of labour might be, and diverse as the products meeting different needs might be in those cases when they are produced for exchange, they are equal and identified by the fact that they are products of labour in general. They are bound together only through their common origin – Man's labour. This labour can generally be measured quantitatively: how much labour and time were required for the production of this quantity of commodities? This common bond makes it possible to equate diverse types of commodities, and prevails over people in such a society. It is an abstract common measure that unites manufacturers on a social scale and turns labour into a social force that rules over individuals.

The common value of any commodity is also rendered in definite things – i.e., is *materialized*. This is money – i.e., materialized value. Gold proved to be the most appropriate form of this materialization. If materialized forms served only as a means to determine human relations, then obviously there would be no alienation and distortion in it. Man remains a subject and master of the situation when he determines himself and his means in his actions. Thus, according to Marx, materialization does not coincide with alienation, and Hegel is basically wrong when he identifies the two and, in this way, immortalizes alienation as something in principle unavoidable. However, for Hegel, Man is not a subject of his own history; genuine history and its universal outcome are made independently of the will of individuals concerned. Hence, in the Hegelian system, individuals are presented just as puppets within the action of some extra-world force. According to the Marxist concept of history, however, alienation must examine its own result – i.e., individuals alienate their relations from themselves, and treat them as something that initially precedes and causes them, determines them, and is primary in their relations towards them.

All these materialized forms that have been created by people, fix and reveal phenomena; this is called fetishism and embodiment – or, to be more exact, 'thingness.' The meaning, content and attributes that Man has fixed in things and processes now alienated, seem to be something not imparted to them by Man, but inherent in their nature. This distortion causes 'fetishes' – idols which people worship. Wealth, in its materialized form (e.g., gold), can be an example of this. World literature, art, and so on, are full of various plots, tragedies and catastrophes connected with the worship of the golden calf as a deity.

We may also infer from this that any alienation of Man's activity from himself is implicitly a self-alienation. Unlike the type of alienation typical of capitalism, the Soviet system dominating in our country of Kazakhstan was characterized by an all-pervasive alienated management. It was no longer the power of wealth that was self-sufficing. The State considered itself to be the beginning of all beginnings (e.g., higher party authorities were in reality supreme state structures), as something absolutely self-valuable, as the subject of people's lives and destinies. This is the very alienated function of managing people. In this situation, the paradox of the management function alienated from its subjects lies in the fact that this function becomes the one that belongs to itself, a subject and master not only of itself but also of the person who carries it out (i.e., Man). Moreover, the alienation of this function lies also in the fact that it renders the subject into a subordinate part. Man is part of this function as a means of its realization. The result is that the function is carried out for the sake of the function and not for Man's sake (i.e., in order to realize and meet his certain needs). This is the reason why, in this respect, function is nothing more than a universal anonymous subject. An anonymous subject, and not Man, carries out the activity where Man is an object of management and impact. Here Man performs a double function: he is both an object and a means of influence.

The intricacy of essential relations likewise lies in the fact that individuals themselves carry all this out, i.e., they remain the subject of the process, viz.: they turn themselves into means and objects; they themselves turn the essential relations inside out. The alienation of management function, which is estranged from their subjects and opposed to them, is typical of all totalitarian systems.

Early types of human organization knew no such alienation. Man merges with his social organization, and relations between individuals are not yet separated from them but constitute their concurrent attribute or manifestation. Individuals just begin the process of self-distinction (i.e., the creation of the world of things and mutual relations, not immediately congruent with them, but nevertheless representing their own aspects and forms of existence, estranged from themselves as their own other selves). The subjectivity of every individual is identical (or congruous) with the subjectivity of another and, in aggregate, of all together. Every individual has a primary and still basic completeness of development since the whole of society is somehow or other accessible to every individual. That's why an adult individual participates together with others in the solution of crucial issues for kin or community.

It was mentioned above that the diversity of mediating inter-individual bonds resulting from division and disintegration of activities was the precondition for the alienation of these bonds to emerge. However the social division of activity is not something external in relation to individuals. It is rather the splitting of an initially common way of individuals' development into a host of separate roads and ways of life, and the beginning of newer and newer forms and fields of life. This is the rise of a new whole with brand new components. Social life has become the aggregate of all spheres of individuals' lives activity that mutually stood apart and withdrew from each other.

With a considerable growth of population and the correlative insignificance of people's productive capacities, economic activity is widened and the rise of private interests and their lack of convergence between different individuals and groups result in continuous collisions among them. In order to preserve and restore the collapsing ties between different groups and separate individuals, there appear the primary institutions that later grew into a state. Though their function was to foster the economic integrity, yet their top priority was to maintain social harmony. Thus, the support of inter-human relations ceases to be an integral part of each individual's activity and is not any longer provided for by established customs and traditions. The separation of this function from people did not, however, mean that through this it becomes alienated from individuals. At its early stage, it is still quite subordinated to and controlled by them. But with the process of the extension and expansion of labour, the separation of various spheres is going on. The need to tie the relations of spheres increasingly moving apart intensifies the management function and strengthens its independence. (Eventually it leads to full transformation of the original relation: a self-sufficing management function emerges that considers itself to be the origin of a social whole). These are the grounds for the rise of despotism.

Yet individuals, without whom it would not exist, continue to carry out the original function of the whole. The whole is the aggregate of their actions and relations – i.e., the thing that is called society. But now they "alienate" this function of tying and establishing relations to an agency set by them. The function has now been alienated; having become the business of the people specially singled out for the purpose. Yet one should not conclude that, at a certain stage of Man's development, his alienation from himself turns into a natural, necessary relation (i.e., in other words, though individuals in a certain way can surpass the fetters of alienation, yet by and large they cannot avoid them). This view is also a consequence of the fetishism of history. The fact that, in history, it was and is like this, greatly hid the vision of a possibly different development. The understanding of freedom will, however, be incomplete and inconsistent if we do not recognize the fact that people can avoid alienation. If we do not consider alienation to be just one of the possibilities that could have been realized by people, then history will be a process where inexorable laws of Nature and not the people themselves determine how and where they will be directed. According to Hegel's and Marx's doctrines, alienation is necessary.

According to Marx, it is obvious that the alienated dominion is created by people, owing to their subjective lack of development. But if one infers that basically people cannot but alienate themselves, then it will be one of the varieties of 'alienation' logic. In this respect, Marx's viewpoint has some discrepancies: people create their history themselves, but do it under certain necessary and unavoidable conditions. They "enter" into definite necessary relations independent of their will. Even if this necessity is not a "crucial" one, it eventually determines and predetermines the general course of human history. One can infer from this viewpoint that a certain stage of social development sooner or later inevitably takes place. Marx considered that the laws of the social process are internal and immanent ones of human activity, but this fact does not change the essence of the matter: Marxism's understanding of freedom remains incomplete. When making the original choice of fundamental ways of being in the world, people virtually have no freedom left.

If we follow the logic of this understanding of freedom that considers it as Man's choice, then alienation is choice in favour of slavery, a choice that denounces all his human purpose on the earth – since freedom only comprises the possibilities for Man to find ways for his harmonization with the world. Alienation is a wrong, misleading way in the search for achieving harmonic development. But whatever grip of necessity Man might find himself in, he always has an opportunity to free himself from it notwithstanding the victims and difficulties it might cause. And thus we return to the primacy of human freedom.

CONCLUSION

What has been argued in this paper is that it is inappropriate to see human existence, its history and development, on a purely legal plane. Nor can the meaning of human being in the world be reduced to the level of the preservation of organic life. Instead, the existence of man is a fundamentally social one.

This social dimension involves freedom and activity, but also alienation. Specifically, we are free, in that we are able to change ourselves and change our relations to the world. It is through activity that we are able to manifest this freedom and create ourselves. And it is in the overcoming of alienation that allows freedom to flourish.

There is, of course, a further dimension – that of the human psyche, which requires an understanding of the nature of thought, of reflection and creative work, and of human consciousness and the unconscious.

Yet by focussing on the social dimension here, we see how social life is not directed simply or primarily to biological survival. Rather, it involves the articulation of values. And while life is the foundation of values, what 'life' amounts to and should be understood as, is itself something that presupposes our search for meaning. It is in the articulation and development of ourselves that we can give meaning to our lives.

The objective basis for this search and for our aspirations is, however, our freedom. But to articulate this freedom, we need to enter into the mental and spiritual universes of human individuals and their communities.

Department of Social Philosophy,
The Institute of Philosophy and Political Science
National Academy of Sciences of Kazakhstan,
Almaty, Kazakhstan

CHAPTER III

HUMAN RIGHTS: AN ISLAMIC APPROACH

MUSTAFA KÖYLÜ

When we consider human rights from a historical perspective, we can say that they began with the laws of Hammurabi, the Decalogue, the laws of Manu, and other holy books. They all tried to formulate the basic rules to be obeyed in order that human life become meaningful and truly human.[1]

However, when we examine human rights from today's perspective, it can be said that it is a relatively new topic. For the first preliminary document of human rights was political – the "Bill of Rights" drawn up in 1689 and imposed by the British Parliament on the new King, William III (1650-1702). The Bill of Rights laid down superiority of law to the King, who was no longer considered as a sovereign ruling by divine right; it enshrined the fundamental rights and freedoms of the people over and against the king. The first substantive document of human rights was again political – the "Declaration of Virginia," drawn up in June 1776 by the British colonists in America who wanted to free themselves from British rule. It led to the War of Independence (1776-81) and the establishment of the United States of America. Another important declaration of human rights was the "Declaration of the Rights of Man and the Citizen" accepted by the French Constituent Assembly on 26 August 1789, which formed a Preamble to the Constitution of 1791. It was followed by two other Declarations. One served as a preamble to the new Constitution of June 1793; it stressed freedom, allowed the assassination of tyrants, and opposed slavery. The other one, proclaimed in August 1795, formulated the duties as well as the rights of man in society, and replaced the statement that men are born free and enjoy equal rights by the formula of men's equality before the law. More recently, we have the Universal Declaration of Human Rights, which was accepted by the United Nations in December 1948. After this Declaration, in 1966, two other Covenants were subsequently drawn up, dealing with social and cultural rights and with civil and political rights.[2]

These declarations of human rights clearly intended to protect the individual against any arbitrary power. While the American one stressed the freedom and independence of man, the French ones sought to establish a

---

[1] Jacques Waardenburg, "Human Rights, Human Dignity and Islam," *Temenos (Helsinki)*, vol. 27 (1991): 152-182, p. 176. In general, see Ann Elizabeth Mayer, *Islam and Human Rights: Tradition and Politics* (Boulder and San Francisco: Westview Press, 1991).

[2] Waardenburg, "Human Rights, Human Dignity and Islam," pp. 152-154.

precise socio-political order opposing any absolutist power and promoting the common well being.

As to Islamic human rights, although there are some modern attempts about this matter in various parts of the Muslim world, there is not any Bill of Islamic Human Rights accepted and implemented by all Muslim countries in the world today. Thus, it can be said that most of the human rights in Muslim countries are applied according to the principles of classical Islamic Law and the traditional understanding of Islam.

In this paper, I will try to describe human rights in light of the Qur'an and Sunna, the sayings and deeds of the Prophet Muhammad. For this purpose, I will divide my paper into two main parts. While the first part deals with human rights mostly based on the views of some traditional Muslims – views that reflect the principles of classical Islamic Law – the second part will try to elaborate some human rights in Islam that are questionable in our modern time when compared to the Declaration of Human Rights of United Nations. The latter will include the rights of women and religious rights (e.g., the case of apostasy and the situation of non-Muslims and their religious liberty).

HUMAN RIGHTS AND TRADITIONAL ISLAM

Human rights in Islam can be placed into four categories: 1) bio-psychological rights, 2) religious rights, 3) political rights, and 4) economic rights. Before examining these basic human rights, let us first discuss some features of Islamic human rights that differ from the other declaration of human rights.

Human rights as conceived by Islam are radically different from those normally associated with a modern approach.[3] According to A. K. Brohi, there is a fundamental difference in the perspectives from which Islam and the West each views the matter of human rights. While the Western perspective may be called anthropocentric – in the sense that the human being is regarded as constituting the measure of everything, since he is the starting point of all thinking and action – the Islamic perspective is theocentric. Here, Allah is paramount and each human being exists only to serve Him.[4] Allah alone sustains one's moral, mental and spiritual make-up, secures the realization of one's aspirations, and makes possible one's transcendence. "It is this which constitutes the decisive distinction between the two attitudes."[5] On the other hand, all regulations related to human rights as made by the West are there only to secure their recognition from some secular authority such as the state. Thus, the first distinction between them is the question of the regulation of human rights.

---

[3] A. K. Brohi, "Islam and Human Rights," in *The Challenge of Islam*, ed. Altaf Gauhar (London: Islamic Council of Europe, 1978), p. 177.

[4] See the Qur'an 51:56.

[5] Brohi, "Islam and Human Rights," p. 180.

The second important distinction between the attitudes of Western and Muslim people is the Qur'anic view of life, which divides its functions into *haqooqullah* – the obligations to Allah – and *haqooqunnas* – the obligations to human beings and society. The former category includes the matters like prayer and the need for ritual purity of mind and body – primarily the personal concerns of the individual; the latter category has a social aspect. Especially in the matters of *haqooqunnas*, no one escapes the penalty for violating the rights of others, and state power is only an earthly agent of the divine power, acting by virtue of delegated authority to enforce the Divine Law.[6] *Haqooqullah* or Divine rights, in the Muslim scholars' view, stand second to man's rights. For example, if a Muslim wants to make a pilgrimage to Mecca but owes something to his fellow men, he has to fulfill first his duties towards his fellowmen. If he acts differently, he will be held responsible in the world to come. It is related that the Prophet himself never offered prayers for those who passed away without paying their debts. In these situations, he paid the debts of those who had died without paying what they owed.[7]

The third difference is that there is no privilege for the ruler over lay people. According to Islamic understanding, the ruler himself, if he betrays his trust, will be punished. Since the Divine Law binds both, there can be no conflict between the state authority and the individual. Even he who handles the affairs of state is under the control of Divine Law and cannot claim any special privileges or prerogatives or immunities. The affairs of the people are to be run for the benefit of the people as a whole. There are many examples in the early days of Islam indicating this view.[8]

The fourth difference is the power of the application of human rights. Islam is primarily interested in securing for its believers "right belief and right conduct" but, in accordance with its teaching, conduct is never right unless it is based on right belief and is consciously willed. Because of this, the Prophet said that the intention of the believer is more important than his or her conduct. Thus, Islam's main purpose is to produce *saliheen* (righteous people), *muttaqis* (self-controlled people), and *sadiqeen* (people who adhere to the truth). On the other hand, according to Brohi, the Western world believes that mechanical conformity to the pattern of

---

[6] Brohi, "Islam and Human Rights," p. 181.

[7] Rashid A. Jullundhri, "Human Rights and Islam," *Understanding Human Rights: An Interdisciplinary and Interfaith Study*, ed. Alan D. Falconer (Dublin: Irish School of Ecumenics, 1980), p. 35; S. M. Sayeed, "Human Rights in Islam," *Hamdard Islamicus*, vol. 9, (Aut, 1986), p. 67.

[8] For example, one of the closest companions of the Prophet Muhammad and the first Caliph of Muslims, Abu Bakr in his first official speech said: "You have made me your leader, although I am in no way superior to you. Co-operate with me when I go right; correct me when I err; obey me so long as I follow the commandments of God and His Prophet; but turn away from me when I deviate." Brohi, "Islam and Human Rights," p. 183.

conduct, prescribed by the law of the State or by some such authority, is sufficient to secure public order and universal peace. In other words, its procedure is to attempt to influence from the outside the inner condition of man, believing that social, political, economic and other institutions are capable of influencing individual character.[9] Thus, it can be said that, while Islam's aim is to create a disciplined society, the West's aim is to produce a permissive society. By disciplining themselves, Muslims rule themselves from within.[10]

Fifth and lastly, and contrary to other worldly systems, Islam wishes to see human beings happy both in this world and in the world to come. To achieve this goal, Islam calls human beings to restore broken relations with heaven. The main object of the Qur'an is to make human beings conscious of their place in the universe as well as of their relations with God.[11] In addition, Islam wants to create a society based on a deep sense of moral responsibility and justice in order to preserve human dignity accorded to human beings by Allah.[12]

Having elaborated some features of Islam concerning human rights, we can now move on to some basic human rights in Islam.

Bio-Psychological Rights

When we speak about bio-psychological rights, we mean that every human being, whatever be the case, has some basic human rights simply in virtue of being a human being; this should be recognized by every Muslim. These rights include the following:

Right to Life. The first and foremost basic right is the right to live and respect human life. Except for a few conditions, such as war or [stopping the] spread of corruption on earth,[13] no one has any right by himself to take a human life. If anyone kills another, it is as if he slays the entire human race. On the other hand, if anyone saves a human life, it is as if he saves all mankind. This instruction has been stated in the Qur'an as follows:

> ...If any one slew a person – unless it be for murder or for spreading mischief in the land – it would be as if he slew

[9] Brohi, "Islam and Human Rights," p. 189.
[10] Allahbukhsh K. Brohi, "Human Rights and Duties in Islam: A Philosophical Approach," in *Islam and Contemporary Society* (London and New York: Longman, 1982), p. 252.
[11] See the Qur'an 17:70.
[12] Jullundhri, "Human Rights and Islam," p. 34.
[13] In these cases too, it can be decided only by a proper and competent court of law. In Islam, no one by himself has the right to take another human being's life.

the whole people. And if any one saved a life, it would be as if he saved the life of the whole people.[14]

In order to preserve the human person and not to shame the human body, Islam prohibits suicide. At this point the Qur'an reads: "And spend of your substance in the cause of Allah, and make not your own hands contribute to [your] destruction; but do good; for Allah loveth those who do good."[15] More importantly, in all the verses related to killing or saving, the word "soul" (*nafs*) is used in general terms without any distinction or particularization. Even some Muslim scholars include other creatures in the meaning of "soul."[16]

Right to the Basic Necessities of Life. Another important human right in Islam is the right to the basic necessities of life. The Qur'an reads as follows: "And in their wealth there is a due share for the beggar and the deprived."[17] This verse clearly indicates that anyone who asks for help and anyone who is suffering from deprivation – irrespective of his or her religion, nationality, color, etc – has a right to the property and wealth of a Muslim. Allah has established this right over rich and powerful Muslims. Islam makes no distinction between Muslims and non-Muslims at this point.[18]

However, it should not be thought that Islam speaks only of the help and charity that is given voluntarily; it has made compulsory charity (*zakat*) the third pillar of Islam. In addition to this, the state is also responsible for supporting needy people. Thus, if one is an orphan or an aged person, a crippled or unemployed person, an invalid or poor, and if has no one else to support him or help him, then is it the duty of the state to arrange for his proper burial. In short, the state has been entrusted with the duty and responsibility of looking after all those who need help and assistance. The Islamic understanding of a state is of a truly welfare state that is the guardian and protector of all those in need.[19]

Right to the Protection of Honor. The Qur'an not only prohibits violation of the life and property of people, but also any

---

[14] The Qur'an 5:32.

[15] The Qur'an 2:195.

[16] Bayraktar Bayraklı, "Kur'ân'da İnsan Hakları," *Din Eğitimi Araştırmaları Dergisi*, sayı 5 (1998), s. 13.

[17] The Qur'an 51:19.

[18] Sayeed, "Human Rights in Islam," p. 74.

[19] Sayeed Muhammad Yusuf, *Economic Justice in Islam*, 2nd ed (Lahore, Pakistan: Sh. Muhammad Ashraf, 1977), p. 9; Masudul Alam Choudhury, *Contributions to Islamic Economic Theory: A Study in Social Economics* (London: Macmillan Press, 1986), s. 168.

encroachment upon their honor, respect and chastity. The Qur'an clearly lays down:

> O ye who believe! Let not some men among you laugh at others: It may be that the (latter) are better than the (former): Nor let some women laugh at others: It may be that the (latter) are better than the (former): Nor defame nor be sarcastic to each other, nor call each other by (offensive) nicknames: Ill-seeming is a name connoting wickedness, (to be used of one) after he has believed: And those who do not desist are (indeed) doing wrong.[20]

According to classical Islamic law, if it is proved that someone has attacked the honor of another person, then irrespective of the fact whether or not the victim is able to prove himself a respectable and honorable person, the culprit will receive due punishment.[21] Thus, Islam declared blasphemy a crime, irrespective of the fact whether the accused is a person of honor, and whether the words used for blasphemy have actually disgraced the victim or harmed his reputation in the eyes of the public. The mere proof of the fact that the accused said such things, which according to common sense could have damaged the reputation and honor of the plaintiff, is enough for the accused to be declared guilty of defamation.[22] Thus, the Qur'an acknowledges the right of human beings to be protected from defamation, sarcasm, offensive nicknames, and backbiting.[23]

Right to Sanctity and Security of Private Life. Islam recognizes the right of everyone that there should be no undue interference or encroachment on the privacy of one's life. This situation is stressed both in the Qur'an and in the *hadiths* of the Prophet Muhammad. The Qur'an states this in the following verses: "O ye who believe! Avoid suspicion as much (as possible): for suspicion in some cases is a sin. And spy not on each other, nor speak ill of each other behind their backs..."[24] The Qur'an even regulated how Muslims should enter each other's homes, saying: "O ye who believe! Enter not houses other than your own, until ye have asked permission and saluted those in them: that is best for you, in order that ye may heed (what is seemly).[25]

The Prophet also instructed his followers that a person should not enter even his own house suddenly or surreptitiously. He should somehow

---

[20] The Qur'an 49:11.

[21] See the verses related to slander and honor: 4:112; 24:4, 18-20,23-25; 49:11-12; 104:1.

[22] Mawdudi, "Human Rights in Islam," p. 72.

[23] See the Qur'an 49:12; 24:16-19; 4:148-149.

[24] The Qur'an 49:12.

[25] The Qur'an 24:27.

or other inform or indicate to the dwellers of the house that he is entering the house, so that he may not see his mother, sister or daughter in a condition in which they would not like to be seen, nor would he himself like to see them in that condition. Peering into the houses of other people is also strictly prohibited. But if a person enters others' houses without permission, then he can be called to account or made liable to prosecution. The Prophet has even prohibited people from reading the letters of others, so much so that if a man is reading a letter and another man casts sidelong glances at it and tries to read it, his conduct is reprehensible.[26]

Religious Rights

One of the basic human rights that the Qur'an stresses is the matter of faith or faithlessness. According to Qur'anic teaching, religion (in the sense of faith) is an affair between the person and Allah, so everyone is completely free in his or her choice of faith. No one has the right to impose his faith on others, including on his children and wife. There is no compulsion in religion. Even the prophet's duty, as stated by the Qur'an, is just to convey his message to people who, on their part, have the right to accept or reject it.[27]

The Qur'an not only enjoins complete religious freedom to all people, but also gives great importance to the preservation of the sacred places that belong to people who have different faiths and beliefs. Thus, the Qur'an tries to protect synagogues, churches, as well as mosques from destruction. It reads as follows:

> [There are] those who have been expelled from their homes in defiance of right, – (for no cause) except that they say, 'Our Lord is Allah.' Did not Allah check one set of people by means of another, there would surely have been pulled down monasteries, churches, synagogues, and mosques, in which the name of Allah is commemorated in abundant measure...[28]

The Qur'anic statement concerning various places of worship reveals the fact that, whether believers be Jews, Christians, Muslims, Hindus, or Buddhists, they should work for freedom of conscience and for the better understanding of each others' faiths.

It is very interesting that Islam not only gives the right to believe or not, but also gives the right to the individual that his or her religious sentiments will be given due respect and that nothing will be said or done

---

[26] Mawdudi, "Human Rights in Islam," p. 72-73.
[27] For religious freedom in the Qur'an, see 2:256; 6:107; 10:99; 16:82; 18:29; 42:48.
[28] The Qur'an 22:40.

which may encroach upon this right. Allah himself in the Qur'an has ordained: "Revile not ye those whom they call upon besides Allah, lest they out of spite revile Allah in their ignorance. Thus, we have made alluring to each people its own doings..."[29] According to Mawdudi, these instructions are not limited to idols and deities, but also apply to the leaders or national heroes of the people.[30] In addition, the Qur'an does not prohibit people from debating and discussing religious matters, though it wants that these discussions be conducted in decency and in a dialogical manner.[31] Moreover, this order is not merely limited to the People of the Book, but is valid for all those who follow other faiths and religions.

Political Rights

Islam not only concerns faith and prayer, but also society. For this purpose, it has set up regulations concerning the running of the state. These can be summarized as follows:

Right to Participate in the Affairs of State. Although Islam does not require a specific governmental form, it gives a great importance to the issue of *shura* (i.e., consultation), that is the main characteristic of a modern democratic system. According to this view, every citizen of a Muslim state has the right to participate in the state's affairs. The Qur'an says: "Those who respond to their Lord, and establish regular prayer; who (conduct) their affairs by mutual consultation..."[32] According to this principle, it is the right of every Muslim that he should have a direct or indirect say in the affairs of the state. Islam never permits or tolerates situations where an individual or a group of people may deprive the common Muslims of their rights, and usurp the powers of the state.[33]

In addition, everyone can criticize the administration and government without being penalized. The task of the head of state is to work for the establishment of peace, justice, and law. People can depose a head of state whom they have elected. The head of the state is required to consult an Advisory Council, and to work for the establishment of justice and law that grants no special privilege to anyone.[34]

As to the rights of non-Muslims living in a country where Muslims constitute the majority, it is evident from classical literature that Muslim jurists hold non-Muslims to be equal to Muslims regarding their political rights. They can take part in government and have access to public

---

[29] The Qur'an 6:108.
[30] Mawdudi, "Human Rights in Islam," p. 79.
[31] See the Qur'an 29:46.
[32] The Qur'an 42:38.
[33] Mawdudi, "Human Rights in Islam," p. 84.
[34] Jullundhri, "Human Rights and Islam," p. 39.

services.[35] The only post confined to a Muslim is the office of the Caliph, i.e., the head of state. This is based on a Qur'anic verse.[36] However, according to the classical authorities, the head of state can nominate a non-Muslim as a minister, a governor, or a secretary. As a result of this, many Christians and Jews have occupied high positions in Muslim governments, including the post of prime minister.[37]

Right to Equality. According to Islamic understanding, all human beings are brothers and sisters in the family of Allah. They all are the descendents of one father and one mother.[38] This means that the division of human beings into nations, races, groups and tribes is for the sake of distinction, so that people of one race or tribe may meet and be acquainted with the people belonging to another race or tribe and cooperate with one another. This division of the human race is neither meant for one nation to take pride over another, nor to regard another with contempt or disgrace, nor to regard them as a mean and degraded race and usurp their rights.[39] The superiority of one over another is only on the basis of God-consciousness, purity of character, and high morals.

The Prophet Muhammad also stated very well the equality of human beings in his address to Muslims on the occasion of his farewell pilgrimage when he said:

> O People! your God is one, your father is one. No Arab has superiority over a non-Arab, as no non-Arab has superiority over an Arab, neither does a man of brown color enjoy superiority over a man of black color, nor does a black man enjoy superiority over a man of brown color, except by piety.[40]

Thus, Islam established equality for all human beings, and struck at the very root of all distinctions based on color, race, language and nationality.

---

[35] Majid Khadduri, *The Islamic Conception of Justice* (Baltimore, John Hopkins University Press, 1984), pp. 162-164; Mohamed Talbi, "Religious Liberty: A Muslim Perspective," in *Muslims in Dialogue: The Evolution of A Dialogue* ed. Leonard Swidler (Lewiston, NY: Edwin Mellen Press, 1992), p. 474.

[36] See the Qur'an 4:59.

[37] Jullundhri, "Human Rights and Islam," p. 40; T. W. Arnold, *The Preaching of Islam* (Lahore, 1961), p. 64; Talbi, "Religious Liberty," p. 474; Muhammad Hamidullah, *Muslim Conduct of State*, 4th ed. (Lahore, Pakistan: Sh. Muhammad Ashraf, 1961), pp. 107-108.

[38] See the Qur'an 49:13.

[39] Mawdudi, "Human Rights in Islam," p. 69.

[40] Brohi, "Human Rights and Duties in Islam," p. 250.

Right to Justice. The right to justice is a universal human right that makes no distinction among people. Many verses in the Qur'an invite people to be just when they deal with worldly issues.[41] The verses related to justice make the point clear that believers have to be just not only with ordinary people but even with their enemies. In other words, the justice to which Islam invites her followers is not limited only to the followers of Islam, but is meant for all human beings. Muslims, therefore, cannot be unjust to anyone. They must treat every human being with justice and fairness.

Right to Protest Against Tyranny. Although the Qur'an commands Muslims to obey Allah, His Prophet, and those in authority over society,[42] neither the authority of the ruler nor the obedience of the subject is absolute or unlimited. Both are subject to the law.[43] Thus, when a person has been the victim of injustice or tyranny, Allah gives him the right to openly protest against the injury that has been done to him. This right is not limited to individuals but may also belong to a group of people. According to the Qur'anic imperative, if an individual or a group of people usurps power and, after assuming the reins of authority, begins to tyrannize, then individuals or groups of men or the entire population of the country have the right to protest against their authority.[44]

Right to Freedom of Expression. Islam gives the right of freedom of thought and expression to all people. However, it sets the condition that it should be used for the spreading of virtue and truth, and not for spreading evil and wickedness.[45] Under no circumstances would Islam allow evil and wickedness to be propagated. It does not give anybody the right to use abusive or offensive language in the name of criticism. The right to freedom of expression for the sake of propagating virtue and righteousness is not only a right in Islam but also an obligation. It is the right of a Muslim – and it is also his obligation – that he should warn and reprimand the evildoer and try to stop him from doing harm.[46]

---

[41] See the verses in the Qur'an related to justice, 2:282; 3:8, 18, 21; 4:3, 58, 127, 129; 5:8, 42; 6:152; 7:29, 159, 181; 12:4, 47, 54; 16:9, 76, 90; 20:2; 21:47; 26:15; 33:5; 57:25; 60:8.

[42] The Qur'an 4:59.

[43] Bernard Lewis, *The Political Language of Islam* (Chicago and London: University of Chicago Press, 1988), p. 91.

[44] Bayraklı, "Kur'an'da İnsan Hakları," p. 17. See also Lewis, *The Political Language of Islam*, pp. 91-116.

[45] The Qur'an says: "Help ye one another in righteousness and piety, but help ye not one another in sin and rancor: Fear Allah, for Allah is strict in punishment." 5:2.

[46] Brohi, "Human Rights and Duties in Islam," pp. 247-248.

While the Qur'an has described the faithful as those who enjoin what is proper and forbid what is improper,[47] it has defined the duties of statesmen as follows: "(They are) those who, if we establish them in the land, establish regular prayer and give *zakat*, enjoin the right and forbid wrong, with Allah rests the end (and decision) of (all) affairs."[48] Thus, the obligation of inviting people to righteousness and forbidding them to adopt paths of evil is incumbent on all true Muslims.[49]

Economic Rights

In the economic sphere, the basic tenet in Islam is that everything belongs to Allah alone. The following verse clearly indicates this principle: "Knowest thou not that to Allah belongeth the dominion of the heavens and the earth? And besides Him ye have neither patron nor helper."[50] Human beings are accepted as Allah's vice-regents on earth. Allah has subjected human beings to service. This is indicated as follows: "And He has subjected to you, as from Him, all that is in the heavens and on earth; behold, in that are signs indeed for those who reflect."[51] This reference is to all humanity.[52] Thus, Islam aims at the distribution of wealth to all people. Wealth must remain in constant circulation among all sections of the society, and should not become the monopoly of the rich.[53]

Islam promotes *neither* a pure capitalism *nor* socialism. It recognizes the diversity of capacities and talents, which is in itself beneficent, and consequently the diversity in earnings and material rewards.[54] It does not approve of an absolute equality in the distribution of wealth, as that would defeat the basic purpose of the diversity, and would amount to denying "the favor of Allah."[55]

The main purpose of the Islamic economic system is to create socio-economic justice in society. If there are some persons who are incapable of looking after their own needs, owing to permanent or temporary incapacity, they have a just call upon the wealth of society. It is

---

[47] See the Qur'an 9:71; 3:110.

[48] The Qur'an 22:41.

[49] Abu al- A'la Mawdudi, "Human Rights in Islam," *al-Tawhid*, vol. 4, no. 3 (Ramadan 1987), pp. 76-77.

[50] The Qur'an, 2:107. See also the Qur'an 3:189.

[51] The Qur'an 45:13.

[52] See the Qur'an 35:39.

[53] See the Qur'an 59:7.

[54] See the Qur'an 4:32.

[55] Muhammad Zafrullah Khan, *Islam and Human Rights* (Islamabad: Pakistan: Islam International Pub., 1989), p. 50; Muhammad Anas Zarka, "Islamic Distributive Schemes," in *Distributive Justice and Need Fulfillment in an Islamic Economy*, ed. Munawar Iqbal (Islamabad, Pakistan: International Islamic University, n. d.), pp. 190-191; see the Qur'an 16:71.

the responsibility of society to ensure such basic necessities as food, clothing, shelter, education, and health care for all, irrespective of their age, sex, color or religion.[56]

Islam has concrete regulations to ensure socio-economic justice and to eradicate absolute poverty. These regulations include positive measures such as working, *zakat*, voluntary spending, and inheritance; they also include prohibitions such as *riba* (usury), unlawful business transactions, and wasteful expenditures.[57]

However, if these regulations do not suffice to answer the needs of the poor and the destitute, then the state itself must meet their needs. Thus, Islam has not left the poor and the needy to the mercy of the rich. Instead, it has given rights and responsibilities concerning the poor directly to the state.[58]

In addition to those rights mentioned above, there are yet other human rights in the Qur'an that must be accepted and applied by Muslims.[59] However, we will not examine those rights here in detail. Instead, we will pass on to the second part of the paper.

SOME QUESTIONS ABOUT CONTEMPORARY HUMAN RIGHTS

While traditional Muslim authors have claimed that Islamic Law is fully consistent with and has always protected human rights, some contemporary Muslim scholars claim that some human rights advocated by Classical Islamic Law – that is, Shari'a – conflict with international human rights standards, and that there are some obvious conflicts between Shari'a and certain human rights. These are Shari'a's discrimination against

---

[56] Brohi, "Human Rights and Duties in Islam," p. 252.

[57] See for more information Mustafa Köylü, *Islam and Its Quest for Peace: Jihad, Justice and Education* (Washington, DC: CRVP, 2003), pp. 82-106.

[58] M. Umer Chapra, "The Economic System of Islam: A Discussion of Its Goals and Nature: Part IV 'The Role of the State'" *The Islamic Quarterly*, vol. 14, no. 4 (October-December 1970), p. 248.

[59] Riffat Hassan lists the following human rights mentioned in the Qur'an. These are 1) the right to a secure place of residence (2:85); the right to means of living (11:6; 6:156); the right to protection of one's personal possessions (2:29); the right to seek knowledge; the right to develop one's aesthetic sensibilities and enjoy the bounties created by Allah (7:32); the right to protection of one's covenant (17:34; 5:1; 3:177); the right to move freely (67:15); the right to seek asylum if one is living under oppression (4:97-100); the right to social and judicial autonomy for minorities (5:42-48); the right to protection of one's holy places (9:17); and the right to return to one's "spiritual center, that is Kaa'ba" (3:96; 22:25-26; 3:96; 2:125). See "On Human Rights and the Qur'anic Perspective," in *Muslims in Dialogue: The Evolution of A Dialogue*, ed. Leonard Swidler (Lewiston, NY: Edwin Mellen Press, 1992), pp. 459-460.

women, the law of apostasy, and the status and rights of non-Muslims. Let us consider these matters in detail.

The Situation of Woman

Some contemporary Muslim thinkers claim that the most important general principle of Shari'a concerning the status and rights of women is the notion of *qawama* (guardianship and authority of men over women). This understanding is based on the following verse (4:34): "Men are the protectors and maintainers of women, because Allah has given the one more (strength) than the other, and because they support them from their means."[60] According to the classical interpretation of this verse, men as a group are the guardians of and superior to women as a group, and the men of a particular family are the guardians of and superior to the women of that family.[61]

Abdullahi Ahmad An-Na'im interprets this verse differently than the classical Muslim understanding. He writes that this verse presents *qawama* as a consequence of two conditions: men's advantage over, and financial support of, women. The fact that men are generally physically stronger than most women is not relevant in modern times where the rule of law prevails over physical might. Moreover, modern circumstances make the economic independence of women from men more readily realized and appreciated. In other words, "neither of the conditions – advantages of physical might or earning power set by verse 4:34 as the justification for the *qawama* of men over women – is tenable today."[62]

Another scholar who does not accept the notion of discrimination between men and women is Riffat Hassan. She writes about this matter as follows:

> Having spent seven years in the study of the Qur'anic perspective relating to woman, I am convinced that the Qur'an is not biased against woman and does not discriminate against them. On the contrary, because of its protective attitude toward all downtrodden and oppressed

---

[60] Roger Garaudy, "Human Rights and Islam: Foundation, Tradition, Violation." *The Ethics of World Religions and Human Rights*, ed. Hans Küng and Jürgen Moltmann (London: SCM Press, 1990), p. 56;

[61] Abdullahi Ahmad An-Na'im, "Human Rights in the Muslim World: Socio-Political Conditions and Scriptural Imperatives: A Preliminary Inquiry," *Harvard Human Rights Journal*, vol. 3 (Spring 1990), p. 37.

[62] Abdullahi Ahmad An-Na'im, "Qur'an, Shari'a and Human Rights: Foundations, Deficiencies and Prospects," in *The Ethics of World Religions and Human Rights*, ed. Hans Küng and Jürgen Moltmann (London: SCM Press, 1990), pp. 61-69 at p. 63.

classes, it appears to be weighted in many ways in favor of women.[63]

In fact, according to the Qur'an, Allah created man and woman from a single life-cell or spirit.[64] Both men and women have male and female components,[65] and both together constitute the human species.[66] In addition, according to the Qur'an, among human beings there is no basis for superiority other than that of piety or obedience to Allah.[67] On eight occasions[68] the Qur'an reminds us that Allah makes no distinction between human beings, be they men or women, except between those who do good and those who do wrong.[69]

The second important general principle of Shari'a influencing the status and rights of women concerns the question of polygamy. According to this common understanding, a Muslim man may marry up to four wives at the same time, but a Muslim woman can be married to only one man at a time.[70] A Muslim man may divorce his wife, or any of his wives, by unilateral repudiation (*talaq*) without having to give any reasons or justify his action to any person or authority. In contrast, a Muslim woman can obtain a divorce only by consent of the husband or by judicial decree for limited specific grounds such as the husband's inability or unwillingness to provide for his wife.[71]

Is the situation related to polygamy really like this? Concerning polygamy, Hassan says that the Qur'an did not institute polygamy; on the contrary, it limited it. The Qur'an imposes conditions that make it almost impossible, saying

> If ye fear that ye shall not be able to deal justly with the orphans, marry women of your choice two, or three, or four; but if ye fear that ye shall not be able to deal justly (with them) then only one, or that which your right hand possesses. That will be more suitable, to prevent you from doing injustice.[72]

---

[63] Hassan, "On Human Rights and the Qur'anic Perspective," p. 460.

[64] See the Qur'an 4:1; 7:189; 16:72; 30:21.

[65] See the Qur'an 49:13.

[66] Hassan, "On Human Rights and the Qur'anic Perspective," p. 460.

[67] See the Qur'an 49:13.

[68] See the Qur'an 3:95; 4:124; 13:23; 17:40; 43:17; 48:6; 57:18.

[69] Garaudy, "Human Rights and Islam," p. 56.

[70] See the Qur'an 4:3.

[71] Polygamy is based on verse 4:3 of the Qur'an. The husband's power to chastise his wife to the extent of beating her is based on verse 4:34 of the Qur'an.

[72] The Qur'an 4:3; see also 33:4.

Thus, although polygamy was intended by the Qur'an to be for the protection of orphans and widows, in practice Muslims have made it a dreadful and dehumanizing instrument for the brutalizing of women's sensibilities.[73]

Then what is the real situation? First of all, we should know that, although the verses related to polygamy were taken to apply to all Muslim women, some of these verses refer only to the wives of the Prophet. Secondly, while the values and customs are supposed to be Islamic or at least consistent with the dictates of Islam, most of them are based on the values and customs of the particular society. Thus, we cannot generalize these rules or exceptions so that they apply to all Muslim women and men. In addition, when we read carefully the verse (4:3) that is related to polygamy, we see that the verse emphasizes not polygamy but monogamy.

Status and Rights of non-Muslims

It is a historical fact that while the doors of many countries were opened by force or *jihad*, as was the general custom then, Islam itself has almost never been imposed by compulsion. On this point, Muslims have followed the Qur'anic teaching. They provided non-Muslims, called *dhimmis*, with a sound protection against the most unbearable forms of religious intolerance.[74] According to Talbi, with two or three historical exceptions, the *dhimmis* have never been prevented from following the religion of their choice, from worshipping, or from organizing their communities in accordance with their own law. It can be even said that, in the beginning, their situation was often greatly improved by Islamic conquest. Thus, they enjoyed long periods of tolerance and real prosperity, very often holding high positions in administrative, court and economic circles. However, it is also a historical fact that at certain times and places (during the reign of al-Mutawakkil [847-861 C.E.] and of al-Hakim [996-1021 C.E.]) they suffered from some discrimination. This discrimination, especially in matters of dress, took an openly humiliating form.[75]

At this point, we should say that although all Muslims are bound by the Qur'anic teaching, Muslim traditional theology developed in a way that for historical reasons did not always fit with the spirit of the Qur'an. Moreover, we must also take account of the situation of medieval times. In the medieval context of wars, hostilities, and treacheries, this policy of discrimination or open oppression was often prompted or strongly backed by the theologians. According to the medieval mentality, it was not a virtue

---

[73] Hassan, "On Human Rights and the Qur'anic Perspective," p. 462.

[74] For a general discussion of this matter, see Osman Güner, *Resûlullah'ın Ehl-i Kitap'la Münâsabetleri* (İstanbul: Fecr Yayınları, 1997), pp. 247-339.

[75] Talbi, "Religious Liberty," p. 474.

to consider all human beings as equal. "How could one consider as equal Truth and Error, true believers and heretics!"[76]

Still, numerous verses of the Qur'an provide for freedom of choice and non-compulsion in religious belief and conscience.[77] These verses have been either de-emphasized as having been "overruled" by other verses which were understood to legitimate coercion, or "interpreted" in ways which permitted such coercion. For example, verse 9:29 of the Qur'an[78] was taken as the foundation of the whole system of *dhimma*, and its consequent discrimination against non-Muslims. An-Na'im suggests that the above-mentioned categorical verse 9:29 (regulating the status of non-Muslims) can be superseded by the more general verses providing for freedom of religion and inherent dignity of all human beings without distinction as to faith or belief.[79]

The Law of Apostasy

Talbi writes that "among all the other revealed texts, only the Qur'ān stresses religious liberty in such an accurate and unambiguous way. The reason is that faith, to be true and reliable faith, needs absolutely to be a free and voluntary act."[80] However, there are some applications concerning religious liberty which do not fit the spirit of the Qur'an. The case of apostasy is an example of this. According to Talbi, in this field too, traditional theology did not follow the Qur'anic teaching. According to this theology, though conversion to Islam must be without coercion, it is not practically possible, once inside Islam, to get out of it. The conversion from Islam to another religion is considered treason, and the apostate is liable to the penalty of death.[81]

At this point, the traditional theologians rely on two justifications: The one is the application of Abu Bakr (632-634 C.E.) who fought the tribes who rejected his authority and refused to pay him the alms taxes. The

---

[76] Talbi, "Religious Liberty," pp. 474-75.

[77] See the Qur'an 2:256; 18:29.

[78] This verse reads: "Fight those who believe not in Allah nor the Last Day, nor hold that forbidden which hath been forbidden by Allah and His Messenger, nor acknowledge the religion of truth, from among the People of the Book until they pay the *jizya* (poll-tax) with willing submission, and feel themselves subdued." The Qur'an 9:29.

[79] An-Na'im, "Human Rights in the Muslim World," pp. 48-49.

[80] Talbi, "Religious Liberty," p. 470.

[81] Talbi, "Religious Liberty," p. 475. While according to the Hanbalits, the apostate must immediately be put to death; to the three other schools of *fiqh*, he or she is given three days to think it over, and it is only if he or she refuses to retract that he or she must be put to death. See Talbi, "Religious Liberty," endnote, 16.

other reason is the *hadith* of the Prophet Muhammad: "Anyone who changes his religion must be put to death."[82]

In fact, when these two reasons for apostasy are examined in detail, it will be seen that apostasy is just a historical and local event. First of all, it should be pointed out that there is no mention of a required death penalty against the apostate in the Qur'an. In all verses related to the case of apostasy,[83] without a single exception, the punishment of the apostate who persists in rejection of Islam after having embraced it, is left to Allah's judgment and to the afterlife. The Qur'an just argues, warns, or recommends the proper attitude to be adopted without ever threatening death.[84]

Secondly, when we see the practice of apostasy in the history of Islam, the penalty of death essentially is – more or less – mixed with rebellion and highway robbery. The cited cases of "apostates" killed during the ruling of Abu Bakr are all without exception of persons who, as consequences of their "apostasy," turned their weapons against the Muslim community. Thus, the penalty of death appears in these circumstances as an act of self-defense in a situation of war. Because of this, some schools of Islam, such as the Hanafit, do not condemn a woman apostate to death "because women, contrary to men, are not fit for war." Furthermore, the *hadith* that orders one to kill those who are apostate is not technically *mutawatir*,[85] and consequently it is not binding. Because of this, Talbi suggests that there are many persuasive reasons "to consider it undoubtedly forged. It may have been forged under the influence of Leviticus (24:16) and Deuteronomy (13:2-19)" – where the stoning of the apostate to death is ordered – "if not directly, then perhaps indirectly through the Jews and Christians converted to Islam."[86]

CONCLUDING REMARKS

In this situation presented above, should Muslims take the Universal Declaration of Human Rights or Islamic Human Rights as the source of human rights standards? To some modern Muslims such as an-Na'im, the Universal Declaration of Human Rights should be taken as a source and base. To him, European law governing commercial, criminal, and constitutional matters in almost all Muslim countries has replaced most of the Shari'a principles. Only family law and inheritance continue to be

---

[82] For this *hadith* see, e.g., Buhari, *Sahih,* Cairo: ed. al-Sa'b, n.d., IX, 19; Abu Dawud, *Sunan,* Cairo, 1952, II, p. 440.

[83] See for example, Qur'an 2:109, 217; 3:85-89, 91, 99-100, 106, 149; 5:57-59; 47:25, 32, 34, 38.

[84] Talbi, "Religious Liberty," p. 477.

[85] A *hadith* is called *mutawatir* when several driving chains of reliable warrantors transmit it.

[86] Talbi, "Religious Liberty," p. 477.

governed by Shari'a, even in countries such as Saudi Arabia which claims always to have maintained Shari'a as its sole legal system; otherwise, these countries have enacted numerous "regulations" based on European law and practice in the commercial and public administrational fields.[87] Thus, An-Na'im believes that "Muslims are obliged, as a matter of faith, to conduct their private and public affairs in accordance with the dictates of Islam, but there is room for legitimate disagreement over the precise nature of these dictates in the modern context. Religious texts, like all other texts, are open to a variety of interpretations."[88] He argues that given the historical contexts of both initial revelation and the subsequent interpretations of the texts of the Qur'an and Sunna, some texts are no longer applicable while others need to be interpreted differently. He believes that divine revelation must be understood and applied in historical context, because it addresses us in our human condition and circumstances which change over time.[89]

When we examine the matter of human rights in Islam we should accept that, as An-Na'im says, first, there is no such thing as *only one possible* or valid understanding of the Qur'an or conception of Islam, since each is informed by the individual and collective orientation of Muslims as they address themselves to the Qur'an with a view to deriving normative implications for human behavior.

> Every person always understands the text in question, and drives its normative implications, in terms of his or her knowledge and experience of the world: perceptions of self-interest in political, economic and social contexts, realities of inter-communal and/or international relations, and so forth.[90]

Thus, a change in the orientation of Muslims will contribute to a transformation of their understanding of it, and hence of their conception of Islam itself.[91]

So, when we interpret the verses of the Qur'an, we should take into account the broad historical, cultural and scientific changes that have taken place in the modern world. Thus, in the words of An-Na'im, the orientation of modern Muslims should be different from that of earlier generations because of the radical transformation of the existential and material

---

[87] An-Na'im, "Human Rights in the Muslim World," p. 20.

[88] An-Na'im, "Human Rights in the Muslim World," p. 15.

[89] See An-Na'im, "Human Rights in the Muslim World," endnote 1, p. 14.

[90] Abdullahi Ahmad An-Na'im, "Toward an Islamic Hermeneutics for Human Rights," in *Human Rights and Religious Values: An Uneasy Relationship?* Ed. Abdullahi A. An-Na'im and Others (Grand Rapids, Michigan: William B. Eerdmans Pub., 1995), p. 233.

[91] An-Na'im, "Toward an Islamic Hermeneutics for Human Rights," p. 233.

circumstances of their life today in contrast to those of the past. Since knowledge and experience tend to change over time, Islam should not be bound by any particular understanding of its scriptural sources.[92]

More importantly, as some contemporary Muslim scholars suggest, Shari'a was constructed by Muslim jurists over the first three centuries of Islam. Thus, although it was derived from the fundamental divine sources of Islam, it is not divine, because it is the product of human interpretation of those sources. Moreover, this process of construction through human interpretation took place within a specific historical context which is drastically different from our own. Consequently, it is possible for contemporary Muslims to undertake a similar process of interpretation and application of the Qur'an and Sunna in the present historical context in order to develop an alternative public law of Islam which is appropriate for implementation today.[93]

As a result, we can say that the fault concerning human rights violations is not that of historical Shari'a as seen in its proper context. Rather, the fault is that of those contemporary Muslims who insist on implementing archaic concepts in modern times. The early Muslims exercised their right and responsibility to interpret the divine sources of Islam in light of their own historical context in order to produce a coherent and practicable system for their own time. It is the right and responsibility of contemporary Muslims to do the same in order to produce concrete solutions to the problems of Muslims today.

Ondokuz Mayıs University
Faculty of Theology
Samsun, Turkey

---

[92] An-Na'im, "Toward an Islamic Hermeneutics for Human Rights," p. 238.

[93] Abdullahi Ahmad an-Na'im, *Toward an Islamic Reformation: Civil Liberties, Human Rights, and International Law* (Syracuse: Syracuse University Press, 1990), pp. 185-186.

CHAPTER IV

"PERSON AND COMMUNITY: RIGHT AND DUTIES": FROM A ISLAMIC PERSPECTIVE

M.S. SUJIMON

My area of specialization relates to the science of the principles of Islamic law *Usul al-Fiqh* – and I will present briefly four points. First, I will propose a definition of the theme, and then give a description of the meaning of dialogue. Following this, I will briefly comment on the harmonious relationship between Tradition and Reason. Finally, I will provide an outline of the procedure of the work undertaken in this volume, which is the direct consequence of the definition and description I propose.

DEFINITION OF THE THEME OF THIS VOLUME

The title of this volume, "The Dialogue of Cultural Traditions: a Global Perspective," indicates that the papers will deal with "Person and Community" and, particularly, with issues related to "Rights and Duties." Does this formulation mean that the theme is founded on a twofold opposition where the person and community would be in the same relation as rights and duties? Or is it that the person and the community – each of them – have the two kinds of attributes related to the rights and duties? The answer depends on how we understand the notion of duty or responsibility. Rights – depending on the conditions under which they may be achieved – may be seen as duties. That is, human beings have to strive in order to obtain their rights: Islam, for example, makes it a duty to defend one's rights. It is also a duty to participate in the life of the community and so to have one's political and civil rights. To be a free citizen is not only a right but also a duty.

SIGNIFICANCE OF DIALOGUE

The term 'dialogue' is a happy one. It signifies the very essence of the human being. As a matter of fact, language – as the specific difference of the human being – is *per se* dialogical. We cannot imagine a mono-logical language. And what is true between two individuals is *a fortiori* truer among peoples, because there we have a dialogue of dialogues: every culture is *per se* dialogical, and human culture as exhibiting a universal bond among human beings cannot be but a cultural dialogue.

Cultural Traditions

In this regard, the Qur'an says, إنا خلقناكم من ذكر وانثى وجعلناكم شعوبا
وقبائل لتعارفوا إن أكرمكم عند الله اتقاكم— which means: Human beings stem from a couple but develop in peoples and tribes in order to acknowledge each other and to be good to each other. This Qur'anic verse means that human relationships are defined by an epistemological and ethical bond; human beings must try to know one another and to do good and avoid evil. This is why the above Qur'anic verse concludes with the notion of moral dignity – an alternative to social and economic hierarchy, which could be regarded as the main source of domination.

A Global Perspective

There are two contradictory visions of globalization: the first seeks free collaboration between equal peoples, and the second presupposes an attitude the unfortunate consequence of which is the enslavement of the weak by the strong. So globalization may lead to a genuine mutual enrichment of traditions which acknowledge each other.

CONVERGENCE OF THE VISIONS

The papers presented in the pages of this volume converge towards the same purpose. For example, Prof. Rolando Gripaldo (of De La Salle University, Phillipines), Prof. Plamen Makariev (of Sofia University, Bulgaria), Prof. Dr. Mustafa Koylu (of the Faculty of Theology of the University of Ondukuz Maiz, Samsung, Turkiye), and Prof. Sirajul Islam (of Visva Bharati University, Santiniketan, India)[1] present papers in which one may find a more precise definition of the ingredients of the crisis we are talking about.

Rolando Gripaldo discusses the relationship between Person and Society. He presents many useful definitions grounded in philosophical and religious thought. Plamen Makariev discusses the relation between identity, social, cultural and economical factors. His balanced conclusion leads to a dialectical definition of the relationship identity of the person and diversity of culture. Furthermore, he presents an original and genuine concept of cultural identity as *per se* multi-cultural identity. We may say that this vision coincides with the acknowledgement of the third generation of human rights viz., human cultural rights. Mustafa Koylu addresses the problem of human rights from a historical and religious perspective.

---

[1] Prof. Andrew I. Isiguzo (of the University of Benin, Department of Philosophy, Nigeria) and Prof. Abu Ya'rub Marzouki (of the International Islamic University Malaysia (IIUM), Department of Usul al-Din and Comparative Religion) also gave papers in the session at which the papers in this volume were initially presented.

Combining these two perspectives in the Islamic tradition, he defines the core of his paper by saying,

> I will try to indicate human rights in light of the Qur'an and Sunna. For this purpose, I will divide it into two main parts. While the first part deals with human rights mostly based on the views of some traditional Muslims' views that reflect the principles of classical Islamic law, the second part will elaborate some human rights in Islam which are questionable in our modern times when compared to the Declaration of Human Rights.

Finally, Sirajul Islam's paper, entitled "Human Dignity and Human Rights: An Appraisal from the Viewpoint of Present-Day Indian Islam," highlights the term 'human dignity' and addresses the question of what are 'human rights' by comparing these notions with the Islamic viewpoint that claims that dignity is an essential human character because human beings are regarded as vice-regents of God. As far as human rights in Islam is concerned, he states, "Islam recognizes that the human being is an embodiment of mind, body and soul."

A PROPOSAL

These questions are important, given the crises of our era. Being a Malaysian, where religious tolerance and peaceful co-existence hold – where the six main ancient traditions of human history (i.e., the religions of Hinduism, Buddhism, Confucianism, Christianity, as well as the religions of Islam and Sikhism) work together in a harmonious and brotherly way – I believe that this fact serves to refute the theory of the clash of civilizations. This result may be understood as a happy combination of tradition and reason. Islam, as a political power, has applied Qur'anic principles which clearly acknowledge liberty of conscience or faith and which explicitly refers to two revealed religions and two non-revealed religions. It also guarantees to believers the protection of their shrines, irrespective of the dogmas and practices of their faith. The vision of Tradition and Person in Islam and how to combine between tradition (tureth) and Reason (naql) in order to adequately define the relation between these two dimensions of social life.

Kulliyyah of Islamic Revealed Knowledge and Human Sciences
International Islamic University
Kuala Lumpur, Malaysia

HUMAN DIGNITY AND HUMAN RIGHTS: AN APPRAISAL FROM THE VIEWPOINT OF PRESENT-DAY INDIAN ISLAM

MD. SIRAJUL ISLAM

The present world has the amazing character of scientific and technological progress, and it is much more integrated – in terms of people from various spheres – than ever before. As a result, the days of isolated civilizations and regional cultures are gradually fading away. There was a time when divergent cultures and civilizations could co-exist and flow simultaneously without any interference from others. But at present, the shape of matters is totally changed. Scientific and technological progress places a high degree of emphasis on materialistic pleasure and satisfaction. Men are little interested in promoting the inner value and dignity of human being. They are focused on individual satiation, as more and more enjoyments and pleasures are offered to people. But, at the same time, more and more disparities among people are also being revealed, and many have raised questions, such as: Are all these materialistic advances real improvements or not? It is obvious that 'humanistic' values are gradually diminishing in the present era. The current statistics shows that in this 'advanced' age, many people are still not even able to fulfill their basic needs – they are not getting just and equal treatment in the various spheres of life. Even today, many people are suffering from unjust wages, malnutrition, restricted health services, and the undemocratic distribution of education, and people also face the problems of war, the arbitrary utilization of chemical weapons, unjust dealings in natural resources, unfair distribution of economic goods, and so on. Not only those who suffer, but even those in the 'developed' world are facing problems of racism, poverty, terrorism, and many other evils. These evils and injustices have gradually spread over the various parts of the globe, violating human dignity and human rights. It is a matter of great pain that, due to their petty interests, the leading political and economic personalities are not taking stronger measures to eradicate such problems. While the concepts of human dignity and human justice have been discussed in many fora, a comprehensive and constructive discussion is still awaited. Some are doing something, but still not enough to address the correlative needs. I think that philosophers, social scientists and political leaders have an enormous responsibility to diagnose these social illnesses and to converse with us regarding the causes and any possible remedies. It is a crucial task because there are diversified forms of injustice and obstruction. However, philosophers have a greater responsibility to assess these structures and steer people towards permanent solutions.

Now legitimate questions emerge: What is human dignity and what are human rights? How far are they interrelated? What role can they play in this ultra-modern world? These are to be discussed in the paper philosophically and dispassionately. This paper will be divided into two sections. At the outset we will indicate something about the historical and philosophical background of human dignity and human rights and then, in the later phase, we will proceed to other relevant points and their link with contemporary Indian Islam.

BACKGROUND OF HUMAN DIGNITY AND HUMAN RIGHTS

The traditional view of human dignity and human rights is partly found in the writings of Plato and Aristotle. In the eyes of Plato, the concept of "justice" is an all-encompassing "political virtue," so that the good society and just society are one and the same. Plato basically used the word "*dikaiosyne*," which is usually translated as "justice." The term "*dikaiosyne*" possessed a very broad meaning in Ancient Greece; this term was often used to indicate "rectitude" or "right conduct." It is true that "justice" cannot be identified with "right conduct," but this idea of "justice" draws our attention to the fact that individuals should receive the treatment which is proper for them. Plato's "justice" is an entire 'virtue' theory, whereas Aristotle believes in egalitarian ideals of justice where "equality" is the main concern. His egalitarian maxim is in favour of a proportional equality, which is related to "share and share alike." After Plato and Aristotle, Hobbes and Mill utilized the notion of "natural equality," and propagated the theory that "all men are equal by nature," calling for the principle of equal treatment for and to all. To maintain natural equality, Hobbes says it is obvious that there are many signs of natural inequalities in society, but man should guide himself in the wise way to provide "equal treatment for equals and unequal treatment for unequals."[1] Mill's ethical theory of utilitarianism is one of the classic statements regarding equality and justice, which envisages that justice is a name for certain moral requirements, and puts collective well being on the scale of social utility, therefore being a paramount obligation.[2] This view received its most influential expression at the end of the seventeenth century in the writings of John Locke. According to Locke, the natural law provided that "no one ought to harm another in his life, health, liberty, or possessions." Therefore this law may be said to give each a natural right to life, liberty and

---

[1] Hugo A. Bedau, *Justice and Equality* (Englewood Cliffs, NJ: Prentice Hall, 1971), pp. 5-6.

[2] Bedau, *Justice and Equality*, p.10.

property.[3] Actually, in the natural condition, men would also possess the right to do what was necessary to protect the rights of others: men would maintain peace by handing over some power to a common authority. In the most recent phase, John Rawls and Bernard Williams have interpreted the theory of justice and equality in terms of logical reasoning. So, from the above discussion, it is evident that people are conscious about human dignity and rights in order to determine their standard of living, as well as maintaining equal treatment in the society.

WHAT IS HUMAN DIGNITY?

The dignity of the human being is an essential concept in society as well as in morality, because through it the quality and honor of a people can be determined, and from the sense of dignity the concept of human rights can also be derived. There is a common belief that the dignity of the human being can be measured through the commercial or economic status of the people in a society and that the G.N.P (Gross National Product) of a particular state may be used as an instrument to measure the quality of human life. But surely this is not absolutely true. The quality of human life is a very complex phenomenon. It is not confined to the commercial or economic system; rather, it touches the various spheres of people's lives – e.g., health, food, education, liberty, equality, the franchise, and so on. We need to know how people are able to live in society in a dignified manner. The sense of dignity makes the difference between human beings and robots. The human being is an embodiment of physical and psychological elements, but the robot is a physical entity only, having no true mind. The life of the human being is closely related to self-respect, through which the dignity of human being can be preserved.[4]

Webster's Encyclopedia Dictionary describes the idea of human dignity as "respect, degree of excellence and nobility."[5] In assessing the universal applicability of human dignity, we have to understand the value of the life of the human being, and it is quite obvious that value-based life is undoubtedly a sign of good life, where equality, dignity and justice are regarded as the powerful instruments of human life. Actually, human dignity is the foundation of each and every right, whether it be political, economic or social. Here, all democratic values are intimately connected with the protection of human dignity and the all-round development of human being. Only human rights and human dignity, when protected by society, are able to afford persons the opportunity to develop their

---

[3] David Miller, *Blackwell Encyclopedia of Political Thought* (Oxford: Blackwell, 1991), p. 3.

[4] Martha Nussbaum and Amartya Sen, *The Quality of Life* (Oxford: Clarendon Press, 1993), pp. 3, 9.

[5] Adam Kuper and Jessica Kuper, *The Social Science Encyclopedia*, 2nd ed. (London: Routledge & Kegan Paul, 1995), pp. 385-386.

personalities in all respects. A bonded slave deprived of even his elementary rights – and, similarly, caste classifications or racism – compel people to live in inhumane conditions. Hence, to preserve human dignity and human rights, it is an essential duty of all societies to evolve a value system. With this intention, the United Nations Charter declares, "We the people of the United Nations determine to reaffirm faith in fundamental human rights, in the dignity and worth of human persons, in the equal rights of men and women and of nations, large and small." This was reaffirmed by the Universal Declaration of Human Rights in 1948: "Whereas recognition of the inherent Dignity and of the equal and inalienable rights of all members of the human family is the foundation of freedom, justice and peace in the world...." All international covenants are to follow this in all aspects of the society, so that human dignity and human rights are preserved.

WHAT ARE HUMAN RIGHTS?

Once upon a time there was no concept of "rights" in society. People were only conscious of the need for food, and they collected it by any means, without having any rules or regulations. They did not bother even for shelter. People lived only in caves or caverns to protect themselves from rain, cold and any natural disasters. In the course of time, they felt the need for laws and principles in order to avoid chaotic situations in society. As a result, many theories have been developed, so that people may enjoy rights in a rational way. Among the various rights systems we have are: the goal rights system, deontological rights systems, utilitarian rights systems, and consequentialist rights systems. All these systems are mainly developed for the preservation of human rights.

Human rights are rights which persons hold by virtue of the human condition. They constitute the common language of "humanity." Actually, human rights are only for human beings and not for the state. Thus, they are not dependent upon the grant or the permission of the state, and also they cannot be withdrawn by fiat of the state or government. The beneficiaries of human rights are individuals. The human rights which each person is entitled to are, for example, the right to a fair trial – and these are the same for a person who lives under a legal system of common law and civil order or not. States have the obligation to ensure that their legal systems offer full protection of human rights. Human rights consist not only of civil and political rights. These rights also cover the economic, social and cultural aspects of human life.[6]

After the Second World War, people felt the need of a universal declaration of human rights, and this was adopted by the United Nations organization on 10 December 1948 at Paris. To protect human rights,

---

[6] S. Abul Hasan Ali Nadwi, *Muslims in India* (Lucknow: Islamic Research and Publications, 1980), p. 72.

international covenants have adopted or ratified extensions of the Universal Declaration of Human Rights (e.g., in the year 1966). In 1989, after the fall of the Berlin Wall, it was decided to convene a world conference on human rights. The conference took place in Vienna in 1993, where it was reaffirmed that fundamental human rights can never be derogated by the state, even during a period of emergency – i.e., no emergency justifies torture, nor can it remove a person's freedom of thought, practice of religion, or acquisition of education.

Contemporary moral and political philosophy is more likely to establish human rights on a commitment to fundamental rules, such as freedom, autonomy, and equality, together with other considerations relating to the essentials of human well being.[7]

RIGHTS AND DUTIES

Rights and duties are reciprocally related to each other. Rights imply duties and vice versa. Without duties, rights cannot be achieved. The term "right" signifies what is "in accordance with what is good and just, which is opposite of any improper action.[8] Moral philosopher Robert Nozick understands a right as follows: "It does not determine a social ordering but insists on setting the constraints within which a social choice is to be made, by excluding certain alternatives, fixing others, and so on."[9] The term duty is that "which one is expected to do by moral obligation," and it is related to value consciousness. Contemporary philosophers like Derek Parfit and Thomas Nagel have interpreted morality in terms of "Agent relative values" and "Agent natural values" respectively. However, the sense of duty is an essential criterion to enjoy rights in a society.

HUMAN DIGNITY IN ISLAM

In Islam, the notion of human dignity is essential. It says that human beings are the vice-regents of God. He bestowed on them power and honor superior to His other creatures (*laqad Khalaqnal insana fi ahsane taqbeem*, The Quran), i.e., "We have indeed created man in the best of moulds."[10] The sense of dignity distinguishes human beings from beasts or animals. Prior to the advent of Islam, men behaved and were treated as animals: racism, untouchability, and apathy were prevalent in society and

---

[7] N.K. Singh, *Social Justice and Human Rights in Islam* (New Delhi: Gyan Publishing House, 1998), p. 33.

[8] Webster's *Encyclopedic Unabridged Dictionary of the English Language*, New Revised Edition (Avenel: New Jersey: Gramacy Books, Random House, 1996), p. 1233.

[9] Amartya Sen, "Rights and Agency," *Philosophy and Public Affairs*, Vol. 2, No. 1 (1981): 20-21.

[10] Al-Quran, (tr. Yusuf Ali), 0, 95:4.

were powerful instruments of discrimination. As a result, a sense of superiority and inferiority had grown in Indian society. People existed for the service of the higher classes. Lower classes had no freedom or dignity in their lives, and the laboring classes were deprived in all matters. Women were treated as commodities of enjoyment; they had no dignity. Most of the young girls were used as concubines of the higher classes. After the emergence of Islam, Prophet Hadrat Muhammad strongly denounced all these social evils, and he had a sense of dignity and honor in society. He fought against all discrimination and social evil, and proclaimed equality and justice towards all. The dignity of women is preserved in Islam in a very reasonable way. No religion had shown similar respect to women before the emergence of Islam. With Islam, the dignity of women received protection by divine prescriptions, and severe punishment is prescribed particularly for those who make scandalous observations about them. Maintenance of property and privacy has been made obligatory in Islam. The holy Quran lays down prescriptions for the honor of women: those who will enter the house of another should seek prior permission before entering and also salute the inhabitants respectfully.[11] In Islam, the lower classes enjoy equal status in all matters. In such a society, a Muslim will have no hesitation in dining with another Muslim or even with a non-Muslim. A group of Muslims can eat together from the same vessel, and one may partake of the others' leftover food or drink with full enjoyment and friendship. The master and the slave may perform *namaz* (prayer) in the same row, standing shoulder to shoulder with each other. Racism and untouchability are completely foreign to Muslim society. Any learned and pious person, however lowborn and economically deprived, can lead prayer, and the highest dignitaries and kings and noblemen will follow him readily. The sense of superiority and inferiority on the basis of black or white skin are completely eliminated in Islam. It does not recognize the past sin of Adam and Eve; rather, it has given equal and reasonable status and dignity to men and women.

It is quite obvious, then, that Islam recognizes the dignity of all human beings and the importance of maintaining a minimum standard of living, so that it can embrace all aspects of the quality of life with full respect and dignity.

HUMAN RIGHTS IN ISLAM

As we noted earlier, the Universal Declaration of Human Rights was proclaimed by the United Nations General Assembly in 1948. This document basically represents the maximum degree of consensus to achieve the final goal of humanity. But Islam has felt the need of such rights from

---

[11] Al-Quran, 2:34, see also S.A. Ali, "Family Life in Islam," in *Islam at a Glance*, ed. Hakim Abdul Hamid (New Delhi: Indian Institute of Islamic Studies & Vikas Publishing House Pvt. Ltd., 1981), pp. 58-59.

the very beginning of human civilization. Islam is highly humanistic in character, because human rights are an integral part of Islam and man is the center of these rights. The holy Quran has clearly stated about man: "certainly we have created in the goodliest fabric, again we abase him (to be) the lowest of the low."[12] According to Islam, man is the highest form of creation (*asraful makhluqat*). The holy Quran attests to this as, "We said to the angels, Bow down to Adam, and they bowed down," which expresses man's superiority. Again, some say man is he "to whom the angels were made to offer obeisance and for whom whatsoever else in the earth is made to do service."[13] The holy Quran again says, "God has created man as his vice regent on earth and placed His trust in him."[14] In Islam, the term 'man' has a broad meaning, which signifies both male and female. It also gives position to all human beings with full respect and dignity and differentiates them from things. Its aim is to attain universality and it extends itself to the whole of mankind as constituting one fellowship. Islam recognizes that the human being is an embodiment of mind, body and soul. Hence, it gives special attention to the basic needs and requirements of human beings, which are not confined entirely to material purposes – but, at the same time, it serves the spiritual aspect of human beings – an aspect which is lacking in the UN Declaration of Human Rights. It also recognizes that the human being is a subtle and noble being, in which various complex sides are integrated into one whole. Its basic belief is that humanity is one and that all human beings are equal. No person can claim superiority over others by virtue of his race or descent or wealth. According to Islam, superiority can be determined only on the basis of a person's good and pious deeds, which are directly related to each human's freedom and responsibility. At the same time, it abolished the system of priesthood and hereditary kingship, and militates for *democratic socialism* to maintain social justice and equality as a whole.

But it is a matter of great regret that Muslims in various corners of the world have deviated from Islam's basic teachings. They frequently violate human rights for personal gain. In reaction to this, some independent thinkers, egalitarian Muslims and non-government organizations have raised their voices to implement and improve human rights in Muslim countries. In supporting this, one of the earliest Muslim human rights organizations was established in Morocco in December 1933. Thereafter, the Iranian committee and some human rights groups have taken special initiatives to defend human freedom and human rights in Muslim countries. Since 1980, the Arab Human Rights organization has become the most important human rights agency in the Muslim world and, through their special initiative, the Universal Islamic Declaration of Human Rights was

---

[12] Al Quran, 94:4 & 95:5.

[13] Al-Quran, 2:34, see also Syed Abdul Latif, *Bases of Islamic Culture* (Hyderabad: Institute of Indo-Middle East Cultural Studies, 1959), p. 13.

[14] Al-Quran 2: 30,6:165.

announced on 19 September 1981. This Islamic Declaration of Human Rights is not only for Muslims but for all; hence, it includes the word "every individual" or "all persons" in its declaration instead of the word "Muslims." The Islamic Declaration contains some rights that are specifically for Muslims, but most of the rights are effective universally.

In Islam, there are huge numbers of rights which are closely related to human needs but, for convenience of our discussion, we will confine our outlook to the most prominent features of it. In my view, the most prominent human rights are as follows:

The Right to Live

Regarding the right to live or right to life, Article 3 of the Islamic Declaration of Human Rights states that Islam envisages the view that the life of human beings is the gift of God. He is the creator of the whole universe and human beings are His vice-regents. According to Islam, human life is valuable and inviolable, so every effort should be made to protect it. Islam as a religion ensures everyone's security in life. In particular, no one shall be exposed to injury or death (though Islam permits execution in some exceptional cases). The holy Quran says in this regard, "Do not kill anyone whom Allah has forbidden, except for just cause."[15] The Prophet says, "The believer in God is he who is not a danger to the life and property of any other and your lives, your property and your honor are as sacred as this day (the day of Hajj) is sacred," and he again says, "your blood and your property are inviolable till the last day."[16] The main purpose of His creation is to awaken in man a higher consciousness in the universe. So, the life and death of human beings are in His hands. The holy Quran repeatedly commands us to protect human life and respect God's sovereignty: for example: (a) "seeing that ye were without life and He gave you life, then will He cause to die, and will again bring you to life[17]; (b) "when they ask thee spirit (of inspiration), say, 'the spirit comes by the command of my Lord'"[18]; (c) "it is God that takes the souls (of men) at death.... He keeps back (from returning to life)..."[19]; (d) "...As for the dead God will raise them up, then will they (man) be turned unto Him"[20]; (e) "...nor can a soul die except by God's leave ..."[21]; in another place, the holy Quran proclaims, "Wa tukhrezul hai-e minal maiete wa tukhrezul maieta minal haie" – i.e., "God is able to take life of the living thing and

---

[15] Al-Quran, 17: 33.
[16] Al -Fatah al Kabir, Vol-3, p. 257; see also Hadith Bukhari Sharif, Vol. 1 (Delhi, 1375A.h), 8, 21.
[17] Al-Quran, 2: 28.
[18] Al-Quran, 17: 85.
[19] Al-Quran, 39: 42.
[20] Al-Quran, 6: 36.
[21] Al-Quran, 3: 145.

also He is able to give life to the dead." Since life is the gift of God, no one can destroy his or her own life by personal wish or choice. Islam does not recognize a right to euthanasia, which violates human rights and also the divine command. The Islamic principle is not only to live but to proclaim, "live and let others live." So, according to Islam, the life of a human being is the gift of God and he has no right to destroy it.

Freedom

The concept of freedom has had an important place in the annals of human history. The Universal Declaration of Human Rights includes the right to freedom in Articles 13, 14 and 18. Article 18 especially recognizes the freedom of thought, conscience and religion. Articles 13 and 14 recognize the rights to movement and to residence in a particular territory, and also recognize political asylum. Islam recognizes both these rights to freedom, and says, "live where you like, but it is an agreement between us that you should not shed blood, commit highway robbery and oppress anyone."[22] God advises all Muslims in the holy Quran: "If (O Prophet) any of them should be polytheists, by protection grant them an asylum that they may know the word of God, then give them safe conduct to their own place of security.[23] Islam recognizes the legitimate freedom of human beings, as – "But ye will accept as God's will"[24] – innate and sacred rights. Islam negates all past sins of men and women.[25] This freedom means "the freedom of choosing and freedom of action." "Man gets only what he strives for."[26] Hence, men and women may choose their religion according to their own free will; so, the holy Quran strongly says, "la ikraha fiddin"[27] (i.e., there is no compulsion in religion), and repeatedly reminds believers that He has sent numerous Prophets prior to Hadrat Muhammad(s) and that they should believe in them and in the holy books revealed through them. According to Islam, no person has the right to sit in judgment over the belief of others. Similarly, no one is responsible for the deeds of others. These principles basically recognize the complete freedom of human beings in performing their deeds. This notion is rightly strengthened by the command of the holy Quran: "...Prevail justice and faith in God altogether and everywhere."[28] In this context, the holy Prophet says, "The best of Jihad is his, who speaks a just word before a tyrannical authority," and "the worst form of class prejudice is to support one's community even in

---

[22] V.A. Syed Muhammad, "Islam and Human Rights," in *Islam at a Glance*, p. 84.
[23] Al-Quran, 9:6.
[24] Al-Quran, 74:56; 76:30.
[25] Al-Quran, 24:26.
[26] Al-Quran, 53:39.
[27] Al-Quran, 2:256.
[28] Al-Quran, 8:39.

tyranny."[29] In another place the holy Quran depicts the idea of freedom as follows: "We have shown him the way; he may accept or reject."[30] And, again, "Truth is from your Lord, so let him disbelieve, who disbelieves."[31] "God does not change the condition of men unless they change themselves."[32] This notion of Islam basically attests to the "non-fatalistic" character of human existence. Islam used the term "*qadr*" specifically for 'luck' here: *Qadr* is the potentiality of a thing or the measure according to which it is created. The notion of *Taqdir* in Islam, therefore, signifies natural law, but it does not mean that human beings have absolute freedom; rather, it implies that men and women are all free agents and they are individually responsible for their deeds. The holy Quran contains innumerable lines which indicate man's responsibility for his or her own actions: "He... who created everything, then ordained for it its measure.[33] Actually, Islam presents human beings within a reasonable religious framework which stresses one's responsibility and accountability. Prior to the advent of Islam, injunctions were prescribed by certain religious agencies as a form of 'Commandments' given to human beings to regulate their conduct. But Islam prescribes only some moral principles and rights, and not in the form of commandments, since there is no external obligation. According to Islam, good and evil (*ma'ruf* and *munkar*) are both created by God, but man is free to choose and move according to his own reason ('*aql*), and that faculty is also given by Him (God), so that he (the active agent) may distinguish between right and wrong. Therefore, the holy Quran attests, "It was not that we wronged them; they wronged their own soul.[34] The Islamic divine principles are accompanied by moral standards in order to protest against political absolutism, oppression and tyranny. It ensures everyone's dignity, security, and freedom in all levels as an embodiment of humanism. Islam also recognizes freedom of opinion, freedom of religion, the franchise, freedom of property, and so on – all of which are necessary to maintain human dignity and human rights.

Equality

The concept of equality is essential in society. The Universal Declaration of Human Rights expresses this notion in Article 1 as: "All human beings are born free and equal in dignity and rights [...] (they) should act towards one another in a spirit of brotherhood." Article 7 provides the notion of equality before the law and equal protection of the law: "All are equal before the law and are entitled without any

---

[29] Hadith Mishkat Sharif, p. 418; see *Islam at a Glance*, p. 83.
[30] Al-Quran, 76:3.
[31] Al-Quran, 18:29.
[32] Al-Quran, 13:11.
[33] Al-Quran, 25:2.
[34] Al-Quran, 11:101.

discrimination to equal protection of the law [and they are entitled to equal protection] against any incitement to such discrimination.[35]

Equality is a primordial principle of Islam. The right to equality is recognized in various verses of the holy Quran. To break down the inequality in society, it proclaims, "all human beings are equal just as are the teeth of a (same) comb."[36] The holy Quran depicts the idea of equality in a way similar to that found in the Universal Declaration of Human Rights. It states: "O mankind! Verily we have created you a male and female and distributed you into tribes and families that you might recognize one another."[37] The holy Prophet also says that one must extend brotherly relation to all human beings, and emphasized: "All creatures of God form the family of God and he is the best loved of God who loveth best his creatures.[38] It strongly opposes any special position being assigned to anybody in society on the basis of race, caste or color. In the farewell address at Ka'bah, the holy Prophet declares, "Neither the Arab is superior to the non-Arab nor the non-Arab is superior to the Arab, except by the degree of piety and righteousness."[39] In the eyes of Islam, all human beings have been born of one ancestor, i.e., Adam, and possess a common nature. A difference in rights based on race, class, tribal attachments, and so on, which existed among certain groups and nations of that time, is entirely rejected by Islam. Islam does not believe that any particular group or class has been born for subjection, nor any other group for mastership. It believes in the motto that "every human being is the part of one another… if any part of the body is afflicted in the daily life, the other parts of the body cannot remain silent" ["bani Adama azaye e yak digarand …. Chun azaye dard award rojekar digar azuha na mande karar" – Sa'adi][40] To maintain equality, Islam discarded the difference between the master and slave and the ruler and ruled before the law. Instead, it depicted the idea of "equal opportunity and protection to all before the law"; here, no one can claim special privilege. Actually, Islam has provided an equality of rights, so that every person can claim equal treatment in accordance with the law, and no person shall be discriminated against before the law while seeking to defend his or her public or private rights. Therefore, in Islam, no one shall be

---

[35] *Journal of Objective Studies*, ed. F.R. Faridi, Vol. 10, No. 1 (January,1998/1418Ah), p. 57.

[36] N.K. Singh, *Social Justice and Human Rights in Islam*, p. 16; Md. Sirajul Islam, "Society and Justice in Islam," in *Problems and Perspectives of Social Philosophy* [International Congress in Social Philosophy, Dharward, Tirupati, ed. Prof. B.P. Siddhashrama, Prof. K.M. Chetty, Dr. B. Krishna Reddy], Vol. 3 (2003), pp. 60-63.

[37] Al-Quran, 49:13.

[38] Al-Fatah al Kabir, Vol. 2 (Beirut Edition), p. 105, See *Islam at a Glance*, p. 81.

[39] V.A. Syed Muhammad, "Islam and Human Rights," p. 81.

[40] Md. Sirajul Islam, "Society and Justice in Islam," pp. 62-63.

deprived of enjoying equal rights. In this regard the holy Prophet says in the Hadith, "O Abu Dhar, you are still a man belonging to pagan (Jahiliyyah) times, lift your head and look. Then know that you are hardly superior to a man of color, be it black or red unless you surpass him in deeds.[41] The right to equality is still further emphasized by the holy prophet, who says: "Wisdom lies in loving each other without depriving the other of his rights. Righteous actions are the only mark of distinction and not wealth, birth or status in life."[42] A society based on complete equality in all respects may only help to make peace and justice prevail in society. The holy Quran says, (a) "Be just: that is next to piety, and fear God; He is well acquainted with all that ye do"[43]; (b) "We sent aforetime our apostles with clear signs and sent down with them the book of the balance (of Right and Wrong) that men may stand forth in justice."[44] Not only in the Quran but also in the Hadith the holy Prophet says, "verily the just shall be nearer to God than the prophets of light, on the right hand of the Merciful (God), if they are just in the exercise of their authority, just to their people, and just to those over whom they are made guardians."[45]

Islam envisages various types of equality in its fold, such as religious equality, political equality, economic equality, social equality, and so on, so that people may receive respect and enjoy equal status in all matters.

Justice

To preserve human dignity and human rights, Islam has accepted justice as an inevitable and essential element of society. Justice in Islam is much more than ritual; rather, it is the foundation of belief ('*Iman*), and reverence to God ('*aqida*). In Islam, justice is called '*adl*,' which is used to express a balanced humanity and healthy community, where each individual is connected to every other in order to maintain universal unity and solidarity, based upon a common good. Justice in Islam acquires such a place of paramount position that being just is a necessary pre-condition for the pious and God-fearing person. It is a concept which is formulated in Islam as comprehensive and which encompasses all aspects of human life. It governs all kinds of relations in life, including those between the ruler and the ruled, between husband and wife, between parents and children, and above all between Muslims and non-Muslims. Hence, justice in Islam is not only a principle or a law but an essential and unavoidable ethical value which touches the everyday life of all Muslims. If any person is deprived of justice in Islam, he may take legal measures for just treatment. The notion

---

[41] N.K. Singh, *Social Justice and Human Rights in Islam*, p. 16.
[42] V.A. Syed Muhammad, "Islam and Human Rights," p. 82.
[43] Al-Quran, 5:9.
[44] Al-Quran, 57:25.
[45] Mishkat Sharif, p.321.

of 'Qada' includes both the judicial process and the arbitration process of common law, and the 'Qadi' is a person who is appointed by the ruler to determine the disputed rights and liabilities of the litigants in civil or criminal matters and to establish public trusts and pious duties.

In the holy Quran, there are many indications regarding justice, which are confirmed by the deeds and sayings of the holy Prophet. The holy Quran repeats the idea as follows:

> (a) "O ye who believe stand out firmly for God as witness to fair dealing and let not the hatred of others to you make you swerve towards wrong and depart from justice. Be just, which is next to piety."[46]
> (b) "Ye who believe stand out firmly for justice, as witness to Allah even as against yourselves or your parents, or your kin and whether it be (against) rich or poor, for Allah can best protect both.... If ye distort (justice), this is as to decline to do justice. Verily, Allah is well acquainted with all that ye do."[47]
> (c) "God commands justice, the doing of good and liberality to kith and kin and He forbids all shameful deeds, and injustice and rebellion: He instructs you that you may receive admonition."[48]
> (d) "The blame is only against those Men who oppress in wrongdoing and insolently transgress beyond bounds through the land, defying rights and justice: For such there will be a penalty grievous."[49]
> (e) "Ye are the best of peoples, evolved for mankind, enjoying what is right, forbidding what is wrong and believing in God....."[50]

In the Hadith, the Prophet Hadrat Muhammad(s) had propagated the idea of justice, and he also warned of the disastrous consequences of injustice, discrimination and inequality before the law for an individual or a community. On several occasions, he established justice even when his decision went against his nearest relatives or descendants. Once he gave a verdict to chop off the hand of a respected lady for stealing. Some of his companions appealed to him to rethink the verdict. But Prophet said, "I swear to Allah, I would have done this (justice) even to my daughter Fatima: she would have been convicted for the same" (Hadith).

---

[46] Al-Quran, 5:9.

[47] Al-Quran, 6:135.

[48] Al-Quran, 16:90.

[49] Al-Quran, 42:42.

[50] Al-Quran, 3:110.

Islam as a religion is very rigid in maintaining justice at various levels, such as the religious level, the social level, the political level, the economic level, the legal level, and so on. This form of justice is not confined to the conduct of Muslims among themselves; rather, Islam makes it an inner obligation for all Muslims in dealings with the faithful of other religions.

Fraternity

Fraternity or brotherhood is one of the important ideals of Islam. In this aspect, all Muslims of the world are integrated as one race and belong to one family. Islam says, "kullu muslemin ikhwanun," i.e., all Muslims are the brothers of one another. These brotherly relationships are expressed in the various spheres of life, i.e., in the performance of prayer, celebrating festivals, in partaking food collectively, in collective charity (*Zakat*), etc. Of brotherly affection the holy Quran says, "O mankind! We created you from a single (pair) of a male and female and made you into Nations and tribes, that ye may know each other..."[51] It is worthy to mention that this idea is not addressed only to Muslims but to all mankind, and that they are all related in one fraternal relationship, for all of mankind is descended from one pair of parents. Their tribes, races and nations are only convenient labels by which we may recognize different characteristics. Before God they all are one, and he gets most honor who is the most righteous. Regarding fraternity the holy Quran says:

> (a) "inna hajehi ummatokum ummatan wahedatun," i.e., Verily this fraternity of yours is a single fraternity."[52]
> (b) "wa inna hajehi ummatokum ummatan wahedatan," i.e., "And verily this fraternity of yours is a single fraternity......"[53]

And in the Hadith the holy Prophet says:

> (a) "Kullu Muslemeen Ikhwanun," i.e., All Muslims are related in fraternal relationship.
> (b) "Ye aiuhannaso kullukum Ibn Adama," i.e., "O Mankind! All you are the descendants of the same Adam."

To extend the concept of brotherhood towards all, the holy Prophet held that all human beings were brothers of one another, and emphasized that all are creatures of God from the family of God and that he is the best

---

[51] Al-Quran, 49:13.
[52] Al-Quran, 21:92.
[53] Al-Quran, 23:52.

loved of God who loveth best His creatures.[54] I think that, in all these points, the term "Muslim" basically signifies righteous people and their fraternal relationship, so that unity and brotherhood may prevail throughout the whole universe. This notion is strengthened by such Quranic notions as, "The brotherhood of Truth is one in all ages. It is narrow men who create sects ..."[55]

Love

Islam thinks that love is the apex of religious and social affairs as well as of human rights; hence, it negates all types of hatred and apathy on religious and social matters. In Islam, the notion of love has acquired a very clear and compelling role. The idea of love has been revealed in several verses of the holy Quran, through the terms "Hubb," "Muhabbah," "Muwadah," and "Wudd." This concept is expressed as follows:

a) "God loves them who turn to him constantly and he loves them who keep themselves pure and clean."[56]
b) "If ye do love God follow me. God will love you."[57]
c) "....Offering them love."[58]
d) "And he is the oft forgiving, full of loving kindness.[59]

Moreover, the holy Prophet is a shining instance of a lover of God. Thus he is called "Habibullah" (the lover of God). In the Hadith, the Prophet has clearly expressed the idea as: "My servant draws high unto me by works of devotion and I love him, and when I love him I am the ear by which he hears, and the eye by which he sees and the tongue by which he speaks."[60] [57]

The holy Quran crossed the boundary of love and asked people to offer over-flowing love (ashaddo hubb al-lillah).[61] Islam believes only in the propagation and extension of love, so that all kinds of hatred and apathy can be removed from society. Hatred and apathy are the curse of society; even today in many societies social evils are practiced in many forms – violating human dignity and human rights relentlessly. Hence, Islam envisages constant love without any discrimination – a love which acquired more depth and popularity in the hands of the Sufi anchorites. Their

---

[54] Al Fatah al Kabir, Vol. III, p. 103, see *Islam at a Glance*, p. 81.
[55] Al-Quran, 23:155.
[56] Al-Quran, 2:222.
[57] Al-Quran, 3:31.
[58] Al-Quran, 60:1.
[59] Al-Quran, 85:14.
[60] Al-Qushyari, Risala (Cairo, 1318 AH), p. 169.
[61] Al-Quran, 2:165.

unsurpassed love is called "Ishq," which is extended to all without any reluctance in order to uphold human dignity and rights.

Education and Shelter

Education. In the Universal Declaration of Human Rights, the right to education is set forth in Article 26:

> Everyone has the right to education. Education shall be free, at least in the elementary and fundamental stages. Elementary education shall be compulsory." "Education shall be directed to the full development of the human personality and to the strengthening of respect for human rights and fundamental freedoms... .

Before the emergence of the Prophet Hadrat Muhammad(s), we have the period of "ayyam-e-jahilliyat" (the age of ignorance). There were no systematic educational institutions, society was backward, and the people roamed around in clans. But we know that education is the cornerstone of the all-round development of personality. No community can be considered as developed unless it is educationally enriched and it can fulfill the ultimate goal of life. Therefore, in Islam, education is an unavoidable and compulsory activity related to human dignity and human rights. In the holy Quran, the absolute necessity of acquiring knowledge is emphasized repeatedly as follows: (a) The holy Quran says "rabby jidny ilman," i.e., "O my lord increase me in knowledge."[62] (b) "Shall they who have knowledge and they who have it not be treated alike?"[63] (c) "Recite thou, for thy lord is the most beneficent, and hath taught the use of the pen, hath taught man that which he knew not."[64] The holy Quran reveals the idea again as "al 'ilmo minal mahde ilal lahde," i.e., education is a continuous process from cradle to grave. In the holy Quran the term "hakim" is also used in the sense of science or wisdom. The holy Quran declares itself as knowledge. In the verse Ya-Sin, the idea is clearly maintained that "Quranil hakim,"[65] i.e., the Quran is full of knowledge or science. In another verse, the holy Quran attests to certified knowledge (ilm al-yaqin). Prophet Hadrat Muhammad insisted upon the acquisition of knowledge or education:

> (a) "talebul ilme farijatun ala kulle Muslemin wal Muslemat," i.e., the acquisition of knowledge is

---

[62] Al-Quran, 20:114.
[63] Al-Quran, 39:9.
[64] Al-Quran, 96:3-5.
[65] Al-Quran, 36:2.

compulsory for each and every Muslim man and Muslim woman. (Hadith)[66]

(b) "utlebul 'ilme kana ilao fissin" i.e., "For acquisition of knowledge people should move towards China." (Hadith).

(c) "The form of devotion to God is to seek knowledge."[67]

(d) "It is the duty of the learned to spread knowledge. They should impart it to those who do not possess it."[68]

The Prophet himself recognized the value and necessity of knowledge and education in life. He repeatedly says that only true knowledge or education can help to differentiate Truth from error, and he gives the suggestion to his companions or followers that knowing and unknowing of Truth can never be treated as "equal." According to him, Truth is itself certain, though the certainty possesses many degrees. There is the probability or certainty resulting from the application of man's power of judgment and his appraisal of evidence. In Islamic terminology, this is called "'ilm al yaqin" (Certainty by reasoning).[69] Islam holds that absolute knowledge is in God only, and so the holy Quran says, "Verily with God is full knowledge and He is acquainted (with all things)."[70] All knowledge is derived from Him, and man should utilize his faculty of knowledge for his improvement.

Shelter. Once upon a time, there were no sophisticated shelters for human beings. People lived in the jungle or in the caves of mountains and always felt troubled about their survival. In the course of time, people felt the need of shelter to help them to live in society in a dignified manner and with security. In Islamic terminology, the place of shelter is called "bait" (house). In Islam, the "kaba" is called the house of Allah (baitullah) and the Prophet says the "kaba" is the house of God and the mosque is my house ("al kaba-o-baitullah wal masjido baity") (Hadith). Hence, Prophet Hadrat Muhammad first built a mosque at Medina on 8th Rabiul Awwal (corresponding to 23 September 622 C.E.), after his migration (hizrat) from Mecca. The Mosque is entitled "Masjid-e-Kuba," and it still survives.

There is an indication of shelter in the holy Quran where God says,

(a) "we gave them both (Mary and her son) shelter on high ground affording rest and security and furnished with [water-] springs.[71]

---

[66] *Journal of Objective Studies*, p. 57.

[67] Mishkat Sharif, p. 37; See *Islam at a Glance*, p. 88.

[68] Bukhari Sharif, p. 35; *Islam at a Glance*, p. 88.

[69] Al-Quran, 69:51. For details see Quranic Footnote No. –5673.

[70] Al-Quran, 4:32.

[71] Al-Quran, 23:50.

(b) "...But if ye enter a house, salute each other – a greeting of blessing and purity as from God."[72]

But it is a matter of great pain that in various countries today many people are still without shelter. The third world countries particularly face this trouble. In Islam, there are many provisions of funds from which educational institutions and shelter can be established for the common people, i.e., Sadqah (optional donation), Zakat (compulsory alms-giving), the Waqaf fund, etc. The construction of homes and the distribution of food for the needy is an eternal and dynamic or higher virtue in Islam (sadqah-e-jariah). It is an unending virtue whose result will be considered by Allah after each person's death. In the dark ages, Islam felt the need of such things so that human beings might live with full dignity in society. Thus, the celebrated Sufi saint Hadrat Nizam-al-din Aulia opined that the devotion to God does not mean detachment from the world, and that the highest form of devotion to God is the removal of misery of the distressed, the extension of a helping hand to the needy, and the feeding of the hungry. He also opined that human submission (ta-at) to God is of two kinds: (a) necessary (lazmi) and (b) communicable (mutaaddi). Those who perform the former submit to God through Shariah, and those who following the latter devote themselves to the service of the common people.[73]

Democracy

Islam is not only a religion but a code of life. Hence, generally, it is related to the political affairs of human beings. It believes that politically deprived people can never be happy and prosperous. Political corruption leads the people towards narrow and dangerous nationalism. The Islamic ruling system is highly democratic, where peoples elect their rulers by exercising their individual franchise, and where the common criterion of nationality in Islam is the "Highest Piety". The Prophet himself discarded hereditary political power. So, he did not nominate any Khalifa or successor from his family to rule the nation; rather, he advised the people to follow a democratic form of government and gave them the freedom to choose their rulers in a democratic way. The Prophet personally utilized this democratic system when he established a city-state at Medina. Hence, the Islamic political system solely depends upon the will and choice of the individual. According to Islam, a king or Khalifa is a constitutional head only – he has no real power. The real power is in the hands of the people (republic), and the head of an Islamic state should maintain a democratic attitude. The holy Quran has ordained another important prescription: "The non-Muslim inhabitants of the Islamic state enjoy a judicial autonomy, each community

---

[72] Al-Quran, 24:61.

[73] Imam Jafar, *Muslims in India* (New Delhi: Orient and Longman Ltd, 1975), pp. 17-18.

having its own tribunals, its own judges, administering its own laws in all walks of life, civil as well as penal."[74]

Abolition of Racial Discrimination and Slavery

To protect human dignity and human rights, Article 4 of the Universal Declaration of Human Rights proclaims: "no one shall be held in slavery or servitude; slavery and the slave trade shall be prohibited in all their forms." In connection with this, Article 23 of the Declaration defends the values of an adequate standard of living, and the dignity of human beings; it asserts, "everyone has the right to work, to free choice of employment, to just and favorable conditions of work and protection against unemployment."[75] It says specifically, "equal pay for equal work."

Islamic society is highly egalitarian. It never permits enslaving people or exploiting a person's labor. In this regard, the holy Quran proclaims, "It is not righteousness that ye turn your faces towards East and West. But it is righteousness to believe in God... And to spend your substances.... For the ransom of the slaves."[76] When Prophet Hadrat Muhammad(s) arrived in Arabia, society was full of inequalities, indignities and superstitions. Nationality and rank were based on language, race, heredity or place of birth, which violated human dignity and human rights. The Prophet fought against all these social evils and he abolished all these inequalities. The holy Quran rejects all claims to superiority based on language and the color of one's skin.[77] Similarly, slavery is rejected in Islam. During the period of the holy Prophet (s), slavery was normal, and slave owners often treated their slaves inhumanely. Even the life and death of the slave was in the hands of his master. And, in general, physical torture, exploitation, and inadequate wages were prevalent. The Prophet Hadrat Muhammad banned these inhumane practices and proclaimed the release of slaves. He advised the people that releasing slaves (ghulam azad) is one of the great virtues in Islam. To abolish this inhumane custom, the Prophet himself released his own slave Zaid bin Harith who had been given to him by his wife Khadija. For this, the Prophet again advised us as follows:

> (a) "Verily wicked are those who purchase human beings."[78]
> (b) "Very wicked are those who trade in human bodies." (Tirmidhi)

---

[74] Al-Quran, 5:42-50,66.
[75] *Journal of Objective Studies*, p. 28.
[76] Al-Quran, 2:177.
[77] Al-Quran, 30:22;49:13.
[78] Bukhari Sharif reference taken from *Islam at a Glance*, p. 85.

(c) "There are three types of people with whom I shall remonstrate on the day of judgement ... the third type of the people are those who hire a laborer, take work from him, but deny him his wages."[79]

(d) "Pay the wages of the labourer before his perspiration dries up."[80]

(e) Forbid "the forcing of the laborer to enter upon his work before settling his wages" (Baihaqi).

(f) "to reduce the wages of the laborer is a grave sin." (Kanz al haqaiq)

(g) "Since when have you enslaved the people while their mothers gave them birth as free?[81]

As far as I am concerned, the Prophet Hadrat Muhammad is a person who raised his voice and who fought first to abolish slavery from the world, so that all human beings may be treated with full dignity and respect.

Humanity

Islam has prescribed excellent humanitarian ideals for society. A pious Muslim must maintain an earnest solicitude for humanity, and show no discrimination. Islam believes that no one is born either unclean into the world, nor can anyone be debarred from anything by the mere fact of his birth. No organization, class or occupation is reserved for a particular section of humanity; rather, a fraternal and humane approach is to be extended to every level of society. Rich and poor can assemble together in religious and social activities. Society is purely classless. The bonds of the then-existing class-ridden society were relaxed to a considerable extent in India. So Pundit Jawaharlal Nehru has rightly commented:

> It [Islam] had pointed out and shone up the abuses that had crept into Hindu society – the petrifaction of caste, untouchables, exclusiveness carried to fantastic lengths. The idea of the brotherhood of Islam and the theoretical equality of its adherents made a powerful appeal especially to those in the Hindu fold who were denied any semblance of equal treatment.[82]

---

[79] Mishkat Sharif, p. 258.

[80] Mishkat Sharif, p. 258.

[81] V.A. Syed Muhammad, "Islam and Human Rights," p. 85.

[82] Jawaharlal Nehru, *The Discovery of India* (London: Meridian Books, 1946), p. 225.

Status of Women

In pre–Islamic Arabian society, the condition of women was very poor, and the birth of a female child was considered as a curse and misfortune in the family. Large numbers of female children were therefore killed. Islam condemned this social evil, as the holy Quran proclaims: "He creates what He wills, He gives daughters to whomsoever He wants and He gives sons to whomsoever He wills."[83]

Female infanticide and killing of the fetus was in vogue in pre-Islamic Arabia. The holy Quran banned this inhumane custom and says, "when the female (infant) is buried alive, the question is for what crime she was killed" [i.e., she had committed no crime meriting this].[84] To maintain equality as well as to show respect to women, Islam has given economic rights to women in society. The holy Quran directs us: "to men is allotted what they earn and to women what they earn."[85]

In this present era, the chastity and purity of women are often violated, and women are treated like a commodity. To guard chastity and purity, the holy Quran says, (a) "for men and women who guard their chastity.... Allah prepared forgiveness and great reward."[86] (b) "women impure are for men impure and men impure for women impure. And women of purity are for men of purity, and men of purity are for women of purity..."[87] Not only this, Islam has given legal recognition to the dignity and rights of women. It holds that women are also human beings; hence, they must be treated as human beings, i.e., in a respectable manner. Islam provides equal rights for women and men at all religious, social, economic, political and educational levels. The Quran presents the basic structure of equality available to all men and women. Thus the holy Quran ordains:

> For Muslim men and women
> For believing men and women
> For devout men and women
> For true men and women
> For men and women who are patient and constant
> For men and women who humble themselves
> For men and women who give in charity
> For men and women who fast
> For men and women who guard their chastity
> And for men and women who engage much in Allah's praise
> For them has Allah prepared forgiveness and great reward.[88]

---

[83] Al-Quran, 42:49.
[84] Al-Quran, 81:8-9.
[85] Al-Quran, 4:32.
[86] Al-Quran, 33:35.
[87] Al-Quran, 24:26.
[88] Al-Quran, 33:35.

The holy Quran is also emphatic and explicit in its declaration of women's rights: "And woman shall have rights similar to the rights against them (men), according to what is equitable."[89]

In the Hatith the holy Prophet says, "fear Allah in the matter of women. Verily women have rights against you as you have rights against them."[90] It permits a widow to remarry in order to retain a dignified and noble place in society. Property rights for women are legal and rationally justifiable in Islam. In Islam, the right of divorce is granted to both husband and wife. In the secular sense, a Muslim marriage is founded on a contract after the free consent of both parties, which forms mutual rights and obligations, and each party is at liberty and free to terminate the contract of marriage reasonably. Husband and wife are free to maintain their individual rights – each can hold, acquire and dispose of their own property according to his or her will. Hence, in Islam, the identity of husband and wife is not merged together. Both have similar importance and value in family life. Therefore, it is clear to us that Islam has given considerable rights to women so that they may live in society with full respect and honor.

Health Services

In a good society, the provision of health services is essential. Earlier, traditional societies were not so developed in this area. Men are the embodiment of body, mind and soul. The body is basically a composition of physical elements which may be affected by illness and diseases. Islam speaks repeatedly of nursing or caring for people with ailments. The Prophet himself several times was engaged in caring for people, even of his opponents. Islam provides for free medical service towards all. The specific medicines of Muslim physicians were among the most advanced of that period. The *Unani* system reaches its peak in India. The indigenous systems faded into insignificance before progress was made. This system was very cheap, simple and in harmony with the Indian climate and environment. It spread in India very quickly, and did a very wonderful service to the people, particularly in the poorer sections. Later on, the Hamdard medical system also prevailed in India, particularly among the Muslims, and this improved the health service towards all.

ISLAM IN INDIA AT PRESENT

At present, Indian Muslims are confronted with various problems. Some of them are of their own creation and some are particularly related to their past heritage. At the present time, in India, Hindu–Muslim relations are extremely bitter. Various Nationalist groups have demanded that religious nationalism control the state. The present [2003] government is

---

[89] Al-Quran, 2:228.
[90] *Journal of Objective Studies*, p. 57.

called the "National Democratic Alliance" – the NDA. It is an admixture of various political parties: the Bharatiya Janata Party (BJP), Visva Hindu Parishad (VHP), Rastriya Svayamsevaka Sangha (RSS), Bajrang Dal (BD), Siva Sena (SS) and some other political groups. They claim the state for Hinduism. To achieve this goal, they have organized many programs which hamper national peace and solidarity, and in connection with this they organized a rally on 6 December 1992, headed by the leadership of the VHP and BJP. Ultimately, huge numbers of fanatical followers (kar sevakas) demolished the Babri Masjid (Mosque) at Ayodhya, Uttar Pradesh. This again fueled Hindu-Muslim conflict, driving it toward a climax. As a result, communal violence has occurred, especially in Mumbai, Ahmedabad, Surat, and Bhagalpur. Many people have been killed in the violence, most of them Muslims.[91] This is not a new thing in India, but it is unusually severe nowadays. Fanatical Muslims are also taking part in anti-Hindu violence, and this situation leads to turmoil throughout the political sphere. In June 2002, violence led to a massacre at Gujarat in connection with the Godhra train-burning, where many ordinary Muslims lost their lives and property. This is a very sad incident in Indian history. It is also known from the media that members of the police and local administration took part in the massacre, attacking Muslims. Today, Muslims of India feel very insecure. The level of employment of Indian Muslims has gradually decreased. They are very few in government service and those who are, are impoverished. Not only this, the Muslims of Kashmir are constantly fighting with the Hindus, and they have killed ordinary Hindus in their struggle for indeoendence. These terrorist activities violate human dignity and the human rights of Indians, and lead to inhumane conditions: malnutrition, barbaric attacks and murder, insufficient shelter, inadequate health service, starvation and an unjust distribution of opportunities for education: These gravely hamper the social order. But this is not a new incident in Indian history. Since the time of independence, this has happened in Indian society quite often. This will be clear from the opinion of Mr. Jaganath Pathey who bravely states, regarding Indian society and the oppression of the downtrodden:

> Since independence through various subtle ways and means it has been incessantly pounded into the people that Indian Nationalism is equal to Hinduism. Not only is the culture of the twice-born Hindus of the Indo-Gangetic plain said to represent the cultural mainstream, but also their language, Hindi, is promoted as the national language…. The Viswa Hindu Parishad activists and the other religious fanatics operate with impunity and with tacit approval of functionaries of the state. But they are

---

[91] Peter Von Der Veer, *Religious Nationalism: Hindus and Muslims in India* (Delhi: Oxford University Press, 1996), pp. 6-7.

never penalized. Indeed not a single 'communal' criminal has been jailed since independence. Through brutal violence and continuous repression, the tribals have been forced into silence.... Those who demand recognition of their inalienable rights to their language, culture and resources, are terrorized. Their houses are burnt down, relatives are tortured and women are dishonored. Their activists are either liquidated in countless encounters or imprisoned without trial.[92]

We know that education has a pivotal role in making people aware of their human dignity and human rights. The Indian national policy of education of 1986 has provided an impetus to continuous and sustained effort to evolve a system of education that will have relevance to the life, needs and aspirations of the people of India. It is true that the growth and the future of the country depends upon the development of its human resources, and education can play a fundamental role in these affairs as well as in increasing the strength of the country. We know from our experience that education plays an important role in meeting the challenges to society. Consequently, it is the duty of the Indian Government to show its commitment and to create confidence in its people as it promotes all-round development in society.[93] And only sound knowledge and awareness can help to mitigate if not eliminate communal tension. Since India is a multilingual and multi-cultural country, the official textbooks and curricula should be prepared in such a way that they satisfy and cover all section interests. But, at present, the official textbooks in college and university curricula convey only the influence of Hindus. India is supposed to be a secular country, where numerous ethnic and religious groups live side by side, and the Indian Constitution has guaranteed freedom of creed and cultural development for all citizens, and has also affirmed the complete equality of all communities irrespective of caste, creed and religion. This Constitution is ideally suited to the condition of our country, which has a heterogeneous character, and it also covers the interests of all minorities in the country.[94] If we will fail to achieve this goal, then fundamentalism will raise its head even more conspicuously and violently in Indian society and will lead to massive destruction. Now is the time to take some effective measures to safeguard the interests of all people.

Here, one major factor in increasing Hindu–Muslim tension is the perception, in the eyes of Hindus, that Muslims are foreigners, and that they

---

[92] Jaganath Pathey, "Tribal Cultural Autonomy and National Integration," in *Indian Society at the Turn of the Century*, ed. N.P. Chaubey (Allahabad: Indian Academy of Social Sciences, 1988), p. 100.

[93] P.L. Malhotra, "Perspective in Social Education at the Turn of the Century," in *Indian Society at the Turn of the Century*, p. 104.

[94] S. Abul Hasan al Nadwi, *Muslims in India*, pp. 128-129.

are not truly Indian. This is not true; history attests that most Indian Muslims are indigenous lower caste Indians, and who converted to Islam because of the egalitarian approaches of the Sufi anchorites. They had equal status in Muslim society. Since they belong to the lower strata of society, they are still somewhat backward. To raise them out of this condition, attention to the economic development of these people is greatly needed. Sometimes Muslims agitate to achieve such a privilege, but the Indian Government has not given any assurance to them. On the other hand, Muslims often say that Hindus are members of the Aryan race – those who conquered South Asia and settled in India and who brought Hindu ideology with them. Such a notion basically relates to the external origin of the Hindu caste system. Such internal 'dirty politics' and mutual blame hampers national unity and integrity. It seems to me that this situation arises mainly from an identity crisis as well as severe economic constraints in society. The unemployment problem among the youth leads to social disturbances of the highest order. Besides this, the radical version of Indian nationalism thinks that Hinduism is the basis of Indian national identity, thereby relegating adherents of other religions to a secondary status. India as a secular state has a moral responsibility as well as a duty to safeguard the interests of all sectors. At the same time, the people of India should strive to improve their brotherly affection for one another and also take part in national development and reconstruction. Therefore, special attention needs to be paid to all these groups by our government, so that India's secular character is preserved. I think it will help the Indian people enormously to achieve peace and happiness, and then human dignity and human rights will necessarily follow.

CONCLUSION

In the contemporary world, and despite the many technological advances, many countries still do not fully guarantee the basic rights of the people. Third world countries are facing the threat of cultural homogenization from the process of globalization. Political corruption, financial constraints and the weaker sections of the ruling class in various countries have contributed to terrorist activities; as a result, the violation of human dignity and human rights occurs with increasing frequency. We have the duty as well as the moral responsibility to save humanity and increase mutual respect, so that people from all the corners of the world, and for posterity, may live with full dignity and be able to build on a secure foundation of basic human rights.

Department of Philosophy & Religion
Visva Bharati University
Santiniketan, India

CHAPTER VI

GROUP-SPECIFIC RIGHTS: A NON-ESSENTIALIST APPROACH

PLAMEN MAKARIEV

In recent years, the traditional dichotomy of "individual rights" and "collective rights" has been challenged by the idea of another kind: group-specific (or, in a different terminology, group-differentiated) rights.[1] This term intends to refer to rights which are more culturally relevant than universal, fundamental human rights, but which are, unlike collective rights, ascribed to individuals and not communities. In international documents, they are referred to by the elegant formula 'individual rights, exercised jointly with other members of the respective community.'

What is most characteristic of group-specific rights is that they guarantee conditions for the realization, maintenance and development of minority cultural identities. The claims for such rights follow the logic of recognizing the value of the cultural identity of national, ethnic and religious minorities – in the sense of the well-known "politics of recognition."[2] The latter presupposes a dialogical model of cultural identity. Without recognition, and in the condition of a humiliating or condescending attitude of the "Others," it is impossible to build or maintain a positive self-consciousness or self-understanding – in other words, it is impossible to achieve the self-confidence and self-respect which are necessary for a proper cultural being.[3]

It is remarkable that, in Charles Taylor's famous article "The Politics of Recognition," the value of cultural identity is inferred from the value of the individual one, i. e., the value of culture as such is not taken as an "independent variable." A group's culture is regarded not as valuable in itself, but as a necessary condition for the well-being of the individuals who constitute the group. Consequently, the recognition of cultural identity in that sense does not lead us to respecting minority rights as collective, but rather as group-specific ones. However, this does not mean that Taylor's methodology of dealing with minority cultures is immune from the charge of the essentialization of cultural differences.

---

[1] See Will Kymlicka, *Multicultural Citizenship* (Oxford: Oxford University Press, 1995), Ch. 3.

[2] See Amy Gutmann (ed.), *Multiculturalism. Examining the Politics of Recognition* (Princeton: Princeton University Press, 1994).

[3] See Charles Taylor, "The Politics of Recognition," in Amy Gutmann (ed.), *Multiculturalism. Examining the Politics of Recognition*.

This term has become popular as denoting the treatment of social phenomena as manifestations of "hard" essences – not subject to historical change, and not intermingling with other social realities. From this point of view, cultural identities are "discrete, frozen in time, impervious to external influences, homogeneous and without internal dissent."[4] For instance, if we are dealing in an essentialist way with the problems of a given minority population, we should be trying to find out what essence is the source of the phenomena that we are encountering on empirical level and, if these phenomena build a rather messy general picture (as is usually the case), we should do our best to establish which of them are manifestations of the "true identity" of this minority, and ignore the others as exceptions, aberrations, anomalies, etc. This approach leads to forcing the rich variety of cultural life into the procrustean bed of a preconceived notion of one or another essence.

The "temptation" to conceive identity in an essentialist way manifests itself when we try to answer the question: what, in principle, is the value of identity? – i.e., not whether it deserves recognition in this or that case (which is Taylor's issue), but why do we consider it important at all? Usually the answer is that to have an identity of your own means to live in an authentic way, to be true to yourself.[5] Or it is that one will therefore have a secure belonging to some social whole, if one is situated in a network of ties of solidarity with other human beings. Or it is that you can overcome your mortality by being linked to something which exists from time immemorial and which continues to exist into the indefinite future. Or it is that, for your actions to have a meaning which transcends the accomplishment of your individual interests, you need to be part of a continuous, collective effort to make and remake your culture.[6] All these arguments refer to ultimate values, from which the value of cultural identity is derived. The latter is valuable as a means of their attainment.

It seems somehow natural that, in order to fulfill this "mission," identity should be nothing else but sameness. It seems that, only by enduring influences and interventions coming from without – i.e., from alien factors – can a cultural entity remain true to itself, and *eo ipso* provide meaning to the individual lives of the human beings who belong to it. However, it is precisely this approach that brings us to the essentialist fallacy. If we insist on the "purity" of identity, this implies isolation from external "input" and resistance to novelty. As historical experience clearly shows, such an identity – isolationist and conservative – has rather poor

---

[4]   Tariq   Modood,   "Anti-Essentialism.   Multiculturalism   and   the Recognition of Religious Groups," *The Journal of Political Philosophy*, Vol. 6, No. 4 (1998), p. 378.

[5]   See the reference to Herder in Taylor, "The Politics of Recognition," p. 32.

[6]   These arguments from various authors, cited by Kymlicka in *Multicultural Citizenship*, pp. 89-90.

prospects of survival. In other words, it is the strategy of preserving identity in its original state that dooms it to decline. This strategy is counterproductive. Besides, it is associated with attempts to overcome the inner diversity of culture – i.e., to base social activity on stereotypes. It is also prone to perpetuating cultural traits which might have an obviously negative impact on the lives of the individuals belonging to the given culture. (If, for example, the traditional mores of a community play an indisputably important role in its life – i.e., if they cannot be considered as a "phenomenon," but are part of this culture's "essence" – then they should be proclaimed inviolable to reform, even if they are a source of tensions and conflicts within the community and between it and its social environment.) And last but not least, the essentialist view of identity ignores well- known facts, which are an evidence of the "constructed" character of many cultural entities, or interprets these facts as cases of the violation and falsification of identity.

If we come back from the overtly philosophical issue of identity to the more politically relevant issue of rights, we should take into account another important factor which makes it even more difficult to justify claims for group-specific rights by referring to an essentialist notion of cultural identity. The rights that the people belonging to a cultural minority really need, cannot be defined only on the basis of their identity in its culturally "pure" form. These rights have to correspond also to specific dispositions and sensitivities of the people in question, which are conditioned by contingent historical facts (e.g., whether there is a record of violence in the history of the relationships with the majority [and, if so, then to what extent]; or, as another factor, the demographic ratio between the minority and the majority, in respect to other minorities [whether we are dealing with a small minority among several others, or with a single large minority]; or, as a third example, the extent to which the minority in question is integrated into society [which also depends largely on historical circumstances], etc.). From an essentialist point of view all these idiosyncrasies should count as phenomena – i.e., as not belonging to the essence of the community's identity. In reality, however, as elements of the minority's collective memory and of the consciousness of its members, they matter quite a bit for the justification of claims for group-specific rights.

Considerations of this kind motivate attempts in recent political philosophy to develop a weaker version of the identity-concept, amounting to replacing the very concept of identity by a related one, which can serve as a standard for attaining, in social life, the ultimate values mentioned above, without providing grounds for essentialist interpretations. For instance, William Sweet proposes to replace "cultural identity" by "cultural integrity" and, consequently, "sameness" by "consistency."[7] If we take into

---

[7] See William Sweet, "Universal Human Rights and Cultural Integrity," in *Collected Papers of the International Conference on Human Rights and*

account that "consistency" implies coherence with the cultural community's own past, we'll see an important commonality between "integrity" and "identity." The difference is, however, that unlike "identity," "integrity" allows for consistency also with the community's environment, including openness to novelty. The argumentation in Sweet's article demonstrates that "cultural integrity" can satisfy the requirement to provide for the attaining of values like authenticity, solidarity and commitment to a cause, which transcends one's individual being. It does so, however, not at the expense of engaging with an isolationist and conservative cultural strategy.

Basing group-specific rights upon a more flexible vision of culture certainly helps to avoid the essentialist fallacy, but raises new problems. The very notion of consistency is a rather slippery ground for minority policy. What are criteria for consistency, and who should decide in which case we have consistency between cultural traits, and in which not? Let us take an example from the recent history of minority issues in Bulgaria.

Until several decades ago, there were three Islamic minorities in Bulgaria, the members of which had, consequently, Muslim names: ethnic Turks, Pomaks (Bulgarians, Islamized in the times when their land was part of the Ottoman empire), and a part of the Roma (Gypsies). The communist regime, striving towards ethnic homogeneity of the population, tried in different campaigns to replace these names by Bulgarian ones (mostly of Slavonic origin). Leaving aside all other interesting aspects of these events, let us consider the following question: in which case was this change consistent with the existing cultural traits of each of these minorities, and in which not? In reality, most of the Muslim Roma accepted this "novelty" rather easily, and now their descendants laugh at the very thought that their grandfathers and grandmothers bore names like Hassan and Aysha. Some of the Pomaks welcomed the change, but the larger part did not, and restored their Muslim names at first instance, after the fall of the regime. With few exceptions, the Turks vigorously resisted the intervention in their private lives; in many cases, the authorities had to use force and, after dramatic events, their names were formally changed, but this change was reversed almost universally after 1989.

Now, what can we say about cultural integrity and consistency in these three cases? The simplest comment would be that the transition from Muslim to Bulgarian names was almost completely consistent with Roma culture, was little less so with Pomak culture, and was entirely inconsistent with ethnic Turkish culture. However, someone might say that this change was equally inconsistent with all three cultures, but cultural integrity was weaker in the Roma case (and was easily reconstructed into a new one, at the expense of violating its consistency with its past), it was stronger in the Pomak community, and strongest in the Turkish one. And logically, as a third alternative, it might also be claimed that the replacing of the Muslim

Dialogue of Civilisations (Qom, Iran: Mofid University Publication Institute, 2001).

names was fully consistent with all these cultures, but the Roma people were most open to novelty, the Turks were too pigheaded (had false consciousness), or in other words, had a wrong, essentialist view of their culture, and the Pomaks were somewhere in-between.

So, how can we judge whether a given novelty would fit into the integrity of the respective culture or would disrupt it? If, instead of integrity, we value identity as sameness, there would be no such problem. It is obvious which change would alter substantially the character of a culture, and which not. In order to preserve the identity, only insignificant changes can be "allowed." By replacing "identity" with "integrity" we avoid this essentialist conservatism, but consequently we confront the problem of deciding what novelty is consistent with a given culture and what is not. Taking into account the infinite variety of culture, it is not realistic to expect that general, "objective" criteria of consistency can be formulated. My suggestion in this respect is that the decision should be taken in each concrete case by the people belonging to the community in question – i.e., by the persons to be affected by the change.

In terms of minority group-specific rights, this would mean that the claims for such rights should not be justified in the light of universal standards, accepted as automatically valid for the concrete cases in the respective countries. If it were so, we would encounter endless problems (of the kind that we just described) concerning cultural integrity. Instead, the claims should be formulated *ad hoc* by the minority in question.

Of course, this solution raises in its turn another sort of problem. What does it mean that the people affected should decide for themselves what group-specific (culture-related) rights they need? Is it only a matter of their specific sensitivity, of their collective psyche – a matter of their "taste"? Isn't such an approach a too arbitrary and subjectivist one? And isn't it possible that some representatives of the minority (e.g., belonging to some kind of community leadership, or to the community's intellectual elite) usurp the role of its speakers and formulate such claims for rights on its behalf, that serve their private interests at the expense of the community's ones? What can guarantee that the claims of this sort are an authentic expression of the attitudes of the minority's members? Can such an expression be realized via public opinion polls or by voting? And besides – perhaps the most important problem in this respect – how do we convince the mainstream public to accept one or another claim for minority rights? What arguments can count as valid in a given cultural setting, if they are formulated in a different one?

First of all, I think that as far as authenticity is concerned, it cannot be guaranteed by arrangements of political nature – e.g., by organizing some forms of will-expression in a "vertical" dimension, i.e., mediated by elected or appointed representatives, leadership, etc. The very idea of group-specific rights is in contrast with the tendency to mediate the relations between the ordinary community members and society as a whole by some kind of leadership.

A possible "mechanism" of rational will-formation and expression, "immune" from manipulations, is public deliberation. The theories of deliberative democracy represent this mode of decision making as a rational discussion among free and equal citizens, which yields solutions that are in the interest of all people affected. Actually, the discussion has the form of an exchange of reasons, which aim to justify one or another alternative of regulating social relations as serving the general interest best.[8] The compelling "force" in this process of decision-making is not the will of the majority (as in the traditional democratic procedure), nor the will of the persons who happen to have the better leverage of whatsoever sort to influence the other participants in decision making (as is the case in ordinary bargaining), but the "force of the better argument." This means that it should be enough to demonstrate rationally that a given solution suits best the general interest, in order to compel everyone to accept it, at least in public.

Of course, public deliberation can serve minority communities as a means of claims-making only in a social environment in which this kind of decision-making is universally accepted. This presupposes a mature public sphere and advanced democracy in general. In such conditions, the deliberation within the minority communities would have the status of functioning of 'sub-publics.'

The differentiation of the public sphere into a plurality of sub-publics is suggested in recent publications which develop a criticism against the theory and practice of deliberative democracy, concerning its treatment of underprivileged (in terms of gender, race or class inequality) groups in society. As Nancy Fraser formulates the problem, socially dominant circles have a monopoly over "the socio-cultural means of interpretation and communication."[9] She regards these means to be:

> the officially recognized vocabularies in which one can press claims; the idioms available for interpreting and communicating one's needs; the established narrative conventions available for constructing the individual and collective histories which are constitutive of social identity; the paradigms of argumentation accepted as authoritative in adjudicating conflicting claims.[10]

---

[8] See, for example, Seyla Benhabib, "Toward a Deliberative Model of Democratic Legitimacy,"in S. Benhabib (ed.), *Democracy and Difference. Contesting the Boundaries of the Political* (Princeton: Princeton University Press, 1996), p. 69; Amy Gutmann and Dennis Thompson, "Why Deliberative Democracy is Different," *Social Philosophy and Policy*, Vol. 17 (2000): 161-180 at p. 161.

[9] Nancy Fraser, "Toward a Discourse Ethic of Solidarity," *Praxis International* 5 (1986), pp. 425-429, at p. 425.

[10] Fraser, "Toward a Discourse Ethic of Solidarity," p. 425.

In other words, the very idea of deliberative democracy gets compromised if we take into account the capacity of dominant groups to manipulate, via public communication, the ability of underprivileged categories of citizens to develop an adequate awareness of their needs, as well as their ability to formulate and justify claims in a convincing manner. If this is the case, the general conditions for public deliberation (such as rationality, openness, equality of the deliberating parties, and freedom from coercion), do not guarantee the fairness of the agreement, which comes as a result of argumentative communication of this kind.

The situation is even worse in the case of interaction between culturally different minorities and the mainstream public. In Fraser's view, the functioning of a single public sphere in a multicultural society would "be tantamount to filtering diverse rhetorical and stylistic norms through a single, overarching lens."[11] And because there cannot be such a lens that is culturally neutral, a minority's participation in public debate would be possible only at the cost of, in Fraser's words, "discursive assimilation."[12]

Fraser argues that, in stratified societies, a competition among sub-publics would "better promote the ideal of participatory parity than does a single, comprehensive, overarching public."[13] She proposes to call them "subaltern counterpublics."[14] In her view, the latter can serve as "parallel discursive arenas,"[15] where members of subordinated groups can develop their own interpretations of their needs, as well as articulate their claims and formulate argumentations in their own terms. With regard to cultural minorities, if they develop as separate sub-publics, this would give them the opportunity to construct and reconstruct their identities without being subject to assimilationist influences. So they would be able to speak in their own voices.

A paradigmatic case of such counterpublics are the feminist ones in the United States in the late twentieth century. As Fraser points out, they have constituted a formidable public sphere of their own, comprising "journals, bookstores, publishing companies, film and video distribution networks, lecture series, research centers, academic programs, conferences, conventions, festivals, and local meeting places."[16] If this "infrastructure" did not exist, we would hardly have to count today with such important terms as, e.g., "sexism" and "sexual harassment," which shape to a great extent the discourse on gender issues.

---

[11] Nancy Fraser, "Rethinking the Public Sphere: A Contribution to the Critique of Actually Existing Democracy," in C. Calhoun (ed.), *Habermas and the Public Sphere* (Cambridge, MA: The MIT Press, 1992), p. 126.

[12] Fraser, "Rethinking the Public Sphere," p. 126.

[13] Fraser, "Rethinking the Public Sphere," p. 122.

[14] Fraser, "Rethinking the Public Sphere," p. 123.

[15] Fraser, "Rethinking the Public Sphere," p. 123.

[16] Fraser, "Rethinking the Public Sphere," p. 123.

Of course, Fraser is aware of the danger that the fragmentation of the public sphere into a plurality of sub- (or counter-) publics would put at risk the communication within it. In the case of multicultural societies the question is: "Would participants in such debates share enough in the way of values, expressive norms, and therefore protocols of persuasion to lend their talk the quality of deliberations aimed at reaching agreement through giving reasons?"[17] She gives a moderately optimistic answer. It refers to the complexity of cultural identities, which allows for overlappings between the identities of representatives of generally different cultural communities. Besides, the "porousness, outer-directedness, and open-endedness"[18] of publics, the plurality of perspectives within them, and the opportunity that one and the same person be member of different publics, are also prerequisites for successful intercultural communication.

The traits of the multicultural societies that Fraser refers to, in order to find prospects for integration of the minority sub-publics into a common public sphere, do exist. However, they are not of a nature that would make possible an argumentative communication across lines of cultural difference. The overlappings, which accompany the relationships between complex identities and also between internally diverse sub-publics, can only be partial and occasional. As such, they cannot contribute much to the "synchronization" among the sets of – to use again Fraser's formulation – "socio-cultural means of interpretation and communication" that are specific for the sub-publics. And without a commensurability of the argumentation that is produced on both sides of the line of cultural difference, a process of inclusive public deliberation is not possible. In the best case, what we can expect from such a development of minority communities as sub-publics is an ideological competition with the mainstream public (and, of course, also among themselves). If we aim at the politicization of cultural diversity, this might be welcome as a means of consolidating the minorities' positions in their unequal political struggle. However, an ideological rivalry is definitely at odds with the principles of public deliberation. Therefore, Fraser's design of sub- (or counter-) publics cannot serve as a solution of our problem – i.e., how to enable minority communities to articulate and justify claims for group-specific rights, which are an authentic expression of their cultural needs, and moreover, which can be convincing for the mainstream public, if they are integrated into a process of public deliberation.

Another approach that recognizes the importance of intracultural discourse for the legitimization of norms and rights is taken by Abdullahi An-Naim. In his paper, "Toward a Cross-Cultural Approach to Defining International Standards of Human Rights," he criticizes the practice of dominant groups within a given society to "monopolize the interpretation of

---

[17] Fraser, "Rethinking the Public Sphere," p. 126.
[18] Fraser, "Rethinking the Public Sphere," p. 127.

cultural norms and manipulate them to their own advantage."[19] If one believes the claims of the government of a given country – that in the context of the cultural traditions of its people, certain norms are legitimate, although they contradict certain international standards (as is the case with, e.g., the issue of corporal punishment in some Islamic countries) – one makes a double mistake. First of all, even if a national culture were a monolithic whole (a rather essentialist assumption in itself), the country's government should not be accepted uncritically as the sole speaker on its behalf. We cannot eliminate from the outset the doubt that a government could represent the situation in its country in a way that suits its own interests, rather than the actual state of affairs.

Furthermore, a cultural tradition is never free of internal contradictions and of competing tendencies, even if the dissent concerns merely the perceptions and interpretations of cultural values and norms (the opinion An-Naim prefers to accept[20]). Having in mind the internal diversity of cultures, we cannot take for granted anyone's claims that he or she knows for sure what is compatible and what is not with the norms of a given culture.

The author maintains that disadvantaged individuals and groups should always have the opportunity to challenge the dominant ones' monopoly on the interpretation of the society's culture. "They should use internal cultural discourse to offer alternative interpretations in support of their own interests. This internal discourse can utilize intellectual, artistic, and scholarly work as well as various available forms of political action."[21]

It is obvious that a claim, addressed to the international public, to respect the cultural specificity of a given society, would be more credible if it is formulated as a result of internal discourse than if it comes directly from some more or less authorized institution. As it is impossible for the "alien" public to evaluate from without the justification for such a claim (because this justification refers to culturally specific relationships), that public can accept the claim only on the basis of trust in the credibility of its "author." In the case of the "internal discourse,"[22] this "author" is society as a whole (because the discourse is an open, not an exclusive one). If, on the contrary, the claim is presented by the country's government or another authorized institution, there can always be doubts whether the claim is a genuine expression of the will of the society as a whole, or has been shaped by dominant groups' interests.

---

[19] Abdullahi Ahmed An-Naim, "Toward a Cross-Cultural Approach to Defining International Standards of Human Rights," in Abdullahi Ahmed An-Naim (ed.), *Human Rights in Cross-Cultural Perspectives. A Quest for Consensus* (Philadelphia: University of Pennsylvania Press, 1992), p. 28.

[20] See An-Naim, "Toward a Cross-Cultural Approach," p. 20.

[21] An-Naim, "Toward a Cross-Cultural Approach," p. 28.

[22] In the sense used by An-Naim.

However, An-Naim does not go into details concerning the characteristics of the "internal discourse" that he recommends as a credible source of claims for recognition of cultural identity. Can any discussion within a cultural community count as a discourse, which could yield claims for recognition that are an authentic expression of the self-understanding and will of that community? Have we not witnessed numerous cases of public discussions which have been compromised by manipulation, propaganda pressure, rhetorical tricks, and more or less discreet forms of coercion? What can guarantee that the "internal discourse" in question would not turn out to be simply a more sophisticated version of the domination of politically or economically powerful groups?

My suggestion in this respect is that the results of a discourse within a cultural community would be credible for the larger public if that discourse proceeds along the "rules" of public deliberation. Moreover, if we regard the community as a sub-public, such a discourse within it can be integrated into a larger process of deliberation, even though a rational exchange of arguments between representatives of the cultural community and the "outer" public is not possible because of the cultural incommensurability (discussed above) in Fraser's idea of sub-publics.

If we return to the issue of group-specific rights, although a claim for such rights on behalf of a minority community cannot be justified rationally to the mainstream public, it can still be made credible in an indirect way – that is, by allowing that larger public to control the "formal" quality of the "internal" deliberation which has produced the claim in question. If the discourse within the community has been a fair one – i.e., the decision has been taken only under the "pressure" of arguments recognized as valid by all the individual and groups affected – the mainstream public can take for granted that the claim is representative for the position of the minority community, even though, from an "external" viewpoint the validity of the arguments that have decided the "internal" discussion cannot be evaluated because of their cultural specificity.

If these conditions are met, a cultural community can function as a sub-public which formulates claims for group-specific rights in a rational way, always open to novelty (including modification of old claims) and inclusive of the positions of all the people affected. The rational consensus among the latter can differentiate between those social changes which are consistent with the minority's culture, and those which are not. Equipped with such protective "mechanisms," minority communities can engage in processes of cultural development and mutual enrichment between cultures without risking their cultural integrity. Thus, the values of authenticity, solidarity and the like can be respected in the minority-majority relations, without resorting to an orthodox, essentialist "identity politics".

Sophia University
Sophia, Bulgaria

B. COMMUNITIES, CULTURAL FOUNDATIONS, AND CIVIL SOCIETY

CHAPTER VII

CULTURAL FOUNDATIONS FOR PERSON AND COMMUNITY: A VIEW FROM THE CENTER

OLIVA BLANCHETTE

There are different ways of viewing globalization. Some view it vaguely as a benign phenomenon that has spread over the globe bringing people together across borders and across continents in new ways of mixing, interacting and communicating with one another, facilitated by "trade, industry, technology, the arts, letters, and music, and religion."[1] In this view, globalization has come in waves starting from Europe in the sixteenth and seventeenth centuries with "concurrent missionary activities of Christianity,"[2] not to mention the impulse to conquer and to amass wealth. This is the view that was found commonly among the colonial powers of Europe, and later on of America, up to World War II, who saw nothing but good as coming from their incursions into the far-flung parts of the globe, while ignoring the consequences of their colonialism on those who were so forcefully invaded – on their culture, on their freedom, and on their very livelihood.

On this view, globalization "has even led to the creation of institutions that are broader than the nation state and which aim at protecting life, liberty, and the security of the person."[3] All this is seen as flowing in a straight line from the European globalizers, as if there had never been slaughter, slave trade, mass impoverishment and destruction of entire civilizations, hardly what one thinks of when one speaks of human interaction and communication in any sort of dialogue. The current wave of globalization is seen as having had only the same sort of positive effects: "individuals and groups have powerful ways of accessing information, communicating, and promoting their cultures and traditions,"[4] as if real dialogue were now the rule of the day for all peoples and cultures.

Then there is the more critical view of globalization that tries to look more precisely into the phenomenon for what it has become institutionally, and for the havoc it is wreaking upon the very institutions, political and cultural, it is alleged to be promoting. This is the view that not only brings out the damages eurocentered globalization has inflicted on all

---

[1] See, for example, William Sweet, "Globalization, Cultural Integrity, and 'Participative Construction,'" in *Notes et Documents* [*Dossier on the Ethics of Globalization*], no. 64 (mai/aout, 2002), p. 14.

[2] Ibid. p. 15.

[3] Ibid.

[4] Ibid.

the different parts of the globe it has affected or infected, but also recognizes that the current wave of globalization is even more insidious in undermining the rich diversity of human institutions and cultures that remain around the globe and reducing them all to its one-dimensional commercial interests. On this view, the current wave of globalization has rendered obsolete the very "political theory which has dominated Western thinking for the past four hundred years."[5]

This political philosophy has been characterized as possessive individualism by C. B. Macpherson,[6] but it can also be seen as leading necessarily to the subordination of all political, national and cultural interests of a people to the economic interests of certain individuals in a state or on a global scale – individuals we can identify as multi-national corporations. That may not be what was intended by the modern political theory of possessive individualism but it is what the postmodern mega-corporations have made of it, by overpowering not just the small states around the world and pulling them into their orbit of control, but even the larger states from which they operate, like the United States, Germany or Japan, and which they now manipulate as part of their cost of doing business throughout the globe at large. Some of the effects of this global takeover by gigantic commercial interests have been a decline of influence of civil associations of all sorts in this post-modern world and a loss of friendly societies in which dialogue took place. Instead of bringing different cultures together, the global takeover has isolated them from one another by manipulation in order to bring each one of them individually under its control or else to eliminate it altogether as one eliminates a competitor. One has only to think of the three or four large companies that control the grain and the seed supply of the globe, whose names are unknown to most people, let alone their existence, or of the McDonalds and the Burger Kings stretched around the globe, to see how this happens not only in the United States and Canada and France, but also in China and India and South Africa. Even French cuisine is disgraced in this competition, or else it is absorbed and diluted in the new processes of mass production proffered by Au Bon Pain.

There is something to be said for the benign view of globalization. One could say that it has given us the United Nations, where some communication among some 125 nations seems to take place, and it has given us the World Congress of Philosophy, and this Conference on the Dialogue of Cultural Traditions. But one has to ask what global perspective is implied in all that. Is it the global perspective of the agents of globalization, or is it some other communitarian perspective that might be developing here or at the United Nations but that the agents of globalization

---

[5] Leslie Armour, "Globalization and Philosophy," in *Notes et Documents* [*Dossier on the Ethics and Globalization*], p. 14.

[6] Cf. *The Political Theory of Possessive Individualism, Hobbes to Locke* (Oxford: Clarendon, 1962).

might be trying to prevent from happening lest their plan for encirclement be subverted? There is not just the UN to be considered, however, but also the World Trade Organization in Geneva and the International Monetary Fund and the World Bank operating out of Washington that are the more powerful engines of globalization, institutions that can bring nations to their court and pass judgment on them to satisfy the demands of the money mandarins of the world, usually at the expense of the blood and sweat and often the cultural patrimony of entire nations. The United Nations and World Congresses of Philosophy may sound good to us, but they are an unpleasant sideshow that the real globalizers would prefer to ignore, if not shut down completely, for fear that a real dialogue among the peoples at the far end of their tentacles might come up with something that they are unable to control.

The better view of globalization is the more critical and the more realistic one, especially if we are thinking of dialoguing about our diverse cultures and what is left of our political and national institutions under this post-modern regime of globalization. There will be no real dialogue unless there is some critical reflection on the reality in which we find ourselves – a reality which is afraid of dialogue because it might become all too liberating for those who enter into such an openness of mind and spirit to other ways of doing things in the world. One of the things we could talk about in a conference such as this is the conditions for the possibility of such a dialogue among cultures or among people of different cultures from around the world, and whether such conditions have been realized in the current wave of globalization. But that is not exactly what we are gathered here to talk about.

We are gathered to talk more about the cultural foundations of person and community, who, of course, are the ones who are supposed to be entering into dialogue. We are to dialogue, first, about how we become person and community in a culture, which is a problem for us because we find ourselves coming from different cultures and speaking different languages. How can we communicate with one another as person and community if we are grounded in different cultures? What is the point of gathering all the information in the world, the way large corporations do, if we can't converse with one another about it and about what it means to us as human beings? And, even more to the point here in our situation of globalization, what is the point of coming together if we come from different sides of a boundary that separates the globalizers and those who are being globalized, where one side may be interested in real cultural dialogue but the other is not? The boundary I am speaking of is a strange one. It can be represented geographically as a demarcation between a center and a periphery, where a power emanates from the center toward a periphery of nations or of persons and communities but is not shared politically or democratically by any at the periphery. It is a line drawn across continents and between north and south by the globalizers for the globalized who are being captured into the system, but are being kept at arms length as human beings, with a monologue on one side and no chance of a dialogue on the other side – at least not with the monologuers or the globalizers who draw the line or control the system. We all come from different sides of this line, some from the side of the globalizers and some from the side of the globalized, but if we are to enter into any sort of dialogue we must transcend this line, recognizing it for what it is and overcoming it politically and democratically at least among ourselves in conversing about our different cultures. We must not remain on the far side of this line, which is often hidden from us and where the globalizers would have us remain, far removed from one another and in silence, as they undermine the very political and intercultural communication we are trying to institute.

As an American I come from one side of this line and many of you come from the other side, for the forces of globalization are seen as coming largely from America with some contingents from Europe and Japan – the so-called G-7 or G-8 nations. But as interlocutors in an intercultural dialogue, we cannot remain divided in this way. The fact is that some individuals on the side of the globalized, in poor countries for example, have been so globalized that they have taken on the role of globalizers in their own countries, that is, have delivered their countries into the hands of the globalizers at the center, namely, the large multi-national corporations that rule over the global economy through the WTO, the IMF and the World Bank. But, alternatively, on the side of the globalizers there are also many who have been left out of this power structure, as in many poorer countries, or who will to opt out of it, and whose number is growing. They too find themselves all too globalized for their human comfort. They are looking for a way out of this straightjacket of imposed globalization in search of a humanization that will embrace all cultures in a free or a fair exchange of ideas, of goods and of spirit among nations, another kind of globalization than the one that has been inflicted on all of us so far.

I speak as one of these protesters from the center here, and I would like to speak of the difficulties we encounter on the side of the globalizers when we find our own political philosophy and the very idea of the nation-state undermined by the globalizing economic interests. Cultural foundations as concentrations of personal and communal life are under threat of obliteration not only at the periphery but also at the center. In fact, the undermining of such foundations may be much more advanced in the comfort of our homes at the center, where we find little real political consciousness and too much willingness to just go along with the charade of a political process that has been reduced to another commercial enterprise of marketing by large corporations with deep pockets who pay for the campaigns, than it is in poorer countries of the periphery, where the imposition of social chaos in negotiations is much more brutal and obvious for all to see in terms of systematic impoverization and disenfranchisement in a culture of silence.

What I would like to express here is how I view this problem of cultural foundation for person and community from the standpoint of one close to the center and perhaps taking too much advantage from it but not wishing to be part of it and its domineering ways, as one who is usually at odds with much of what goes on at the center, let alone at the periphery, at the behest of multinational corporations, in order to invite others to express their view of the problem who may feel further removed from this insidious center, more on the periphery, than perhaps I do. Let me do this by indicating four important points of contention in this complex of ideas concerning person, community, cultural foundations and cooperation among peoples that post-modern globalization calls into play for us, starting from the perspective of possessive individualism mentioned earlier.

First, with regard to the idea of person that we invoke so casually (as if it were uppermost in the mind of globalizers), we should recognize that it is very contentious in the way it comes out of the modern thinking of the center. On the one hand, this thinking fixes on the individual as absolute, and an end in itself in isolation from all other individuals and from any association with other human beings, something that has only self-interests in competition with other individuals with only self-interests, without any sense of community to begin with. On the other hand, we speak of what we call personal relations and mutual recognition of one another as values that transcend this kind of absolute individualism and which grounds human rights. This is where our political sense of community comes from, as it did for the Greeks and for most traditional societies, namely, as something that should take precedence over isolated individualism at the expense of all other individuals in what was described by Hobbes at the beginning of modern political theory as the war of everyone against everyone.

In fact, it is this very political sense of community itself that has become contentious in this post-modern globalization. The idea of community is often used loosely by people of the center to designate any grouping or collection of individuals, such as a crowd of consumer-revelers in Times Square or a conglomerate of banks that stretch around the globe, without regard as to whether there are personal relations involved at all, as if they were just numbers to be counted in projections for market timing. Such ways of grouping individuals who essentially remain isolated in their individuality endow them with a phony aura of personality or community that they do not have except in the mind of planners who, for their part, only bunch them all together as they would individual fish swimming in a market pool. When we think of community more precisely, however, we think of people coming together on a basis of mutual recognition, mutual respect and mutual regard for one another and for common interests shared by all – in other words, people with a real personal interest in one another, no matter what the differences, without excluding relations of justice and friendship. This is what the Greeks spoke of as *koinonia*, Hegel as *Volk*, and we as a community or a people. I'm sure that people all over the world have such an idea for themselves and for people with whom they feel associated in a special way as persons.

Third, when we introduce the idea of cultural foundations into this mix of ideas, we find ourselves even more perplexed in this contention about person and community. Cultural foundations are built up historically by particular communities, as persons consolidate themselves in relations of justice and friendship among one another and (to include the religious dimension that is usually found in these cultural traditions) in relations to the divine. This has to include a very rich understanding of the many different ways in which different peoples have humanized themselves through very personal relations indeed.

However, it also happens that cultural foundations take on a life of their own in civil society, independently of particular individuals and in abstraction from the community that brought them into existence. When this happens – when some aspect of a cultural foundation takes on a life of its own (and it does more often than not) – these cultural foundations can be used by individuals, not just to lord it over the community, but even against the community and its common good. This is what happens when some people speak loosely about community to cast an aura of absoluteness about a particular way of organizing society and then to have this particular way spill over into other communities that already have another way of organizing of their own. These globalizers take one particular cultural foundation, such as the absolute right of private property in a framework of competition, for example, and then try to make it, not only the sole cultural foundation for their own community, as in possessive individualism, but also the cultural foundation for all other communities around the globe in the process they then call globalization, thereby stripping all other peoples of their own traditional cultural foundations for communal life among persons.

This brings me to the fourth level of contention in our theme for discussion here, the very idea of cooperation among peoples as a form of globalization. Some people like to think of globalization as a new way of coming together, as in a community based on mutual recognition, respect and regard for one another. This is the idea that underlies such expressions as "cooperation among peoples." It is an ideal that we should strive for in the context of common interests we all share and want to participate in, an ideal we try to institutionalize in things like the UN or what we call an international community. But is that in fact what post-modern globalization has become, or is it not rather the imperialistic expansion of a particular cultural foundation spreading out from a center to dominate and exploit all other cultural foundations for its own competitive advantage? Western-style capitalism is a cultural foundation now well established and spreading to all parts of the globe. It is the only cultural foundation that is universally established, but it is one that is established at the expense of other cultural foundations and for its own exclusive benefit. It works by standardization of all goods and values to comply with the requirements of its means of production and distribution. This is a betrayal of the very idea of international community, and a reduction of all cultural foundations to something that will serve only the private interests of the individuals who have names and who sit, unbeknownst to most people, at the centers of control for globalization.

This is hardly a program for cooperation that will benefit all peoples who take part in justice and friendship. Nor is it a program that will foster dialogue among cultures that create personality and community. It is a program that only manipulates language and social regulation for its own ends of profit taking, and that drowns out all other voices by the din of its aggressive advertising. If we are to enter into any sort of dialogue, inter-cultural or just plain cultural, as persons belonging to different communities, we will have to overcome the perversion of language that has come about as a result of the current wave of globalization. We will have to reaffirm the priority of persons and of community – indeed, of different communities – and of the political over the economic as well as over every attempt to reduce all these terms, such as person, community and cultural foundations, to meaningless babble. We will have to reaffirm our personality, not just our individuality, which can still be manipulated by the purveyors of globalization, and even our different personalities in all our differences. True dialogue is capable of encompassing all these differences we find among persons and communities in the mutual recognition of a shared humanity in the world, but only if it resists being hypnotized by the false allurements being served up by the agents of globalization to keep us from looking at it from a critical human standpoint.

The problem for us then is to figure out whether the idea of a real cooperation based on mutual recognition, respect and regard for one another among peoples is only an illusion or a pipe dream, as those in the center who have controlled globalization so far would have us believe, or is it instead something we can still work out cooperatively in mutual respect and regard for one another with everyone participating on a footing of some equality – what I have referred to as mutual respect and regard – in what is to become a common good for all the cultural foundations that sustain the different communities around the globe, east and west, north and south. Is this the way people at the periphery see the problem or is it still just another way of manipulating the debate so that it will serve once again the interests of those at the center who are the agents of the on-going post-modern globalization?

Boston College
Boston, USA

CHAPTER VIII

PLURALISTIC CULTURE AND THE OPEN SOCIETY

TRAN VAN DOAN

In this paper, I advance the thesis that the determinate factor of social progress is an open attitude. Such an "open society" is one which is able to receive different cultural traditions and is able to incorporate them into its own institutions.

To demonstrate this thesis, I will partly adopt Sir Karl Popper's views, arguing that the open attitude is more than a scientific attitude, and that it would lead to a rational society. However, I will contest his tendency to reduce society and its activities to the scientific community and scientific knowledge. Popper stubbornly and dogmatically believes in the force of reason – though he understands it slightly differently from the rationalist view of the modern age – and he attempts to treat scientific activity as the ultimate human activity. Starting with a critique of Popper's reductionism, I will go a step further by showing that the open society, due to its dialectical character, should not be understood in terms of 'science-doing' alone, but rather more in terms of 'society-making.' History testifies that human beings have consistently attempted to synthesize all that may be of use to preserve and, further, make life more perfect. The term 'useful' is understood here in a broad sense of making human life more secure, comfortable, and enjoyable (i.e., much broader than "the effectiveness of problem-solving" in science). The 'useful' can be fully grasped only in human life and the human world. Here I adopt Gadamer's theory of the 'fusion of horizons' to support my arguments.

INTRODUCTORY REMARKS

The idea of an open society is as old as the history of humankind. An open society is a society in which people are tolerant of others' ideas, life-styles and ideologies. An open society, thus, is known by its members' behaviour of respecting others' ideas and even taking them into consideration. In a word, an open society can be known by its ability to receive other cultures, and by its capacity to bring them together into itself, and so becoming more ideal. In this sense, many Confucians have claimed that ancient China was once an open society with a democratic practice – found in the regimes of Yao and Shun, the two legendary kings. These two knew how to listen to their people, how to satisfy their needs and how to harmonize conflicts.[1] Similarly, some have boastfully exalted the *"chin-ming"* or "love for people" of Mencius as the best example of democracy, an essential aspect of an open society.[2] Of course, Western apologists would challenge Eastern scholars by crediting Socrates and Plato as the forerunners of the idea of an open society. The killing of Socrates certainly inspired Plato's allegory of the cave: only the ignorant, the autistic ego would be intolerant to truth. Plato's idea of a republic in fact aimed at correcting the intolerance and cynicism of the oligarchy which was responsible for the death of his master. It is, however, neither my intention to support or question these claims, nor my wish to look for an exact definition of 'open society.' Neither claim seems completely founded or justified, and the idea of an open society seems to be as vague as controversial. We know well that the prophets for an open society may be its worst offenders, as seen in the case of Platonists and even of Confucians. Similarly, the most ardent opponents of the feudal system may turn out to be its most fanatical defenders. Popper has exposed this paradox in his classic, *The Open Society and Its Enemies,*[3] which I will discuss in the next section. Thus, I will not embark on a search for a definition of open society. There is one thing that we may agree on – and which Popper himself would concede – namely, that the idea of an open society is born and constructed slowly and progressively in the process of human history – in Popper's own vocabulary, via 'piecemeal social engineering'[4] – and, as such, it is by no means definitive. And this provides my starting point for arguing for the internal relationships among human tolerance towards other cultures, their receptivity of different ideas, and the emergence of an open society.

POPPER'S CONCEPTION OF THE OPEN SOCIETY

Many readers of *The Open Society and its Enemies* would be deeply angered by Popper's violent attack on Plato, Hegel and Marx, to mention a few, whom he calls the open society's greatest enemies. This anger may be similar to that of the captives in the cave at the moment they were told about the truth of an outside world. Plato's account of this anger is insightful. He demonstrates that what we regarded as absurd in the past might turn out to be what we automatically take for granted later. For this reason, despite its provocative character, *The Open Society and its Enemies* is worthy of a careful re-evaluation.

---

[1] Cf. Liu Shu-hsian and A. Allinson, eds., *Harmony and Strife* (Hong Kong: The Chinese University Press, 1993).

[2] Kim Ñònh, *Cöũa Khoảng (Gate to Confucianism)* (Sài Goøn: Ra Khôi, 1967), ch. 2.

[3] Karl Popper, *The Open Society and its Enemies*, 2 vols. (Princeton, NJ: Princeton University Press, 5th ed. rev.,1971).

[4] *Open Society*, I, p. 3.

Let us suppose for the moment that Popper is right. I would like to begin with the question of how great and open-minded thinkers – ones who have decisively contributed to the progress of mankind – can make a 180 degree turn to become the enemies of the open society. This is also Popper's main concern. Popper himself never doubts the greatness of these immortal thinkers, and he does not question their enormous contribution to the building of human society.[5] Plato's far reaching vision of a republic, Hegel's forecast of the coming of the absolute state, Marx's attempt to give flesh and blood to Hegel's absolute spirit (i.e., the Proletariat) – all have served to push the world forward. (Similarly, Martin Heidegger's tireless digging into human being, and his relentless critique of Western philosophy, have inspired generations.)

Now, the question of whether Popper is right to blame them for the closedness of society, for dictatorship, for being the enemies of the open society, must be carefully examined. Here, we have to examine his arguments, or at least his explanation of the shift of great philosophers from men of enlightenment to enemies of reason. Popper's arguments – found mainly in *The Open Society*, in a previous work, *The Poverty of Historicism*, and in his later *Conjectures and Refutations*[6] – could be resumed in the following points.

First, the claims for science and for being scientific are very questionable and, in many cases, unfounded. These claims are based on a biased conception of science, according to which science is a certain kind of knowledge of universal and necessary characteristics, and scientists are those who possess this kind of knowledge. As seen in the case of Plato and, later, Descartes, only ideas that are universal and necessary can be "scientific." Descartes had no doubt that such knowledge is mathematical and, therefore, science is identified with mathematics, and scientific methods are none other than the mathematical methods of deduction or analysis and geometrical intuition. On the other hand, John Locke, by following Francis Bacon, would favour induction as the best method for all the sciences. Such a claim is rarely challenged. It is taken for granted by

---

[5] Popper was, early in life, a Marxist, and became a member of the Austrian Communist Party in 1919. However, dissatisfied with the failure of the Party to assume responsibility after a fatal accident in a demonstration in Vienna during which 6 young members were shot to death, Popper quit the ACP. See Karl Popper, *Lessons of This Century* - Interviewed by Giancarlo Bosetti (London and New York: Routledge, 1997), pp. 16-17. Despite his severe criticism of Marxism, he still openly acknowledged its influence in his *Open Society*, p. 275: "All modern writers are indebted to Marx, even if they do not know it. This is especially true of those who disagree with his doctrines, as I do."

[6] Karl Popper, *The Poverty of Historicism* (London: Routledge & Kegan Paul, 3rd ed., 1972); *Conjectures and Refutations: The Growth of Scientific Knowledge* (London: Routledge & Kegan Paul, 4th rev. and enlarged ed., 1972).

most scientists and even philosophers up to our day. Popper objects to such a claim. In his view, if science is defined by the criterion of truth, and if its method is analytic, then there are hardly any scientific discoveries at all. All of what mathematicians and philosophers have done and are doing is only a confirmation and reconfirmation of the fact; or, in Marx's quite reasonable critique, all that philosophers have done is only a kind of interpretation[7] of the world.

Hence, it is time to rethink science. Starting with his examination of Marx's view of social critique, Popper holds that the business of science is, first, to discover the problems of knowledge and of the world, and, then, to solve them. And in order to solve the problems or to change the world, criticism – relentless criticism – is the *conditio sine qua non*.[8] From such a conviction, Popper conjectures a new understanding of science:

> The criterion of the scientific status of a theory is its falsifiability, or refutability, or testability. Every genuine test of a theory is an attempt to falsify it, or to refute it… As scientists we do not seek highly probable theories but explanations; that is to say, powerful and improbable theories.[9]

A similar understanding of science is applied to the social sciences and humanities as well, as he writes in his thesis on the social sciences:

> Thus the method of science is one of tentative attempts to solve our problems; by conjectures which are controlled by severe criticism. It is a consciously critical development of the method of trial and error.[10]

Second, as a consequence of the view of science as an endless process of "trial and error" (i.e., as rational criticism), Popper rejects any kind of scientific theory that claims absolute truth. If science is acquired by "mistake-learning," and if the process of "mistake-learning" is endless, then (as a logical consequence), no truth could be final. Therefore, any belief in the absolute form of science (i.e., in an absolute truth or in a perfect society

---

[7] Marx, *Theses on Feuerbach*, Thesis 11.

[8] Popper consciously quoted a very famous passage from Marx as the motto of his *Open Society*, insisting on criticism as the necessary condition to change the world. In a letter to Arnold Ruge, Marx once wrote: "We do not anticipate the world dogmatically, but rather wish to find the new world though the criticism of the old."

[9] *Conjectures and Refutations*, pp. 36, 37, 58.

[10] Karl Popper, "The Logic of the Social Sciences" in Theodor W. Adorno, *The Positivist Dispute in German Sociology*, tr. Glyn Adey and David Frisby (London: Heinemann, 1976), Thesis 6, p. 90.

– as once claimed by Plato, Hegel and Marx) is dismissed by him as historicism.[11] Historicism is the belief that history would end in an absolute state, that the historical process would follow a certain logical pattern, and that such a history is within our reach. Plato's absolute state based on the eternal *eidos* and *arche*, Hegel's on absolute *Geist* and its impeccable dialectic, Marx's dream of a classless society as the final stage – all point to the belief of a culmination of human history and all share the dogma of a final, absolute logic of history. It is precisely in this sense that Popper understands Marx's historicism as the belief in "the method of a science of society" (i.e., the belief that "the study of history, and especially of the tendencies inherent in the historical development of mankind").[12] According to this belief, historicism is implicit in human activities and, of course, in all human social structures. And in conformity with Marx's division of social structure into the super-structure and the infra-structure, historicism expresses itself in its two most fundamental forms: the economic and the moral. On Popper's view, the first one is embraced by Marx,[13] while the latter is embraced by Christianity (from which Marx inherited his ideas, even if he denied it).[14] Such a historicism contradicts itself, not because the premise of Hegel's logic was false (no proof is sufficient), but because a progressive society contradicts any claim of an absolute. Any claim of an absolute truth constitutes an objection to any form of historicism.

Having unmasked the essentially hypocritical character of such logic, Popper goes to draw the conclusion that historicism is the chief enemy of an open society. Then Popper goes a step further: to defend the open society, one has to unmask the fallacy of Hegel's and Marx's logic. (Here he strictly follows Marx's radical criticism, by unmasking his own master.) Only if we succeed in doing it may we have the chance to regain the freedom once lost in the land of historicism.[15]

Third, Popper sides with David Hume by arguing that there is no logical connection between fact and norm, between the "is" and the "ought." Popper writes: "It is impossible to derive a sentence stating a norm or a decision or, say, a proposal for policy, from a sentence stating a fact."[16] This is his direct confrontation with the great Kant, even if he is, in a certain measure, a Kantian (as seen in his stubborn insistence on the autonomy of ethics). In Popper's view, fact belongs to the order of the first world, while

---

[11] *The Poverty of Historicism*, op. cit.

[12] *Open Society*, II, p. 303, note 2.

[13] *Open Society*, II, pp. 296 ff.

[14] *Open Society*, II, p. 386.

[15] *Conjectures and Refutations*, p. 338. Here Popper wrote: (Historicism is the) "view that the story of mankind has a plot, and that if we can succeed in unravelling this plot, we shall hold the key to the future."

[16] *Open Society*, I, p. 64.

norm to that of the second world.[17] Fact is "natural" while norm is often constructed after a certain model of nature or, in most cases, artificially at the whim of rulers. Policy, for example, could be made in accordance with, or in response to some facts (the case of natural disasters) but, mostly, arbitrarily.[18] The norms adopted by socialism are surely not identical with those found in the capitalist system, even if both claim the rightness of their norms, simply because their factual (actual) life is different. Popper argues: "That most people agree with the norm 'Thou shalt not steal' is a sociological fact. But the norm 'Thou shalt not steal' is not a fact, and can never be inferred from sentences describing facts."[19]

Fourth, Popper follows Kant in insisting on the autonomy of ethics. As a rational individual, fully conscious of his or her own acts, man has the right to determine his own fate. Here is the main reason for Popper's "passionate belief in the right of individuals to criticize their rulers and the institutional framework of their societies."[20] Here is also the reason for Popper's bitterness against Plato's concept of justice – which he dismisses as "a synonym for 'that which is in the interest of the best state.'"[21]

Fifth, Popper accuses Plato, Hegel and Marx of being prophets of historicism, in the sense that they were trying to build a utopian society (i.e., a society with no foundation and unrealisable). In contrast, Popper conceives of an open society (i.e., a society in the process of being constructed step by step and by means of critique). In his words, his is a

---

[17] In *Objective Knowledge: An Evolutionary Approach* (Oxford: Clarendon Press, 1972) and earlier in two important scientific papers "Epistemology Without a Knowing Subject" (1968) and "On the Theory of the Objective Mind" (1968), Popper puts forth the thesis of the three worlds: "(1) the first world is that of matter and energy, i.e. the material world (inorganic and organic, including machines and all living forms), (2) the second world is that of conscious experience, and (3) the third world is that of objective knowledge. Of course, norms could belong to the third world if it is kind of natural law in the sense that it is coded symbolically in the actual structures that serve as the vehicles for this knowledge." (See J. C. Eccles, "World of Objective Knowledge," in *The Philosophy of Popper*, ed. Paul Arthur Schilpp (La Salle, IL: Open Court, 1974) , Vol. 1, p. 351.

[18] *Open Society*, I, p. 61: "Critical dualism merely asserts that norms and normative laws can be made and changed by man, more especially by a decision or convention to observe them or to alter them, and that it is therefore man who is morally responsible for them; not perhaps for the norms which he finds to exist in society when he first begins to reflect upon them, but for the norms which he is prepared to tolerate once he has found out that he can do something to alter them. Norms are man-made in the sense that we must blame nobody but ourselves for them; neither nature nor God."

[19] *Open Society*, I, p. 64.

[20] Edward Boyle, "Karl Popper's Open Society," in *The Philosophy of Karl Popper*, ed. Paul Arthur Schilpp, op. cit., Vol. 2, p. 845.

[21] *Open Society*, I, p. 89.

piecemeal social engineering.[22] Here, a further clarification of Popper's conceptions of utopian society and "piecemeal social engineering" is needed in order to avoid possible misunderstanding. Utopian society is the ideal but unreal state which Plato and the Platonists sought to build on earth. The utopian is often conceived as the perfect, the absolute, the ultimate which never existed before, and which need not ever be replaced by another state. If Plato had tried in vain to build his ideal republic, and if Hegel had attempted futilely to reincarnate the absolute *Geist*, then Marx's ideal of an absolute proletariat would also have been a rather hopeless project, since all these are in fact utopian. In a word, the ideal of an absolute, final state remains as vague as it is unreal and, consequently, unrealisable. In contrast, "piecemeal social engineering" is a realistic attempt to build our society. Piecemeal engineering is described by Popper as follows:

> Any rational action must have a certain aim... Only when this ultimate aim is determined, in rough outline at least, like a blueprint of the society at which we aim, only then can we begin to consider the best ways and means for its realization, and to draw up a plan for practical action... I wish to outline another approach to social engineering, namely, that of piecemeal engineering. It is an approach which I think to be methodologically sound. The politician who adopts this method may or may not have a blueprint of society before his mind, he may or may not hope that mankind will one day realize an ideal state, and achieve happiness and perfection on earth. But he will be aware that perfection, if at all attainable, is far distant, and that every generation of men, and therefore also the living, have a claim to it; perhaps not so much a claim to be made happy, for there are no institutional means of making a man happy, but a claim not to be made unhappy, where it can be avoided... The piecemeal engineer will, accordingly, adopt the method of searching for, and fighting against, the greatest and most urgent evils of society, rather than searching for, and fighting for, its greatest ultimate good.[23]

For all of these reasons, and also because of an obsession with these gigantic ideas, Popper concludes that Plato, Hegel and Marx were seduced by their own logic into accepting the dogma of a unique truth, a unique ideal state, etc. And consequently, almost against their better

---

[22] Boyle, pp. 884-45.
[23] *Open Society*, II, pp. 157-158.

judgement, they indirectly advocated for a closed, monolithic society. In short, this is how they could become the enemies of the open society.

PLURALISTIC CULTURE AND ITS RELATION TO THE OPEN SOCIETY

There is no doubt that Popper may have gone too far with his rather lavish critique, and many criticisms have been raised against him. Nonetheless, one can hardly dismiss his principal point – namely, that an open society is marked by its capacity of receptivity and by its trait of non-conformity. Furthermore, social progress proceeds step by step, by means of constant correction, and not by any external force or supernatural idea. I will develop his idea further by extending the two characteristics of receptivity and non-conformity beyond the sphere of scientific research.

On the one hand, one has to recognize Popper's intention behind his devastating critique. His merciless attack on Plato, Hegel and Marx does not in fact aim at these great personalities, but rather at what they might have been responsible for, namely a certain ideology, the so-called historicism which Popper regarded as the stronghold of the enemies of the open society. Historicism, with the ideology of tribalism as its legitimate product, is an ideology founded on the belief that only a certain ethnos, a certain race, a certain country, or a certain culture has the privilege or the gift of possessing the whole truth and the right to claim (or, better, the right to dictate to) the world. And as such, it entertains the view of a unique, predetermined history which belongs to one race, country, religion, political party, etc.

In the same context, scientific tribalism is the uncritical view that only a certain view, a certain method (e.g., induction), or a certain science could warrant truth, stimulate discovery, and change the world. This ideology is, regrettably, wholeheartedly taken by many scientists and philosophers – ones who claim for themselves the possession of truth and its method. Here is the main reason why Popper starts his arguments against the claim of a 'unique truth.' In his view, the belief in a unique truth and in the illusion of possessing it, are too strong and too uncritical, so that almost all Western philosophers, especially modern ones, have taken it for granted. Such a belief strongly persuaded scientists and philosophers to search for it. They came to the view that there is a "best" method, which is the most effective instrument in the search for truth and which warrants truth. Consequently, their main concern is with who has the right method. Such reasoning leads to a corollary; the search for truth is identified with the search for the best method, and vice-versa – and, of course, this method must be scientific in nature. Scientific discovery is identified with an elaboration (or manufacture or construction) of method. Descartes built his philosophy in this context. On Descartes' view, if truth is to be possible, we need the correct method. To him, the correct method has a scientific character. As we all know, this method is none other than mathematics (with geometry and arithmetic as the models). We have no need to reiterate here what Bacon, Locke, and Newton achieved with their search for the exact method. It is sufficient to note that, for all of them, their scientific work is identified with their elaboration of scientific method. However different they might have been, they shared the same belief – that only *their* method is correct and effective.

Popper remarks that, if their method is the only one correct, and if their truth is the only unique one, then what we have to do is to put their claim to the test of reason. Not quite in the line of the great Kant, Popper takes the two principles of falsification and justification as the criteria for the test. He argues that, if a view could be easily "falsified", then we can successfully prove the claim of unique truth to be untenable, and then we can demonstrate that such and such a method may be questionable. In a word, such a view can be easily refuted. Here, Popper deploys pincer-tactics by attacking from two sides.

First, in the case of the claim to a unique truth, there is perhaps only one correct method which may reach this truth. However, each scientist may adopt different methods. That means that they tacitly accept that there are many methods to reach it. If so, then Popper argues that these philosophers and scientists commit either a self-contradiction or they have to accept a new view of science. In Popper's view, they have misunderstood science and, hence, the conception of truth. Science is not marked by the criterion of universal and necessary truth, but by constant criticism.[24] Second, if truth is unique, then one should have a clear-cut definition of truth. The fact is that no one can arrive at such a definition. Thus, one has to concede that truth cannot be defined. If so, then all ideologies are absurd. Ideologists tend to turn a blind eye to the fact that, as an inclusive concept, 'open society' is too vague. It is not identified with truth, and certainly much less defined by truth criteria. By not discovering the difference between *theoria* and *praxis*, and by entertaining the illusion of a perfect society in accordance with the principle of mathematical truth, they have been led to seek the realisation of such a society. And, as a result, they have opened the door letting the enemy sneak in. "Open society" becomes, therefore, a mere slogan or, rather, simply an instrument for the opposite purpose. As seen throughout human history, under the guise of the idea of an open society, dictators have transformed the notion into an ideology to grab power, and then to cement it. Worse, they suppress their opponents and destroy the open society itself. The case of a Maximilien de Robespierre or a Jean-Paul Marat is by far not an exception; it is, pitifully and deplorably, a common case, regularly repeated by great "leaders" like Adolf Hitler, Joseph Stalin, Mao Zedong, Chang Kai-shek, and a horde of

---

[24] Karl Marx; Popper, *Open Society*, II, p. 261; *Conjectures and Refutations*, "We learn a great deal from mistakes"; Also in "The Logic of the Social Sciences", thesis 6, in Theodor Adorno, *The Dispute in German Sociology*.

similar "great leaders." They proclaimed with great fanfare a coming democracy but, at the same, they cynically extinguished the burning desire for freedom of their people.

On the other hand, we also discover in Popper's logic certain fallacies; one is that he has insufficient grounds (or data) to universalize the critical method as the only scientific one; another is that he commits a category mistake (i.e., his tendency to apply the same method to a diversity of different subjects). And, as such, Popper seems to be on a par with those whom he attacked: he is still a faithful believer in a certain ideology, i.e., that of rational criticism. As a consequence of his unquestioned belief in the magical power of criticism (i.e., in his method of "trial and error"), he is prevented from recognising the true intention of Plato, Hegel, and, especially, Marx. I will elucidate my critique as follows.

First, one cannot take the so-called method of "trial and error" as a panacea, applying it to all sciences, not to mention to the human sphere beyond the sphere of the exact sciences. Can one test the love of a mother? Can one verify her love by employing so-called objective criteria? Or must we recognise the fact that love cannot be defined, that there is not the same love, that love has its own logic (as Pascal once brilliantly showed)? Here is evidence of what we can identify as a category mistake (i.e., the error of applying the same criteria [or the same method} to different categories, or in the Kantian view, of applying the same categories to different subjects).[25] Second, even if such a method may be of a scientific character, it is still far from immune from the accusation of being a "dogmatic" belief. The fact is that any choice or any conjecture of a thesis (premise) cannot be a kind of *creatio ex nihilo*. It is born (or constructed) in our life-world, where it aims at addressing a certain problem. And our life-world is shaped by traditions, habits, beliefs and so on. This means that any conjecture can be possible in a certain life-world, and influenced by pre-scientific views. Just as the claim of reason is often nourished in the womb of irrational belief, the scientist's claim of science is often grounded on non-scientific belief. Here is the reason why no one, including Popper himself, could avoid the so-called Mannheim paradox – namely, any critique of ideology is in itself ideological. All criticism is born in an uncritical belief (i.e., an unverified premise).

Second, Popper seems to be convinced by the belief that anyone – anyone who produces a kind of "meta-narrative" (in the terminology of post-modernists) or grand theory – commits the same mistake (i.e., of being utopian and determinist). Such a belief, however, prevented Popper from making a fair assessment of these great theoreticians. The fact that Marx

---

[25] Cf. Peter Winch, *The Idea of Social Science and Its Relation to Philosophy* (London: Routledge and Kegan Paul, 1957); See also Tran Van Doan, *Reason, Rationality, Reasonableness* (New York/ London: University Press of America, 1989; Reprinted: Washington, DC: The Council for Research in Values and Philosophy, 2001).

had rightly discovered the double face of the claim about the open society hidden in the uncritical claim of truth, is simply ignored by Popper. Indeed, Marx had dismissed Bauer, Proudhon, Feuerbach and Bakunin for their lack of criticism and for their contentment with the mere rhetoric of an open, utopian and unscientific society.[26] On Marx's view, the danger of the utopian society advocated by Proudhon was as great as the irresponsible adventure of an anarchistic state championed by Bakunin. In the same line as Marx, and yet ironically against Marx, Heidegger's attack on the traditional conception of truth could be interpreted as his objection to Marx's prophecy of an absolute truth incorporated in the dictatorship of the proletariat. And the neo-Marxist Jürgen Habermas would play the same game, chiding the postmodernists for their aimless adventures, and doubting the extravagant claims of absolute truth coming from the self-declared guardians of socialism from the Kremlin or from the newly forbidden city (Peking). To be sure, Heidegger, Habermas, and the like are returning to the path once opened by Socrates – namely, that it is not the truth, but the search for truth, that counts. That is the path once insisted upon by modern philosophers like Descartes and Locke when they claimed to possess the truth and the method of truth-acquisition. Seen in this context, it appears that Popper scratches where he does not itch: his criticism of Marx, Heidegger, and the others ultimately leads nowhere, since he himself has followed the same path once cleared by Hegel, Marx and Heidegger. In this sense, he may understand reason not in the sense of modern philosophy, but as a rigorous and non-conformist attitude. That means that, however different his conception of reason may be, he still believes in the force of reason. Thus, Popper continues to share the belief laid down by modern philosophers like Kant.

THE OPEN SOCIETY AND ITS CHARACTERISTICS:
THE DIALECTICAL FORMATION OF PLURALISTIC CULTURE

Following the main thesis presented in *The Open Society and its Enemies*, one may put forth another thesis as its corollary – namely that, as long as the transition from the tribal or closed society to the open society does not obey the principle of the 'critical power' of man, it encourages reactionary movements which try to overthrow civilization and return to tribalism. Here, Popper elevates the power of criticism to the rank of a non-

---

[26] Marx wrote: "It is therefore the duty of history, the beyond of truth having vanished, to establish the truth of this world. Philosophy is in the service of history. Its primary duty, once the sacred image of human self-estrangement has been unmasked, is to unmask self-estrangement in all its unholy forms. Criticism of heaven is transformed thereby into criticism of earth, criticism of religion into criticism of right, criticism of theology into criticism of politics." *Marx-Engels Gesamtausgabe* (1927-1932), I, 1, p. 608. See also K. Löwith, op.cit., pp. 97 ff.

negotiable condition.[27] According to Popper, the worlds imagined by Plato, designed by Hegel, and constructed by Marx were lacking this critical force, and therefore, fell prey to tribalism. Thus, they were at best pseudo-champions of the open society. I find Popper's thesis very challenging but, at the same time, very "dangerous," in the sense that, as a result of this, we may lapse into a certain kind of scepticism or radicalism. The point I wish to press against Popper is that his view is quite plausible insofar as it is applied in a certain field – say, in the field of logic – but it would become a mere slogan if it were applied to the real world. My own thesis is different; a society makes progress only if it has a clear purpose that benefits it, and provided it knows how to attain this goal. In this section, then, I will challenge Popper's view by arguing that criticism alone is insufficient to constitute the open society. At its best, criticism can safeguard our path by not letting us wander and get lost in the woods. The open society cannot grow out of criticism, but requires a permanent construction and reconstruction (i.e., a tireless dialectical synthesis of all elements of life). Criticism is only a means helping us to be clear about our purposes, to correct our methods, and sometimes even to adjust our purposes. Without a certain purpose in sight, any criticism would be empty and meaningless. Criticism makes sense only when it is concerned with the rightfulness or the usefulness of some purpose, when it helps to find a correct method to attain this goal, and when it challenges us – forces us to be, not at rest, but to discover the problems which we often, out of ignorance, may take for granted as non-problems. Thus, I contend that the main force which makes society progressive is not just criticism but, rather, the human power of dialectically synthesizing all elements of life (i.e., elements which may contribute to human survival, human self-preservation and human progress). Furthermore, the richer the world is, the more encompassing a knowledge and set of practical ideas and methods one needs. That is true in our present world, the so-called globalized world – a world of innumerable problems and needs that no single idea, no single method, and no single bit of knowledge can adequately respond to. Plato would respond differently to

---

[27] *Open Society*, I, p. 3. And, faithful to this principle, Popper passionately developed his life-long philosophy. In *The Logic of Scientific Discovery* (*Logik der Forschung*, 1934; tr. London: Hutchinson, 1960), Popper argued for a new approach to science, or rather, to a new understanding of science by means of permanent criticism. Such an idea was developed further in *Conjectures and Refutations*, in other more popular but less rigorous works (notably *The Poverty of Historicism*, and *The Open Society and its Enemies*), and much later in other less known works, like *The Open Universe* (London and New York: Routledge, 1982) and *All Life is Problem-Solving* (London and New York: Routledge, 1999), etc. Since the idea of criticism is the only one factor which contributes to the progress of knowledge (science), and since it is universal, Popper conjectures that only an open society (i.e., a society not determined by any factor, but by criticism alone) could be the ideal one.

our world, just as Hegel and Marx would have second thoughts before venturing any conjecture. They have to know what our world is, what the people need, whence we are coming and where we are going, and so on. In other words, they would reiterate the same question that a thoughtful Kant once posed: What are contemporary human beings?

The Hegelian Model and its Principles: The Rational Law of Aufhebung[28]

Hegel has been regarded as a false prophet – as a soothsayer or as a "charlatan." Many of his rivals have attempted to bad-mouth him; Schopenhauer is one and Nietzsche is another. But if Hegel is a "dead dog" (the way contemporary intellectuals like Schopenhauer, and even Friedrich Schelling, treated him), then how can we explain the survival and even the irresistible attractiveness of his dialectics?[29] The assault of these prominent figures on his philosophy seems to go nowhere, except to hurt the detractors. Schelling, for example, ended up using a very Hegelian manner, consciously widening dialectics to the sphere of religion, while Schopenhauer tarnished his image with a mystical and pessimistic philosophy of will. Yes, to be fair, Hegel scored a point – a very important point indeed – namely, that history progresses precisely by means of a dialectical *Aufhebung*.[30] According to this view, human history is a long, endless process of negating the negative elements, conserving the positive ones, and synthesizing the new elements with the old ones, making society more perfect, and more progressive. This logic led him to suggest that the

---

[28] The German term *Aufhebung* used by Hegel cannot be easily and adequately translated into other languages. Originally, by *Aufhebung* (verb: *aufheben*), Hegel means a dialectical activity which consists of three moments: the moment of affirmation (thesis), that of negation (anti-thesis), and that of sublimation (synthesis). Karl Popper himself has translated *Aufhebung* as "conservation, abrogation and sublimation" (*Open Society*, part on Hegel's Dialectic). In this paper, I consciously keep it intact in its original German.

[29] Marx was famous with his remark in the Afterword of the second edition of his *Capital* (1873) that "Aber grade als ich den ersten Band des 'Kapital' ausarbeitete, gefiel sich das verdriessliche, anmassliche und mittelmassige Epigonentum, welches jetzt im gebildeten Deutschland das grosse Wort fuehrt, darin, Hegel zu behandeln, wie der brave Moses Mendelssohn zu Lessings Zeit den Spinoza behandelt hat, nämlich als "toten Hund." In K. Marx, *Das Kapital*, Vol. 1 (Hamburg, 6th edition, 1909).

[30] In the lecture on the philosophy of history (1822-23, 1830-31), Hegel explains the principle of his investigation of history: to unfold the spirit, and to discover freedom in different stages of history. In fact, Hegel's philosophy of history traces the whole historical process from the Oriental world through the Greco-Roman world to the Christian-Germanic world. The end of history is the final stage represented by the French Revolution (1789). See G.W.F. Hegel, *Vorlesungen über die Philosophie der Weltgeschichte*, ed. Georg Lasson (Leipzig: Felix Meiner, 1930 [1917]), p. 779.

spirit of his times (*Zeitgeist*) and the spirit of his society (*Volksgeist*) as well as the arts (romantics) and religion (Christianity) would lead to the final synthesis of human history, since they conserve and sublimate the best elements of Eastern cultures (religions) and Western civilisations.[31] The romantic arts, he said, are the synthesis of the pre-classics and classics, of the subject and object, just as Christianity is the final synthesis of all religions, since in it one finds the elements of feeling and reason, and of immanence and transcendence. Of course, this philosopher would conjecture that philosophy is the final synthesis of all kinds of knowledge (arts, religions, etc.).[32] As Karl Löwith brilliantly puts it,

> The outline of the Hegelian system consists in its measuring the course of history according to temporal progress; that is, on the basis of the final stage, it argues backwards to those preceding as necessarily leading to it. This orientation toward an historical sequence presupposes that the only valid aspect of world history is that which has many consequences, that the sequence of world events should be evaluated according to the rational principle of its success.[33]

Hegel's vision seems to be quite plausible if there is only one unique truth, and if the power of reason really overwhelms the world. The question is, if reason and truth cannot be known a priori, but only a posteriori, then how can Hegel, the thinker par excellence, know beforehand what will happen? This kind of speculative thinking does not help much in cementing the absolute power of reason. As a matter of fact, Hegel dogmatically gives to reason what he has found in God. Furthermore, if reason and truth reveal themselves in different ways, even diversely and self-contradictorily – the kind envisaged by Heidegger and later by postmodernists – then Hegel's conclusion is rather premature and dogmatic. My critique of Hegel's speculative reasoning does not rest on the above-mentioned point, but goes farther, attacking the dangerous game of dualism

---

[31] G.W.F. Hegel, *Vorlesungen über die Philosophie der Religion*, ed. G. Lasson, 3 vols. (Leipzig, 1929), III, pp. 229. See also B. Bauer, *Hegels Lehre von der Religion und Kunst, vom Standpunkt des Glaubens beurteilt* (Leipzig, 1842), pp. 222 ff. Note that the Hegelian prophecy of the end of history has become recently a source of inspiration for Daniel Bell (*The End of History*), Gianni Vattimo (*The End of Modernity*), and, of course, for postmodernists like Jean-Francois Lyotard.

[32] G.W.F. Hegel, *Phänomenologie des Geistes*, ed. G. Lasson (Leipzig, 1907), pp. 483 ff.

[33] Karl Löwith, *From Hegel to Nietzsche: The Revolution in Nineteenth Century Thought*, tr. David E. Green (New York/Chicago/San Francisco: Holt, Rinehart and Winston, 1964), p. 218.

which Hegel and most of Western philosophers have played so far. The argument that there is either a reason or a non-reason, and that this reason is possessed by them, logically leads to an exclusion of any culture, civilisation, belief, or practice which does not conform itself to the "reason" of modern philosophers. That Hegel dares to claim that his Christian-Germanic civilisation is the final stage, that "his" philosophy is ultimate knowledge, and so on, is in fact a logical consequence of such an extravagant claim. We know (by learning from Hegel's over self-confidence and optimism) that any claim of a unique reason seems to be far fetched and even "irrational." Max Horkheimer and Theodor Adorno have ironically demonstrated this "truth" in their now-classic *Dialectic of Enlightenment*.[34] Conscious of this error, Neo-Hegelians (either rightists or leftists) have developed the idea of *Aufhebung* in a more acceptable manner, by searching for a scientific ground to justify it. For our purpose, I will explore the model of "the fusion of the horizon" of Hans-Georg Gadamer (1900-2002), a disciple of Heidegger but with a true Hegelian spirit,[35] to back my thesis.

The Model of the Fusion of the Horizon: Gadamer's Thesis

The fact that human history (and human culture) do not follow a unique path, but many diverse (if not contradictory) ways, and the fact that reason is expressed not uniquely but in different manners, force us to cast doubt on the claims of modern philosophy and to search for a new model. The point is, how are we to *aufheben* so many different and contradictory elements into a new, more complete, more reasonable synthesis? Heidegger suggested a new understanding of identity in the sense of "belonging together." Only if this is so, can one fully grasp the paradox of "identity in difference."[36] *Aufhebung* here is a kind of Oriental thinking (by which Heidegger is heavily influenced),[37] expressing how one constructs his life-

---

[34] Max Horkheimer and Theodor W. Adorno, *Dialektik der Aufklärung* (1944, Frankfurt a.M.: Fischer, 1969); tr. John Cumming (New York: Herder and Herder, 1972), p. xvi: "myth is already enlightenment; and enlightenment reverts to mythology"; and p. xvii: "Its 'irrationalism' is deduced from the nature of the dominant *ratio* itself, and the world which corresponds to its image."

[35] Hans-Georg Gadamer, *Hegels Dialektik: Fünf hermeneutische Studien* (Tuebingen: Mohr, 1971).

[36] Martin Heidegger, *Identitaet und Differenz* (Pfullingen: Neske, 1957); See also Martin Heidegger, *Unterwegs zur Sprache* (1957-8).

[37] See Paul Hsiao, "Wir traffen us in Holzmakt" in *Heidegger zur Erinnerung* (Pfullingen: Neske, 1978). In the article "Der Satz der Identität," Heidegger explicitly draws out the similarity between the Oriental concept of Tao and the Greek concept of Logos: "Das Wort Ereignis soll jetzt, aus der gewiesenen Sache her gedacht, als Leitwort im Dienst des Denkens sprechen. Als so gedachtes Leitwort läßt es sich sowening übersetzen wie das griechische

world from a pool of different elements and lives. That is also the kind of thinking rooted in the Christian tradition, as expressed by Nicholas of Cusa in terms of *coincidentia oppositorum*, of how man relates himself to God, and God to the world; of how the infinite discovers itself in the finite (and, in reverse, the finite in the infinite). Of course, such a way of thinking has been fully developed (and distorted) as mediation and synthesis (as seen in the philosophy of Leibniz, Kant, Fichte, Schelling and Hegel). Gadamer develops this principle in a more concrete way. He takes the model of the fusion of the horizons to be a proto-model to cast light on how cultures shape themselves, how our consciousness formulates itself, and how knowledge comes into its proper form.[38]

Let us begin first with what we understand as horizon, especially the horizon of life. Looking forwards, one easily finds a line which gives us the impression that it would be the point (line) linking the sky and the earth. Such a line is called by us the horizon. The point is, of course, that such a line is not real, in the sense that it does not exist as a thing even if it appears before our eyes. We really do see it. Everyone sees it. It is not an effect of illusion or hallucination. Thus, its existence is beyond any doubt. However, it cannot be verified by the same external facts, by the same data or by a set of criteria, as required by science. It is in our mind that this line constitutes itself as what we call the horizon. The horizon means, therefore, not only a real line, but a real world which emerges with our presence, and which constitutes our actual and conscious world. Yet this world never exists as some *thing*. It gradually emerges as more encompassing, wider, and deeper. It is our world, but we are unable to grasp it completely. The more closely we approach it, it maintains the same distance between us. Thus, the only one thing that we discover, in our constant approach, is that our knowledge is widening, deepening and perhaps, becoming more intimate. From this observation, one may say that the same line seems to be extended, appears quite differently, and is often richer in the sense that it encompasses the past lines and the past worlds which surround the line. Secondly, we are not really advancing farther, since the distance remains the same. However, we are getting more encompassing knowledge about it. The distance in terms of the space between us and the line is narrowed, and yet, curiously, widened in our mind. In this sense, one can say that our constant effort to approach the horizon produces a richer knowledge about it. Third, the newly acquired line does not exclude the past lines, just as newly acquired knowledge and the newly acquired world do not exclude old knowledge,

---

Leitwort Logos und das chinesische Tao." Republished in *Identity and Difference*, tr. Joan Stambaugh (New York: Harper Torchbooks, 1969), p. 101. Bilingual edition.

[38] Hans-Georg Gadamer, *Wahrheit und Methode: Grundzüge einer philosophischen Hermeneutik* (Tübingen: Mohr, 1960); tr. John Cumming as *Truth and Method* (London: Sheed and Ward, 1975).

worlds and traditions. It encompasses all of them in it. Thus, it may appear as the same, but certainly with richer and more encompassing content.

To apply this thesis to our discussion, I would venture to argue analogously that, the more contact we pursue, the more encompassing is our life world; the more *rencontres* we have, the richer is our life. Our life world is, thus, in a permanent process of self-enrichment, providing that it is open to possible contacts.

CONCLUDING REMARKS: THE INSEPARABILITY OF PLURALISTIC CULTURE AND THE OPEN SOCIETY

Since my main focus is the relationship of pluralistic culture and the open society – or, better, that pluralistic culture is the most expressive and concrete form of an open society – I will not delve into the detail of the long process of the formation of either Vietnamese culture or Chinese culture. It is sufficient to make some brief notes about what I mean by pluralistic culture. By pluralistic culture, I understand a culture which is open to all possible cultures and which may try to incorporate into its own body their quintessence, with the purpose of enriching its own treasure of values. Pluralistic culture is far from the newly-emerging ideology of pluralism – the so-called cultural pluralism with a policy of *laisser-faire*. Here, all views are possible, they are not open to critique and all views have their own right. Since I have already raised my critical voice against such an ideology, I will not delve into the matter here, and will rest content with my argument that only an open society is in a position to enrich itself; and only by means of the so-called 'fusion of horizons' can our life-world be able to respond to newly-emerging needs and human desires. To conclude, I would formulate my thesis in the following way:

First, 'open' means the capacity of receiving new elements, which one digests and integrates into one's own body.

Second, 'open' indicates one's ability to use new elements to solve existing problems and to discover new ones.

Third, 'open' expresses a human way of living, a way of making life better, in terms of being more encompassing, more perfect and more enjoyable.

Fourth, our society today is one of constantly emerging needs and desires which, due to the rapid expansion of high technology and its products, are beyond our control. Any rigid attitude or narrow policy dictated by a closed mentality would produce more harm than benefits. It could not solve the problems emerging in and from modern society and, of course, it would be unable to satisfy newly emerging needs and desires.

Fifth, with the facilities given to us by high technology, one easily recognises that our needs and desires are implicitly hidden in our different and diverse cultures. Hence, new desires and needs are the direct products of the so-called cultural fusion.

Sixth, therefore, cultural fusion is the necessary condition for a truly open society.

National Taiwan University
Taipei, Taiwan

CHAPTER IX

ETHNICITY AND GLOBALIZATION

FRANCIS GIKONYO WOKABI and *STEPHEN OMONDI OWINO*

INTRODUCTION

Ethnic antagonism and tribalism are evils that have proven to be both disastrous and endemic in many nations of the world, especially in Africa. Lives have been lost, property destroyed and many people displaced and disabled – all in the name of ethnic chauvinism. Ethnicity is contentious in social, political, religious and even economic discourse. Thus, ethnicity is a topic that cannot be ignored in any discussion about cross-cultural interaction. In this paper, we present two popular approaches to ethnicity, namely toleration and celebration, and endeavour to distinguish two opposed meanings of each of these approaches.

The popular meanings of toleration and celebration are widely advocated by leaders as a remedy for ethnic chauvinism. Popular toleration involves "putting up with" ethnic differences. Ethnicity is regarded as a necessary evil. A defeatist attitude towards ethnic antagonism is therefore condoned. Popular celebration involves uncritical praise and adoration of one's ethnic roots and practices. Those who advocate popular celebration as a remedy for ethnic antagonism take ethnicity as a fact of life that is above criticism. In practice, however, popular celebration may lead to ethnocentricity. The paper shows that popular toleration and celebration of ethnicity do not offer a viable solution to ethnic conflicts.

This paper also attempts to relate three philosophical perspectives namely; pluralism, monadism, and monism to the debate of cross-cultural interaction in a globalized context. Pluralism will enlighten the popular toleration of cultures. Monadism will be used to analyse the popular celebration of cultures. Monism will be used to discuss the pessimistic view of globalization. The position proposed in this paper is that critical toleration and celebration of ethnicity is the most reasonable alternative for handling ethnic matters in this era of globalization. We call this position cultural synergism and suggest some possible ways of realizing it.

ETHNICITY AND CULTURE

Eriksen[1], Haralambos[2], and Brown[3] agree that ethnicity is to be

---

[1] T. Eriksen, *Ethnicity and Nationalism* (London: Pluto Press, 1993).

[2] M. Haralambos, M. Holborn, and R. Heald, *Sociology: Themes and Perspectives*. 5th ed. (London: HarperCollins Publishers Ltd, 2000).

understood in contemporary times as a social concept referring to the cultural distinctiveness of a social group. An ethnic group can therefore be identified using socio-cultural rather than physical-biological characteristics. These characteristics include: shared beliefs, language, religion, race, common origin, a common name and an attachment to a common homeland. These characteristics may occur singly or in combination. The shared values may be real or mythical. Material aspects of culture (for instance, crafts, food, dress, and architecture) and non-material aspects of culture (for instance, music, laws, customs and institutions) are used to develop, perpetuate and preserve the feeling and belief of ethnic belonging. Since ethnicity is defined in terms of culture, the two concepts are therefore inseparable.

Culture can be understood as the total way of life of a people. It comprises the ideas, habits, skills, and knowledge that are learned, valued, shared and transmitted from one generation to another. "To a large degree culture determines how members of society think and feel: it directs their actions and defines their outlook on life. Members of society usually take their culture for granted."[4] Culture as the sum-total of human activity is a central aspect of human existence. Though people rarely reflect on it, its implications on their interaction and aspirations are enormous. Ethnicity has often been associated with inequality and conflict in many parts of the world – for instance, in Rwanda, Burundi, East Timor, Northern Ireland, Sri-Lanka and Yugoslavia among others. Social problems like poverty and crime have been blamed on ethnic minorities. The conflicts may be expressed violently or non-violently. According to Brown, ethnic conflicts can arise due to the following: malicious myths and prejudices about other social groups, the inability of political institutions to protect ethnic minorities (this may be real or merely perceived), and the proximity of ethnic groups in relation to one another and the democratization of multi-ethnic societies.[5]

The focus of this paper has to do with the way people (especially political leaders) have responded to ethnicity and its attendant conflicts in Africa. Without careful examination of the cultural dimensions of ethnicity and their implications on social relationships, political and even religious leaders have tended to either celebrate or tolerate ethnicity in a cheap and uncritical sense. This, in the long run, has promoted ethnic suspicions and antagonism.

---

[3] Michael E. Brown, "Causes and Implication of Ethnic Conflict" in *The Ethnicity Reader: Nationalism, Multiculturalism and Migration*, M. Guibernau, and J. Rex, eds. (Cambridge: Polity Press, 1997), pp. 80-100.

[4] Haralambos, Holborn, and Heald, *Sociology*, p. 3.

[5] See Brown, "Causes and Implication of Ethnic Conflict."

POPULAR TOLERATION AND CELEBRATION OF ETHNICITY

The popular sense of 'toleration' of ethnicity regards cultural diversity as a necessary evil. Ethnic differences are taken for granted as understandable bases of social indifference. People become resigned to social tensions and hostilities. The apartheid policy, which was pursued for a long time in South Africa, could be understood in this light. Different cultural groups were encouraged to "co-exist in isolation." This isolationist policy was claimed to preserve the purity of ethnic groups, but it ended up entrenching discrimination and other social injustices. Popular toleration failed to be a sustainable approach to inter-ethnic interaction.

Popular 'celebration' involves uncritical praise and adoration of different cultures. Each cultural group regards itself as perfect and complete. Yet each stands opposed to others, which also harbour similar claims. Those who advocate popular celebration as a remedy for ethnic antagonism take ethnicity as a fact of life that is above reproach. Paradoxically, however, in practice, popular celebration may lead to ethnocentricity – whereby ethnic groups become self-centred and exclusive. In some instances, ethnic nationalism has made some groups become bold enough to demand recognition as independent political entities.

Yet the popular versions of toleration and of the celebration of socio-cultural differences run contrary to the distinctive characteristics of human persons. As rational and self-conscious beings, humans ought to reflect impartially on their condition. This reflection should penetrate the real and imagined values of every culture. Critical appraisal should reveal the shortcomings as well as the strengths of individual cultures. This should further lead to the identification of cultural universals that can be useful as a basis for cultural dialogue. Through cultural dialogue, ethnic groups can understand, enrich, respect, and complement one another. In the contemporary social context characterized by globalization, it is the opinion of the authors of this paper that popular toleration and celebration of ethnicity is inadequate as an approach for addressing inter-ethnic relations.

GLOBALIZATION

Globalization is quite a controversial concept. In nearly every discipline where it is employed to analyse or explain current political, social, economic and cultural trends, the concept attracts varied responses. There are those who regard globalization as a concept that captures the subtle and varied attempts by the developed countries to dominate and exploit economically under-developed nations. According to Wasike, globalization is a form of re-colonization of the poor nations of the world by the rich and militarily superior nations.[6] The process has disastrous

---

[6] In M. Getui, and M. Theuri, eds. *Quests for Abundant Life in Africa* (Nairobi: Acton Publishers, 2002).

implications on the majority of poor peoples and nations. It promotes Euro-American values and lifestyles and undermines local cultures in a systematic and uncritical manner. The integrity and independence of local and national social organizations tend to be diminished by forces of globalization. Understood in this light, globalization is an evil that needs to be resisted at all costs. This can partly account for the numerous anti-globalization demonstrations in many parts of the world. We regard this as the pessimistic view of globalization.

Some writers have portrayed globalization in a more optimistic light. According to Albrow, globalization is a process that integrates the diversities of humankind.[7] This process is based on and justified by the social and rational nature of human beings. As social and rational beings, humans increasingly become aware of their interdependence. Globalization is the logical culmination of this increasing awareness. It involves the deliberate dissolution of impediments to human interaction and the promotion of opportunities for cross-cultural dialogue. Such a process is regarded as anticipated by the very constitution of human beings. It is a means of realizing the vast potential of human persons. As such globalization is desirable. We regard globalization as an inevitable process characterized by intensification of socio-cultural relations on a worldwide scale. This process is catalysed by technological, economic and political trends operative in the contemporary world. The wholescale condemnation of globalization (i.e., the pessimistic view of globalization) fails to appreciate the positive possibilities of the process. Uncritical celebration of globalization (i.e., the optimistic view of globalization), on the other hand, fails to come to grips with the limitations and vulnerability inherent in the human condition. We therefore advocate a position which we call cultural synergism, that aims at avoiding the pitfalls of the extremes described above. We attempt to clarify this position by discussing some relevant philosophical perspectives.

PHILOSOPHICAL PERSPECTIVES

We now attempt a brief discussion of some philosophical perspectives, which we consider paradigmatic of the above approaches to ethnicity and globalization.

Pluralism

This philosophical perspective refers to the abandonment of attempts to reduce all reality to one or two ultimate forms of being. Historically, we can associate it with Empedocles in antiquity, when he

---

[7] M. Albrow, "Globalization" in *The Blackwell Dictionary of Twentieth-Century Social Thought*, W. Outhwaite, and T. Bottomore, eds., (Oxford: Blackwell Publishers, 1994).

suggested that reality is made up of four ultimate elements namely: fire, water, earth and air. Plato, too, was a pluralist when he attempted to reduce all reality to a plurality of eternal ideas. In its broad outline, pluralism emphasizes discreteness, separateness, independence, and novelty. Reality is perceived as distributive rather than collective. Going hand in hand with a pluralistic world-view is the realization that, besides physical and mental things, there is a plurality of socio-cultural phenomena.

A dominant pluralistic conception of socio-cultural reality in our contemporary world is postmodernism. Broadly, it emphasizes variations in socio-cultural world-views, thus urging a tolerant and flexible attitude towards cross-cultural interaction. This toleration commits the postmodernist to prefer the microanalysis of cultures to macroanalysis. In other words, it prefers "each form" rather than "all form" of cultures. Postmodernism thus embarks on a project of radical and systematic decentring of values and insists that there is no reason to assume that any culture exists that is the centre and paragon of values. Consequently, postmodernism upholds a relativistic world-view, which engenders cultural relativism. According to Rachels,[8] cultural relativism has the following characteristics:

a) that different societies have different moral codes;
b) that there is no objective standard to judge different codes;
c) that no moral codes have any special status;
d) that there are no universal truths;
e) that the moral code of a society determines what is wrong and right in that society, and
f) that it is arrogant to judge others. Instead we should tolerate.

Postmodernism, therefore, over-emphasizes difference, fragmentation, plurality, and heterogeneity of cultures. This socio-cultural pluralism coupled with politics of self-determination has negatively reinforced and heightened ethnic antagonism. Uncritical assertiveness of individual cultures condoned and justified by postmodern perspectives underlie the popular toleration of ethnicity discussed earlier in this paper.

Monadism

This is a metaphysical doctrine associated with the philosopher Leibniz. But more than just being a doctrine of Being and substance, it represents a model of thinking which underlies another socio-cultural perspective. In brief, monads in Leibniz's system were characterized as substances with dynamic force and, hence, capable of action. Each monad is different and absolutely independent of the others. They have no causal

---

[8] J. Rachels, *The Elements of Moral Philosophy* (New York: McGraw Hill Inc., 1995).

relation to each other and are self-sufficient. This means that they are their own internal source of action. Above all, the monads are window-less; hence, the rest of the world does not influence or affect them. This view is certainly paradigmatic of ethnic and cultural enthusiasts who perceive their own ethnic groups and cultures as perfect, complete, and simply the best. Accordingly, they view other cultures as simply irrelevant and inferior to their own. They therefore emphasize the need for being proud, upholding and conserving "our culture against foreign influence."

Monadism, therefore, encourages a view of society as a mere aggregation of different, independent and complete socio-cultural units. This, too – compounded with the aforesaid politics of self-determination – tends to encourage conservative glorification of ethnic groups and cultures, thus obstructing a fertile cross-cultural interaction. It thereby engenders the popular celebration of ethnicity and globalization referred to earlier in this paper.

Monism

This is a philosophical view that sees all reality as ultimately reducible to one single whole or unity. This may take a materialistic or an idealistic form – for example, the philosophies of Karl Marx and Hegel respectively. With regard to globalization, it underlies a conception that is abhorrent to many. This is pessimistic globalization interpreted as the neo-imperialism of Western capitalism over impoverished peoples in the guise of benevolent advances in communication technology. It bears the tendencies of the domination of the individual, the elaboration of macro-theories, and the totalising tendencies and the centring of values. These tendencies are at cross purposes with pluralistic and monadistic ideals. Monism implies, therefore, that ethnicity and globalization are mutually exclusive concepts and processes.

However, we propose that a critical toleration and celebration of ethnicity would result in what we call 'cultural synergism.' This would create the conditions conducive for the realization of humane globalization – a perspective that is not oblivious to both the benefits and burdens of globalization.

CULTURAL SYNERGISM

In this paper, we regard cultural synergism as the capacity of cultures to enrich one another qualitatively and quantitatively by opening up and talking *with* one another as opposed to talking *to* each other. Cultural synergism is based on the assumption that individual cultures, though functional in quite unique aspects, are incomplete and in need of perfecting. This perfecting, however, cannot be achieved if they remain isolated and hostile or indifferent to other cultures. The isolationist tendency results in "cultural entropy." Entropy is the tendency of elements to decay over time. Cultural entropy, therefore, refers to the gradual decay of cultural systems. The decay consists in an indiscriminate annihilation of cultural values.

The perfecting of a culture hence calls for systemic interaction with other cultures. This enables them to bring in new energies, hence reversing the process of cultural entropy. We view individual cultures as generative elements that result in a higher social-cultural synthesis. This is analogical to the timeless philosophical adage which we reconstruct as: "the whole is both better and greater than the sum of its parts." It would promote mutual affection and dependence between cultures. This perspective would resolve the apparent contradiction between ethnicity and globalization by creating a condition in which individuals and ethnic groups show both autonomy and a need of completion. The diversity and differentiations of socio-cultural life should serve the realization of a higher and more comprehensive integration of humanity. As Beck observes, "...it would imply a living unity of mutual appreciation and completion in the diversity and variety of ways of life."[9]

TOWARDS THE ENHANCEMENT OF CULTURAL SYNERGISM

We now suggest possible ways of promoting cultural synergism at the personal, local (intra-ethnic), national (inter-ethnic) and international levels.

Cultural Synergism at the Personal Level

At the personal level, cultural synergism can be enhanced by the promotion of the habits of self-examination and the making of reflective judgements. This is aptly captured in the Socratic maxim "know thyself." Human beings tend to be disposed more towards looking outward to others rather than inward. In looking outward, they easily and selectively notice the frailties of others. It is also important to cultivate a sense of individuality rather than individualism. By individuality, we mean a reasonable sense of assertiveness, autonomy, and resourcefulness, whereas individualism means the exclusive concern for oneself even at the expense of legitimate interests of others. Individuality is desirable and justifiable because of the limitations as well as the perfectibility of human beings. As the adage goes, "there is a lot of bad in the best of us and a lot of good in the worst of us." It is therefore necessary for individuals to examine themselves in order for them to recognize the need of and the means to the cultivation of individuality.

---

[9] H. Beck, "Europe-Africa-Asia, the Creative Proportion Between the World Cultures" in G. Presby, et al. eds., *Thought and Practice in African Philosophy* (Nairobi: Konrad Adenaeur Foundation, 2002), p. 63.

Cultural Synergism at the Local (Intra-ethnic) Level

At the intra-ethnic level, cultural synergism can be promoted by encouraging intra-ethnic dialogue as opposed to intra-ethnic indoctrination. The latter refers to the dogmatic transmission of ethnic heritage that includes its myths and prejudices. Intra-ethnic dialogue should include the de-classification and interrogation of what we refer to analogically as "ethnic heresies." These serve to glorify, justify and perpetuate traditional positions and practices while derogating so-called "alien values." In Kenya, for instance, equality for women is dismissed in many ethnic communities as foreign propaganda that can never work in an African homestead.

Ethnic groups should also open up to each other and be ready to learn from one another. The hitherto windowless monads should sense the necessity and urgency of creating windows big enough to allow ethnic 'osmosis' that facilitates both the survival and the improvement of the different groups. According to Fanon, culture is apprehended as a process of becoming rather than a state of affairs, which seeks always to accommodate reality lying in the present and unfolding in the future as a perpetual creation.[10] A common hindrance to intra-ethnic dialogue is what we identify as conventional hierarchies that may have gender, generational, hereditary or even matrimonial dimensions. Traditionally, constructive contributions were believed not to be able to come from certain quarters, chief among which were the young, women, lower castes and unmarried persons. Cultural synergism demands the revision of these conventional hierarchies to enable the members of an ethnic group to evaluate its condition and contribute towards its amelioration.

Cultural Synergism at the National (Inter-ethnic) Level

Ways and means of promoting social justice should be explored to ensure a fair distribution of available resources. This can be expedited by the integration of law and morality. Without morality, law runs the paradoxical risk of becoming prejudicial to justice. As such it fails to realize its noblest objective and spirit. Democracy as popularly preached has majoritarian overtones. In practice, it tends to favour major ethnic blocks and oppress and even create new minor ethnicities. This heightens ethnic tensions. We therefore recommend inclusive democracy that takes into account the interests of minority groups as integral to the interests of the entire nation at large.

The advancement and expansion of communication technology have engendered rapid diffusion of knowledge and information. However, this knowledge is skewed towards benefiting the originators of the technology. This leaves indigenous knowledge and expertise marginalized. Cultural synergism contends that globalization cannot be humane if it

---

[10] F. Fanon, *The Wretched of the Earth* (Harmondsworth: Penguin, 1974).

ignores the positive contribution of indigenous ethnic knowledge and expertise. There should also be a rigorous and sustained search for cultural universals that can form a basis for cross-cultural dialogue instead of emphasizing cultural differences.

Cultural Synergism at the International Level

Dichotomies such as developed/underdeveloped countries, civilized/uncivilized nations, first-world/third-world, and so on, are commonplace in international social-cultural discourse. Underlying such dichotomies is a power component that facilitates discrimination and exploitation. This may account for the negative perception held by the detractors of globalization. Cultural synergism recommends a critical interrogation of the assumptions underlying these dichotomies as well as their attendant stereotypes. One obvious feature of the contemporary world is the prominence of the neo-liberal doctrine that prescribes free enterprise as the ideal avenue to economic prosperity. This economic model tends to emphasise materialism, technologism, consumerism and individualism as absolute universal values that are self-justifying. This is often in total disregard of other human values, such as the spiritual. Cultural synergism calls for a rational evaluation of all values in order to identify those that can inform policies and practices that prioritise integral human well-being.

Implications of Cultural Synergism for Philosophy

Perhaps one of the most devastating criticisms that is levelled against philosophy is that it is merely theoretical and devoid of any relevance to socio-cultural reality. This criticism, if pursued, leads to the condemnation of philosophers as hypocritical, that is, persons who preach water and take pure wine. Cultural synergism calls for honest attempts aimed at bridging the gap between theory and practice. It may also help to bring philosophical practice from the ivory tower to the local level. The problem of detaching theory from practice was clearly perceived by thinkers as diverse as Plato and Karl Marx. Plato noted that unless rulers became philosophers or philosophers became kings, the world would never benefit from the wisdom of philosophy. Karl Marx also observed that the business of philosophy is not merely to interpret reality but also, and most importantly, to transform it. As evident in our recommendations above, essential philosophical elements and dispositions – for instance, evaluation, criticism and analysis – ought to inform socio-cultural life starting from the personal to the international levels.

Finally, cultural synergism calls for an interdisciplinary approach to philosophical inquiry. It is not uncommon to find "philosophers of science" who have bare knowledge of science, "philosophers of religion" devoid of the most basic theological knowledge, and so on. This hinders the adequate achievement of the philosophical objective of attempting to understand reality in its entirety.

CONCLUSION

Critical toleration involves an empathetic understanding of ethnic orientations leading to enlightened inter-ethnic respect. Critical celebration involves an impartial appraisal of our ethnic orientations. We have argued that globalization demands that we tolerate and celebrate our ethnicity in a critical way so that the essential aspects of human identity in ethnicity can be appreciated, preserved, and perfected. This enlightened approach is inclusive, adaptive and humane. It integrates the rational, moral, social, and creative resources and dynamics of mankind. The paper has suggested some ways of enhancing critical toleration and celebration of ethnicity, which we refer to as cultural synergism.

Department of Philosophy
Kenyatta University
Nairobi, Kenya

BETWEEN FREEDOM AND PATERNALISM AS DISCURSIVE ETHICAL PRACTICES: THE UKRAINE ON THE ROAD TO CIVIL SOCIETY

ANATOLIJ KARAS

My aim here is to present some thoughts and provide some information on Post-Communist Ukraine in connection with a "Civil Society" perspective. I would like to start with a quotation from Jacques Maritain, a famous French philosopher of the twentieth century, who spent part of his life in America. He said: "As I grow older I realize more and more how fundamental for mankind political activity is, and how deeply it depends on the most disappointing contingences."[1] This was said after the Second World War.

A little more than a few decades ago, it was a contingent fact that three persons in the world were handling their jobs at the same time: Pope John Paul II, the President of the USA Ronald Reagan, and the President of the former Soviet Union Mikhail Gorbachev. The world was not disappointed by this contingency. As a result of a well-done job, a new world appeared at the turn of the millennium. This new world appeared after the collapse of the Soviet Union, which was the embodiment of the totalitarian kind of social and political relations.

Among the countries which can now be found on the map of the new Europe, we can see the Ukraine. This independent state, with a population of just under 50 million and area of 603 thousand square kilometers, has a significant place in the continent's stability and development. Everybody who is acquainted with the history of Europe could ask the question, How do the two World Wars relate to the Ukraine? Would the Second World War have been possible if the Ukraine had preserved its independence after World War One?

History cannot answer this question. But human beings can think and make demands on society according to their mode of thinking and understanding. Communists and nationalists have made such demands on the social system, for example. The independence of the Ukraine and the union of its lands into a national state has been a political ideal for Ukrainians for centuries. This ideal has its origin in the national memory of the great Kyivan-Rus State of the tenth and eleventh centuries, when the name "Ukraine" first appeared in the old chronicles. It has its tradition in the powerful and independent Ukrainian Kingdom of King Danylo (in the

---

[1] See Jacques Maritain, *Reflections on America* (New York: Charles Scribner's Sons, 1958), foreword.

thirteenth century). This ideal was at its highest point during the careers of Hetman Khmelnytskyj in the seventeenth century and Hetman Mazepa in the eighteenth century (the "Hetmans" in the Ukraine were elected political leaders during the sixteenth to eighteenth centuries). In the nineteenth century, a modern national movement developed in the Ukraine. Russia's response was repression, the denial of Ukrainian nationality, and a ban on the Ukrainian language (in 1863 and 1876). But a freer atmosphere for Ukrainian self-expression existed under Austrian Galicia.

After the collapse of both the Russian and the Austro-Hungarian Empires at the end of World War I, the two divided Ukrainian regions were briefly reunited in an independent state. In 1921, however, Galicia and Volynia were occupied by Poland, while smaller areas in the west were annexed by Romania and Czechoslovakia. The eastern Ukraine, conquered by Soviet Russia, became the Ukrainian SSR. In the east, Stalin's forced collectivization and the artificially introduced famine in 1932-33 led to the loss of at least seven million lives. World War II brought massive destruction and a further loss of about 12 million lives, as the Ukraine became the main battlefield between the USSR and Nazi Germany.

The idea of independence for the people's development was embodied during World War II in the proclamation in Lviv of the Ukrainian State. All the principal leaders of that time were imprisoned by the Nazi regime, but were also persecuted by Soviet authorities. Manifesting their aspiration for freedom under the German occupation during 1941-45, Ukrainians created their own armed resistance groups in 1941, which were united into a big and powerful Ukrainian Insurgent Army under one supreme command. It was supported by the entire Ukrainian people and greatly contributed to the destruction of the German armed forces in Western Ukraine and continued the struggle against the Soviet Army until 1955.

Indeed, modern Ukrainian history is the history of the Ukrainian movements for freedom and democracy. Political changes proceeded rapidly after 1989, the year that saw the rise of mass organizations – most notably the Rukh (People's Movement of Ukraine) – which pushed for definitive autonomy in the last years of Soviet rule. Following the failure of the Moscow coup d'etat, independence was proclaimed on 24 August 1991. This was confirmed by 91% of the voters in the referendum held on 1 December 1991.

DEMOCRACY AND ITS STATE SUBSTITUTION

The breakdown of the totalitarian Soviet system brought with it a democratization of life that facilitated the creation of numerous new nongovernmental organizations. This process developed in the Ukraine under the influence of nationally and culturally-oriented demands that came from within that society. When networks of civic organizations aimed at cultural autonomy appeared, the demand for economic private property was raised. This was at the time when Ukrainians not only proclaimed their political independence but also adopted a new Constitution (1996), guaranteeing democracy and equal human rights and liberties. Its main provisions dealt with guarantees of the rule of law – by which all citizens of the Ukraine, regardless of their ethnicity and religion, are protected – and the permission of private property. The Constitution established the fundamental laws of the country and, therefore, confirmed its new statehood. The implementation of constitutional laws in daily life required the strengthening of democratic reforms. The main task was – and still is – to maintain and broaden the democratization of society by introducing human and civil rights. But this task appeared difficult to resolve.

Some observers had noted that our Constitution showed some vestiges of its Ukrainian communist past, such as a fear of the capitalist system and the importance of guaranteeing full employment, housing, and health protection. Others had noted that some "fine tuning" might still be needed to provide an effective system of checks and balances to guarantee the impartiality and independence of the judiciary, and even to clarify who has ultimate responsibility over the executive branch – i.e., the President, the Prime-Minister, or the Cabinet of Ministers. This issue has not been resolved yet (i.e., by 2003), and many people say that the President's power is increasingly authoritarian (I shall explain this later).

In any case, the fact of adopting a democratic constitution shows the existence of political consensus in the Ukraine. And in doing this, Ukrainian society has taken its place among other democratic societies in Europe. But, unfortunately, in the Ukraine things have not gone well with the implementation of the new Constitution and other laws. Since the collapse of the Soviet Union and the achievement of political independence in 1991, the people of the Ukraine have been engaged in the construction of a new social life in which the supreme values are freedom, human rights and democracy. This demands the development of a wide range of civil society institutions. From the very beginning of this social reconstruction, the process of democratization was understood by many politicians in its fundamental sense. But, all in all, democratic politicians have not been in the majority. On the contrary, the main reins of power remain in the hands of former communists. Thus, in a short time, the political rhetoric changed from democracy to the free market, which has been considered as the main end of the government policy regarding social transformation. It is true that, without developing free markets (which had not existed earlier in the Ukraine), democracy would not be a realistic option. Under the pressure of the need for free market reforms, the task of transforming the whole social political life has been supplanted by the rhetoric of economic transformation. The government (consisting mostly of former communist bureaucrats) was interested only in holding political power and controlling the economy by transforming only the forms of administration. At the same time, society had to undertake absolutely new tasks: to assure public stability and preserve peace, to hold down economic inflation, and to maintain living standards. A very low level of productivity has been reached by the workers, who were forced to use the old Soviet engineering technology built mostly for the military purposes. The need to achieve a whole social reconstruction has been replaced by an interest in the redistribution of state resources. For the political authorities, it has focused on the privatization of the main economic wealth of the young state. The old bureaucracy was not removed from power. It focused on redistribution in the economic sphere, but was not interested in spreading democracy. It has not wanted to pass the reins of power to the new national-democrats.

The Soviet system was perhaps the most perfect form of closed society made by man. It penetrated into virtually everything; all spheres of human activity were under the pressure of bureaucratic requirements, and for its transformation the powerful will of social groups was needed. There has been a need for developing civil society with civic activity. The need for civil society is urgent, but the people who make up Ukrainian society know little about it. On the eve of independence in 1991, only a few intellectuals had discussed the theme of civil society – and there, only in a few magazines. Mainstream discussion has brought about the possibility of free market and economic transformation. Hence, alongside political and economic reconstruction, the need for a new type of state has become a main force in shaping the development of life in Ukraine. From the government's point of view, the main purpose of the power of the state is to redistribute property. Thus, instead of democracy, civil society, and even free markets, society remains in the control of bureaucrats.

FROM DEMOCRACY TO MARKET FUNDAMENTALISM

The contemporary democracy movement in the Ukraine had its sources in the 1960s, when Stalinist terror was revealed, and there appeared rare springs of communist opposition. This is about the so-called dissenters who, in the Ukraine, were nationalists as a rule and who brought both an intellectual opposition and a democratic movement into the Soviet state. It is important to realize that during the communist rule in the Ukraine, it was extremely dangerous for somebody to be called a "bourgeois nationalist" by authorities. This meant imprisonment and often death. This kind of repression extended only to non-Russian nationalists, and was a subtle form of political and social discrimination. In this we can find one of the sources of the decay of the USSR. And this can help us explain why the most powerful opposition against the totalitarian regime in the Soviet Union was combined with national democratic forces in the Ukraine and in other former Soviet republics. The national democratic intention to construct an independent Ukrainian state coincided with the task of building a new type of democratic society. Under these circumstances, the new democratic forces – mostly consisting of people with very different social convictions – appeared to be divided by its own ideas and illusions, in comparison with old, well-entrenched 'Red type' nomenclature, which held its administrative ground.

Now, in 2003 – after twelve years of independence – we in the Ukraine may say that Red-type bureaucracy – but not national-democracy – has won the battle for state power. Those of us who are particularly concerned to see democracy realized, see that this seed was sown at the very moment of gaining political independence. First of all, this happened because old secret service structures, the police, and the armed forces were not disbanded or overhauled. The second reason was that national-democratic leaders and parties became allied with former Soviet officials during the move to an independent state. This involved the relativization of morality and ethics in order to gain power and to promote a free market and private property. The third reason can be discerned by the fact that a free market was for many the main factor for democratizing the country. This latter was largely supported from abroad, contrary to other intentions to spread national-democracy – namely, that initiative from 'below' should be encouraged to create free cultural and related organizations.

In the time of the great crises of the mid-1990s, the former Soviet (and now, the new Ukrainian Party) nomenclature met the problem in ways which would ensure they would hold political power (in order to keep control over the economy) and, at the same time, transform power without being deprived of the status quo. Thus, rhetoric about the free market and the temptations of private property came to take first place instead of freedom and human rights.

This was the road to oligarchic forms of economic and political power. It was well supported by the mass media, which by then already belonged to a few so-called "new Russians" or "oligarchs." The movement in this direction was headed by President Kuchma, who won the first election in 1994 owing to: a) state administrative resources in the places where power was in antidemocratic hands; b) oligarchs; c) mass media manipulation; d) Russian interest in preserving control over Ukraine; and e) collaboration of national democrats with the state administration and oligarchs. This was the road to strengthening state power around the President's administration, and aimed not at free market reforms but control over the main economic possibilities. People say the political authorities became allied with economic forces and vice versa. In this way, instead of a "velvet revolution" (as in Poland and Czechoslovakia, which had been introduced by each's national democracy movement), a so-called "nomenclature" has emerged in the Ukraine. The interiorization of totalitarian social habits continues to exercise an influence on society, mostly at the administrative level. Because of this, the intention to have a strong independent Ukrainian state – which is indeed needed for strengthening the functioning of the free market – has turned into a restoration of all old Soviet type ethics and, related to it, new but closed forms of social relations. A culture of legal ignorance has become the general practice. Today, only a few in society control more than 95% of the country's wealth that, only a short time ago, belonged to "nobody." This was assisted by funds given by international financial organizations to various Ukrainian governments – a process that never worked well until Victor Yushchenko became Prime Minister. Such social relations, as those George Soros noted in 2002, may be characterized as a rapacious capitalism, since the most effective way to increase private capital in the absence of good starting conditions is the privatization of the state (administrative) resources. Foreign help provided by the International Monetary Fund and the World Bank did not achieve its objectives as often it should have. We can judge this, for example, from the case of Pavlo Lazarenko – a former prime minister of the Ukraine – who was imprisoned in the USA.

The situation of implementing a free market in the Ukraine was more difficult and sophisticated than anyone could have predicted. On the one hand, the classic approach did not allow the state to interfere in free market development. On the other hand, in the circumstance of a lack of 'civil society' values, a free market cannot be entirely independent of state authority. The question is what kind of authority can we expect? As I have tried to show, without consideration of this question, the rhetoric about democracy and the free market could lead towards market fundamentalism (a term used by George Soros).

The Ukraine now has a rather feeble model of state capitalism based on political power, limited administrative resources, and a monopoly of the few over the many. This control of the economy is carried out by the tax administration, the police, the secret service, the prosecutor's office and also by criminal elements. Market development free from state administration and from the oligarchs has become impossible in the contemporary Ukraine.

The Ukrainian economic environment has been entirely deprived of any significant Western investment. The attempt of Yushchenko's government to change the situation and make it transparent ended with massive attacks on the government. Because of this, the Ukraine does not have any civilized form of free competition. It does not have a free market yet. Thus, bureaucracy has appropriated in its own interests, not only initial capital but the rules of the economic game and the state with its budget. This "new-old" bureaucracy has changed its stripes only a little, and it continues to hold onto political and economic means of state and social control.

National-democratic groups and political parties appear not to have been able to put into practice any significant economic changes, and have become the hostages of their dreams of freedom and an independent state. Ukrainian independence has been virtually given to former Soviet empire and openly anti-Ukrainian forces. The latter seized power, and tried to persuade chauvinistic people not to believe the democrats and nationalists, who were turned into the main culprits of the low standard of living and social instability. The conjuncture of administration and oligarchy has become a very effective obstacle to the free market and, as a result, to democracy and civil society. Thus, the oligarchs, who are very close to political power, may be called the 'stagnarches,' and their form of ruling as the 'stagnancies.'

NEED OF DEMOCRACY AS NEED OF CONFIDENCE AND SOCIAL ACTIVISM

Unfortunately, in the Ukraine things have not gone so well with regard to prosperity, human rights and freedom. There is difficulty with the implementation of the Constitution. The standard of living is very low. There is hidden unemployment. Many people (about 5 million) go abroad looking for a job but nobody from abroad (or very few) comes to the Ukraine to work as a simple worker or employee. As a rule, factories, mass media (TV and the press) and the market place belong to oligarchs or those with administrative power. But the chief problem is the slow rate of change in society, and it has many aspects: economic, financial, political, moral, and ethical. The main reasons for this slow rate of change are related to the diminishing confidence between society and authority, or between people and government. This is on the one hand, an old sickness, inherited from the communist past, but it has not diminished over time. On the other hand, this is reflected in the manipulation of political parties (of which there are at least 120), indicating a decline in the level of social and political trust and responsibility. It is an unbelievable fact that the government of Victor Yushchenko – which was the first in the last several years to have been able to pay salaries on time (earlier salaries had been delayed to 3 to 6 months) – was dismissed by the parliament. This was the first Prime Minister who gained the trust of people and who continued to have the confidence of more than 58% of the voters after his forced dismissal – a removal caused by an aggressive clique of oligarchs closely cooperating with Russian political and economic concerns.

As a result, the threat of violence and the lack of public confidence have increased. The level of criminality is very high as well as the level of abusive treatment and the abuse of power. The people suffer greatly from organized crime. Major crime often goes unpunished. Political crime is taking place daily in the country. There have been politically-motivated assassinations of Ukrainians who were active in public life, demanding transparency and accountability on economic and political issues and who defended the values of democracy. This particularly has been directed towards some journalists and leaders of nonpolitical and nongovernmental civic organizations. One such person was the journalist Georgij Gongadze who was murdered almost three years ago, and this case has not resulted in any indictments in spite of the bad light under which President Kuchma has been put.

The case with Gongadze has greatly influenced society and put it into deep frustration that has been strengthened by the so-called "tape-gate" around the President and his close advisors. At the same time there is an army of police in the Ukraine – of about 400,000 members – in addition to a huge number of people belonging to the judiciary and the prosecution branches. Because of this, many people consider that the threat of violence, the decline of the dignity of the person, and the lack of confidence in the state are now greater than even at the beginning of the road to independence. There is a gap between political life and new social needs, which remain hidden behind the mask of the authority's 'declaration' of democracy.

There is one very interesting lesson that Ukrainian society could be taught – and perhaps others would find it interesting. It is well known that the main goal of communists and communism was to eliminate private property. This goal was reached in the former Soviet Union in virtue of a very strong central authority. But now, all those, who not so long ago had acquired their authority by fighting against private property and by fiercely struggling against Ukrainian nationalism and independence – especially during the time of the imaginary independence of the Ukraine – have shown no wish either to refuse private property or to retire.

The next equally important problem confronting Ukrainian society is the bitterness related to national and ethnic issues. Recently much thought has been given to the paradox that the vision of a modern, multicultural Ukraine prolongs, rather than undermines, the colonial process – even more than the agenda that Soviet Russia pursued. Many Ukrainian intellectuals are frightened by new forms of 'assimilation,' carried out by government administrators together with the oligarchs. Even in the thirteenth year of independence, events have taken place that threaten the material basis of the existence of the Ukrainian nation as well as its language, culture, and spirituality. One famous document adopted in 1997 by the Congress of the Ukrainian Intelligentsia declared: "External and internal forces, which in the course of the last years have blocked and sabotaged in every way the process of the Ukraine's transformation into a strong, rich, socially just, and sovereign state, have today launched an all-out assault aimed at our 'Belarussianization'." Many people are anxious about the conscious refusal by political leaders and oligarchs to recognize such concepts as the national dignity of the people – and that they allow the Ukraine to be openly abused and humiliated in the eyes of the world. At the same time, some official political forces in Russia are adopting imperialistic attitudes, and even the government looks forward to the ideology of Russian exclusiveness and 'missionary' Russification. They and allied political groups in Ukraine aim at the destruction of Ukrainian society under cover of the "pan-Slavonic" and "pan-Orthodox" ideologies. For example, in a recent book, *Civil Society: origin and contemporary character* (published by the Russian Federation Institute of Public Prosecutors in Saint Petersburg in 2000), we read: "The road to Russian development in its geopolitical aspect (and on this point we can agree with I. Frojanov) is to revive the Russian Empire," which can be understood as the form of existence of peoples, united in and on a single territory and led by the Russian people." These are the words of Mr. Frojanov: "I am deeply convinced that Russia cannot exist in any form except as an Empire. No Empire – no Russia!"[2] I would like to underscore that these words were written in a book giving the perspective of civil society in the Russian Federation! Its authors consider civil society as a positive basis for imperialistic development.

It is not an accident that today's Ukrainian state has effectively threatened the national identity of its people and of Ukrainian culture. The Constitution demands: "No one shall use benefits and privileges not established by law." But democracy, even under the Ukrainian Constitution, is not observed in government practice, and there is an absence of government good will to spread democracy in society. This has created a climate of injustice and it has resulted in deep frustration throughout society. And this, in turn, raises a question about the reality of human rights in an independent Ukraine.

In recent years, time and opportunities have been wasted, and the trust of the people has been lost because governmental authority has not carried out radical action against corruption and crime. Unfortunately, President Kuchma does not take a firm position regarding Western policy, continues to make advances to Russia, and promotes mostly Russian investment in the Ukrainian economy. Although celebrating the emergence of free markets and democracy in words, there is nevertheless destabilizing avaricious corruption in the Ukraine, accompanied by the unleashing of private initiatives under the cover of an administration that ignores common standards of human decency.

CIVIL SOCIETY ISSUES

I would like to take a look at civil society as a semiotic phenomenon. It has (according to the works of George McLean) three inseparable parts related to subjectivity or humanity as active in social life. It is about: a) *arche* or the origin of action, or of freedom as the properly human exercise of life and being; b) the pattern of values and virtues as constituted in cultural traditions which gives form to freedom; and, c) the structure of relations between people and social institutions.[3] On the whole, civil society is constituted as a process of semiosis in which the generation and the rejection of signs, significations and symbolization take place,

---

[2] *Civil Society: origin and contemporary character*, ed. J. I. Kalnoj (Saint Petersburg: Russian Federation Institute of Public Prosecutors, 2000), p. 159 (in Russian).

[3] George McLean, "Philosophy and Civil Society: Its Nature, Its Past and Its Future," in *Civil Society and Social Reconstruction*, ed. George F. McLean (Washington, DC: The Council for Research in Values and Philosophy, 1997), p. 14.

involving language-speech communication as well as discursive ethical practices.

Discourse means the assembly of signs, significations, symbols, objects, and codes which are organized in verbal, lingual, musical, and narrative texts present through speech and communication. Discourse serves as the basis for choice, selection and giving priority to one category of significations over another. Discourse is present in communities, social groups, and social and cultural traditions. Discourse works as a semiotic act which appears in events, affairs and actions that outline signs, the symbolic and objective framework of actuality, and its human perception.

Because human life takes place in a common space of freedom and necessity, there are reasons for discerning at least two discursive actions having ethical patterns, arising around contradictorily-directed social relations. Some exhibit so-called horizontal, and others vertical and hierarchical, relationships. It is possible that the values of human existence become the means for achieving another 'ethical action' or purpose. Actuality consists of at least two-dimensional discursive ethical practices.

Discursive actions or ethical practices are realized by laying stress on signs and significations in relation to: a) freedom, free will, benevolence, voluntary and self-identifying actions and, b) coercion, compulsion, necessity, subjection, submission, subordination and patron-client relationships. Not all semiotic stipulated discourses and correlated ethical practices exhibit the intention of increasing the freedom and dignity of human beings. Some ethical and cultural traditions may be promote submission or personal advantage.

If we look at Ukrainian history, we see that two contradictions in discourse-ethical practices and social-cultural traditions have come into being: those dealing with a) the freedom and dignity of human beings, and b) paternal-client relations.

The realization of democracy is not only the recognition of its formal principles into the constitution of a country. Highly organized and deeply rooted civil society is needed for democracy to become a reality. The danger of particularity and the atomization of Ukrainian society as its real condition were caused by artificial social and political values and, related to them, the "narcissism" of groups supported by the state's authority and the economic elite or oligarchs. Under today's conditions, Ukrainian society seems to be a conglomerate of "workers for salary," but in general social, public and private life has changed to a great extent.

On the one hand, observers have noted very little popular concern for the new possibilities created by political change. For example, according to polls, only a very small part of society is interested in supporting political parties and civic associations. But, on the other hand, citizens of the Ukraine generally take part in elections (the rate is about 70% of all eligible voters). Most of the population tends to conformist positions in relation to authority, both during elections and in everyday life. Because of this, the idea of justice does not mean much in society. People very seldom and only unwillingly appeal to courts to defend their dignity or civil rights. In this way, they show a distrust in authority and, at the same time, they continue to rely on power at the local level, considering the latter like the Party before independence. On a private level, though, relationships among people are getting more trusting and close.

Ukrainian society is greatly affected by the memory of past repression, which was particularly sinister in this part of the USSR. According to statistics, one out of every three Ukrainians perished between 1914 and 1953. This concerns primarily the peasant society in the Ukraine that, during the long history of colonization, created some kind of local authority and local institutions which lay outside of government control. Institutions of peasant society in the Ukraine, before the Soviet radicals destroyed them in the 1930s, included: ritual institutions, political institutions, and commercial institutions. As a matter of fact, Ukrainian agricultural and social practices related to the local community – and the creation of so-called *hromada*, which was a voluntary association where leaders were elected for terms of one, two or three years. These elected officials decided a wide range of problems, including relief for widows and for some categories of the poor. But *"hromada* was not concerned with a leveling of wealth within the community. On the contrary, characteristic of Ukrainian peasants was a drive to create wealth, largely through an increase in the family's land holdings, through the sale of surplus agricultural products and through various home industries and services."[4] Based on agricultural production, the family was key to this system, in which there was a tight link between cultural and economic norms. Because of this, William Noll has suggested that here we have the existence of institutions of civil society in the Ukraine before Soviet collectivization, because these institutions lay outside of state control. According to the Communists, collectivization was intended not only to transform the agricultural system of the peasantry, but to alter or entirely destroy peasant culture that was the basis of all Ukrainian cultural society. One of the most far-reaching social consequences of collectivization was the famine of 1932-33 (with about 7 million victims) and the famine after World War II (with one to two million victims). One of the main aims of collectivization was "to break the civil society of peasant culture of such longstanding and to replace it with a newer Soviet culture."[5] The destructive outcome of such Soviet policy is still to be found in our society. It is worth noting that now, in 2003, the Ukraine does not have any significant monument to the memory of the victims of collectivization. The number of victims is in the millions, but their memory was acknowledged by the government only in 2003 (and not by the Communist Party, which was responsible for all these crimes).

---

[4] William Noll, *Transformation of Civil Society. An Oral History of Ukrainian Peasant Culture of the 1920-1930* (Kyiv: Rodovid, 1999) (in Ukrainian), p. 10.

[5] Noll, *Transformation of Civil Society*, p. 11.

In addition to this kind of social passiveness there are, outside of the Western area, numerous monuments, street names, factories, etc., dedicated to the main culprits responsible for Soviet terror in the Ukraine. Instead of fully eradicating all vestiges of that terrible Communist past, many Ukrainian authorities and members of the so-called "intelligentsia" simply say, "this is our history." Unfortunately society seems to be indifferent, and people have become habituated to such a view.

Social tradition and ethical intentions within the frame of discourse of freedom and dignity –which can be identical with values of civil society and democracy – have strongly influenced the Ukrainian cultural actuality (*Lebenswelt*). Ethical traditions which show a paternal-client pattern (as distinct from freedom and democracy) have historically been the product of non-Ukrainian languages and cultural political institutions, and therefore exhibit an indifference, if not hostility, to the Ukrainian cultural actuality. Two distinctive ethical traditions came to be in the actuality of social and political history, and they were not brought into it by force.

It is, therefore, significant for those of us interested in the notion of civil society to recognize the importance of national consciousness-raising. This is the creation of a society that is politically aware, rather than just existing passively under the state's yoke, and so it involves pressing for reforms in areas such as intellectual life, religion, mass media, the freedom of assembly and, of course, the protection of civil rights. Since the view that "the state is above all" has been inculcated into people's consciousness in the Ukraine, it has hindered the development of civil society, but the emergence of the latter will prevent social life from oligarchic stagnation.

From the time of independence onwards, the Ukraine has travelled a road where there is an increasing number of organizations, associations and funds that have been created through the initiative of its citizens. According to data from the Center of Innovation and Development, in 1999 the Ukraine had about 30,000 registered public organizations, 800 of which had a country-wide status. But among them are those that use this persona as a mask for illegal activity. Public organizations may be classified into three main groups: a) organizations with state support and protection; b) organizations created thanks to foreign funds and dependent on ongoing investment; and c) organizations created by individual initiative, aimed at gaining and protecting their private and public interests throughout society and the state. These latter activities belong to the authentic development of civil society and now opposition state oligarchies. This has created an urgent need for a new examination of what has been termed "civil society." It is social rather than individual, for it provides the immediate context required for personal growth, interaction and fulfillment. It is civil, rather governmental, because it has a personal and humanizing character.[6] It requires personal activity, and goes beyond any particular dimension: economic, political, religious, national. Nevertheless, it includes all of the

---

[6] See, here, the work of George McLean.

above, and this active engagement and creative expression of the people constitutes an authentic democratic process.

The development of civil society in the Ukraine, therefore, is a desirable option, and this perspective can be identified with the discourse of freedom and the corresponding ethical tradition. This is also historically related to the maintenance of Ukrainian socio-cultural patterns of the *Lebenswelt*. Rhetoric about civil society that is indifferent to discursive-ethical freedom is also possible, but in this case, we will have a dominant political regime spreading a non-Ukrainian cultural actuality – and this will inevitably lead to the dominance of a semiosis of paternal-client ethics. This kind of civil society will fail to go all the way in promoting democracy and the primacy of human rights.

The Ukraine emerged as a civilization based on the principles of freedom, democracy, and human rights, and on belief in the Holy Spirit. Owing to an analogous belief, the great American Thomas Jefferson was able to say: "I have sworn upon the altar of God eternal hostility to every form of tyranny over the mind of man."[7] And we might add that he put this attitude to work in American social life. Ukrainians believe in these values too. The Ukraine has tasted the freedom of belonging to Europe, to be where she has already been in her past history, and now there is 'no turning back.' This is the main hope for the Ukraine today, as it continues on the difficult road to civil society.

Franko Lviv National University
Lviv, Ukraine

---

[7] Letter to Benjamin Rush (September 23, 1800).

CHAPTER XI

ON THE INTIMATE RELATION BETWEEN SOCIAL FACT AND THREE TYPES OF VALUES[1]

GONG QUN

INTRODUCTION

Since 1900, a considerable number of philosophical works have been published on the relation between fact and value. Is fact totally separated from value, or is there some intrinsic or intimate relation between them? The traditional division between "is" and "ought," outlined by David Hume, suggests one major approach to this issue. Yet while a number of scholars have worked on this subject, research continues, and the possibility of a new way to approach the subject is still open. My opinion is that in order to discuss the issue – the relation between fact and value – first we need to divide "fact" into "natural fact" and "social fact." If we focus on this division, we can find that fact and value are not totally separated from one another, for there is an intrinsic entangling relation between social fact and value.

TWO SENSES OF VALUE

What is a fact? And what is a social fact? Fact can be defined as that which human beings can know and feel through sense experience (the object of human sensibility) or through the mind (the object of human consciousness or thinking). There are two types of facts: one is natural fact, and the other is social fact. Natural facts exist in nature; they are things such as mountains and rivers. Social facts exist and have existed in the social field or the social world, and so there are historical facts as well as present facts in the world.

Social facts can be divided into two types: spiritual fact and fact designated by material objects. It is impossible, however, that any fact is purely spiritual – for a spiritual fact is expressed in language, and every

---

[1] [Abstract] A social fact is a type of fact which humans can recognize and experience. The basic distinction between social facts and natural facts lies in the values embodied by the social facts. Therefore, values either lie in social facts or determine their different features. To be specific, according to their relation to social facts, values can be classified into three categories: the first is the value which is implied by social spiritual affairs, the second is behavioral value related to spiritual social facts (i.e. oughtness), and the third type is the value which lies in social facts embodied in social material affairs.

language needs a certain kind of physical shell (which we call a "material object" in physical nature). There is, then, a kind of social fact that is expressed by material objects but which has spiritual content. (If this is not so, then either such facts are not social, or there are only natural objects in the world.)

Clearly, we also need to define the conception of value. "Value" deals with the meaning of human spiritual culture. The term "value" may refer to conventions, moral ideas, religious ideas, and even those wild spiritual and cultural ideas that are found in all human pursuits, as well as to the understanding of spiritual existence and the relationships between human beings or between humans and nature. In other words, only notions which are found in and kept, respected, and pursued by the human mind imply value. We can call this Value I. Value I is the conception that indicates human spiritual meaning. Value for human behavior – namely, "oughtness" value (which distinguishes itself from "what is") – is Value II. Finally, the value elements in those things in which we can find the presence of the human spirit have cultural meaning; such value elements we can call "Value III." These three kinds of values have different relations to social facts.

In human society, cultural phenomena include both spiritual facts and facts expressed through physical matter. In a sense, value is the central conception of culture. What makes human existence different from natural existence? We hold that it is culture. The existence of a human being is that of a cultural being. What, then, is culture? Different thinkers have different conceptions of culture. However, I think that the conception held by Samuel P. Huntington is just what I have in mind. Huntington writes:

> [c]ivilization and culture both refer to the overall way of life of a people, and a civilization is a culture writ large. They both involve the 'values, norms, institutions, and modes of thinking to which successive generations in a given society have attached primary importance.'[2] A civilization is, for F. Braudel, 'a space, a 'culture area,' 'a collection of cultural characteristics and phenomena.'[3] Wallerstein defines it as a 'particular concatenation of worldview, customs, structures and culture (both material culture and high culture) which forms some kind of historical whole and which coexists (if not always

---

[2] Samuel P. Huntington, *The Clash of Civilizations and the Remaking of World Order* (London: Simon & Schuster, 1996), p. 41.

[3] F. Braudel, "The History of Civilizations: the past explains the present," in *On History*, ed. F. Braudel (Chicago, IL: The University of Chicago Press, 1980), pp. 177–218.

simultaneously) with other varieties of this phenomenon.'[4]
A civilization is according to Dawson the product of 'a
particular original process of cultural creativity which is
the work of particular people,'[5] while for Durkheim and
Mauss, it is 'a kind of moral milieu encompassing a
certain number of nations, each national culture being only
a particular form of the whole'.[6]

From the quotations above, we can see clearly both Huntington's
definition of culture, and also the definitions of culture and civilization
given by other thinkers (whom he quotes). In any kind of culture,
institutions, rules, moralities, conventions or customs are necessary factors.
Culture is the living space and living field of human beings, and so there
are obviously objective (material) elements in it, such as churches, temples
and so on. Still, if the facts in culture can be divided into different levels,
spiritual facts can be said to be on the first level, and the facts expressed
through material objects are on the second level. Why is spiritual fact on the
first level? It is because spiritual facts appear directly as value. In different
kinds of spiritual facts, conventions and moralities are seen as pure spiritual
phenomena; this is also seen in religion. Religion is the important cultural
phenomenon whose internal center consists of religious ideas and whose
external forms are such symbolic things as religious organizations, religious
communities, churches and temples. In a sense, religious ideas are typical
values because religion holds belief to be a holy thing which is above all
else. Human beings live with their belief, by their belief, and on their belief,
which indicates that they take their belief as the most valuable thing in their
lives. The pursuit of beliefs and ideals gives meaning to one's existence.
Conventions and moralities provide order and a structure in life and society.
In H. Rickert's eyes, value is the root of life; "without value, we are not
alive. In other words, without value, we would no longer have desire and
action because value gives us direction for our will and action."[7]

However, religious values and moral notions have an intrinsic
relation. In religion, transcendent existence is its value focus. But if you go
deep into the ideas of any religion, you will find that the transcendence of
values is in fact present in the following situation: namely, a transcendent
super existence is used to protect and support real social norms. We know
that one of the functions of religion is to justify secular morality or, in other

---

[4] Immanuel Wallerstein, *Geopolitics and Geoculture: Essays on the Changing World System* (Cambridge: Cambridge University Press, 1991), p. 215.

[5] Christopher Dawson, "Toynbee's Study of History: The Place of Civilizations in History," *International Affairs*, Vol. 31, No. 2 (Apr., 1955): 149-158.

[6] Huntington, *The Clash of Civilizations*, p. 41.

[7] H. Rickert, *System der Philosophie I* (Tubingen, 1921), p. 120.

words, to let human morality have a religious centre and to teach human beings that our secular behavior can be moralized by following a morality that reflects the commandments of God; we see this in Christianity, Judaism, Buddhism and Islam. We all know the Ten Commandments, the 'Love your neighbor' command given by Christ, the Eight Precepts in Buddhism, and so on. I think if there were no secular moralities to serve as a foundation, religious belief would just be a castle in the sky. Recently, Hans Küng has been advocating "A Global Ethic" that looks towards the common secular morality implicit in different religions. If there were no such secular morality present in religions, Hans Küng could not possibly have put forward his proposal.

Morality is not only enforced by religion, but it is rooted in society. Throughout human history, moral phenomena and social institutions have always been integrated, and we can hardly separate them by saying that '*this* is morality, not a mere institutional norm,' and '*that* is an institutional norm, not morality.' All moral systems involve at least parts of a social system. One's duty, mission, and task by which people can evaluate one's performance to determine whether one is good or not – all come from the social responsibilities that one has. Our social duty is determined by the social system and by our status in this system. Indeed, behind morality we can always find deeper factors – which are those of social institutions or institutional norms.

All human social institutions are based on norm systems that define human beings in terms of their particular social status, rights, duties and obligations. Jürgen Habermas argues that:

> a social world consists of a normative context that lays down which interactions belong to the totality of legitimate interpersonal relations. And all actors to whom the corresponding norms have force (by whom they are accepted as valid), belong to the same social world.[8]

These are norms that Habermas says involve (for actors or social actions) legally valid systems, rules, and principles, which construct the context of the norms through which society "determines what interactions belong to the totality of legal interpersonal relations" and which show the interrelations among intersubjectivities and social world. Or, in Heidegger's words, it is the relation of *Ereignis* in both the subject and the social world.

---

[8] Jürgen Habermas, *The Theory of Communicative Action*, tr. Thomas McCarthy (Boston: Beacon Press, 1984), Vol. 1, p. 88. ["Eine soziale Welt besteht aus einem normativen Kontext, der festlegt, welche Interaktionen zur Gesamtheit berechtigter interpersonaler Beziehungen gehören. Und alle Aktoren, für die entsprechende Normen gelten (von denen sie als gültig akzeptiert werden), gehören derselben sozialen Welt an." Jürgen Habermas, *Theorie des kommunikativen Handelns* (Frankfurt, 1988), Bd. 1, p. 132.]

Therefore, Habermas says, the social world belongs to the totality of all interpersonal relations. However, if there were no norms in the social world, there would be no definitions of value in personal interactions. What, on this account, is normal behavior? We can understand it as:

> the concept of normatively regulated action does not refer to the behavior of basically solitary actors who come upon other actors in their environment, but to members of a social group who orient their action to common values. The individual actor complies with (or violates) a norm when in a given situation the conditions are present to which the norm has application. Norms express an agreement that obtains in a social group. All members of a group for whom a given norm has validity may expect of one another that in certain situations they will carry out (or abstain from) the actions commanded (or proscribed).[9]

A norm is a social existent that universally constrains or directs members of a social community in some mode of action. The central content of a norm is constraint or that which makes people's actions conform to some pattern. If a norm has no constraint or coercive effect, or is rejected by people, or erodes social life, it cannot be regarded as a norm. All institutions, rules, and conventions that constrain social action can be called norms; in this sense, 'norm' has the meaning of a social mechanism which involves not only behavior, but the context of social behavior.

From the perspective of social action, norms play the role of constructing social life. For instance, norms (moral norms) in the family and in the clan system determine social order – e.g., how man and woman come together, and which ways are reasonable for male and female to relate. Norms, such as duty, sense of mission, and conscience, embody the individual side of social duty. Conscience is that which preserves social and legal order in the human heart and which embodies the constrictive effect of the social norm. In terms of legal order, a norm is a kind of institution with the effect of producing communal constraint. In many societies, norms are universal, valid, and legal. A norm inside and outside the human mind is, in its essence, one and the same thing. What is more, in relation to social institutions, Habermas argues: "In the terminology of Max Weber ... we can say that in a certain way sociology presupposes the value-interpretation of the hermeneutical science, but is itself concerned with cultural tradition and value-systems only insofar as they have normative power in the orienting of action. Sociology is concerned only with institutionalized values."[10]

---

[9] Habermas, *Theorie des kommunikativen Handelns*, Bd. 1, p. 127; *The Theory of Communicative Action*, Vol. 1, p. 85.

[10] Jürgen Habermas, *On the Logic of the Social Sciences*, tr. S.W. Nicholsen and J.A. Stark (Cambridge: The MIT Press, 1988), p. 75.

It is not only that an institution is a value, but also that all conventions, customs, religions, moral norms and the inner workings of cultural and spiritual phenomena are values. These values are basic for human beings and necessary for human respect. Therefore, in order to define the concept of value, we must first focus on the characteristics of human existence. What is more, those facts implying values are "natural" facts that are part of the human world, and they come into our practice in the context of our social and practical activities, they underline practical activities, and they affect our practical activities. We can undoubtedly evaluate them as "good" or "bad" by some kind of social standard.

Nevertheless, it is important to recognize that each type of social institution or basic construction entails duties, missions and tasks. In other words, it is the social institution or the basic construction that regulates the subject of social behavior and that gives the reason of "oughtness" – namely, the reason why the subject of social behavior should act in this way. The power of the imperative sentence, "You ought to...... ," comes from the value implied in the social fact. In fact, the route goes from factual value to behavior value; the former generates the latter. We can call the value of the former, "Value I," and the value of latter "Value II." The distinction between Value I and Value II is the distinction between "what is" and "what ought to be" – a distinction which people often recognize.

The value of "ought" appears in both institutional norms and in ideas of norms in general. The moral concept "ought" may be used in two senses. One is that which is present when we prescribe actions to people in social practice – such as when we say "You ought to do that, because you are ...", or "You ought to do that, because it is moral" according to institutional facts (norms), the duties and missions of social institutions, or the general norms of morality. The other sense is that where we use the above presuppositions or make a general demand (where we evaluate people's conduct in moral terms) in order to point out that some particular action ought to be carried out or not. For example, we say that a policeman ought to do certain things in his work, and that he ought not to do such things as striking others or being rude or tough. In this sense, "ought to" entails the sense of that which is right. The proposition that "stealing conduct" [theft] is not "ought conduct" implies that the moral man ought to respect the property of others. Therefore, understanding the value of "ought" cannot be separated from the social fact of institutional norms or from moral norms as general cultural facts. In other words, it is impossible to break the relation between the value of "ought" and Value I. Value I not only implies a demand (an ought) imposed on human behavior, but is the root of behavioral value.

Why can such facts become the root of behavioral value? Simply because there are values or factors of value implied in those facts. Of course, not every use of "ought" is equal to value. But we cannot deny the characteristic of "ought" as an evaluative word, given that we say things like "You ought to... because you are ...". In this sentence, "because" points to the root of value. The content that appears after "you are" is always some kind of social fact implying value, and a fact defining the value of the action. In other words, the ideas of values, evaluations, and value judgments are never just kinds of psychological, emotional or spiritual needs, but things rooted in social convention, morality, and an institutional background. Value notions, which appear in statements about human motivation, attitudes, and intentions, can be found in certain cultural backgrounds and social contexts. If we think that the sources of action value are simply attitudes, desires, or the motivations of acting agents, then we cannot answer the question of changes of attitudes and desires in history. Social basic construction and other aspects of cultural context are the deep sources whose changes necessarily affect the desires of agents. If we look at the differences between the period before "Open China" or "Reform in China" and afterwards, we see that there are totally different values. (Before this period, people respected spiritual values; now, people no longer do so, and respect utilitarian values instead.) This is the result of a historical cause involving a change of social context.

How do we understand what people say in general concerning the distinction between "what is" and "what ought to be"? In order to answer this question, first we need to know what Hume said. Hume argued in his *Treatise on Human Nature*:

> I cannot forbear adding to these reasonings an observation which may, perhaps, be found of some importance. In every system of morality, which I have hitherto met with, I have always remark'd, that the author proceeds for some time in the ordinary way of reasoning, and establishes the being of a God, or makes observations concerning human affairs; when of a sudden I am surpriz'd to find, that instead of the usual copulations of propositions, *is*, and *is not*, I meet with no proposition that is not connected with an *ought* or an *ought not*. This change is imperceptible; but is, however, of the last consequence. For as this *ought*, or *ought not*, expresses some new relation or affirmation, 'tis necessary that it shou'd be observ'd and explain'd; and at the same time that a reason should be given, for what seems altogether inconceivable, how this new relation can be a deduction from others, which are entirely different from it. But as authors do not commonly use this precaution, I shall presume to recommend it to the readers; and am persuaded, that this small attention wou'd subvert all the vulgar systems of morality, and let us see, that the distinction of vice and virtue is not founded merely on the relations of objects, nor is perceiv'd by reason.[11]

---

[11] Hume, *Treatise of Human Nature* III, 1, 1.

Many understand from this that Hume is arguing that there are two kinds of judgment – factual judgment and evaluative judgment – and that neither has a logical connection to the other. For these scholars, Hume is regarded as having made an important claim – one that has had a key role in later moral philosophy. We know that Hume indeed raised the question of the difference between "what is" and "what ought to be." But a close examination of his moral writings reveals that this distinction is not the same as the distinction between a factual judgment and an evaluative judgment, nor does it entail that the two kinds of judgments are logically incompatible. What Hume actually said was only that moral writings in his age used "ought" rather than "is" in connecting propositions, and that this new relation was entirely different from the prior one.

How should we understand Hume's "discovery"? Why had description in moral philosophy undergone such change? We consider that any answer here must first take note of the social milieu, culture, and thought in which Hume lived. As we know, the political conception of divine power had been definitively challenged by the theory of natural right. Though the influence of Christianity was still very strong, people had no longer viewed the state as a kind of divine institution. Secondly, before Hume, Hobbes – and Mandeville – had twice already raised the issue of egoism. Therefore, though there were some very famous theological moralists (such as Shaftesbury, Hutcheson, and Joseph Butler) who still advocated moral principles drawn from ethics of Christian benevolence, God's status in relation to moral authority had been serious attacked. Hobbes and Mandeville explained moral phenomena without depending on God, but rather through the egoistic psychology of the human being. For Mandeville, the fundamental motivation of social development was not the morality advocated by Christianity, but the egoism in human nature. This was quite unlike the view in the Middle Ages, where the ultimate origin of moral value was regarded as being only God. Of course, at this time the existence of God still had not been radically challenged. But by Hobbes's time, the development and change in social notions was so great that moralists – and even common people – would no longer try to infer anything directly from existence of God, and could not know what "ought to be," starting with the goodness of God, because the relation between human beings and God had been broken. Hence we have to see, in context, why it was that Hume was troubled by the transformation from "what is" to "what ought to be." And this shows, in that historical period, God's authority as the source of value had been shaken.

Although God was no longer the source of value, people could not shake off social conventions, institutions, and their norms and rules. To take the ought value (Value II) of behavior as rooted in social conventions, institutions and so on, is the viewpoint of neo-naturalism. Philippa Foot argues that we can derive evaluative conclusions from factual presuppositions. John Searle points out that conventional facts, social-institutional facts and value are intrinsically connected. As noted above, the sentence "You ought to do that, because you are ..." omits the position or duty of the agent (which is an institutional fact) and that cannot been separated from relative value. For example, from the factual proposition "He is the head of the ship," we can effectively derive an evaluative judgment: "He ought to do what the head ought to do." Every subject has a certain role or roles; his duty or mission (Value I) determines the value of his action (Value II). If the institutional duty or cultural values carried by one social subject were taken away from him or her, the subject of value would become a ghost – with no characteristics, no identity, and no personality. Therefore, the human being has not only a psychological existence, but a social existence. What is more, his psychological contents are not merely individual ones, but include elements of historical culture and embody a whole background rooted in social history. Further, we can understand a normal person only by social-communicative actions. Human beings are properly understood in their social action, not in abstraction. The human being is just a series of actions in an interpersonal, social context. In other words, we understand human beings as existing in social life; this means that individuals are never isolated; he or she is integrated into social-interpersonal relations. And at the same time, the intersubjective relation as such is one kind of life-world relation in a greater social context. When we look at the background composed of social institutions, cultural constructions, and the characteristic of subject action in the background, Value I (which lies behind the subject-object relation) will appear before us. It is the real source of the value of action. The root of the value of "ought" or "ought not" can be found in the social-institutional background or in the cultural background. Therefore, if we recognize the real nature of the social subject of conduct, we can know what an "ought value" is.

VALUE III

Spiritual social value is not only the root of Value II, but also the root of Value III. In social life, the spiritual pursuit of human beings is embodied in some kind of physical form. Some kinds of physical things made by human beings will always embody ideas of cultural value. Max Weber argues that the phenomena of social culture are significant ones. Why is this so? His answer is

> the concept of culture is a value-concept. Empirical reality becomes "culture" to us because and insofar as we relate it to value ideas. It includes those segments and only those segments of reality is colored by our value-conditioned interest and it alone is significant to us. it is significant because it reveals relationships which are important to us due to their connection with our values. Only because and

to the extent that this is the case is it worthwhile for us to
know it in its individual features.[12]

The viewpoint of Weber here illuminates our understanding of
Value III. The nature of social fact expressed by the physical elements in
human experience and in the perspective of the natural physical world, is
still physical and is a part of a rich natural world. There are various social
facts – such as buildings, highways, planned greenspace, and any natural
thing that has been "humanized" – and these are natural phenomena, though
they are dependent upon human strength and will. However, the natural
characteristics of these things are not objects of research of the social
sciences. Only a very small part (implied value) of the elements of reality
has a special significance for our research. Implied value in reality has
significance if we need to understand or recognize the cultural meaning of
the social object in question. Furthermore, we must pay attention to its
relation to values in researching the cultural meaning of social fact that is
carried by physical material in the perspective of culture; in other words, we
can understand and recognize them only when we put them in the context of
value. And when we put them in the context of value, we will find value in
these cultural things. We call this kind of value "Value III," due to the
implied value in social fact carried by physical materials.

Compared with spiritual social fact, we know Value III better.
Spiritual fact stays and is contained in the human mind or human heart; in
other words, it exists in the way that human consciousness or understanding
is aware of it. Of course, people cannot avoid experiencing some kind of
effect from conventions or social systems and, in general, people have deep
experience and knowledge about them because these factors regulate or
constrict people's actions, and determine what is good and what is bad.
Therefore, they are the factors that construct the social world. Of course, we
need to employ some visual objects (such as a crown for 'king,' and a stick
for 'power') in order to have ideas for them. But the knowledge we get is
through consciousness. Spiritual fact presupposes spiritual relationships of
human beings, and spiritual relations lie in the intersubjectivities of social
life. This relationship differs, depending on the nation, culture, and period
of history.

Value III lies in social facts transmitted through physical materials
– or, better, Value III defines the nature of the social fact. Of course, the
existence of social facts presupposes natural objects or materials of the
natural world. In other words, it is in physical substance. But, how we can
call such a thing a "social fact"? We do so just because there are elements
in the object, namely value factors. Therefore, we can distinguish such a
thing from a natural fact. However, though it is a very small part of a social

---

[12] 马克斯·韦伯：《社会科学方法论》，中央编译出版社，1999年，
第27页 [Max Weber, *The Methodology of Social Sciences*, trans. Edward A.
Shils and Henry A. Finch, New York: The Free Press, 1949, p. 76.]

fact, it is very complicated, and the degree of complication is not less than that of materials. What's more, the substantial nature of social fact and the value of the nature of a social fact lies in one fact – and not in a corresponding relation to law. What kind of value it is, and how large the value is in what kind of natural things, do not depend on natural things as such, but on its status in the context of social culture. In this sense, the very small part in reality or in social fact, its color, and its significance, are very different for different individuals or different cultures and civilizations. The form that human beings have, and the physical nature of the buildings in which they live, are very common throughout the globe. The physical nature of the materials used in architecture does not change in different nations and different cultures. The system of the circulation of blood in the human body is common for all human beings; blood circulation has a universal character for all people. The things which have value do not depend on any correspondence to law, because the nature of the elements of a social fact, which has special significant for social science, is not determined by its relationships with other majority elements.

In fact, the value significance of a social fact is defined by its position in the context of social culture or by the agent's position in social relations. Social fact carried by physical materials has not only an intrinsic physical construction, but also some features of social value. A physical social fact takes a physical form, such as a love letter. Its existence in this world requires matter as a physical foundation. This is important to the construction of its value or significance. The value of a love letter, for a particular individual, is priceless. It is a testimony of love. Love is one kind of conception, so it is Value I – and the love *letter* is a testimony of that love and is its physical foundation. We can see both as existing in a relation: Value I produces Value III.

The value factor (Value III) of social fact transmitted by physical materials is one kind of social meaning construction. If we want to know exactly what Value III is, we must show its relation in context – i.e., with an institution or a culture, and relative to people's values and their purpose. In other words, we can understand its value significance and its rationality of existence, only through the background of social culture and in the context of interpersonal relations. Alfred Schutz points out that the common world in which we live

> is from the outset an intersubjective world of culture. It is intersubjective because we live in it as men among other men, bound to them through common influence and work, understanding others and being understood by others. It is a world of culture because, from the outset, the world of everyday life is a universe of significance to us, that is, a texture of meaning which we have to interpret in order to find our bearings within it and come to terms with it. This texture of meaning, however – and this distinguishes the

realm of culture from the realm of nature – originates in and has been instituted by human actions, our own and our fellow men's, contemporaries and predecessors.[13]

We still need to point out that the texture of meaning must reflect the social relationships among people. However, we understand social relationships, not only from the perspective of the ontology of social existence, but also from the value perspective. Therefore, we can interpret its value meaning, and find rich value implied in social fact.

The construction of Value III forces us to take the social fact into the texture of intersubjectivity in which we can find its real nature. In the Chinese life world, gift-giving is a very well-known social fact. As a social fact and a social reality, the implications of a gift can be understood only from the perspective of the particular interpersonal relation. A gift – such as a carton of cigarettes, a car, and so on – has only the status of a thing or of goods before it becomes a gift. As a kind of objective reality, it does not carry any implications other than its usability. However, when it becomes a gift, it functions to express someone's feelings, or has the value significance of exchange (e.g., in taking the gift, there is a change in the status or power that is held in the hands of a person of high social status). Chinese gifts move in two kinds of contexts: one is the horizontal or transverse direction – among classmates, friends, and relatives; the other is the vertical direction – namely, between those of a higher social status (leaders) and those of lower social status (those to be led), or between a leader and the masses. The masses or lower officers send gifts to their leaders when the latter celebrate important events, such as holidays, or illness, suffering, mourning, or marriage, and so on:

> lower officers or the common masses give a leader a gift, and in this way they express their respect and loyalty, which in turn reflects the leader's power and authority in the eyes of lower officers and the common masses. Cadres often compare the numbers of guests who are invited to share in the important activities of a family, and they feel that a greater number of guests reflects their authority and achievements. Therefore, if some lower officer did not send a gift when his leader or his family celebrated or commemorated an important event, his behavior could be understood as an offence to his leader.[14]

---

[13]许茨：《社会实在论》，华夏出版社，2001年版，第36-37页. Alfred Schutz, *The Problem of Social Reality*, (Beijing: Huaxia Publishing Co., Ltd., 2001), pp. 36-37. For this English translation, see Schutz's *Collected Papers*, ed. Maurice Natanson (The Hague: Martinus Nijhoff, 1971), p. 10.

[14]阎云翔：《礼物的流动》，上海人民出版社，2000年版，第158-159页.

If a gift does not have a value, or does not have other value implications, can we call it a "gift"? Of course not. A social value implied by a gift is in fact one kind of social construction. Value significance takes the role of constructing a social relation. It is because there is such social construction, through movement and transference, that a common thing becomes significant and a gift.

The existence of Value III and its constructing role are often embodied in symbolic things. What is a "symbolic thing"? A symbolic thing is a thing that is bestowed with a special meaning of cultural value. For example, a gravestone or a church is a symbolic thing that has a meaning of value. The meaning construction of Value III is an intrinsic function of certain value (cultural meaning) systems. In other words, it comes from Value I. This means that, without the relevant knowledge of the culture or the background knowledge of human spiritual life of some society, we cannot understand the value implied in that symbolic thing. What's more, the feelings stimulated by the symbolic thing are very different, depending on whether you are (or are not) in some interpersonal or spiritual relation. An observer standing before a gravestone of someone he does not know may have no feeling about it. But if the gravestone belongs to a dead relative, the feeling in his heart would be totally different. The feeling for a church in the heart of one person who does not believe in Christianity may be the same as that which he or she has for other buildings; at most, his feeling about the church may simply be based on something about in its shape. If he hates Christianity, his will may be to destroy the church, even all the churches in the world. However, for an alien from outside of the Earth, what meaning does a church have? He does not know what it is, because he has no knowledge of its cultural value on Earth. He cannot distinguish the value meaning of a church from that of any other building. We all know that a church is not an ordinary building because we know about the history of Christianity, and we may be moved by Christ, or are touched by Christians and understand the actions of Christians. Of course, another example of a symbolic thing in Christianity is the cross. But if we do not know about the death of Christ and the Christian interpretation of it, we cannot understand the very rich symbolic implication of the cross. Suppose we found some ruins of the Mayan civilization, where the position of the ruins was similar to that of a church in Western countries. Suppose that we also see there something like a cross – though we would not know if it was a sign of some religion because we do not have any information about that religion. In such a case, we would have no any feeling about the cultural meaning and have no feeling about the ruins and the like, for they are only a collection of materials (supposing that knowledge of the civilization that built them had disappeared). The materials indeed exist, but they lose all cultural meaning; we cannot even take them as ruins. The 'symbolic thing' is too small to have any significance to us.

The significance of Value III that is carried by physical materials may change with the change of the social-cultural system, and some holy meaning may be lost in the course of history. The construction and transformation of social value (Value III) is carried out among intersubjectivities, and meanings of Value III need to be read into the thing by some subject. Furthermore, a change of subject necessarily has an implication for the understanding of value.

Take the example of the 'earth' temples in the countryside of China. Before 1949, we could see earth temples in almost every village; the earth temple was considered to be the most holy thing, and nothing could challenge its divine authority. Peasants worshipped the god of 'earth' and prayed to the god of earth for his blessings and protection and for a greater harvest. The meanings of Value III were here illustrated in the collective ceremony of worship, reverent activities for the earth god, and the devout attitude towards the earth god. In a sense, the earth god was the center of both the farm and spiritual activities. Peasants believed that a good harvest solely depended on their reverent attitude toward the earth god. Its meaning construction lay in peoples' behaviors. If I wrongly moved one light in a temple, villagers would punish me – but this was not because I had mistaken what it was in its objectivity, but rather (for those who participated in the meaning community and who identified the construction of social meaning) what I did offended the value meaning which they constructed. It was, as it were, an activity of rebellion against its holiness. Therefore, my action was not only unreasonable, but also illegitimate in the context of their value system.

However, if we examine the situation during the period from the 1950s to the 1960s, attitudes concerning objects in relation to the earth god were totally different. Communism and atheism had constructed a new value system. If someone thought the earth god was divine, people would take him away – which was just like taking away the earth god and pulling down the earth temple – because the old value system no longer functioned. The new value system that people had constructed left no position for the earth god and thus the earth god had no value significance. It is just as Habermas says: "The reconnection of *Verstehen* to the initial hermeneutic situation is linked with value-interpretation, which has to direct itself to historically objectivated cultural meanings from within the irreducible value relationships of its own situation. ... For cultural values not only serve to regulate social systems; they also function as goals within the system, goals that are not reflected in the values themselves." [15] Cultural values are the values of meaning-contents objectified as such.

The value systems that people live by have an objective meaning for them. We can experience the meaning or significance not only of Value I in the social world, but also of the order for action ('ought' value), and of the Value III in objective things of the human world. These three kinds of

---

[15] Jürgen Habermas, *On the Logic of the Social Sciences*, p. 86.

value constitute the system of value life. Human beings live in the world and take part in the construction of value meaning. The system of value meaning maintains the life and spirit of human beings. The system of value meaning gives meaning to one's life, goals and ideals. In each person's eyes, the value meaning is a real one, which cannot be denied because each lives in such a system of value meaning. In this sense, to understand any text or social fact is to understand the 'self.' Self-understanding must take the form of understanding one's value world. Meaning construction embodies some kind of value direction. If meaning construction is different from the value direction held by some particular person, value understanding will make the person unable to identify with the outward value system, resulting in a crisis of existence. In other words, if some value system identified by a person has been destroyed, the destruction is equal to that of his spiritual life.

A good example is Wang Guowei's death during the transformation period of China from the Qing dynasty to modern times.[16] Human beings bestow rich meanings on this world and, at the same time, they are interpreters of meanings of this world. But when society has changed the construction of value meaning, a new interpretation is needed. People living in the system need to change their understanding of social reality. Otherwise, the social system that has a new order or a new construction cannot personally involve you as a member of it, because the very life construction of the interpreter is a meaning construction. Whoever can understand can know how to plan his future in terms of his possibilities. To plan one's self is to plan one's history and social future. To construct oneself means to construct the value meaning of and for one's society. There are always human beings, so constructing the value meaning of human history does not come to an end. The meanings of this world are bestowed by people, and the bestowing activities and the meanings are real events – indeed, they are the meaning of human existence as such. Life is one vast river of meaning. If the river of meaning stops at some point in time, it signifies only that one value meaning world has been closed by the past. If the river continues to flow, it means that the human life-world nonetheless continues to advance. We continuously build and rebuild 'things' of meanings. We can end our discussion by quoting Hans-Georg Gadamer:

> What is at issue is not only the well-known distinction between fact and value that is especially dominant in southwest neo-Kantianism and the way it influences the social sciences (Max Weber). The present-day discussion shows that this distinction is pointless on the level of

---

[16] For the story of the suicide of Wang Guowei (1877-1927), see for example Q. S. Tong and Xiaoyi Zhou, "Criticism and Society: The Birth of the Modern Critical Subject in China, *boundary 2*, vol. 29.1 (2002) 153-176.

reflection we have reached today – especially after the dogmatism of the concept of 'fact' has been critiqued by theory of science, hermeneutics, and ideology critique.[17]

Department of Philosophy
Hubei University and Renmin University of China
Beijing, P.R. China

---

[17] Hans-Georg Gadamer, *Hermeneutics, Religion, and Ethics* (New Haven, CT: Yale University Press, 1999), p. 58.

CHAPTER XII

HUMAN STUDIES IN VIETNAM AT THE BEGINNING OF 21ST CENTURY

HO SI QUY

INTRODUCTION

Thinkers from both the West and the East have delved deeply into the study of human nature, and there have been several schools of thought – such as Confucianism and Taoism in ancient China, those of Socrates and Aristotle in ancient Greece, those of Freud and the existentialists in modern times, and many others – which have paid close attention, and made impressive contributions, to the complexity of human existence. The understanding of the complicated relationships between the individual and society is rooted in cultural traditions from the earliest times.

The idea of the unity of man and the universe has often been understood as belonging to the East – but this is a mistake, for this idea has also been found among the most ancient theories of the West. In atomism, for example, Democritus referred to the "microcosm," meaning the homogeneity of man and the external world. According to him, after a man died, "spiritual atoms" were released and disappeared into the air.[1] We should, therefore, avoid making generalizations, such as that the East is more advanced than the West in terms of considering man as a microcosm of the universe, or that the West is more advanced than the East in developing the idea of the importance of the autonomous individual. And so, human studies in modern times should not go looking for easy answers, such as that the West needs to turn to the East, or vice versa. Of course, both the East and the West have their contributions to make in trying to understand man in modern society. Moreover, cultural traditions can be the source of useful suggestions in planning for the future. But the many challenges involved in understanding human existence do not allow any community to isolate itself from new ideas, even it has a great tradition or heritage.

THE VALUE OF HUMAN STUDIES

For mankind, there is nothing more interesting than itself. Even in ancient times, Socrates understood this and awakened the hunger for truth about human nature by emphasizing that one must "understand oneself"

---

[1] Философский энциклопедческий словарь, Сов. энциклопедия. М. (1989), p. 157.

(gnothi seauton). But man is not only a subject that has knowledge, understanding, and a good will, as Socrates imagined. Nor is he just a political animal as Aristotle affirms, or an economic animal as F.W. Taylor (1856–1915) would say.[2] Man is an animal that can create tools with which to work, as Benjamin Franklin understood -- but this understanding is still too simple. Man should be considered as a cultural animal. This means that the man is "a bio-social reality;" and that "in its reality it is the ensemble of social relations" (Karl Marx; Theses on Feuerbach, 6).

In reviewing all of the preceding concepts, we see that what has been known about the self so far – although it is rich and profound – is still one-sided and does not provide us with sufficient understanding of ourselves. Looking at the achievements of medicine, medico-biology, the social sciences – and especially new achievements in genetic mapping, transplants, the analysis of brain activity, the managerial sciences, cultural factors, and so on – many scholars consider the twentieth century as the century of the discovery of human nature. The World Conference on "Science for the Twenty-First Century: a New Commitment," organized by UNESCO in Hungary in June 1999, assessed the contributions of the sciences and technology to human progress in the twentieth century – and there is no doubt that scientific knowledge has brought the greatest benefits to humanity. Life expectancy has been improved substantially, and has passed the limit (of three score years and ten) mentioned in the Bible.[3] Many diseases are under control or can be controlled rapidly. Agricultural production can provide more and more products, even as the population increases. There is a marvelous increase in the amount of energy available. Human beings have been liberated from hard work. The present generation is enjoying more products and services in comparison with previous ones. Knowledge of the universe's origin, the origin of life, and the origin of man and mankind, allows man to adopt new approaches to solving problems concerning human life. The sciences have had a great impact on human behaviour and on man's expectations of himself. Man occupies a central role in development once again.[4]

It is easy to note the significant progress in human studies that has been made in the twentieth century. However, compared to other research areas, especially those outside of human nature, do the achievements made in human studies satisfy us? In this regard, Professor Pham Minh Hac points out that, so far, "humanity knows very little about itself: ... two brain human hemispheres, like the globe, contain a number of mysteries... man,

---

[2] This comment is to be found in his *Principles of Scientific Management* (1911).

[3] "And the days of our years in them are three score and ten years. But if in the strong they be fourscore years" (Psalm 89:10).

[4] "Conference of Nobel Laureates: Facing the 21st Century: Threats and Promises; Paris, 1988," in *Nguoi dua tin*, UNESCO, No. 5 (1988).

as a microcosm, is just as unknown as space or the universe.[5] Elie Wiesel, in the opening speech at the Meeting of Nobel Prize Laureates of 1988, said: "we should recognise that, in respect to social ethics, we are groping as we go ahead. Our priorities are not properly oriented. We are concerned more about the nature of the universe than in looking for an acceptable ethic. Man went to the moon, but did not step any closer towards his fellows. Man is exploring the sea bottom and the limits of the universe, but his neighbours are still strangers. We live until an old age, but old age becomes a burden and a curse."[6]

It is difficult to deny the fact that there is no theory which can answer the questions: What is man? and What is the meaning of life? Studies of natural man are not in accordance with research on social man. Human development indices proposed by the United Nations Development Programme (UNDP) are important and are steadily being improved upon, but at best they can reflect only the quality of life, not happiness. A life with high quality is not the same as a happy life, especially in the eastern understanding of the term. The concept of "quality of life" is one-sided and cannot replace "happiness." Man and his happiness are still as mysterious as they were thousands of years ago. Both reason and non-rational cognition about man lead one to a paradoxical situation – i.e., in ordinary life, rational knowledge is not always the most effective; sometimes non-rational knowledge and intuition are more useful. The fact that more people are concerned about emotion, religion, spiritual life and mysterious forces shows that high living standards, social and health facilities, information technology, and so on, are not enough for people to feel assured about their lives or to be satisfied with their prospects in the future. Moreover, an approach based on the sub-conscious and on intuitive knowledge does not seem to be an appropriate way to discover truths about human nature. Guesses about the possibilities open to human life are generally unreliable sources of knowledge. Many theorists study human factors in isolation and the definition of man according to one approach is frequently different from that which we find in another approach. E. Morin and A.B. Kern warn that today's "concept of man is torn into pieces."[7]

The discoveries of science contribute to a more comprehensive understanding of natural and social man. As a scientific enterprise that is also of great value to us, studies on human nature should change, and they should seek to bring the various separated pieces of knowledge about human beings together and, thereby, explain human nature through a comprehensive approach that shows human beings as they really are – including their individuality, their activities, and the physical conditions of

---

[5] Pham Minh Hac, *Bai phat bieu tai le cong bo quyet dinh thanh lap Vien nghien cuu Con nguoi* (Hanoi, 24/01/2000), p. 4.

[6] *Nguoi dua tin*, UNESCO, No. 5 (1988), p. 18.

[7] Pham Minh Hac, *Bai phat bieu tai le cong bo quyet dinh thanh lap Vien nghien cuu Con nguoi* (Hanoi, 24/01/2000, p. 3.

their lives.[8] When evaluating the achievements of the human sciences, Jean Dausset, the French Nobel Laureate in physiology, states: "Man has a new task. Man is no longer an object that is subject just to chance. Man no longer is governed by fate, because he can go toward a certain future. In brief, man takes his fate into his own hands. We don't have the right to be optimistic or pessimistic; we simply have to be wise."[9]

This is the direction for a new science of man. In Russia, when acknowledging the contribution of the journal *Human Studies* in pursuing this approach, Academician V.E. Davidovich wrote: "In recent years, the series of investigations that have led researchers to revolutionize the established integrated anthropology (or social anthropology, cultural anthropology, philosophical anthropology, etc.), have also shown that we do not yet have a comprehensive picture of mankind. In Russia, and indeed in the whole world, the task of understanding mankind in its comprehensiveness, its nature, and its diverse appearances, once again is given to each generation."[10] Therefore, the direction we must take today is to form a new science (or new field of knowledge – to use a more modest term) – and this is a research direction taken by my own Institution, the Institute of Human Studies of the National Centre for Social Sciences and Humanities, in Vietnam.

VIETNAM AND HUMAN STUDIES

In Vietnam, human studies have many purposes, but one of them is to understand, more deeply and comprehensively, the Vietnamese of the past and present in comparison with the peoples of the West and East and Southeast Asia. This is a new task, but it has long been considered by Vietnamese scholars. In the past, studies of literature, history and philosophy were not separated. During the one thousand years in which Confucianism dominated, knowledge of Confucian culture was mostly knowledge about man, and the major theme here was that of teaching and learning to be a man. At the beginning of the twentieth century, this interpretation of man was compared with that which we found in the West and in East Asia. From that moment on, investigations were made into specialised areas of understanding man and, specifically, Vietnamese man; evidence of this is found in a diversity of sciences such as history and archeology, medicine and ethnology, sociology and psychology, and so on. Since the 1980s, national cultural characteristics have become an important aspect of this study. Human studies, then, have attracted a good deal of

---

[8] C.Mac va Ph.Angghen, *Tuyen tap.* t.I, Nxb Su that (Hanoi, 1980), p. 267.

[9] *Nguoi dua tin*, UNESCO, No. 5 (1988), p. 18.

[10] В.Е.Давидович, *В зеркале философии* (Феникс. Ростов-на-Дону, 1997), p. 99.

research, and we see the efforts of social activists who strive to identify the characteristics of the Vietnamese people.

In many publications, however, knowledge of the Vietnamese people remains simple and anecdotal. Of course, basic research in medicine, biology, the social sciences and the humanities cannot help in the identification of distinctive characteristics of the Vietnamese people. Indeed, what we can say about the Vietnamese people is divided among the various social sciences and humanities, and so is rather fragmented. It is difficult to imagine Vietnamese man as such in these studies. The emergence of a new science of human studies at this moment responds, then, to a genuine cognitive need. For the Vietnamese, then, Vietnamese man was born in Vietnamese history with its distinctive challenges, and he has specific characteristics that are very different from the people of the West, of Russia, of China, and of Southeast Asian. Nevertheless, we must acknowledge that the Vietnamese people have been a product of cultural integration. Geographically, Vietnam belongs to Southeast Asia and has such characteristics; culturally, Vietnam remains under the influence of Confucianism, and belongs to East Asia. Defining the development of the Vietnamese people and of Vietnamese society in general, then, is very complex, and this must be taken into account in carrying out human studies.

Faced with new challenges to its development in the present era of globalisation, the Vietnamese people have social, psychological and culturally-specific characteristics which have been accumulated during thousand years of struggling to establish the nation and to protect the country from foreign occupiers. This has been reaffirmed in many official documents. Of course, these specific features are not unique. "Specific" does not mean that we will not find these characteristics in other places; it means, rather, that the Vietnamese people have a number of distinctive values. In this spirit, however, we understand that the values specific to the Vietnamese are not only part of our heritage as we begin the 21st century, but they are also part of the heritage of all of humanity.

The Institute of Human Studies
Vietnamese Academy for Social Sciences
Hanoi, Vietnam

CHAPTER XIII

ETHNIC DIVERSITY AND CULTURAL CLASH IN THE SAINT PETERSBURG PRESS

S. VINOGRADOVA and *T. SHALDENKOVA*

From the moment of its foundation, Saint Petersburg has been a multinational city. Iogann Georgi, the author of a detailed description of Saint Petersburg during the last decade of the eighteenth century, wrote that the advantages that Peter the Great and his successors granted to foreigners attracted them to Saint Petersburg, not only because they could worship according to their own system of belief, but they could freely engage in arts, crafts, and indeed any other form of commercial activity.[1] Writing about the "distinction of inhabitants or tribes," the author names the Finns as the most ancient local inhabitants. Among the "foreigners" (in Georgi's words), the most numerous were the Germans. Dutchmen, Frenchmen, Swedes, Italians, Spaniards, Poles, Armenians, Georgians, Tatars, Kalmyks and "negroes" who also lived in Saint Petersburg. All together they formed "the eighth or the ninth part of the Russians."[2] Among the non-Orthodox population Protestants prevailed, but there was also a Catholic parish. There was no Islamic mosque at that time, but services in the Arabian and Tatar languages were conducted in households. Among the many scientists, artists and musicians there were Englishmen, Frenchmen, Italians, Finns, Czechs, Hungarians, and Serbs.

In spite of the fact that modern sociologists regard Saint Petersburg as "quite mononational," in comparison with the Russian population overall, the ethnic picture of the city and area is rather varied. National associations in Saint Petersburg include the Abkhazians, Assyrians, Bashkirs, Byelorussians, Bulgarians, Buryats, Greeks, Georgians, Jews, Cossacks, Kazakhs, Karaites, Koreans, Kirghizes, Komi, Latvians, Lithuanians, Germans, Ossets, Poles, Tatars, Turkmen, Ukrainians, Chechens, Estonians, and representatives of many other nationalities. Various faiths are present in the city. There are a number of schools where education is conducted in national languages; moreover, some ethnic groups publish newspapers and magazines.

Such a variety can only serve to please, since it gives a powerful impulse for socio-cultural development, without averaging, leveling or impoverishing its resources; the concern of UNESCO for the disappearance

---

[1] I.G. Georgi, *Description of the Russian Imperial Capital of Saint Petersburg and sightseeing in its vicinities, 1794-1796* (Saint Petersburg, 1996), p. 146.

[2] Georgi, p. 147.

or fading of small cultures can be mentioned here. At the same time, one cannot deny that today ethnic relations are one of the leading challenges in social reality: "Ethnic conflicts, ethnic violence, forced migration – society today pays for the earlier lack of interest in ethnic groups, and now suffers from an exaggerated attention to them, to the detriment of dealing with other serious problems."[3]

Some scientists speak about the "ethnic paradox of modernity." For some time, Western social scientists predicted a convergence but, instead, we have seen a powerful process of divergence. In the opinion of a number of Russian political scientists, many fractional or local conflicts (including those having an ethnic "cover") reflect a global conflict in which centrifugal and centripetal tendencies collide. The centripetal tendency (with a view to the creation of a united "world community") is reflected in the USA, Europe, NATO and the United Nations; the centrifugal, by Russia. There is also a conservative tendency by South Asian, Far Eastern, Central Asian and Euroasian civilizations.[4] If one looks closely at these areas, the "explosion" of ethnic problems can be readily observed.

Several decades ago, ethnic problems seemed to be concentrated in regions of the so-called "Third World" – in particular, in Africa; nowadays, they have become active in Belgium, Italy, France, Scotland, Canada, Yugoslavia and in "the post-Soviet space." Moreover, each "explosion" possesses a unique capacity and orientation. At the end of the 1990s, sociologists in Russia noted the increase of ethno-psychological uneasiness among Russians, caused by an instability of interethnic relations both within the country and abroad. During this period, we also find problems in ethnic relations in Saint Petersburg. Sociologists have confirmed that 20% of the inhabitants consider this to be the main problem of the city. A third of the national minorities in Saint Petersburg have identified this as the first and foremost problem.[5] Sociologists have connected this phenomenon, first, with the increase of external migration, along with certain negative features accompanying it (a high share of migrants among the homeless, and the existence of "ethnic-based" criminal groups).

Surveys have shown a clear discrepancy in the attitudes of various groups of Petersburgers to other nationalities. 21% of the Russians living in the city preferred to work in ethnically diverse workplaces; 58.3 % did not oppose interethnic marriages. Russians believed that they were more concerned for other peoples than other peoples for them. "Non-Russians" (especially the Azerbaijanians, Armenians, and Ossets), in their turn, accused Russians of prejudice. On the basis of extensive sociological research, scientists concluded that there has been some decrease in anti-

---

[3] G.U. Soldatova, *Psychology of Inter-ethnic Intensity* (Moscow, 1998), p. 3.

[4] A.A. Kotenev, *Ethnic Conflictology* (Saint Petersburg, 1996), p. 27.

[5] Z.V. Sikevich, *Sociology and Psychology of National Relations* (Saint Petersburg, 1999), p. 123.

Semitism in Saint Petersburg but a significant increase in "Caucasus-phobia." Old ethnic prejudices have begun to be replaced by new ones. "Persons of the Caucasian nationality" have come to be stereotyped, and associated with such features, as cruelty, arrogance, and aggression. Sociologists have noted an "unfriendly attitude to Chechens by 8,4% of the city dwellers, to Azerbaijanians by 8,3%, to Georgians by 3,2%, to Armenians by 3,0% – and on the whole, towards "a person of Caucasian nationality," by 70,7%.[6]

Several years ago, researchers analyzing the Osset-Ingush conflict came to the conclusion that, given the negative character of much of the information transmitted by the mass-media, any solution to this conflict would be complicated:

> Extreme negative examples, associated with this or that ethnic group, incline the readers of newspapers to forget the fact that these cases are very rare and are more likely an exception. Criminals come from all classes of people ... but such generalizations can provoke conflict. Emotionality and subjectivity in the depictions of social problems by journalists are also results of such an "emotional infection," and contribute to ethnic conflict.[7]

Sociologists also note that the press can politically "heat up" various forms of nationalism (for example, nationalistic newspapers may kindle anti-Semitism). The influence of political factors on portrayals of this or that nationality is incontestable (the stereotypical image of the Pole has been formed in Russian literature since the times of 'the great distemper' in the 17th century, and as a result of the conditions of Russian-Polish relations); geopolitical moments are no less significant. Today, we see a desire to strengthen (or at least to prove) the "European" status of Saint Petersburg. This desire for integration into the international community, however, is reflected in the consciousness of some of the ethnic groups in Petersburg and the surrounding area, and has had an effect on an interest in sovereignty or (at least) the strengthening of regional independence. For many, the hope is that, through this integration, the sense of the existence of a commonwealth with neighboring countries will grow, tourism will develop, an inflow of investments will begin, and there will be a new ethnos that preserves "the Slavonic-Finnish nucleus." Yet, at the same time, today in Saint Petersburg the number of inhabitants from the Caucasus has grown and, in state-farm fields in the area, we can already see (writes the magazine *Neighbors*[8]) "the yellow faces of the Chinese and Tadjik's tyubeteykas."

---

[6] Sikevich, p. 127.

[7] Soldatova, p. 295.

[8] *Neighbors* (August 1999), p. 6.

The reaction of Saint Petersburgers to the creation of German settlements is similarly inconsistent. The reason for conflict is not national hostility. Instead, the interests of the families of military men and their new neighbors have collided here and there because of the absence of accommodation and space for housing. The proximity of the Baltic countries and the tensions connected with the relations with them have resulted in an enhanced attention among Saint Petersburgers to the position of Russians abroad.

According to sociologists, the prevalence of ethnic hostility is directly age-related: among youth (from 18 to 25 years) 71.1% of those surveyed had negative views about representatives of other nationalities.[9] As Sikevich writes, "the formation of a radicalized, nationalistic youth in Russia is one of the most disturbing facts which have been uncovered in research on the influence of the ethnic factor on the mass consciousness of Russians."[10] Thus, despite its reputation as the "peaceful city," Saint Petersburg has not been able to escape the hostility which has come to characterize inter-ethnic relations in our country as a whole. This ethnic problematic has been reflected in the Saint Petersburg press, and the study of this activity, with its successes and failures, can be interesting and instructive.

Certainly, the general principles involved in this situation depend on many circumstances. These events occur in concrete conditions of place and time; how they are portrayed is connected to the traditions inherent in this or that kind of mass-media or the in the individual media outlet. Not the least is the role played by the creative individuality of the journalist, reflecting his moral and professional formation. To show to what degree the mass-media uses its opportunities in the noble business of encouraging (or discouraging) ethnic tolerance in society, we have chosen three newspapers from Saint Petersburg: the "Sankt-Petersburgskye Vedomosty" [Saint Petersburg Gazette] (at the time of the writing of this article, its founders were a labor collective and the city mayoralty; it has a circulation of over 83,000 copies); "Vetcherny Petersburg" [Evening Petersburg] (published by the Joint-Stock Company "Daily newspaper Evening Petersburg," with a circulation of 37,150 copies); and "Smena" [Change] (founded by the Legislative Assembly of Saint Petersburg and the Joint-Stock Company "Change," it has a circulation of over 19,000 copies). These papers – among the oldest in the city – aspire to maintain their prestige and quality while simultaneously taking account of market conditions and competition.

Within the framework of our research, we have analyzed the complete set of newspapers for August 1999. The choice of this month is not arbitrary: in August 1999, significant changes occurred in the country, and political and military conditions had become aggravated in a number of regions of both Russia and "the post-Soviet space." Materials containing

---

[9] Sikevich, p. 129.
[10] Sikevich, p. 130.

"ethnic" information made up approximately one-sixth of the overall number of articles in the *Saint Petersburg Gazette*; in *Evening Petersburg*, we see the same ratio, and in *Change* it is about one-eighth. The overwhelming majority of these articles were written by staff journalists or came from national news services. The greatest part of the "ethnic" information found in the three Petersburg newspapers did not directly concern life in the city and area. In some cases, mentions of the burning problems of modern Russian society (e.g. the problem of war and peace) were not only connected with military subjects, but to a large degree were embedded in it. For example, practically all articles of the *Saint Petersburg Gazette* where the region of Dagestan was mentioned, were devoted to the military conflict there. We found a similar pattern in *Evening Petersburg*. The amount of "local color" was a little bit stronger in *Change*, which informed us about the meeting of Dagestan representatives in Petersburg (though this actually never took place; the newspaper had wanted to express indignation about actions in the Chechen Republic), and about the Petersburg OMON, carrying out the task in Dagestan (see the issues of August 19 and 25). But does this mean that "the Caucasian break" had safely bypassed Saint Petersburg, and that the ethnic problematic had lost its importance for the mass-media of the city?

In the Saint Petersburg press in August 1999, one finds a number of responses to a series of stories about national relations broadcast by the TV programme "Sobytyie" [*Event*; the fifth channel in Saint Petersburg] at the end of July of that year. This is remarkable, and demands serious analysis. In the psychology of journalism, the "boomerang effect" is well-known. According to social scientists, if we address an audience, using false or inadequate information or employing poorly-argued rhetoric, we get a reciprocal effect. Precisely this situation arose in the Saint Petersburg mass media. The purpose of the programme was probably noble – to draw attention to interethnic relations in the city and region, and to condemn nationalism. But the result turned out to be quite the opposite.

The first broadcast dealt with "the Azerbaijan motive," where journalist S. Chernjadjev tried to comment on a conflict which had arisen in the market in Podporojie (Leningradskaya oblast). The question was a serious one, and in fact more economic than political; the city and region depend on deliveries of foodstuffs, its own agricultural sector is in recession, and trade is poorly organized and corrupt. But at the forefront there was, alas, a suggestion of ethnic problems. Moreover, it was suggested to TV viewers that they call in to vote on whether ethnic cleansing was necessary in city. The question was ethically and politically tactless and, from a scientific point of view, it should not have even been raised: sociologists have to be especially careful about questions touching on ethnic issues. And in carrying out such investigations, subtlety and delicacy are necessary. Any answers obtained through the 'poll' conducted following the programme can hardly be considered accurate. But the majority of respondents (it is impossible to determine exactly how many they were) supported "ethnic cleansing." Thus, the journalist struck a spark of malevolence, only worsening the situation.

A week later another broadcast took place. Here, S. Chernjadjev addressed "the Jewish theme," based on a very weak knowledge of the history of national culture. And again (in his own words) he "dictated" to the city an obviously provocative question about "pogroms." The third broadcast did not bring any clarity to audience understanding. Chernjadjev's interlocutor, the famous scientist V. Skvirsky, determined that the discussion of these issues on Saint Petersburg television went on to cause serious problems. And through such innuendo and manipulation ethnic clashes were nourished. The indignation of the Saint Petersburg public was expressed by the writer N. Katerli in his article "Non-native A. Blok" and in other similar articles, and in a letter of protest to the northwest regional management of the State Committee for the Press in the Russian Federation. Sharply negative opinions on the broadcasts were made by scientists, writers, and members of some juridical organizations. On the basis of the law of the Russian Federation "concerning mass media," an official warning has been sent to the "Petersburg" broadcasting company.

In connection with these broadcasts, an article by M.M. Chulaki, a writer and Chairman of the Saint Petersburg Governor's Committee on Human Rights, was published in the *Evening Petersburg* on August 24 and 25. This highly publicized article was written boldly, sharply and completely fairly, condemning such methods of journalistic provocation as vicious. Unfortunately, however, this author too did not avoid national stereotypes. "If you are the wisest, My God, reconcile with Allah!" – is a line from a diary of the twelve-year Bosnian girl who, during the ethnic conflict there, lost both her (Catholic) mother and her (Muslim) father. This line became not only a headline in the notes of B. Ohtinsky (*Evening Petersburg*, August 1999), but also an epigram for many other statements from the mass-media on the theme of inter-ethnic relations.

We note that there was a certain perspective repeated throughout the various articles in the Saint Petersburg press concerning the ethnic problem. For example, in the *Saint Petersburg Gazette*, the issue was connected with a story about Russians living in distant countries, where they have become national minorities and where the question of ethnic tolerance is reversed. Such articles are numerous and varied. In some (for example, in J. Simonjan's lengthy sketch, "Moscow/Tbilisi," in the issue of August 5, 1999), nostalgia for the former friendship among peoples is expressed. In others, we come across horrifying tales about the trade in Russian slaves: in 1998, that number was 1,415. This was written about by A. Arakeljan, Vice-President of the Congress of National Associations of Russia, an expert associated with the Saint Petersburg center "Strategy," and a representative on the Council on Human Rights in Russia (August 20, 1999). In some publications, the position of Russians in Latvia (August 21 and 28, 1999) was discussed. All these materials stressed the division of people into "us" and "them."

Perhaps a more optimistic note can be found in a story written by the journalist E. Belenkova, about the restoration of the Cathedral in Kaliningrad; a number of Petersburgers participated in this work. In this case, the categorical imperative of Kant, which insists on the moral necessity of acting in a way that one could will that all others act, has come close to practical realization. Representatives of different nationalities and creeds took part in the restoration of the Cathedral (see *Saint Petersburg Gazette*, August 21, 1999).

How can journalists today contribute to that continuity and connectivity without which a culture cannot exist? By the destruction of stereotypes. Attempts by journalists to overcome their own prejudices and the negative views of their audience are certainly worthy. On August 14, *Change* published a human interest story entitled "Gipsy with an exit in the park of Ekateringof," which was devoted to the festival of gipsy art. In another story, by the journalist I. Bondarenko, we have the stereotype of the gipsy (as dirty, guilty of larceny and every other perfidy, with gold tooth-capping and wearing a mohair jacket and worn-down bedroom slippers); we read: "with a crash came the sight of a woman in strict black narrow clothes and beautiful, well-groomed hair. A proudly-raised head, high and thin heels, and a flying gait. And her eyebrows, eyes…" A popular artistic image, familiar to the readers, illustrated the text; it was of the semi-legendary character of Hodja Nasreddin, who is known as someone crafty, wise, and able to win in any situation. The journalist A. Mezentsev titled some correspondence about the Russian (and Tadjik) writer Timur Zulfikarov (b. 1936), "Hodja Nasreddin walks in Petersburg" (see *Change*, August 14, 1999). The author of "Hodja Nasreddin's Letters to Yeltsin and Clinton," predicts that in the 21st century we will discover the genius of poetry which synthesizes the achievements of representatives of all modern literary traditions and which will be directed, not just to the elite, but to all.

On August 15, 1990, the well-known Russian singer Victor Tsoy passed away. A tale about this "last" hero was given by the journalist K. Cherbakova (August 13, 1999). For her, this musician was one of the landmark figures in Russian history, the founder of a direction in Russian rock-and-roll close to that found in Britain. At one point, the author mentions "a familiar Korean structure" as a symbol of originality and recognition. This "Korean theme" appeared on more than one occasion in *Change* (August 4, 1999.). We also have a report on an exhibition by Korean artists, containing interesting ethnographic information and art criticism, and expanding our understanding of Korean culture.

The most extensive articles with "international" content tend to be devoted to sports. They dazzle their readers with the names of the countries, capitals, and frequently the nationality of the sportsmen; mentioning this is perceived as a natural, organic and necessary part of the articles. The great principle of noble competition founded in Ancient Greece has turned out to be one of the most powerful reflections of the European mentality and global culture. *Change* writes a lot about sports and sportsmen – and this is very clear: this newspaper is primarily for the youth. In most cases, it finds original ways of communicating information. But annoying errors connected with ethnicity sometimes appear in the statements of journalists. For example, stories about a Black forward, playing for the football team "Spartac," repeatedly appeared in the pages of the press. Describing a great victory of the team (incidentally, one of the leading Russian broadcasting companies recognized this event as being more important than the military action taking place in the Chechen Republic), the journalist A. Shevtsov wrote: "the Black forward did not neglect doing draft work" (*Change*, August, 13 1999). This phrase is repeated in a headline as follows: "Black Robson is not afraid of draft work," bringing into focus the racial origins of the sportsman even though there was no necessity for it. And in the spirit of the gutter press we see the headline: "Zenith buys black caviar. And the black forward?" (*Change*, on August 17, 1999).

Apart from puns concerning skin color, we find, in a magazine published in Paris, the following story. Here, an article was published under the heading, "Russia is Africa!".[11] What arguments are provided for this thesis? The existence of an abundance of natural resources is noted together with the absence of something imperceptible, difficult to determine, that impedes Africa and Russia from realizing the opportunities of liberalizing their economies. This "something" is "explained" by the psychology of Russians and Africans – their mentality, their desire to receive instead of to make, and (in the "understandable" view of the world) genetic laziness (see pages 76 and 77). "Young Africa" predicts that Russia will make a quiet and confident return to the nineteenth century (p. 78). Then comes a question about the character of the Russian economy: Tatarstan is compared to Nigeria, Yakutia is compared with Zaire (p. 79), and some similarities are drawn between Moscow and Ouagadougou; in general, the main point is that Russia and Africa are doomed to remain far from the highways of civilization. The author argues that Pushkin's African roots made him the spokesman of Russian nation since "the Russian soul is an African soul." Let's hope that this French observer was mistaken with his forecasts, that Tatarstan like Nigeria (the richest African country) will not be far from the highways of civilization, and that we can be proud about the great Russian poet Pushkin – but let's be careful with how we express this, when the question is about one's skin colour, even if it is only a little bit different from our own.

On the sports pages of *Change* (August 21, 1999), we find two interesting and extensive interviews. One was written by J. Hrustovskoj, on stories in the French press, under the heading "Lilian Thuram: when Panov runs, the French go crazy." In this story, world champion footballer Lilian Thuram talks about himself. Within the framework of a discussion of ethnic tolerance, his answer to a question on citizenship is quite interesting: "I was born on Guadeloupe, became a person in France, and now I work in Italy.

---

[11] See October 5-11, 1995. pp. 72-73.

And everywhere it is pleasant for me. Probably, I am the citizen of the world". He said this with pride. Another article is an interview by B. Hodorovsky, who spoke with Sarkis Ovsepyan, an Armenian football player who played for the Saint Petersburg club "Zenith," and who had begun to learn English. (This usually indicates that one has decided to go abroad.) But, interestingly, this Armenian football player also called himself a citizen of the world, and with the same pride as his colleague from Guadeloupe. But the interview has the headline: "Russian foul language unites football players" and the subtitle "Better they should swear in Armenian." The contrast between these articles, devoted to the same theme is obvious.

Thus, an analysis of the publications *Saint Petersburg Gazette*, *Changes*, and *Evening Petersburg* confirms that journalists writing about ethnic issues are successful if they are competent, if they manage to rise above using stereotypes, and if excessive emotion does not overwhelm them. First of all, the civic position of the journalist reveals the degree of his social responsibility. Frequently, the publications do not provide precise and scientifically verified information illuminating interethnic relations. Sometimes a newspaper describes events and phenomena which are only incidentally related to the issues of the moment. That's why, on the pages of the press, we don't have a sense of the ethnic diversity which is typical of Saint Petersburg and which can serve as one of the bases for future cultural dialogue. It is necessary for journalists to study this dialogue. And it isn't an accident that today, in Saint Petersburg, there is an increase in the attention paid to the preparation and retraining of journalists writing on ethnic themes.

At the National Institute of the Press, briefings, press conferences, discussions, and presentations of books and films have become regular events. They promote an expansion of the journalists' knowledge through providing interesting and extensive information – and the journalists are forced to look at the problems of inter-ethnic relations more seriously. Here are the themes of some of these meetings: "Aims and problems of representation of nations in mass media", "Illumination of ethnic conflict in mass-media", "How journalists cover the problems of diversity in society", and "To unity through culture." The International Federation of Journalists (based in Brussels), together with the Center for War, Peace, and the News Media at New York University, have developed the project "Illuminating minority problems." Special lectures and seminars, devoted to the place and role of mass-media in an ethno-cultural context are organized at the Faculty of Journalism of Saint Petersburg State University. An exchange of opinions on the activities of the press on ethnic and cultural issues is becoming a tradition during annual conferences.

Thus it seems likely that research programs in these areas will have an urgency into the foreseeable future, and that they will help journalists to report more competently on ethno-cultural and ethno-social reality in the pages of their newspapers and magazines, in television, and in radio broadcasts.

Saint Petersburg State University
Saint Petersburg, Russia

CHAPTER XIV

THE MYSTICISM OF ASIA IN
THE PHILOSOPHICAL MIRROR

HO SI QUY

> We should turn to the overwhelming mass of mysticism of
> Asia.   – Teilhard de Chardin

ASIAN PHILOSOPHY

Asian philosophy (or philosophies) is not a genuine philosophical concept. It is just a term that some use simply for convenience. The term Asian philosophy is rather a vague one, it is not obvious what it means, it has no definite implications, and it can be understood rather differently in different contexts. (It is, in fact, even more vague than the term 'Oriental philosophy.')

Still, the term 'Asian philosophy' seems to be increasingly popular in international academic and political-social fora. Because the concept of Asia has nowadays become a focal point of almost all "hot issues" of our time – ranging from the nuclear crisis on the Korean peninsula to the legal dispute between the US and some Asian countries over trading shrimp and catfish; from political issues between the two sides of the Chinese straits to Islamic cultural issues in Malaysia, Indonesia, Pakistan and the Middle and Near East; from globalization to the epidemics of chicken influenza and acute respiratory disease (SARS); from the struggle against terrorism to the claims about the limits on human rights in some Asian countries; from the change of Asian-European continental relations following the collapse of the Soviet Union to the difficulties met by Turkey during its process of attempting to join the EU; from the dizzying speed of economic growth in China to the sexual exploitation of women in some south-east Asian and eastern European countries. All this seem to involve a notion of Asian peculiarity – what Teilhard de Chardin called "the mysticism of Asia." All these things need to be explained philosophically. And Asian Philosophy is, therefore, what must be considered.

Of course, Teilhard de Chardin was not the first who talked about the mysticism of Asia. He was, however, one of the few who used this term in a positive sense. Before and after Teilhard, many people – even Hegel (who considered Asia as a land of no freedom) – have used the term 'the mysticism of Asia,' or expressions similar to it, in a negative sense. In the nineteenth century, Europeans influenced by 'Orientalism' and by the illusion that they had a sacred mission to civilize non-European lands, aggravated prejudices about Asia – about an Asia that is wise but sluggish in scientific development, skilful in trading but unsuccessful in building market relations, hard working but lacking technical thinking, rich in books to teach people how to live but lacking those to teach them how to do.[1] Even at the beginning of the twentieth century, Max Weber, while discussing the Protestant ethic in Europe, was still doubtful of the prosperity of Asia and considered that this region did not have a cultural basis in which capitalism would flourish.

Now, at the beginning of the twenty-first century, we see that Asia has changed greatly, even in comparison with 30 years ago. However, such change has not made Asia any less mystical. Asian capitalism has sometimes been criticized as arbitrary and paternalistic. The struggle against globalization has been violent almost everywhere else, while Asia remains quiet. It seems that Asia accepts globalization but, at the same time, does not agree with it. Socialism in China seems to resemble Confucian capitalism more than socialism in Singapore, and Confucian capitalism in Singapore is, ironically, more similar to socialism than is the case in China.

The reasons why the concept of Asian philosophy (together with the concept of Asian culture – that is, in comparison with Western culture) has been frequently referred to in international symposia during the last 10 years are:

1. It is impossible to explain recent events in Asia without mentioning so-called Asian peculiarity. But what is Asian cultural peculiarity if it is not the fact that Confucian and Buddhist culture stand beside and come between other ways of thinking and cultural types? In other words, in speaking of Asian cultural peculiarity, one has to mention Asian philosophy or philosophies that make up the spirit of Asian culture. Even though it may not be easy to define, Asian philosophy always appears in Asian culture: the more people try to neglect it or to deny it, the more it appears as something very basic – it is intrinsic to it.

2. The growth and importance of the East Asian region, starting in the 1980s, has become, during recent years, more and more remarkable, overwhelming all aspects of politics, economics, and culture – here, China may be seen as a special Asian phenomenon – and it has made Asia both interesting and difficult to explain. To explain modern Asia or to forecast its future requires understanding the origins of philosophy in this region. The understanding and application of ancient Indian philosophy as well as Confucian and Taoist philosophies have, however, greatly changed. While it is only in schools and universities that researchers can understand thoroughly the philosophies of *original* Confucianism, Buddhism and

---

[1]   *Восток-Запад.Современный философский словарь* (1998), Изд. Панпринт. London, Frankfurt/Main, Paris, Luccemburg, Москва. Minsk. p. 159-163 [*East and West: Modern Dictionary of Philosophy* (London, Frankfurt/Main, Paris, Luxemburg, Moscow, Minsk: Publ. House Panprint, 1998)]. See also Dinkar Shukla, "Indian diplomacy down through the ages," *India Perspectives* (July 2002), pp. 17-19.

Taoism, Confucian, Buddhist and Taoist *cultures* are very popular in the spiritual life of society. Just by a gesture of nodding for greeting, for example, people can, everywhere in the world, recognize one another as being of the same Confucian cultural origin.

3. This is not to mention the presence of philosophical ideas, albeit on a smaller scale, in indigenous cultural traditions, such as those of the Philippines, Malaysia, Vietnam, and Indonesia. It may be controversial to call these traditions philosophies. But it is quite reasonable to say that they contain philosophical ideas. And it is not easy at all to deny the stable existence of traditional philosophical ideas in similar peoples and similar nations. The time of depending on European colonists has passed, and in the former European colonies European culture is no longer as dominant, or even as popular as it once was. It is, however, true that many traditional ideas in Asia seem to have gone; only lately are some of them being revived and coming to have a new existence in modern Asian society. The term "Asian Philosophy" does not exclude these philosophical ideas, although Asian philosophy is much more than that. Much has been written on this subject in non-philosophical papers. And from a philosophical viewpoint, we would like to mention the views of Mme. Ioanna Kucuradi, former President of the Federation of International Societies of Philosophy (FISP):

> What we experienced in the past few decades in various African and Asian countries is a reaction to "Western culture," a reaction which has led each group toward the search of its "cultural identity" or its own "values"; and, since it was not possible to identify what they wished in the existing state of affairs, they looked backwards and tried to find, in order to resurrect it, what they felt, or assumed, to be their own, i.e. the world-view, the conception of man and the conception of what is valuable (the value judgments) prevailing in each of these groups before their industrialization efforts began or before their encounter with the "Western culture" to which they reacted.[2]

In the present context, philosophy should not and cannot evade the issue of 'Asian mysticism.' Living in the 'information age' – and in societies permeated by globalization – modern philosophers, of course, not only cannot, but should not be intentionally scholastic, standing apart from social life. The problem is that, while one may disapprove of what is called "the mysticism of Asia," one has to explain exactly what one means. Is it "the mysticism of Asia" or Asian peculiarity? Which is illusion, and which is reality? We really can no longer embrace Western ethnocentrism and

---

[2] Ioanna Kucuradi, *Philosophy Facing World Problems*. The XXI World Congress of Philosophy. Istanbul, Turkey, August 10-17, 2003.

reject all that does not follow European academic ideals – though this is sometimes done. There was a time when the concept of the Orient was a heuristic tool for Eurocentric scholars, but this does not justify using the concept of Asia as a heuristic tool for Asians.[3] Of course, an Asian philosopher's research need not have a relation with Asian culture, but issues about Asia should not be easily put aside. Discussing the mysticism of Asia and Asian philosophy is now necessary. Later might be too late.

REAPPROPRIATING ASIAN PHILOSOPHY

What would be substantially involved in speaking of Asian philosophy? We could imagine that the following issues would arise:

1. Asian-originated philosophical ideas (that focus on orienting human behaviour and a world-view) are considered by many Asian philosophers to have had a very significant effect on the Asian region. Ancient Indian philosophy, Confucian philosophy, Buddhist philosophy, and Taoist philosophy, for example, are fundamental philosophical positions that are necessary in explaining Oriental phenomena. Among ancient Oriental philosophies, Confucianism has to be recognized as having had a very special role. It seemed to fall into oblivion as a result of criticism in China during the time of Lu Xun (during the 1920s) and, later, during the time of "criticizing Lin, criticizing Confucius" in the 1960s. But Confucianism not only did not die, but was revived in the form of "Confucian capitalism." Expansion in Newly Industralizing Countries (NICs) in Asia, accompanied by the rapid growth of continental China, have led non-Asian scholars to praise the concept of Confucian capitalism, explaining the prosperity of modern Asia by the "revival of the Confucian tradition." But there are still scholars in regions impregnated by Confucian culture, such as China, Taiwan, Vietnam, and Korea, who are suspicious of this view: there are too many points in Confucianism that are found not to be positive in the modern world. Moreover, if Confucianism really has the effect of promoting the development of Confucian societies, why did the hibernation of Confucianism in continental China and Vietnam last so long?

---

[3] "Originally there was no concept of the Orient anywhere in Asia. There was no sense of Orientalism in the Asian consciousness. The Orient or Orientalism is nothing but a term created by the Westerner's desire for hegemony since modern times. The Orient existed not in Asia but in the West. The Orient exists only in the mind of the Westerner. The Orient has always been on the outside existing to the east of Europe and the West's satellite partner whose value has been evaluated solely by the European standard. What has made the Orient was not the East but the West and Western values." Jae-Youl Kim, "What Are Asian Values in the Twenty-First Century?," *Proceedings of International Conference on "Research on culture, man and human resources at the beginning of the 21ST century,"* Hanoi, November 27-28, 2003, p. 621.

It cannot be denied that there is some reason for relating the changes in Asia to Confucianism per se. Nevertheless, Confucianism is not everything. Neither is Confucian culture, but it is no doubt vital to the development of modern Asia.

2. As referred to above, Confucian-Buddhist-Taoist philosophy has changed greatly from its origins in how it is understood and applied into daily social life and how it is manifested in human behaviour. Thus, that which has the greatest social significance in the spiritual life of modern society does not stand on the principles of classical Asian philosophy as such. The refraction of classical principles into daily human culture has, in fact, a more concrete significance. What people say about Asian philosophy is, in fact, often about Asian *culture*. Confucian culture, Buddhist culture, Taoist culture and so on, orient human activities – and this is the basic content of the term 'Asian philosophy.' This, of course, is not something where we can expect to find a coherent presentation of philosophical concepts. Yet we may accept this, at least temporarily, if we recall Martin Heidegger's comments about 'what is philosophy?':

> What is philosophy? With this question we are touching on a theme which is very broad, that is, widespread. Because the theme is broad, it is indefinite. Because it is indefinite, we can treat the theme from the most varied points of view. Thereby, we shall always hit upon something that is valid. But because, in the treatment of this extensive theme, all possible opinions intermingle, we are in danger of having our discussion lack proper cohesion.[4]

3. One of important elements that the term Asian philosophy refers to is the native philosophical ideas of peoples, communities, and nations in Asia. In fact, in almost all peoples and nations that are rich in traditional culture, the issue of whether or not there exists a native philosophy is rather complicated. In comparison with Western academic standards, the philosophical ideas of Asian peoples are neither systematic and complete in their organization of concepts and categories, nor united in methodology and practice. Most Oriental philosophical ideas are incomparable and uncategorizable in terms of classical European notions such as materialism-idealism versus dualism, ontologism versus gnoseology, dialectic-metaphysic versus eclecticism, gnosticism versus agnosticism. Thus, it is not easy at all to prove whether philosophy really exists in Asia. It is

---

[4] M. Heidegger, *Что такое философия?* Вопросы философии, No 8 (1993), p. 113 [M. Heidegger, *What is Philosophy?* In *Philosophy Problem* [Russian Philosophy Review], No. 8. (1993)]. See *What is philosophy?* Tr. with an introd. William Kluback and Jean T. Wilde (London: Vision, 1958), p. 19.

understandable why, even now, there are philosophers who deny that Confucianism, Buddhism and Taoism are philosophical systems.

On this point, recall the view of the Russian poet and thinker Fyodor Tyutchev (1803-1873). With his famous phrase "You cannot understand Russia, you can only believe in her," Tyutchev violently criticized the mechanical application of European rationality to understanding Russian distinctiveness. As we know, only half of Russia is Europe – although its contribution to European rationalist thinking is considerable.[5] Consequently, we need to take a more reasonable view in discussing the native philosophical ideas of Asia. Philosophy is created from real life, and if life cultivates and develops an idea or thought so that it reaches the level of a world-view or a framework for human activities, such thought may be called philosophy. According to N.I. Konrad (1891-1970), a Russian Orientalist, what is worth noticing about peoples from countries such as Gruzia [Georgia], Armenia, Turkey, Korea, and Japan, is their method of bringing the native philosophical ideas into life and their powerful ability in orientating activities.[6] We feel that is a feature that can be found throughout all Asian countries. In his study comparing ideas that originated in Europe with ideas that originated in Asia, Konrad found that native philosophical ideas, especially about human life, though less systematic and not in a sophisticated form, are likely to influence great numbers of people, and to be carried out into action. In Vietnam, besides those authors and intellectual traditions which clearly express developed systems of thought, we find, in the public mind, many philosophical ideas from Confucians and from poets and persons of like kind.[7] And the majority of people *apply* such ideas so that they become the working philosophy of their lives.

ASIAN PHILOSOPHICAL IDEAS AND PHILOSOPHIES

So what enabled philosophical ideas originating in Asia to be shaped into Asian philosophies? Several comments may be made here.

To begin with, philosophy, in the Western traditions, has no complete concept of 'life-view.' Or, to be more precise, from primitive ages until now, in European philosophies the notion of 'life-view' has usually been expressed in relation to the concept of 'world-view' – and this has been addressed only in some schools of philosophical anthropology, for

---

[5] Ф.И. Тютчев, *Знание, верность и нравственность*. В кн: *Прошлое и мы.* (1991) [Fyodor Tyutchev, Knowledge, Belief and Ethics. *Past affects us.* Politizdat (Moscow, 1991), p. 164].

[6] Cf. Н.И. Конрад, *Запад и Восток* (Москва, 1972) [N.I. Konrad, *East and West* (Moscow, 1972)].

[7] Cf. Dao Duy Anh, *Vietnam van hoa su cuong* (Nxb Hoi Nha van, 2000) [Dao Duy Anh, *Fundamentals of Vietnamese Culture* (The Council's Writers Publishing House, 2000)].

instance, those of Socrates, I. Kant, Teilhard de Chardin, M. Scheler, and J.-P. Sartre. In European philosophies, the only concept of the same order as world-view is methodology. But this is not the case in Oriental philosophies; there, 'life-view' is a major concept that plays an important role, especially in Confucian-Buddhist-Taoist philosophies. 'Life-view' is a concept of the same order and on a par with 'world-view.' In the Orient, both very well-known philosophers such as Confucius and Meng-zi and those who have a distinctive way of thinking, such as Nguyen Trai (1380-1442), M. Gandhi and Son Wen, have dealt with the notion of life-view and exhibited this view in their own lives. This is a feature of Asian philosophies.

One's life-view is a viewpoint, a conception of life, and a system of human and social values that orient behaviour; it includes conceptions closely attached to the way of living, the style of living, and behaviour, by defining the meaning of life and the meaning of being a man. As a matter of fact, Asian philosophies have always been philosophies about man. Philosophies of existence, of mere ontology or gnoseology, have no place in Asian thought. Asia has its own conceptions of life, with a system of values of "being man" and "living life" (terms used by Ho Chi Minh[8]) that are remarkably different from the West. This has been recognized in works by Dan Waters, David Hitchcock (United States), Mahathir Mohamad (Malaysia), Chen Fenglin (China), Francis Fukuyama (United States), Phan Ngoc (Vietnam), Tommy Roh (Singapore), Richard Robinson (Australia) and many other authors.[9]

If we summarize the work of specialists in the field, we find that the Asian life-view has the following characteristics:

It recognizes:

---

[8] Ho Chi Minh, *Toan tap* (Nxb CTQG. Ha Noi, 2000) [Ho Chi Minh, *Complete works* (Hanoi: The National Politics Publishing House, 2000)].

[9] Dan Waters, *The ky XXi. Phuong thuc quan ly vuot tren ca nguoi Nhat va nguoi Trung Quocc* (Nxb. CTQG. Ha Noi, 1998) [*The 21st Century - Methods of Management beyond the Japanese and Chinese* (The National Politics Publishing House, Hanoi, 1998)]; David I. Hitchcock, *Factors Affecting East Asian Views of the United States: The Search for Common Ground* (Washington, DC: CSIS, 1997); Mahathir Mohamad, *Politics, Democracy and the New Asia. Selected Speeches by Dr Mahathir M.* (Subang Jaya: Pelanduk Publications, 2000), Volume 2, pp. 139-146; Chen Fenglin, *May suy nghi ve quan niem gia tri.* Dong A, Tai lieu Vien TT KHXH so TN 99-44 (1999) [Chen Fenglin, *Some Ideas on Asian Values.* Data from Institute of Information for Social Sciences, No. TN 99-44 (1999)]; Francis Fukuyama, "Asian Value and the Asian Crisis," *Commentary* (Feb. 1998): 23-27; Francis Fukuyama, Sanjay Marwah, "Comparing East Asia and Latin America. Dimensions of Development," *Journal of Democracy*, Vol. 11, No. 4 (2000): 80-94; Tommy Roh, "Asian Values and Vietnam's development in comparative perspectives," in *Proceedings of the International Symposium*, ed. Le Huu Tang (Hanoi, March, 1999).

- the value of diligence and the love of work,
- the value of studiousness,
- the value of the family and of one's kin,
- the value of community and one's responsibilities to the community.

Along with, and following from, these values, there are a number of other virtues that are part of the Asian life-view. Social and individual virtues are often mentioned (such as industriousness and thrift, respect of obligations between the government and citizens, interest in being a member of a moral society, and the disapproval of extreme individualism – according to Tommy Roh's work; respect of power and praise of authority – according to Francis Fukuyama; self-reliance, discipline, and responsibility toward others; endurance, loyalty [towards the family, party and company], love of appearance, and conservatism – according to Dan Waters; modesty, freedom from torment of material needs, and care of children more than of oneself – according to Phan Ngoc, and so on).

One might object, however, that all of these virtues are found in non-Asian people, for every people is diligent, studious and industrious – so how can they be considered as values proper to Asia? The answer, however, is that, after having carried out extensive comparative research (both qualitative and quantitative), we find that – both in Asian philosophies and in Asian popular culture (especially in east and south-east Asia), the four values of diligence, studiousness, family, and community are always placed in the top rank. Americans and Europeans, however, consistently give priority to other virtues, especially to individual rights, individual well-being, autonomy, and creativity. That diligence, studiousness, and valuing the family and community are given such a high priority is distinctive of Asian values – and of Asian philosophies.

It is unfortunately necessary to say that, there are still many – especially those influenced by Eurocentrism or Orientalism – who are biased against Asia as a cultural region and consider Asian culture to be inherently negative. Dualism (in a bad sense), pragmatism, an emphasis on economic well-being and the attempt to sort things out through trial and error – all have been regarded as negative characteristics of Asian philosophies. Doubts about Asian virtues especially appeared in 1987-88 when the financial crisis occurred in Asia. At that time, a question was put: Why is an Asia that professes such a respect for diligence, studiousness, community values, responsibility, and its own traditional culture, not powerful enough to address the financial crisis? Is there something inherent in such values that caused the financial crisis to occur – namely, an excessive respect for authority, conformity, pragmatism, and so on? Fukuyama is right to say that: "From being the cause of Asia's success,

Asian values are now seen as the root of last summer's currency crisis and of the ensuing economic meltdown across nearly the whole region."[10]

We think the issue is not so simple. To suggest Asian culture can be understood in black and white terms would be naive. In fact, for some decades, there have been Western scholars, bored with classical European rationalism, who turned to write about Asia and who thereby led Westerners and even some Asians to see Asian traditions as simply full of good values. There are even those who think that there will come a time when the world is Asia's world. These views have led to regrettable mistakes.[11]

A number of leading scholars in Asia have been on the alert to avoid such mistakes. Asians are proud of the good in their traditions, but also know to avoid adopting an extreme ethnocentrism. At the Sorbonne, at the University of Paris, in 1983, Mrs. Indira Gandhi, a former Indian Prime Minister who was inspired by Indian philosophy, frankly acknowledged: "Not only the wisdom but also the insanity of the past centuries burdened us. It is dangerous to be their successor."[12] More recently, in 1996, at the 29th Session of Asia-Pacific Economic Committee held in Washington, Mahathir Mohamad, a Malaysian politician who is considered as an enthusiastic defender of Asian values, also made observations worth heeding:

> Some Asian values should obviously be unlearned. God only knows how hard we have struggled against so many of these harmful values in the past. Many parts of Asia are plagued by excessive materialism while other parts suffer from excessive anti-materialism. There is, of course, extreme spiritualism too; spiritualism carried to the extreme, paradoxically, usually manifests itself in the most unspiritual of ways, either through violence or the oppression of certain groups in society. And there is its opposite, too. While some Asian societies espouse the

---

[10] Francis Fukuyama, "Asian Values and Asian Crisis".

[11] Magoroh Maruyama, *Phuong thuc tu duy voi cac nen van hoa.* UNESCO, No. 2 (1996) [Magoroh Maruyama, *Methods of Thinking on Cultures.* UNESCO, No. 2. (1996)]; Ерасов В.С., *Проблемы сомобытности незапатных цивилизаций.* Вопросы философии. No. 6 (1987) [B.C Eraxov, "Characteristics of non-Western civilizations," *Philosophical Problem* [Review], No. 6 . (1987)]; Ерасов В.С., *Концепции культурной встранах третьего мира.* Вопросы философии. No. 11 (1971) [Eraxov. B.C, "Concepts about the Culture of the Third World," *Philosophical Problem*, No. 11 (1971)]; Jae-Youl Kim (2003).

[12] Indira Gandhi, *Tu duy An Do,* Van Nghe 22/01/1983 [Indira Gandhi, *Indian Thinking* (Address at the University of Paris, Sorbonne, on the occasion of receiving the degree of Doctor Honoris Causa), *Art Newspaper*, 22/01/1983].

ethic of fatalism, others admire domination, contentment, smugness, and even arrogance... Though much of these is a result of ignorance and poverty, some may be due to greed and an uncaring attitude. There is also much adherence to superstition and magic, and in many places, widespread corruption and tolerance thereof... Asian values are neither inherently good nor bad; if 'Asian' does not necessarily mean 'good' exclusively, 'Western' does not necessarily mean 'bad' exclusively either. Asia obviously has much to learn, both from its own process of development and economic struggles and from the West. There are some worthy Western values which we may adopt or internalise more deeply in the future.[13]

With all that we have seen through the mirror of Asian philosophy, the Asian life-view obviously has both a theoretical and a practical concern.

CONCLUSIONS

Asia has never been as developed as it is now – and Asia will certainly have a new status in the twenty-first century. Asia also has an interest – more than ever – in decoding its attractive enigmatic qualities. Asian philosophy, which is the origin of these qualities, is rightly the first concern of non-Asian and Asian scholars alike. Interest in Asian philosophy is not only for its ancient "classical" philosophies (such as Confucianism, Buddhism, Taoism, and some of the ancient Indian philosophical schools), but also for native Asian philosophical theories or ideas, i.e., what are often called "non-classical" theories and which may be systematic or non-systematic, coherent or non-coherent, cognitive or non-cognitive, materialist or spiritualist, and so on. All such things are part of Asian philosophical values.

Therefore, can we really raise the question: Does there exist an Asian philosophy? Surely we cannot ignore the philosophical characteristics of an Asian thought-system that has played so large a role as to be called "classical." The issue is, besides Confucianism, Buddhism, Taoism, and so on, what other philosophical ideas or systems have developed in Asia? And, once we take these latter as philosophies too, should we change our definition of 'philosophy,' or should we leave it unchanged as our current "academic" definition?

It is easy to see that considerable roles have been played by Confucianism, Buddhism and Taoism in the development of modern Asian societies. But other native philosophical ideas have also played a role.

---

[13] Dr. Mahathir Mohamad, *The Asian Values Debate. Politics, Democracy and the New Asia. Selected Speeches by Dr Mahathir Mohamad* (Kuala Lumpur, 2000), Volume 2, p. 142.

Clarifying the identity and distinctiveness of such types of "non-classical" philosophies is a responsibility of both Asian and non–Asian scholars – and here Asian scholars who live in the West have such a special role for, standing outside Asia, they can sometimes see it more objectively, while all the while recognizing that there many things which only insiders can perceive. Asia, as discussed, is no longer just a geographical or geopolitical concept but a cultural-philosophical concept. From the cultural view, Asia can be seen to have a distinctiveness and a particularity. The basic characteristics of so-called Asian philosophy lie in the Asian life-view. It is a life-view and not a world-view. In Asian philosophy, the life-view is a concept of the same order as that of a world-view.

The Institute of Human Studies
Vietnamese Academy for Social Sciences
Hanoi, Vietnam

CHAPTER XV

PERSONS AND COMMUNITIES

WILLIAM SWEET

Persons and communities have been thought by some – particularly in the modern West – to be in tension if not in conflict; certainly, much of modern political philosophy is concerned with the issue of safeguarding the individual from the state. In the essays in this volume, however, we have seen that the positive relations between the person and the community far outweigh the differences. To discuss the meaning of these notions, and how they can be in a constructive and mutually supporting relation to one another, the authors have explored two sub-themes: rights and duties, and the cultural foundations of civil society.

These two sub-themes are related. The former suggests a challenge: How are we to balance people's rights and duties? The latter proposes a context within which such a balance might be able to be arrived at – namely, within a genuinely civil society that respects cultural foundations. As both sub-themes are developed in this volume, we come to see that 'person' and 'community' are not in fundamental conflict at all.

When we speak of rights and duties, the key underlying notion is that of the person – that is, the one who is the subject both of rights and of corresponding duties. Western philosophical traditions have long understood the "person" to be – in the words of Boethius – an "individual substance of a rational nature"[1]; more specifically, the person has often been regarded (as Descartes expressed it) as a "res cogitans" – a "thing that thinks."[2]

This concept of the person has, however, been challenged; several of the authors in this volume explain why. Some, such as Rolando Gripaldo, argue that one must go beyond the so-called 'Cartesian' notion of the 'isolated subject.' As a result, Boethius's definition has been enhanced by adding that persons are also self-conscious subjects, who are autonomous and have dignity, but who are also social beings (see Kazhimurat Abishev's essay). In the context of speaking of rights and duties, then, it is important to have a comprehensive view of the person that reflects both the social and the individual dimensions. How we understand

---

[1] Boethius: "persona est naturae rationabilis individua substantia." In "De persona et duabus naturis", ch. 2, in *Patrologia Latina*, ed. J.P. Migne, vol. 64, cc. 1342–5 (Paris 1847); see Thomas Aquinas, *Summa Theologiae*, III, q. 2, a. 2.

[2] Descartes: "Ego sum res cogitans, id est dubitans, affirmans, negans, pauca intelligens, multa ignorans, volens, nolens, imaginans etiam & sentiens," in *Meditationes De Prima Philosophia*, Meditation III.

the notion of person bears on what rights – and duties – we have. If our account of personhood is inadequate, we risk either a too-individualistic theory of rights, or a too collectivistic theory of one's duties.

What are the rights that persons have? In modern Western thought, the emphasis has tended to be on 'natural' human rights, such as rights to life, liberty, the security of the person, private property, equal protection of the law, freedom of conscience and thought, and peaceful assembly and association. And, in the development of charters and constitutions in the west, rights have focused on the civil and political sphere. Most of the first twelve articles of the Universal Declaration of Human Rights (promulgated by the United Nations in December 1948) focus on these civil and political rights, and this also seems to be the case in many charters and human rights documents.

But there have been a number of challenges to placing such an emphasis on rights. To begin with, some argue that rights should not have a central role in political and social life. For rights, particularly in the late twentieth and early twenty-first centuries, have frequently been the first thing that individuals appeal to in making claims on others and on the community, and such claims have often led to conflict. The insistence on individual rights – particularly the right to private property – has, for example, been used as a justification for maintaining exploitative systems. And so, if we are to defend the notion of rights, it seems to need to be tempered or contextualized in some way.

A second challenge to the emphasis on civil and political rights is that such rights are far too narrow, and that more attention should be paid to other rights that reflect a more complete picture of the human person. Thus, some would insist that because the human being is a social being, we need to recognise corresponding social and economic rights. Others would maintain that the human person is a being whose value is rooted in principles that transcend the natural order. Thus, in Islam and Christianity, the source of human dignity is found in the relation of the person to the divine (see the papers of Sirajul Islam and Mustafa Koylu). Finally, some (for example, Plamen Makariev) would argue that collectivities as well as individuals have rights.

Such views lead us beyond the traditional list of natural and civil rights to a 'second generation' of rights – a model that includes social, economic, and cultural rights, such as rights to the free development of one's personality, to participate in the cultural life of the community, to social security, to work and to receive just remuneration, to rest and leisure, to housing, to a standard of living adequate for the health and well-being, and to education. And we should note that, given the social dimension of the person that is emphasised here, there are corresponding duties. (A model of such an attribution of rights and responsibilities is to be found in social institutions such as the family, and it is reflected in Article 29 of the Universal Declaration.)

One consequence of the arguments of the authors in this volume, then, is that we need to look for a richer, more robust understanding of rights or, at the very least, to refuse to separate rights from duties.

Still, if we are to provide a more comprehensive view of rights and duties, one may well ask how they are to be balanced.

One solution to this question may be found in the notion of civil society, and several of the authors in this volume have focused their discussion on civil society and its cultural foundations.

What is 'civil society'? The term 'civil society' is admittedly vague, if not an ambiguous; it was used by Hegel, in his *Philosophy of Right*, to describe a social union founded on contract and the exchange of rights of a fundamentally commercial character, but not as ethically developed as the State. Some have understood civil society as a society that is 'secular' – i.e., as distinct from a religious society or community – in which civil rights are established. But generally we might say that civil society is a social structure that reflects and seeks to satisfy basic human needs and interests, involves people recognising shared concerns and interests and taking responsibility to address this, and which has a grassroots or popular democratic character. It is something that can exist on a national or even an international scale. To quote Alfred Stepan: civil society exists "where multifold social movements ... constitute themselves in an ensemble of arrangements to express themselves and seek to advance their interests."[3]

The authors in this volume acknowledge, and take as a given, the values of civil society and of cooperation. Civil society is a structure that reflects and preserves the freedom, autonomy, and dignity of persons. It involves, and is the occasion for, dialogue. It is an effective way to identify needs and to encourage responsibility. It also is a means of making morality concrete – that is, to establish it as a social fact (see Gong Qun). And, further, it reaffirms that ethics is not something independent of the public sphere, but essential to it.

If one looks at the essay by Anatolij Karas, for example, one sees that civil society is a good – and even obligatory – because it is an institution that recognises the dignity (i.e., the freedom and autonomy) of human persons. A civil society is also an open society, which is able to exhibit different cultural traditions without forcing them to assimilate. It has a pluralistic dimension, but it is not an empty pluralism. As Tran Van Doan points out, it is because of this pluralistic character that an open, civil society exhibits social progress. Nor is it a monolithic notion, for it also has to take account of the different life views of the cultures in which it is to take root (Ho Si Quy). One way in which this can eb done is suggested by H.G. Gadamer's notion of "the fusion of horizons" (see the essay by Tran Van Doan).

---

[3] Alfred Stepan, *Rethinking Military Politics: Brazil and the Southern Cone* (Princeton, NJ: Princeton University Press, 1988), p. 4.

Civil society draws much of its strength and dynamism from its roots in culture and traditions – from its cultural foundation. As Ho Si Quy points out, we have to be attentive to the particular history, traditions and conditions of communities, and let them determine their own particular structures with their own identity. But this is not all. In supporting civil society, a number of conditions have to be met – or, at least, have to develop. We need to ensure that there is a mutual recognition of parties as far as possible on a level of equality (Blanchette). We may need to recover or retain the virtues – via a focus on cultural synergy rather than cultural identity (Wokabi and Owino) – for there is more to a culture (and so more to civil society) than its uniqueness.[4] We need to avoid an easy and superficial 'toleration' of difference, and engage difference in a constructive way – and in so doing search for cultural universals or a fusion of traditions. This is a particular challenge in places that are only recently freed from totalitarian or colonial regimes, where civil society may need to be created. We can see examples of where attempts have been made to do just this: in the Ukraine (Karas), in Africa (Wokabi and Owino), and in Russia (Vinogradova and Shaldenkova).

But how, concretely, is such civil society to be nourished or achieved? We might, for example, follow the models of some groups (such as the Catholic Church in Hungary[5]), which have been engaged in reviving civil society in post-Communist states. Or we might simply work to have the notion of civil society discussed – among our academic colleagues (particularly philosophers, sociologists, political scientists and educational theorists) and our students. Yet we also have to think of practical ways of encouraging civil society, particularly within existing nation states. Each of us must, of course, throughout be conscious of our 'place' in such discussion and action – that is, whether we are speaking from the centre or from the periphery (Blanchette). For all too often it has been those at the 'centre' – in London, or Paris, or Washington, or Boston – who have been

---

[4] I have argued for a rather similar view in "Cultural Integrity and Liberty Rights," in *Indian Philosophical Quarterly*, Vol. XXX, No. 4 (October 2003): 479-494. See also the discussions in Makariev and in Wokabi and Owino, above.

[5] See the (unpublished) paper presented at this conference by Miklós Tomka (Hungary), "Emergence Of Civil Society and its Obstacles in Post-Communist Europa. Some Small Reflections." Some of Tomka's related work may be found in his recent books *Church, State, and Society in Eastern Europe* (Washington, DC: Council for Research in Values and Philosophy, 2005); *Religion During and After Communism* (ed. with Paul M. Zulehner; London: SCM Press, 2000); *Religion and Nationalism* (ed. with John Coleman; London: SCM Press, 1995) and *Religion und Kirche in Ungarn: Ergebnisse religionssoziologischer Forschung 1969-1988* (Wien: Herausgegeben vom Institut für Kirchliche Sozialforschung: Ungarischen Kirchensoziologischen Institut, 1990).

inclined to sit back and tell others what they need to do in order to be 'good citizens of the world.'

In advocating for change, however, the key is dialogue; even the most passionate advocates for radical change have to be attentive to context and the aims of their interlocutors and intellectually honest. The self-righteous arrogance of the do-gooder is a particular impediment here. Civil society requires genuine and mutual respect, for without it no dialogue and no reconciliation can occur.

There are challenges to building civil society, and yet some of these challenges may bring with them a means to overcoming them. Perhaps the major challenge is globalization. Globalization can erode and even destroy local cultures, but simplistic opposition to it plays very well into the hands of anti-globalizers of 'the center' and 'the periphery,' who oppose trans-national organisations, such as an International Criminal Court. Instead, we need to avoid both isolationism and universalism and seek a more integral and synergistic response.

An effective account of civil society, with its emphasis on open participation, shared concern and responsibility, and critical dialogue, may provide the basis for guaranteeing the dignity and respect of persons, for ascribing rights and duties, and for keeping these rights and duties in balance. It may also serve to recognise the social dimension of the person, and the value of the contributions of persons to the community, without becoming servile to it. In all too much of contemporary politics, the community is portrayed as a threat to the person; the essays in this volume reaffirm that 'person' and 'community' need not be in conflict or tension at all.

St Francis Xavier University
Antigonish, Nova Scotia
Canada
and
St Thomas University
Fredericton, New Brunswick
Canada

PART II

ETHICS, VALUES, AND DIALOGUE

CHAPTER XVI

DIALOGUE AND JUSTICE

TADEUSZ BUKSINSKI

INTRODUCTION

The development of ethics and morality is connected with the development of social structures and the rise of social problems. In the ancient period and in the middle ages, ethics was microethics. It was created for persons living in the relatively small communities – villages, towns, the polis – and regulated the relations between neighbours, in families, and among citizens. It was grounded in the restricted calculi of good and evil, when the consequences of human activity were rather clear and evident.

In the modern period, with the rise of large nations, empires, factories, organizations and institutions, such as legal systems, banks, corporations, systems of public service, governances in different areas of social life, a new kind of ethics developed – the ethics of the 'middle level.' The norms of this ethics determined the behaviour of people through their roles: workers, business people, entrepreneurs, and administrators. The consequences of their activities were in these cases much wider and more difficult to forecast than in small communities. The influence on activity depended on many institutional factors and conditions and on cooperation among people who did not know each other. At that time there came into being two specific forms of this middle level ethics: the first, so-called bourgeois morality, which allowed one to take care of private interests only when the established frame of general moral norms and laws were observed – honesty, formal equality, freedom, truthfulness; and the second, so-called constitutional ethics, which reduced the morality to faithfulness and observation of laws of the state and institutional regulations as a precondition of moral behaviour. This ethics collapsed with the crimes of the Second World War, the corruption of institutions, and the widespread increase of clan and mafia relations.[1]

Now, on the eve of the period of globalization, we find that human actions have global effects, and these are filtered through a massive array of cultures. We are no longer able to foresee the important consequences of our activities. Some of them could be terrible for mankind. In the hands of man are technologies which could demolish the whole world. The growing inequality and injustice between regions, cultures and individuals have given reasons for hatred between cultures and religions. Therefore we have

---

[1] M. Ossowska, *Moralność mieszczanska* [*Middle-class morality*] (Warszawa: PWN, 1960).

a duty to act with special caution. Ethical reasoning has to be changed. The responsibility for one's activity is much larger than ever before but, at the same time, much more difficult to determine.

In this paper, we concentrate only on one problem of the contemporary epoch: the minimal presuppositions of dialogue between the cultures. Dialogue is a precondition of the peaceful development of our societies. Therefore we should strive to understand it and determine the conditions for it. By the dialogue between cultures we mean, on the one hand, the communication among the representative major cultures dominating their different regions of our globe ("the eight civilizations," to follow Samuel Huntington[1]); and, on the other hand, the relations among the cultural (national, ethnic, moral, and religious) majorities and minorities living together in different countries. All societies are multicultural, and dialogue must be continued day by day among large and small cultures everywhere. Dialogue strives to create that which is acceptable to all societies: common values, norms and attitudes as the basis for peaceful cooperation, as well as justice and global economic and political structures. But honest dialogue is not possible without some moral rules and values accepted by the representatives involved in the dialogue; these exist already at the moment the representatives decide to take part in the dialogue.[2]

We would say that dialogue presupposes some kind of elementary (basic) justice and its aim is, at first, to develop this justice, to make it deeper, more sophisticated, and broader; its second aim is to go beyond this justice to build social relations and structures based on the principles of solidarity.

One cannot reduce today's justice to charity or humanitarian aid, either. To contend that individuals or institutions have only humanitarian obligations – that it is only of their own good will that they are to aid others who have been afflicted with misery – we must assume that the fundamental social and political principles and mechanisms are already right and proper, and that there is only a temporary inefficiency in their functioning. However, in today's world the moral principles in international relations cannot be limited solely to norms drawing on one's good will and the intentions of people acting in their private or public capacities. Assistance to the wretched, poor and persecuted is not an act of supererogation, but a duty arising out of the principles of justice. It cannot be conditioned politically. The morality of justice is narrow and stricter than the morality of charity. It triggers social restrictions in the moral sphere, and legal and physical coercion to perform specific activities.

---

[1] Samuel P. Huntington, "The Clash of Cultures," *Foreign Affairs*, Summer 1993, pp. 22-49.

[2] J. Habermas, *Theorie des kommunikativen Handelns*, 2 vols. (Frankfurt/Main: Suhrkamp, 1981); Karl-Otto Apel, *Das Apriori der Kommunikationsgemeinschaft und die Grundlagen der Ethik*, in K-O. Apel, *Transformation der Philosophie*, Vol. 2 (Frankfurt/Main: Suhrkamp, 1973).

Charity has a private dimension and belongs to the realm of personal virtues, while justice requires institutional commitment.

Solidarity, in turn, demands faithfulness to the principles of cooperation among free people of equal dignity, and their readiness to sacrifice themselves for these principles and for the victims of injustice. It means the full internalisation of the principles of free, peaceful cooperation without any coercion from the outside.

Justice is a normative idea. It requires an equitable (impartial, neutral, and just) treatment of subjects, in spite of their actually unequal status. Individuals and social groups are treated in an equitable way, provided they are all granted the same value, the same status and the same amount of attention. This is a postulate, a norm of social behaviour and institutional mechanisms. At the same time, however, an analysis of this norm cannot disregard concrete facts connected with the implementation of the principles of justice, since it is in practical application that the strength and weakness of axiological and normative premises become fully evident.[4] Justice is a moral minimum in relations among people, irrespective of their nationality or origin, and in relations among institutions and states. This is the indispensable, required minimum, and that is why it is legally and institutionally sanctioned. Just judgements are different from judgements about needs, about people's suffering, or simply about inequalities. They determine whether or not social relations are correct and specify accountability in those relations. Justice grants authority and imposes on all sane subjects the duties of observing equal and equitable rights, the principles of exchange, the redress of damage, and the distribution of goods. Justice posits a certain hierarchy of values and goods and imposes the necessity to abide by this hierarchy in action. It makes it possible for the owners of rights to place demands on those who are bound by obligations. And actions stemming from duties and rights are right and proper.

Justice, then, creates conditions for the dignity of individuals and the minimum conditions and standards for the adequate functioning of public, political, economic, governmental and non-governmental institutions. By the same token, it legitimises domestic and international social relations. It provides a framework for and delineates the limits of acceptable and legitimate activities and relations. For instance, individual rights limit the negative effects of the action of the state and of political authority, while the principles of re-distribution curb the detrimental effects of the market. In the cultural sphere, cultural rights (for example, minority rights) make possible the flourishing of culture and limit outside intervention in its internal affairs. Those who do not comply with these rights act without legitimacy. Particular duties between individuals,

---

[4] See B. Barry, *Theories of Justice* (Berkeley and Los Angeles: University of California Press, 1989); J. Rawls, *Teoria sprawiedliwości* [*Theory of Justice*] (Warszawa: PWN, 1994); J. Rawls, *The Law of Peoples* (Cambridge, MA: Harvard University Press, 1999).

members of communities, or cultural groups are only secondary and subject to the principles of justice. Injustice, in turn, is not only wrong in itself but makes dialogue impossible because of its consequences: suffering, backwardness, disrespect for human dignity, instilling the sense of inferiority and of being wronged, degradation of individuals and communities, restriction of freedoms, autonomy, activities of some by (the privileged) others, and so on.

BASIC JUSTICE AND THE JUSTICE OF EQUAL OPPORTUNITIES

As mentioned above, elementary (basic) justice is presupposed as a condition for dialogue. Without unconditional observance of basic justice, there could not be real dialogue, i.e., a dialogue which could promote mutual understanding, and whose results are freely accepted by the participants in the dialogue and by the other subjects whom it may concern. Basic (elementary) justice consists of minimal values and norms valid in the three realms of life. On the material (economic) level, it demands provision of the following goods: security of life, provision of shelter, avoidance of suffering, freedom from slavery and serfdom. These minimal values imply a list of prohibitions. These are: prohibition of murder, fraud, torture, and physical restraint. The list of prohibitions may be supplemented with a list of positive norms, i.e., those that impose actions directed at the implementation of fundamental values where those values are violated: assistance to the poor, care for the suffering, protection of the persecuted, fighting against those who murder, rape, and torture. In the sphere of politics and public life, the elementary values consist in freedom of movement, freedom from arbitrary arrest and imprisonment, the right to an open and unbiased judicial process, and the absence of aggression towards foreign cultures. In the area of culture, the most important values are religious and ethnic tolerance and the absence of racism. Norms which prohibit coercion to change nationality, religious belief and political opinions are prerequisites of personal and social life.

If the above-mentioned values and norms are not observed, at least one partner in the dialogue has no possibility to express her (his) desires, needs, will, basic interests and opinions. Then she (he) is not a real partner in dialogue. According to this view, partners need not be formally or actually equal, but they have to have at least the chance to express their basic wants without the fear of persecution or the danger of aggression or war. Starving nations do not now have the possibility of taking part in dialogue. Societies living under a strong totalitarian political regime are in a similar situation.[5] It seems that the direct goal or aim of communication and

---

[5] H. Shue, *Basic Rights: Subsistence, Affluence, and U.S. Foreign Policy* (Princeton: Princeton University Press, 1996); J. Rawls, *The Law of Peoples* (Cambridge, MA: Harvard University Press, 1999), pp. 65ff.

discussion today among the representatives of different cultures is establishing (creating) the rules of peaceful cooperation and mutual recognition as equal subjects. The kind of justice the partners in dialogue are striving for we may call the 'justice of equal opportunities'.

Materially, this justice consists in setting the rules of distribution of material goods. Formally, it only calls for a relatively equal distribution of goods among the societies of the entire globe, but in a substantial sense it requires (stipulates), for instance, an unequal distribution of manufactured goods in order to offer equal opportunities for those currently underprivileged or afflicted in the past on account of their race, religion, or class background. In this sense, the imbalance in trade relations between industrialized countries and exploited, economically 'backward' ones, should be rectified.

In the sphere of politics and public life, people fight for equal rights and freedoms to determine their political systems and create laws regulating the public and private life. What is important is not only tolerance of different political opinions and attitudes in the private realm, but also the recognition of the freedom to formulate and express political opinions in public life (for example, by different political parties), and equal access to public offices for those from all social groups.

In the sphere of culture, the problem consists in the introduction of norms and rules assuring the freedom (not only the tolerance) of cultural practices, expressions of national and religious identity in public life, and the freedoms of education and of language. It means the recognition of the specificity of different cultures representing cultural minorities and so-called 'weaker' (or 'passive') cultures. The justice of opportunities in the cultural area could be understood in either a formal or a factual way. In the first case, what are needed are norms and laws which treat all groups in a neutral way; in the second case the norms and laws treat groups unequally, which means they give privileges and advantages to those groups persecuted in the past, and to the weaker ones today. For example, it pays attention to the cultural context of minorities from the point of view of equal opportunities in life, such as the role of language or social background for education or social prestige. The guarantee of equal recognition of cultural identities is the most difficult problem from a theoretical approach and for practical implementation. In the areas of religion, morality, spirituality, and nationality, justice of equal opportunities consists rather in the recognition of the unique and incomparable value of cultural differences. Unique elements of cultures can be preserved and developed on the condition that each of them is granted special (not equal) conditions. A problem arises: how is it possible to guarantee the equality of numerous divergent, incomparable axiological systems and spiritual identities that claim to be absolute? Each small culture requires special treatment for itself. [6]

In many cases conflicts arise also between the principle of recognizing the autonomous value of cultures and human rights. Human rights stipulate that all individuals have a moral value and should be equally respected, while the theory of the autonomous unique value of cultures assumes that cultures (and small communities) as such carry specific rights and values and that, within those communities, interpretations are formed and implementation of human rights is effected. According to this approach cultural communities possess a greater value than particular individuals. Different communities define the rights and duties of their members differently. To reconcile individual rights with the rights of cultural communities is one of the most difficult problems of our time. This problem is especially evident in authoritarian, fundamentalist, or traditional communities and cultures, which aim at absolute rule and expansion through the use of physical and mental violence. Justice requires collective recognition, but at the same time calls for defending the weaker (groups, individuals) against the stronger. We should, therefore, recognize the sovereignty of some cultures in a particular territory, but simultaneously must not allow discrimination against other cultures (or individuals) in their territory, nor their expansion by the use of force into the territories of other cultures. Accordingly, a liberal culture also must be subject to certain restrictions. One cannot allow it to impose liberal laws on the whole world, since this would be tantamount to the destruction of non-liberal communities and the uniformisation of societies. Modernization and economic globalization are detrimental to the majority of communities and cultures. This is why they need to be defended through the recognition on a global scale of their freedoms, rights, and values.

THE PROSPECTS FOR SOLIDARITY

The proper management of dialogue provides a chance for the reasonable development of social life on the globe. Justice should form the underlying principle for global, spiritual, and institutional order. A need arises for the development of a more and more sophisticated justice, namely one that will include all major areas of social life around the globe, take into consideration axiological problems, and – most of all – will refer to the

---

[6] S. Caney, "Cosmopolitan Justice and Equalizing Opportunities," in ibid., p. 126; S. Caney, "Cosmopolitanism and the Law of Peoples," *The Journal of Political Philosophy*, 10 (2002): 95-120; C. Flinterman, "Three Generations of Human Rights," in J. Berting (ed.), *Human Rights in a Pluralistic World* (London: Meckler, 1990), pp. 75-82; see also C. Taylor, *Negative Freiheit?* (Frankfurt/Main: Suhrkamp, 1995), pp. 145-187; C. Beitz, *Political Theory and International Relations* (Princeton: Princeton University Press, 1979), pp. 125ff; T. Pogge, *Realizing Rawls* (Ithaca, NY: Cornell University Press, 1989).

diverse hierarchies of values and norms of different societies, regions and communities.[7] When development is achieved, we can give up institutional justice and replace it with solidarity.

In the dimension of relations between large and small cultures, the main problem concerns the recognition of cultural identity. Besides those societies which do not observe the elementary norms of justice (i.e., the totalitarian and aggressive societies), all others are able to take part in dialogue with the aim of constituting, in a democratic way, a truly global order. In this way, justice could be done to and for all subjects, taking into consideration their great numbers and the axiological differences among them. The main objective of justice construed in this way is to guarantee equal dignity to all groups' subjects by safeguarding them from the arbitrary hegemony of one or several groups or of one overriding model of social life. What is necessary is, of course, abstention from the use of force and violence in the solution of conflicts among subjects and groups. This kind of justice creates the preconditions for solidarity, It means that the attitudes of social and cultural groups are directed towards assisting each other and cooperating without the compelling force of the laws, institutions, or the presence of particular egoistic interests.

The experience of the last few decades in the countries of Central and Eastern Europe indicates the inadequacies of external help in the provision of justice. In turn, this experience points to the importance of the participation of those countries interested in the trans-national (in this case trans-European) decision-making process; this process applies to them directly, and here a major role is played by domestic forces striving for dialogue and cooperation with other subjects (other nations). In an authentic democratic dialogue of real subjects situated in real conditions, the rules and mechanisms of just cooperation are created for all fields of social life. In other words, what is at stake is the common creation of a genuinely global order of equal partners through the liquidation of monopolies and other forms of economic, political and cultural domination on a global scale.

The stability of the global order in turn, needs, in the long term, a global civil society and the feeling of solidarity with all people on the globe. Without this kind of support, the global system will collapse. And only the democratic way of building it can evoke this kind of support for a society governed by democratic principles and rules.[8]

In political philosophy, justice is frequently contrasted with democracy. A thesis has been put forward that liberals recognize the

---

[7] R. Robertson, "Social Theory, Cultural Relativity and the Problem of Globality," in A.D. King (ed), *Culture , Globalization and the World–System* (New York: Macmillan, 1999), pp. 69-90.

[8] D. Miller, "Justice and Equality," in A. Hurrell, N. Woods (eds), *Inequality, Globalization and World Politics* (Oxford: Oxford University Press, 1999), pp. 187-210.

priority of justice (especially when it concerns rights) over the sovereignty of the people, while republicans grant priority to the sovereignty of the people. On such an approach, law remains in conflict with the freedom and autonomy of the community; either we have a morally motivated priority of justice over subjects or an autonomy of subjects in establishing and justifying norms of justice and solidarity. In the former case, morally justified global justice puts limits on democratic decisions; in the latter, consensus is a creation legitimising collective decisions and is 'above' justice. This conflict poses a significant problem for political philosophy and for legislative practice. On the one hand, we are certain that not all decisions or collective statuses are right, even those accepted unanimously; on the other hand, we witness a variety of opinions on justice and universal values and norms.

Principles of global justice and global solidarity can be established and accepted only when they are not imposed on subjects from the outside. They need to be developed in democratic dialogue, or from within, from the bottom up, in the course of rational argumentation, persuasion, and setting examples. They need to be accepted by the subjects they relate to. Only then can they accept and respect those principles and rules. Global subjects (states, cultures, communities, institutions) cannot be deprived of their dignity and identity in this process. In other words, only in dialogue that respects cultural differences can the partners establish just principles for regulating international and internal relations. This is a requirement of the present era. A world order based on a strategy of menace and scare tactics would be fragile and dangerous. Proliferation of weapons of mass destruction and other means of killing would eb suicidal. Global dialogue cannot exclude those who think in other ways – for example, opponents of liberalism (as Rawls would claim) or those deemed irrational (as was postulated by Habermas). On the contrary, dialogue only makes sense when it takes place between radically different cultures, regions, and states, in real (not ideal) conditions. Arbitrary exclusion of those who think differently or represent other values (but respect elementary justice) is dangerous as it disrupts communication and obstructs the democratisation of relations in the world. Dialogue with other societies enables the West to realize the particularity of its own interpretations of human rights, democracy, and culture. What is at stake, then, is a common creation of global laws and principles of coexistence and solidarity – and not the conversion of others to liberalism. The potential of rationality and solidarity is inherent in the beliefs of all cultures. The establishment of a system of global solidarity via the method of 'dialogue' is a long process. We are at the beginning of it, but it is the philosophers who have the task of creating the axiological foundations for it.

Institute of Philosophy
Adam Mickiewicz University
Poznań, Poland

CHAPTER XVII

EVOLUTION AS A FOUNDATION OF ETHICS AND MORALITY

JERZY A. WOJCIECHOWSKI

Morality is not fun. Whether we like it or not – and mostly we do not like it – we are confronted with the moral choice between good and evil. In other words, we are always faced with a moral dilemma. Consequently, questions of ethics and morality are an unavoidable fact of human life. The intriguing question is why this is so. Where do ethics and morality come from? Why do they seem to be binding upon us?

Usually we explain the fact of the existence of ethics and morality by means of rationality. We are rational animals, and therefore we are moral agents. This explanation sounds plausible, but the initial question is easily pushed one step further. Why are we rational animals? Why do we have the capacity to distinguish between good and evil? We usually get off the hook by invoking religion. Religion comes in handy, providing us with the Old Testament and the Ten Commandments. For believers, the questions are answered and the problem is solved. Unfortunately, there are fewer and fewer believers in today's world. How, then, is it possible to justify ethics and the need for morality? The purpose of this paper is to do just that.

If the situation of humanity were, by and large, satisfactory, there would be no urgent need for a justification; the question would have mainly only a theoretical importance. This, however, is manifestly not the case. We live in an era of growing shortages of natural resources, but what we need most is an ability to exist peacefully, and this ability requires acceptance of ethical principles and moral behaviour. Thus a justification of morality and ethics becomes an urgent necessity. To provide a justification, let us return to the fundamental question: Why are we moral agents? How is it that our brains are capable of moral choices? Human brains are, as far as we can tell, the product of evolution, just as the rest of our body is. Is it therefore logical to conclude that morality and ethics are a result of evolution? This surprising statement seems contrary to our deep-seated convictions. Not only does it appear to contradict the personal nature of moral choices, but moreover it seems to transform morality into a physical phenomenon; otherwise, it identifies evolution as a moral process. How does we solve this dilemma?

Let us analyse, first of all, the notion of evolution so as to do justice to this phenomenon. Of all observable phenomena, evolution is the most significant one, and the most extensive. It is coextensive in time and in space with the Universe. It began with the Big Bang fifteen billion, seven hundred million years ago, and has continued ceaselessly ever since. It is incredibly complex, producing increasingly more advanced beings and forms of behaviour beginning at the subatomic level, and it has further organized sub-atomic particles into atoms, atoms into molecules and then strands of DNA, thus enabling the formation of a living cell – the building blocks of life. With the emergence of life, evolution has produced not only radical novelty, but also a radically superior level of complexity. The complexity of life forms has carried with it the potential for an astounding variety of differentiations of these forms. Evolution has become increasingly more complex. One can therefore speak of the evolution of evolution. The more evolution progresses, the more and more varied are the relations between beings, and the more complex the universe becomes. Concurrently, the pace of evolution itself increases.

The relationship existing between the degree of complexity of beings and the pace of evolution is fundamentally interdependent. It can be formalized in the following manner:

Law I   The pace of social evolution is proportional to the complexity of beings evolving.

Therefore, among others:

Law II   a) The pace of social evolution is greater than that of biological species. Hence:
Law II b) Social evolution is more rapid than biological evolution.
Law II c) Social evolution has greater potential to accelerate its pace than biological evolution.

We accept social evolution as an obvious fact. We partake in it, are proud of it, and are not surprised by it. And yet, social-cultural evolution is surprising, to say the least. As far as we know, in the visible universe there is nothing like it. It is an absolute novelty in the history of evolution, and of major importance not only to humanity but to the entire Universe. The human species is the most advanced of species in existence, and social/cultural evolution is the pinnacle of the evolutionary process.

It is one thing to stress the importance of the social/cultural development, but it is another to try to understand it. How does it happen? What explains it? To say that it is the product of human rationality is at the same time true and insufficient. All humans are rational, but there are great differences in the manner and speed of development of various social groups and epochs of history. These differences have to be explained.

To make sense of human history, it is essential to realize the role played by the capacity to retain knowledge outside of those who know ("knowers"). The capacity of the brain to know and to remember is finite, while knowledge and culture are a collective product which grows by leaps and bounds. What makes it possible? The answer is writing. The invention of writing was the epochal discovery which liberated the development of knowledge and the advancement of culture from the limits of the capacity of individual brains. This fundamental fact can be expressed in the form of a law:

Law III The system = the knowers' body of knowledge (the knowledge construct, KC) has:

a) a greater potential of evolving faster than the knowers themselves.

b) a faster rate and far more varied way of evolving than the knowers alone have.

c) been aided by the human evolutionary process, which produces ever more varied, numerous and efficient tools for externalization, communication and preservation of knowledge outside of individual brains.

It becomes more and more evident that evolution is increasingly knowledge-centred and intellect-generated. Thus, the intellect becomes, to a greater extent, the main engine of the evolutionary process, producing ever more advanced forms of existence. It continuously opens up new avenues for ever faster developments of knowledge. The development of knowledge in turn generates competition on ever higher levels and offers advantages for those who produce knowledge and use it efficiently. In other words, by means of the intellect, evolution engenders by and from itself the necessitation of more evolution in general, and more *intellectual* evolution in particular.

The evolution of knowledge is not only quantitative but also qualitative. Generally speaking, knowledge is a life-enhancing device. It enables and facilitates life and, notwithstanding its destructive capacities (amply demonstrated in the past century), it makes possible the continuous expansion of the human species. It is because of knowledge that the earth can support now over six billion humans together with an increasingly larger number of animals bred to feed people. It would be tempting to conclude that, through the development of knowledge, humans produce continuously more evolution. Such a conclusion would be certainly pleasing to our ego, but it would lead to a false impression that we are the true makers of evolution. This is not the case. The process of evolution is far greater than us and, no doubt, more important.

In fact, far from being the makers of evolution, we are much more likely the product of evolution. This is a fundamental fact, easy perhaps to state, but difficult to grasp, because of the active role played by humans in the process of evolution which we have described. It is important to grasp that if we can contribute to evolution so effectively, it is not really because of our deliberate intentions, but because we are the product of the evolutionary process which enables us to behave creatively.

We are like people in a boat carried by a mighty current. We do not create the current. The current makes us move in a certain direction which it – not we – determines. It is not we who make us what we are; nor do we determine our capabilities. It is the current. It is important to realize that there is an intrinsic logic to the current. It does not advance haphazardly. It moves in an obvious direction. It goes from less to more, from less complex beings to more complex ones, from less capable agents to more capable ones, from less perfection to more perfection.

Perfection is a loaded notion, avoided by many because of its theological implications. But it is unavoidable in the discussion of evolution. Short of being blind or dishonest, any student of evolution has to admit that evolution is a directional process and progresses from less being to more being.

We began this paper by stating that questions of ethics and morality are always with us. They are the noblest achievements of the human species. Evolution cannot but make them more necessary, more important, and more complex. We are facing – and not of our own will – a more intensely moral future. It does not mean that we will automatically become more moral. But, it means that the questions of morality will play an increasingly greater part in human life. It may not be a very pleasant conclusion, but it is an unavoidable consequence of being human and of being involved in the process of evolution.

University of Ottawa
Ottawa, Canada

CHAPTER XVIII

GANDHI'S SOCIAL-POLITICAL PHILOSOPHY: THE EFFICACY OF NON-VIOLENT RESISTANCE

PURABI GHOSH ROY

In today's world, the need for cultivating non-violence is becoming more pronounced. In the context of the current violent global scenario, Gandhi's thought and practice provide a basis for (re)generating non-violent cultures. Gandhi offered non-violent alternatives in both the social and political fields. The ideal of non-violence professed by Gandhi was not a novel proposition. He says, "I have nothing new to teach the World. Truth and non-violence are as old as the hills. All I have done is to try experiments in both on as vast a scale as I could."[1] Edward Thompson testified, "[H]e will be remembered as one of the very few who have set the stamp of an idea on an epoch... that idea is non-violence."[2] Gandhi extrapolated an ideal society based on non-violence. Gandhi's social philosophy encompassed all of humanity and had a very strong human base. To quote Einstein: "Generations to come, it may be, will scarce believe that such a one as this ever in flesh and blood walked upon this earth."[3] For Gandhi, two cardinal principles of life – non-violence and truth – were the essence of social good. He, however, focused his attention on the principle of non-violence. To him, non-violence was "the most active force in the world."[4] Once, he said, "It is love, pure and simple."[5] Non-violence is not only a personal virtue, but also a social virtue. Forgiveness is a virtue born out of love. In forgiveness and tolerance lies the supreme talisman of man's happiness. Another acme of love or non-violence is fearlessness, perhaps the most positive of all the social virtues. Gandhi asserted that the fearlessness is the natural outcome of the law of truth, love and non-violence.

---

[1] M.K. Gandhi, *My Non-Violence* (Ahmedabad: Navajivan Publishing House, 1960), preface, p. iii.

[2] Edward Thompson, *Ethical Ideals in India To-Day* (London: Watts and Co., 1942), p. 14.

[3] Albert Einstein, *Ideas and Opinions* (New York: Bonanza Books, 1954), p. 78.

[4] Gandhi, *My Non-Violence*, p. 78.

[5] M.K. Gandhi, *Satyagraha in South Africa* (Ahmedabad: Navajivan Publishing House, revised second edition, 1950), p. 105.

Love is the abundance of divine energy, and "energy is divine."[6] In other words, love is energy personified. The opposite of love is fear: "lack or failure of energy."[7] In the context of today's increasingly global unrest, divisive forces of fear, anger, and hatred are at work. Ethnic and religious conflicts threaten to tear apart more and more societies and "tend to cut off our awareness or realization of the unity of mankind."[8] Freud maintained that "Infancy matters";[9] Gandhi's political philosophy had religious and spiritual bearing because of his childhood experience. The act of self-denial was deeply ingrained in him; this he had imbibed from his mother. In order to achieve India's independence, he focused on the law of suffering. Strategies of protest – namely the non-cooperation and civil disobedience movement adopted by Gandhi – came under the purview of the law of suffering. He wrote, "No country has ever risen without being purified through the law of suffering... [P]rogress is to be measured by the amount of suffering undergone by the sufferer. The purer the suffering the greatest is the progress."[10]

Gandhi differentiated passive resistance from active resistance. Active resistance is tantamount to violent action as it tends to resorting to unfair means producing hatred. Gandhi declared that brute force had no place in his conceptions of Truth and non-violence. After practicing Satyagraha (non-violent resistance) in South Africa, Gandhi accorded Satyagraha "a domestic analogy"[11] which, during the course of action, however, "yielded harsh and violent deeds"[12] such as the burning of foreign clothing. Gandhi treated the burning of foreign clothes as a part of Satyagraha, and made it clear that he had ruled out secrecy from the book of non-cooperation.[13] An avowed pacifist, he saw non-cooperation as a training in self-sacrifice. In Gandhi's dictum, non-violent, non-cooperation was "a method of search for social truth."[14] Progressive non-violent, non-cooperation was one way to secure justice free from violence. When the Indian poet Rabindranath Tagore, a Nobel laureate, condemned non-cooperation on "spiritual grounds"[15] (saying Gandhi was transforming

---

[6] Richard Gregg, *Gandhiji's Satyagraha or Non-violent Resistance* (Madras: S. Ganesan, 1930), p. 164.

[7] Ibid.

[8] Ibid., p. 165.

[9] Quoted in D.G. Tendulkar, *Mahatama, 1869-1920*, Vol. 1. Vithalbhai K. Jhaveri and D. G. Tendulkar (Bombay, 1951), p. 7.

[10] Ibid., p. 355.

[11] P. Spratt, *Gandhism: an Analysis* (Madras: The Huxley Press, 1939), p. 56.

[12] Ibid.

[13] B.G. Kunte, *The Non-Cooperation Movement in Bombay City 1920-25*, Vol. VI (Government of Maharashtra, Gazetteers Department, 1978), p. 17.

[14] Gregg, *Gandhiji's Satyagraha or Non-Violent Resistance*, p. 146.

[15] Tendulkar, *Mahatma*, Vol. 2, p. 59.

moral force into a manifest force), Gandhi replied that non-cooperation was "a protest against unwitting and unwilling participation in evil."[16] Its basic tenet is self-control and discipline. He called it also "a religious purification movement."[17] He cautioned that non-cooperation does not apply to service under private individuals. Its efficacy lay in voluntary withdrawal from the affairs of the State, an expression of popular discord, causing discomfort to government. "My goal is friendship with the World and I can combine the greatest love with the greatest opposition to wrong,"[18] he said. Gandhi suspended the non-cooperation movement due to an outbreak of violent incidents at Chauri-chaura in Uttar Pradesh as it challenged the underlying principle of peaceful protest, thus reaffirming his faith in non-violence.

The civil disobedience movement launched by Gandhi was based on Ahimsa. He started a non-violent civil disobedience movement to fight injustice and untruth. It showed strict adherence to non-violence. In Bardoli, the peasantry successfully carried out a non-violent tax-resistance campaign against the Government of the Bombay Presidency and the imposition of unjust taxes. It highlighted the success of Gandhi's civil disobedience movement. The basic tenet of the movement was to educate people in the state's happenings. Thoreau, whose writings had influenced Gandhi, also proclaimed that, by not paying taxes, "I am doing my part to educate my fellow countrymen."[19] Richard Wasserstrom held the view that "... every act of civil disobedience is an attempt at civil education,"[20] which also meant that there must be "a willingness to accept the penalty."[21] Civil-disobedience is justified on the ground that it is the violation of unjust laws – laws which are "out of harmony with the moral law of universe."[22] On the other hand, he says the practitioner of non-violent social action feels a "moral responsibility to obey just laws."[23] He thought that the civil disobedience movement was a device to be applied only in a corrupt tyrannical state.

Gandhi kept fasts for both anti-violence and communal peace and harmony. His idea was that of universal brotherhood. His political life records numerous fasts undertaken. Fasting as a means of self-restraint was a religio-political weapon used by Gandhi. He called it a "potent weapon in the Satyagraha armoury."[24] He first undertook public fasts in South Africa

---

[16] Ibid., p. 60.

[17] Ibid., p. 42.

[18] Kunte, *Non-Cooperation Movement in Bombay City 1920-25,* Vol. VI, p. 3.

[19] Quoted in Hugo Adam Bedau, Ed., *Civil Disobedience: Theory and Practice* (New York: Pegasus, 1969), p. 20.

[20] Quoted in Bedau, p. 18.

[21] Ibid., p. 99.

[22] Ibid., p. 101.

[23] Ibid.

[24] Harijan, 18.1.1948.

in connection with the sufferings of the indentured labourers. To Gandhi, to fast meant "personal cleansing"[25] against a moral lapse either on the part of the individual or the government. In this, the young Gandhi was deeply influenced by his mother who observed religious fasts steadfastly, a part of the socio-religious characteristic of the Indian ethos which his Western counterparts looked upon with curiosity. He kept fasts against the moral lapse of two of his inmates in the Phoenix Ashrama.[26] To settle the dispute between the striking mill-workers and employers in Ahmedabad, Gandhi asked workers not to resort to violence. He himself undertook fasts in support of the mill-workers. This put pressure on the mill owners, and they agreed to meet the workers' demand for an increase of 35% in their wages.[27] In the socio-political context, the efficacy of fasting lay in self-denial, awakening the conscience of the people. He reported that, as a result of fasting, "a splendid esprit de corps grew up among them."[28]

In Gandhian discourse, the ideal state was a non-violent society based on democracy. When an American friend asked Gandhi why he said "Democracy can only be saved through non-violence," Gandhi's reply was that "Democracy, so long as it is sustained by violence... cannot provide for or protect the weak."[29] Gandhi's notion of democracy did not include violence and was instead concerned with "service to the weakest."[30] He rejected Machiavelli's justification of the "method of force"[31] to achieve this end. His was akin to Thoreau's views that "government must have the sanction and consent of the governed."[32] Gandhi expressed the opinion that the state should be secular. The state borne out of mankind's need was an "ethical association,"[33] its chief function being the welfare of all. He stressed the fact that "in no part of the world are one nationality and one religion synonymous terms."[34] In *Hind Swaraj* or *Indian Home Rule*, Gandhi wrote:

> India cannot cease to be one nation because people belonging to different religions live in it... In reality, there

---

[25] *Young India*, 23.2.1921.

[26] M.K. Gandhi, *An Autobiography* (Ahmedabad: Navajivan Publishing House, 1927), p. 285.

[27] Sumit Sarkar, *Modern India-1885-1947* (Madras: Macmillan India Limited, 1983), p. 186.

[28] Gandhi, *An Autobiography*, p. 278.

[29] Gandhi, *My Non-Violence*, p. 115.

[30] Ibid.

[31] Niccolo Machiavelli, *The Prince*, tr. Luigi Ricci (Bombay: Jaico Publishing House, 1957), p. 79.

[32] Henry Thoreau, *Selected Writings on Nature and Liberty*, ed. Oscar Cargill (New York: The Liberal Arts Press, 1952), p. 32.

[33] Ernest Barker, *Greek Political Theory* (London: Methuen, 1925), p. 7.

[34] M.K. Gandhi, *Hind Swaraj or Indian Home Rule* (Ahmedabad: Navajivan Publishing House, 1938), p. 49.

are as many religions as there are individuals but those who are conscious of the spirit of nationality do not interfere with one another's religion. If they do so, they are not fit to be considered a nation.[35]

He opined, "My patriotism is not exclusive, it is calculated not only not to hurt any other nation but to benefit all in the true sense of the word."[36] Thus, it can be said that Gandhi interpreted the movements of the Indian struggle for freedom in a universal frame of reference.

Gandhi's philosophy of Satyagraha was born in South Africa in 1906. Reminiscing about his days in South Africa, Gandhi wrote:

> Up to the year 1906, I simply relied on appeal to reason. I was a very industrious reformer.... But I found that reason failed to produce an impression when the critical moment arrived in South Africa. My people were excited; even a worm will and does sometimes turn and there was a talk of wreaking vengeance. I had then to choose between allying myself to violence or finding out some other method of meeting the crisis and stopping the rot and it came to me that we should refuse to obey legislation that was degrading and let them put us in jail if they liked. Thus came into being the moral equivalent of war... the conviction has been growing upon me, that things of fundamental importance to the people are not secured by reason alone but have to be purchased with their suffering. Suffering is the law of human beings; war is the law of jungle. But suffering is infinitely more powerful than the law of jungle for converting the opponent and opening his eyes, which otherwise are shut, to the voice of reason. Nobody has probably drawn up more petitions or espoused more forlorn causes than I and I have come to the fundamental conclusion that if you want something really important to be done you must not merely satisfy the reason. You must have the heart also. The appeal of reason is more to the head but the penetration of the heart comes from suffering. It opens up the inner understanding in man. Suffering is the badge of the human race, not the Sword.[37]

---

[35] Ibid.

[36] Quoted in Tendulkar, *Mahatma,* Vol. II, p. 169.

[37] *Young India*, 5 November, 1931.

"Satyagraha literally means insistence on truth."[38] Gandhi also called it the Truth-force or Love-force. In the West it was known as passive resistance. From the outset, Mahatma Gandhi was clear in his belief that the term "passive resistance" was a misnomer. At the Johannesburg meeting, in September of 1911, Mr. William Hosken's speech defined passive resistance in a way completely divergent to Mahatma Gandhi's definition of Satyagraha. Hosken said:

> The Transvaal Indians have had recourse to passive resistance, when all other means of securing redress proved to be of no avail. They do not enjoy the franchise. Numerically, they are only a few. They are weak and have no arms. Therefore, they have taken to passive resistance which is a weapon of the weak.[39]

However, the power of the Transvaal Indians was not one of passive resistance, but was the basis of intense activity. The Indians of South Africa believed that the Truth was their object, that Truth alone triumphs, and with definiteness of purpose they persistently held on to Truth. They put up with all the suffering that this persistence implied. These people were Gandhi's true Satyagrahis. Mahatma Gandhi made a clear distinction between passive resistance and Satyagraha. He pointed out that Satyagraha was essentially different from what was generally meant in English by the phrase "passive resistance." To explain the deep and fundamental differences between the two forces, Gandhi cited the example of the suffragette movement in England. He emphasized that, in this case, passive resistance was a weapon of the weak, voteless and hence voiceless. The suffragettes had no franchise rights, they were weak in numbers as well as in physical force. Also, the suffragist movement did not eschew the use of physical force. Passive resistance conveyed the idea of the suffragist movement in England. Burning of houses by women was called passive resistance, as was their fasting in prison. All such acts might very well be "passive resistance" but they did not come within the ambit of Satyagraha. Thus passive resistance was the weapon of the weak. Gandhi declared that brute-force had no place in his conception of Satyagraha. In his view, Soul-force and brute force were completely antagonistic in nature. He had fully realised the significance of this antagonism even at the time of the advent of Satyagraha.

Gandhi had no idea of the exact time when the phrase "passive resistance" was first used in English and by whom. However, he observed:

> But among the English people, whenever a small minority did not approve of some obnoxious piece of legislation,

---

[38] M.K. Gandhi, *Satyagraha in South Africa*, p. 68.
[39] Ibid, p. 103.

instead of rising in rebellion they took the passive or milder step of not submitting to the law and inviting the penalties of such non-submission upon their heads.[40]

Non-conformists offered passive resistance against the passing of the Education Act by the British Parliament. They took recourse to this measure since, being a minority within Parliament, they found that it was not possible to prevent the passage of the Education Act. This episode of passive resistance may be taken as containing elements of commonality with the suffragette movement in England, referred to earlier. Among the groups, such as above, who were committed to the concept of passive resistance, use of arms for the attainment of aims was permissible. However, it should be noted that this was mainly a theoretical paradigm. In practice there was very little prospect of success by force of arms. Moreover, "in a well organized state, recourse to arms every now and then in order to secure popular rights would defeat its own purpose."[41] Again, some segments of non-conformists would generally object to taking up arms even if it had been a practical proposition. Gandhi was not fazed by the issue of numbers or numerical weakness. In his Satyagraha in South Africa he wrote, "I was perfectly indifferent to the numerical strength of the fighters on our side."[42] Gandhi emphasised three aspects of Satyagraha: viz., Self-help, Self-sacrifice and Faith in God.[43] In his definition, the very nature of Satyagraha was such that the fruit of the movement was contained in the movement itself. Gandhi felt that the element of inaction had no place in theory and practice of Satyagraha. In his words

> ...[S]ince Satyagraha is one of the most powerful methods of direct action, a Satyagrahi exhausts all other means before he resorts to Satyagraha. He will, therefore, constantly and continually approach the constituted authority, he will appeal to public opinion, educate public opinion, state his case calmly and coolly before every body who wants to listen to him, and after he has exhausted all these avenues will resort to Satyagraha. But when he has found the impelling call of the inner voice within him and launches out open Satyagraha he has burnt his boats and there is no receding.[44]

---

[40] Ibid, p. 104.
[41] Ibid.
[42] Ibid.
[43] Ibid, p. 168.
[44] *The Selected Works of Mahatma Gandhi*, Vol. 6, 1968, p. 186.

Gandhi defined Satyagraha as the power "born of Truth and Love or non-violence,"[45] which contained significant elements of self-purification and self-reliance. These two elements found their reflection in women's participation in the Indian freedom struggle. The very self-sacrificing nature of women made them able satyagrahis. Women acted courageously and joined their menfolk in the satyagraha movement in South Africa. In Tolstoy, the farm women protesting Asiatic Registration Act courted arrest and were sentenced to three months imprisonment.[46] This had greatly stirred the heart of the Indian community in South Africa and also deeply touched the people of India. In this, Gandhi had enlisted the support of European women to India's cause.[47] The cause of women was dear to his heart. He stated that his own contribution to the problem of women's role in society was the practice of truth and non-violence in every walk of life. The presence of the "Mother-archetype" and the "feminine-archetype"[48] was prominent in Gandhi. In the words of B.R. Nanda:

> The strongest formative influence on young Mohandas, however, was that of his mother Putlibai... [W]hen there was sickness in the family, she wore herself out in days and nights of nursing... Something of her maternal love he came to possess himself, and as he grew it flowed out in an ever increasing measure, bursting the bonds of family and community, until it embraced the whole of humanity. To his mother, he owed not only a passion for nursing which later made him wash leper's sores in his ashrama, but also an inspiration for his techniques of appealing to the heart through self-suffering...a technique which wives and mothers have practised through time immemorial.[49]

Mrs. Millie Graham Polak, a close associate of Mahatma Gandhi in South Africa, wrote this about him:

> Another of the many pictures of life in South Africa arises clearly in my mind. It was during the early years of life in Phoenix. Mahatmaji had at this time come to definite conclusions about sex-abstinence. He had written and

---

[45] M.K. Gandhi, *The Collected Works of Mahatma Gandhi* (Delhi: Publication Division, Ministry of Information and Broadcasting Government of India, 1961), Vol. 29, p. 92.

[46] Gandhi, *Satyagraha in South Africa*, p. 258.

[47] Ibid., pp. 164-166.

[48] B.N. Ganguli, *Gandhi's Social Philosophy: Perspective and Relevance* (New Delhi: National Gandhi Museum and Radha Publications, 2000), p. 6.

[49] Quoted in Aruna Asaf Ali, *Resurgence of Indian Women* (New Delhi: Radiant Publisher, 1993), p. 13.

spoken on the subject very decisively. I had several
discussions with him about the continuance of human life
on this planet, and had, on one occasion, remarked that he
must surely consider that God was wrong in having
created men and women with their senses and emotions,
since, were they to accept and adopt Mahatmaji's dictum,
then God's expression through creation would cease; self-
control, I contended, being the goal of developed humanity
and not the denial of God's method of peopling the world.
Very soon after this conversation, one of the members of
the little settlement at Phoenix gave birth to a child. I
purposely refrained from speaking of the matter when I
visited Phoenix two or three days later. I thought that
perhaps Mahatmaji might feel the fact displeasing. After a
short while, and having talked of other things, he said in a
surprised voice, "You have not asked about the mother and
babe. Do you not want to see them?" He then came with
me to see the baby and talked in a quiet, joyous way to the
mother; and I realized in a flash that, even as a woman
does, he differentiated between abstract principles and
human needs and affections.[50]

Gandhi's social experiments using Tolstoy's farm method were of
a unique nature. For him, education was the real emancipator of woman. He
introduced co-education in Tolstoy's farm-model, formidable a task though
it was. This was an experiment he cherished as "the most fearless of its
type."[51] Gandhi brought the gamut of Tolstoy farm experiments to the
Indian national scene, and there lies the efficacy.

Gandhi was in full consonance with the utopian philosophy of "the
practice of virtues."[52] His series of experiments with Truth can be seen as
"experimental existentialism."[53] When asked, "Is it not necessary that
individuals should practice non-violence first in their own person, in their
relations with other individuals," Gandhi's reply was:

It would be a delusion to think otherwise. If one does not
practice non-violence in one's personal relations with
others and hopes to use it is in bigger affairs, one is vastly
mistaken. Non-violence, like charity must begin at home.

---

[50] Quoted in Nirmal Kumar Bose, *Lectures on Gandhism* (Ahmedabad:
Navajivan Publishing House, 1971), pp. 61-62.

[51] Gandhi, *Satyagraha in South Africa*, p. 222.

[52] Thomas More, *Utopia* (New York: Washington Square Press,1965), p.
81.

[53] Erik H. Erikson, *Gandhi's Truth: On the Origins of Militant
Nonviolence* (London: Faber and Faber Ltd, 1970), p. 10.

But if it is necessary for the individual to be trained in non-violence, it is even more necessary for the nation to be trained likewise. One cannot be non-violent in one's own circle and not outside it. Or else, one is truly non-violent even in one's own circle; and often the non-violence is only in appearance. It is only when you meet with resistance, as for instance, when a thief or a murder appears, that your non-violence is put on its trial. You either try or should try to oppose the thief with his own weapons, or you try to disarm him by love. Living among decent people your conduct may not be described as non-violent. Mutual forbearance is not non-violence. Immediately you get the conviction that non-violence is the law of life, you have to practice it towards those who act violently towards you; and the law must apply to nations as to individuals. Training is no doubt necessary. And beginnings are always small. But if the conviction is there, the rest will follow.[54]

A "practical idealism,"[55] the non-violent means adopted by Gandhi to achieve ends were efficacious. Thus wrote Gandhi on the power of passive resistance or Love-force:

The fact that there are so many men still alive in the world shows that it is based not on the force of arms but on the force of truth or love. Therefore, the greatest and most unimpeachable evidence of the success of this force is to be found in the fact that, in spite of the wars of the world, it still lives on.[56]

In his analyses, Gene Sharp saw non-violence or satyagraha "as a concrete expression of the principle of moral approximation of the ends and means relationship,"[57] which "can be regarded as the most unique contribution to the philosophy and technique of revolution in our time."[58] Indeed, in a centrifugal world, Gandhi's views on non-violence and love are needed more for today's global situation than for any other time in history.

Maharshi Dayanand College
Bombay, India

---

[54] Tendulkar, *Mahatma,* Vol. 5, p. 14.

[55] Gandhi, *My Non-Violence*, p. 4.

[56] M.K. Gandhi, *Hind Swaraj or Indian Home Rule*, p. 78.

[57] Quoted in R.R. Diwakar, *Gandhiji's Life, Thought and Philosophy* (Bombay: Bharatiya Vidya Bhavan, 1963), p. 58.

[58] Ibid.

CHAPTER XIX

ORGANICISMIC ETHICS:
AN INDIAN SPIRITUAL PERSPECTIVE

S. R. BHATT

One of the most significant implications of the Organicismic view of Reality is the acceptance that the cosmos, rather than the cosmic process, is a totality of occurrences and not of things alone. It is a highly complex and intricate but planned and purposive networking of events and not a mechanistic arrangement of preexistent entities. Every existence, living or non-living, has a dependent origination out of a causal complex characterized by mutuality and openness, inter-relatedness and reciprocity. Each one has a specific nature, place, role and function in the cosmic setup as determined in the scheme of the universe. The cosmos is a vast and subtle inter-netting of multiple interrelated and interdependent existences which are in a constant flux. It has physical, mental and spiritual dimensions. There is determinism at the physical level but freedom and spontaneity at the spiritual level. The mental realm is partly determined and partly free. The human being is an organic unity of psycho-physical processes animated by the spiritual element. It is thus a complex of body, mind and spirit.

With these metaphysical premises one can work out Organicismic ethics. An ethical system purports to provide the norms to regulate human conduct in relation to other human beings, their social organizations, other living beings and the natural environment. This is because all are dynamically interrelated and interdependent and the functioning of one affects the rest. However, the human being is at the center stage of ethical considerations as it is the most evolved being, having freedom and spontaneity, creativity and a capacity for manipulating reality. The human being has the prerogative to exercise free-will and thus feels responsible for his or her conduct. Freedom necessitates norm-prescription and this implies norm-adherence as well as norm-violation.

Human life in the world is incomplete and imperfect and points beyond itself. It has a goal to achieve, a purpose to fulfill, and an end to realize. It is establishment of a society of perfect individuals where the sorrows and sufferings of the world may cease to exist. This is the longing intensely cherished by every human being. The release of human beings from the travails and travesties of worldly life is not effected by mere wish. Nor it is an idle or ideal apprehension through abstract speculation. It is a realization through properly planned, executed and accomplished endeavor. It requires rigorous discipline of knowledge, will and conduct and the fruits of conduct in mutual sharing, mutual cooperation and mutual collective enterprise. It demands harmonious organization and skillful management of end, means and modalities. It implies just and distributive sharing of the fruits without selfish considerations which is possible only through equanimity of mind and the feeling of self-sameness. This can be achieved by self-control and self-sacrifice. But this is not self-abnegation. It is self-fulfillment through corporate living and partaking.

A spiritual approach to ethics is not rights-based but duty-oriented. It involves performance of one's obligations as per one's station in the total cosmic setup without any attachment to consequences. In order that an individual can perform one's duties properly, faithfully, efficiently and disinterestedly, one must know one's nature and capabilities as well as what is to be performed, how it is to be performed, when it is to be performed, why it is to be performed, etc. An unwavering skillful performance depends upon rightness of knowledge and firmness of will.

Activity is the law of life. Conation is an essential feature of consciousness. Cessation from action in thought, words and deeds is impossible for a human being. Action alone confers the required all-round growth and development. Every individual contains within him- or herself immense potentialities which, when fully developed and properly cultured, open up the center of infinite energy, unbounded expansion and limitless bliss. In this state, the individual identifies one's whole essence with the universal center of energy and feels oneself as only an instrument through which the universal center of energy is manifesting itself. No longer does one feel one's limited existence as a separate individual possessing limited energy, a limited span of consciousness and a limited degree of enjoyment. This is ego-less-ness. This is equanimity or *samadh.* This realization of feeling of oneness with the totality is possible when the actions are performed with a spirit of sacrifice without attachment to their fruits, and with full knowledge and skill. This is self-realization through self-sacrifice.

In Indian culture, philosophy and religion, views and ways of life, theory and practice, and knowledge and conduct are not divorced and segregated. They are named as *Darsana,* which is not mere reflection upon the nature of reality but also a quest for and a realization of values. Basically it is a discipline for realization of 'perfection' (*moksa sastra*). There is a definite purpose in life and reality if we care to know it, and a definite goal to achieve if we have a will to do so. Our existence is not meaningless. It has a value and significance. But we must first of all know what we are, what the nature and purpose of life are, what we should be in our life, and how we can be so, etc. The aim of human existence should be spiritual perfection through material progress. But material progress is only a means, not an end. The end is self-realization, which is achieved through the removal of karmic matter and liberation from *samsara.* This is the ultimate teaching of all schools of philosophical thought in India.

In Indian philosophy great emphasis is laid on proper knowledge. Knowledge is the only and surest way to material progress and spiritual perfection. It, therefore, emphasizes that we must draw a clear distinction between truth and falsity. Falsity entangles us in the vicissitudes of worldly life. It is bewitching and bewildering and it springs from ignorance. In order to have right knowledge, a right attitude or right mental make-up is necessary. This is a prerequisite for a proper view and way of life. This is authentic existence. Opposed to this is falsity with which we generally suffer. Falsity does not serve any genuine purpose and hence it must be discarded. For an aspirant of perfection only the right type of knowledge is helpful. This is the main theme of the teachings of all the schools. Knowledge always leads to good conduct. The value and purpose of knowledge is not theoretical but necessarily practical. Right conduct ensues only from right knowledge. *Conduct without knowledge is blind and knowledge without conduct is lame.* The two are complimentary. Knowledge has to lead to the corresponding conduct. Without right conduct, deliverance from worldly miseries and from trials and tribulations is impossible, and without complete deliverance from these no permanent happiness can be achieved. Right attitude, right knowledge and right conduct are the three jewels of life which every human being must wear. But this wearing is not decoration; it is an actual practice and concrete realization. However, this is not easy to achieve. It requires austerity and rigorous discipline, a rigorous control of body, will and mind. Its essential prerequisite is right faith and firm belief in the words of great seers and sages as expressed in their life and teachings. The seers and sages are those who have conquered all passions and internal enemies, and have attained omniscience, so to say. Faith in the efficacy of their teachings as the only guide for spiritual progress and deliverance is the *sine qua non* of the spiritual mode of living. Right faith diverts the attention of the individual self from worldly affairs and directs the self to spiritual progress, which alone is the real purpose, meaning and goal of life. Right faith is the only way to get rid of worldly bondage and to direct our attention, thoughts and actions to the spiritual perfection which is a necessary condition of and prerequisite to liberation.

Seers and sages attain right knowledge from their subliminal intuitive realizations and from the scriptures, and impart that knowledge to the householder and laity. But the householders should remember that knowledge without conduct is useless. Merely listening to discourses is waste of time and futile. It does not help us in any way. What is needed is the ensuing conduct. But unfortunately most of us forget this. We listen to the sermons of the spiritual persons but do not practice them. We take it as a pastime or a matter of routine of life. Our knowledge remains mere information at the mental level. The *Dasavaikalika sutra* (IV) compares a person having knowledge without practice to a donkey who carries a load of sandalwood without knowing its value or utility. As the donkey bears the load of sandalwood but has no share in the wealth of his load, similarly a person without practice merely bears the burden of his knowledge. He cannot enjoy spiritual progress, which is the real fruit of knowledge. Instead he indulges in evanescent and fleeting worldly pleasures which invariably end up producing pain and suffering or mental unhappiness or a feeling of vanity of life. The Vedas and the Upanisads also aver that knowledge is useless without conduct and conduct is useless without knowledge.

Knowledge pertains to the real. The real is multifaceted and multidimensional. It has infinite properties and relations and therefore it can be approached in infinite ways. This is perspectivalism at the levels of reality, thought and language. As there are many aspects of reality, there can be multiple approaches to reality. Each one is true in itself but it is only partially true. It is true from a particular perspective. From another perspective it may not be true. We may have a total or holistic perspective, known as *pramana*. But if we have a partial perspective it is known as *naya*. Both *pramana* and *naya* are true and valuable. This type of understanding leads to mutual complementarity, mutual cooperation, mutual trust and co-existence and, above all, to non-violence (*ahimsa*) which is the highest truth and highest virtue in Indian ethics. The perspectival approach to reality alone can lead to non-violence and coexistence, and this in turn can guarantee peace, progress, prosperity and perfection in the world. That is why non-violence is regarded as the highest virtue (*paramo dharmah*).

The real has three phases of existence. In it something endures, something originates and something passes away. So it is both permanent and changing. But we must know what is permanent and what is changing. We have to attend to both in proper proportion and in proper perspective. More often than not we do not do so under the spell of ignorance and the sway of passion. The seers and sages have shown the way, which is the right path to be emulated by us. Proper knowledge, proper will and proper effort on our part alone can yield the desired result.

We must know the nature of reality, the world of living beings and non-living things, and also their interrelation. We must know the nature and the role of karma and the ways for the cessation of the karmic flow. We must know the distinction between good and evil along with their respective results. We must know how and when to practice right conduct. We must know the requirements of the practice of a householder and a retired person. Spiritual progress is a gradual and graded realization, and therefore the theory of gradual progression should also be properly understood so that we may march on this path smoothly and without falling. But all this is not a bookish knowledge which some of us possess by our readings of the classical texts either fully or partly. Such knowledge, as we have seen earlier, is only a burden and does not help.

Organicism, with its corollary of perspectivalism, provides for democracy in ideas and in living. It inculcates the spirit of peaceful co-existence, tolerance and mutual support. This alone can ensure universal peace, solidarity and harmony. It is a unique contribution of Indian spirituality, which is noble and sublime, deep and subtle. It is not very easy to understand it and to practice it. But if this can be achieved the world will be an ideal place to live in and to realize spiritual perfection. Another significant implication of Organicism is the practice of vegetarianism and environmental protection, which are the needs of the day. Everything in the world is interrelated and interdependent. Every thing has its unique existence and value. So nothing should be destroyed by a human being for his selfish ends. Indian ethics not only regulates human conduct in relation to one's own self and in relation to other human beings but goes a step further in bringing human conduct into relation with all living beings and the natural environment. Every existence has intrinsic worth and it must be given due respect. In case some misconduct occurs due to ignorance or negligence, or is even willed, there is a provision for forgiveness and repentance. The Indian ethical tradition advocates selfsameness in all existence in spite of its inherent variability. It thus has the unique feature of synthesizing quantitative and qualitative monism and pluralism, and monadic uniqueness and modal dependence. In fact, Organicism is the cardinal tenet of Indian thought and it is impregnated with immense possibilities of drawing out newer and newer implications and corollaries for cosmic well-being. But this should not be a mere intellectual exercise. It must involve programmatic action at the individual and corporate level on a cosmic scale. This may not be easy, but it is not impossible.

Indian thinkers have put forth the concept of 'dharma'. It is another unique contribution, which is highly valuable in the spheres of thought and action. In spite of the vast literature available on this rich and complex concept, its tremendous implications are yet to be brought to the fore by saints and scholars. It provides a strong base for relativism, perspectivalism and situationalism which are needed for pluralistic worldly life. It helps in avoiding the pitfalls of absolutism, dogmatism, obscurantism, ego-centricity and narrowness of all types. The concept of dharma stands for the unique and distinct nature of each entity, its place, function and value in the scheme of reality and also the principle, which has to regulate its behavior and interrelationship. Thus dharma has both constitutive and regulative aspects.

In the context of spiritualistic ethics, it is desirable to analyze the notion of 'Quality of Life' as it has been projected and nourished in different cultural and sub-cultural traditions of India so that all that is true, good and beautiful in them, and which is worth emulating, may be brought together and synthesized for pursuit of world peace and cosmic well-being which are the ideals cherished by humankind at all times all over the world. In the context of the present day quest for globalization and universal harmony in the strife-ridden and divisive world such an attempt at the theoretical level may help in generating a beneficial climate and congenial mind-set through proper and adequate education and other means of mass communication. Thought motivates action and good thoughts will certainly ensure good deeds. It is pragmatic to live by ideals even though they may not be easily or fully realizable. Ideals need to be projected and pursued. There have been seers, sages, saints and knowledgeable persons in every known historical age and in every region who – on the basis of their subliminal intuitions – have given us noble ideas and ideals for universal well-being. It is prudent to go by their precepts and practices, which have eternal relevance and utility.

The pursuit of excellence, the striving for betterment and the attainment of quality of life, have been perennial human concerns and aspirations. All human endeavors in diverse fields of culture and civilization have been directed towards the realization of this goal. The search for freedom from imperfection and consequent suffering has been the main motivating factor for all-cognitive enterprises and technological advancements. Though every human individual cherishes and strives for this and posits it as the ideal of life, its realization requires planned corporate efforts. It cannot be an individual enterprise. A single individual may work out a plan, but its execution has to be corporate. Moreover, quality of life concerns the individual as well as the cosmos since the two are interrelated and interdependent and constitute an organic whole. This apart, one cannot attempt to realize a good quality of life for an isolated individual, society, nation or region. It has to be a global vision and a universal realization without any privilege to any one section of the universe. Everyone has to participate and partake in this venture, which is a collective enterprise. Everyone should be able to contribute by manifesting one's capabilities through a dynamic discovery of one's potential, being assisted in this process by society and the natural surroundings.

The universe is an undivided whole. There is Organismic interdependence, cooperative partnership and supportive mutualism in community living. All beings have to coexist in the universe, but this co-existence must be regulated just like a bird's nest, wherein the young ones coexist in a regulated way. The bird-parents operate with the attitude of distributive justice and selfless sacrifice, and the young ones coexist in mutual co-operation and co-sharing. They do cry for food, but do not quarrel with one another. The parents see to it that their needs are satisfied, but they do not feed their greed. If little creatures can have such a harmonious living, why can we, who claim to be rational, not have the same?

Human existence is multi-dimensional, multi-layered and multi-relational. As stated earlier, it is a mind-body complex animated by a principle of consciousness called soul or spirit. Human identity, therefore, cannot be determined by any one of these facets. It is the totality and intricate unity of all these, with subtle and fine inter-netting and interdependence of the three, which constitutes human personality. Added to this is the social dimension, which is a highly complex, complicated and intricate network of relations. Society provides the ground and sustenance for human existence and also the basic structure and materials for human evolution. But there is no dichotomy or chasm between individual existence and the social environment. Further, each human being is essentially 'natural' in the sense that he or she is an inalienable part of nature, is sustained and nourished by nature and ultimately reaches his or her culmination and consummation in and through nature. Nature surrounds the human being, and provides a basis for human evolution as well as for excellence. But in spite of all this, nature does not exhaust human existence, nor does human existence exhaust nature. Human being is bound by nature and yet he or she can transcend the bonds of nature. He or she is aware of being natural, but also of the capacity to overcome and go beyond nature. Even though dependent upon nature, he or she can become liberated from nature with the help of nature itself. Thus, he or she has a paradoxical awareness of dependence on nature and, yet, a possible freedom from nature. It is a prerogative of a human being to acquire this self-awareness and shape his or her life and existence accordingly.

Human life is a prized possession, and humanity is the most evolved being that has emerged so far. It has been a remarkable biological evolution through ecological interaction and cultural transformation, through innate competence and overt performance. On the basis of their planned endeavor and successful behavior, human beings have been able to achieve wonderful feats. A mechanistic understanding of human ontology and human evolution cannot do justice to the spontaneity, creativity and goal-oriented character of human pursuits. Experience has shown reality to be through and through telos-embedded, and human life, being part and parcel of it, has to reflect this feature. A teleological approach alone can support a viewpoint which co-ordinates work, welfare, possession, and enjoyment with a spirit of sacrifice, social progress social justice, material well-being, and spiritual enhancement.

Quality of life is the *summum bonum*, and globalization is its essential corollary. Its realization therefore requires the propagation and profession of global ethics. The principle of the universalizability of ethical norms and their adherence without exception stem from this very consideration. But globalization is not only to be understood in materialistic terms, in the sense of liberalization of trade and commerce. Basically, it is a spiritual ideal. It is an inculcation of the attitude of seeing self-sameness everywhere, leading to global unity. It is the realization of the fundamental unity of the entire cosmos. It is a mode of co-existence with a spirit of mutual support, mutual sacrifice, and mutual caring and sharing. It enlightened conduct, like that of a Bodhisattva or a Jivanmukta who is constantly engaged in universal well-being, who is happy in the happiness of others and feels miserable in the miseries of others, and who always thinks of the good of others and acts for their welfare. The moral codes prescribed in all the cultural and religious traditions of the world aim at cultivation of this mindset of universal affinity and self-sameness.

Matter and the materialistic approach are primarily divisive and depriving without being distributive, in the sense that consumption of material goods by one deprives all others from that consumption and consequent enjoyment since it is not possible to share them. But if the spiritual element is added to this consumption in the form of sacrifice, as the sacrifice of a mother in making her child consume good food even if she has to remain hungry and deprived, then there would be no feeling of injustice and deprivation. The regulative principles of self-centered enjoyment and enjoyment with sacrifice or in sacrifice are not the same. The latter alone can provide a basis for global ethics. According to the Indian creation-mythology, the cosmos is created out of sacrifice and it is sustained by a spirit of sacrifice only. But ignorant and selfish human beings forget and ignore this cosmic principle in their conduct. The message of the Bhagavad-Gita is that success lies in sacrifice and in the performance of one's obligations in the world without any selfish considerations. Apart from cosmic service it enjoins us not to usurp what does not belong to us and not to deprive others from what legitimately belongs to them. The nature which nurtures us functions through the principle of sacrifice. In Indian culture, it is regarded as 'mother' precisely to bring home this truth. It is bountiful and enjoyable, it is benevolent and merciful, but it is to be enjoyed with care and consideration, and with a spirit of sacrifice and distributive sharing. Then only real joy is obtained; otherwise it is only sadistic pleasure. The example of a bee can offer us the best guidance. A bee gets sustenance from a flower but it does not harm its beauty, diminish its fragrance, or destroy its reproductive power. It gathers pollens from the flower only to turn it into sweet and nourishing honey for the betterment of others. This is the model of caring and sharing which we have to put forth for our conduct.

Globalization is not the bulldozing of the multitude or multiplicity in an overt or covert manner, but the accommodating and harmonizing of them within the organic unity of the entire cosmos. It stands for coordination rather than for uniformity of thought and action. It envisages no antagonism or incompatibility between one part and the other, like organs in an organism, since all are conceived as interconnected, interrelated and interdependent elements of one and the same whole constituting a single field or continuum. That is why the analogy of a living organism or a field is put forth where there is 'multiplicity-in-unity' – many situated in one – not as separated, segregated and scattered elements, but in mutual openness and reciprocity supplementing as well as complementing one another. Here conflicts and disorders may not be unnatural but their resolutions and harmony may also not be unrealizable.

Globalization is both a viewpoint and a course of action, a policy instrument and a world-wide movement for a new world order based on enlightened principles of conduct aiming at enhancement of 'Quality of Life' not just of human beings but of the entire cosmos. This calls for a new formulation of global ethical norms which may regulate the entire gamut of human conduct in relation to one another and also between human beings and the rest of the cosmos. This is the precursor to the emergence of a global society in which the entire world can be experienced as one single family. This is possible through the realization of self-sameness and cultivation of the spirit of sacrifice. But this necessitates a trans-valuation of values, a paradigm shift in values, a changed mind-set, an enlarged vision of cosmo-centricity, and an enlightened view and way of life actuated through the proper training of body and mind by illuminating knowledge and liberating wisdom. It calls for a total transformation of matter and mind and realization of spiritual oneness. It is a widening of the self as totality, from 'I' to 'we', from oneself to total self, from individual to cosmic. Here there should be no deprivation and exploitation, no sorrows and sufferings that are unmitigated, no injustice and discrimination unabated. This is realization of heaven on earth, to use figurative language. The cosmos is full of splendors and can provide sustenance to all its inhabitants in a just, fair and equitable manner. But this is possible only through the postulation of a new value schema and a new ethics which cares for all and tends all. This has been the cherished desire of the enlightened mind. It is not a utopian dream but an ideal realizable in actual practice through proper education. This has been the message of all great religious traditions of the world.

Globalization is a mode of coexistence with a spirit of mutual sacrifice and sharing in which enjoyment with sacrifice is practiced as a matter of routine rather than as a binding force or injunction. The moral codes prescribed in Hindu, Buddhist and Jaina ethics, and for that matter in the ethical ideals of all cultures of the world, aim at cultivation of this mind-set of universal affinity and self-sameness. This is the *anatmabhava* of the Bhagavad-Gita and Buddhism. This is the *sarvatmabhava* of the Vedas and the Upanisads.

In a meaningful consideration of global ethics, there is a need not only for a new vision and a new intuition for a newer paradigm, but also for a widening of attitude. In a global ethics put forth in a holistic perspective there is no antagonism between individual and society, between egoism and altruism, between human beings and the rest of the cosmos. It is multifaceted and multi-layered such that it accommodates both absolutistic rules and situational or contextual rules. Both are needed in different situations, and acceptance of both as per the demands of the situation does not involve any contradiction. There may be situations wherein different sets of moral rules may appear as presenting a dilemma, but these dilemmas can be resolved by taking into account the perspectives of the differing norms.

Depending upon the nature and types of the *relata*, there can be many branches of global ethics like individual ethics, social ethics, bio-medical ethics, professional ethics, work ethics, environmental ethics, political ethics, religious ethics, etc. There are multiple aspects of human conduct which need to be regulated and there can be as many facets of ethics. Human existence is multifaceted both in its individual and socio-cosmic dimensions, and there is a vast network of human conduct the whole of which has to be regulated by moral principles. The sphere of ethics can be widened and multiplied as per the needs of the changing situation, and there is nothing static about it.

In the changed situation of modern times there is a need to reformulate the basic moral principles suited to the demands of globalization. Then only we can hope to have the emergence of a global society in which the entire world can be experienced as one family. This is realizable, given a proper cultivation of knowledge, will and action in a harmonious framework. It is possible to plan out such a framework provided there is a will to do so. This will involve the education of a required type, which alone is the key to bring about this awareness through the refinement and heightening of consciousness and the transcending of narrow confinements. This has been the cherished desire of the enlightened human mind. But this requires a proper and well-planned endeavor on the part of human beings. For this, a newer ethics is called for which must go beyond traditional ethics. It will be an ethics based on spirituality – an ethics for totality – in which there are no considerations of rights and demands but only of obligations and sacrifice. It will be an ethics of duties. All beings, human and non-human, exist in this field in intimate relation to one another, having an assigned nature, status and role. We have to know our nature and status, and roles and functions assigned to that status.

The proper performance of our duties and discharge of obligations requires 'management of action' and 'management of results of action'. Both are necessary and important. Management of action implies three things:

1. we must know what actions to perform, why to act and how to act
2. we must have a will to act as per the knowledge acquired
3. we must act in the most skillful manner so as to realize the desired result.

All these three requirements may be worked out in detail. But the point to be emphasized is that, though every action is motivated, it should not be intended. That is to say the agent should know why the action is to be performed and what will be the result of the action. This apart, he/she should also have the will and skill to perform the action. So there is a definite motive to perform the action. But the act is to be performed without attachment to the consequences or irrespective of the consequences. This is how a soldier fights for his/her country. He/she knows what action to perform, why to act and how to act, but when engaged in action he/she is not mindful of the consequences. Here there is engagement in action, but withdrawal from or non-attachment to the fruits of action. There is a subtle but clear distinction between motivated and intended action, and this needs to be appreciated.

For the performance of action, the human agent is not the only responsible factor. There are several factors responsible for this. There is a causal collocation in which there is a multiplicity of factors, but every factor has a definite place and role in the totality of the collocation. In their operation, there is an order. Thus, for example, apart from human endeavor, supporting instruments, natural circumstances, positive and negative conditions, etc., partake in the causal collocation. So the human being is not the only cause, though generally we tend to assign causal agency to human beings only. Of course, the human being plays a dominant and decisive role and that is why the onus of responsibility is generally put on him/her. In the management of action, all these factors also need to be managed.

So far as management of the results of action is concerned it is enjoyment with sacrifice that is the guiding principle. It is enjoyment with the totality in together-ness, in the spirit of sharing and caring following the rules of distributive justice. This alone is the legitimate enjoyment of the results of action. The guiding principles of the management of results should be such as to ensure justice and fairness to all existences as every one has a rightful place in this cosmos. Peaceful coexistence is the only proper way of existence. But this has to be ensured by all legitimate means. No one should be permitted to disturb the cosmic course, and for this deterrent measures can also be undertaken. The rule of law, justice and righteousness need to be protected, preferably by proper education and persuasion. Deterring measures should be the last resort. The human being is prone to evil, but evil propensities can be prevented and checked by suitable means. It should be one of the tasks of global ethics to regulate human conduct in such a way as to lead to and ensure universal peace, prosperity and harmony. Performance of action is necessary, ensuing of result is inevitable, but sharing of result is desirable. Skillful performance of action is ideal, proper management of results is obligatory, and its distributive enjoyment is conducive to total well-being. The objective of a healthy and meaningful global ethics should be material prosperity with spiritual enhancement.

University of Delhi
Delhi, India

CHAPTER XX

IN DEFENSE OF RELIGIOUS PLURALISM

VIBHA CHATURVEDI

One thing which cannot be denied in the contemporary world is the presence of difference and diversity in outlook, be it with respect to ontological, moral, cultural or religious questions. Singularism, the view that there can be only one right or correct or true view on any such issue, is neither an attractive nor an acceptable option for the modern liberal mind. Pluralism, the view that there can be more than one point of view on these important issues is better suited to the cognizance of diversity. Pluralism poses philosophical and epistemological difficulties, but in certain areas these difficulties do not seem as insurmountable as in some others. One would not hesitate to accept that literary or artistic interpretations of an object vary. Similarly, cultural differences pertaining to dress, eating habits or social customs are also comparatively less problematic, though we do have evidence of the tendency of one culture to assert its superiority over others, and of the conflicts generated by this tendency. In general, it can be said that wherever a viewpoint makes or involves ontological commitments, pluralism raises serious philosophical problems relating to the concept of truth, the nature and validity of knowledge, and the relation between language and reality, and so on. The challenge is that one cannot assert in a straightforward manner that something 'X' is both 'A' and 'not A' at the same time.

Here, I shall limit myself to the issue of religious pluralism. The question I wish to address is whether we can build up an argument with the help of the notion of interpretation in order to create room for such pluralism. I think we can and, drawing inspiration from the Indian philosophical tradition, I will briefly indicate how this can be done. I will also try to indicate briefly the implications of this proposal. It seems that a full-fledged acceptance of religious pluralism has important consequences for understanding faith and for certain religious practices like proselytizing.

Let me first clarify the presuppositions inherent in my proposal.

First, statements pertaining to the belief system of a religion are assertions and have ontological import. Supporters of the Verification theory of meaning argue that all putative assertions about a transcendent reality or a reality not accessible in sense experience are devoid of cognitive meaning and are what Carnap calls, 'pseudo-statements'. Flew comes to the same conclusion by adopting the criterion of falsifiability. According to this view, the problem of conflicting truth claims of religions does not even arise, since the putative assertions do not make truth claims. I do not think that non-cognitive analyses of religious belief and language are adequate. To say that a statement like 'God loves his creatures' or 'A man experiences rebirth after death' is merely an expression of an attitude towards life, as for example Carnap and Wisdom suggest, does not appear to be an adequate analysis of these sentences. Braithwaite's proposal that religious language should be seen merely as expression of a commitment to certain moral principles, and Hare's analysis of such assertions as 'bliks' is also not adequate.[1]

The belief system of a religion is an integral and important part of that religion. Wittgenstein, in his later works, draws our attention to the distinctive features of use of language in religious contexts.[2] He insists that religious assertions should not be understood as scientific hypotheses and that questions of evidence and supporting reasons are not relevant here in the way they are in the context of scientific claims. He emphasizes the importance of the affective and commissive force of a religious belief. His point that that an analysis of religious belief and language must pay due attention to these aspects of believing is well-taken. But I would like to add that the ontological import of a religious world-view cannot be ignored. The affective and commissive force of religious beliefs is linked closely to the ontological import of the world-view in question.[3]

Second, there can be genuine conflict between the truth-claims of different religions. We can cite examples of such conflict. We find different claims about the nature and attributes of the ultimate reality, about the status and creation of the World, about the place of man on earth, about the destiny of man after death and about the ultimate goal of life. For example, Islam and Christianity assert that God and the world are two ontologically distinct realities, whereas Spinoza asserts that these are identical. Christianity maintains that the God creates the World out of nothing. Nyaya monotheism asserts that matter is eternal and Isvara creates the world out of such matter. Adherents of Islam, Christianity and Judaism believe this world to be real, but Advaita Vedanta of Samkara holds that only Brahman is ultimately real and that the world of plurality is an illusion. We find conflicting viewpoints on the question of rebirth. Such doctrinal differences

---

[1] A. Flew, R.M. Hare and B. Mitchell, "Theology and Falsification", R.B. Braithwaite, "An Empiricist's View of the Nature of Religious Belief" and I. M. Crombie, "The Possibility of Theological Statements" in Basil Mitchell, (ed) *The Philosophy of Religion* (Oxford: Oxford University Press, 1971).

[2] Ludwig Wittgenstein, *Lectures and Conversations on Aesthetics, Psychology and Religious Belief*, ed. C. Barret (Oxford: Basil Blackwell, 1966) and *Culture and Value, ed.* G.H. von Wright & Peter Winch (Oxford: Basil Blackwell, 1980).

[3] Vibha Chaturvedi, *Wittgenstein's Fideism, Belief, Reason and Practice* (New Delhi: Om Publications, 2002). Wittgenstein's analysis of religious belief and language is discussed and examined in detail in this book.

and their power to give rise to conflicts among believers of different religions need to be acknowledged.[4]

RESPONSES TO RELIGIOUS PLURALISM

The exclusivist response, or "singularism," would assert that only one religious standpoint is true or correct; all others, insofar as they do not agree with it, are false or incorrect. A milder position of this kind may maintain that other standpoints are only approximations to truth or are valid up to a point. In most of the religious traditions of the world, such exclusivist claims can be found, sometimes explicitly and sometimes implicitly expressed. The exclusivist tendencies are more pronounced in religions based on claims of divine revelation as articulated by a divine messenger or a prophet. Divine revelation, if genuine, has to be infallible. The traditional propositional view of revelation regards the scripture as a record of divine revelation – as literally God's Word, in other words. An exclusivist stand about one's own religion is a logical outcome of such an approach. A somewhat different analysis of the concept of divine revelation is also available within the Christian tradition. According to this analysis, the object of revelation is not propositions but certain events in human history. Scripture is a record of attempts by people to articulate and interpret their revelatory experiences in a certain segment of human history.

It is clear that most religions today are trying to come to terms with diverse religious traditions, even if in a feeble or superficial manner in many cases, it is also equally evident that exclusivist claims about one's own religion have not been given up. Such claims provide the foundation of evangelist enterprises. I personally think that, as far as revealed religions are concerned, exclusivist claims cannot be totally eradicated. The exclusivist approach is totally opposed to pluralism. Human history provides ample evidence of the conflict such an approach can lead to.

I will now discuss some models to accommodate religious pluralism, which are available in the Indian philosophical tradition. I will begin with those that I do not find completely adequate.

One response is to assert a kind of identity of function among different religions. Swami Ramakrishna compares different religions to the different banks (*ghats*) of the same pond. The followers of these religions draw and partake of the same water from these different *ghats*. They may, however, call this water by different names.[5] Swami Vivekananda, in a similar vein, compares different religions to different rivers, all leading to

---

[4] V. Chaturvedi, "Believer versus Unbeliever: Reflections on the Wittgensteinian Perspective," *Indian Philosophical Quarterly*, 20 (1993). This paper critically evaluates various ways to interpret Wittgenstein's remark that an unbeliever does not contradict a believer.

[5] *The Gospel of Sri Ramakrishna* (New York, 1907), p. 151.

the same sea.[6] Different religions are sometimes compared to different paths leading to the same destination. The important point in this model is that different religions are believed to share a certain goal and are held to be equally efficient for that purpose. This is definitely an attractive idea, but it does not withstand critical scrutiny. It is debatable whether all religions can be said to share a goal. The ultimate aim of life and the path to achieve this goal endorsed in different religions vary. However, sometimes it is argued that religion as a whole has one goal or quest. This goal may be defined as a move away from worldliness and towards other-worldliness or as the development of a spiritual outlook. It is indeed correct to say that religions perform certain similar functions for their followers. Religion provides a sense of identity to its followers and regulates the thinking and conduct of the believers according to a certain shared world-view. But this very identity also becomes the basis for perceiving the followers of different religions as 'the other' and generating antagonism towards them.

Sometimes it is claimed that different religions speak of the same reality but use different names for this reality. When Muslims talk of 'Allah,' Christians of 'God' and Hindus of 'Isavara', they refer to the same reality. According to this view the difference is at the level of language and not at the level of reality. Radhakrishnan, for example, observes

> Differences in name become immaterial for the Hindu, since every name, at its best, connotes the same metaphysical and moral perfections. The identity of content signified by different names is conveyed to the people at large by an identification of the names. Brahma, Visnu, Siva, Krsna, Kali, Buddha and other historical names are used indiscriminately for the Absolute Reality[7]

It is debatable, however, whether this statement can be said to be accurate about Hinduism. It certainly is not obvious that all the different names mentioned here refer to the Absolute. However, even if it be granted for argument's sake that, within Hinduism, different names refer to the same reality, the same cannot be said to apply to differences among various religions. Given the vastly different and often conflicting descriptions put forward by different religions about the ultimate reality, its nature and relation to the world, the claim that these refer to the same reality is not

---

[6] Swami Vivekananda, *The Complete Works* (Calcutta: Advaita Ashrama, 1985).

[7] S. Radhakrishnan, *The Hindu View of Life* (London: George Allen and Unwin, 1961) p. 34.

plausible. I agree with the criticism that this view 'does not take religion seriously' and is rather 'simplistic'.[8]

Drawing inspiration from Jainist *anekantavada*, one could argue that different religions present different aspects of the same reality. Each is true, but each is only a partial understanding of the reality, an understanding of one aspect of the reality. This model is also problematic. Firstly, these different understandings cannot be combined to present a more complete picture of the reality. At the same time, our common view of reality does not allow us to treat vastly different claims about reality as presenting aspects of the same reality in a straightforward sense. Moreover we have to recognize that each religion makes a claim to complete truth. Any suggestion that each religion gives only partial truth or presents one of the many aspects of reality is likely to be found unacceptable and offensive.

A very different strategy to deal with religious pluralism is to ascribe validity to each religion at a certain level but deny it at another higher level. We find such an approach reflected in discussions of Swami Vivekananda and Radhakrishnan. According to Vivekananda, ultimately only Brahman is real, and all plurality is to be negated. The goal of religion is to reach self-realization, to become one with Brahman, and at this level all plurality and all distinctions are negated. He grants validity to all different religions up to a point. However, beyond a point these religions lose their validity. He says that:

> ...the science of religion becomes perfect when it would discover Him who is the one life in a universe of death, Him who is the constant basis of an ever-changing world, One who is the only true Soul of which all souls are but delusive manifestations. Thus is it through multiplicity and duality, that the ultimate unity is reached. Religion can go no farther.[9]

Radhakrishnan states that intellect is subordinate to intuition, dogma to experience, and outward expression to inner realization.[10] One could argue, then, that the differences exist at the level of the intellect but at the higher level of experience (*anubhava*) or insight into reality (*darsana*) such differences do not matter. According to him, 'The bewildering polytheism of the masses and the uncompromising monotheism of the classes are for the Hindu the expressions of one and the same force at

---

[8] M. Amaladoss, "Tolerance and Religious Faith: Some Models and Problems," in *Tolerance in Indian Culture*, ed. R. Balasubramanian (New Delhi: I.C.P.R., 1992).

[9] Swami Vivekananda, *Chicago Addresses* (Calcutta: Advaita Ashrama, 1992), p. 25.

[10] S. Radhakrishnan, *The Hindu View of Life*, p. 13.

different levels.' The different sects of Hinduism, Radhakrishnan adds, represent a hierarchy with respect to improved knowledge of God.

> The worshippers of the Absolute are the highest in rank; second to them are the worshippers of the personal God, then come the worshippers of the incarnations like Rama, Krsna, Buddha; below them are those who worship ancestors, deities and sages, and lowest of all are the worshippers of petty forces and spirits.[11]

If this gradation were to be applied to different religious traditions, the monotheistic traditions like Christianity and Islam, etc., would figure at the second level, below the monistic tradition. This model thus relegates different religious traditions to a secondary status, reserving the pride of place for one standpoint – in this case, Advaita Vedanta. It thus falls short of a wholehearted acceptance of religious pluralism.

I will now discuss a proposal, which can be developed to explain and accept religious pluralism. The Rg Veda says that the reality is one, but the learned speak of it differently.[12] This idea can be developed to give a model where different religions are seen as different interpretations of the same reality. It may be noted that the intention is not to take them as presentations of different aspects of reality or as approximations to truth, but to accept these as genuinely different interpretations of reality, each complete in itself. How do we account for this possibility?

I would like to argue that no understanding of reality is possible without some element of interpretation in the light of the knower's conceptual structure. The conceptual structure in different knowers may vary. One might object at this point and claim that the conceptual structure of all persons is almost the same. After all, perceptual judgments of people correspond to a great degree. Immanuel Kant argued that the forms of human sensibility and categories of understanding shape all knowledge of objects. He, however, believed that these forms and categories are the same in all persons. My response would be that there could be various kinds and levels of interpretation. The higher the element of interpretation, the more the likelihood of diversity. A religious worldview is one such higher level of interpretation and admits of diversity. I would like to argue that the interpretative apparatus of people might vary. Once we accept this, it follows that the reality can be understood and interpreted differently. Vivekananda's example of the same light being reflected through glasses of different colours is a metaphor to illustrate this difference.[13] For a full-fledged acceptance of pluralism one would need not only to accept the

---

[11] *Ibid*, p. 24.
[12] Rg Veda, 164, 46.
[13] Vivekananda, *Chicago Addresses*, p. 31.

possibility of different interpretations; one would need, further, to accept that all different interpretations are at par and equally valid.

Most religions are either based on revelation or on mystical or religious experience. In the case of both, the role of interpretation cannot be ignored. Religious experience is indispensable for revealed religions. Religious experience is involved in the receiving of revelation. Interpretation enters at two levels here: firstly, at the level of articulation of the religious experience by the person who has had the experience, and secondly at the level of people's understanding when they hear or read such articulations. Those who take a propositional view of revelation may argue that, in the case of revelation, there is only a faithful recording of experience, and not interpretation. But this claim can be challenged. Even in simple perceptual judgments there is some element of interpretation. The non-propositional view, however, does admit the element of interpretation in the understanding of revelatory events in human history.

It is not within the purview of this short presentation to present effective arguments against the contention that all persons share the same conceptual structure. It should suffice to mention that it is reasonable to accept the possibility of multiple interpretations in the case of religious experience. Quite often the interpretations, the vocabulary used to describe the nature of the experience, and the object of the experience are drawn from the socio-religious background of the person or the mystic in question. The diversity of mystical interpretations of reality has been noted by scholars and is well recorded. As far as a revealed text or scripture is concerned, the possibility of different interpretations is accepted within most religious traditions, at least in a limited sense.

The Indian philosophical tradition clearly admits of multiple interpretations of the same scripture. All the orthodox systems of philosophy accept the validity of the Vedas and yet put forward very different, often conflicting, metaphysical and religious systems. A very clear example of diverse interpretations of the same scriptural text is seen in the Vedanta philosophy. 'Vedanta' means 'the final portions of the Vedas'. It has, however, come to signify 'the settled conclusions of Vedas taken as a whole'. Schools of Vedanta refer to the same scripture (*sruti*) and yet present greatly divergent interpretations of the Vedic philosophy. Samkara, Ramanuja, Vallabhacarya and Madhavacarya have very different metaphysics. The *advaita* of Samkara and *dvaita* of Madhvacarya seem to be diametrically opposed.

The Indian philosophical tradition provides ample evidence of debate and dialogue among different philosophical traditions. Each school presents the view of the other schools and gives extensive arguments to show their weaknesses. An attempt to understand the other is quite evident in such discussions. Yet this does not imply that each school is prepared to accept all diverse points of view as equally valid. On the contrary, each school tries to establish its philosophy through a rebuttal of others. Jain philosophy appears to be an exception because of its *anekantavada*. But despite its tolerant attitude towards different perspectives, even Jain philosophy does not go to the extent of openly saying that all other schools are at par with it. However, we do find that the diversity of philosophical standpoints is generally acknowledged within the Indian tradition and debates among these are encouraged.

What is a plausible stand in the face of multiple interpretations? Can we account for all intra-religious and inter-religious differences in this way? And if so, what can be said about the validity of these views? These are some of the questions that need answers. At present I would like to emphasize that an exclusivist approach, or singularism, does not remain an option. Once we admit that a knower's conceptual structure has a significant role in his/her understanding of a text or experience, it follows that there is no way to adjudicate between different understandings/interpretations. There is no neutral, presupposition-free point of view that could enable one to judge and evaluate various points of view. Every evaluation would necessarily be conditioned by the interpretative apparatus of the person doing the evaluation. There is no view from nowhere, so to say.

Multiplism or pluralism, the view that there are different, equally valid religious interpretations, seems to be the obvious suggestion. This position, however, raises serious questions about our understanding of religious faith and practices. If all different interpretations are equally valid, it is difficult to explain and justify the total commitment inherent in religious faith of the believers. Every religion demands from its followers that they obey and practice its teachings. Proselytizing or persuading followers of other religions to convert to one's own faith are an integral part of many religious traditions. If we look at the history and practice of two major religions of the world, namely Christianity and Islam, it is evident that these cannot accommodate a full-fledged pluralism. In case of most of the practiced religions today we find that different sects or streams exist within a religion with overlapping similarities and differences. Even here each one of these in most cases derives its strength from singularist claims about itself. Once a religion grants that all other sects or religions are equally valid, it makes no sense to argue that people must believe and do what it prescribes. Within the Hindu tradition there is a reasonable degree of flexibility to accommodate different religious sects. A large section of Hindu population continues to be polytheistic and worships several gods and goddesses. Different sects of Hinduism share practices, moral perceptions and beliefs, such as in the doctrine of karma and rebirth. However, as far as monotheistic and monistic Hinduism is concerned, singularism is ultimately inevitable. These accommodate divergent views as valid up to a point but ultimately need to be superseded by a higher insight. The Hindu tradition does, by and large, emphasize religious tolerance. Yet one cannot conclude that the Hindu tradition accepts religious pluralism with all its implications. To the best of my knowledge, only the Bahai faith preaches that praying matters, whatever be the object of worship.

Most religions demand their more serious devotees to spread their message far and wide. Proselytizing and conversion have been the tools through which large sections of populations in different regions of the world have been brought into the fold of a faith. Such practices even today are a major source of tension among different religions in pluralist societies. But this is not the present concern of this paper. I wish to emphasize the point that, once we grant that all religious interpretations are equally valid, no theoretical basis can be provided for proselytizing. The only viable option would be to undertake a descriptive analysis of these traditions, as recommended by Wittgenstein in his later works. It is a fact of life that people do not start their lives in a religious vacuum. One is gradually initiated into a religious way of life within the family and society. This explains why some feel comfortable with a certain religious way of life while others identify with another way.

One of the major challenges for multiplism or pluralism would be to guard against the consequence that 'anything goes' in the name of a religious interpretation. I admit it is not clear how this challenge is to be met. Yet it seems intuitively clear to me as a rational human being that a theoretical basis for internal criticism of a religion, as well as for an external evaluation of it, must be open. Every religion needs to change its practices and perceptions in the light of changing conditions. People do recognize the validity of such an exercise. Almost every religion has gone through a process of reform and change over a period of time, though in varying degrees. Evaluation of a religion would require some common standard acceptable to human beings, despite differences of race, colour, and nationality, and so on. It is as true to say that different human beings think differently as to say that we can find overlapping similarities among their thinking on fundamental issues. I admit that I cannot explain at this juncture what might provide a basis for such common criteria of evaluation. Our general perception of the requirements of human dignity or general agreement about human rights may, however, be taken as a starting point.

The diversity of religions certainly does not entail that there are no shared ideas. It is to be seen how far and in what respects different religions agree. Nor is it plausible to hold that different religions cannot communicate with each other. The demand of pluralism is to avoid hegemonic tendencies and to communicate and interact with each other with a healthy, mutual respect. The possibility of dialogue and understanding always remains. The need of the present time is to strengthen the attempts in this direction and discourage those tendencies which generate conflict and strife among different religions. A wholehearted acceptance of religious pluralism inevitably leads to the conclusion that no religion has a monopoly over truth and morality. Instead of working towards hegemony and power, different religious traditions need to work towards empathetic understanding and co-operation. Dialogue, not conflict, is the need of the time.

The conflicts among religions generally arise with respect to the role of religion in socio-political matters. Indian society gives ample evidence of peaceful co-existence of different religious traditions, as well as of conflicts. Religion in most cases says something about every aspect of an individual's life. The moral code prescribed by a religion generally lays down rules about different aspects of both personal and social life. Religion is also increasingly being used as an instrument of social and political power. Since people feel strongly about their religion, leaders and politicians find it easy to arouse their feelings by creating a 'threat-perception' and gather huge, often blind, support from them. The divisive and conflict-generating dimension of religions must neither be ignored nor downplayed by scholars. In the contemporary world, the hold of religion on people's personal and public life has to be restricted within reasonable limits. Religion should primarily be a way to search spiritual goals and in this basically and ultimately every religion has the same goal.

To conclude, I would like to say that it is the need of the hour to acknowledge and respect the variety of human outlooks. But we also have to find ways of understanding and communicating across them. The value of different models to accommodate religious pluralism discussed earlier lies in the fact that these make an effort in the right direction. The models, certainly, are not free from theoretical difficulties, but these at least shift the focus towards sharing and commonality. If each religion approaches another with a spirit to understand it on its own terms, much of the strife and conflict generated by religious differences would disappear. We need to recognize that the basic function of religion consists in a spiritual quest, and its role in secular matters needs to be downplayed. Globalization should provide an occasion to celebrate the diversity of human outlooks in every area, including the religious, and find ways of understanding and communicating across it. A concern for human welfare – for the poor, underprivileged and suffering of humanity – can act as a strong bond among the different religions and civilizations in the world. Finally the last lines of Swami Vivekananda's poem titled 'The Living God,' he exhorts us not to forget man, the living God, in our concern with the divine:

> Ye fools! who neglect the living God,
> And his infinite reflections with which the world is full.
> While ye run after imaginary shadows,
> That lead alone to fights and quarrels,
> Him worship, the only visible!
> Break all other idols.[14]

University of Delhi
Delhi, India

---

[14] Vivekananda, *The Complete Works*, vol. 8, p. 169.

CHAPTER XXI

THE ETHICAL MEANING OF "TIAN" (HEAVEN) AND CONTEMPORARY "ETHICS WORSHIP"

LI DONGNI

What characterizes Chinese culture is the undisputable heaven-human unity as embodied in the heaven-human relationship. In this paper, I wish to focus on the intense ethical implication here, as reflected in Chinese ideas about the concept of the heaven. This has much to do with what I call "ethics worship" in contemporary China.

In *Shuo Wen Jie Zi* ("Explaining written language and parsing words"), Xu Shen defines heaven as "zenith," meaning "the top." Its etymological meaning is "the first." It is also inferred from inscriptions on bones, tortoise shells, and bronze to refer to a human-shaped god that is bigger than man.

Two American scholars have recently compared the dictionary definition of "tian" and its translation.[1] They note that, in a standard Chinese dictionary, "tian" means: "1. the sky; 2. air; 3. day; 4. the movement of the sky and astronomical phenomenon; 5. the sun; 6. god; 7. nature, natural; 8. the emperor; 9. father; 10. indispensable; 11. a period of time; 12. positive; 13. fate; 14. inclination, the body; 15. great." They then note that, in a standard Chinese-English dictionary, the term is translated as: "1. heavenly bodies, the outer space, the sky; 2. weather; 3. day; 4. Zion, fatality, God, (personified) nature; 5. husband; 6. indispensable."

The major difference between the two lies in the fact that, in the standard Chinese dictionary, "tian" is not defined as Zion, fatality, or God (with a capital 'G'). The Chinese notion of "tian" has no transcendence. It can be the *fornix*, lording over the earth via the natural laws; it can be integrated with man, never divorced from him in time or space and never reaching [a Buddhist] *Paramita*.

Such an absence dates back to remote antiquity. Scholars of Chinese mythology have noticed that there was not a universal god in ancient Chinese mythology, which did without a well-developed theogony. Nor was there a supreme god. There were many regional arch-gods in the early myths, a reflection of the multiple origins of Chinese civilization. There had been gods that were "Jiu Zhou" and "Jiu You" in pre-Qin literatures, but they were no more than arch-gods of individual clannish tribes, and there was not a universal theogony. The mythology is instead rather scattered, and this shows that the myths had been created to enhance

---

[1] Hao Dawei and An Lezhe, "Tian Di" in *The Cultural Source of Chinese Philosophy* (Jiangsu People's Press, 1999).

the cohesion and the political strength of particular tribes. This is why the Chinese myths had not been able to bring about a social network under an arch-god, let alone primogenitors like Adam and Eve. Accounts about Fuxi and Nuwo, two legendary figures, date back to the pre-Qin era. They are not primogenitors. Nor was there any connection between the two. In the East Han dynasty, there were two primogenitors with half-human images: either a snake with human head or a crocodile with a human head. This indicates that the Chinese myths at that time were tinted with a heavy, primitive human-animal combination. In the sequence of the evolution of myth, animal images, such as animal and plant totems, predate human-animal combinations, such as the human-headed snake in Chinese myths and the Sphinx in ancient Egypt, followed by theanthropism. Fuxi and Nuwo were treated in Chinese literature as brother and sister, or as lieges, rather than spouses, let alone the primogenitors characterized by procreative myths. They were treated as spouses until the Tang dynasty, by which time Buddhism, together with its myths, had been in China for more 800 years. Nothing testifies to its Chinese origin.

According to cultural research, another important fact is that there is no supreme god in Chinese mythology. An arch-god can be either an idol for adoration or a source of sagas, whereas the idea of a supreme god implies religious worship. An underdeveloped arch-god or supreme god implies that transcendence had not been formed in China. Mythology is seemingly contradictory to reality. The Western theogony resembles the Chinese social pattern in many respects, with the arch-god commanding the thearchy that grew through kinship or incest. In human society, however, the role that kinship plays is not well defined. Chinese society is formed on the basis of personal relationships. The Chinese social order is strict while its mythology is in great confusion. This is where the difference is. Human society, no matter what culture it belongs to or what form it takes, has gone through a clannish stage. Western society stepped out of clannish society, leaving it to the thearchy, while the Chinese culture retained clannish society. Chinese culture pays attention to human society and builds it on the basis of natural relationships. The non-affinity world of mythology is counter to the affinity world of human beings.

In the early days of Chinese civilization, one does not find a well-developed theogony. Compared with the arch-god, the primogenitor occupied an important place. This accounts for the lack of transcendence in the idea of "Tian" in ancient China. The absence of transcendence is indicated by the focus on the union of man and "Tian." Heaven is nothing more than the zenith, the greatness, closeness to the highest god. The Chinese also have a different interpretation of the notion of "paramount." Historically, heaven in its paramount sense stemmed from the emperor. During the Shang dynasty, there appeared in China a word, "Di", which is equivalent to "God." The highest ruler of human society is known as "the "Di", while "Di" is the title of the supreme god. The emergence of "Di" signified the evolution of the mythology into theanthropism. In this period, a distinct line could be drawn between Chinese ideas and Western ideas. The Chinese mythology excluded the primitive religious element and historicized the mythology. Xie Xuanjun, in his book *Society and National Character*, gave a comparative analysis of "The Classic of Mountains and Seas" (*Shan Hai Jing*) and "Generation-Clan" (*Yao Dian*), which illuminated the process in which mythology excluded the religious.

According to the *Shan Hai Jing*, Huang Di wed Lei Zu, who gave birth to Chang Yi. And Chang Yi gave birth to Han Liu. Han Liu wed A Nu, who gave birth to Zhuan Xu. Hence, Duang Di was the great-grandfather of Zhuan Xu, who was the son of Chang Yi and the great-grandson of Huang Di. According to *Yao Dian*, Zhuan Xu was son to Chang Yi and great-grandson to Huang Di. Han Liu was missing.

The *Shan Hai Jing* relates many ancient myths with strong primitive religious tints. Primitive religion was characterized by the worship of animals – which runs contrary to the belief that god had qualities that transcended human beings. Han Liu was the father to Zhuan Xu, who was a great god in history. To treat him as holy is to empower him with the power of a god. There was no physical description of Chang Yi, father to Han Liu and grandfather to Zhuan Xu in the *Shan Hai Jing*, but there was a detailed physical description of Han Liu. This is unique to animal spirits, which were transformed from historical figures. According to the *Shang Hai Jing*, Han Liu had a long neck, small ears, a human face, a pig's muzzle, the torso of a kylin (a mythical chimerical creature), and hoofed feet. These traits of gods in primitive religions showed that this theanthropism lacked rationality. An exception to the Chinese historical myths is Qui, who, in his early days, was a regional god of thunder and was said to be able to be heard within 500 *li* [Chinese miles]. In some historical legends, he became the god of music while retaining some animal traits. Han Liu, father to Zhuan Xu and a figure in a line of "Di," could only be wiped out as he could not afford to bear an animal image as in primitive religions.

There were many other primitive gods with fates similar to that of Han Liu. They were placed at the bottom of theogony, without forming a heavenly theogony similar to human society. Apotheosized "Di" were all "Di" in ancient times. "Di" in historical myths bore some characteristics of personhood while "Di" in human society bore some divinity. Divinity nevertheless lacked transcendence. Natural persons, however, "acquired" some supernatural power due to apotheosis, so the "Di" became the spokesmen for god. In Chinese cultural history, the transformation of primitive religious gods into historical legendary gods is equivalent to the transformation of "Di" into "Tian." Such transformation was completed sometime between the Yin and Zhou dynasties. The establishment of Tian is the formation of "affinity culture" in its conception.

During the Yin dynasty, the Zhou were a small backward tribe in the west – austere, hardworking and practical – that believed in Tian. After conquering the Yin, the Zhou met with a problem that is common in the conquest of powerful tribes by small tribes: they had to reinforce their rule with a cultural as well as a political conquest. The "Di" of the Yin was also their primogenitor god, and the people looked on themselves as the primogenitory offspring of their "Di," and so held a conspicuous superiority to the Zhou people. As a result, the Zhou considered it necessary to establish a new belief system based on the primitive religious system of the Yin so as to justify its ruling. The Zhou rejected the mythical "Di" in favor of "Tian" and "fatality" – more ethical concepts – so as to account for the rise and fall of the Yin. This accorded with the political needs of the ruling class. Zhou Gong, when talking about the rise and fall of the Yin, attributed the prosperity of the Yin during the long reign of Tai Wu, Wu Ding and Zu Jia to their cautious political control and attention to the needs of the people rather than their identity as the offspring of god. And the fall of the Yin, given their ignorance of farming and indifference to the suffering of the people, is attributed to the indulgence of the later kings. Here the concept of Tian is used to denote that one's fate is determined by one's moral and political behavior and is under one's own control. If one's action does not conform to certain moral standards, one will become a slave of foreigners. The Yin were destined to collapse. And the Zhou could not defy the decision made by Tian. This "Tian" is nothing more than an expression of the needs of the ruling class. Shang Shu-Jun Shuang pointed out that Tian was not reliable and that the Zhou relied on virtue of the king Wu rather than Tian. The king Wen achieved success by his virtue. Confucius was sharp-witted enough to see the transition of the primitive religious "Di" of the Yin to the historical mythological "Tian" – that is, the difference between the Yin and the Zhou in their interpretation of the concept "Tian."

The definition of "Tian" in position and content determined the adoption of Confucianism in the history of the Chinese culture and revealed that Confucianism is a result of culture rather than the origin of Chinese culture. Yet, owing to Confucianism, "Tian" has never been divorced from its ethical sense throughout the long history of Chinese thought. Nor does it imply absolute command. The philosophical realm of the heaven-human union has gone through the human-human animal gods of primitive religion and the theanthropical gods of historical myths. There have not been many disputes over the philosophical argumentation and conceptual evolution of the heaven-human union. Attention should be paid to several points from the cultural and philosophical perspectives.

Firstly, a distinct line cannot be drawn between "Tian" and the human, whether in time or in space. In China, "Tian" no doubt plays a role that deserves attention. But the principal of the role is not of something ontologically independent. "Tian" dominates everything on the earth and everything on the earth develops under heaven. "Tian" is the origin of everything and everything *per se*; it is the creator of everything and itself. It exists in an endless and timeless existence. "Air" permeates everything and transcends the meaning and position of "element." It reflects the Chinese idea of heaven-human relationship. It encompasses life and non-life, consciousness and non-consciousness, nature and human society, rules and things that embody them, motion and rest, time and matter, and time and space.

Secondly, the heaven-human union is the theorized notion of the ontological "Tian." This has the same cultural origin as the inseparable heaven-human union. There are no fundamental differences among the various theories of different scholars about the notion of "Tian." Philosophically, they differ greatly as there were fierce debates over the issue. But the differences are not fundamental. Their common ground is to acknowledge socialization and theorization. This differs greatly from the Greek and Hebraic ontological theories. In speaking of Confucian "Tian" or Taoist "Tian," we have a social philosophy that goes well beyond natural philosophy. It is difficult to tell whether the figures in ancient times are from myths or from history. When the ancient myths became historicized, the ethical relationship in the deified world was transformed into human history. The ontological idea about the world was accordingly theorized. As the world was seen to originate from the social activities and ethical relation of human beings, the focus on naturalness faded away. The story of a person from the state of Qi, who worried all day about the collapse of the heavens, was told in jeer and jest. It is, however, a reflection of the Chinese quest of nature. Lao Zi is widely regarded as the author of a classic work of natural philosophy, but it is more a work of social and political philosophy. It is true that, in addition to its major concern about governance and human life, part of it has been interpreted as natural philosophy. Yet it focuses on ethical relationships; the individual exists only in the sense of having a role as a link in the social network. This accounts for the lack of individuality of the deified figures and historical figures. The ancient kings and emperors are either of ambiguous personality and appearance or of a particular stereotype. The historical legends and artistic works themselves have been conceptualized and formalized, to serve as a tool for moralization.

Thirdly, we see a unity of the human mind and reason. "Tian" is man, and man is "Tian." Man is the social man, and ethics is the social order based on affinity. "Tian" thus gives way to "reason." "Reason" as sociality is an extrinsic requirement for man as an individual. The dissolution of the individual by the affinity culture made reason a necessity for the kind of existence that includes the individual. The way to interpret reason is not extrinsic. This transition of the heaven-human union to the unity of the mind and reason began with the pre-Qin era, through Dong Zhongshu, to the idealist philosophy of the Song and Ming dynasties. Thus, the affinity culture matured.

The ethicization of "Tian" makes China receptive to atheism and "Tian" has been worshipped under the mainstream ideology of atheism. Unlike theism and ordinary religious beliefs, the object of worship is the ultimate "Tian" or other supremacies. The focus is a particular ethical system or principle. We may refer to this practice as "ethics worship".

Under this "ethics worship," ethical principles have supremacy. As can be seen in the numerous peasant uprisings in Chinese history, few leaders of these uprisings claimed themselves to be waging a war in the name of "Tian Zi," the son of the heaven. Rather, they claimed to be performing the principles of "Tian." These principles are supreme, and "Tian" became valued because of its principles, not vice versa. One of the most common ethical principles is "equality of wealth." "Justice" is another one of the principles of "Tian." After years of atheist ablution, ethics does not require "Tian" as a justification. The supremacy of ethics can only be seen in its worship. Due to the supremacy of ethical principles, "ethics worship" is nothing less than the worship of "Tian." "Tian" and reason have become united in the mind, so that "ethics worship" can be more profound than the worship of god. One of the typical examples is Fa Lun Gong.

This notion of "ethics worship" will be the object of a future study. The notion is introduced here as a preliminary outline of its cultural roots. The nature of worship engaged in by the public can be understood only in the light of "ethics worship" and its cultural roots.

Nanchang University,
China
and
Centre of Applied Philosophy and Public Ethics,
University of Melbourne,
Australia

APPROPRIATING THE OTHER AND TRANSFORMING CONSCIOUSNESS INTO WISDOM: SOME PHILOSOPHICAL REFLECTIONS ON CHINESE BUDDHISM[1]

VINCENT SHEN

In responding to today's urgent situation full of conflicts created by the self-enclosure of different disciplines, cultures, political and religious groups, etc., we humans should be more concerned with one another and the possibility of mutual enrichment. In order to overcome antagonism by appealing to effective dialogue, in recent years I have proposed "strangification"[2] and "language appropriation" as viable strategies. The term "strangification," a neologism that might appear odd in English, makes sense in Chinese; *waitui* 外推 means, etymologically, an act of going outside of oneself to the other, or going outside of one's familiarity to the strangeness, to the stranger. This act presupposes the appropriation of language by which we learn to express our ideas or values in the language either of others or understandable to others. "Strangification" and "language appropriation" presuppose an original generosity toward the other, without limiting oneself to the claim of reciprocity, quite often presupposed in social relationship and ethical golden rules.

Philosophically speaking, before we can establish a sort of reciprocity (emphasized for example in Marcel Mauss's *Essai sur le don*) as the principle of human society, there must be a generous act of going outside of oneself to the other, so that a relation of reciprocity can be established accordingly. The new principles for society and ethics that we are looking for should be based on original generosity and strangification as the act of going outside of oneself to the other.

In this paper, I will provide some philosophical reflections on Chinese Buddhism based upon strangification, language appropriation, and

---

[1] This article was originally published in *Dao: A Journal of Comparative Philosophy*, III.1 (Winter 2003): 43-62. It was reprinted here with the permission of its publisher, Global Scholarly Publications.

[2] The concept of "strangification" was first proposed by F. Wallner, University of Vienna, as an epistemological strategy in interdisciplinary research. I later developed this concept to include the domains of intercultural interaction and religious dialogue.

generosity to the other. [3] I do not make the distinction, as Yu-lan Fung did, between "Chinese Buddhism" and "Buddhism in China." Rather, I use the term "Chinese Buddhism" to denote broadly those Buddhist tendencies introduced and developed in China without basing their "Chineseness" upon any criteria whatsoever.

Fung took Weishi 唯識, or the Conscious-Only School, as his example of "Buddhism in China," and the Middle Path School and Chan or Zen Buddhism as the best examples of "Chinese Buddhism." He said:

> There were certain schools of Buddhism which confined themselves to the religious and philosophical tradition of India, and made no contact with those of China. An example is the school known by the Chinese as the Xiang Zong or Weishi Zong, which was introduced by the famous pilgrim to India, Xuanzang (596-664). Schools like this may be called "Buddhism in China." Their influence was confined to restricted groups of people and limited periods. They did not and could not reach the thought of every intellectual, and therefore played little or no part in the development of what may be called the Chinese mind. [4]

On the other hand, Fung thought that Mādhyamika, the Middle Path School (or in Chinese, the *Sanlun Zong* 三論宗), belonged to his category of "Chinese Buddhism" because of its similarity to Daoism, especially as regards the Daoist method of moving always to higher levels of discourse, as well as to the Daoist achievement (which for Zhuangzi 莊子 was "sitting in forgetfulness (*zuo wang*_坐忘)" and for Jizang 吉藏, Nirvāna). [5] But, according to Wing-tsit Chan, both the Three Treatise School and the Consciousness Only (Weishi) School lasted for only several centuries and failed to exert a lasting influence on Chinese thought. For him, the Weishi School was completely alien to Chinese tradition and, together with the Three Treatise School, was merely an "Indian system transported onto Chinese soil." [6] Nevertheless, Wing-tsit Chan pointed out something much deeper in saying that "both were introduced into China by

---

[3] This text was first delivered as the keynote speech at the International Symposium on Yogācāra Buddhism in India, Tibet, China, and Japan; the conference was organized by Prof. Leslie Kawamura at the University of Calgary, September 6-8, 2002.

[4] Yu-lan Fung, *A Short History of Chinese Philosophy* (Toronto: Collier-Macmillan, 1948), p. 242.

[5] Fung, pp. 245-246.

[6] Wing-tsit Chan, *A Source Book in Chinese Philosophy* (Princeton: Princeton University Press, 1969), p. 373.

outstanding philosophers. Both have something profound and subtle to offer which China had never known."[7]

I have no intention here of disputing Fung on his distinction between "Chinese Buddhism" and "Buddhism in China," or in arguing against Wing-tsit Chan's judgment of these two schools as "alien to Chinese tradition." What intrigues me is the supposed "strangeness," "alienness," or "otherness" in Chinese Buddhism, especially with respect to the dimension of the other in Weishi Buddhism, which, for me, instead of being taken as alien to the Chinese Mind, could come to be seen as an enriching resource for Chinese philosophy. What interests me here is the problem of how we go outside of our own familiarity and go to the other – to the strangers – and learn from them.

I would take Buddhism in general and Yogācāra or Weishi Buddhism in particular as a case par excellence of strangification and the appropriation of language. Buddhism has well strangified itself to South Asia, Tibet, China, Korea, Japan, Europe, North America, and now to the whole world. In Chinese history, Buddhism has become an essential part and an inner dynamism of Chinese culture itself. However, before we discuss Buddhism, let me make a detour to discuss my concepts of appropriation of language and strangification.

STRANGIFICATION AND LANGUAGE APPROPRIATION

The concept of strangification – first proposed by Prof. Fritz Wallner, my colleague in Constructive Realism, as an epistemological strategy for interdisciplinary research[8] – has been extended by me as a strategy of cultural interaction and religious dialogue, so as to be applicable not only to different micro-worlds constituted by different scientific disciplines or research programs, but also to different cultural and religious worlds.[9] According to Constructive Realism, different scientific disciplines, because of their methods and languages, construct accordingly different micro-worlds, only to be bridged by the strategy of strangification. There are three types of strangification.

The first type is linguistic strangification, by which we translate one discourse about the findings or supposed truth in the context of one particular discipline or research program into the language of or one understandable to other disciplines, to see whether it works there or, alternately, becomes absurd. If the latter case occurs, then reflections must be made concerning the methodology and principles by which one has established the first discourse. If one discourse is translatable into and

---

[7] Chan, p. 357.

[8] Fritz Wallner, *Acht Vorlesungen über den Konstruktiven Realismus* (Wien: WUV-. Universitätsverlag, 1992).

[9] Vincent Shen, *Confucianism, Taoism and Constructive Realism* (Wien: WUV-. Universitätsverlag, 1994, 1997, 2002).

thereby understandable to other disciplines, it should be said to have a larger truth because of its universalizability and ability to be shared with other micro-worlds.

The second is pragmatic strangification. Since science is also culturally and socially bound, if we can draw the truth of one particular discipline from its social and organizational context and put it into another social and organizational context, we can make clear its pragmatic implications and enlarge its applicability to a different social context. If it can still work and develop in the new context, this means that it has a larger or more universalizable truth. If it cannot work in the new social context, then it is limited only to a particular socio-practical context and is not to be seen as universalizable.

The third is ontological strangification. I tend to think that, when an act of strangification is conducted with an ontological detour to a direct experience with Reality Itself in order to understand another's micro-world, then there is an ontological strangification.[10] This means our direct experience with Reality Itself can nourish our language and our dialogue with others.

When extended to the cultural and religious worlds, I should say that, if a value/cultural expression/religious belief is universalizable by being able to be translated into a value/cultural expression/religious belief claimed by another culture or religious community, then it has a larger or universalizable validity. Otherwise, its validity is limited only to its own world and reflection must be made on the limits of one's own value/expression/belief. Also, if one value/expression/belief is universalizable and applicable in other social and pragmatic contexts, this means it has larger validity than in its own context of origin. Finally, a value/expression/belief, when universalizable by a detour of experiencing Reality Itself, (for example, a direct experience with other people, with Nature, or even with the Ultimate Reality) would be very helpful for mutual understanding among different cultural and religious worlds. Thus, especially when we come to religious dialogue (which presupposes ontological strangification by its own nature), one's experience with Ultimate Reality is very helpful for understanding others' religious discourses and practices.

---

[10] On this point I differ from F. Wallner, who understands ontological strangification by the fact that we can travel from one microworld to another, which for me is merely ontic and can become ontological only when, in the access to the other micro/cultural/religious world, there is a detour through Reality Itself or Ultimate Reality. Apart from this, I have modified Wallner's two realms of reality – the "Reality Itself" and "Constructed Reality" – into three by adding the "Life-World" which mediates the Reality Itself and Constructed Reality. Also I have modified his pragmatist vision of science; see my *Confucianism, Taoism and Constructive Realism*.

Further, strangification presupposes language appropriation. As we can see, a person, as you and I, from infancy to adulthood, has to learn various kinds and different levels of language. In the beginning of our lives, we learn language via the generosity of our significant others who are generous in talking to us. Because of language appropriation, we begin to open up a world of meaningfulness. When grown up, we learn all kinds of disciplinary, knowledge-related, technical, and cultural expressions; all these occur through some sort of language appropriation. Language appropriation enriches our lives with knowledge and meaningfulness. Through appropriating a language understandable to others, we shall be able to strangify ourselves via that kind of language. This is also applicable to the collective process of learning. For example, when China began to open itself to Buddhism during the Han Dynasty, or more recently, to Western philosophy and science, this opening up could be seen essentially as a process of language appropriation.

For me, the most fascinating phenomenon about Buddhism consists in its strangifiability or universalizability, as it was initially introduced into the Asian world, and now into almost the whole world. As a student of Chinese philosophy, I take Buddhism's conquest of China as a case of successful strangification. Buddhism entered China during the Han Dynasty, arguably around 2 BCE according to the earliest record, beginning as a popular religion and facing a lot of hostile criticism. Buddhist monks cut their hair and left their parents, going against Chinese ethics, especially the concept of filial piety. Likewise, they paid no respect to political leaders (the emperor and his officers) and made no contribution to economic production. Buddhism was a "barbarian or strange cult." However, it succeeded finally in becoming an essential element of Chinese culture and, together with Confucianism and Daoism, constitutes one of the three Great Teachings of China. Since the beginning of the 4th century CE there have emerged progressively different schools of Chinese Mahayana Buddhism, such as the Sanlun 三論 School, Tiantai 天台 School, Faxiang 法相 or Weishi 唯識 School, Huayan 華嚴 School, Pure Land or Jingtu 淨土 Buddhism, and Chan 禪 Buddhism.

BUDDHISM AND STRANGIFICATION

This great success comes from the fact that Buddhism, in the long history of its conquest of China, has adapted itself to the context of Chinese culture by taking different measures of strangification and language appropriation.

First, we shall concern ourselves with linguistic strangification. There were successive translations of Buddhist scriptures and intellectual dialogue with Daoism and Confucianism through a process of language appropriation. The translation of Buddhist scriptures was not easy in the beginning, and the quality of translations was quite low, so much so that Kumārajīva (343-413) once criticised "translation" as "chewing rice for others, which would not only lose its original taste, but also make people feel like vomiting."[11] Yet later, in the Tang dynasty, especially with Xuanzang 玄奘 (596-664), translation became a systematic and rigorous institution, having its own special spaces, regulations, functions and procedures. Because of this, we can see Weishi Buddhism, and especially its founder Xuanzang (who conducted the largest translation project in Chinese history until now), as an excellent model of strangification. In his *Report of Returning Country*, it is said that:

> Xuanzang noticed that Buddhism emerged in the West and that the Buddha's posthumous teachings propagated to the East, though its best scriptures have yet to come to us [and] we're still in need of its perfect teaching. Therefore I always thought of visiting there to learn it, despite my own life. That's why in the April of the third year of Zhenguan I traveled to India, stepping on the immense desert of Tianzhu, crossing the highest Mount Xueling,... traveling through fifty thousand li... and explored the enlightening thought of strange countries.[12]

This text shows that Xuanzang saw the meaning of his trip to India as exploring "the enlightening thought of strange countries." This tells us that he truly realized the idea of learning from the other. It is also interesting to notice that Xuanzang conducted double strangification in having translated not only 75 Buddhist scriptures, mostly Yogācāra works, into Chinese, but also the famous *Dasheng Qixinlun* 大乘起信論 or "Awakening of Belief in Mahayāna" (arguably attributed to Aśvaghosa), from Chinese back to Sanskrit. Indeed, Xuanzang shows the virtue of gratitude by making a contribution to their intellectual generosity in return.

Further, there was also the so-called *geyi* 格義, which was intended to appropriate Daoist and Confucian concepts in order to render Buddhist concepts understandable to Chinese intellectuals. This was done by Zhu Faya 竺法雅 (c. 4th century) and Kang Falang 康法朗 (c. 3rd century). Even though Dao'an 道安 (312-385) criticized *geyi* as "running against Buddhist doctrine," he himself used Laozi and Zhuangzi's terms for analogical understandings of Buddhist doctrine. Also, he allowed his disciple Huiyuan 慧遠 (334-416) to use Zhuangzi's terms in explaining Buddhist Scriptures. This could still be considered as *geyi* in a broader sense.

---

[11] *Taishō shinshū daizōkyō* 大正新修大藏經, Vols. 1, 30, 45, and 48, ed. Takakusu and K.Watanabe (Tokyo: Taisho Issaikyo Kankokai, 1924-1932); Vol. 50, p. 332.

[12] Xuanzang (Hsuan Tsang) 玄奘, *Ch'eng Wei-shih Lun*, trans. Wei Tat (Hong Kong: Dai Nippon Printing Co, 1973), p. 7.

There was also doctrinal re-contextualization; for example, Daosheng 道生 (355-434) posited that "All sentient beings can become Buddha," something confirmed by the later translated Mahāparinirvāna Sūtra. This thesis thereby made itself compatible with the Confucian doctrine that "Everyone can become Yao 堯 and Shun 舜." In the Tang dynasty, Zhanran 湛然 (711-782) proposed the idea that "Even non-sentient beings have Buddha nature," an important concept for today's ecological thinking in that it sees all beings, sentient or non-sentient, as the manifestation of the immanent, universal, absolute, true Buddha as such.

Unfortunately, this line of thought was not followed by the Weishi School, which made the distinction of five natures and in which we find a category of "sentient beings without Buddha nature (*youqing wuxing* 有情無性)." This idea has its origin in the Lankāvatāra-sūtra. Xuanzang, who was sensitive to its potential conflict with Daosheng and the Mahāparinirvāna-sūtra's doctrine of Buddha nature, was in the beginning reluctant to introduce it to China. However, under the command of his Indian Master, the Venerable Śīlabhadra, he nevertheless kept to it in his writings. This distinction of five natures and the doctrine that some human beings could not attain Nirvāna and therefore could not become Buddha, was continued by Kuiji 窺基 (632-682), in his *Cheng weishilun shuji* 成唯識論述記 and his commentary on the Avtamsaka-sūtra. Kuiji's disciple Huizhao 慧沼 (650-714) developed it systematically and thereby criticized other schools, rendering, therefore, more vehement the conflict that already existed between Weishi and other Chinese Mahayāna Buddhist schools. This was also one of the reasons that the Weishi School failed to become more popular among Chinese people, who seemed to be much in need of encouragement from the saying that "All sentient being has Buddha nature."

The second sense of strangification is pragmatic strangification. It was necessary for Buddhism to withdraw from its Indian context and to adapt itself to the Chinese socio-politico-ethical context. Envisaging criticism from Chinese elitists, Buddhists took different measures of strangification. For example, Buddhism faced the critique of anti-filial-piety by translating, commenting on or even inventing some Buddhist scriptures on filial piety. The early translated *Liudu Jijing* 六度集經 (*Collected Sutras on Six Pāramitrās*) already featured the importance of filial piety by saying that filial piety was more important than charity. The second part of the Brahma-jāla-sūtra (*Fanwanjin* 梵網經), attributed to the translator Kumārajīva, also emphasized the filial piety of Sākyamuni and combined filial piety with Buddhist *śīlas* (commandments). The Buddhist scholar Qi Song 契嵩 (1011-1072) in his very influential *Xiaolun* 孝論 (On Filial Piety) said that Buddhism, more than other religions, emphasized filial piety. Qi Song also equated the five Buddhist *śīlas* (*wujie* 五戒) with the Confucian five cardinal virtues: ren 仁, yi 義, li 禮, zhi 智, and xin 信. In the Tang Dynasty, an invented sutra in Chinese, the *Fumu Enzhong Jing* 父母恩重經 (*Sutra on the Weighty Grace of Parents*) appeared to feature a Buddhist value of filial piety.

The Ullambanapātra-sūtra (盂蘭盆經), said to be translated into Chinese by Dhamaraksa 竺法護(266-313), is often seen as the *Xiao Jing* 孝經 of Buddhism, in which we find the story of Maudgalyāyana (Mulian 目蓮), a disciple of Sākyamuni, who enters purgatory to relieve his mother from suffering. This led to the biggest national Buddhist festival – All Souls – which has been held on about the 15th of the seventh moon, from the 6th century until now, with the joint participation of Confucianism and Daoism. Together with innumerable Chinese commentaries and related literature, images and dramas, all these transform Buddhism into a religion of filial piety.

Buddhism also faced the critique of disrespect for the emperor and his officers. To this Huiyuan 慧遠 (331-414) answered in his *Samen bujing wanzhe lun* 沙門不敬王者論 (*On Why Buddhist Monks Don't Pay Respect to Political Leaders*) by distinguishing common believers from Buddhist monks. Buddhist common believers in the secular world should pay respect to and obey the emperor, his officers, and social ethics, while Buddhist monks should go beyond worldly ethics and rituals so as to concentrate on Buddhist truth and enhance their spirituality. Once a monk has perfected his virtue, he saves by the same token, not only his parents, brothers and relatives, but the whole world. Therefore, the ultimate purpose of Buddhist monks leaving their homes for spiritual cultivation is much the same as those of Confucians.

Unfortunately, not all pragmatic strangification communicated the right message to the Chinese. For example, concerning ethics, the ordering of terms in Indian Buddhist Scriptures expressing ethical relationships – such as "mother and father" and "wife and husband" – when translated into Chinese, were rendered as "father and mother" (sometimes modified as "paying filial piety to father and mother"), and "husband and wife." The phrase "marry one's wife" was quite often rendered as "marry one's wife and concubines" in Chinese. As to political relations, "republican relation" might be rendered as "imperial relation". A good example of this can be found in Volume 2 of the Dīrghāgama, where Sākyamuni praises the country of Vraja people, who often held meetings to discuss righteous affairs in a republican way. Yet, when rendered into Chinese, it reads "the Emperor and his subjects are in harmony and the superior and inferior respect each other" (君臣和順，上下相敬).[13] The consequence of this is that the messages contained in Buddhist Scriptures of more egalitarian ethics and republican politics were turned into hierarchical and totalitarian terms in order to adapt to Chinese culture and, as a result, the people were unable to learn for their own long term benefit.

---

[13] *Taishō shinshū daizōkyō*, 1, p. 12.

Finally, we shall look at ontological strangification. "Emptiness" could be seen as the Ultimate Reality of Buddhism. With their account of Ultimate Reality, Buddhists were able to make Buddhism understandable to other endogenous philosophies such as Confucianism and Daoism. The Buddhist experience of emptiness, the Daoist experience of dao 道 and wu 無, and the Confucian experience of ren 仁 (humanness, humanity, and cosmic interconnectedness) and cheng 誠 (sincerity and true reality), though quite different in themselves, still exhibit some similarity and complementarity as experiences of Ultimate Reality. Therefore, much effort has been made to meet one with another, through which a Confucian or a Daoist might be able to understand a Buddhist discourse on "emptiness" and Ultimate Reality. From as early as Mourong's 牟融 *Lihuolun* 理惑論 (*On the Correction of Doubt*, c.196 BCE), different kinds of complementarity have been proposed relating these three teachings. Also, by proposing various versions of the doctrine of the Common Origin of Three Teachings (*sanjiao tongyuan*三教同源), Buddhism made an effort to accommodate itself to the intellectual milieu of traditional Chinese culture.

WISDOM, MIDDLE PATH AND THE OTHER

Now I would like to come to the second part of my thesis: that concerning wisdom, especially Weishi's concept of transforming consciousness into wisdom. By "wisdom" I mean the Buddhist concept of prajñā. According to Xuanzang in his regulations on translation, the fifth category of "terms not to be translated" (*wu bu fan* 五不翻) concerns the term prajñā because "the use of the term prajñā shows respect, whereas the use of the term zhihui 智慧 (wisdom) turns out to be superficial" (般若尊重，智慧輕淺).[14] Nevertheless, we still use the term "wisdom" here to render its meaning, especially concerning Weishi's concept of *zhuanshi dezhi* 轉識得智 or *zhuanshi chengzhi* 轉識成智 – the conversion of consciousness into wisdom or to get wisdom. In fact, wisdom was the common concern of both the Sanlun School and the Weishi School; this originated in the two Indian Mahayāna Buddhist schools, the Mādhyamika and the Yogācāra respectively, but have been judged by Wing-tsit Chan to be alien to Chinese tradition. The difference between them consists in the fact that, for the Sanlun School, prajñā means emptiness, whereas for the Weishi school, wisdom is based on the marvellous being of Alaya-vijñāna.

I would say that both Sanlun and Weishi retain a certain dimension of the other, which makes them alien to the immanentist tendency of Chinese Buddhism. Here I do not want to indulge myself in comparison. It

---

[14] These five categories are: 1) those that represent secrecy; 2) those that represent multiple meanings; 3) those that represent objects not found in China; 4) those that are in accordance with ancient usage; 5) those that bring about better respect.

suffices to say that, for the Sanlun School, the other is that which lies always beyond in denying or rendering void that which one arrives at in negative dialectics – rendering void in order to show the non-substantial character of the Ultimate Reality. The Middle Path, which is prajñā, consists in understanding interdependent causation in the sense of non-substantiality. After destroying any dualistic situation in the process of negative dialectic, even the reality of interdependent causation should be denied.

The Sanlun School, basing itself on three treatises – that is, Nāgārjuna's Mādhyamika-śāstra (Treatise on the Middle Doctrine, 中觀論), Dvādaśanikāya-śāstra (*Twelve Gates Treatise,*十二門論), and Nāgārjuna's disciple, Āryadeva's Śata-śāstra (*One Hundred Verses Treatise,* 百論) puts its emphasis on prajñā and sees wisdom in emptiness.

The Buddhist term Śūnyatā or emptiness could have many meanings. I would suggest that we can discern three main layers of meaning. On the ontological level, "emptiness" (*kong* 空) means that all things come and go by interdependent causation and therefore are without any substance of their own. Second, on the spiritual level, 'emptiness' means that the spiritual achievement of a sage consists in total freedom whereby he attaches himself neither to being nor to non-being, neither to dualism nor to non-dualism, nor even to any form of spiritual achievement, no matter how high and deep it is. Finally, on the linguistic level, 'emptiness' means that all words we use are but artificially constructed, without any fixed correspondence to reality.

Although Indian Buddhism puts much emphasis on the ontological and the linguistic senses of emptiness, Chinese Mahayāna Buddhism, generally speaking, emphasises mostly the spiritual sense of emptiness. For example, although we can find all three meanings in Sengzhao's 僧肇 *On the Emptiness of the Unreal*不真空論, Sengzhao himself would interpret "emptiness," in appropriating Daoist philosophy, as the spiritual achievement of a sage. For example, we read:

> Unless one possesses the wisdom and special penetration power of a sage, how can he harmonise his spirit with the realm of neither being nor non-being?
>   The sage moves within the thousand transformations but does not change, and travels on ten thousand paths of delusions but always goes through.[15]

This spiritual achievement of a sage – who has no attachment to the realm of either being or non-being, and no attachment to his own spiritual achievement whatsoever – belongs to the marvellous function of his mind/heart, which on the one hand is non-substantial and empty, but on

---

[15] *Taishō shinshū daizōkyō,* 45, pp. 152-153.

the other hand is marvellous in its function and self-transcending. Because of this, both the Dao (the Ultimate Reality) and the Sage are not far away from us, but realised all of a sudden at the moment of enlightenment. "Things when touched become real... Man when enlightened becomes marvellous."[16] In order not to attach oneself to being or non-being or to any horizon of spiritual achievement, a negative dialectic is necessary to move from any fixation or presumed foundation. In Jizang's 吉藏 (549-623) *Treatise on the Double Truth* (二諦義), we find a negative process of levelling up. The first level, according to Jizang, is the worldly view of being, on the one hand, and the true view of non-being on the other. Then, through a negative dialectic, one moves on to the second level, where both being and non-being belong to the worldly view, whereas non-duality (or middleness) belongs to the true view. Then, again through negative dialectic, comes the third level on which both duality and middleness are worldly views, whereas 'neither-duality-nor-centrality' is the highest truth.

In his *Short History of Chinese Philosophy*, Fung interprets the theory of double truth in a misleading manner. Fung saw the point of this theory to be the denial of all one-sided truths.[17] However, according to Jizang's argument, the real point of this theory is to overcome any dualism rather than merely the one-sidedness of the worldly view and the true view. The negative dialectic consists in first denying the dualism between you 有 (being) and wu 無 (non-being); then, that between two one-sided views; and finally that between the one-sided view and the middle (central) view. The true middle path is thus interpreted as neither one-sided-nor-middle, and is realised in the process of negative dialectic as emptiness, which is freedom from all kind of dualism constituted by sophistic or playful discourse.

It is clear, then, that in this negative dialectic, the refutation of mundane views is identical with the elucidation of the true view. However, when a true view is held in place of a mundane one, it has to be refuted again. It is only through an endless dialectical process of denial that the enlightened can keep to the real Middle Path. In Chinese Philosophy, the concept of the Middle Path comes down from the category of the Great Ultimate in the Book of Documents, which interprets it as "impartiality" or "non-onesidedness." In the fifth (therefore middle) category of the "Royal Ultimate" (*huangji* 皇極), interpreted by Zhu Xi 朱熹 as the Great Middle (*dazhong* 大中), we read:

> Without deflection, without unevenness,
> Pursue the splendid righteousness.
> Without any selfish preferences,
> Pursue the middle path;

---

[16] *Taishō shinshū daizōkyō* 45, pp. 152-153.
[17] Fung, pp. 245-246.

Without deflection, without partiality,
Broad and long is the middle path.
Without partiality, without deflection,
The middle path is level and easy;
Without perversity, without one-sidedness,
The middle path is right and straight.[18]

In the case of Sanlun Buddhism, the concept of the Middle Path, inherited from Nāgārjuna, is interpreted as the "emptiness" which can be arrived at only through unceasing negative dialectic, free from all names; it is "inexplicable in speech and unrealisable in thought," and therefore rid of all discursive sophistry or playful discourse. There emerges then the universal principle of spiritual equality according to which all dharmas, conceived from the viewpoint of emptiness, would show no sign of difference and are, therefore, equal one to another, and seen as different facets and manifestations of the same Bhūtatathatā. Summing up the spirit of the Mahāprajñāpāramitā sūtra, Jizang said:

> Such a doctrine is recondite and abstruse, deep and profound as to be unfathomable. ... the primal theme of the sūtra under discussion is to entertain the Dharma-nature with nothing particular to dwell upon and the ultimate fulfillment of the Dharma-nature is to attain nothing whatever that has been gained.[19]

Here all dharmas are equal, not because all of them are the "irreducible other," or that their otherness is worthy of our unconditional generosity, but rather because ultimately speaking they are empty, without substance and without gain. The true meaning of prajñā therefore accords well with the philosophy of emptiness. I myself am quite amazed by the three typologies of wisdom according to Jizang: first, the Ultimate wisdom (*shixian prajñā* 實相般若), which penetrates genuinely into the Ultimate Reality, or the emptiness of all things; second, the illumining wisdom (*zhenguan prajñā* 正觀般若), which throws light upon the Ultimate Reality in all its different facets and manifestations; third, the linguistic wisdom (*wenzi prajñā* 文字般若), with powerful linguistic expressions elucidating the perfect congruence between the Ultimate Reality and its manifestations. Unfortunately, the Sanlun School's negative dialectic that aimed at emptiness and no-gain, though rich in the abstract art of refutation and negation, was unable to give the common people any positive values for everyday life and was therefore divorced from the Chinese mind. This explains the reason that it declined in the 9th century.

---

[18] *The Shoo King, or the Book of Historical Documents*, tr. James Legge (Oxford: Clarendon Press, 1893-1895), pp. 331-332.

[19] Fang, p. 199.

THE DIMENSION OF THE OTHER IN YOGĀCĀRA

In the case of Weishi Buddhism, prajñā consists in moving away from the two extremes; there is neither the grasper nor the grasped, and yet still there remains the nature of depending on others, which, though non-substantial and still to be purified, is not to be annihilated. For the Weishi, non-discriminating wisdom realizes the true thusness and the Bhūtatathatā, depending on the marvelous being of consciousness. Yogācāra attains wisdom not by the method of negative dialectic, but by its yoga praxis that purifies and finally transforms consciousness into wisdom. The idealistic doctrine of this school is quite often exaggerated, so that there is no self, no dharmas, but Consciousness Only, and everything else is merely a definite form of the manifestation of Consciousness. For me, the most interesting philosophy of the school of Consciousness Only is its analysis of consciousness, which serves as a praxiological program and the conversion of consciousness into wisdom as the final goal of spiritual achievement.

Weishi is famous, not to say notorious, in its awesomely detailed analyses and minute classifications, presented most completely in the so-called 100 dharmas, which are classified into five categories: Citta-dharma (mind), Caitasika-dharma (mental contents), Rūpa-dharma (material elements), Citta-viprayukta-samskāra (things not associated with mind) and Asamskrta-dharma (non-created elements). These were elaborated out of the 75 dharmas of the Abhidharma-kosa.[20] All these minute distinctions lead to what Dr. Hu Shi 胡適 called "a tedious scholastic philosophy."[21] This could be seen as one of the reasons that Weishi was not easily accessible to the people, except for a few sophisticated intellectuals.

We have to understand that Yogācāra's minute distinctions and classifications are not purely intellectual inventions, as they appear in the process of yoga praxis. They are very useful in discerning where one is and where to proceed in one's spiritual itinerary. Even if we could find intellectual pleasure in these kinds of minute conceptual distinctions, without spiritual progress all kinds of distinctions prove themselves to be in vain and without gain.

Yoga praxis itself, though not to be seen as an intellectual invention, is very much related to Buddhist Scriptures and, therefore, to a "textual other" in order to appropriate it in a process leading to wisdom. This is very clear in its Indian origin. For example, in the Mahāyānasūtrālamkāra of Asanga, a special regard was paid to Scriptural texts and the hermeneutic understanding of their meaning. We find this in the teaching and lesson explored in the fourteenth chapter of the Mahāyānasūtrālamkāra, which (in describing the way of praxis towards the

---

[20] Junjiro Takakesu, *The Essentials of Buddhist Philosophy*. 3rd ed. (Honolulu: Office Appliance Co., 1956), pp. 72-74.
[21] Hu Shi, *A Short Intellectual History of Mediaeval China* 中國中古思想小史 (Taipei 台北: Academia Sinica, 1969), p. 106.

fullest unfolding of Bodhisattvahood), seems to emphasize the textual other and the hermeneutic procedure of treating it, by starting with linking one's mind to the names of sūtras, then censuring gradually the categories of words and their meaning (*artha*), both individually and collectively.[22] There, dharma seems to be found in the sutra, *geya*, and so on.[23]

In the Mahāyānasūtrālamkāra, six kinds of thought are discerned in the study of texts: fundamental thought, consecutive thought, thought of pondering, thought of affirmation, thought of subsumption, and thought of expectation. Some of these have their own subdivisions of steps or methods. For example, in the case of pondering thought, we have methods such as calculation, comparison, reflection, and perspicacious observation of Buddhist texts. These hermeneutic considerations and understandings of textual meaning lead eventually to the self-awareness that "the thought is the only foundation and there is nothing other than thought."[24]

The practitioner then should go through eleven kinds of mental acts[25] and nine steps of elaboration,[26] which show gradual progression to enlightenment and are, therefore, very interesting from the point of view of spiritual praxiology and pedagogy. For my part, what is most remarkable is that, once one arrives at supra-mundane wisdom, one achieves equality of oneself with others. There is five-fold equality: equally no-self, equally suffering, equally working, equally lacking of payment in return, and equally like other Bodhisattvas. In his compassion for all creatures, the practitioner does all his best for their welfare; he employs himself in the *artha* of their life, and he is tireless for his work, for which he has no anxiety and expects no return from others. This shows unconditional generosity towards others. In Chapter 14 of Mahāyānasūtrālamkāra, we read the following two verses:

Verse 38:
Those who, without the view of self, have here the view of self,

---

[22] Read for example verses 4, 5, in Chapter 14 in Asanga, *Mahāyānasūtrālamkāra*, trans. S. V. Lamaye (Delhi: Sri Satguru Publications, 1992). From time to time this translation needs corrections. Here I pick up this Scripture to serve my purpose of comparing Indian Yogācāra with Chinese Weishi in respect to the problem of the other.

[23] This is very similar to the Yogācāryabhūmi-śāstra. See for example Yogācāryabhūmi-śāstra in *Taishō shinshū daizōkyō*, 30, pp. 418-419.

[24] Asanga, p. 262.

[25] These include discursive thought, judgment, non-discursive thought, judgment alone, non-the discursive and non-judgmental mental act of pacification, the mental act of inspection, the mental act of tying and checking, the mental act of retaining, the mental act of causing pacification, the mental act of causing apathy, the mental act of continuation, the mental act of good deeds, etc.

[26] These steps include holding thought, restraining, retaining, supporting, taming, appeasing, appeasing more, rendering unified, and waiting.

Those who without suffering, are extremely afflicted for others,
Those who develop the work of all without waiting for returns.[27]

Verse 41:
The sons of the victor have affections for the creatures;
They have employment, and they are tireless,
He (Bodhisattva) is the supreme marvel in the worlds; or rather
not!
As the others and self are identical for him.[28]

We should point out that this kind of unconditional generosity towards the other is preponderant in Asanga's writings. Take another example: in Chapter 4 of the Bodhisattva-bhūmi, where Asanga discusses the problem of knowing reality (Tattvartha), it is written:

> The Bodhisattva has many benefits: he rightly engaged in
> thoroughly ripening the Buddhadharmas for himself and
> for others, in thoroughly ripening the Dharma of the Three
> Vehicles. Moreover, thus rightly engaged, he is without
> craving for possessions or even for his own body…. You
> should know that the Bodhisattva thus rightly engaged
> carefully attends all virtuous beings with worship and
> reverence. And all un-virtuous beings he carefully attends
> with a mind of sympathy and a mind of supreme
> compassion. And in so far as he can and has the strength,
> he is engaged in dispersing their faults. He carefully
> attends all harmful beings with a mind of love. And in so
> far as he can and has the strength, being himself without
> trickery and without deceit, he works for their benefit and
> happiness, to eliminate the hostile consciousness of those
> who do evil because of their faults of expectation and
> practice.[29]

It was probably because of his respect for the "textual other" that Xuanzang made the effort to travel to India and bring 657 Buddhist scriptures back – and why he translated 75 of them into Chinese. However, generally speaking, the Chinese Weishi School did not much discuss the hermeneutic procedure of treating the textual other. Even less discussed was the "ethical other" as the subject of unconditional generosity. Rather, it put more emphasis on the purification of consciousness and its transformation into wisdom. Even when "equality" was mentioned, it did not evoke so

---

[27] Asanga, p. 274.
[28] Asanga, p. 275.
[29] Asanga, p. 156-157.

much an unconditional generosity towards the other, but rather mentioned it as a spiritual horizon to be attained.

I tend to think that the dimension of the other might have begun to be reduced in the development of Indian Yogācāra, but its reduction becomes more evident in the Chinese Weishi School: from ontological otherness to constructed otherness, to transcendental emptiness of the other. This is what is implied in Professor Thomé Fang's argument that Yogācāra begins with a kind of descriptive phenomenology taking the one hundred dharmas as description of reality, thus sharing some views of the Abhidharmakosa. Then, it is developed into a constructive phenomenology in the form of critico-epistemological idealism. Finally, it culminates in the transcendental phenomenology that might well be reconciled to some extent with the philosophy of sunyata based upon the Mahāprajñāpāramitrā sūtra.[30] In this process of appropriation, the other might be reduced to a transcendentally constructed otherness or even an empty otherness, giving rise to no unconditional generosity. The focus, therefore, is now on the purification of one's consciousness.

STRUCTURE OF CONSCIOUSNESS AND ITS PURIFICATION

The purification of consciousness takes the form of consciousness analysis. We find there is an analytic progression from the five consciousnesses to the empirical self-consciousness, to the transcendental self-consciousness, and then finally to the ontological origin of all consciousness, the Alaya-vijñāna. Five sense perceptions – seeing, hearing, touching, smelling, and tasting – are seen as the five consciousnesses. Consciousness properly speaking follows; this is empirically the center of the five sensations or the sense-centered consciousness, which could be called the empirical self-consciousness.

For my part, it is philosophically questionable to separate these six "consciousnesses," or to separate the five consciousnesses from the sixth, because, when there is consciousness of their activities, the five senses always work with empirical self-consciousness so as to form a conscious perception of the object. The five senses – or, at least, some of them – have to work together to reach the object perceived. Phenomenologically speaking, the object of perception appears in profiles, and we always perceive it with a certain "imagined totality." This is the effect of the co-working of the senses in body-movement and their passive synthesis in our empirical consciousness. The use of such a distinction consists only in the praxiological discernment; therefore, the distinction is itself methodological, not ontological.

Now, the seventh consciousness – as the thought-centered consciousness (the manas-vijñāna) from which come all willing and thinking, and which often attaches itself to its own imagined centeredness

---

[30] Fang, pp. 167-168.

as its own true self – is quite similar to the Cartesian *Je pense*, or the Husserlian transcendental Ego. Although the *Je pense* for Descartes and the transcendental Ego for Husserl are seen as the ultimate constituent of our self and the transcendental constituting dynamism of all our empirical experience, for the Weishi School, they are not the ultimate self, but only a derivative transformation of the eighth consciousness.

Finally, the eighth consciousness, the "storehouse consciousness" (alaya-vijñāna), contains all seeds or potentialities of right/wrong thoughts and good/evil deeds to be manifested and thereby effected in the former seven forms of consciousness, and it receives their influences. That is to say that alaya-vijñāna exercises a double process: on the one hand, it realizes the seeds into deeds and thoughts in the process of manifestation; on the other hand, it receives the influence or is fumigated by the former seven consciousnesses in its actual operation. All these distinctions in psychic layers are meaningful (but eventually abandoned) in the process of Yoga praxis for the benefit of the enlightened and the multitude of others; they should not to be imagined as real distinctions.

THE TRANSFORMATION OF CONSCIOUSNESS INTO WISDOMS

For me, the most interesting part of the philosophy of consciousness in the Weishi School consists in the conversion of consciousness into wisdom. This presupposes that we enter into the Ultimate Reality, either as alaya-vijñāna (according to the tradition of Xuanzang) or as bhūtatathatā itself (according to the tradition of Paramārtha), both related to but detached from all other dharmas and from the determination of all specific representations and names. From this Ultimate Reality, the eighth consciousness is transformed into mind/heart, corresponding to the wisdom of the grand perfect mirror. Then, based upon this, one could transform the seventh consciousness into mind/heart corresponding to the wisdom of equality. Then, upon these two, one could transform the sixth consciousness into mind/heart, corresponding to the wisdom of marvelous observation. Finally, basing upon all these, one could transform the five actual consciousnesses into the wisdom of achieving all deeds.[31]

---

[31]According to the Buddhabhumi, we are to "transform the eighth consciousness into the heart corresponding to the wisdom of grand perfect mirror, which is thus called because it could retain in itself all seeds of merits and virtues, and manifest and give birth to all representations of all bodies and lands; transform the seventh consciousness into the heart corresponding to the wisdom of equality, which is thus called because it is far away from the two extreme distinctions of self and other, and attests to the equality of all things. Transform the sixth consciousness into the heart corresponding to the wisdom of marvellous observation, which is thus called because it could regard all things without any hindrance. Transform the five actual consciousnesses into

There is a double process in the transformation of consciousness into wisdom. On the one hand, there is the process of retracing self-awareness, going back to deeper and more original layers of self-awareness from the five consciousnesses to the sixth, to the seventh, and to the eighth consciousness, until we arrive at the Original Ground, either the alaya-vijñāna or the bhūtatathatā. On the other hand, there is the process of purifying manifestation, which transforms first the eight consciousnesses into the wisdom of the grand perfect mirror, and then purifies and realizes the seventh consciousness into the wisdom of equality; next, it purifies and realizes the sixth consciousness into the wisdom of marvelous observation; finally, it purifies and realizes the five consciousnesses into the wisdom of achieving all deeds.

According to the tradition of Paramārtha in the 6th century, "The so-called original nature of heart is the true noumenon. The heart of all sentient being is imbued with equality. All sentient being is bhūtatathatā; all sentient being owns Buddha nature."[32] Yet according to the tradition of Xuanzang, not all sentient beings are capable of converting consciousness into wisdom and becoming Buddha.

We could say that the state of perfect wisdom, if any, is nothing but the functioning of the nature of consummate perfection (*parinispanna*). Weishi's theory of the three natures reveals to us a successive progression from the nature of imagined discrimination to that of dependence on others (*paratantra*) and then to that of consummate perfection. As the *Cheng Weishi Lun* says,

> One does not see the *paratantra* as long as one has not seen the *parinispanna*; when one has not perceived and realized *parinispanna* (by a prajñā that discerns immediately), one cannot discern the 'nature of *paratantra*,' for, not having yet understood that

---

the wisdom of achieving all actions, which is thus called because it is capable of realizing and achieving all external activities" (Buddhabhumi, in *Taishō shinshū daizōkyō*, 26, p. 302; my translation). On the other hand, according to Xuanzang's *Cheng Weishi Lun*, it is for the reason of encouraging sentient beings, and not for ontological reasons, that one should cling to wisdom and relinquish consciousness so that these four wisdoms are attained by the transformation of the eighth consciousness. "The four wisdoms are attained by the transformation of the mental attributes of the eighth, the seventh, the sixth, and the first five consciousnesses respectively.... In order to encourage sentient beings to cling to Wisdom and relinquish consciousness, we say that one attains the four wisdoms by virtue of the transformation of the eighth consciousness" (Xuanzang, p. 770 (1973).

[32] *Taishō shinshū daizōkyō*, 26, p. 305.

parikalpita is void (non-existent), one cannot in reality know the manner of existence of *paratantra.*[33]

The realization of the nature of consummate perfection, with which one comes to be in the Ultimate Reality, begins from the realization of the nature of depending on others: "That *parinispanna* is neither identical nor separated form *paratantra,*" and "this *parinispanna* is neither different nor non-different from that *paratrantra.*"[34] This is to show that the other, or the dependence on the other, and the world of dynamic relationship in which one depends on the other, are quite essential to the understanding of the Ultimate Reality and the attainment of consummate perfection.

It is very interesting to notice here that this relation between the three natures is quite similar to, though philosophically speaking still different from, the Heideggerian distinction of *Vorhandenheit,* *Zuhandenheit,* and *Dasein.*[35] According to Heidegger, those "beings-present-at-hand," in the mode of *Vorhandenheit,* are taken as substances without any connection to human existential concern, whereas those beings-ready-to-hand, in the mode of *Zuhandenheit* – as *Zeug* or tools around us referring one to another – would be able, under existential analysis, to show our existential concern. Finally, human beings as *Dasein,* by questioning concerning Being and by an authentic act of existence, could become manifestations of Being and serve as the "there" of Being. It is only by understanding through existential analysis beings-ready-to-hand in their mutual reference that we can understand Being's manifestation in human beings as *Dasein.* This Heideggerian notion is helpful for us to understand Xuanzang's notion of the relation between dependence on others and consummate perfection, in the sense that *Zuhandenheit*'s reference to one another could be understood as dependent on others, and that an existential analysis of *Zuhandenheit* may lead to the emergence of understanding *Dasein.*

CONCLUSION: REDISCOVERING THE DIMENSION OF THE OTHER

Chinese Buddhism's openness to the textual other and the ethical other culminates with Xuanzang's appropriation of Yogācāra Buddhism, even if the status of the other, from Indian Yogācāra Buddhism to Chinese Weishi Buddhism, has changed. Unfortunately, this openness to the other has undergone a process of reduction in Chan Buddhism. When Chan Buddhism came on the scene, it radicalised the proposition "All sentient beings can become Buddha" into "all sentient beings are originally

---

[33] Xuanzhang, p. 637.

[34] Xuanzhang, p. 635.

[35] Martin Heidegger, *Being and Time,* tr. J. Macquarrie and E. Robinson. (New York: SCM Press Limited, 1962), pp. 95-107.

Buddha," supposing that the Buddha nature or the absolute mind/heart is the same in everyone and everywhere. For Chan Buddhism, the bhūtatathatā reveals itself in the selfsameness of the absolute mind/heart and the everydayness of its manifestation. Since the self-nature of everyone, the bhūtatathatā, reveals itself in the self-sameness of the absolute mind/heart, there is no place for the other. In the Platform Sūtra, transformation of consciousness into wisdom is merely nominal, not noumenal. It reads:

> It is the nature of the wisdom of a grand mirror to be pure and calm; the wisdom of equality means no sickness of one's mind/heart; the wisdom of marvellous observation sees no merit of one's own; the wisdom of achieving all deeds is the same as the grand mirror. The fifth and the eighth transformations work on the side of cause, and the seventh and the sixth transformations work on the side of effect. They are all but transformations of names, not transformations of noumenon.[36]

For Chan Buddhism, there is no need to refer to the Scriptures.[37] Those who practise Chan Buddhism use *dhyāna* to attain their Buddha nature and combine it with the *prajñā*, going so far as to identify the two as one.[38] There is the primacy of practice over any argumentation and hermeneutics of texts. Chan masters use situational methods of teaching in order to let their disciples penetrate into their own Buddha nature, sometimes even by beating and shouting, such as in the case of Linji Chan. Although this method might lead to a direct insight into the unfathomable emptiness without the need to discern any progressive steps,[39] it tends to deny the function of language and texts, which is very important for human civilization and philosophy. Chan's denial of language and texts leads to shouting and beating, the effect of which on human understanding is still

---

[36] *Taishō shinshū daizōkyō*, 48, p. 356.

[37] For example, we read, in the Platform Sutra, "Therefore it is known that we possess prajñā in our own nature, and we should always contemplate by using our own wisdom, without going through scriptures (故知本性自有般若之智，自用智慧，常觀照故，不假文字)" (*Taishō shinshū daizōkyō*, 48, p. 350).

[38] We can see this point clearly in Huineng's 慧能 saying that "Calmness and wisdom are the foundation of my method... In the case of those whose hearts and words are both good and in whom the internal and the external are one, calmness and wisdom are identified. Self-enlightenment and practice do not consist in argument (我此法門以定慧為本。...心口俱善，內外一種，定慧即等。自悟修行，不在口諍)" (*Taishō shinshū daizōkyō*, 48, p. 352).

[39] *Taishō shinshū daizōkyō*, 48, p. 357. In Chinese: 聖諦尚不為，何階級之有?

hard to determine; unfortunately, the Scriptures are thereby abandoned without being carefully read.

Buddhism has long since penetrated both the intellectual and everyday life of the Chinese. This might have been pushed by Chan Buddhism, which has even gone so far as to become immanent in people's everyday life. As the Platform Sutra says:

> If one's heart is even, there is no need of obeying obligations. If one's act is right, there is no need of practicing dhyanāya... Prajñā is to be sought in one's heart; there is no need of searching for metaphysical truth in the external world. Just to listen, to say and to cultivate one's self in this way, the Western paradise appears just in the present moment.[40]

We should say that the loss of the dimension of the other in Chan Buddhism has brought huge changes to Buddhism in China. According to Nāgārjuna and Asanga in the Indian tradition, the Buddhist way of life should lead to compassion and altruism, to a way of existence for the enlightenment of the other, and of all sentient beings. Yet Chan Buddhism would interpret it as the enlightenment of one's own heart in everyday life. In everything great or small of everydayness there is the Dao of enlightenment. Though this has the merit of transforming Buddhism into being accessible in everyday life, by the same token it has taken Chinese life and philosophy into the realm of immanence, without being open to the other, or going outside of one's self and to the stranger, to the other.

This, among other characteristics, has a huge impact on capturing Chinese thought within the philosophy of immanence. Today, more contributions should be made to Chinese culture by bringing it back to the dimension of alterity or the other. We need the strategy of strangification and the virtue of generosity toward the other in order to transform Chinese culture, already rich in immanent resources, into a renovative cultural dynamism complemented by resources from alterity.

I believe that the Chinese mind in general and Chinese Buddhism in particular, like our ideal model Xuanzang, should be able to go outside of its familiarity and go to the stranger, to the other. It should learn again from the other and be generous towards the other. Such people of the Weishi School as Yang Rensan 楊仁山 and Ouyang Jingwu 歐陽竞無 have made an effort to modernize Buddhist studies and have paid much attention to Weishi's relation to science and speculative philosophy. Now, we should understand that praxis is more fundamental to Weishi than are science and

---

[40] *Taishō shinshū daizōkyō*, 48, p. 352) In Chinese: 心平何勞持戒，行直何用修禪。恩則孝養父母，義則上下相憐。讓則尊卑和睦，忍則眾惡無諠.... 菩提只向心覓，何勞向外求玄。聽說依此修行，西方只在目前。

speculative philosophy. In praxis, there is always the dimension of the other. We should continue to appropriate the other by translating unceasingly the other into our familiarity, and, on the other side, by unceasingly going outside of our selves and our familiarity to the side of the other, of strangeness and alterity, with an original and unconditional generosity. In this way, we could truly realize a process of mutual enrichment.

Lee Chair in Chinese Thought and Culture
Department of Philosophy and Department of East Asian Studies
University of Toronto
Toronto, Canada

REFERENCES

Asanga. *On Knowing Reality: The Tattvartha Chapter of Asanga's Bodhisattvabhumi*. Tr. with introduction, commentary, and notes by Janice Dean Willis (New York: Columbia University Press, 1979).

Asanga. *Mahāyānasūtrālamkāra*. Tr. S. V. Lamaye (Delhi: Sri Satguru Publications, 1992).

Chan, Win-tsit. *A Source Book in Chinese Philosophy* (Princeton: Princeton University Press, 1969).

Fang, Thomé 方東美. *Chinese Philosophy: Its Spirit and Its Development* (Taipei: Linking Press, 1981).

Fung, Yu-lan 馮友蘭. *A Short History of Chinese Philosophy* (Toronto: Collier-Macmillan, 1948).

Heidegger, Martin. *Being and Time*. Tr. J. Macquarrie and E. Robinson (New York: SCM Press Limited, 1962).

Hu Shi 胡適. *A Short Intellectual History of Mediaeval China* 《中國中古思想小史》, (Taipei 台北: Academia Sinica, 1969).

Jizang 吉藏. *Rambling Thoughts about the Mahaprajnaparamita Sutra*, in Taishō sinshū daizōkyō, Vol. 38.

Legge, James, trans. *The Shoo King, or the Book of Historical Documents* (Oxford: Clarendon Press, 1893-1895).

Mauss, Marcel « Essai sur le don. Formes et raison de l'échange dans les société archaïques » 1923-1924, in *Sociologie et anthropologie* (Paris: PUF, 1968).

Shen, Vincent. *Confucianism, Taoism and Constructive Realism* (Wien: WUV-. Universitätsverlag, 1994).

Shen, Vincent. "Inter-religious Dialogue Between Buddhism and Christianity Conceived with Strangification and Contrast." In *The Movement of Constructive Realism*, edited by Thomas Slunecko (Wien: Wilhelm Braumüller, 1997).

Shen,   Vincent.   *Contrast,   Strangification   and   Dialogue*
《對比、外推與交談》(Taipei 臺北: Wunan Publishing Company
五南出版社, 2002).

Taishō shinshū daizōkyō (Abbreviated as TSD) 《大正新修大藏經》,
1924-1932. ed. Takakusu and K.Watanabe. Vols. 1.30.45.48. Tokyo:
Taisho Issaikyo Kankokai.

Takakesu, Junjiro. *The Essentials of Buddhist Philosophy*. 3rd ed.
(Honolulu: Office Appliance Co., 1956).

Wallner, Fritz. *Acht Vorlesungen über den Konstruktiven Realismus* (Wien:
WUV-. Universitätsverlag, 1992).

Xuanzang (Hsuan Tsang) 玄奘. *Ch'eng Wei-shih Lun*, tr. from the Chinese
texts by Wei Tat (Hong Kong: Dai Nippon Printing Co., 1973).

Xuanzang (Hsuan Tsang). "Report of Returning Country 陳還國表." In
Selected   Materials   for   Chinese   Buddhist
Thought《中國佛教思想資料選編》. Vol. 2. Book 3 (Beijing 北京:
Zhonghua Shuju 中華書局, 1989).

CHAPTER XXIII

DAOISM AND SUSTAINABLE DEVELOPMENT: AN INTEGRATIVE PERSPECTIVE[1]

CHEN XIA and *CHEN YONG*

INTRODUCTION

When humanity entered the second half of the twentieth century, a series of problems related to population, resources, environment and development appeared or intensified worldwide. How to tackle such problems has been a great challenge facing numerous countries and the world as a whole. In the early 1980s the World Commission on Environment and Development was established under the sponsorship of the General Assembly of the United Nations and in 1987 it published a significant report, "Our Common Future," in which the classic definition of "sustainable development" is given and a series of related issues are discussed. The World Conference on Environment and Development held in Rio de Janeiro in 1992 marked the maturity of the concept of sustainable development and its acceptance by the world community. Although it originated in the science of ecology,[2] it has now become an interdisciplinary concept linking economics, politics, society, culture, technology, natural resources and the environment. Since its appearance in the mid 1970s, this concept has evolved and is still being enriched by various disciplines.

Sustainable development is a vision of development which differs from that defined by traditional economists which has GNP as its sole indicator.[3] What is most significant about the concept is its emphasis on conservation of natural resources and environmental protection for the sake of human and social development. The pursuit of human welfare is the ultimate purpose of sustainable development. It is becoming clear that the

[1] *Acknowledgements:* We are grateful to Ms. Maria Grazia Quieti from the United Nations Food and Agricultural Organization, who encouraged us to write this paper and showed a constant concern for the completion of it. We also appreciate the help of Ms. Camilla Krueger in proofreading and correcting the paper. Prof. Deng Peng's encouragement and a reviewer's comments helped us to finish this paper. Comments from the Conference on "The Dialogue of Cultural Traditions: A Global Perspective" August 8-9, 2003, Istanbul gave us much insight into this topic.
[2] C.J. Barrow, "Sustainable Development: Concept, Value and Practice," *Third World Planning Review*, 17 (1995): 369-386.
[3] M. Little, "The Liberation of Development," *Geojournal*, 35.2 (1995): 123-35.

environmental crisis is a manifestation of a social and spiritual crisis. We need to change our attitudes to nature and the aims of life if we want to return to the balance between development and natural preservation. A macro-shift of worldviews and a philosophy based on different traditions are urgently required. Though religion has been comparatively late in initiating its involvement with these issues, it is now quite active in discussing ecology. Religions offer interpretations of the world and shape the human being's relationship with it. If we re-interpret these teachings on human and nature and make small changes in the lives of individuals, salvation can come to mean different things.

Daoism absorbed many ideas from Daojia (philosophical Daoism) and evolved into a religious tradition. Since its inception over 1800 years ago as China's indigenous religion, and through its history of interaction with Buddhism, Confucianism, and other religious traditions, Daoism has evolved a system of concepts and practices uniquely relevant to the relationship between man and nature. Daoism contains, in its creeds, tenets, and practices, many ideas compatible with the concept of environmental protection.

"DAO FOLLOWS SPONTANEITY" (DAOFA ZIRAN), AND THE PROTECTION OF ENVIRONMENT AND NATURE

In pursuing sustainable development, mankind must abandon the traditional road of development that has overemphasized economic profit without considering the supporting capacity of the environment. As we attempt to satisfy the needs of the present generation, we should leave space for the development of future generations. In this regard, our forefathers have left us a heritage, and Daoism has left notions such as the "Unity of Heaven and Man" (tianren heyi), and the ideas that "The Heavenly Way is Non-interference" (tiandao wuwei) and that "the three realms draw resources from each other" (sancai xiangdao); these are all worthy of our attention.

"The Unity of Heaven and Man": A Concept of Totality

"Dao" is the transcendent concept of Daoism. In Daoism all things originated from "Dao", and "Dao" is the basis of the existence of all beings. In the *Book of Dao and its Virtue* (Daodejing), it is said: "Dao begets one. One begets two. Two begets three. Three begets all things."[4] In the "Immortals' Book of Salvation of the World by the Manifestation of Dao from the Supreme Concourse" (Taishang huadao dushi xianjing), a Daoist scripture, it is stated that Dao is the Mother of Heaven and Earth and of

---

[4] *The Book of Dao and its Virtue* (Daodejing; Tao Te Ching): Foreign Language Teaching and Research Press, Beijing, 1998

Yin-Yang, and the origin of the Five Agents and of the myriad beings[5]. Man and all other beings are born from the same primordial Breath (Qi)[6], so that all beings emanate from Dao and obtain their essence from Dao. Meng Anpai proposed in his *Daojiao yishu* that all sentient beings, and even fruit, wood and stones, partake of the essence of Dao.[7] Similarly, the Book of Western Ascension (*Xisheng jing*) considers that Dao not only exists in me, but in all things.[8] All things in the world are inseparable and interdependent. Thus a Daoist poem sings that "Heaven and Earth have the same roots as me, all things share the same body with me. The human body is the micro-cosmos, Heaven and Earth are the macro-cosmos."[9] In the Book of the Hidden Talisman of the Yellow Emperor (*Huangdi yinfu jing*), people are instructed to follow the heavenly Dao, as it is said that "Both birth and death are the ways of Dao. Heaven and Earth are drawn by the myriad beings; the myriad beings are drawn by human beings and human beings are drawn by the myriad beings. If the three forms of drawing are in harmony, the three types of beings (Heaven and Earth, human beings, and the myriad beings) will be in peace." The notions of Heaven and Earth "sharing the same body as human beings" and "Heaven, Earth and Man exploiting each other" represent Daoist concepts of totality. Daoism seeks the lofty realm of nearness to Dao and sharing one body with the cosmos.

Under the influence of the Judaeo-Christian tradition and the mechanistic thought represented by the English philosopher Francis Bacon and the French mathematician Rene Descartes, the Western world has succeeded in dominating nature to a degree unprecedented in human history.[10] Industrial civilization has liberated human beings from nature. However, it has been accompanied by a growing ecological crisis. Regarding this situation Aurelio Peccei, the chairman of the Club of Rome, once commented that, while using science and technology in different ways, people have forgotten the spiritual principles, ethics and beliefs that can teach them how to use these things appropriately.[11] Most importantly, the present generation has lost the concept of holism. Our present society

---

[5] See the *Daoist Canon* (*Dao Zang*) [The Book of Western Ascension (*Xishengjing*)] (Wenwu Press / Shanghai Bookstore Press / Tianjin Ancient Book Press, 1988), vol. 11, p. 403.

[6] The Immortals' Book of Salvation of the World by the Manifestation of Dao from the Supreme Concourse (*Taishang Huadao Dushi Xianjing*): in Daoist Canon, ibid., vol. 22, p. 382.

[7] *ibid.*, vol. 24, p. 832.

[8] *ibid.*, vol. 11, [The Book of Western Ascension (*Xishengjing*)], p. 510.

[9] *ibid.*, vol. 33, p. 129.

[10] Yingzhang Li, *The Fall of Nature and Its Salvation (ziran de chenglun yu zhengjiu* (Beijing: China Social Science Press, 1996).

[11] See Philippe Braillard, "New Political Values for a World in Crisis: The Approach of the Club of Rome," *International Political Science Review / Revue internationale de science politique*, 3 (1982): 238-245.

should revitalize this concept. The Daoist concept of totality implied in "the Unity of Man and Heaven" and the idea that "The Three Realms exploit each other" can be a basis for establishing a modern environmental ethics.

"The Heavenly Way is Non-interference" (tiandao wuwei): The Daoist Attitude towards Nature

Since nature and man are a harmonious whole and mankind is an integral part of it, man should take into account the eternity of heaven and earth and pass on his ancestors' traditions to future generations, while assisting Heaven in the process of Creation and Earth in giving Form to beings.[12] Man can only survive and develop by being in harmony with his environment. So Daoism advocates that humans must be natural and do no harm to nature. It tells people to follow the laws of nature and not to "go against its Way." In the Book of Dao and its Virtue, it is said that "Man abides by Earth, Earth by Heaven, Heaven by Dao, Dao by Nature." In the eyes of a Daoist, Man, Earth, Heaven, Dao and Nature are bound together in an organic chain. In this chain Nature plays a very important role, for everything ultimately abides by Nature. "Nature" in Daoism means "to be spontaneous, to be genuine, not to be artificial." It also refers to the natural environment outside the human body. Daoism advocates "allowing things to be in their natural way" (*renwu ziran*), "letting things follow their natural phases" (*yinying wuxing*); "the Heavenly Way is Non-interference" (*tiandao ziran wuwei*). All of this is advocated in order to let everything fully develop and maintain a world of bio-diversity. In the Book of Great Peace (*Taiping jing*), "affluence" is defined as follows: "Affluence means that every creature is maintained. When everything is born, heaven regards it as rich. In ancient antiquity, at the beginning of recorded history, there were 12,000 species, indicating wealth. In middle antiquity (three thousand years ago), the number of species declined a little, and there were fewer than 12,000 species, indicating relative poverty. In the period of lower antiquity, the number of species declined further, indicating even greater poverty. If you wish to know the effect, just imagine your house without any rare articles or valuables, just like that of a poor family. If there are fewer than ten thousand creatures, there is extreme poverty, indicating the poverty of Heaven and Earth.... Heaven is our father and Earth is our mother. If the parents are extremely poor, the children will be worried with poverty."[13] In modern times, thousands of species are disappearing from the world each year. The worries of the Book of Great Peace remain highly relevant today.

---

[12] Ming Wang, *Taipingjing he jiao* (Beijing: Chinese Book Press, 1960), p. 36.

[13] Wang Ming, *Taipingjing he jiao* (Beijing: Chinese Book Press (zhonghu shuju), 1960), p. 30.

According to its tenet of "Let things be natural," Daoism opposes the destruction of the natural environment. Daoism considers that man and nature are interrelated and bound by ties of reciprocity and retribution. If man is in agreement with nature, and nature is well treated by human beings, the world will be peaceful and harmonious, and all things will be prosperous – a situation beneficial to man. If nature suffers from human beings, it will retaliate against man, causing calamitous suffering and the extinction of species. The disastrous floods which occurred in the middle and the lower reaches of Yangtzi River in the summer of 1998 are a good example of nature's retaliation. As Mr. Zhuang Guotai, an official in the Chinese State Environmental Protection Bureau, commented: "The occurrence of the great flood is related to the destruction of the ecosystem in the upper reaches of the Yangtzi River."[14] In the early 1880s Friedrich Engels mentioned the great damage that the people on the Po Plain in Italy suffered from torrents and floods due to the clearance of the trees in the Alps. Man should learn from the Daoist tradition of ecological wisdom, following the laws of nature to live in harmony with it.

DAOISM'S ATTITUDE TOWARDS LIFE: "VALUE HUMAN BEINGS AND EMPHASIZE LIFE" (GUIREN ZHONGSHEN)

Sustainable development is a vision of development that puts human beings at its center. In the Rio de Janeiro Declarations on the Environment, it is stated that human beings are at the center of concerns for sustainable development, and that they are entitled to a healthy and productive life in harmony with nature. This human-centered idea of development is also put forth in the Population and Development Program of Action adopted at the International Conference on Population and Development held in Cairo in 1994. Sustainable development is a denial of the traditional development model that is solely based on economic attainment. The experience of developing countries in the past decades has shown that traditional development has put them in even heavier debt without alleviating their poverty. While traditional development emphasizes the process of development, it tends to ignore its ultimate aim and purpose. On the other hand, sustainable development is concerned with both the process and the end goal and fruits of development. Considering the requirements of sustainable development, we should reconsider the traditional pattern of development.

Daoism, in doctrines similar to the philosophy of sustainable development, puts humans at the center and pursues the value of human life. Daoism is a human-centered religion. Having attached great importance to life, Daoism always attempts to prolong life and improve its quality. All Daoist sects stress human life and value life. The philosophical

---

[14] Jianwu Liu, "We Cannot Blame God for the Big Flood this Summer," *Workers' Daily (gongren ribao)* (August 1998).

Daoist school of Yang-Zhu in the period prior to the Qin Dynasty (221-206 BCE) considered the most important thing in the world to be life. Of all things in the world, Daoism considers human life to be the most precious thing, and of all good things, longevity ranks the uppermost. Both Daoism and sustainable development share the idea that human life is the most important thing in the world. In order to enrich the concept of sustainable development, it is necessary for us to return to and learn from the old religious traditions.

LAOZI'S IDEA OF "SMALL NATIONS WITH A SMALL POPULATION" (XIAOGUO GUAMIN): AN EARLY VIEW OF POPULATION CONTROL

Since population was closely related to the strength of a state in the ancient times of China, most Chinese rulers tended to encourage the growth of a large population. Under the influence of Confucianism, the Chinese used to believe in popular sayings such as "More children, greater happiness" and "Of the three types of filial impieties, no offspring ranks first." Contrary to the mainstream culture of Confucianism of ancient and modern China, Daoism advocates giving birth at an appropriate age. Laozi opposed overpopulation, advocating states with a small population.

Concerning human reproduction, Daoism does not approve of abstinence. In the Book of Great Peace, men and women are considered to be manifestations of Yin and Yang (male and female); therefore, marriage and reproduction are seen as the foundation of human society. On the other hand, Daoism is opposed to indulgence in sensual pleasures and excessive sexual activity. According to the Daoist art of Cultivation and Refinement, people should value their Primordial Breath (*yuan qi*). Excessive ejaculation and childbirth were considered to use up one's 州 Primordial Breath. Daoist techniques of "Controlling Desires and Keeping the Essence" (*jieyu baojing*) aimed at storing up Primordial Breath for the sake of attaining longevity. As a result, the population would not increase so fast and the quality of the population would improve.

Nowadays most countries in the world agree with the goal of limiting the population while improving its quality. As early as the late 18th century, T. R. Malthus realized that since the amount of cultivable land on this planet is limited and the productivity of the land restricted, increase in food production couldn't keep up with an increasing population. Although Malthus's theory and the methods of controlling population have aroused much criticism, it is well known that the supporting capacity of the earth is limited and the planet cannot support an indefinite number of human beings. It has been recognized that the issue of population control is at the center of sustainable development. Since human beings are important consumers of natural resources and producers of waste, population increase and the improvement of people's living standards have a direct impact on natural resources and the environment. On one hand, an increase in population will exert a greater pressure on the ecosystem, leading to depletion of natural resources. On the other hand, the increase in population will degrade the environment of human habitats due to pollution. The United Nations has called on all governments to contribute to an early stabilization of the world population. Laozi's idea of "small nations with a small population" is still relevant to the present situation of overcrowding and overpopulation.

"THE HEAVENLY DAO DIMINISHES THE EXCESSIVE AND REPLENISHES THE DEFICIENT" (TIANZHIDAO, SUNYOUYU ER BUBUZU): THE VIEW OF SOCIAL EQUITY IN DAOISM

The Daoist concept of inherited merit or guilt (*chengfu*) is related to the equity between generations. It warns people not to leave debts to future generations, lest their descendants suffer hideous disasters. Merits and evils inherited from the past are called *cheng*, while those passed down to future generations are called *fu*. According to the Book of Great Peace, our ancestors once lived in accordance with the will of Heaven. Unaware of their small errors, they passed them down to later generations, and now the present generation is irresponsible towards its descendants. Hence, *chengfu* reveals that evils may accumulate between generations through the inheritance of sin. If sins caused by former generations accumulate, the later generations will experience retribution; if former generations accumulate merit, the later generations will benefit from them. This is true of the problem of environment. People used to say: "One generation plants trees, the next generation can rest under the shadow." This is *chengfu* with respect to the environment in a positive way. The fact that large-scale deforestation in the period from the Qin dynasty (221-206 BCE) to the Han dynasty (206 BCE-220 CE) left us endless troubles is a good example of such an inheritance. The Daoist concept of *chengfu* counsels people to protect the environment, which is beneficial to future generations. In the process of exploiting natural resources, we should not kill the hen to get the eggs or drain the pond to get the fish: we should give future generations the opportunity to develop.

Besides emphasizing equity among generations, sustainable development stresses equity among people of the present generation. Is it not irrational to care for the welfare of future generations, while ignoring the poor and suffering of our own generation? Up to now industrialized nations have consumed a great amount of the world's resources and energy, and have exerted a great influence on global environmental change. Since they still occupy an advantageous place in the international economic system, the industrialized nations are and will continue to occupy and consume most of the world's resources and energy. The developed nations, then, have a strong responsibility in solving global environmental problems, and they have an obligation to help to enhance the capability of developing nations in conserving natural resources. More and more people have recognized that poverty is a big environmental problem. In developing countries, many people have no other way but to rely on local resources in order to survive, leading to the inevitable over-use of resources and degradation of the environment. Since the global ecosystem is an organic entity, the destruction of any part of it may result in a series of reactions threatening the survival of people and development in other places. As pointed out in the Rio Declaration on Environment and Development, in order to reduce the gap in living standards in the world and better satisfy people's needs, all nations and individuals should cooperate in fighting poverty, which is a prerequisite to achieving global sustainable development. Daoist ideas of helping the poor and relieving the distressed embody the principles of equity and commonality in the concept of sustainable development.

In the *Book of Dao and its Virtue*, it is said that the heavenly Dao diminishes the excessive and replenishes the deficient. In the *Wenchang dijun yinzhi wen*, a Daoist moral tract, it is said that "to help the needy is like saving the fish in a dry river; to rescue the endangered is like relieving the bird caught in a net. Show pity to the orphan and take care of the widow, respect the aged and have compassion for the poor. Give clothes and food to the hungry on the way.... Help your relatives when your family is rich, and aid the neighbors when famine comes." Daoism advocates sharing treasures among people, not to hoard them as one's own. The *Book of Great Peace* says that goods are the property of Heaven, of Earth and of the Central Harmony, which together make use of them in order to nourish mankind. Money and other riches in the treasury are not destined to provide for the needs of a single man; all those who do not have enough are entitled to draw on them. It is necessary to let these goods circulate. It also says that it is a sin to accumulate riches and refuse to give them to the poor, letting them die of starvation and cold. Those guilty of this sin cannot be excused.

Sustainable development calls for social equity and gender equality, which are essential to achieve sustainable development. Any development model which disregards equity and equality will increase the gap between the poor and the rich, and has no dynamic sustainability.[15] Development achieved on the basis of discriminating against women and children or without considering their needs, is not sustainable. In its attitude to women, Daoism is quite different from some other cultural traditions. Daoism values softness and modesty. In Daoism, man and woman are both important components of the world. Equality between the sexes comes from the idea of the "balance between yin and yang." In the Book *of Great Peace* it is said that the nature of Heaven and Earth is half yin and half yang. Ever since the world distanced itself from Dao, discrimination against women has become widespread, leading to the diminution of yin and the loss of equilibrium between Heaven and Earth. The lonely yang element, without a companion, began to wither and dry up. Through its behaviour, society as a

---

[15] G. Annix, "Sustainable Development," *Development, No. 1* (1991).

whole shows its scorn for the original Mother and exterminates the terrestrial Energies. As the female element corresponds with the Earth, so the Earth is unhappy; natural disasters occur and the king's government does not find its balance.[16] Thus Daoism prohibits the ancient custom of despising and killing daughters. In a Daoist tract it is said that "drowning daughters is a great sin. The muddle-headed don't know, because no one warns them with moving words. Your mother is the daughter of someone, and your wife is the daughter of someone. Without daughters, how can you have a mother and a wife? Killing daughters is the most serious sin."[17] Daoism's concept of the equality between man and woman may be a contribution to the ethics of sustainable development.

"TO REDUCE SELFISHNESS AND RESTRAIN DESIRES" (SHAOSI GUAYU), AND SUSTAINABLE CONSUMPTION

Daoism considers that the orientation of life is to return to simplicity and go back to reality. One should live a simple, quiet and natural life. Daoism believes in a plain and simple lifestyle. It suggests that one not be selfish, but rather have few desires, and that one should live a life with plain tea and simple food. Daoism advocates frugality, maintaining that contentment with what one has brings happiness, making one's mind peaceful and free of troubles. The Xianger Commentary on Laozi (*Laozi Xianger Zhu*) reads: "Do not labor your mind to get more money to nourish your body, do not usurp power to glorify your self, do not indulge in the five flavours to satisfy your cravings. Though your clothes be tattered and your shoes ragged, you should still not strive for fame and gain."[18] *The Inner Book of the Master Embracing Simplicity* (*Baopuzi Neipian*) reads: "To learn to be immortal, one needs to live simply, to reduce desire, to look inside and to live with few desires." The *Book of Western Ascension* also has a negative attitude towards desire, saying, "Desire is the root of disasters; absence of desire is the origin of Heaven and Earth. If you don't know the Origin, you will not know the Root. The sacred person discards desire to cultivate himself." The *Book of Tranquility* (*Qingjing jing*) says, "If you keep away from desires, your mind becomes tranquil. The tranquil mind cleanses the spirit naturally." Daoism yearns for spiritual freedom and pursues spiritual satisfaction, free of the burden of material desires.

The Daoist idea of "reducing selfishness and restraining desires" is compatible with the lifestyle proposed by sustainable development. Nowadays, the main difficulty facing sustainable development is the unsustainable pattern of production and consumption. In developed countries and among rich people in the developing countries, excessive

---

[16] See Wang.

[17] *Zangwai Daoshu*, Vol. 28 (Chengdu: Bashu Book Press), p. 400.

[18] *The Xianger Commentary on Laozi* (*Laozi Xianger Zhu*): in the *Daoist Canon*, ibid., vol. 31.

consumption, especially the consumption of natural resources, is a common phenomenon. Today, as little as 25 percent of the world's population in the industrialized nations consumes 80 percent of the world's commercial energy, and the remaining 75 percent of the population, living in 128 countries, consume only 20 percent of the world's energy. In modern society, consumption is usually regarded as the symbol of success and social status. Wealth and luxury are considered to be signs of success. However, it is widely recognized that, above a certain level, wealth has no direct relation with happiness.[19] As a matter of fact, excessive consumption may accelerate the exhaustion of natural resources and exert a great pressure on the environment. In his book *Our Country, the Planet*, S. Ramphal, President of the World Conservation Union, states that the question of consumption is central to the issues of the environmental crisis. Human impact on the biosphere is producing environmental stress and endangering the planet's capacity to sustain life. Essentially, that impact is made through the energy and raw materials that people use or waste worldwide. For the interest of our descendants and the survival of the poor, it would be better to change our consumption pattern, to have a new concept of consumption, and to choose a simple life style. The Daoist concepts of "reducing selfishness and restraining desires," "returning to simplicity and going back to perfectness" and "discerning plainness and embracing simplicity" are important inspirations to modern people.

THE DAOIST PURSUIT OF "A LAND OF PARADISE ON EARTH" (DONGTIAN FUDI) AND SUSTAINABLE DEVELOPMENT OF THE HUMAN HABITAT

Daoism, like other religions around the world, yearns for an ideal realm. While it devotes itself to the construction of otherworldly realms, it works for this world's mortal dwellings as well. The ideal Daoist dwelling should have winding paths leading to pagodas and pavilions with numerous springs, abundant in animal and plant life. The environment is beautiful. In harmony with nature, man will have no worldly worries. The Daoist ideal dwelling is a model for the beautiful residence that human beings are seeking. In real life, Daoist temples are generally located on quiet mountains, far from noisy cities. They suffer no pollution and the ecology is good. At present in developed countries some people are tired of the noisy and busy urban lifestyle, preferring to go to the remote countryside to live a simple but environmentally sustainable life. "The centralization of population in great cities exercises of itself an unfavorable influence," wrote Friedrich Engels in 1844. "All putrefying vegetable and animal substances give off gases decidedly injurious to health, and if these gases have no free way of escape, they inevitably poison the atmosphere ... [the poor] are obliged to throw all offal and garbage, all dirty water, often all

---

[19] A. Maslow, *Motivation and Personality* (New York: Harper, 1954).

disgusting drainage and excrement into the streets, being without other means of disposing of them; they are thus compelled to infect the region of their own dwelling."[20]

Although what Engels described here was the life of the working class in the 19th century, the same situations can be still observed in the slum areas of some developing countries. The 21st Agenda, adopted in the Environment and Development Conference of the United Nations in Rio de Janeiro in 1992, has proposed the following overall aim of human habitats: to improve the social and economic environment of all human habitats, especially the living and working conditions of both rural and urban citizens. The Daoist ideal dwelling and the concept of building a heavenly land on earth provide an example for us to build a sustainable human habitat.

CONCLUSION

Established during the Eastern Han dynasty (25-220 CE), Daoism has become an important part of China's traditional culture. Daoist ideas on conservation of nature and development have had much influence on the Chinese and their society. Due to its unique ecological ideas, Daoism is expanding westward, exerting an increasing influence on Western society. The West is now beginning to benefit from the concept of the Unity of Heaven and Man, with the conservation of nature being one of the fruits. Cui Dahua argues that in modern times Daoism will show that it may contribute to lofty cultures and rational philosophies while it is interpreted in new ways and gains popular recognition.[21] In this paper, we have attempted to articulate a new interpretation of Daoism, linking it with the modern concept of sustainable development.

We acknowledge that there are limitations and weaknesses of Daoism's contribution to the environmental movement; it has not always, for instance, faced up to environmental problems nor did it address some concrete ecological issues directly. It failed to play its role in stopping environmental deterioration in China. But if we hermeneutically interpret its cosmology and teachings under new circumstances, make it a new, integrative culture through modern science and philosophy, embed it into Chinese daily life as it was in the past, and let its voice be heard by politicians, Daoism will show that it may contribute to contemporary culture and gain popular recognition.

---

[20] Friedrich Engels, *The Condition of the Working Class in England*, ed. Victor Kiernan (Harmondsworth: Penguin Classics, 1987), pp. 128-129.

[21] Cui Dahua, "Daoist Thought and its Implications in Modern Times," *Literature, History and Philosophy (wenshizhe)* Vol. 1 (1995).

Institute of Religious Studies
and
Institute of Population Research
Sichuan University
Chengdu, China

JAVANESE-ISLAMIC VALUE CONSENSUS: A NOTE ON THE LIBERAL COMMITMENT TO PLURALISTIC VALUE

DONNY GAHRAL ADIAN

Some proponents of liberal political philosophy have come up with the idea of "value pluralism," a principle that recognizes the diversity of value held by human beings as moral subjects. This results in a new agenda proposed by Rawlsian liberal philosophy called an "overlapping consensus" – i.e., a consensus in which everyone must share some socio-political values in order to actualize their own ethical conception. This consensus is a delicate matter since society often builds upon major ethical conceptions won precisely by marginalizing or discriminating against other conceptions.

Most ethical conceptions tend to be for the rule of a society as a whole. This happens when it turns out to be not just one among many conceptions but a "single-ruling" or founding doctrine. It is a "comprehensive doctrine," according to Rawls – i.e., a doctrine which deals with all parts of human affairs, from personal to political. By doing this, it often deals with other doctrines confrontationally. The main agenda is always proposing its ethical conception as the comprehensive doctrine to be held by the rest of society; and it takes over or influences the state apparatus.

According to liberal political philosophy, religion might be regarded as a form of ethical monism which has three major weaknesses. *First*, it is the seed of totalitarianism due to its commitment to a highest good (*summum bonum*). *Second*, it cannot reach consensus upon which the democratic culture is built. Its agenda is always ethical homogenization by integrating the individual into society. *Third*, it blurs the private/public distinction by privatizing the public sphere which is supposed to be pluralized by varieties of interests, values, ideologies and perspectives.

These are strong critiques of the ethical conception. The question then is whether these critiques are theoretically and historically true. Is it true that religion and the liberal way of life will always be in so great a tension with each other? In this paper I would like to show how the liberal critiques can be proven to be not absolutely correct. My argument is based upon the historical Islamicization in Java which results in a harmonious consensual relationship between Islam and Javanese ethical conceptions. The consensus leads to my hypothesis that religion (Islam, in this context), despite its comprehensiveness, can undertake an overlapping value consensus in relation to any other belief system. My paper will be written in three main parts: *first*, religion and value pluralism; *second*, Islamicization in Java: tension and integration; *Third*, Javanese-Islam "overlapping value consensus."

RELIGION AND VALUE PLURALISM

"Value pluralism" is a concept that many liberal philosophers hold as a basic principle. It is what they think distinguishes liberal philosophy from communitarian, conservative or socialist philosophy. Isaiah Berlin came up with the concept. He differentiated between "value pluralism" and "value monism."[1] The first is the doctrine that there are many values or good things in life and, as a result, there is no rational basis for concluding that one is best. Value monism, on the other hand, insists that there is, in principle, a rationally best way for us to live. Berlin said that the world we encounter in ordinary experience is one in which we are faced with choices between ends equally ultimate, and claims equally absolute. The commitment to value pluralism in such a world is inevitable.

The "value pluralism" principle bases itself on the idea of community. Community nonetheless is a fictitious body, composed only of individual persons who are considered as constituting, as it were, its members. Community is simply a name we use to describe the actions, traits and interactions of individuals who are real. Every social explanation must take account of individuals as starting point. Pluralists like Rawls take this idea of community and propose a principle that each person possesses an inviolability founded on justice that even the welfare of the whole society cannot override.

The social philosophy developed during the nineteenth century brings about strong resistance to that social ontology. Society is not simply an aggregation of individuals; it has a culture and customs that shape the individuals born into it. The individual's life only expresses the common will of society, and in extreme cases may have to be sacrificed for the good of society. An atheist, for example, may have to relinquish his belief for the common religious belief.

The concept sounds clear enough, but reality shows how many moral doctrines regard themselves as general and comprehensive doctrines.[2] A doctrine is general when it applies to a wide range of subjects and is the limit to all subjects universally. It is comprehensive when it includes conceptions of what the "value" in human life is, as well as the ideals of personal character, friendship, familial and associational relationships, and of much else that is intended to inform our conduct, establishing the limits to our life as a whole.

---

[1] Gerald F. Gaus, *Political Concepts and Political Theories* (Boulder, CO: Westview Press, 2000), pp. 58-59.

[2] See John Rawls, *Political Liberalism* (New York: Columbia University Press, 1996), p. 13.

These two latter characteristics cannot be accommodated by commitment to value pluralism when it comes to politics. Rawls shows how the political conception needs to free itself from any comprehensive moral doctrine. When it fails to do that, political affairs will be ruled by a single doctrine and results in marginalizing other doctrines. Political affairs must be founded on liberal tolerance and value neutrality. However, those value pluralism-based principles are, for most of the third world countries like Indonesia (which upholds moral homogeneity), remote and alien. But before we get to that issue, let us go over the theoretical dispute between these two principles.

Liberal tolerance is a principle that insists that it is wrong of government to use its coercive power to enforce ethical homogeneity on the community through a shared ethical code.[3] Many arguments have been proposed to challenge this principle. *First* is an argument from democratic theory associating the good of the community with the will of the majority. The community has the right to use law to support its vision of ethical decency. In other words, it has a right to impose its views about ethics just because it is the majority. *Second* is an argument from paternalism. It holds that in a genuine political community each citizen has a responsibility to protect the well-being of other members and should therefore use political power to reform those whose defective practices will ruin their lives. *Third* is the argument of self-interest. It rejects the atomism that holds that individuals are self-sufficient beings, and so emphasizes that people need community, materially, intellectually and ethically. *Fourth* is the argument of integration. The argument rests on the belief that the value of the goodness of any individual citizen's life is only a reflection and function of the value of the life of the community in which he lives. This means that, in order to make their lives valuable, citizens must vote and work to make sure that their fellow citizens lead decent lives.

All of these arguments rest on the priority of community over individuals, the same social ontology that strongly opposed the liberal commitment to value neutrality. The principle of neutrality in political affairs is rejected by communitarian nations, which want to sustain an account of what it is to live well. Communitarian nations oppose the notion of a political realm that is free from any comprehensive moral doctrine. Liberal value neutrality faces three strong challenges: *first*, the challenge from the romantics, who accuse liberalism of insensitivity to the importance of individuals breaking free of petty morality; *second*, the challenge from Marxism that strongly opposes the alienated and impoverished character of life in liberal capitalist democracy (for the value neutrality of liberals is, according to Marxism, a mask for support of bourgeois morality); *third*, the challenge from the conservatives that accuses liberalism as failing to understand that life can be satisfying only when it is rooted in a community

---

[3] Ronald Dworkin, *Sovereign Virtue: The Theory and Practice of Equality* (Cambridge, MA: Harvard University Press, 2000), p. 211.

defining norms and traditions. These three challenges share the same belief that political community must be subordinate to one single ethical conception. The value pluralism is just unthinkable.

Religion as an ethically comprehensive doctrine is usually associated with the idea of ethical homogenization. It is based on the idea that the religious conception of the good is that of the highest good (*summum bonum*), so all other goods must be subdued and converted to that one. It denies value pluralism. This attitude leads to the need for a political hand to bring about its agenda, a political hand that converts the dissident by punishment-reward mechanisms. The freedom for one to choose his or her own ethical conception is limited. The individual must integrate herself fully into the community's moral doctrine.

Recently, there has been strong resistance to the monolithic character of religious moral doctrine. Brian Hebblethwaite, in his essay "The Varieties of Goodness,"[4] writes that the idea of a *summum bonum* is by implication totalitarian. It puts aside the recognition and positive affirmation of the varieties of human goodness. From the perspective of Christian theological ethics, Hebblethwaite emphasizes the necessity of welcoming other forms of religiously motivated goodness. Christianity has no monopoly of the ways of God with humankind, since there may well be forms of the religious life that encapsulate and manifest values understressed in the Christian tradition.

The same resistance emerges from the Islamic intellectual world. Dale F. Eickelman strongly states that it would be incorrect to say that there is a single, dominant view among Moslems concerning religious and value pluralism. This is restated by Khalid Masud, who says that there have always been several moral traditions in Islam, some of which – as in other religious traditions – are more tolerant and open to alternative ethical positions. The Qur'an, as the Moslems' holy guide, offers itself a distinctly modern perspective on the role of Islam as a force for tolerance and mutual recognition in a multiethnic, multicommunity world. There are several Qur'anic verses endorsing this view. "To each among you, We have ordained a law and assigned a path. Had God pleased, He could have made you one nation, but His will is to test you by what He has given you; so compete in goodness" (5:48); "O mankind! We created you from a male and female and made you into nations and tribes, that you may know one another" (49:13). Historically, Islam has been remarkably open to the outside world. Fazlur Rahman, a prominent Moslem scholar, argues that the prophet Muhammad recognizes without a moment of hesitation that Abraham, Moses, Jesus and other Old and New Testament religious

---

[4] See Joseph Runzo (ed.), *New Ethics, Religion, and the Good Society Directions in a Pluralistic World* (Louisville, KY: Westminster Press, 1992), p. 3.

personalities are God's messengers like himself.[5] Their different messages, which are contextually bounded, were truly universal and identical. Muhammad even said in the Qur'an that "I believe in whatever book God may have revealed" (42:15). It shows that the idea of "book" (*kitab*) is a generic term in the Qur'an denoting the totality of divine revelations.

Historically, the Islamic tradition has been intensely interactive with other beliefs. We witness how Islam has incorporated many preexisting and coexisting cultural elements. It encompasses a variety of civilizational and cultural forms of life. By the tenth and eleventh century, for instance, the Islamic world showed a remarkable variety of institutional forms ranging from North Africa to South Asia. In terms of moral tradition, Islam has incorporated many pre-Islamic tribal values. There is something in Islamic moral doctrine called literary moral tradition (*adab*), which derives its ethical values from multiple sources, both Moslem and non-Moslem. However, we also witness a rupture in the history of the Islamic attitude toward value pluralism. A nadir of intolerance within the Moslem community was the inquisition (*mihna*) of 833-848 CE. Within the period of fifteen years, the four successive caliphs implemented an authoritarian imposition of single doctrine through the state apparatus. It soon met strong resistance and was abandoned after 848 CE. The sociologist Robert Bellah argues that the authoritarian version of Islamic moral teaching is due to what he called "stagnant localisms" of tribe and kinship.[6] These "stagnant localisms" strongly resist the pluralist version of community found in seventh-century Islamic society, a society built upon the very principle of egalitarianism.

The above arguments lead to the thesis that the Islamic aversion to value pluralism is not based upon the holy guide itself but the infiltration of cultural chauvinism. Islam as moral tradition favors pluralism on two grounds. This is first evident in its appeal to human reason. Islamic moral tradition highly values individual rational choice and responsibility, as seen in verses such as "There is no coercion in religion. The truth stands out clear from error" (2:256); "By the soul, and the order given it, He has inspired it to its wrong and to its good" (91:7-8); and "To each is a goal to which He turns it. Then, strive for what is good" (2:178). These emphasize ethical values as reasonable and understandable by all humans. Different levels of understanding from one person or one community to another are inevitable. This is evident, second, in the social acceptance of Islamic values. Islamic values are understood by different persons and communities that result in different regulations of the permissible "room to maneuver"of dissent. It is the social dialectics that determine and enforce the acceptable definition of ethical values.

---

[5] Sohail H. Hashmi (ed.), *Islamic Political Ethics: Civil Society, Pluralism, and Conflict* (Princeton, NJ: Princeton University Press, 2002), p. 118.

[6] Ibid., p. 117.

ISLAMICIZATION IN JAVA

Historically, Islamicization in Java did not begin in a cultural vacuum. Java had already a great civilization based on a Hindu-Buddhist metaphysical and value system. Some called it a Javanese belief system (*kejawen*). So, according to Clifford Geertz, the well-known American anthropologist, Islamicization in Java did not construct a civilization – it appropriated one.[7] The appropriation itself, however, failed to make a good start. Islam did not win the hearts of many Javanese aristocrats who strongly upheld the Javanese belief system (*kejawen*) as their ultimate spiritual and practical guidance.

In *Babad Tanah Jawa*, a story about the history of Java, it has been told how the king of *Majapahit* (one powerful kingdom in Java) refused to take Islam as a new belief system. This refusal represents the aversion of Javanese aristocrats toward Islam. It is based on the idea of superiority of Javanese belief system compared to the others. Due to this refusal many Islamic missionaries went to the villages, especially along the coastal area, to spread Islamic teaching. Those missionaries were quite welcome there and built many Islamic schools (*pesantren*) which became a counter-culture to the dominant Javanese culture.

After the fall of *Majapahit*, Islamicization started to get a grip on the belief system of Javanese society. By the end of the eighteenth century, almost the whole of Java had been Islamicized. At the beginning, the central development of Islamic culture was founded in the cities on the north coast of Java. From there, it moved deeper into the central area of Java. But the tension was still great between the world views. Even though many places in Java had officially accepted Islam, the way of life of most aristocrats was still based on the Javanese worldview. Many were still conducting Javanese spiritual rites like the *wayang* performance, dances, and other spiritual ceremonies.

More frequent contact between Islamic movements in Java and those in the Middle East brought tension to another level. The demarcation became more vivid as the Middle East movement's orientation of purifying Islam infiltrated into the culture of *pesantren*. It strongly opposed Javanese mysticism, which was regarded as a non-Islamic belief system. The *pesantren* society's main agenda then was to implement the purest character of Islamic teaching as it was understood in Egypt through the influence of Muhammad Abduh. They emphasized the rigid implementation of Islamic *shariah*[8] like that practiced during the period of the prophet Mohammed. This purification resulted in "consciousness-raising" for many Javanese

---

[7] Clifford Geertz, *Islam Observed: Religious Development in Morocco and Indonesia* (Chicago: University of Chicago Press, 1971), p. 11.

[8] Law constitutes a divinely ordained path of conduct that guides the Moslem toward a practical expression of his religious conviction in this world and the goal of divine favor in the world to come.

followers. They started to realize their uniqueness compared to Islam and tried hard to preserve their ancestral worldview. The schism between *pesantren* and non-*pesantren* culture began to take its form.

This schism echoes up through to the modern period. Clifford Geertz's anthropological research in Mojokuto, a small village in East Java, shows a tension between the so-called *santri* and the *abangan*.[9] *Santri* is a category for those emphasizing the ritual aspects of Islam. A true Moslem, according to them, is the one who performs all those rituals as God's absolute imperatives. *Abangan*, on the other hand, leads to a mystical way of life that emphasizes the spiritual aspect of religion. They do not seem to put much emphasis on the ritual aspect of religion. For them, the most important thing is controlling inner drives and doing good deeds.

That schism was emphasized by the anti-colonial movement, which was very political in nature. In the year 1913, a political organization called *Sarikat Islam* (Islamic Union) was born. During the first ten years there was an internal conflict between the puritan group and the socialist-based group. Since then the development of Indonesian politics has been based upon that polarization. After the nation's declaration of independence, the polarization became stronger and stronger and led to many crises. There were certain Islamic groups which strongly opposed the new-born nation, a nation which according to them is a non-Islamic (*kafir*) nation. Many revolts conducted by Islamic puritanical groups happened during the 1950s.

The conflict between Javanese and Islamic culture is only one side of the story. There has also been an integration of the Islamic and Javanese belief systems on the esoteric level, an integration which can be seen in many literary works. In terms of literature, many Javanese men of letters absorbed the wisdom of Islamic mysticism to Islamicize the ancient literature inherited from the period of Hinduism. They wrote many beautiful literary works about mystical teaching. Many literary works are still being written. They include *Wedhatama, Wulangreh, Serat Centini, Wirid Hidayat Jati,* and *Paramayoga Serat Centini.* The last is a work written by Ronggowarsito, a prominent Javanese man of letters, about the journey of reaching the highest knowledge and becoming one with the ultimate reality.

Many men of letters thought that Islamic mysticism could enrich and perfect the culture of the ancients. What is so extraordinary about these men of letters is their openness, adaptability, and flexibility toward other cultural elements, something that cannot be found in *pesantren* religious figures. What we find there is nothing other than the strict orthodoxy of *pesantren* culture based on Imam Al-Gazali's religious teaching, the teaching which is being held by *pesantren* as guidance to purify Islam from the infiltration of the Javanese belief system. The cultural gap will never be narrowed if none of the rival believers relinquish their orthodoxy. The openness of Javanese men of letters has made the integration possible. They

---

[9] See Clifford Geertz, *Abangan, Santri, Priyayi dalam Masyarakat Jawa* (Pustaka Jaya: Jakarta, 1970), p. 165.

have opened the bridge between those two belief systems within the context of esoteric teaching.

INTEGRATION OR VALUE CONSENSUS?

Some scholars think there was an integration of the Javanese and Islamic belief systems, metaphysically and practically, resulting in a newly-born religion of Java. However, I have some reservations about that thesis. There are two basic reasons. *First*, the Javanese and Islamic worldviews are quite distinct. The Javanese believe in a cosmic order into which a man must fit himself. The Javanese idea of God is not of a transcendent deity, but a mysterious one who can be found only in personal experience. God is not a God of knowledge but of feeling. When we can discard our self-interest and integrate harmoniously with the cosmic order, we will feel God's presence in our day-to-day conduct. The Islamic worldview, of course, is a monotheistic worldview, a worldview that posits God as a transcendent being who is the centre of the universe, and the course of history is His volition; man is a mere creature who should live attuned and subjected to the will of God. In other words, a transcendent God is the measure of all things, and man is a mere servant who derives satisfaction and legitimacy from following the rules and religious obligations set by God. *Second*, the religion of Java is not identical with religion in Java. Followers of the Javanese belief system clearly distinguish themselves from the followers of Islam. The so-called integration is just a political construct created for the sake of social stability. It was deliberately done by the kingdom of Mataram to neutralize revolts from the *pesantren* communities. The integration, thus, is not a natural integration, but a forced one.

It happened that each belief system, respecting the other's integrity, developed some kind of value consensus for social and political affairs. The question then becomes: how can the Islamic and Javanese belief systems develop such a consensus if both of them claim to be comprehensive? My thought about this is that both belief systems, no matter how comprehensive, remain at peace toward each other. It is politicization that stimulates the tension. Through politicization, each would like to authorize its ethical conception as the ruling conception of society. Meanwhile, what happened in grass-roots society is quite different. There was a value consensus between Islamic and Javanese teaching in regulating public affairs. In a Javanese family consisting of a Moslem father, an *abangan* mother, one Moslem daughter and two *abangan* sons, there would never be any significant fissure between them.

The question is whether there can be such an overlapping value consensus between two ethical conceptions claiming to be the highest good (*summum bonum*) – a claim which is shared by both Javanese and Islam belief systems, since both propose some ultimate ethical code of conduct regulating everything from personal to social affairs derived from each metaphysical doctrine. History has taught us about the difficulty of such a consensus between two conceptions of the *"summum bonum."* In the sixteenth century we witnessed a religious conflict due to the lack of consensus between Catholics and Protestants. Both faiths held that it was the duty of the ruler to uphold the true religion and to repress the spread of heresy and false doctrine.

Rawls thinks that such an ethical consensus between two comprehensive doctrines is possible. The consensus about values held in social-political affairs need not be any more indifferent than, say, truth in comprehensive doctrine. It must be true or reasonable from the standpoint of each comprehensive doctrine.[10] The value of toleration, for instance, must be backed up by the truth in each belief system. Similarly, overlapping value consensus is also open to Javanese and Islamic ethical conceptions as each providing a *summum bonum*. But, first of all, we must explore each ethical conception to find the overlapping value consensus.

The Javanese ethical conception is based upon the idea of the sacred order of the cosmos where man must find a way to fit in. In order to do that, he must repress his self-interest and become one with the macrocosm. Based on the unity of cosmos, there are three elements in the Javanese ethical conception. The *first* is *sepi ing pamrih*. It means that we as human beings must cleverly control our self-interested impulses for the sake of harmony. Self-interest is what hinders us from developing compassion for another being. The basic idea of the *sepi ing pamrih* principle is solidarity and harmony as a result of management of our self-interest. The *second* is *rame ing gawe*. It can be translated as "actively doing good deeds for the welfare of humanity." As Javanese, we are not only asked to manage our impulses, but also actively to do good to one another. When people from other belief systems want to hold a ceremony, for instance, a Javanese obligates himself to offer help. It is an ethical obligation to help one another sincerely, and it can only be done when one has managed his self-interest. *Third* is *mamayu hayuning bawono*. It is an ethical imperative for the Javanese to beautify the world. Beautifying the world can only be reached by continuously checking our self-interest and doing good to one another. In other words, it presupposes an ethic of solidarity, not just solidarity among human beings, but also the entire cosmos.

The Islamic ethical conception is based on the notion of the unicity of God (*tawhid*). It means that, for Moslems, no other thing besides God deserves worship. One must remember that everyone and everything is one's equal as fellow creatures of the one and the same God. If one worships one's own self-interest, one finds oneself distant from one's fellow creatures and discards God from one's life. The remembrance of the unicity of God must illuminate the whole life of a Moslem, making life not merely a life, but a life full of meaning: the meaning of trial and doing good. The remembrance of one true God reinforces that men live in

---

[10] Rawls, op. cit., p. 150.

harmony while including all the elements of their humanity: living in harmony means to be linked with the values of goodness, justice, and solidarity,[11] values which transcend reductionist individualism and commodity fetishism. The Prophet Mohammed himself told Moslems to speak in the best manner and to remember to treat one another with generosity, goodness and kindness, something that can be fulfilled only by the continuous remembrance of God, self-restraint and the linking oneself with an ethic of solidarity.

Both Islamic and Javanese ethical conceptions, as we see, uphold the value of solidarity over individualism, remembrance (*eling* in the Javanese belief system) over forgetfulness, being over having, finality over means, and quality over quantity. Consensus regarding that principle is what I believe to be the social integrator of post-*Majapahit* Javanese society. Conflicts only arise when the orthodox Moslem from the *pesantren* community blindly follows Islamic *shariah* and forgets the universal ethical message behind the Qur'anic revelation. Such people forget that *shariah* is supposed to be a legal conversion of ethical principles found in the Qur'an. What they struggle for is only legalizing *shariah* through the positive law, which means proposing the Islamic ethical conception as an official conception – an agenda which discards any effort of natural overlapping consensus which, I believe, happens during the absence of all those social engineering processes. Without the "political make-over," the Islamic and Javanese ethical conceptions – despite their differences in metaphysical worldview, and far from being totally excluded from one another – manage to have consensus upon values such as solidarity, justice, self-restraint and generosity.

CONCLUSION

Overlapping consensus is the most advanced agenda proposed by liberal political philosophies to back up theoretically the very concept of a democratic society: a society built upon the principle of equal concern and respect. What can endanger this consensus is the politicization of belief systems. Politicization is something that triggers the conflicts which are also provoked by the strong orthodoxy held dear by fanatics, an orthodoxy that so easily creates a demarcation line between puritans and heretics. The combination of politicization and orthodoxy leads to ethical homogenization which, from the perspective of liberal political philosophy, blurs the distinction between an "association" and a "democratic society" – between society which is single-handedly run by a comprehensive doctrine and that which treats the whole society with equal concern. In other words, ethical homogenization stands diametrically opposed to the liberal commitment to value pluralism.

---

[11] See Tariq Ramadan, *Islam, the West and the Challenges of Modernity* (Leicester: The Islamic Foundation, 2001), p. 234.

Historically, religion as a *summum bonum* finds difficulties for developing an overlapping value consensus with other belief systems. However, the value consensus between Islamic and Javanese belief systems proved to be otherwise. What happened between them was not a true integration. Even when it did happen, it was an integration forced for the sake of political interest. It was an overlapping consensus constructed as a social mechanism to maintain order and stability, a consensus upon values such as solidarity, justice and self-restraint. This consensus shows how far Islam can walk hand-in-hand with the principle of value pluralism in a liberal society. The contemporary echo of this historical message is the need for Islam to give up its agenda of ethical homogenization and focus instead on finding out the overlapping value consensus with other belief systems within the framework of democratic society.

Department of Philosophy
University of Indonesia
Jakarta, Indonesia

CHAPTER XXV

HUMANIST VALUES IN LOCAL MANUSCRIPTS: BETWEEN THE PAST AND THE FUTURE

IRMAYANTI MELIONO

INTRODUCTION

Indonesian local manuscripts are one of many items of cultural heritage found in the Indonesian archipelago. At first they were read and understood only by those who love that heritage. Now, as we enter the era of globalization, the existence of these manuscripts needs to be analyzed thoroughly from the perspective of heritage and its functions. Are these manuscripts still relevant to us? As long as we still care for these local manuscripts, we need to rethink their hidden values. The exploration of these values will lead us to a reinterpretation of these values. In doing so, the message in the local manuscripts can be enacted through reinterpretation, and then disseminated in the various mass media (print and electronic) so that society at large can read and understand the message better.

I shall examine the values of truth, goodness, and beauty, found in the local manuscripts, in relation to their relevance to society and its needs. It is expected that these local manuscripts can have an added value: that is, to play a role in a modern society characterised by globalization.

WHAT IS A LOCAL MANUSCRIPT?

A 'local' manuscript is a written text with special characteristics; it bears certain meanings. In Indonesia, local manuscripts can be found in many societies that practice certain cultures; such societies are the Javanese, Sundanese, Balinese, etc. A text must meet certain requirements to be called a 'local manuscript.' First, it must be hand written on paper or leaves, or carved on wood. Second, one theme must be written in one manuscript only. Third, the theme must be that of the writer or commissioned by someone (usually the ruler of a local society such as a king, sultan, etc). Finally, the story usually tells of a situation, describes the society in a certain period, or predicts its future based on the society's philosophy, customs and traditions as well as religion.

HUMANISM IN LOCAL MANUSCRIPTS

What is humanism in local manuscripts? To answer that, we first need to define humanism. Humanism is an idea that tries to explain human values in a given culture. Historically, Humanism emerged in the Renaissance (from the fourteenth to the seventeenth century) in Europe. During that time, Humanism appeared in many forms such as literature, sculpture, architecture and painting. By expressing themselves in these works, the people of the 'Renaissance' demonstrated their humanism, e.g., by respecting the individual who has capabilities and the recognition of humans as having creativity which may express itself in the form of art.[1] With this analogy to the European Renaissance, we may ask whether local manuscripts have the form and values of humanism. Research into some local manuscripts in Java like *serat Wehatama* [in Wehatma script] of KGPAA Mangkunagoro IV[2], *serat Cabolek*[3] [in Cabolek script] and others show that they can carry strong messages. In other words, humanism does exist with relation to local manuscripts. The next question concerns form. This depends on what is present in a society at a given time. The writing of local manuscripts has been positive for certain societies like the Javanese, Sundanese and Balinese. At a certain stage, the society finds or develops 'creators' who have a certain way of thinking that enables them to express themselves imaginatively in written works.

As a human being, one's ability to create indicates several things: (1) rationality – as expressed in the ideas, (2) philosophy – way of life, (3) freedom, and (4) work ethic (the spirit of ethos) – hard working and persistence. One can see how creators demonstrate their high level of rationality. They can think, learn, and search for knowledge and have the ability to classify this knowledge. Through ideas written in a systematic and logical way, they produce a work. 'Way of life' has always been a theme in local manuscript writing. As an example, Mangkunegoro IV (The Royal Family of Mataram-Javanese Kingdom) reflected his ways of life in his teachings concerning goodness, ethics and morality in *serat Wedhatama* (Wedhatama script). The writer exhibits freedom; he is free to create, and express his ideas. This freedom of expression is manifested in the writing of manuscripts. This is possible because of hard work and a high level of discipline. The spirit of ethos appears in hard and good work.

From a different perspective, some literary figures demonstrate a shift in their behaviour from that of observer to writer. Written traditions, with their distinctive letters, have given birth to writers such as Mangkunegoro IV, Yasadipura I and many others with whom we are

---

[1] See Charles G. Nauert, Jr., *Humanism and the Culture of Renaissance Europe* (Cambridge: Cambridge University Press, 1995).
[2] Mangkunagaro IV. *Wedhatama (terjemahan)* (Surakarta: seksi Dokumentasi dan Perpustakaan Yayasan Mangadeg, 1975).
[3] S. Soebardi, *The Book of Cabolek* (Leiden: KITLV, 1975).

acquainted because of their masterpieces. Thus, the factors mentioned above become tools for a writer and indirectly give meanings to the manuscripts – local manuscripts in particular. Within this context, we can see a humanistic message. The message must be understood in a correct and precise manner. Through accurate understanding, humanist values can grow in a given society. People will be interested to understand local manuscripts and learn the values implied therin; those ideas which are in accordance with the ways of present society can then influence behaviour.

THE MEANING OF LOCAL MANUSCRIPTS

In this section, I shall discuss humanistic values as they can be found in local manuscripts. These are the values of truth, goodness and beauty. In this context, value is necessary to make sense of something. Here, we shall consider certain norms and criteria which encompass these values. For example, one will have a goodness value provided that he or she obeys and practices the teachings of his or her religion. An aesthetics value will have to do with the polarity of beauty and ugliness, as well as interesting and uninteresting aspects found in artworks. Goodness, truth and beauty will bring various judgements of norms or criteria for the three values based on the way of life in a given society. The truth value is related to the understanding of how one comes to knowledge. In philosophy, the search for truth is always done through epistemology. Therefore, one recognizes basic theories of truth, such as the correspondence theory, the coherence theory, pragmatics, and the semantic theory. A correspondence truth will emerge when knowledge enables somebody to form a perception of what is good from an empirical and conceptual point of view, while a coherent truth exists when there is a consensus among the subjects of what they see. In addition, a pragmatics truth appears when one can show the use of an object. For instance, a manuscript full of values of the good life learned and practiced may become one's guide in life. This shows that the manuscript has a pragmatics truth. Finally, there is the semantics truth. The truth will emerge if one can show the meanings of the words used in his or her research.

How are values manifested in the local manuscripts? At first, the truth value appears, as the writer knows exactly what to write (apart from tangential problem statements and basic questions). In other words, what interests him or her is nothing other than the object. Through various ideas, a writer starts to write words in a systematic and logical way, which later becomes a manuscript. When it is read, the readers may have different responses. If the readers have no need to question the validity of the content, or the substance in the manuscript corresponds with the readers' ideas, then coherence truth is achieved. The second value is the truth. The truth always corresponds with wisdom. Why? Historically, both of them stem from the same root, that is, 'ethics.'[4] Ethics always questions where the wisdoms and truth are. Are they in behaviour or ideas? For me, behaviour and consciousness are the foundations of goodness and human wisdom. By goodness I mean a character embedded in a human being. In this sense it is distinctive and humane. Through a good deed a human being is expected to demonstrate his or her goodness. Sometimes, one does not reveal one's goodness, and only bad things prevail. By nature, human beings always show their goodness. Goodness stems from good deeds and avoidance of bad deeds. As discussed above, goodness takes its root from ethics and emerges as one listens to one's heart and decides to behave well towards others. As one puts forward one's own interests without thinking of others' interests, one will only demonstrate one's bad deeds. Thus, many phenomena in life – such as education, religion, custom, tradition and culture in a society – can be a foundation for an ethics that encourages good deeds.

The third value is aesthetics value. Aesthetics always corresponds to arts (literature, dancing, painting, sculpture, etc). It is also related to reality, empirical experience and the involvement of the senses. Is it always about what we can see? This question instigates our interests to reflect on beauty. Philosophical contemplation takes us to see beauty as a part of our existence. Through their rationality human beings contemplate – and even question – the beauty of the cosmos and the works of the Creator: The Supreme One, God, *Hyang Widi, Gusti Allah*. As life goes by, men see beauty differently. It starts to become part of their lives.

DIALOGUE BETWEEN THE "PAST" AND "THE PRESENT"

This dialogue takes place when a local manuscript is put in the present context. Local manuscripts can make a significant contribution to present-day life, particularly in the context of diversity of cultures and ethnicities. The question is whether the manuscript is relevant to today. Local manuscripts, with their advice and teachings, reveal deep philosophical and moral values. It can inspire contemporary writers to write about goodness. The teachings of goodness can be found in many Indonesian manuscripts like *Serat Centini* (Centini script), *Serat Cabolek* (Cabolek script), and so on. Many good teachings, such as children's respect for their parents, students for their teachers, a wife's for her husband, as well as the love of a mother for her children, and the wisdom of a king in ruling his kingdom, can be found in local manuscripts. In brief, the goodness will stem indirectly from the ethics which will be revealed in their daily life.

The dialogue can start with a reflection on aesthetic value. Differing from aesthetics in the West, which emphasizes positivism,

---

[4] See Franz Magnis Suseno, *Etika Jawa* (Jakarta: Gramedia Pustaka Utama, 1996).

rationalism and a strict scientific tradition as in the works of Kant, Fechner, Croce and others, Eastern aesthetics places more stress on feeling (*roso* in Javanese) – a deep feeling and emphasis on intuition, emotion, and personal interface with the truth of life. It emphasizes inward-looking perception. In Indonesia, aesthetics can be seen in the thinking of Ki Hadjar Dewantara, Ki Ageng Suryomentaram, Sutan Takdir Alisyahbana, YB Mangunwijaya, Umar Kayam, etc. In general, aesthetic thinkers can be divided into three main groups:[5] (a) those who stress the importance of morality; (b) those who stress images and originality founded upon aesthetic values; and (c) those who make aesthetics a part of signifying practices (culture, religion, arts, etc).

In contemporary society, one can find that beauty appears in men's consciousness (in this case a writer's) and has a metaphysical aspect. It brings out human transcendentality and actualizes it in concepts and thinking. Aesthetics values emerge with contemplation of harmony, and through nature, through philosophical/ethical/moral teachings, and through the signifying practices of symbols as commonly found in the manuscripts. For a particular society, like the Javanese, cultural symbols are important as they contain messages that are meant to be interpreted accurately and correctly. For present-day society, the messages in the local manuscripts are often claimed to be old-fashioned. They require re-reading and re-interpreting. The re-interpretation of local manuscripts gives inspiration to advance the elements of culture, such as education. Some sayings from the old manuscipts are:

> Spiritual intelligence leads to prosperity.
> Purity and orderliness lead to unity.
> All that obstructs will disappear.

These provide a message regarding how one becomes a better person, and they will be useful if exercised in daily life. "Taman Siswa" is an example of how the Indonesian education system is based on those sayings; it provides sayings in which great Indonesian moderate thinkers like Sukarno (former President of the Republic of Indonesia) and Ali Sastroamidjojo were educated.

CONCLUSION

This paper concludes with a question: With so many influences coming from Western thought and in the era of globalization, do we still need local manuscripts? This leads us into a philosophical reflection: as long as there are still those who study and concern themselves with local manuscripts, they will still exist. The problem here is how to use the

---

[5] Agus Sachari, *Estetika – Makna, Simbol dan Daya* (Bandung: Penerbit ITB, 2002), pp. 37-49.

manuscripts for the benefit of their readers and not merely as part of a collection of old books on a bookshelf. Local manuscripts will be revitalized, provided that the intellectuals and the translators of local manuscripts are able to deconstruct the substance of the scripts in their translation. By deconstruction I mean a re-interpretation of the manuscripts. It can be done through a new, multidisciplinary paradigm. By employing methods like semiotics, hermeneutics and literary criticism, we may expect to find messages and use them in new situations.[6]

Modernity is considered by some critics to be just a Western product or a demand of globalization, but it does not have to be completely rejected. The use of local manuscripts can provide a meeting point between two worlds – the traditional (the past) and the modern (the future). The use of local manuscripts allows a more progressive modern thought because of the values of truth, goodness, and beauty.

The signs in the local manuscripts will be more meaningful if they are related to the world by way of humanistic associations: truth, goodness and beauty. Their relevance will be made manifest if the three values, and the humanism present within the local manuscipts, can be explored through re-interpretation. In doing so, the correct re-interpretation will bring about positive effects. The humanist values of local manuscripts will arise through a study of the humanities and practical learning for people who live in the era of globalization. Local manuscripts are not just something found in the library and read by a small number of scholars, but also something that can be read and understood – something beneficial (a pragmatical function) – to all Indonesians through a humanistic cultural transformation.

Diagram

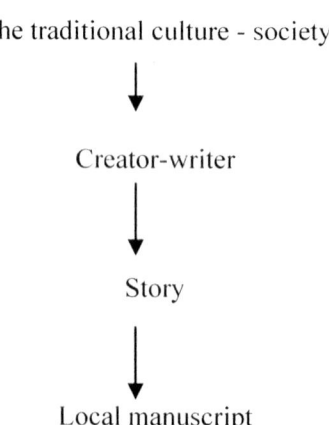

The traditional culture - society

Creator-writer

Story

Local manuscript

---

6 See Jean Grondin, *Introduction to Philosophical Hermeneutics*, foreword by Hans Georg Gadamer, tr. Joel Weinsheimer (New Haven, CT: Yale University Press, 1994).

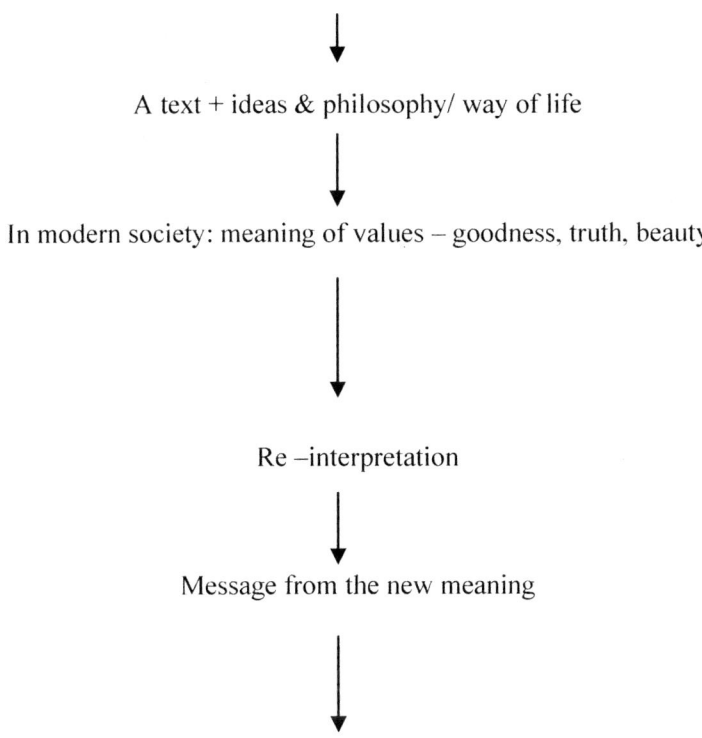

A text + ideas & philosophy/ way of life

In modern society: meaning of values – goodness, truth, beauty

Re –interpretation

Message from the new meaning

Humanism for the new era, the era of globalization

Faculty of Humanities
University of Indonesia
Jakarta, Indonesia

CHAPTER XXVI

CHRISTIAN ETHICS IN MODERN EUROPE

ALFRED RAMMER

In the first half of the 20th century, the number of philosophical approaches to ethics was largely related to neo-Aristotelian, neo-Kantian, neo-Hegelian and various forms of Marxist thought. Again, a trend in approaching ethics is marked by strong criticism of such lines of thought as materialism, positivism, empiricism and scientism. A second trend is constituted by axiological forms of ethics. A third trend is formed by Humanism. A fourth trend is called situation ethics, a conception prevailing in the works of those philosophers who proceed from a religious perspective. These scholars hold the view that each moral problem is unique and can only be solved by the person directly confronted with the specific problem.

Perhaps the two dominating schools of philosophical ethics in the second half of the 20th century were the hermeneutic conception of ethics and the conception of communicative ethics. Hermeneutic philosophy proceeds by searching for meaning that exists outside the framework of history – for meaning that is given at any time. Therefore the hermeneutic philosopher attempts to "retrieve" the grand ideas about human conduct from tradition. Communicative ethics drafts a transcendental anthropology of knowledge from which the basic insight(s) necessary to understanding the basis of science and of our moral and social behaviour can be developed. The fundamental norms of an ethics of communication and deliberation are to be found by means of a transcendental reflection upon those norms that we necessarily must have already accepted as norms. ("Value" was first used as a philosophical and technical term by Kant.)

Some remarks on history may open the way to a better understanding of this problem.

THE RISE OF MODERN EUROPEAN PHILOSOPHY

The European Enlightenment dismissed the paradigm of a comprehensive God-given world order. Within the project of modernity, Europeans began to subdue the world under their own will. Scientific progress and the political-military impulse for expansion led to a Eurocentric interpretation of the world, which had never been seen before in such scope. The growing confidence of Europeans in their own power undermined the relevance of religious security and increased the emancipation of man from clerical guardianship. During this time the impetus of leading the pagan world to Christian redemption evaporated. A vindication for conquering and shaping the world and dominating the lives of other peoples could not be found outside mankind any longer. Being part of the human race became the last bastion for moral valorisation.

The devastating impact of two world wars in the 20th century and other disturbing developments (e.g. pollution of the environment) shattered the optimism of a society functioning as its own final jurisdiction. The modern grand ideologies of the last centuries, working as general scientific explanations and pseudo-religions, were shattered. The core of the crisis of confidence in progress is the crisis of the modern understanding of reason. Technical-industrial progress, which has become an absolute value, is being unmasked as an idol.

Humanism and Modern Identity

Even though the term is ambiguous, "Humanism" may arguably be the central concept of European modernity. It is important to take into consideration that for Europeans it is impossible to think about modernity or humanism from an "outside point of view". Whether they approve or disapprove of their respective notion of modernity, all participants of the discussion are involved and are part of this modern identity, which is to be seen as a structure of self-interpretation. The way of thinking about one's self, about life and about how to evaluate these aspects depends on this kind of self-interpretation imbedded in modern culture. To grasp the idea of modern identity, it is necessary to trace its history and look for its base.

Charles Taylor identifies three elements in the modern notion of identity: the inner self, the distanciated subject, and the affirmation of normal life.[1]

The inner self: the first element is the conviction that our Self is something internal. The conception of the source of morality lying in man's reason comes from Plato. According to him, the ability of acting good in a moral sense comes from the domination of reason over passion and emotion. In this new ethics, the purpose of action is decisive for morality – not its success. In a special sense the moral sources do not lie within man's soul but outside, in the Good itself (see the Allegory of the Cave).

Augustine took over Plato's doctrine of the Ideas and his conception of a higher incorporeal reality. Augustine recognizes an important parallel between the Christian God and Plato's idea of the absolute Good: both are the basis of being and of cognition. For Augustine, however, the way to God does not lead through the world of objects, but rather, God can be found within ourselves. Not only is God the transcendent object mankind tries to recognize, he is also the source of our cognition. There is a great shift from Plato to Augustine, who shifts our attention from the realm of discernible objects to the act of discernment. You may call the

---

[1] Charles Taylor, *Sources of the Self: the making of the modern identity* (Cambridge, MA: Harvard University Press, 1989).

standpoint of "being with one's self" a "radical reflexivity" which can be seen grammatically in the first person singular pronoun.

Augustine introduced the idea of radical reflexivity to accidental thinking and the theory of cognition. Although he proceeds from the metaphysical theory of Plato, there is a great difference: Augustine's theory leads from the exterior to the interior and from the interior to the superior.

The distanciated subject: The distanciated subject emerges with Descartes. Descartes, an Augustinian in many respects, moved the moral resources into the human being. Descartes presents a new understanding of reason and a new interpretation of how reason reigns over passion. According to the new developments in science (e.g., Galileo), the universe is seen from a mechanical point of view, which entails changes in anthropology. Modern science since Galileo aims to construct a correct conception of reality, a correct interior picture of the exterior reality. But these conceptions have to be situated in an appropriate order to assure their correctness. For Descartes there is an ontological gap between body and soul.

Descartes' new conception of reason is also the base of his approach to ethics. His conception appears to be similar to that of the Stoa; it differs, however, in decisive aspects. The wise man now has to pursue rational control over passions to exploit them according to their functions. For Descartes the human being does not need to free himself from his passions. The hegemony of reason is now seen as rational control, as potency to objectivize body, world and passions, and to encounter them from a thoroughly instrumental standpoint, which is only possible if the sources of morality lie within man himself. The hegemony of reason as rational control means that we are in accordance with the order of things, an order that is not inherent in a cosmic order but in our own lives, and thus is shaped from an order which is constructed according to rational means. The rational desire for cognition causes our construction of arrangements of conceptions and these require us to correspond with the things outside; in the same way practical reason requires the use of these objects, thus maintaining and strengthening rational control. From now on the order of objects is not the means of rationality; the last criterion of rationality is not in accordance with this order. Rationality now is not defined by its contents, but is procedural. This step from substance to procedure, from pre-existing to constructed orders represents an enormous intensification.

The affirmation of normal life: The notion "normal life" comprises aspects of human life dealing with production and reproduction such as work, production, sexuality, marriage and family. Whereas for the Greeks the preservation of life was only the condition for a good life that consisted of theory and politics, for modern people ordinary life has become a priority. From now on, science has to be useful, has to show how things function (Francis Bacon). The "artificers" became more important than the philosophers. In the 18th century trade became the leading activity.

This notion of "civil ethics" obviously has an egalitarian impact on modern liberal society, thereby playing an important role in its development.

The origins of the affirmation of modern life lie in Christian spirituality, and the so-called Protestant reformation played a crucial role in conveying it. Refusing the mediating role of clerics leads to spiritual revalorisation of the world and everyday life. This positive estimation experienced a decisive transposition in secularized forms. And this humanism forms a synthesis of this affirmation with the idea of the distanciated subject. The best way of living requires one to take an objectivized and distanciated stance towards one's self and towards nature.

Leaving their Christian origins, both the affirmation of everyday life and the distanciated subject conform to the doctrine that life is affirmed and best served through instrumental reason. The "reformers'" rejection of ascetic vocation turned into a rejection of Christianity itself. And not only is instrumental reason seen as the best way to serve human success, it is also seen as the only way to recognize the real value of nature.

Ethics in Religious Surroundings

Despite the process of secularization it has been subjected to in the 20th century, Christianity has not come to an end. There are still a lot of religious sources in philosophy, and even those who reject their obligations often show traces of religiousness in their thinking. But similar to the spread of philosophy as a whole during the second half of the century, theism and theistic ethics cannot be reduced to one single source. They can be divided into categories such as: divine command ethics, natural law ethics, virtue ethics, and narrative ethics.

Divine command ethics: For a divine command moralist, the standard of right and wrong is constituted by the commands and prohibitions of God. Only because it is commanded or forbidden by God is an action right or wrong. It is important to see the core argument: for those who adhere to the divine command theory, God does not command a particular action because it is right (or prohibit it because it is wrong) – rather, the action is right or wrong because God commands (or prohibits) it. A new interest in divine command ethics emerged during the last quarter of the twentieth century, but the idea goes back to ancient Greek philosophy.

Purely voluntaristic versions of the divine command morality, in which the divine will (without the divine intellect) issues the commands constituting the moral law, are confronted with the objection that it makes morality arbitrary. But this criticism does not apply to a version according to which the divine will that establishes the command is seen as identical to the divine intellect. Others do not see God's commands as arbitrary, because God's will is in accordance with other divine attributes, such as knowledge, justice and love.

There are different ways of supporting the theory of divine command ethics. Some relate the acceptance of divine commands as normative for human conduct to mankind's dependence on God as the creator. Others regard the Divine command ethics as a correlation to the divine power. In the realm of metaphysics an analogy may be seen between the metaphysical notion of God as first being and the ethical notion of God as predominant value. The dependence of morals on divine commands can be connected with God's status as first und uncaused cause, morality being treated as one instance of this more general problem.

There other problems as well. Theists may disagree among themselves about the content of divine law. How can we determine what God permits and forbids? If there is no way to determine what the divine commands are, Divine command ethics cannot be used as an action guide and will at last lead to scepticism about morals. Another problem is that Divine command ethics does not permit the formulation of a coherent account of the moral attributes of God. It is rather trivial to explain an action as morally good because it is God's will, which means nothing else but "God does what God wills".

Natural law ethics: Natural law is the body of moral norms and other practical principles that provide reasons for action and restraint. The most basic precepts of natural law direct people to choose and act for intelligible ends and purposes. These precepts refer to the range of basic human goods for the sake of which people can intelligently act. Natural law is not to be conceived as analogous to legislation. The prescriptivity of moral and other practical principles are a matter of rational bindingness or necessity.

For Francisco Suarez (1548-1617), knowledge of the reasonable, the good and the right, is derived from prior knowledge of human nature. For Thomas Aquinas something in the moral domain is "natural" for human beings and in accord with human nature in so far as it can be judged to be reasonable; it is "unnatural" and morally wrong in so far as it is unreasonable. For contemporary thinkers in the tradition of Aquinas, practical knowledge is a source of our knowledge of human nature.

Theories of natural law should be distinguished from Kantian theories which neglect or even deny the basic human goods to which the first principles of practical reason direct choice and action. Likewise should theories of natural law be distinguished from theories of the "intuitionist" sort and from utilitarian, consequentialist, proportionalist and other theories which propose aggregative accounts of justice and moral goodness.

All natural law schools of thought emphasize the "intransitive" significance of morally significant choices for human goods – they are never seen as mere means to other basic goods, but as self-shaping. For most natural law theorists, human beings have their duties because they have been created with a particular nature. For the theological exponents of natural law, God directs people to their proper ends, not by instinct, but rather by practical reason.[2] Christian natural law theorists interpret St. Paul's reference to a "law inscribed in [our] hearts" (*Rom.* 2:15) as a reference to the natural law, which can be known by unaided reason. Hence the moral law is "natural", which means that it does not depend on supernatural revelation. Human beings then participate in God's providential direction of the whole of creation according to a plan conceived in wisdom and love. But according to Aquinas, reason has been weakened and distracted by sin. Revealed moral teaching reinforces and illuminates what can be known of moral truth by reason alone.

Virtue ethics: Moral philosophy began with reflections on the nature of the virtues and their place in an overall conception of human excellence. With the rise of modernity, the concept of virtue gradually lost its central place in moral reflection. In her essay "Modern Moral Philosophy,"[3] Elizabeth Anscombe reinvents the theme. She argues that the central concepts of the moral philosophy of her time – duty and moral law – are no longer credible. Having abandoned the belief in a divine lawgiver and recognized the incoherence of Kant's self-legislating reason, she turned to an Aristotelian account of the virtues to provide a starting point for an alternative moral philosophy. Alasdair MacIntyre points out that contemporary morality consists of fragmentary survivals from earlier traditions and cannot sustain rational discourse. For him, coherence in moral discourse can only be attained within the context of particular traditions. According to Anscombe and MacIntyre, a new interest in the classical authors as resources for contemporary moral thought emerged. Aristotle in particular became important as a source for moral reflection. For both, the point of virtue ethics seems to be the revival or construction of a framework for normative analysis, within which rational, cogent moral discourse would be possible.

Apart from the traditional themes, some conceptual problems are central to the contemporary discussion: what do we mean by a "virtue", and how is this virtue related to notions such as habit and disposition? Despite the consensus that virtues cannot be reduced to tendencies to perform certain kinds of actions, it is not clear which criteria are suitable to determine whether a person has a given virtue or not. Another conceptual issue concerns the relationship between having or practicing the virtues and

---

[2] See Charles E. Curran and Richard A. McCormick, *Natural Law and Theology* (New York and Mahwah: Paulist Press, 1991).

[3] "Modern Moral Philosophy," *Philosophy*, 33 (1958): 1-19; reprinted in *The Collected Philosophical Papers of G. E. M. Anscombe*, Vol. III: *Ethics, Religion and Politics* (Minneapolis: University of Minnesota Press, 1981), pp. 26-42; more recently reprinted in *Human Life, Action, and Ethics: Essays by G.E.M. Anscombe*, ed. Mary Geach and Luke Gormally (Essex: Imprint Academic, 2005), pp. 169-194.

following moral rules. For some, virtue can be reduced to a disposition to follow moral rules; for others, moral rules are at best rough guidelines; for still others, rule-governed behaviour has an independent place in the moral life.

Another set of issues can be seen as normative. One question here is whether the traditional identification of prudence, justice, temperance and fortitude can still be defended today. Which virtues are central for us? How far should we take the virtues to be morally desirable qualities?

A third set of issues can be described as social. Here the question arises as to whether the traditions of the virtues offer a sufficient basis for a thoroughgoing social critique. Do the traditions of the virtues offer sufficient resources for mediating social conflict in complex societies? Do they lead to a sectarian morality?

Interestingly, most philosophers of religion tend to pay most of their attention to divine command theories of morality. But there has been a revival of a distinctively theological exploration of the virtues since the 1970s. Many scholars have turned their attention to a retrieval of Aquinas' virtue ethics.

Narrative ethics: The concept of narrative has gained prominence recently. A narrative is a verbal account of a temporally connected series of events and shows connections between the past, the present and the future. By depicting their actions, interactions and reactions, a narrative probes into a character's continuities and changes. Narratives can be historically true or fictional. To a significant extent a person's identity is constituted of his or her history. Talking about one's self requires talking about the connections with other people, relations with institutions, things which were done or not, things which happened to one. Much of this account will take narrative form. The identity of a person has a "narrative structure", which does not mean that it is a narrative, but that it is in part a history which can only be properly displayed in narrative form.

More than in the past, contemporary ethics has been approached psychologically, which has increased an emphasis on narratives. At the same time, this interest tends to make ethics more richly and concretely psychological. Character ethics is a return to the notion that the philosopher is in the business of discovering and purveying ethical wisdom – the knowledge of the good life for human beings. Unfortunately, philosophers often are not good story-tellers and story-tellers are often not good philosophers, hence a coordination between philosophical and narrative presentations of the virtues and vices is needed.

According to Wittgenstein's "grammar," the grammar of a trait term determines the kind of actions, emotions, motives, and reasons that characteristically exemplify the trait. The narrated incidents that display a virtue mark grammatical features of it. Philosophical analysis of the virtue consists in identifying its grammatical features. The narrative provides a basis for philosophical analysis superior in some ways to everyday life in that it enlivens the philosopher's imagination.

The narrative not only gives an account of particular moral persons and displays virtues, but also comprises aspects that are culturally distinctive about a set of virtues, by entering into the very grammar of those virtues. The narrative of the Hebrew exodus from Egypt basically recounts the actions of God in owning the people of Israel; it is the story about Israel's formation as a people, about the people's identity as belonging to God. Similarly constitutive for Christians is the story in the four Gospels. The narrative of the incarnation, death, and resurrection of Jesus as the Son of God displays a set of virtues with a special grammar, and, maybe more importantly, it is taken up in the grammar of the virtues of those who accept the story and become members of the community. The main function of the narrative in the Christian community is not to display the Christian virtues, but to take a place in the grammar of those virtues.

CURRENT REQUIREMENTS

What is required today is a new realistic, well-founded and long-term world order, a new orientation, a new macro-paradigm. In the search for a post-Euro-centric, post-capitalist as well as post-socialist, post-patriarchal, pluralistic-integral culture, the leading force must not be a decay of values, but rather a change of values. Whereas postmodernism confines itself to radical pluralism or relativism, society is threatened with the loss of the last remaining values followed by the attitude of "anything goes" or anarchy.[4] What is to be avoided, however, is the fundamentalist request for installing "conquest" orientations. What remains possible and promising is a critical walk through the history of the mind, so that we can trace back the ways of how ethics and values came into being and find out what there is to vindicate at present and preserve for the future. There is reason to expect that Christian ethics will be sustained without being destructive while also not giving up its *proprium*.

As modernity prevails, humanity experiences the loss of the conviction of being embedded in a cosmic order of ideas. This conveys the requirement to affirm life and to find resources of values by man himself. This strongly depends on human beings accepting their existence as good. But a naturalistic humanism cannot refer to an ontology beyond science. Therefore, naturalism remains insufficient and one-dimensional. Consequently, a lot of competing opinions have emerged, exploring ways of creative imaginative power or of radical freedom of activity. All these are continuations of the modern project and accept that glorification is the responsibility of man himself.

---

[4] See Frederick Ferré, *Living and Value. Toward a Constructive Postmodern Ethics* (New York: State University of New York Press, 2001).

The difficulties and "aporias" of modern humanism do not indicate the necessity or even the possibility of abolishing it, of leaving it behind, or going back to pre-modern drafts of world-explanation. We all are too much involved with and within our culture; we are inevitably accustomed to ordering our lives with instrumental reason, to looking for glorification through creative fantasy and to adhering to free self-determination. But the question should be raised whether humanism points beyond the world of human beings.

Looking for possible ways to regain plausibility for Christianity – in the middle of the current philosophical discussion, without passing over its achievements but, on the other hand, without accepting the alleged "end of metaphysics" (which Habermas proposes[5]) – in regard to the requirements of modern reason, two drafts seem to offer promising perspectives: the theory of Natural Law and that of Narrative Theology.

Reason of Man

There is only one "rationality" in the world, which unfolds itself through history in the dialogue between men and its use. Reason is inherent in every person. But it is not available for all at any time in the same way. It arises from the collective activation of theoretical cognition and moral practice and goes in different directions with diverse speeds. In principle, reason never and nowhere comes to an end. It is forever bound to the historic process of practicing of reasonable human self-realization in theoretical cognition and moral activity. Though one can trace back its roots to the very beginning of human history, reason, as a free kind of philosophy which has its foundation and justification through itself, does not emerge before the 6th century B.C. ("the axial period"), and reaches its first peak in the Greek classical period.

Philosophy is human reason which has come to self-consciousness. Philosophy, too, unfolds itself in dialogue. Philosophy requires that each cognition and moral insight is generated and justified by reason. Because reason exists only in men, both reason and philosophy can only come to themselves through dialogical confrontation.

A great step forward on the way to the internalizing (*Verinnerlichung*) and civilizing (*Versittlichung*) of reason was made by the emergence of monotheistic religion. But without an intrinsic self-critical philosophical reflection, these monotheistic religions are still in danger of falling into dogmatism and fundamentalism. In fact, when monotheistic religions came into power, they claimed an absolute access to truth and established a hierarchical clergy, codifying and controlling the thoughts and actions of people.

---

[5] See Jürgen Habermas, *Nachmetaphysisches Denken. Philosophische Aufsätze* (Frankfurt am Main: Suhrkamp, 1988).

The relations of the three great monotheistic religions to philosophy are quite distinct. For Christianity with its huge debt to mythology, the development towards monotheism required the incorporation of philosophy. Thus Christianity is rooted in (1) the message of Jesus and (2) philosophical dialectic. From a theological point of view, the Christian religion appears to be a philosophy; seen as a people's religion, it remains a mythology. The Renaissance and Enlightenment emancipated philosophy from religious conduct. Day-to-day life became more and more secular, while religious belief – far from being destroyed – was driven back into the private sphere.

Rationality in Europe appears in two figures.

First, emerging from ancient Greek philosophy, the figure of rationality appears as self-critical philosophy with the aim to explore the borders of human reason, to give orientation towards sense and morality, and to call on man's historical responsibility. Though philosophy is supposedly independent from religions and political burdens, it does not deny the "question of God". Critical philosophy exposes this "question of God" as an indispensable "limit-problem" which human beings cannot evade without getting trapped in an absolutistic fetish. Therefore, philosophy is ready for dialogue with all non-fundamentalist religions.

Second, the other figure of rationality is one-dimensional reduced rationality. The scientific-instrumental rationality and the utilitarian-economic ideology lack all self-critical reflection. One-dimensional rationality does not acknowledge truth and morality, nor, of course, does it acknowledge God. But this one-dimensional rationality creates a new God: the economic law of profit. And all human morality and all human determination of meaning are sacrificed to it.

Contemporary Christianity

The one-dimensional rationality can only be overcome by critical philosophy, and this critical thinking does not necessary bear an atheistic attitude. The openness towards critical dialogue with theological traditions could lead to a strengthening of critical philosophy.

The theory of natural law: For a long time natural law was under fire from many Protestant moralists, who prefer a Christocentric ethic. Even some Roman Catholic moral theologians refuse to ground ethics on natural law. But as I see it, the rethinking of the Natural Law concept could pave the way to link Christian and non-Christian morals. It also could open the door to revive the connection between philosophy and Catholic theology, which Catholic theologians discerned to be disrupted due to Kant.

Nearly all theological schools place an emphasis on the humanity of Christ. Abandoning traditional approaches, they start from Christ's humanity and move towards his divinity. In this light, Christ does not contradict, but rather fulfils humanity. He contradicts man's actual condition but fulfils what we have already recognized deep within us as true human personhood. These Christological considerations are of high relevance, when trying to relate Christian ethics to the moral aspirations of people who are not Christians.

Suggesting that Christ fulfils the potentialities of man, so that this Christhood can be considered as a kind of self-transcending humanity (which is also the very image of God), does not claim to present Jesus as perfect man. It is rather a matter of his decision to give up all other possibilities for the sake of the most distinctively human possibility of all: self-giving love. And because this love is the most creative thing in human life, Christ manifests the "glory of man" by becoming transparent to the ultimate creative self-giving source of all: God. Thus, if Christ is understood as the revelation of God, then this surely strengthens the argument for a basic affinity between Christian and non-Christian morals – for what is revealed or made clear in Christ is also implicit in the whole creation. In this way, Christian and non-Christian morals can be linked on the ground of a doctrine of creation and not of redemption.

What is natural law?: Natural law, as an ethical concept, is quite distinct from any scientific law of nature. Moral laws cannot be derived from biological laws. The notion refers to a norm of responsible conduct, and suggests a kind of fundamental guideline or criterion that is prior to all rules or particular formulations of law. Like natural theology, natural law has its roots in the Greek contribution to Christian and Western reflection (Anaximander, Heraclitus, Aristotle).

A complete natural law theory has to identify a) the basic human goods which provide non-instrumental reasons for acting, b) the moral norms which follow from the integral directiveness of the principles which prescribe these goods, c) the virtues which sustain morally good individuals and groups in upright choosing, and d) the explanation for and defence of the possibility of free choice. Thus, a complete natural law theory provides practical propositions identifying certain choices, actions, and dispositions as reasonable or unreasonable, good or bad, right or wrong, permitted or forbidden, as well as theoretical propositions about the truth, objectivity, and epistemological warrant for the practical propositions and the real possibility of freely choosing them.

The theological/ontological foundations: I want to suggest that there is an intrinsic connection between religion and morality, and that natural law provides the link. Natural law claims to be founded in ultimate structures, but these do not necessarily require a theological or religious interpretation. Natural law is an ontological ground, common to the various forms of morality, and receiving a religious or a secular interpretation. Natural law is implicit wherever an unconditioned moral obligation is recognized.

That most people seem to believe in something like natural law may be seen in the fact that every single law can be seen as unjust. There seems to be found among most people the conviction that there is a criterion, beyond the rules and conventions of human societies, by which these may be judged. That each judgement, even that of a highest court of appeal, can be seen as unjust, suggests that justice does not have a purely empirical origin. Even Hans Kelsen, a proponent of a positive theory of law who was most influential in the construction of the Austrian constitution, has made considerable use of the natural law concept; so did the lawyers of Germany, Italy and Japan after World War II. The concept of natural law is a safeguard against the usurpation by the state of unlimited power.

It is important to state that a doctrine of natural law does not necessarily commit one to a theistic belief. It is possible to hold a natural law doctrine without a theological formulation, but it seems to be impossible to do so without some ontological or metaphysical formulation. And such ontological interpretation of morality has at least some kinship with the religious interpretation. In both cases the moral demand has about it an ultimate character.

Natural law in a contemporary dynamic conception: Natural law is unwritten and cannot be formulated precisely. It is our inaccurate way of referring to those most general moral principles against which particular rules have to be measured. Therefore it has to be fixed according to the thinking of each era. And so referring to it in our times requires us to reinterpret the idea of natural law in a way that allows for flexibility and growth, so that it really will protect and foster the fulfilment of human possibilities.

While the notion of the unchangeableness of natural law was rooted in the idea of an unchanging nature, both in man and in the cosmos, we now have to acknowledge that man's nature is open, and that he is always going beyond or transcending any given state of himself. Further, we have to acknowledge that this open nature of man is set in the midst of a cosmos which is likewise on the move and is characterized by an evolving order. Natural law itself is on the move and cannot have the immutability once ascribed to it. In particular, the conviction that there was a kind of original human nature to which everything subsequent is an accretion has to be abandoned.

Conceding the variability of natural law does not necessitate the loss of any reliable criterion. We still have a criterion, but its constancy is not that of a law but of a direction. In this sense "natural law" means rather a constant tendency, a built-in directedness. Whereas the movement in the cosmos is unconscious evolution, the movement in man is a conscious moral striving. In the case of man's development, it is a question of what ought to happen. At least in general terms, we know where we ought to be going because to exist as a human being is to exist with a self-understanding, an understanding both of who we are and of who we might become. In theological language we may speak of the *imago Dei* both as fundamental endowment and as ultimate goal. Natural law changes in the sense that the precepts we derive from it change as human nature itself changes; likewise, man's self-understanding changes as he sharpens his image into maturity. This directedness of moral striving has a constancy that inhibits any step into pure relativism.

Christians define mature manhood in terms of Jesus Christ, especially his self-giving love. But Christ himself is not a static model. He is an eschatological figure and his return "with glory" implies that there are dimensions of Christhood not manifest in the historical Jesus and not yet fully grasped by the disciples. Thus discipleship does not restrict human development to some fixed pattern, but summons it into freedom. The "natural" (non-Christian) understanding of morality leads to similar conclusions. If man's nature is to exist, then he exists most fully when he goes out of his own self. And only the man who is prepared to venture beyond himself – and even to empty himself – attains the truest selfhood.

Narrative theology: Christian theology has to deal with underivable, original experiences whose linguistic articulation shows narrative features. The core themes of the Jewish-Christian religion break the borders of pure argumentation and resist the full decomposition or transposition of their narrative frame. The questions of the beginning and the end – and even more the question of the new which is to come – are only to be presented and to be born in mind through narrating. A reason which shuts its eyes to the narrative interchange of such experiences of the new exhausts itself in reconstruction and becomes 'pure technique.'

There is no need for rendering narrative speech in favour of pure argumentative speech in order to reach freedom and enlightenment. There are stories which contain a sense of freedom and encourage imitation. And this critical-delivering force of such narratives can be *a priori* neither proven nor reconstructed. You must encounter them, listen to them and, perhaps, present them to the others as well.

It is important to stress that we are talking about narratives as a profound structure of theology. Hence, such a story is not only an "example", a supplement to theological argument. We thus speak about the theological meaning of narratives and about the indissoluble connection between narratives and arguments. In such theology, salvation and historical life have to be connected without detriment to either. History includes the experience of reality with all its conflicts and contradictions. The theological notion of salvation refers to the reconciliation of these conflicts and contradictions through God's act within Jesus Christ. The narrative remembrance of salvation opens the possibility of presenting salvation within history without shortshrifting either. Hence there is no need either to let drop the subject of salvation into pure unhistorical paradox, nor to subdue it under the coercion of a logical identity that is to be obtained by a dialectical mediation between history and salvation. This does not mean that theological argument has come to an end. But it should be made clear that narratives are inherent in all theoretical attempts to present the connection between history and salvation.

Narratives and remembrance appear as critical instances towards a historical reason without narratives. This critical instanciation asks for new respect for the history of the suffering within our critical consciousness. For such critical reason, history gets a special frame of tradition: it is passed on in a narrative way, in "dangerous stories" and is not merely argumentative.

HTL-Leonding
and
Universität Linz
Linz, Austria

CHAPTER XXVII

THE DIALOGUE OF CULTURAL TRADITIONS, ETHICS, AND PUBLIC SERVICE

WORKINEH KELBESSA

INTRODUCTION

The world has faced countless problems including social and political conflict, civil unrest, religious conflicts, global ecological problems (such as rising sea levels, melting of the polar icecaps, shortage of fresh water, ozone layer depletion, and global warming), absolute poverty, the HIV/AIDS epidemic, threats of terrorism, the domination of the poor by the rich, imbalances in international trade, and the like. What we have been observing is the growing pauperisation of the poor and the increasing affluence of the well-off. The gap between the "developing" and the "developed" world in economy, information and communications technology seems to be unbridgeable. The flow of capital in the global economy leads to uneven development and radical inequalities, not a convergence of living standards.[1] Rich countries dominate the key global economic structures such as the International Monetary Fund (IMF), World Bank, G-7, G-10, G-22, Organisation for Economic Co-operation and Development (OECD) and World Trade Organization (WTO), whereas poor countries have very little influence and voice in today's global policy-making forums, either for lack of membership or for lack of capacity for effective presentation and participation.[2]

Furthermore, the present social and economic system promotes organised greed, commodification of all life, monoculture, monopolies, and the centralised global corporate control of people's lives. Nation states are deprived of their cultural and often political sovereignty. Power and capital are concentrated in corporate hands, and the security of investors takes precedence over the livelihood of citizens. The creation of global-regional economic blocs and the globalisation of relations of production and exchange have led to the erosion of the nation-state and the shrinking of state power. Regional blocs around the United States, the European Union and Japan through agencies such as the World Bank, the IMF and the World Trade Organisation are collectively exploiting the world.

---

[1] Robert Went, *Globalisation: Neoliberal Challenge, Radical Responses* (London: Pluto Press with IIRE, 2000).

[2] United Nations Development Programme, *Human Development Report* (New York and Oxford: Oxford University Press, 1999), pp. 8, 11.

Western countries and transnational corporations (TNCs) have dominated developing countries through unequal terms of trade, debt and other instruments of exploitation. They have created dependencies, scarcity, misery, and have undermined the self-help capacities of the people in developing countries, although the leaders of developing countries are also responsible for these problems. They have controlled world markets and have fixed the prices for "Third World" products. They have forced "Third World" countries to open up their markets to TNCs. Market forces have not enabled developing countries to control the exploitation of their mineral and other natural resources. Instead, they have undermined their resource bases. Excessive focus on export-oriented production has also led to a decline in food production.

Moreover, industrialised countries have used multilateral international trade instruments such as the General Agreement on Tariffs and Trade (GATT) and the WTO to extend their intellectual property rights regimes to plants, animals and microorganisms. Transnational corporations use intellectual property rights to lay claim to indigenous practices used in "developing" countries. State institutions in different countries have become protectors of the property and profits of corporations at the expense of the health and rights of people.

So, what is required is a change of the present situation. It is not physically possible for powerful self-interested states and transnational corporations to continue to grow indefinitely without adverse global repercussions. Different cultures need to come together and address global problems. This paper argues that dialogue of cultural traditions is a means of building bridges of respect and understanding across cultures. In the first part, I will examine the significance of dialogue among cultural traditions and ethics. In part two, I will briefly look into ethics and public service. The last section gives the conclusion of the paper.

DIALOGUE OF CULTURAL TRADITIONS AND ETHICS

The co-existence of different cultural and social groups, and the continuous movement of people and information across cultural and civilisational borders make the dialogue of cultural traditions necessary. Moreover, a global dialogue of cultural traditions is desirable in order to influence TNCs and address the above-mentioned and other related global problems. Only in this way can we respond to the new challenges that have changed our world. In today's world, a great deal can be achieved by working on coalitions of common cause. Without cross-cultural dialogue global problems may not be solved.

It can be objected that the global dialogue of cultural traditions is likely to prove less useful than most people hope, because the problems that we face are largely problems that originated in the West with which other traditions have little experience. Moreover, the global dialogue of cultural traditions is not likely to solve the deep problems created by capitalism. And, certainly, this issue resists short and simple answers.

Still, although dialogue among traditions may not solve all problems we have been facing in a short period of time, it is a good thing to have it. Mutual dialogue among civilisations and cultures is a process that is emerging in the contemporary world. The process emerges where different civilisations in the world come together and allow the Earth to be in control; this becomes a very group-oriented process where there are no authoritarian leaders. That is the process that has to work. Thus, people should relinquish the colonisation mentality of control and take their fate into their own hands. As Heinz Holley observes,

> [M]issing today are the values of communality and reciprocity which have been widely displaced by those which foster competition and extreme individualism within and among nations. In order to realize a world order which has at heart the values and interests of all nations, there is a strong need for all cultures and nations, big and small, rich and poor, to appreciate this requirement so that these values and principles are agreed upon unanimously and ultimately enshrined in the respective institutions of all particular nations and the international institutions of the United Nations. This will make it more difficult and probably impossible for global economic players to impose their will and dictates upon weaker societies, as is the case today. To arrive at this objective, it [is] necessary that the globalization process, which in the main goes hand-in-hand with the expansion of Western values to the rest of the world, be changed into one of dialogue involving the values of all world cultures without distinction.[3]

Samuel P. Huntington also suggests that "[i]nstead of promoting the supposedly universal features of one civilization, the requisites for cultural coexistence demand a search for what is common to most civilizations. In a multi-civilizational world, the constructive course is to renounce universalism, accept diversity, and seek commonalities."[4] In this connection, it is worth noting that global dialogue generated the Earth

---

[3] Heinz Holley, "The Emergence of Nationalism, Ethnic Clashes and Fundamentalist Movements in the Light of Globalization: Some Reflections for Ethical Principles," *National, Cultural and Ethnic Identities: Harmony Beyond Conflict,* Jaroslav Hroch et al (eds) (Washington, DC: Council for Research in Values and Philosophy, 1998), p. 52.

[4] Samuel P. Huntington, *The Clash of Civilizations and the Remaking of World Order* (London: Simon & Schuster UK Ltd, 1996), p. 318.

Charter, which is an authoritative synthesis of values, principles, and aspirations that are widely shared by growing numbers of men and women in all regions of the world:

> The Earth Charter is the product of a decade long, worldwide, cross-cultural conversation about common goals and shared values. The drafting of the Earth Charter has involved the most open and participatory consultation process ever conducted in connection with an international document. Thousands of individuals and hundreds of organizations from all regions of the world, different cultures, and diverse sectors of society have participated. The Charter has been shaped by both experts and representatives of grassroots communities. It is a people's treaty that sets forth an important expression of the hopes and aspirations of the emerging global civil society.[5]

I believe that dialogue among traditions helps us to rethink our place and future on the planet Earth. It helps us to understand diversity as constitutive of reality. As Denis Goulet has noted: "That differences exist, must not be seen as something abnormal, aberrant or scandalous, a condition merely to be tolerated. On the contrary, plurality is the very standard of reality, to be cherished by all."[6] A creative cross-cultural dialogue can help us recognise and reveal the importance of difference, and enable us to hear and benefit from important voices which would otherwise be unrepresented or underrepresented. "We hold that it is precisely this recognition of significant differences that provides an opportunity for mutual enrichment by suggesting alternative responses to problems that resist satisfactory resolution within a single culture."[7] Dialogue will enable us to cultivate understanding of each other's point of view, to be more sensitive to the needs and aspirations of others, to better appreciate our differences and embrace our diversity, to look beyond differences and work together on matters that are crucial for the survival of all beings, and

---

[5] *The Earth Charter Initiative*, www.earthcharter.org.

[6] Denis Goulet, "Global Community: Its Ethical Basis," *Planet Earth: Emerging Global Values* (Spring 1985), Menlo Park, CA: Planetary Citizens, p. 12. See also his "The World of Underdevelopment: A Crisis in Values," in *The Christian Century*, 61 (1974): 452-455; and "The Moral Basis of World Solidarity", in Leonard Berry & Robert W. Kates (eds.). *Making the Most of the Least: Alternative Ways to Development* (New York: Holmes & Meier Publishers, Inc., 1980), pp. 227-240.

[7] D. H. Hall and R. Ames, quoted in Sheelagh O'Reilly, "Reason as Performance: A Manager's Philosophical Diary," *Reason in Practice: The Journal of Philosophy of Management*, 1 (2001): 38.

thereby to recognise that we are one human family and one Earth community with a common destiny.

Human beings can reveal their collective historical destiny to actualise and express all their rich potentialities through their diversity of cultural, political and symbolic forms. That, in turn, would help them to appreciate the historical and cultural background of peoples living in different circumstances and areas of the world. Accordingly, the mutual relation among cultures is an important issue in today's world. "Nowadays there is no room for civilizing missions of one culture at the expense of others."[8] However, as the participants of the International Congress on Dialogue among Civilizations from the Viewpoint of the Young People, held in Tehran between 30-31 October 2002, stressed, a true and fruitful dialogue has certain prerequisites, conditions, and rules which are necessary to be understood, recognized, believed in and practically observed by the parties of dialogue, and thus they should be paid attention to. Among these rules are knowledge, understanding of each other's point of view, avoidance of unreasonable hostility and prejudice, criticism and reasoning, acceptance of differences, critical assessment of one's self as well as of others, and acceptance of truth, and in short, emphasis on the commonalties and avoidance of disparities. "Forced exchanges between civilizations, in particular if based on the economic dominance of one civilization over the other, have little potential to develop into a meaningful dialogue."[9]

Mutual respect and tolerance are required in the process of the dialogue of cultural traditions. Three ethical elements can be identified from an analysis of past inter-civilisational encounters: a common interest in engaging in an exchange across cultural or civilisational boundaries, a sound recognition and understanding of other cultures and civilisations; and mutual respect among different civilisations or cultural groups.[10]

An ethical approach to the dialogue of cultural traditions will clarify the responsibilities of the concerned parties and help them to be accountable for their decisions. Common ethical principles underlying the specific value systems and the common cultural features and similarities in values among different civilisations will contribute to the development of global ethics that will help us to address global problems. The role of ethics for the guidance of human behaviour should not be underestimated. Environmental ethics, development ethics, and business ethics can influence "developed" and developing nations and transnational corporations to participate in inter-civilisational dialogue. Environmental and business ethics contend that the trade regime needs to pursue its economic goals by showing sensitivity to other important goals and values,

---

[8] Goulet, "Global Community: Its Ethical Basis," p. 12.

[9] United Nations University, *Observations and Recommendations*, UNU Workshop on "The Contribution of Ethics to the Dialogue of Civilizations," 24-25 May 2001, p. 4.

[10] United Nations University, p. 4.

such as poverty alleviation, environmental protection, the promotion of public health and the encouragement of good working conditions. Ethics can thus help us build a just, sustainable and peaceful global society.

ETHICS AND PUBLIC SERVICE

In this section, I wish to examine whether ethics can contribute to the dialogue of cultural traditions and public service. "Public service" refers to the activities of individuals dedicated to delivering work and service in the pursuit of the public interest and common good. Some scholars have suggested that moral force rather than coercive authority is essential to persuade countries to respect international environmental law. For instance, Holmes Rolston said that a vital part of international law is "the moral force, just because the coercive legal force is reduced ... No nation wishes to stand morally condemned by the rest of the world (as South Africa has been with its apartheid)."[11] Attfield for his part maintains that some kind of ethic (a theory of right and responsibility) is necessary to solve problems whether global, environmental or otherwise, for it provides us with guidance and direction.[12]

Nigel Dower also argues that we need to accept a global ethic and to see ourselves as world citizens. He stresses that what is required is global governance rather than global government. He remarks that, "[t]o the extent that citizens accept a level of identity as world citizens, to that extent their states will be directed to the global common good anyway."[13] Although Dower has noted the environmental problems of the present world, he is of the opinion that some of the trends in the world can be checked through transformations of attitude and of ethical priority.

Although I acknowledge that ethical pressure is important, I have some reservations. Despite the good principles formulated by ethicists and countries during international conferences on various subjects, the world is not yet on a path toward socially just and environmentally sound development. As has been stated earlier on, transnational corporations and various countries have continued to promote their interests at the expense of the natural environment and poor countries. Moral force does not influence transnational corporations and powerful countries to limit their exploitation. Powerful countries may make use of the dialogue of cultural traditions to further their interests. Motivations for dialogue can sometimes be conditioned by power relations. If the two parties do not have equal power, very little can be achieved.

---

[11] Holmes Rolston III, *Conserving Natural Value* (New York: Columbia University Press, 1994), p. 214.

[12] Robin Attfield, *The Ethics of the Global Environment* (Edinburgh: Edinburgh University Press, 1999), p. 27.

[13] Nigel Dower, *World Ethics: The New Agenda* (Edinburgh: Edinburgh University Press, 1998), p. 196.

As Went has persuasively argued, in spite of the continuous reshuffling of the responsibilities and authority of organisations like the OECD, the World Bank, the IMF, the WTO, the G7, the EU and the UN, none of them will have the resources, facilities, room and authority to impose international regulations and controls against irresponsible countries and TNCs.[14] Although the 1970 UN Declaration on a New International Economic Order (NIEO) called for a radical redistribution of resources from North to South,[15] this project has been wishful and unfulfilled.

Although ethics is important and may influence power and its exercise, we still cannot rely on moral pressure alone to tackle environmental, developmental and political problems. Many Western governments are not living up to what they have promised. There is no way for developing countries to avoid dependency, ecological destruction and poverty as long as the present power structures remain unchanged. At the same time global environmental problems will be increasing in the years to come. To be really effective, the question of power relations should be looked at in a different way. Political and legal regulations in international law should be in place in order to control the negative effects of globalisation. To this end, dialogue among civilisations will serve as a fruitful way of tackling global problems.

As a matter of fact, in spite of what has been stated above, we can make moral progress. It is true that sometimes we move one step forward and two steps back. We may lose many battles and win some. In spite of this, I believe that moral progress is possible. Goulet's view may help us to understand this: "[A]s long as societies accept, even implicitly, the dictum that 'in war there is no substitute for victory' – whether in military, economic or political warfare – they are condemned to perish by the sword."[16]

Ethics is essential in tackling global problems and in making wise choices. It can change the way people behave, because it helps individuals to be responsible citizens that will seek constructive solutions to complex moral problems. Goulet contends that ethics can be a "means of the means." "Ethics has a twin mission: to identify the values which ought to be promoted, and to collaborate with these societal actors who can safeguard these values while simultaneously transforming institutions and behaviour in ways which keep human and cultural costs within tolerable bounds."[17] Also, ethics enables us to test practices, conventions and conduct.

In this connection, it is worth noting that, during China's Cultural Revolution, Mao Zedong advanced the following slogan: "Values

---

[14] Went, *Globalisation: Neoliberal Challenge, Radical Responses.*

[15] Dower, *World Ethics: The New Agenda*, p. 138.

[16] Goulet, "Ethical Strategies in the Struggle for World Development," *Sociological Inquiry*, 46 (1976), p. 290.

[17] Goulet, "Obstacles to World Development: An Ethical Reflection," *World Development*, 11(1983), p. 620.

command politics, politics command economics, economics command technique."[18] It seems that this dictum is still acceptable. I fully endorse the view that "[n]either technology nor economics – and a fortiori mere corporate profit-seeking – must be allowed by any society to assume primacy over the higher demands of politics, charged with the common good and, in turn, over the values to which politics itself must be subordinated: the inviolability of the person, and open-ness to transcendence or ultimate meanings."[19]

In today's world, we need more awareness of the full spectrum of values in nature; we need more regulation that can be effective across national values; we need participatory democracy, better technology, sources of energy that are not polluting, and more tourism. People need to travel around the world and appreciate heritages of beauty and wildlife. Thus, individuals should bring an ethical perspective to their role as citizens and professionals. This would help them to value public service, show concern for the common good, and bring moral theory to bear on issues in public life.

Individuals who work in public administration should know how to be sensitive to ethical problems that arise in the course of their service, because they are decision makers in positions of power. They must analyse the moral consequences of the economic and political systems that their society institutes. They should have discussions about whether people in public service are sufficiently visible, and sometimes they have to publish accounts of what stocks they own. They should support transparent decision making processes, in which positions are openly disclosed and debated. Truthfulness and honesty are required in handling expense accounts. Thus, public service should be accountable to the citizenry it serves.

Another important point is the relationship between ecology and public service. What must be noted here is that public service is primarily concerned with use of natural resources. Various government ministries including agriculture, environment and the like are greatly concerned with the conservation of natural resources. Ecological wisdom has a paramount role in managing global resources. So people in public service have to talk to ecologists, and find out what kinds of interventions in natural systems can be successful and unsuccessful. They need to have ecological knowledge to prevent the depletion of natural resources and thereby to improve the quality of public services supplied. They need to reflect upon global problems by confronting the ethical dimensions of historical and contemporary environmental issues. Every public service employee should be trained to strengthen his or her capacity for ethical judgment.

---

[18] Quoted in Goulet, "Creating Wealth, or Causing Poverty?" in *Ethics and the Multinational Enterprise: Proceedings of the Sixth National Conference on Business Ethics*, ed. W. Michael Hoffman et al. (Lanham, MD: University Press of America, Inc., 1986), p. 205.

[19] Goulet, "Creating Wealth, or Causing Poverty?" p. 205.

CONCLUSION

It has been argued that dialogue among civilisations is desirable in today's world. A common concern for survival, and our concerted efforts to build both an environmentally and socially sustainable world and a just and developmental world order, force us to be cautiously optimistic and to work on the dialogue of cultural traditions. But, creative dialogue conducted in the mode of reciprocity between "old" and "new" societies and old and new models of rationality "can only be achieved if all patterns of domination, cultural no less than economic, are abolished."[20] The dialogue of cultural traditions contributes very little to a world that is divided into donors and recipients of charity. It will not give rise to constructive communication and cross-enrichment. What has been going on in the present world indicates that cross cultural dialogue does not have any future. In particular, the unauthorized intervention in Iraq, with the concomitant attempt to marginalise the United Nations, and the unlimited expansion of TNCs, show that there is little hope in the future. It seems that the United States will use its power in ways that it judges right, without the approval or consent of other nations.

Although ethics can teach corporations that they should pursue wealth in an ethically acceptable manner, ethics alone is not sufficient to address global problems. The concerned parties should address the question of power relations. As Goulet rightly noted, without a cultural revolution within the United States, the American society will become unlivable and no just world order can be forged.[21] The American people should force their leaders to examine their policies and listen to other nations. The former should remember that a dialogue within nations as well as among nations is desirable and beneficial. Other citizens should also oppose governments that support undemocratic governments that invest in, produce and sell morally questionable weapons and use these weapons to kill innocent people the world over.

The dialogue of cultural traditions will help us to build a more civilised and a more just world for human and nonhuman beings. It is a tool of betterment and growth. It would help different traditions to gain new insights about their own principles of life and those of others. Thus, we need to participate effectively, efficiently, and appropriately in the dialogue of cultural traditions. We must utilise our cultural, historical and political wealth to create systems of organisation that are morally responsible, humane and democratic. What is required is shared responsibility in finding global and local solutions to global and local problems. To this end, we need to continue to raise awareness about the significance of the dialogue of cultural traditions and the future of the world. Small changes are possible,

---

[20] Goulet, "Global Community: Its Ethical Basis," p. 11.
[21] Goulet, "Ethical Strategies in the Struggle for World Development," p. 289.

in spite of opposing forces. We have to be cautiously optimistic, because we lose many battles and win only some.

Finally, the following questions require our attention: What is the role of ethical reflection and commitment for the dialogue of cultural traditions? What is the practical objective of a dialogue among civilizations? What had been done to other civilisations? How would the dialogue continue and who would control it? Does creating wealth cause poverty? Is it enough to generate profits if we are not also accounting for the human and environmental costs? Can the demand for ecological integrity ever become strong enough to offset the "profit imperative"? How can we make ethical decisions about our environment in the face of increasingly conflicting needs and opinions? What type of world do we want to live in? What will be the goals of this world, and what is the role of history's poor in defining its shape?[22]

Department of Philosophy
Addis Ababa University
Addis Ababa, Ethiopia

---

[22] On this theme, see also my other recent work: "Indigenous Environmental Ethics in Ethiopia", in Katsuyoshi Fukui, et al. (eds.), *Ethiopia in Broader Perspective: Papers of the XIIIth International Conference of Ethiopian Studies*, Kyoto, 2-17 December, Volume III (Kyoto: Shokado Book Sellers, 1997), pp. 264-303; "Globalization and Indigenous Environmental Knowledge in Ethiopia", in Taye Assefa et al. (eds.), *Globalization, Democracy and Development in Africa: Challenges and Prospects.* Addis Ababa: Organization for Social Science Research in Eastern and Southern Africa (OSSREA), 2001, pp. 275-306; *Traditional Oromo Attitudes towards the Environment: An Argument for Environmentally Sound Development. OSSREA Social Science Research Report Series*, No. 19 (Addis Ababa: Commercial Printing Enterprise, 2001); "Indigenous and Modern Environmental Ethics: A Study of the Indigenous Oromo Environmental Ethic and Oromo Environmental Ethics in the Light of Modern Issues of Environment and Development," Unpublished Ph.D. Thesis, University of Wales, 2001; "Globalisation: Friend or Foe to the Youth of Today and Tomorrow?," Paper presented at the African Regional Conference on Youth and Human Values held in Accra, Ghana , 8-10 July 2002; "Dialogue Among Civilizations and the Process of Globalization", Paper presented at the International Conference on Dialogue Among Civilizations from the Viewpoint of Youth," Tehran, 30-31 October (2002..

PART III

WAYS OF THINKING AND

WAYS OF INTERPRETING

CHAPTER XXVIII

WHO ARE WE, AND
WHERE ARE WE HEADING?

JERZY A. WOJCIECHOWSKI

Biologically, the human species is a roaring success. It populated the earth, reached to the moon, and intellectually embraced the furthest reaches of the universe. Aristotle's belief that human mind is "as if it were everything" is being realized before our eyes. Other species live in ecological balance with the environment and have a more or less well-defined ecological niche. Nature does not allow them to trespass its limits. Excesses are not tolerated and are swiftly eliminated when the species transcends the feeding capacity of the niche. Humans are in a different situation. Thanks to their rationality they do not seem to have a defined niche of their own. If such a niche existed in the time of Adam and Eve, their descendents have dramatically extended its limits. Not only did they spill out of their original habitat, but they transformed themselves externally and internally. They formed various races, adjusted to a multitude of very different conditions of life, and evolved into a plethora of cultures.

Strange as it may sound, because of their rationality, humans are not only a changing object of knowledge, but, moreover, an increasingly complex one. Does it mean that Aristotle's definition of humans as rational animals is no longer valid? The answer is simple: yes, and no! Let us explain. As far as definitions go, humans are in a very particular situation. Generally speaking a definition is as valid as its object is unchanging. The definition of a molecule of water, H_2O, is indefinitely valid because its nature does not change with time. Our belief in the permanence of aspects of the physical universe is the foundation of our belief in the a-temporal validity of science.

If this is the case, we can draw an important conclusion about humans. There cannot be a science of humans similar to physics, chemistry or astronomy. Does it mean that there cannot be any science of the human phenomenon at all? Fortunately this is not the case, either. We have many sciences of the rational animal from archeology to psychiatry. Moreover, with every advancement of knowledge, in whichever field it may be, we can learn more and more about humans, and we do learn constantly more. This is not surprising. After all, what is there more interesting to know for us than ourselves!

In general, knowledge gives us a reassuring feeling; it protects us against the unknown. The word "paradise" comes from an old Persian word meaning a walled (i.e., secure) place. The wall protects us against the threatening unknown. It would seem logical to conclude that the more knowledge we have the more secure we should feel. Unfortunately this is not the case. Humanity has never been more knowledgeable than now. Never before has the development of knowledge been as rapid and as global as it is presently. And yet, the future of humanity has never been as uncertain as at the present moment. Why?

The very question is surprising, to say the least, and the answer is equally strange. The incertitude which we experience presently about our future is due to the development of knowledge, i.e., to the very factor which should make us secure. Such a sweeping statement demands an adequate explanation. It so happens that the present writer has been trying, for the past thirty years, to furnish the answer by means of his theory of the Ecology of Knowledge. The theory is concerned with the relationship existing between knowers and the body of knowledge (the knowledge construct – KC for short), seen as a distinct, *sui generis*, entity.

The theory is based on three affirmations, namely:

1. knowledge exists
2. intellectual knowledge expands
3. intellectual knowledge is, as stated above, a *sui generis* entity distinct from knowers

The first two affirmations are, I believe, self-evident. The third should become also self-evident upon a moment of reflection. It is important to realize its meaning because it is the keystone of the theory of Ecology of Knowledge – EoK for short. This affirmation accounts also for the strangeness of the EoK. It allows us to view intellectual knowledge in a novel and surprising light, very different from how intellectual knowledge has been viewed before.

It sounds illogical, but knowledge as an object of knowledge is obscure, opaque and difficult to know. The best proof of this is the history of philosophy itself. Traditionally, since the beginning of philosophy, thinkers looked at intellectual knowledge as a glorious product of the intellect, a harmonious extension of the intellect, but and were all in agreement in their praise of the value of intellectual knowledge. They all considered the intellect as the highest, most perfect human faculty, the specific mark of humans, distinguishing them from animals and forming the essence of humanness. To suggest to them that intellect and its product could be the source of problems endangering the future of humanity would be beyond imagination. And that is precisely what the EoK suggests! Once we grasp the distinction existing between the KC and knowers, it is easier to understand that whatever the intentions of knowers, knowledge (KC) exists on its own and produces positive as well as negative effects. Knowers do not master externalized knowledge.

We live in strange times indeed. To understand the situation we are presently in, it is necessary to grasp the strangeness of it. It is not the very fact of being threatened that is unusual. Humans have always felt threatened, but in the past the threat has always come from the outside: a deluge or a drought, earthquakes or plagues, or other natural calamities. And if they were man-induced, like wars or persecutions of various sorts, they were limited in time and space and did not threaten the future of humanity as a whole. The present development of knowledge, however, does.

Let us be more specific. The dangers facing humanity are of two very different sorts. One is more obvious, the other more hidden. The dangers of the first and, I dare say, less important sort are the weapons of mass destruction. Not surprisingly, they are the product of the development of knowledge; their danger is therefore proportional to the level of knowledge. The more advanced knowledge is, the more varied and accessible they become. If today they are in the hands of, say, half a dozen countries, tomorrow a dozen countries will have them, and the day after tomorrow two dozen. Likewise, groups of people (not just countries) with adequate knowledge and financial means come to have access.

In a foreseeable future almost everybody will be able to produce them in his basement or back yard. Will this herald the end of humanity? On the contrary. It will result in the exclusion of warfare from the available choices of human behaviours. When these arms will become universally available, the potential adversaries will become assured of mutual destruction and the chances of winning will become non-existent. Thus, we will have to learn to live in peace, not because of a sudden improvement in morality, but because the instinct of self-preservation will force us to limit our aggressive instincts.

Let us realize that the development of science and technology will give us not only more sophisticated means of mass destruction but also more advanced means of defense against them. Humans may deploy ever-greater ingenuity in developing constantly more sophisticated means of aggression, but the law of action and reaction is not of human making, and it is more fundamental than human wishes and desires. Fortunately, we are not the only kids on the block when it comes to the play of destruction. This is why the present writer believes that the means of mass destruction are the lesser of two sorts of threats confronting humanity.

Let us now turn to the second, less obvious but more serious sort of dangers facing humanity. They are of the environmental kind. We became aware of them after the Second World War, even though their sources are older. The most important new insight that emerged in the last half century is the awareness that we are denizens of a finite earth system. We have, of course, always been aware that we inhabit this planet. But we were not aware of the consequences of the finitude of the earth system. Until the mid-twentieth century, we behaved as if nature were infinite, i.e., inexhaustible. It was on this assumption that we based our economic theories and expectations. Whether it was John Stuart Mill or Karl Marx, people on the social right or left, all were certain that we could live off nature indefinitely, without inducing any negative consequences, let alone endangering the future of humanity. We believed that natural resources would never run out.

We may look with condescension on these naïve assumptions but we must not forget that they were held generally until very recently. If they seem so naïve and so distant from us, it is merely a proof of how fast our knowledge progresses and how rapidly the conditions of our existence change. Earlier we said that rational activity makes the human phenomenon more and more complex. Further, the more humans think, the more problematic they become for themselves. They are the only ones to have problems with themselves. This happens for two reasons. First they possess the intellect. But the intellect in itself does not explain why humans have more and more problems with themselves. In order to explain this situation, we have to consider not just the intellect but also its product, namely intellectual knowledge and its development. In other words, we have to explain why and how knowledge expands as it does and what the consequences of its development are.

The first thing we have to realize is the fact that the KC can expand indefinitely while the intellect cannot. The capacity of the individual brain is finite. I can learn so much, I can remember so much, I can understand so much and no more. The discrepancy existing between the indefinite additivity of the KC and the limited capacity of the brain leads to a paradoxical but true conclusion which can be expressed in the form of a law: "Knowledge produces ignorance." The greater the KC, the greater the field or amount of existing knowledge which the individual knower ignores. This fact has multiple and far reaching consequences which we will now try to explore.

In the first place, let us explain that the expansion of the KC is made possible not just by the capacity of the intellect to think. This capacity is a necessary but insufficient condition of the expansion of the KC. The crucial condition making this expansion possible is the storing of knowledge outside the brain. This is achieved by means of writing. The invention of writing and the subsequent improvements in the technique of externalization, communication and storing of knowledge, were crucial steps in the development of knowledge. Without the invention of writing, its simplification by the introduction of alphabet, the invention of print and, finally, the electronic means of communication and storage of knowledge, the world would not be what it is today.

The constant intercourse between the intellect and the KC is the essential condition of not only the development of knowledge, but the evolution of the human species. This has far reaching consequences. The evolution of humanity is an element of general evolution. We usually view evolution as a biological phenomenon, but, as we have realized recently, it is a cosmic phenomenon as well. It is in fact the most fundamental and universal of all material phenomena that we know of. It began with the big bang and continued through the formation of atoms to the formations of molecules, the double helix of DNA, the first living cell, the multiple cell organisms, to ever more sophisticated animals, to Adam and Eve, and from them to us. The process of evolution has been progressing inexorably and at an ever-faster pace.

Since the appearance of humans the rate of evolution has been attached to the evolution of intellectual knowledge. This fact can be expressed by means of a law: "The rate of human evolution is proportional to the rate of evolution of intellectual knowledge." In general, the history of the pace of evolution since its beginning may be expressed as follows: "Cosmic evolution is slower than biological evolution, which is slower than human evolution." Human evolution is speeding up proportionately to the evolution of intellectual knowledge, which advances proportionately to the development of the means of externalization, communication and storage of knowledge.

The French say "the dead travel fast."[1] The same is true now of the living. It would be interesting to speculate whether the rate of evolution of the living could be accelerated much longer. The present writer is not a prophet, but it seems to him that we are reaching quickly a limit of our capacity to absorb change. If this is the case, then we are close to a profound intellectual, psychological and social revolution. The future will be very unlike the present. Does it mean that the future is only for the lionhearted? I do not think so. Maybe thinking about the future requires a certain amount of intellectual courage because it demands our getting off the beaten track and thinking in a new key, but it does not mean that we are facing an end of humanity.

By and large, the human race is not a collective candidate for suicide. On the contrary, the average human wants to live, abhors death and desires happiness. Candidates for suicide are few and far apart. It has always been so and most probably will remain so. Suicides have always had a bad press. Dante placed them in one of the lowest places in hell. It is true, however, that the development of knowledge multiplies our demiurgic powers, which can threaten our future. Consequently, it is certain that the more we know, the more we have to think about the future, i.e., the more we have to evaluate our condition and the consequences of our activity.

It may come as a surprise, but the future is the realm of values. Future thought is value thought. We perceive it as a field of possibilities, i.e., a domain of choices facing us. To make choices, inexorably we have to make value judgments. Thus, the more we have to think about the future, the more we have to be concerned with values. The problem is that we are not well equipped for that because modern science has shied away from values. Its astounding success is due to choosing measurement as the miraculous key for prying open the secrets of nature. But measurement yields number-measures; it explores the quantitative aspects of the world,

---

[1] See the painting "Les morts vont vite (d'après une ballade de Bürger)" by the artist Ary Scheffer (1795-1858).

not the qualitative ones. Powerful as it is, to the extent that it is quantitative knowledge, it is of little help when it comes to the most important of all judgments, namely the moral ones.

Traditionally, we associate morals with religion and with Sunday preaching. Morals were the domain of the Ten Commandments and vouchsafed by the authority of the Almighty. The Ten Commandments regulated the relations between God and humanity, and were sufficient in the time of Moses. But they had nothing to say about the relationship of humans to the environment. If Moses went on Mount Sinai today he would have come down with many more than Ten Commandments. So why did he or God not add the commandments which we now badly need?

I think the answer is simple. Adding commandments which would be needed in a distant future would not only have been unnecessary but confusing for the contemporaries of Moses, i.e., counterproductive. Today the regulation of highway traffic is an understandable necessity. To tell the cameleer on the Sinai desert in the time of Moses to stop at red lights would be not only superfluous but incomprehensible, and it would discredit the other commandments. For a commandment to be authoritative it has to be meaningful, that is, it must apply to an existing situation. It may be a surprising conclusion, but modern science and technology, non-qualitative as they are, are forcing us now to be value-oriented and ever more moral for seemingly non-religious reasons, such as the dependence on the environment. Had we lived in an infinitely big earth system, we would not have the concerns which we now have, and we would have no need to expand our ethical system. The following chart illustrates the situation.

Differences in Perception of the Earth System and its Consequences

Nature is	Infinite, i.e. inexhaustible	Finite, i.e. exhaustible
Hence:	No exploitation of nature	Exploitation of nature
	No negative effects of the use of nature for (a) nature, (b) humans	Negative effects for (a) nature (b) humans
	No responsibility for the development of powerful knowledge	Responsibility for the development of powerful knowledge
	Knowledge does not threaten nature	Knowledge threatens nature
	The development of knowledge does not create a human/nature moral	Presence of a human / nature moral problem; need to enlarge the moral

problem; no need to enlarge the moral problematic	problematic
Scientific (quantitative) knowledge is sufficient; no need to complement it by enlarged knowledge of qualities and values; humans may imagine themselves as masters of the world.	Scientific (quantitative) knowledge insufficient; need to complement it by enlarged knowledge of qualities and value; humans are NOT masters of the world.
No concern about effects of scientific knowledge on nature	Concern about effects of scientific knowledge on nature
Ethics is secondary	Ethics is primary

We have come a long way from the discussion of the KC, but the distinction between the KC and knowers was that which made possible our reaching of the problems of morality and illuminating the situation of humanity.

Evolution is always a co-evolution. The more complex the evolving entity, the faster it evolves. The evolution of humanity is the result of a system composed of humans, the KC and the surrounding nature and human products – some of which are material, like dwellings, vehicles, and tools; others are immaterial, such as customs, laws or systems of values. Humans are the most active element of the system. Because of them, the system is dynamic and implosive, self-stimulating and form-creating, growing in size and complexity and evolving ever faster. The interactions occurring in the system structure human existence, thereby inducing increasingly higher forms of behavior and organization. This is achieved through the generation of constraints of a material and intellectual sort (information and problems), forcing humans to live up to them. The system transforms lower, material energy into higher, intellectual energy which gives humans the power to act more and more rationally. Through rational activity, the system grows in size, complexity and rate of change. So does its impact on all elements of the system. The Evolutionary System of Mankind is an evolution-producing device. It forces humans to evolve toward higher levels of 'humanness', and toward a more rational, conscious, self-directing and synergistic, globalized humanity.

University of Ottawa
Ottawa, Canada

CHAPTER XXIX

THE PRESENT MOMENT

JERZY A. WOJCIECHOWSKI

We live in the most revolutionary time in history. The revolutionary nature of the present is neither the result of terrorist activities, nor the 9-11 types of events. It is not caused by negative feelings or a protest against an existing situation. On the contrary, it is the result of positive attitudes and actions. The reality around us changes ever faster because of the explosion of knowledge. It is the result of increasingly more massive, conscious and systematic rational activity of legions of researchers: scientists and technologists of various sorts engaged in the broadening of the field of knowledge. The present day revolution is animated by positive feelings and intentions, directed not against somebody or something, as was the Marxist revolution, but by a positive desire to improve the existing situation, to know more, to do more, and to be more.

Never before has the rate of change been so rapid, so much desired, and so much approved of. The impact of knowledge is nothing new. But presently, because of the level of knowledge, it is more powerful than ever before, and is a factor that makes life constantly more complex. It may sound strange, but knowledge – which was supposed to facilitate life and solve problems – is fast becoming a source of growing problems. Has something gone wrong? Have we worked ourselves into a blind alley? Not really. Knowledge facilitates life for our muscles. It liberates us from tedious manual chores, but it makes life constantly more demanding for our intellect. Knowledge demands constantly more knowledge from us. The more knowledge there is, the more we have to know to succeed in life, to compete with others, to be rational animals. The present situation is the logical result of human evolution and a means of furthering this evolution.

One of the most important consequences of the development of knowledge is the disappearance of physical distances separating us from each other. This radically changes our existential situation. Since the beginning of humanity we have lived as individuals and societies in a given place which we called our own, distinct and distant from others. The distances between these places made communication difficult, and contributed to the evolution of distinct personal and societal identities with all their complex consequences.

The emergence of instant, world-wide communication abolished the spaces among us. Suddenly, we became next-door neighbours while remaining ourselves, outwardly unchanged. Although no physical change can be noticed in our appearance, our mental condition has changed dramatically. We have become physically and mentally interdependent, influencing each other more and more, realizing Marshall McLuhan's idea of the global village. More importantly, we have become morally interdependent. A shining example of this is the decision of Indian authorities to accord Mother Teresa the honour of a state funeral. Whether it realized it or not, the Indian government indicated for humanity the direction evolution has to follow. Thus, the humble nun became in her death the beacon indicating the road from the present day morass into a sustainable future.

In an ever more crowded world, with knowledge giving us constantly more accessible and varied means of mass destruction, the only chance for humanity and for a viable future is more evolution. It entails the moral development of the ability of global coexistence. This, in turn, requires better knowledge of our close and distant neighbours. The need to know each other, to understand us as we are, with all our peculiarities, and to accept them as positive factors accounting for the richness of the human phenomenon, are fundamental conditions of human advancement.

Solidarity was the name of a Polish workers union. But "Solidarity" is an idea expressing the basic need of interhuman relations for the future. Its strength and its radical novelty lie in its nonviolent nature, as did its ability to overcome the most armed and violent regime in existence – the Communist empire – and to do it in a peaceful way. Like the Indian government honouring Mother Teresa, like Mother Teresa herself, solidarity shows humanity the direction to follow. May we heed their example.

Moral responsibility is proportional to the level of knowledge of each one of us and to the awareness of the situation we find ourselves in. As philosophers, we have a particular duty to comprehend our times and the moral responsibility to act accordingly. If we act in communion with each other, we create synergy which multiplies our forces and our impact on the world. This is why the meeting, of which this present volume is the fruit, was so significant. It was the beginning step on the road which we should follow. Our meeting was to enrich philosophy and make important contributions towards finding a way out of the ever more complex problems of the present moment.

University of Ottawa
Ottawa, Canada

CHAPTER XXX

NATURALISM, SUPERNATURALISM, AND DENATURALISM

PABLO LÓPEZ LÓPEZ

INTRODUCTION

Our study encompasses a renewed view of the history of philosophy (and science) and the corresponding philosophy of history, including the connected history of religion (and art). All possible world-views, with their general rationalities and anthropologies, are taken into consideration. Such a speculative and general topic can make an important contribution to a concrete intercultural and "interepochal"[1] dialogue. Here a crucial concept will be "Modernity" since it involves a key appreciation of cultures rather than a descriptive and neutral concept. "Modernity" can no longer be regarded as exclusive of Denaturalism. We have to be very cautious, because our claims are ambitious. We are aware of the risk of oversimplification. In fact, this is one of our main claims. All past, present and future world-views and religions, all existing or possible general philosophies, belong to one of these three models: Naturalism, Supernaturalism and Denaturalism. Moreover, since philosophy is a basis for the sciences, these models also constitute the general framework of all scientific developments. Art has always expressed and promoted these panoramic views and their multifarious divisions or trends.

---

[1] By *"interepochal dialogue,"* I mean *the deep communication or empathy between people of very distant times or historical circumstances.* There are epoch-making events creating general situations which are difficult to understand by people of different epochs. History's goal is to overcome those difficulties by understanding past times and their different mentalities. But this historical approach can be exclusively seen in a unidirectional way. Instead, since a mutual and real communication and understanding between diverse contemporary cultures is highly desirable, we also propose a highly desirable dialogue between people of different epochs – an interepochal dialogue. Even though it is not possible in a literal sense to have a dialogue with deceased people, we can experience a real closeness to people of the past and an exchange of feelings and ideas. We can feel that we understand what they really meant and that they understood our views by anticipating our own perspectives and ideas. In the same way, we experience closeness to very different cultures, even without physical contact or a concrete feedback.

NATURALISM

The Naturalist world-views and religions[2] have a circular perception of reality, according to the natural model. The term "nature" keeps its etymological meaning of "what is given by birth."[3] In Naturalism everything is natural, given by nature, given by birth. Therefore Naturalism implies at least some tendency towards determinism: everything is determined by birth and within a circularity. This destiny remains within a general circular order abundantly observed in nature (seasons, day and night, tides, deaths and births, periods, etc.). Naturalists see everything as nature: an anonymous, living and well-characterised strength turning around on itself. Even gods belong to nature, since they did not create it out of nothing. Divinity is widespread and hence not well distinguished, although there are usually natural elements venerated as particularly sacred, like a river, a tree, a mountain, a star or an animal. In Naturalism, divinity derives from natural phenomena. In consequence, the Naturalist world is heavily sacralised. This is sacralism, which involves politics and every aspect of life.

But this does not necessarily imply pantheism. Paradoxically, this basically anonymous and impersonal identity of nature (which is not a personal design of a personal being) is combined with recurrent anthropomorphisms. There cannot be real theocentrism or anthropocentrism, since neither divine nor human "persons" are yet properly distinguished (in spite of some meritorious attempts). This view is a confusing mixture of anthropomorphism and sacralism, but within the

---

[2] A distinction between secular world views or philosophies and religions is done in our culture on the basis of the Judeo-Christian differentiation of what is, on the one hand, a global supernatural revelation turned into human concepts and words, and, on the other hand, mere human thinking about the fundamentals of everything. After Occam (14th c.) this key distinction was increasingly emphasised. After the "Enlightenment" (18th c.), and its implicit or explicit Denaturalism, such a subtle differentiation became a severe separation and opposition.

As an example of this typical Naturalist indistinctness, let us recall what Sue Hamilton writes in *Indian Philosophy: A Very Short Introduction* (Oxford: Oxford University Press 2001), p. 1: "What Westerners call religion and philosophy are combined in India in people's attempts to understand the meaning and structure of life–in the broadest sense. This is comparable more with the approach of Socrates than with religion as faith in revelation and philosophy as an academic discipline." This is so because Socrates and all Greece's and all India's world-views (philosophy and religion combined) are Naturalist.

[3] *"Nature"* is the Anglicized form of the Latin *"natura"* which comes from the Latin verb *"nascor" (I am born)* and more precisely from its past participle *"natus-a-um"* (a form derived from a putative supine "natum").

impersonal atmosphere of circular nature. It represents a time of pre-humanism and pre-deification.

This age-old view has two major stages: first, Mythical Naturalism and then, starting with the Greeks, Intellectualist Naturalism. Naturalism in the first stage was conceived in the free fantastic way of myth. Myth was also a rational production and played the crucial role of giving sense to major environmental and social phenomena. Obviously in myth areas or aspects of reality are not well distinguished; in exchange they are represented in a free and attractive use of fantasy.

The Greeks became progressively enthusiastic with the general view of a perfectly aesthetic, rational and vitalist world, ruled by a "logos." Everything was still natural, but this nature or "physis" was believed to be fully arranged according to a divine "logos" (or "nous" or "eidos"), i.e., a divine intelligence. The universe was a "cosmos," a beautiful order; everything had soul, life. Such a passionately poetic and intellectual approach was the inspiration, the real Muse of Greek religion, philosophy, art, science and general culture or way of living. Rome gave Greek intellectualism permanency, balance, unity and spread. "Logos" became "lex" and then "imperium": in philosophical terms, we have a broad, solid and millennial universalization of a supranational, consistent and systematic rationality.

There is confusion among many scholars with respect not only to Supernaturalism, as we will see, but also to Naturalism or paganism. We can only understand Supernaturalism if we understand Naturalism, and vice versa. And to understand both of them is the condition for understanding Denaturalism. But unfortunately Naturalism is usually mistaken for Denaturalism, as if this were a mere Neo-naturalism or neo-paganism (like Plotinianism). Gus di Zerega supplies a good example, when he tries to distinguish – throughout his whole book – Christianity and Paganism. His basic mistake is that he only differentiates these two. According to this Brazilian writer, "pagan spirituality may be distinguished by the five following characteristics: (1) Pantheism or Panentheism; (2) Animism; (3) Polytheism; (4) The Eternal Present (with a primary emphasis upon spiritual reality's cyclical and mythical, rather than linear and historical, character); (5) No equivalent of Satan or ultimate evil.[4] However, panentheism is a Judeo-Christian distinction which cannot be identified or assimilated to pantheism. The pagan Greeks went far beyond mythical explanations. In most Naturalist religions there is an evil principle or diabolical agents.

Another example of radical confusion in a presumed specialised scholar is that of Jean-Claude Barreau: "I am still a pagan because of my affective reactions as well as my complete lack of sense of guilt, and

---

[4] Gus di Zerega, *Pagans and Christians, The Personal Spiritual Experience* (St. Paul, MN: Llewellyn Publications, 2001), p. 5.

because of my absolute curiosity for whatever doctrine."[5] What would be "pagan affection"? The lack of sense of guilt is not pagan at all, but precisely Secularist. And is a great curiosity a distinctive pagan feature? Nobody should write so frivolously.

SUPERNATURALISM

Christianity, especially by those who are non-Christians, can be understood as a philosophy or a world-view, which is not necessarily revealed, but able to contribute rationally to deep truth. In this context, a revolutionary Judeo-Christian general contribution is the clear discovery of the supernatural. A generalised anachronism is confusing the idea of divinity (obviously very present and relevant in Naturalism) with the idea of the supernatural (the radical novelty in Judeo-Christian philosophy). "Divinity" expresses the notion of a supreme being or beings. Such a being or beings can be a part of nature (in Naturalism) or constitute a new realm over nature, as the absolute and unique Creator of nature (in Supernaturalism). There are no definitive scientific grounds to accept the first or second option, or to deny either. Despising beforehand the second one (the supernatural perspective), as it is customary to do in Secularist countries, is simply absurd and an irrational unfairness.

It is politically correct to assume that if an Ancient Greek (a Naturalist) or a post-Cartesian (e.g., a Denaturalist) thinker states something about god(s), he may be doing philosophy, while if the author speaks as a Christian, he can only do a sort of dogmatic theology. But every ideology and each person's way of life is based on beliefs, on a particular "creed": some beliefs are more reasonable and others are less consistent; some are recognised as such beliefs, while others are boldly presented as "scientific" (e.g. "scientific Socialism" and "Positivism"). Jews and then Christians conceived of the supernatural realm, as well as of the corresponding human supernatural vocation. Human beings could think of themselves as images or reflections of the supernatural Being. The revolutionary starting-point is the idea and the historical experience of a wholly transcendent, absolute and personal, supreme Being. He created everything out of nothing, and is fully involved in the providential recreation of all people as his children, provided they are active and involved in creative collaboration. The Creator of nature could no longer be a part of nature. As children of such a supernatural Being, people could discover their potential suitability for and their vocation to supernatural life both here and after death.

Human time was liberated from natural circularity, because there is a beginning (creation) and an end (historical and eschatological recreation): a full perception of the specific human historicity was born. That is the framework of a civilization of humanism as well as of deification

---

[5] Jean-Claude Barreau, *No todos los dioses son iguales* [*Tous les Dieux ne sont pas égaux*] (Madrid: Editorial Acento Editorial, 2001), p. 8.

(distinction and mature experience of God in human life). Supernaturalism is not at all a rejection of nature. Even more so, nature is revaluated as the work of such an Artist and is progressively rediscovered in its astonishing autonomy and complex order. The Creator of nature cannot reject his own work. The Creator and his creative creatures assume responsibility for nature. Human beings are conscious of being a part of nature (though they cannot be reduced to nature), and the transcendent God, by means of Incarnation (a central Christian claim of the most radical humanism) becomes a part of his own work. Nature is the human basis of the way to supernaturality, and the way is history, i.e., freedom through time.

The world is entirely the fruit of a will, of a wise and personal will. It is a personalised work which has an aim, a project. All men and women can understand themselves to have dominion in this voluntarist and personalised reality: they have the dignity, the will and the intelligence of persons. Such is the origin of the Volitionalist perspective (different from the Voluntarist one), united to the best Intellectualist tradition of the Ancient Greeks (different from the Rationalist one). As a whole, this is a Personalist view of reality and human dignity, and an overcoming of anthropomorphism and impersonalism.

The central Christian idea of Incarnation implies a balanced secularisation of God, an actual balanced union between the natural and the supernatural. Surprisingly, the most transcendental God becomes secular, and the supernatural joins the natural, in harmony with it and without creating confusion. Between the extremes of Sacralism (among Naturalists) and Secularism (among Denaturalists), Christianity (with its Supernaturalism) represents a balance consisting at once of a deep sense of both secularity and sacrality. That is why we cannot confuse secularisation (of a Christian origin) and Secularism or Laicism (Antichristian and opposed to every religion).

DENATURALISM

Denaturalism is the third world view and is represented by Secularism, which is different from secularisation or secularity. Nevertheless, "secularity" and "laicity" are usually mistaken for "Secularism" and "Laicism." Secularists or Laicists are not simple upholders of the independence of the State from Church interference. Their initial impulse is not even a clear delimitation of the autonomy of religion, politics, science and civil ethics. Supernaturalist reason fully agrees originally with that. Secularism consists in a "theophobia" or systematic opposition to any religious philosophy (almost all previous Philosophy) and particularly to Christianity; it also consists in the corresponding chasm regarding the rational or intellectualist Hellenic-Christian tradition. Not only was transcendental faith a victim of Secularism, but reason, the Greek theoretical "logos," has been generally reduced to a pragmatic or instrumentalist rationality since the "Enlightenment." However, Secularism is a pseudo-religion, as is made clear in the writings of authors like Comte or Feuerbach, and it claims to be the purest rationality. The Illuminist or "Enlightened"[6] "goddess Reason" was a rhetorical figure with little rational

---

[6] We prefer *the term "Illuminist" rather than the usual "Enlightened,"* as in Italian, where "Enlightenment" is represented by the word "Illuminismo" ("Aufklärung" in German, "Philosophie des lumières" in French, "Ilustración" in Spanish). The English, German, French and Spanish terms take for granted that this particular tendency or ideology of the 18th c. is indeed the intellectual light par excellence, the actual and unique light of reason, the historical climax of human culture. "Illuminism" keeps the same root meaning: the idea of "light." The ending of "-ism," however, points out the fact that we are dealing with a tendency or ideology, which is actually the case. We do the same with most schools or trends of thought: "Existentialism," "Idealism," "Platonism," "Marxism," etc. Regarding "Illuminism," this distinction is even more important. If we say "Platonic" or "Scholastic," we are not necessarily assuming a positive connotation. But, "Enlightened" implies this positive connotation, which is specially despising of other ways of thinking. Do we have to believe acritically all that a group of thinkers claims about its own achievements and absolute supremacy? Even if we like them, we should keep a critical distance. This prudent attitude is particularly necessary with Illuminists, since humility is not their virtue.

Illuminist authors also claimed, and so it has been believed, that their ideology represented a whole new era, a new age of unpredecented progress. They call it "le siècle des lumières." Of course, they were trying to introduce a different world-view (which I recognize as Denaturalism), but not a rationally superior new age. And, it is a fallacy that the 18th c. was as a whole the "Illuminist" century, like the fifteenth and the sixteenth can be said to be "Renaissance centuries." Illuminism did not even have a peculiar art style. And let us not forget that Illuminism was by definition a very élitist movement. The Illuminist influence in history has been intensive (and not always as positive as Illuminists prophesied), but this influence was not so present in their own century. I agree with Thomas Munck when he writes that "we have to be cautious in regarding the enlightenment as a decisive turning point. Few governments were genuinely keen on the idea of freedom of opinion, and the relaxation of censorship was frequently half-hearted. The spiritual environment of the great majority of Europeans was even more resistant to change." See his *The Enlightenment: A Comparative Social History* 1721-1794 (London: Hodder Arnold Publication, 2000), p. 162. Illuminist influence was intensive in the following centuries, but not as much in its own century. "Le siècle des lumières" did not exist. We have explored the first reason: Illuminism was not a movement involving the majority of people and governments and the core of culture. A more basic reason is that such a claim would mean that there was no rationality in other centuries, which is an absurd boast. There are no solid reasons to speak about the "Enlightened century." We can just say that Illuminism was born and had an initial influence in the 18th century.

The term "Illuminism" has another advantage: it also suggests the subtle closeness to the mystical Illuminist movement, as I am about to explain.

content except for drastic self-criticism and self-confinement and for a demanding social efficiency. "Goddess Reason" was rhetorically effective in order to create a dilemma between their Illuminist views, as the only possible rationality, and religious "faith," as interpreted in a merely fideistic and reductive way. Humanity was proclaimed to be "reason" (as a full self-consciousness and absolute self-determination or conscience), and therefore humanity, in an abstract and ethnocentric sense, was deified. "Goddess Reason" meant "goddess Humanity" (in a very partial sense of humanity). Besides, instead of a real separation between Church and State, the Church was intended to be absorbed so as to found the Church-State, a deified State[7]. Clear examples of this "Church-State" are found in Hobbes, Hegel and Marx (pre- and post-Illuminist thinkers). Secularism arises against Supernaturalism. It is often regarded as a sort of paganism or neo-paganism, but is a far more complex ideology and is also opposed to Naturalism and to nature. This is why Secularism is Denaturalism: a theoretical and practical reduction or denial of the importance or even of the reality of nature in many fields. This process of denaturalization has been very gradual. In the words of the first Denaturalists, nature (a mechanical and absolutized conception of nature) was even claimed as a standard of judgement; it was, rather, a way of expressing opposition to Supernaturalism. The philosophy

---

[7] We mean "State" in the broadest sense of human organisation of political and economic power. Thus also anti-state theories like Anarchism and the Capitalist rhetoric of "Free Market" are perfectly suited to be included in the general project of a Church-State (though obviously not with this name). Anarchist atheism cannot stand up to the idea of God, because an absolutely free humanity must be divine and does not admit another divinity (forms of Anarchism were born in monotheistic societies); Capitalist "free market" is providential and therefore divine. Let it be clear, we are not speaking of a State-Church or a confessional State, which is only a first stage for a Church-State.

Today a net of international (or global) lobbies is building its own world-wide Church-State, with an agenda of genocide and mind control over populations; only one State or government for the world, where freedom would be a mere virtual feeling; only one religion of a self-idolatrous humanity, opposed to all traditional religions seen as "dogmatic fanaticisms."

This Church-State model is not a simple return to the ancient, pagan and pre-Christian supremacy of collectivist values and to the naturalist confusion between religious and political powers. All ancient and Naturalist "States" (or the equivalent political organisations) sought to be on the best terms with divinity, with a superior realm having supremacy over human society. On the contrary, the Secularist State tries to substitute itself for divinity. Roman emperors or Pharaohs, for example, were deified as new gods among other and more powerful gods. Secularist States, like the Fascist, Communist and Masonic ones, demand to be considered the only divinity on earth as well as in heaven. This demagogic human deification is not a real anthropocentrism, but is, in practical terms, a deification of the rich and powerful élite.

derived from the first Denaturalist and Secularist authors shows very clearly the innermost core of those initial proposals of the "Enlightenment." It is difficult to change the whole terminology in one or two generations. It is enough to change the meaning of important and prestigious terms ("reason," "nature," "substance," "transcendental," etc.). In any event, after consciously denying the new outlook of Supernaturalism, it is no longer possible to go back to the "innocent" penumbra of Naturalism.

In the previous paragraphs we see that Illuminism is not so "irreligious," not so "rational" and not so "natural" as it is believed. Illuminist theophobia is compatible with a multifarious subjectivist "religiosity," ranging from different deisms up to agnosticism and atheism. Even deisms, which are supposed to be another way of affirming God's existence, drift easily into a sort of self-deification. If one's own reason establishes by itself what divinity is and what good or evil is, this reason and the individual will be assumed to be divine. Deists do not worry about the fact that they hardly agree among each other except for refusing as superstitious popular and traditional religions (especially the Catholic faith and reason). However, many of these religions are indeed much more rational than the minimalist Deism.

The drift to self-deification is clearer in forms of atheism,[8] in particular when they include any kind of social utopia. Atheists just refuse a divinity other than themselves, because they believe to be gods themselves (and good by themselves). Both Deist and Atheist self-deification can be understood in the artificial Kantian dilemma between religious "heteronomy" and rational "autonomy." Such a sophism appeals to a deep pride rather than to a balanced and deep rationality. Such a partial approach derives from ignoring the subtle and modern argument between Molina and Báñez (16th c.) on human freedom and divine omnipotence. The final result of this debate was not a precise formula, but at least was much more complex, balanced and profound than the simplistic and 'Manichean' Kantian dualism.

---

[8] Here Modern pantheism can be included. Modern or post-Christian pantheism, like Spinoza's and Hegel's, differs from the Naturalist tendency of confusing the divine and the non-divine, as in animism. After a clear historical differentiation of divinity as supernatural, a return to pantheism cannot but mean a human self-deification through the deification of reason (of a particular conception of reason, which rationally does not convince everyone). Modern pantheism can state the existence of a divinity, and even though this divinity seems to be applied to everything, it is lastly ascribed to human reason, particularly to the philosopher's reason. More basically, *if everything is divine (pantheism), nothing is really divine (atheism)*, because the minimal concept of divinity involves the idea of a great superiority. But if everything is uniformly superior, nothing is superior. However, feeling one's own divinity sounds nice for personal vanity. That is why the diffuse propaganda of the Gnostic "New Age" movement, another fashion of "mystical" Illuminism, is so successful among the consumerist population.

Illuminists and Secularists in general share different sorts of pseudo-religiosity (either individualist or collectivist) rather than being merely "irreligious." It is pseudo-religiosity (and not any type of real religiosity) because one's own self-deification is a falsification of the universal human religious impulse – i.e., an open mind and heart to a greater otherness. What kind of basic pseudo-religiosity do Illuminists share? They share a sort of "mystical" Illuminism, which has precisely been called "Illuminism." It has remarkable precedents in the manifold Gnostic tradition and in Pelagianism. But in modern times it adopts a more persuasive face which combines both extremes according to the public to be addressed – from a scientificist rhetoric or a sentimentalist and "mystical" wording. This is our surprising thesis: at bottom, the Illuminist proclaims that the "goddess Reason" and "mystical" Iluminism are one and the same thing, the two horns of the same bull. The common Illuminist core is the idea that a human individual has, by himself and within him, the fullness of life and truth: the "light" for everything. The way to discover this "fullness" can be expressed in seemingly "Rationalist," or in ecstatic, terms. Each "horn" has many branches, especially since the eighteenth century. Sometimes they are outwardly opposed to each other.

The Gnostic and theosophical tradition always had this double talk of an extolled rationalism and a very sentimental and esoteric ecstasy.[9] This second and pseudo-religious dimension is the real Illuminist identity. Its "Rationalist" face is rather propaganda against the Supernaturalist world-view. Illuminism is ultimately irrational and anti-natural and, therefore, denaturalising and dehumanising. The "Enlightenment," the 18th century Illuminism, was even the main enemy of real Rationalism (Descartes, Leibniz, Wolff, etc.), in spite of the common Immanentist epistemology. Kant despised it as "dogmatic." Spinoza is usually considered a Rationalist, but he is rather a pre-Illuminist. Both extreme sides, the Rationalist and the "mystical," are very visible in his writing.

A good modern example of this twofold Illuminist message is Masonic ideology, which embraces pragmatic and rationalist thought as well as a ritualistic and "mystical" orientation. Another example in modern times is the Illuminist Order, founded by the German Adam Weishaupt (1748-1830). Weishaupt and his followers, the "Perfectibilists," addressed

---

[9] This twofold and dualist talk is fully different from the complexity and poeticity of many Naturalist philosophers like Plato and especially from the Church tradition where a very rational, clear and organized theology and philosophy are consistent with a poetic and profound mysticism. For example, St. Augustine and St. John of the Cross were as orthodox and rational in their theology and philosophy as they were free, intimate and personal in their mysticisms. Their rational doctrine and their religious feelings were like the two wings of one eagle. Instead, the very heterogeneous Illuminist movement can show a rationalist face (an extremist, partial and exclusive use of reason) or an ecstatic proposal, which is the real irrational nature of Illuminism.

their Deist doctrine to German Rationalists. They presented their message as "anti-dogmatic" and "anti-ritualistic" because they had their own dogmas and rituals. Goethe, Herder and other writers welcomed this movement. Rosicrucians since the 16th century also claim to be "Illuminates." Emmanuel Swedenborg represents another example in this individualistic way.

The most meaningful example of the twofold Illuminist appearance is to be found in Pietism and its substantive influence in Kant. Pietism appears as another "anti-dogmatic" and "anti-institutional" movement derived from the Lutheran Church and led by Philipp Jakob Spener. Through the Pietist Crusius, Kant received his main ethical inspiration, although the Prussian thinker was more willing to publicly admit an influence from another reputable philosopher like Rousseau. Key theoretical examples of denaturalization are the so-called "naturalist fallacy" of Hume and Kant and the "pure law" theory of Kelsen. As a wide practical example, we see everywhere the massive and unprecedented destruction of nature through an unwise use of technology and a consumerist way of living produced by Secularist values. The usual militant Ecologism claims respect for nature in general, but shares the ideology of annulling the specific dignity of human nature, like the Animalist movement voiced by Peter Singer. At present, the esoteric and very diffused "New Age" mentality supports those views among increasing masses of people in rich, capitalist countries. For more scholarly and ironic tastes, so-called "Postmodernism" leads the contemporary fragmentation and destruction of rationality, but in a very similar way as Hume and Nietzsche did centuries ago in "modern" times. The different branches of Secularism and Denaturalism continually claim to exhibit "novelty," but this is often superficial or a mere ostentation, not a fact. It is marketing.

Secularism has been visible, growing, and organized since the eighteenth century, and it has been much more influential the world over since the end of the twentieth century. It tries to push aside, in different ways and grades, religious communities – especially Christian communities. The term "Laicism" implies rather the political, legal, economic and media dimensions (i.e., power dimensions) of this social exclusion, while "Secularism" points out the deepest levels of cultural dimensions: art, philosophy and ethics, celebrations, and so on. Secularisms are arbitrary mixtures of Naturalist, Christian and even Anti-naturalist elements. Secularists go back in some aspects to Ancient Naturalism or paganism, but in general they have a proud, mechanical and denaturalised view of humankind and reality. They deny a real supernatural perspective, although they may play around with some spiritualistic beliefs (e.g., the Gnostic and popular "New Age"), as well as with a Naturalist way of life.

In spite of its rhetoric of "modernity" and "scientificity," Secularism represents a merely instrumental rationality, but is irrational at bottom. Secularism uses science, but is not scientific. As is clear in areas like bioethics, it tries to impose an anti-humanism which also shows a lack of all respect for nature. Never before was it necessary to demand such a respect for nature, because never before has nature, both general and human, been so harshly attacked. Secularism rejects nature as well as the supernatural, and represents therefore a denaturalisation. Its innermost tenet is a self-deification of human beings (those well-off and powerful) and an instrumentalization of large numbers of people. Due to their Christian origin, Secularists have brought, on the one hand, Intellectualism to the extreme of Rationalism (which gave into Empiricism or merely instrumental Rationalism) and, on the other hand, Volitionalism to the extreme of Voluntarism. Voluntarism is the real final perspective of secularism, because even Empiricism is nothing but Voluntarism; extremely self-limited reason gives way to an unlimited and arbitrary will.

An instrumental rationality is a fragmentary and self-limited rationality, as is clear in so-called "Postmodernity," a simple reproposal of Illuminist scepticism. Thus Secularism is not only an open attack against a traditional and civilising religious faith and morals, but also a subtle denial of reason itself. Seen as a whole process and in its roots, Secularism may exalt reason in some moments, but finally destroys reason.

HYBRID WORLD VIEWS

Let us consider two important hybrid cases concerning the three main cosmovisions. Supernaturalism embraces and enhances the value of nature, but clearly goes beyond Naturalism. Denaturalism is, to a certain extent, a mixture of Naturalist ideas and the Supernaturalist perspective, and combines both terminologies, but it embodies a very different world-view. It uses Naturalist and Supernaturalist elements in order to deny both. Denaturalism uses for its advantage its enemies' "weapons." There are two main hybrid world-views. The first would be classified as "philosophical" ("Neoplatonism"); the second would be conventionally classified as "religious"(Islam). "Neoplatonic" thinkers do not prove more of their tenets or dogmas than Islam, and they permanently also appeal to divinity. So they are not less religious than Muslims. "Neoplatonists" even regard truth as divinely revealed. And Islam can be explained in general terms as a philosophy or world-view, encompassing not only religion and morals ("din"), but also politics, law, art and culture as a whole. We can combine both aspects in the two world-views. Like many other general life proposals, "Neoplatonism" and Islam are two religious philosophies.

The amount of Platonism in so-called "Neo-Platonism" is quite disputable and, hence, this very name is questionable. Not even the Academy, founded by Plato, was very Platonic soon after Plato's death. Plato is probably the most influential philosopher in history, but like many other great philosophical teachers, he had no significant and faithful disciples after his death. Later his Academy became even the direct contrary of Platonism: a sceptical school. There is no doubt that Ammonius Saccas, Plotinus, Porfirius, Jamblicus, Julianus, Proclus and others were closer to Plato than to Aristotle, for instance. But it does not mean that they were just putting forward a Platonic revival, with some secondary additions. Plotinus and Porfirius were synthesising much of the whole Greek philosophy and religion. From Athens, the Platonists harshly criticised Plotinus and saw him rather as an imitator of Numenius of Apamea, the real founder of "Neo-Platonism," according to authors like Guthrie. There are also Christian authors like Augustine and Nicholas of Cusa, who received a particular influence from this Platonic and Plotinian tradition, but they were basically of a Supernaturalist viewpoint. Since Ammonius is not very well known, we should name the so-called "Neo-Platonism" simply "Plotinianism," and perhaps refer to later theory as "Neo-Plotinianism." In other words, this school has enough autonomy and importance so as not to be considered merely a "neo-proposal" among other philosophical schools. Every school learns something from the past, but this Plotinian school, and its branches in Rome, Syria, Pergamon, and Athens, are original enough to be independent. However, Plotinus was leading the revival of something greater than a particular philosophical school: it was the first revival of the first world view, Naturalism, but in a peculiar and hybridised way.

The Plotinian school has not been well understood in its context because its Platonic affiliation has been overstated to the detriment of its most peculiar source within a pagan or Naturalist world: a non-pagan and Supernaturalist source like Philo, the Jewish thinker from Alexandria, the same city of Plotinus' teacher, Ammonius Saccas. Philo himself could be easily assimilated because he was close to the Platonic tradition. Nevertheless, above all he was a thinking Jew. The connection with Numenius of Apamea strengthens the Philonian and supernaturalist source. Numenius, who considered Plato to be a Greek Moses, used Philo's doctrines together with teachings of the Gnostic tradition. Amelius, a disciple of Plotinus, upheld the autonomy and difference between Plotinus and Numenius. But even if there was actually this twofold and autonomous way, the result is the same: the Philonian source.

Only from this Philonian perspective can we understand the high speculation and the relative closeness to Supernaturalist metaphysics of Plotinus and his followers. The Plotinian School later became a rich inspiration for many Supernaturalist thinkers who soon recognised an unusual closeness among reputable pagan thinkers. But first of all the Plotinian school was the most qualified intellectual enemy of Christian philosophy. Its subtleness and strength against Supernaturalist rationality is specifically derived from Philo's teaching. They were using their enemy's strength. As a whole, Plotinianism was a very interesting hybrid world-view. As we said, it was the first revival of Naturalism: Plotinianism is the first neo-paganism or Neo-naturalism, with remarkable elements of Jewish supernaturalism. This first revival of Naturalism was highly sophisticated, thanks to the influence of subtle oriental religions, but its highest inspiration came from the Jewish sense of transcendence. It only lacked in the more complete Christian sense of Incarnationist humanism, which makes every person God's child.

We say "the first" Neo-naturalism, but properly it was the only one. Before Judeo-Christianity, "neo-paganism" or "Neo-naturalism" was not possible, since all cultures were Naturalist. After the long presence of Christianity and its Supernaturalist perspective, Neo-naturalism is not possible again. The emergence of the Jewish people was very slow and gradual, a long process of historical maturing, whose main witness is the Bible. The Jewish people were comparatively small in number and often lived in exile or were persecuted; they had no proselytizing activity. Therefore Jewish Supernaturalism could not have such a big influence so as to bring about a remarkable anti-supernaturalist reaction. This reaction could only arrive after the universal Supernaturalism of Christianity, rapidly increasing at the expense of paganism. With the Hellenistic Jew, Philo, the seed of a Supernaturalist viewpoint (with some Naturalist Greek elements) was planted. When Christianity arose and spread, some Naturalist scholars simply had to merge Philo's ideas and his Greek Naturalist tradition. In those days Naturalism was still so near and hegemonic that it could have possibly been considered a Neo-naturalism or Neo-paganism – for the first and the last time. On the contrary, when a culture has been Christianised for many centuries, it is no longer possible to go back to Naturalism. As we said before, Denaturalism is even much more complex than a Neo-paganism, which is still in the realm of Naturalism. "Neo-Platonism" or Plotinianism was the first and the last trial of a real Neonaturalism. Thus it could be rightly called "Neonaturalism" par excellence, at least in the Hellenic-Christian civilization.

Of course, there are still now many other Naturalist cultures, like the Hindu and the Japanese ones. Particularly in the Hindu culture, there is a strong reaction against Muslims and Christians living in India. This could be called a Neo-naturalist movement, but it is a nationalist and political force (sometimes with violent extremists involved), rather than a well-thought intellectual reply using some of their opponents' ideas, like the Plotinians did. Japan has kept its own identity to a certain extent, but it is moving quickly from a Shinto-Buddhist Naturalism to a Secularist society. Naturalist cultures have to face an alternative between embracing Supernaturalism or Denaturalism. Naturalism cannot stop Denaturalism by itself. It is even very difficult for Supernaturalists. Communism and Capitalism are both Denaturalist and Neo-Malthusian ideologies and are hegemonic almost everywhere.

If Plotinianism is a Neonaturalism with some Supernaturalist elements, Islam is the Supernaturalist world view (a sort of Neo-Judaism), but with a background Naturalist vein.[10] We can explain this specific hybrid character here very briefly.

---

[10] As before, when talking about Christianity, here we do not assume the truthfulness of a particular religion. We respect all believers' consciences and

The supernaturalist message of absolute divine transcendence in the Qur'an is as emphatic as in the Bible. Islamic revelation follows this vertical pattern. God as providential creator is absolutely above all nature and human thought. From this starting-point a very precise and legalist morality emerges in the same Semitic style as a strict Judaism. Sufism or Islamic mysticism usually can only soften such religious legality. Judaism as well as Islam demand a large number of concrete rules, ranging from great principles up to many physical details in all fields of life (e.g., in praying, politics, law, or cooking and dressing). Physical bonds are irreplaceable. Life is unthinkable without a complex net of sacred procedures and places. A concrete, unique holy language plays a central role among all those physical bonds and rules.

The need of those many physical bonds and the multitude of concrete commandments and prohibitions, mentioned in connection to Judaism, retain a Naturalist attachment, even in Judaism. Although Judaism and Islam are explicitly opposed to the Incarnation, they are more bound to material-precise procedures and places. Christian Incarnationism, implying a concentration on the sacrality of every human body and soul, is a release from those many concrete duties in favour of a more spiritual contemplation and more social commitments. The only main feature specifically shared between Christianity and Islam – and not Judaism – is universality, and this world-wide mission leads them to go out to every individual and culture, although each offers a different way. Even though Islam is plural according to each culture, it tends to be culturally and politically more unifying than Christianity, especially in its use of a common and unique sacred language, Arabic, and the *sharia*.

What Christians call "conversion" (to Christ) is called "recognition" in Islam: to be a Muslim is simply regarded the "natural" thing – the Naturalist way, as we would say it. Nature itself is considered to be "Muslim." Instead, to become a Christian involves a free act within a process of maturing; both a divine supernatural grace or gift and a human free and radical acceptance (leading to a continuous inner revolution of

---

simply try to give a philosophical explanation of each main kind of world-view, both religious and non-religious.

This does not exempt our criticisms from a commitment to open dialogue. We are also free to express that a world-view can embody an advance. Of course we expect to hear the opposite, but we would at least be within the same logic of understanding.

For instance, Supernaturalism is clearly a rational progress, but this does not oblige one to accept by faith the mysteries of Judaism and Christianity. Supernaturalism is absolute freedom from Naturalist determinism and from Denaturalist social uniformism. Denaturalism has an extraordinary appearance of freedom, but indeed makes people think and talk in a very uniform way. Denaturalist dogmas are much more subtle and are often imposed in a very subliminal and implicit manner.

customs and thought) are necessary. It is the free gift of a spiritual presence or inhabitation of God in a free soul, freely welcoming day by day this grace. There are more Christians than Muslims, but, according to their respective theologies, to be a Christian is an extraordinary, a supernatural event, while to be a Muslim is the natural and ordinary event.

Another key Naturalist feature in Islam is the general tendency towards confusion between the religious dimension and other fields like politics and law. Political confessionalism is generally practised and "justified," even to the point of theocracy. Sometimes one cannot know whether religion is politicised or politics are sacralised. Judaism and Islam have their own tendencies to sacralism. What we call "confusion" may be seen by Muslims as a compact and positive unity of all aspects in life. No matter the valuation we may give, this "unity" or confusion, sacralism itself, is a Naturalist characteristic. Muslims are making the same mistake as most Christians and ex-Christians in Europe and in the American continent: none distinguish the Hellenic-Christian heritage – a supernaturalist civilization enriched with the best of the best Naturalist cultures (Greece and Rome) – from its very opposite – Secularism and Denaturalism (radically confronted with Greek and Roman rationality and Christian faith and reason). Both extremes are confused in a geographically meaningless term: "the West" – as in the so-called "Western" culture.

Many Muslims complain about its "Western" enemy. Many "Western" patriots claim to defend "Western" civilization.[11] But the real and imminent enemies of Islam are, on the one hand, Secularism and Denaturalism, coming from outside (and not Christians, who are rather victims suffering from the lack of religious freedom in most Islamic countries) and, on the other hand, Islamist forces bringing in extreme sacralist and theocratic tendencies which seek to justify brutal violence and suicide (Here, there is a dramatic confusion between martyrdom and fanatical and criminal suicide.).

DIALOGUE AND CONFRONTATION AMONG THE THREE WORLD VIEWS

We need to introduce these and other distinctions in speaking about our cultural identity. If we do not know ourselves, we will not be able to

---

[11] One of the many confused "patriots" is Samuel P. Huntington, who writes in this way: "The preservation of the United States and the West requires the renewal of Western identity." See *The Clash of Civilizations and the Remaking of World Order"* (London: McGraw-Hill, 1997), p. 318. This use of the term "Western" is a gross misnomer. It is meaningless. Do Eastern countries like the Philippines or Australia and New Zealand not belong to the so-called "Western" culture? But the term is worse than meaningless: it hides the real and deepest identity of the Hellenic-Christian civilization in many countries in the East and in the West, in the North and in the South.

understand others or be understood by others; dialogue will be impossible. However, scholars and professional politicians are still using as a dogma the meaningless term "Western," referring at the same time to Secularist Denaturalism and to the Hellenic-Christian civilization, which synthesises the best of Naturalism (Intellectualism) and of Supernaturalism (Volitionalism). Most of us are not Greek, but we must know that Greece is the basic source of our civilization. Similarly, many people in Europe, Australia or America are no longer Christians, but we should all be aware of the central relevance of Christian values and ideas in our world-views. Even Denaturalism, being a whole alternative to Hellenic-Christian civilization, can only be understood on the basis of Christianity, where it was born. In our times, these three world views coexist and their dialogue is difficult, but we need such dialogue in order to live together.

We should avoid interpreting these distinctions of concepts (Naturalism, Supernaturaism, Denaturalism, etc.) as if they were applicable to very clear and concrete blocs of people or institutions in society, i.e. in a 'Manichean' sense. On the one hand, there are many Atheists, Agnostics and Deists who do not share the militant Denaturalist agenda. They follow at least some natural principles. Perhaps they still keep the Jewish or Christian principles of their education. It is not necessarily and immediately the same to be an Atheist or an Agnostic and to be involved in a fully Secularist and Denaturalist way of living.

On the other hand, Secularism is found in many members of the Church and other religious communities, in varying degrees. "The main reason for the velocity with which the Church is in decline, derives from its own internal secularisation, from its voluntary and largely unconscious adoption of the ideas and practices of the benign adversaries who came to it with friendly countenances and largely innocent intentions," writes Edward Norman in an Anglican context, though his words are quite suitable for other Christian contexts.[12] Of course, by "secularisation" he means "Secularism." He further seems to drop an ironic hint by generally talking about "largely innocent intentions." Nowadays, not even religious sects proselytize as much as Denaturalists. However, instead of being again in the cultural vanguard, as it was customary along the history, many Christians suffer an inferiority complex in the face of what they naïvely believe to be "the modern world." Little by little they leave their Hellenic-Christian culture in exchange for leading "a pleasant life." Denaturalism can still accept that a mass of people think themselves to be Christian and celebrate their rituals, as long as they are obedient and do not criticise the dominant Secularist culture.

By controlling the larger part of the mass media, many educational systems and the most influential culture and entertainment industry in the world, Denaturalism has made many people blindly and thoughtlessly

---

[12] Edward Norman, *Secularisation* (London: Continuum International Publishing Group, 2002), p. ix.

believe that Denaturalist values are exclusively "the modern ones." Of course, there are social groups who deserve the negative category of "integrist," "conservative," "fundamentalist," etc. But Denaturalists compulsively qualify Supernaturalist culture and values as "anachronistic," "pre-modern," "Medieval," "integrist," "conservative," "fundamentalist," and so on. Almost no one openly criticises this one-sided thinking, including those who appear as the official representatives of Anti-globalism and Anti-one-sided thought. However, Illuminist and Secularist values, dear to Denaturalists, are only one of the alternatives in Modernity. Denaturalism can no longer claim to represent the only possible modernity, rationality and progress for humanity.

This is even worse than the paternalist ethnocentrism of colonialism. It is ultimately the world-wide imposition of the pseudo-religion of self-deification, which is a tendency as old as humanity. I do not think this is very "modern." But I could accept it as another kind of modernity for other people, provided that Denaturalists also respect different ways of moral and religious modernity, and further provided that real human rights are not compromised (e.g., the systematic and commercial killing of babies in their mothers' wombs can no longer be said to be "Modern" or "Progressivist"). This is a perversion of language and of humanism. Dialogue and coexistence, even a universal fraternity, should not be very difficult with most people: all sorts of Naturalists (Animists, Hindus, Buddhists, etc.) as well as Muslims, Jews and Christians, and even many Atheists, Agnostics and Deists keep some basic natural moral principles. I am very optimistic about human potentialities. On the contrary, to expect dialogue from the élites who are the leaders of Denaturalism is nonsense. As long as they possess their power, they will never give up, unless each of them experiences a radical humanist conversion.

If we seek a real intercultural and inter-epochal dialogue we cannot be "irenic" or merely complaisant. Confucius taught that the first urgent reform was calling things by their proper names. Before the re-establishment and the renewal of a constructive dialogue, we have to recognize and analyse the actual confrontations between the main world-views and other important variants. We do want to build a profound and sincere dialogue, a mutual understanding and respect among all peoples. And the first steps are to stop the gross manipulation of language and to go beyond every superficial approach. Agreeing with these clear conditions, let us meet with every kind of people, freely listening to each other, and discussing 'face to face'.

Instituto Superior de Filosofía
Valladolid, Spain

CHAPTER XXXI

ON EINSTEIN'S IMAGINARY DIALOGUE BETWEEN POINCARÉ AND REICHENBACH

SAMET BAGCE

Einstein had a deep respect for Hans Reichenbach's work on space, time and relativity. Reichenbach, too, valued Einstein's studies. He saw the results of the theory of relativity as having revolutionary impacts on the discussions of long-debated philosophical issues, but at the same time he believed that the theory of relativity revolutionised the way we have conducted philosophy.[1] In his essay, "The Philosophical Significance of the Theory of Relativity," Reichenbach makes this explicit by saying that:

> It is a privilege of our generation that we have among us a physicist whose work occupies the same rank as that of the man who determined the philosophy of space and time for two centuries. If physicists present us with implicational philosophies of such excellence, it is a pleasure to be a philosopher. The lasting fame of the philosophy of modern physics will justly go to the man who made physics rather than to those who have been at work deriving the implications of his work and who are pointing out its impact on the history of philosophy. There are many who contributed to the philosophy of Einstein's theory, but there is only one Einstein.[2]

In the same article, Reichenbach states some of the central theses of his book, *The Philosophy of Space and Time* (henceforth abbreviated *PST*). In his reply, Einstein brings in an imaginary dialogue between Poincaré and Reichenbach.[3] After the dialogue, Einstein remarks:

> I can hardly think of anything more stimulating as the basis for discussion in an epistemological seminar than this brief essay by Reichenbach.[4]

---

[1] cf. Introduction in Hans Reichenbach, *The Philosophy of Space and Time* (New York: Dover, 1928, rep. 1958).

[2] In P. Schilpp (ed.), *Albert Einstein: Philosopher-Scientist* (New York: Tudor Publishing Co., 1949), p. 311.

[3] Schilpp, pp. 677-679.

[4] Schilpp, p. 679.

This dialogue is the topic of my paper, the aim of which is to undo the injustice which seems to be done to Poincaré in this imaginary dialogue.

Now what I would like to do first is to outline Reichenbach's general epistemology, which is given in his *Experience and Prediction* (*EP*).[5] However, that is his later epistemological position, which constitutes the very philosophical basis of his *PST*. His former position was somewhat different. Although Reichenbach was closely associated with the development of logical positivism, he was not a member of the Vienna Circle. In fact, he was a leading member of the Berlin School, which preferred the designation "logischen Empirismus". The arguments exhibited in *EP* are, according to him, not refutations, but certainly corrections of standard positivist doctrines. For him, the aim of separating facts from conventions constitutes an "integral part of the critical task of epistemology." In addition to that, there is another aim of the book: to show what an indispensable role the concept of probability has in the theory of knowledge. He explicitly points out in *EP* that it is not possible to provide a full elaboration of an epistemology such as his without a well-developed theory of probability and induction. This developed theory, he felt, had been presented in his *Theory of Probability* (*TP*).

Reichenbach formulated two different versions of conventionalism, one earlier and one later. The former is developed in *The Theory of Relativity and A Priori Knowledge* (*TRAK*) of 1920, and the latter in his *PST* of 1928. Each of the two types of conventionalism was motivated by different epistemological concerns. Briefly, the difference between his earlier and later conventionalism is that the first is largely motivated by Kantian themes, even though it is aimed at refuting Kant by appealing to the theory of relativity. However, this thesis also has a far more interesting consequence: the relativity theory also provides a reinterpretation of Kant's notion of *a prioricity*, a reinterpretation that points out what is right about Kant's epistemology.

However, in his later epistemology, Reichenbach makes an effort to reject Kant completely. In *PST*, Reichenbach seems to have given up his association with neo-Kantianism.[6] Thus, the epistemology underlying his later conventionalism is basically non-Kantian and empiricist: the conventional elements in science are just non-observational or theoretical ones. The only facts are observable facts; all the rest is the "contribution of reason." The conventional/factual distinction corresponds to the theoretical/observational distinction. But in the earlier conventionalism, the former distinction is not identical to the latter; instead it had been drawn within the realm of the theoretical: certain elements of theoretical structure – for example, the choice of rest system and of inertial system – were

---

[5] Reichenbach, *Experience and Prediction* (Berkeley: Chicago University Press, 1938, rep. 1970).

[6] Reichenbach, *Philosophy of Space and Time*, p. xii.

conventional; other theoretical elements, such as the choice of the metric system, were not.

Although there are differences between his earlier and later conventionalism, in both cases the starting points of Reichenbach's general philosophy and epistemology are the same: his position in favour of the theory of relativity, his probabilistic and inductivist orientation, and (hence) his critical attitude towards Kant. Reichenbach's epistemology is mainly concerned with the presence of conventional elements in human knowledge. The fact/convention distinction is held to be essential for epistemology and for the philosophy of science. He refers to this task of separating facts from conventions in science as constituting "an integral part of the critical task of epistemology."

As for Reichenbach's accounts of space and geometry, they are given in his two major books, *TRAK* and *PST* written in the period 1920-1928.[7] Since Reichenbach iterates some of the central theses of *PST* in his essay on the theory of relativity, as it appeared in Schlipp's volume, Reichenbach's second major book, *PST*, is relevant to our discussion here. So, I now would like to consider this book.

In the first chapter of *PST*, Reichenbach clarifies the relationship between mathematical systems of geometry and physical space. He answers

---

[7] Actually between these two books Reichenbach wrote another major book, *Axiomatization of Theory of Relativity* (Berkeley & Los Angeles: California University Press, 1924 (1969)), which carries out a relatively formal axiomatic reconstruction of Einstein's special and general theories of relativity, based on axioms that express the elementary physical facts upon which those theories rest.

One could possibly claim that our theories seek to explain and predict the properties of material process and events by relating them to the geometrical structure within which they are contained. On that view, one tends to take the more abstract geometrical entities as primitive and to attempt to define the more observational entities in terms of them. But this claim contrasts with Reichenbach's philosophical formulation in the above mentioned book, where his view characteristically takes more observational entities, such as reference frames, light rays, particle trajectories, material rods and clocks, as primitive and attempts to define geometrical structure in terms of the behaviour of such relatively observational entities.

About *ATR*, Salmon [*Hans Reichenbach: Logical Empiricist*, Dordrecht: D. Reidel, 1977, p. 23] writes that "the axiomatisation is not mathematically elegant, nor is it intended to be. It is intended rather as a logical analysis that would enable one to locate precisely the distinctions among physical facts, mathematical truths, and conventional definitions which are thoroughly intermingled in the usual presentation of the theory". In this respect, there is a close analogy between what Hilbert (1902) had done regarding the foundations of geometry, what Russell and Whitehead (1910-1913) had done, and what Reichenbach was doing for the *physical* theory of relativity. The motivations in all these cases are certainly closely allied.

the following question: "What is the geometry of physical space?" Reichenbach also reiterates the well-known claim that the very existence of non-Euclidean geometries refutes Kant's view on the nature of space. He then offers an elegant analysis of the important epistemological role of the concept of visualisation. By showing the indispensable role of a coordinative definition of congruence, he develops his important theory of equivalent descriptions. He then claims that, once a coordinative definition of congruence has been given, the geometric structure of physical space can, in principle, be ascertained empirically. He also maintains that if certain suitable changes or adjustments are executed, then we can preserve a particular geometry (say, Euclidean) as the correct description of physical space. This leads to his conclusion that one may choose either a definition of congruence or an abstract system of geometry as a matter of convention. But once we have made one of these choices, the determination of the other requires the ascertainment of physical facts regarding physical space. He also shows that there are equivalent descriptions which are equally adequate physically, but that nonetheless there are other non-equivalent descriptions, which are therefore not empirically acceptable.

In the second chapter, Reichenbach turns to time. Among the most important issues that he examines there is the problem of ascertaining simultaneity relations in a single inertial frame – before getting involved in the relativity that arises when we look at reference frames in motion with respect to one another. He elaborates on the status of simultaneity in a single reference frame and relates it to the maximality of the velocity of light. There we see again the fundamental role of equivalent descriptions. However, in this case, their possibility depends not merely on some logical or semantical considerations, but also upon the physical fact that light is, in Reichenbach's own term, a "first signal", that is, a signal whose speed of propagation cannot be exceeded by a signal of any other type.

In the third and final chapter, he deals with the problems that arise when the considerations about space and time are combined with the problems of the theory of relativity proper. This chapter is more technical, and based on the results of his *ATR*. It is divided into three parts, the first of which examines the space-time manifold without gravitational fields, i.e., the special theory of relativity; the second part takes up gravitation within space-time manifolds, i.e. the general theory of relativity; the last part deals with the most general and abstract properties of the space-time manifold.

Reichenbach articulates and defends a distinction between conventional and factual components within a scientific theory. For example, he argues that the axioms of geometry are factual whereas the coordinative definitions for geometry are conventional. Such a distinction is the core of his theory of equivalent descriptions and of his philosophy. Much of his technical work in the philosophy of space and geometry is essentially directed to the goal of separating the conventional from the factual or empirical elements in physical geometry and in the theory of relativity.

As it was said above, Reichenbach's "theory of the relativity of geometry" plays an important role not only in this book, but in his whole account of geometry and in his epistemology. One sees how important this theory is for him because of the fact that he repeatedly states the same thesis under different names. For example, he calls it "Mach's principle in the wider sense" in the case of accelerated inertial systems,[8] and "the philosophical theory of relativity" in application to space-time.[9] He regards his relativity thesis as the most fundamental insight and achievement of modern philosophy of science.

The geometrical version of his thesis is that a geometry can be true or false only relative to the coordinative definitions which have been laid down beforehand as conventions. That is, the statements of geometry are empirical provided that the coordinative definitions for geometry are laid down as conventions. These coordinative definitions are to determine how geometrical quantities, such as length, are to be measured and how geometrical relations, like those of congruence, are to be ascertained. So, for example, one may claim that physical space is Euclidean relative to certain coordinative definitions as conventions which postulate universal forces. In addition, one can obtain the same "empirical consequences" when a different set of conventions is combined with a different geometry. Thus, one can obtain factually or empirically equivalent descriptions by combining different conventions with different geometries. However, the choice of coordinative definitions always remains conventional.

Let us first consider the problem of physical geometry. The mathematical discovery of non-Euclidean geometries did not make it impossible for one to maintain that Euclid's was the "true" geometry. But later it was shown that non-Euclidean geometries were logically consistent relative to Euclidean geometry. With the proof of consistency came a new understanding of the status of the axioms of geometry: these are not true or false, but arbitrary statements. The discussion of truth or falsehood of the axioms of geometry was not a question for logic or mathematics to answer, but one about properties of the physical world; i.e., it became a physical question. Then the distinction that grew out of the discovery of non-Euclidean geometries was introduced between pure or mathematical geometry and applied or physical geometry; i.e., the problem of space was divided into two parts: the problem of mathematical space and the problem of physical space.[10]

Reichenbach accepts this distinction. Moreover, he claims that there is another problem: if several kinds of geometries are regarded as

---

[8] Reichenbach, *Philosophy of Space and Time*, p. 216.

[9] Cf. *Philosophy of Space and Time*, p. 177, where he defines "the philosophical theory of relativity" as "the discovery of the definitional character of the metric in all its details."

[10] Cf. Reichenbach, *Philosophy of Space and Time*, p. 6.

mathematically possible and equivalent, then which of these geometries is applicable to physical reality? His answer to this question is this:

> Mathematics shows a variety of possible forms of relations [mathematical spaces] among which physics selects the real one [physical space] by means of observations and experiments.[11]

He then asks the following question: "What methods should physics employ in order to make a decision?" He maintains that "the answer to this question will at the same time supply an answer to the question why we are justified in speaking of a specific physical space."[12] Before answering this question, Reichenbach engages in considering another issue: that of the analytical treatment of geometry. With respect to the problem of physical geometry, he claims that the geometry of physical space is an empirical question; that is, it is the task of physics to single out the actual *physical* space among the possible *mathematical* spaces by empirical means. But how should it proceed? His answer is:

> The method for this investigation is given by Riemann's mathematical procedure: the decision must be brought about by practical measurements in space.[13]

The geometry to be ascribed to physical space depends on our method for measuring length. Reichenbach provides a very clear example, which seems to be inspired by Poincaré's parable in *Science and Hypothesis* (*S&H*).[14] It can be illustrated in the following way: imagine two surfaces – one has a hemisphere on top, and the other is the plane below. Imagine that there are two-dimensional creatures living on each of the surfaces, and that they try to determine the geometries of their respective worlds by means of two-dimensional measuring rods. The intrinsic geometry of a space depends completely upon the metric of that space.

[11] Reichenbach, *Philosophy of Space and Time*, p. 6.
[12] Reichenbach, *Philosophy of Space and Time*, p. 6.
[13] Reichenbach, *Philosophy of Space and Time*, p. 10.
[14] H. Poincaré, *Science and Hypothesis* (New York: Dover, 1902, rep. 1952), pp. 64-68.

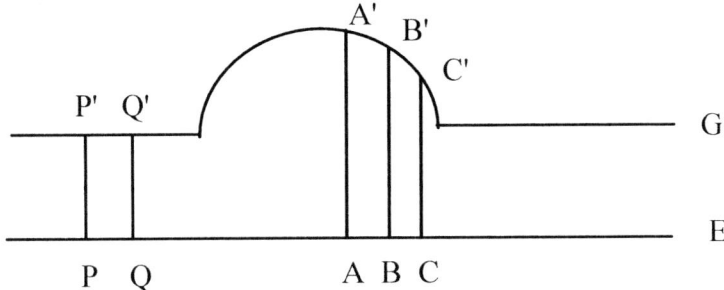

Figure 1: Projection of a non-Euclidean geometry on a plane

The creatures on the hemisphere measure length in the normal way, by assuming that rigid rods retain their length under transport. They find, say, that A'B' is congruent to B'C'. Moreover, they discover thereby that the geometry of their surface is non-Euclidean (for example, by comparing the radii and the circumference of the circles).

On the other hand, if the creatures on the plane also measure length in this normal way, of course they will find out that the geometry of their surface is Euclidean. But, suppose that the creatures living on the plane adapt their methods of measurement in such a way that two intervals are regarded as congruent iff they are the projections of congruent intervals on the hemisphere. This method involves the assumption that rigid rods expand as they are transported toward the boundary of the hemisphere. They will find, for example, that AB is congruent to BC, and therefore that the geometry of their surface is spherical and non-Euclidean.

Reichenbach, after this example, introduces the notion of force, and makes a distinction between:

(i) Universal forces, and
(ii) Differential forces.

He then asks the following question: if the nature of the geometry of a surface is not known, how can the effect of the force that is acting upon that surface be discovered? He states that if the acting force is a differential, say, heat, then direct indications of its presence can be found without making use of geometry as an indirect method. Indeed, direct evidence for the presence of heat is based on the fact that it affects different materials in different ways. However, "universal" forces are defined by Reichenbach in such a way that their presence cannot be demonstrated directly. They have two properties:

(i) They affect all materials in the same way, and
(ii) There are no insulating walls against them [*PST*, p.13].

After these considerations, he asks the following questions:

> [W]hat can be stated about the shape of the surfaces E and
> G? G has been described as a surface with a hump and E
> as a plane which appears to have a hump. By what right do
> we make this assertion? The measuring results are the
> same on both surfaces. If we restrict ourselves to these
> results, we may just as well say that G is the surface with
> the "illusion" of the hump and E the surface with the
> "real" hump. Or perhaps both surfaces have a hump. In our
> example we assumed from the beginning that E was a
> plane and G a surface with a hump. By what right do we
> distinguish between E and G? Does E differ in any respect
> from G?[15]

Reichenbach points out that this peculiar characteristic of the
problem of physical geometry is the indication that something was omitted
in the formulation of the problem, since the determination of geometry
depends upon the definition of congruence. He then claims that, in order to
inquire into the epistemological assumption of measurement, an
indispensable concept, the concept of a coordinative definition, must be
introduced. The introduction of such a concept is, he thinks, essential for
the solution of the problem.

Reichenbach says that if we want to use a term in science, we must
first define it. For example we can introduce a new term into a theory by
offering a stipulative definition of it in terms of previously accepted
meaningful terms of the theory: "Defining usually means reducing a
concept to other concepts. In physics, as in all other fields of inquiry, wide
use is made of this procedure."[16] However, it is not analytical definitions
one is concerned with in science:

> There is a second kind of definition, however, which is
> also employed and which derives from the fact that
> physics, in contra-distinction to mathematics, deals with
> real objects. Physical knowledge is characterised by the
> fact that concepts are not only defined by other concepts,
> but are also coordinated to real objects. This coordination
> cannot be replaced by explanation of meanings, it simply
> states that this concept is coordinated to this particular
> thing. In general this coordination is not arbitrary. Since
> the concepts are interconnected by testable relations, the
> coordination may be verified as true or false, if the
> requirement of uniqueness is added, i.e. the rule that the

---

[15] Reichenbach, *Philosophy of Space and Time*, p. 13.
[16] Reichenbach, *Philosophy of Space and Time*, p. 14.

same concept must always denote the same object. The method of physics consists in establishing the uniqueness of this coordination, as Schlick has clearly shown. But certain preliminary coordinations must be determined before the method of coordination can be carried through any further; these first coordinations are therefore definitions which we shall call coordinative definitions. They are arbitrary, like all definitions; on their choice depends the conceptual system which develops with the progress of science.

Wherever metrical relations are to be established, the use of coordinative definitions is conspicuous. If a distance is to be measured, the unit of length has to be determined beforehand by definition. Here the duality of conceptual definition and coordinative definition can easily be seen.[17]

We need to provide a definition of congruence as a coordinative definition; for example, taking "the geodesic curve between two points" to be the "path of a light ray in vacuuo connecting those points" is a coordinative definition. Or one can choose rigid bodies for this purpose, and define it in the following way:

Rigid bodies are solid bodies which are not affected by the differential forces, or concerning which the influence of differential forces has been eliminated by corrections; universal forces are disregarded.[18]

The following two questions about coordinative definitions naturally arise:

(i) Why do we need them?

His answer is this: If one wants to make measurements, one has a logical need for a unit. It is logically impossible to measure a distance without having first such a coordinative definition.

---

[17] Reichenbach, *Philosophy of Space and Time*, pp. 14-15.
[18] Reichenbach, *Philosophy of Space and Time*, p. 22. He says that we do not actually neglect universal forces, but we merely set them equal to zero by definition. Reichenbach claims that "without such a rule, the rigid body cannot be defined. Since there is no demonstrable difference produced by universal forces, the conception that the transported measuring rod is deformed by such forces can always be defended. No object is rigid relative to universal forces."

(ii) Why should we think that our methods for measuring length are arbitrary, as Reichenbach suggests?

Reichenbach's argument is epistemological: there is no way of verifying any assumptions about the behaviour of rigid rods by direct observation; for example whether or not they retain their length under transport:

> Assume two measuring rods which are equal in length. They are transported by different paths to a distant place; there again they are laid down side by side and found equal in length. Does this procedure prove that they did not change on the way? Such an assumption would be incorrect. The only observable fact is that the two measuring rods are always equal in length at the place where they are compared to each other. But it is impossible to know whether on the way the two rods expand or contract. An expansion that affects all bodies in the same way is not observable because a direct comparison of measuring rods at different places is impossible.[19]

But why is the normal assumption of length retention unverifiable? This is because the possibility of universal forces makes it possible to have an alternative description which is "empirically" equivalent to the normal one. Reichenbach further maintains:

> The problem does not concern a matter of cognition but of definition. There is no way of knowing whether a measuring rod retains its length when it is transported to another place; a statement of this kind can only be introduced by a definition. For this purpose a coordinative definition is to be used, because two physical objects distant from each other are defined as equal in length. It is not the concept equality of length which is to be defined, but a real object corresponding to it is to be pointed out. A physical structure is coordinated to the concept equality of length, just as the standard meter is coordinated to the concept unit of length.[20]

For Reichenbach, the great significance of the realisation that congruence is a matter of definition lies in the fact that with its help the

---

[19] Reichenbach, *Philosophy of Space and Time*, p. 16.
[20] Reichenbach, *Philosophy of Space and Time*, p. 16.

epistemological problem of geometry is to be solved: the determination of the geometry of a certain structure depends on the definition of congruence.

With regard to the problem of geometry, Reichenbach states that the question which geometry holds for physical space must be decided by measurements. Furthermore, this decision is dependent upon the assumption of an arbitrary coordinative definition of the comparison of length.

Consider his "Theorem Θ" which expresses the central principle of "the relativity of geometry":

> Mathematics proves that every geometry of the Riemannian kind can be mapped upon another one of the same kind. In the language of physics this means the following:
> Theorem Θ. "Given a geometry G' to which the measuring instruments conform, we can imagine a universal force F which affects the instruments in such a way that the actual geometry is an arbitrary geometry G, while the observed deviation from G is due to a universal deformation of the measuring instruments."[21]

He clarifies this theorem in the following way:

> The force F is a tensor. If g'$\mu\nu$ are the metrical coefficients of the geometry G' and g$\mu\nu$ those of G, the potentials F$\mu\nu$ of the force F are given by
>
> $$g'\mu\nu + F\mu\nu = g\mu\nu \quad \mu\nu = 1,2,3$$
>
> The measuring rods furnish directly the g'$\mu\nu$; the F$\mu\nu$ provides the "correction factors" by which the g'$\mu\nu$ are corrected so that g$\mu\nu$ results. The universal force F influencing the measuring rod is usually dependent on the orientation of the measuring rod.

The principle of the relativity of geometry, formulated in Theorem Θ, thus asserts that Euclidean geometry is not a priori preferable on epistemological grounds, for the theorem shows that all geometries are equivalent. There is another but very important consequence of this theorem: we can get a statement about physical space only if in addition to the geometry G of the space, its universal field of force F is specified. "Only the combination G+F is a testable statement."[22] That is, only G+F has verifiable consequences. Given that, we can change, say, Euclidean

---

[21] Reichenbach, *Philosophy of Space and Time*, pp. 32-33.
[22] Reichenbach, *Philosophy of Space and Time*, p. 33.

geometry G into, say, a non-Euclidean geometry G' by making compensatory adjustments in F so that F' results: G+F is empirically equivalent to G'+F', but not to G'+F. If various combinations of different coordinative definitions and different geometries give us empirically equivalent descriptions, then why could we not regard the choice of a particular geometry as being conventional? If we first adopt coordinative definitions by convention, then the geometry we combine with it will appear to be a factual part in the whole system. On the other hand, if we first adopt a geometry by convention, then the coordinative definitions we combine with it will appear to be the factual component of the system. However, he chooses one among many possible empirically compatible systems by appealing to experience, e.g., through requiring that $F\mu\nu = 0$, as providing the right geometry of physical space.

Now let us come back to Einstein's imaginary dialogue. The dialogue is initiated by the desire of finding the correct answer for the following question: "Is a geometry – looked from the physical point of view – verifiable (viz., falsifiable) or not?" Einstein goes on to say that "Reichenbach, together with Helmholtz, says: Yes, provided that the empirically given solid body realizes the concept of 'distance'. Poincaré says not, and consequently is condemned by Reichenbach."[23]

What Poincaré claims here is that the solid bodies around us are not really rigid, and thus, they cannot be employed to define geometric intervals. Therefore, the axioms and theorems of geometry are alone in no way empirically verifiable. In his reply, Reichenbach admits that he accepts that "there are no bodies which can be immediately adduced for the 'real definition' of the interval."[24] Nevertheless, he maintains, by taking into account several correcting factors, they can do so. Since this, he claims, does not lead into any contradiction, this is really possible as classical physics had demonstrated.

Einstein continues the dialogue by letting Poincaré reply as follows: In order to have the real definition you have made some improvements; in doing so you have made use of physical laws which, in turn, require a geometry – in this case it is Euclidean – for their formulation. Thus, one cannot here speak of an empirical verification of geometry but of the whole system of physical laws and geometry. It follows from this that the empirical assessment of geometry by itself is then not possible. We thus ask: "Why should it consequently not be entirely up to me to choose geometry according to my own convenience (i.e., Euclidean) and to fit the remaining (in the usual sense 'physical') laws to this choice in such manner that there can arise no contradiction of the whole with experience?"[25]

Einstein then halts the dialogue:

---

[23] Schilpp, pp. 676-677.
[24] Schilpp, p. 677.
[25] Schilpp, p. 677.

The conversation cannot be continued in this fashion because the respect of the [present] writer for Poincaré's superiority as thinker and author does not permit it; in what follows therefore, an anonymous non-positivist is substituted for Poincaré.[26]

There is another important point which Reichenbach makes a bit later in the dialogue:

Against Poincaré's suggestion it is to be pointed out that what really matters is not merely the greatest possible simplicity of the geometry alone, but rather the greatest possible simplicity of all of physics (inclusive of geometry). This is what is, in the first instance, involved in the fact that today we must decline as unsuitable the suggestion to adhere to Euclidean geometry."[27]

As I have said above, the aim of this paper is to undo the injustice which seems to be done to Poincaré in this imaginary dialogue. In order to remove the injustice, I would like to consider Reichenbach's criticisms leveled in Einstein's imaginary dialogue on Poincaré's account of geometry. They are basically directed against Poincaré's so-called "geometrical conventionalism" and they revolve around three points. In order to have a better understanding of Reichenbach's criticisms of Poincaré, I would like to consider them in detail.[28] However, there is one thing I would like to note, viz., that Reichenbach was writing in a context in which the general theory of relativity had already been accepted. Thus, the problem he was concerned with was whether the adoption of a system of geometry for space-time is a matter of deriving a hypothesis from observational data, or merely making a conventional choice. Although Poincaré never contemplated the possibility of non-Euclidean space-times, the application of his doctrine to this new "manifold" of the world seems to be clear.

I would like first to consider Reichenbach's criticism of the so-called "geometrical conventionalist" position. Reichenbach believes that the philosophical discussions of conventionalism, "misled by its ill-fitting name", did not always present the epistemological aspect of the problem

---

[26] Schilpp, p. 677.

[27] Schilpp, p. 678.

[28] Reichenbach criticises Poincaré in some other studies of his as well, such as especially in the first chapter of *Philosophy of Space and Time* and in *The Rise of Scientific Philosophy* (Berkeley & Los Angeles: California University Press, 1949) (*RSP*) and in *TRAK*. Since they are not the ones I am concerned with at the moment, I shall omit them.

with sufficient clarity.[29] He claims that "this is also true of the expositions by Poincaré, to whom we owe the designation of the geometrical axioms as conventions and whose merit it is to have spread the awareness of the definitional character of congruence to a wider audience."[30] Reichenbach maintains that "Poincaré overlooks the possibility of making objective statements about real space in spite of the relativity of geometry and deems it impossible to 'discover in geometric empiricism a rational meaning.'"[31] From this, Reichenbach maintains, the consequence is derived that we are dealing only with subjective arbitrariness, and that the question of the true geometry of physical space would be meaningless. This is, Reichenbach says, a misunderstanding. He further maintains that although the statement about the geometry is based upon certain arbitrary definitions, the statement itself does not become arbitrary. For, once the definitions have been laid down, it is determined through objective reality alone which is the actual geometry.[32]

For Reichenbach, the significance of coordinative definitions is not to make both geometry and the choice of the actual geometry conventional; on the contrary, it is to lend an objective meaning to physical measurements. As long as it was not noticed at what points of the metrical system arbitrary definitions occur, all measuring results were undetermined; only by discovering the points of arbitrariness, by identifying them as such and by classifying them as definitions, can we obtain objective measuring results in physics. "The objective character of the physical statement is thus shifted to a statement about relations."[33] According to Reichenbach, there is an objective statement about the geometry of physical space: "It is a statement about a relation between the universe and rigid rods."[34] The geometry chosen to characterise this relation is only a "mode of speech". However, he maintains, our awareness of the relativity of geometry enables us to formulate the objective character of a statement about the geometry of the physical world as a statement about relations. The only path to objective knowledge leads through conscious awareness of the role that subjectivity plays in our methods of research.

As a reply, I would like to say the following: Poincaré did not unify his philosophical views into a single coherent system. For this reason, some passages of his philosophical writings do not fit together consistently. Not surprisingly then there are many different and incompatible interpretations of his philosophy of science and geometry. According to some philosophers, including Reichenbach, Poincaré's philosophy is conventionalist. Thus Reichenbach misunderstands Poincaré's position:

---

[29] Reichenbach, *Philosophy of Space and Time*, p. 36.
[30] Reichenbach, *Philosophy of Space and Time*, p. 36.
[31] Reichenbach, *Philosophy of Space and Time*, p. 36.
[32] Reichenbach, *Philosophy of Space and Time*, p. 37.
[33] Reichenbach, *Philosophy of Space and Time*, p. 37.
[34] Reichenbach, *Philosophy of Space and Time*, p. 37.

Poincaré, though he employed the term convention when he spoke of the postulates of geometry, never used the appellation "conventionalism" either for his general philosophy or for his account of geometry.[35]

Reichenbach also criticises Poincaré's claim that Euclidean geometry would always be the simplest geometry come what may. Reichenbach states this in the dialogue[36] and also in *PST* as follows:

> This point of view can be answered as follows: Physics is not concerned with the question which geometry is simpler, but with the question which coordinative definition is simpler. It seems that the coordinative definition F=0 is simpler, because then the expression G+F reduces to G. But even this result is not essential, since in this case simplicity is not a criterion for truth. Simplicity certainly plays an important part in physics, even as a criterion for choosing between physical hypotheses.
>
> Geometry is concerned solely with the simplicity of a definition, and therefore the problem of empirical significance does not arise. It is a mistake to say that Euclidean geometry is "truer" than Einstein's geometry or vice versa, because it leads to simpler metrical relations. … The simpler system is always preferable; … Properties of reality are discovered only by a combination of the results of measurement with the underlying coordinative definition. …The significance of this simplicity should not be exaggerated; this kind of simplicity, which we call descriptive simplicity, has nothing to do with truth.[37]

It is of course true that the combination of a geometry and a physical theory is important – not the simplicity of a single geometry. So Poincaré, as Reichenbach claims, may seem to be mistaken on this point. However, this is not the case; in fact, this is exactly what Poincaré means, though not in a very straightforward manner.

In order to see this is so, one has to take into account two things: first the way Poincaré constructs (geometrical space) geometry out of spaceless sense-perceptions, that is, out of sensible (representative) space

---

[35] For more on this point, see E. Zahar, "Poincaré's Structural Realism and his Logic of Discovery," in *Henri Poincaré: Science and Philosophy*, J-L Greffe, G. Heinzmann and K. Lorenz (eds.) (Berlin: Academie Verlag, 1996) and *Poincaré's Philosophy: From Conventionalism to Phenomenology* (Chicago and La Salle: Open Court, 2001), as well as S. Bagce "Poincaré's Philosophy of Geometry and Its Relevance to his Philosophy of Science," in *Henri Poincaré: Science and Philosophy, op. cit.*

[36] Schilpp, p. 678.

[37] Reichenbach, *Philosophy of Space and Time*, pp. 34-5.

(remember his disc example, i.e., his parable,[38] in which he would not definitely choose the physical theory stated in Euclidean geometry with the universal force as the simplest or the most natural geometry). Second, there is the fact that Poincaré never adhered to a distinction between physical and pure geometry. On the contrary, he was totally against it. His opposition to such a distinction can easily be seen in his discussion in his *S&H* against the *a priorist* account of geometry.

Moreover, in gaining the real definition of the geometric intervals, one has to make use of physical laws. So, the empirical confirmation or falsification here refers not merely to geometry itself but to the entire system of physical laws which constitute its very foundation. Thus, the distinction between pure and physical geometry is untenable. That distinction Reichenbach accepts – and he is certainly in no position to defend it as well as to know whether the geometry in question or physical theory – gets the empirical confirmation. Thus, Reichenbach's claim that physical geometry is empirically verifiable, and thus his empiricist account of geometry becomes certainly vulnerable.

Lastly, consider Reichenbach's thesis of relativity of geometry that implies that "if we change the coordinative definition of congruence, a different geometry will result."[39] However, as we know through Grünbaum's study, this is not the case.[40] Take an ordinary table-top as a surface. Consider our horizontal table-top equipped with a network of Cartesian coordinates x and y, but now metrise this surface by means of the non-standard metric ds2=sec2 dx2 + dy2, where sec2 is a constant greater than 1.[41] This metric, like the standard metric, i.e., ds2=dx2 + dy2, yields a Euclidean geometry for that surface, but is not the customary one since it makes the length of a rod dependent on its orientation and/or position. Thus, there can be different congruence definitions yielding the same geometry, i.e., every change in the coordinative definition of congruence relations does not result in a change of geometry.

This result has a very important outcome for Reichenbach's claim that when you have chosen your coordinative definition of congruence, which physical geometry will result is a matter of empirical investigation. Now given Reichenbach's empiricist account of geometry and his relativity thesis of geometry, it seems to me that one cannot empirically determine the physical geometry at all in his framework.

Let us say that we have adopted A as our coordinative definition, and after some empirical investigations we have found out that the physical geometry is Euclidean. Nothing is wrong with this, because it is either

---

[38] Poincaré, *Science and Hypothesis,* pp. 64-68. See also his "On the Foundations of Geometry," *The Monist* (1898), pp. 1-43.

[39] Reichenbach, *The Rise of Scientific Philosophy*, p. 132,

[40] Cf. his *Philosophical Problems of Space and Time,* 2nd ed (Dordrecht-Holland: D. Reidel, 1973), pp. 98-105.

[41] Cf. Grünbaum, *Philosophical Problems of Space and Time,* pp. 98-101.

Euclidean or not Euclidean. However, Reichenbach's relativity theory implies that when we change A into A', then the resulting geometry, i.e., Euclidean, should change into a new geometry – in this case, a non-Euclidean one. However, A' can still be Euclidean, i.e., making the length definition depends upon, say, orientation and/or position. So there seems to be a contradiction here. Thus, it does not seem possible in Reichenbach's philosophy of geometry that one can empirically determine the physical geometry. Of course, this is the case only within Reichenbach's philosophy, not refuting altogether the claim that one can determine geometry empirically.

Department of Philosophy
Middle East Technical University
Ankara, Turkey

EPISTEMOLOGICAL DUALISM AND THE PRIMAL OTHER: TRACING THE CONTOURS OF THE ENCOUNTER, AGAIN

A.O. BALCOMB

In his introduction to the 1994 publication of Descartes' *A Discourse on Method, Meditations and Principles*, Tom Sorell writes the following:

> Descartes broke his journey in Germany in the winter of 1619, and in a house near Ulm he gave himself over completely to reflection on methodological questions. His near obsessive meditations seem to have led, on 10 November 1619, to his experiencing a day-time vision, and that night three dreams, which revealed to him, as he thought, his task in life: to unfold a wonderful science.[1]

This little insight into the circumstances surrounding Descartes' celebrated discovery of his *cogito ergo sum* is one that we seldom hear about. This is probably because we cannot conceive of the father of modern rationalism coming to his "revelation" through visions and dreams! Yet it tells a story about the way human beings used to view the world and themselves before the Cartesian revolution. Descartes' "discovery" about himself took place in the context of a worldview that was totally different from the worldview that developed largely as a consequence of his discovery. The primal worldview had been in existence, in one form or another, from the earliest records of 'Homo Sapiens' – in other words, from the upper Palaeolithic period, about 35,000 years ago. Indeed, what differentiated Homo Sapiens from the Neanderthals was the former's ability to conceive the existence of a spiritual universe which was, metaphorically speaking, separated from the physical by the thinnest of membranes. The spirit world, according to the cognitive archaeologist David Lewis-Williams, was an immanent reality "interdigitating" with the material world.[2] The entire existence of the earliest human beings was shaped by this alternative reality. "All life, economic, social, and religious, (took)

---

[1] R. Descartes, *A Discourse on Method, Meditations and Principles,* Tom Sorell (ed.) (London: J.M. Dent, 1994), p. xix.

[2] David Lewis-Williams, *The Mind in the Cave* (London: Thames and Hudson, 2002), p. 209.

place within and interacted reciprocally with (this) specific conception of the universe." [3]

Such a state of affairs existed universally amongst the human race, to one degree or another and in one form or another, until the advent of what is now called the European Enlightenment. And while Descartes' visions and dreams over that forty-eight hour period have gone almost completely unnoticed in history, what is now called the "Cartesian cogito" is feted as one of the most important milestones in the philosophical journey of the human race. This is because his "wonderful science" has become associated with none other than the modern scientific project and the so-called objectification of reality.

The question must be asked, however, whether there is an alternative tradition within the Western paradigm that fits more comfortably with the worldview in which Descartes himself lived and thought and in what forms this worldview continues to exist today.

MODERNITY AS DISENGAGEMENT

At the heart of modernity, according to Gunton, is what Taylor calls "disengagement." Gunton describes disengagement thus:

> Disengagement means standing apart from each other and the world and treating the other as external, as mere object. The key is the word instrumental: we use the other as an instrument, as the mere means for realizing our will, and not as in some way integral to our being. It has its heart in the technocratic attitude: the view that the world is there to do with exactly as we choose. [4]

Gunton argues that Descartes destroyed the notion that the "social order ... (is) rooted in some way in an insight into ... the order of being as a whole." [5] "Without a philosophy of engagement", says Gunton, "we are lost." And here Gunton gives the first hint of a yearning for the primal past:

> Plato in effect shows us ... that pure philosophical or metaphysical speculation, a demythologising of the gods in the name of pure rationality, is the beginning of disengagement. Underlying the anthropomorphism of the Greek gods, however irrational and morally unacceptable, there lay a quite proper concern for a universe which made some sense of the human moral condition. ... The

---

[3] Williams, p. 209.

[4] C. Gunton, *The One, The Three, and The Many – God, Creation and the Culture of Modernity* (Cambridge: Cambridge University Press, 1993), p. 14.

[5] Gunton, p. 15.

Presocratics and their sceptical successors, in losing the anthropomorphic, also lost the personal. Ethos was lost to environment, and so person and world were torn apart.[6]

In the Western tradition an alternative to such a worldview can be found in the Phenomenological school.

EDMUND HUSSERL AND THE PHENOMENOLOGISTS

According to David Abram, the philosophical tradition of Phenomenology is a natural place to turn when trying "to understand the strange difference between the experienced world, or worlds, of indigenous, vernacular cultures and the world of modern European and North American civilization." [7] According to the phenomenologists, the world in which we live is not "an inert or mechanical object but a living field, an open and dynamic landscape subject to its own moods and metamorphoses."[8] Abram rejects a materialistic and mechanical view of the universe on the basis that it marginalizes direct "pre-conceptual" experience by relegating it to a secondary, derivative dimension – a "mere consequence of events unfolding in the 'realer' world of quantifiable and measurable 'facts'."[9] Stripping the pulse of subjective experience from the things that we "objectively" study cannot be done, according to Abram, without "the things themselves losing all existence for us." The phenomenologists come to the rescue here because they do not seek to explain the world as much as to describe it as closely as possible in such a way as to "pay attention to its rhythms and textures, not to capture or control it."[10] Phenomenology is the rigorous science of experience that opens the way for other sciences to do their work. The French phenomenologist Maurice Merleau-Ponty put this most emphatically:

> All my knowledge of the world, even my scientific knowledge, is gained from my own particular point of view, or from some experience of the world without which the symbols of science would be meaningless. The whole universe of science is built upon the world as directly experienced, and if we want to subject science itself to rigorous scrutiny and arrive at a precise assessment of its meaning and scope, we must begin by reawakening the basic experience of the world, of which science is the

---

[6] Gunton, p. 15.
[7] David Abram, *The Spell of the Sensuous* (New York: Vintage Books, 1996), p. 31.
[8] Abram, p. 32.
[9] Abram, p. 34.
[10] Abram, p. 35.

second-order expression ... To return to things themselves is to return to that world which precedes knowledge, of which knowledge always speaks, and in relation to which every scientific schematization is an abstract and derivative sign-language, as is geography in relation to the countryside in which we have learnt beforehand what a forest, a prairie or a river is.[11]

Husserl took this a step further and developed the concept of intersubjectivity. How, he asked himself, was it possible that in our subjective experience we would be able to experience the reality of other experiencing selves. We do so through our bodies. The body is a multifaceted phenomenon that always accompanies one's awareness. But one can only experience one's body from the inside. The phenomenal field contains many other bodies which one experiences from the outside. Other bodies move around your body. There is a deep affinity between your body and these other bodies. One's own body is experienced from within. These other bodies are experienced from without. But these experiences echo and resonate with each other in such a way that there is mutual recognition of other bodies as centres of experience. In other words there were other subjects out there responding to you as subject. These multiple subjectivities meant that "the phenomenal field was no longer the isolate haunt of a solitary ego, but a collective landscape, constituted by other experiencing subjects as well as by oneself."[12]

If Husserl and others laid the foundation within the philosophical tradition of Phenomenology, John Macmurray picked it up in the field of ontology.

MACMURRAY AND RELATIONAL ONTOLOGY

In his *The Self as Agent*, the published version of his Gifford lectures given in 1953, Macmurray systematically dismantles the Cartesian and Kantian schema. The West is facing, he says, a "crisis of the personal":

Modern philosophy is characteristically egocentric. I mean no more than this: that firstly, it takes the Self as its starting point, and not God, or the world or the community; and that, secondly, the Self is an individual in isolation, an ego or "I", never a "thou". This is shown by the fact that there can arise the question, "How does the Self know that other selves exist?" Further, the Self so premised is a thinker in search of knowledge. It is

---

[11] In Abram, p. 36.
[12] Abram, p. 37.

conceived as the Subject; the correlate in experience of the object presented for cognition.[13]

The self, says Macmurray, should not be conceived of theoretically as subject but practically as agent. Human behaviour, he says, is comprehensible only in terms of dynamic social reference. In other words the idea of the isolated, purely individual self is fiction. The problem with adopting "I think" as the central reference point in Cartesian philosophy is that it "makes it formally impossible to do justice to religious experience."[14] The Self "is part of the world in which it acts, and in dynamic relation with the rest of the world. ... To be part of the world is to exist, while to be excluded from the world is to be non-existent."[15] While Macmurray is fairly merciless with Descartes he is more sympathetic with Kant. Kant's revolutionary hypothesis – that instead of asking how it is that we understand the world we should be asking how it is that the world comes to be understood by us – is given sympathetic treatment. However, in Kant's two-world hypothesis Macmurray detects once again the Cartesian dualism that he detests. Kant believed that there is a phenomenal world – that is the world as it appears to us – and the world as it is in itself, or the noumenal world. The former is accessible through "practical reason" and the latter through "pure reason". But pure reason, even though Kant argues that it is primary, is pure indeed in the sense that it remains in the realm of the theoretical and not the practical. So Kant acknowledges the theoretical existence of a world that we can speculate about but denies that we can know anything about it in terms of practical experience. In other words, we cannot experience the world as it is; we can only experience it as it appears to us. And it must appear to us in terms that we ourselves rationally determine. This means that if the world as it is has God in it then we cannot experience God except in terms that we have already prescribed, and Macmurray is not prepared to countenance this because it brings us back once again to the Self as subject and not as agent.

Macmurray's critique of Descartes and Kant – the two pillars on which modern philosophy is built – is obviously crucial when we consider the possibility of a worldview that countenances precisely what each respectively discounts: that is, that the Self is agent, not subject, and that the experience of the numinous is real, not imaginary.

FURTHER DEVELOPMENTS: HOPPER AND THE NON-RATIONALIST TRADITION

Hopper has described a paradigm shift in science, philosophy, and

---

[13] J. Macmurray, *The Self as Agent* (London: Faber and Faber, 1953) p. 31.

[14] Macmurray, p. 71.

[15] Macmurray, p. 91.

theology away from the dominance of Logos (classical logic) to Mythos (rootedness in experience).[16] In science, the movement is discernible in the shift from Newtonian to Quantum physics, in philosophy from rationalism to dynamism, and in theology from dogma to process. The consequence of such a shift has been a recognition of the open-endedness of the universe, a fundamental unity between the knower and the known, and open-ness to the divine. In other words the movement is from a mechanistic to a vitalistic view of the universe. Such a shift, because it is radically different from the rationalism of modernity, has been described as "non-rational."[17]

Restoring to the non-rational (that is the antithesis of the rational), "its own unique and particular frame of reference" is a project that must be embarked upon.[18] Three features of the non-rational need especially to be rehabilitated, namely the experience of the world around us in terms of the numinous, the personification of the "map of the psyche", and the re-mythologising of our lives by "rereading ... the stories we tell of our lives in the light of archetypal stories which have come to us in our corporate tradition."[19]

THE NUMINOUS

Rudolf Otto's famous description of the numinous as *mysterium tremendum et fascinans*[20] has been described "as an experience of an unknown and uncontrollable, yet awesome and enchanting, takeover of the everyday self by a force so sheerly other that we can speak of it only by denying it our words."[21] Such a definition, however, belies the fact that the numinous contains an epistemological dimension. Otto associated with the numinous what he called a heightened sense of "creature-feeling" or self-abasement before an overpowering, absolute might of some kind. This denotes the acknowledgement of the presence of an Other, outside the self, that makes the self feel at the same time abased as well as uplifted. Thus one may speak of an "objectivity" of the numinous in which both knower and known become self-consciously related. It is the reverse of the instrumentalist objectivity of the disengaged modern. It is the "thou" of Martin Buber which is held in awe by the "I" of the beholder.

Epistemologically this means that we no longer see ourselves as "subjects" that scrutinize a range of "objects" in the world in a detached

---

[16] David H. Hopper, *Technology, Theology, and the Idea of Progress* (Louisville, KY: Westminster/John Knox Press, 1991), p. 116.

[17] J. Heisig, "The Mystique of the Nonrational and a New Spirituality" in *Archetypal Process – Self and Divine in Whitehead, Jung*, and *Hillman*, D. Griffin (ed.) (Evanston, IL: NorthWestern University Press, 1989).

[18] Heisig, p. 185.

[19] Heisig, p. 185.

[20] R. Otto, *The Idea of the Holy* (London: Oxford University Press, 1959).

[21] Heisig, p. 187.

manner. Torrance rather strongly calls this approach an expression of "open-mouthed imbecility." Instead he advocates that we allow the world to "disclose itself to us … in its own reality and nature."[22] And when we do this we stand, with Einstein, "in awe of the eternal mystery of the world in its comprehensibility." This attitude, according to Torrance, leads to a truer picture of the world.

PERSONIFICATION

Personification, according to Jung, is to do with the "habitual, instinctual, ineluctable demand of the psyche to transform all of life into the image of persons so that it might have 'real' meaning for us."[23] Mental events are imagined as persons and players who people our dreams, and fantasies are the symbolic representation of those events. Personification in dream psychology is suggestive of it existing in the human psyche at a more fundamental, epistemological level. This is, in fact, argued by Macmurray. He asserts that it is impossible to become aware of "existents" other than ourselves when we objectify them in terms of the Cartesian Cogito. True apprehension, according to Macmurray, depends on two things: the primacy of the tactile over the visual and the primacy of person over object. Sight is associated with cognitive, passive acknowledgement of an object. Through touch, on the other hand, we become aware of the Other-than-self by means of physical resistance. It is on the basis of the primacy of the tactile as opposed to the visual that Macmurray develops his notion of the Self as agent and replaces "I think" with "I do". But establishing the existence of the Other through touch does not mean that we have yet established the *behaviour* of the other. This we can only do by attributing to the Other the form of activity that we attribute to ourselves. "My understanding of the behaviour of the Other," he says, "is always mediated through my understanding of my own." In this sense, asserts Macmurray, all human knowledge is necessarily anthropomorphic. To use the categories of Jung, apprehension is through personification.

A more moderate variation of this is found in Thomas F. Torrance who, while he does not speak about personification, suggests that objectivity should not be confused with objectification and advocates the need for an active engagement between subject and object in which the subject is "prepared and ready for whatever it (the object) may reveal in the give-and-take of investigation."[24]

REMYTHOLOGISING

One of the first casualties of the modern project was the belief that

---

[22] T. Torrance, *God and Rationality* (Edinburgh: T&T Clark, 1997), p. 10.

[23] Heisig, p. 192.

[24] Torrance, p. 9.

truth could be conveyed through myth. Myths and traditions were to be "brought into the supreme court of reason in which the solitary ego ... (passed) judgement on the meanings behind the surface meanings of things."[25] The modern project, in other words, was quintessentially about demythologising the stories and traditions that had been passed down from the elders and ancestors. But the remythologizing advocated here is not so much to do with reinstating myth as historical explanation of reality, but as a means of discovering a collective unconscious embedded in the history of a people. Ordinary ideas, for example, are charged with archetypal significance through images found in myths and thus transported to a more universal realm. In this way myths "draw the individual out of the isolations of personality into the collective drives of the race."[26] It would appear that Gabriel Setiloane has drawn on such a Jungian interpretation of myth which he describes as "a communal memory of the group as it has grappled with the questions of its, and all human origins, life on earth, being ... and even the hereafter."[27]

Mention of Setiloane brings us to the subject of African understandings of reality.

AN AFRICAN WORLDVIEW AND POST-CARTESIAN REALITY

Richard Tarnas describes the prototypical human being, stepping out of seventeenth-century Europe, as a product of the Enlightenment in this way:

> A newly self-conscious and autonomous human being – curious about the world, confident in his own judgements, sceptical of orthodoxies, rebellious against authority, responsible for his own beliefs and actions, enamoured of the classical past but even more committed to a greater future, proud of his humanity, conscious of his distinctiveness from nature, aware of his artistic powers as individual creator, assured of his intellectual capacity to comprehend and control nature, and altogether less dependent on an omnipotent God.[28]

Compare this human being with a human being stepping out of a worldview that has been described in the following way:

---

[25] Heisig, p. 195.

[26] Heisig, p. 197.

[27] G. Setiloane, *African Theology – an Introduction* (Braamfontein: Skotaville, 1986), p. 14.

[28] Richard Tarnas, *The Passion of the Western Mind* (NY: Ballantine Books, 1991), p. 282.

First, a sense of kinship with nature, in which animals and plants, no less than human beings, have their own spiritual existence and place in the universe, as interdependent parts of the whole.

Second, the deep sense that humankind is finite and weak and in need of a supernatural power.

Third, that humankind is not alone in the universe, that there is a spiritual world of powers and beings more ultimate than itself. This is a personalized universe where the appropriate question is not *what* causes things to happen but *who* causes things to happen.

Fourth, that human beings can enter into relationships with the benevolent spirit world.

Fifth, an acute sense of the afterlife usually expressed in belief in and respect for the ancestors who may be referred to as the "living dead".

Sixth, that humans live in a sacramental universe where there is no dichotomy between the physical and spiritual and that the physical can act as a vehicle for the spiritual.

This is Turner's celebrated six-feature analysis of what he and others have called the "primal" worldview, which worldview Kwame Bediako and others have identified as basically reflective of the African worldview.[29] That there are resonances between this and the post-Cartesian worldview is clear. What remains is to pinpoint the similarities as accurately as possible. This will be done by reflecting on three of the key features of the primal worldview that seem to link with the shifts that have taken place in post-modern science, philosophy, and theology as described above. These features are, conversely, seen also to be most at odds with the old paradigm.

The first is the fundamental unity between subject and object, observed and observer, God and world, knower and known, and with this the interconnectedness of all being. The second is the posture of the human being toward the world as one of open-ness, engagement, and vulnerability. And the third is the belief in a personal universe.

UNITY BETWEEN SUBJECT AND OBJECT

One of the most graphic descriptions of unity between subject and object in the primal worldview is given by J.V. Taylor. He describes an experience he had on Lake Victoria, where he assisted some fishermen bringing their nets. As the fishermen draw in the two ends of the net to enclose the fish, and themselves, within it, the net itself becomes a metaphor for an "unbroken circle" that characterizes the primal universe. He feels "the edges of separateness evaporating" as he experiences the one-ness of this universe in the one-ness of all things in and around him. His

---

[29] K. Bediako, *Christianity in Africa: The Renewal of a Non-Western Religion* (NY: Orbis, 1995).

graphic account of this experience ends with the following description of what he calls the "primal vision":

> Not only is there less separation between subject and object, between self and not-self, but fundamentally all things share the same nature and the same interaction one upon another – rocks and forest trees, beasts and serpents, the power of the wind and waves upon a ship, the power of a drum over a dancer's body, the power in the mysterious caves of Kokola, the living, the dead and the first ancestors, from the stone to the divinities an hierarchy of power but not of being, for all are one, all are here, all are now.[30]

Every scholar of primal thought, from Lucien Levy-Bruhl in the late nineteenth and early twentieth century to Placide Tempels in the mid-twentieth century, to Alexis Kagame, to V.Y. Mudimbe, and John Mbiti, has commented on the oneness of the universe in primal thinking.

The first person to recognize this phenomenon as *the* distinctive feature that differentiated Western and primal thought was Lucien Levy-Bruhl. The essence of this way of thinking, according to Levy-Bruhl, was a mystical orientation in which "objects" were fused with an intangible power which meant that the "object is both itself and a spirit; the spirit both itself and an object."[31] This led to what he called "participation", a term that has developed into the celebrated concept of "vital participation" which has been widely described by both African and European scholars of primal thought.[32]

Placide Tempels was the first to articulate the African worldview in terms of a philosophical system and his *Bantu Philosophy*[33] has become a departure point for discussion amongst many African philosophers since then, especially in Francophone Africa. "[The] concept of separate beings," he says, "which find themselves side by side, entirely independent one of another, is foreign to Bantu thought":

> Bantu hold that created beings preserve a bond one of another, an intimate ontological relationship, comparable with the causal tie which binds creature and Creator. For

---

[30] J. V. Taylor, *The Primal Vision: Christian Presence and African Religion* (London: SCM, 1975), p. 64.

[31] R. Horton, *Patterns of Thought in Africa and the West: essays on magic, religion, and science* (Cambridge: Cambridge University Press, 1993), p. 65.

[32] See, for example, K. Dickson and P. Ellingworth, *Biblical Revelation and African Beliefs* (London: Lutterworth, 1969), Chapter 7.

[33] P. Temples, *Bantu Philosophy* (Paris: Presence Africain, 1959).

the Bantu there is interaction of being with being, that is to say, of force with force. Transcending the mechanical, chemical and psychological interactions, they see a relationship of forces which we should call ontological.[34]

Most African philosophers (one exception being Kagame) have taken issue with Tempels's identification of "being" with "force," but few have denied his assertion that African ontology valorizes the interconnectedness of all being. The most articulate of these philosophers has been Alexis Kagame who set out consciously to test Tempels's theories in linguistic analysis. In his monumental *La Philosophie Bantu-Rwandaise de l'Etre* (1956) he linguistically analyzes the term *ntu*, which is roughly translated as "being." Mudimbe's summary of Kagame's conclusion is "that the Bantu equivalent of 'to be' is strictly and only performed as a copula. It does not express the notion of existence, *and therefore cannot translate the Cartesian cogito.*"[35]

This observation of Mudimbe's is remarkable. That the Nguni word for 'being' can only be performed as a copula, and that within this schema the Cartesian *cogito* cannot be translated, is probably the most radical way of stating that the essence of African ontology, usually adumbrated in the expression "I am because others are, and because others are I am", is diametrically opposed to the Cartesian schema. Mudimbe's summary of Kagame's analysis of *ntu* is a fine expression of African ontology:

> In sum, the *ntu* is somehow a sign of a universal similitude. Its presence in beings brings them to life and attests to both their individual value and to the measure of their integration in the dialectic of vital energy. *Ntu* is both a uniting and a differentiating vital norm which explains the powers of vital inequality in terms of difference between beings. It is a sign that God, father of all beings ... has put a stamp on the universe, thus making it transparent in a hierarchy of sympathy. Upwards one would read the vitality which, from minerals through vegetables, animals and humans, links stones to the departed and God himself. Downwards, it is a genealogical filiation of forms of beings, engendering or relating to one another, all of them witnessing to the original source that made them possible.[36]

---

[34] Tempels, p. 58.
[35] V. Y. Mudimbe, "African Gnosis Philosophy and the Order of Knowledge: an Introduction," in *African Studies Review* 28.2/3 (June/September 1985), p.189. Emphasis mine.
[36] Mudimbe, pp. 189-90.

The interconnectedness of the universe, beginning with the creator and going all the way down to rocks, can surely not be more strongly stated. Here is a system that is indeed a Cartesian nightmare and a Whiteheadian dream.

OPEN-NESS, VULNERABILITY, AND ENGAGEMENT

The second feature, regarding a posture of open-ness, vulnerability, and engagement has many manifestations. There is open-ness, vulnerability, and engagement with respect to the transcendent, with respect to the Other, and with respect to the novel. The African experience of the transcendent is as pervasive as it is common-place. The profound difference between the transcendence of modernity and the transcendence of the primal is that, in the former, it is distant and, in the latter, it is immediate. There is a divinity that is indeed distant, but this is not the divinity that is influential and that pervades everyday existence. The Sotho word for the ancestors, *badimu*, is a variation of the Sotho word for God, *Modimo*. In other words, it is the plural form of God. The one is manifest in the many and, though the one is absent, the many are present – a phenomenon which Idowu called "diffused monotheism."[37] Turner and others have pointed out that it is this "imminent" transcendence that makes the African approach so different from the Western approach. The emphasis on *this* world and not some world to come means that the primal world finds it difficult to conceive of the transcendence of God as believed in classical Christianity. Bediako makes the point that such this-worldliness "encompasses God and man in an abiding relationship which is the divine destiny of humankind, and the purpose and goal of the universe."[38] The fact that this world is so suffused with the transcendent means that humankind comes to participate in the transcendent. For Bediako this is the true meaning of vital participation:

---

[37] Ngoetjana has argued, however, that the term "monotheistic" is questionable when used in the context of describing *Modimo* because by definition it valorizes a notion of one-ness that does not exist in *Sotho* religion. See L.M. Ngoetjana "Critical comparison of the concepts of God in Sotho traditional religion and the concepts of the Christian God as a missiological problem" Unpublished PhD thesis, University of KwaZulu-Natal, 2003.

[38] Bediako, p. 101. The statement coming out of the Ecumenical Association of African Theologians in Accra, 1977, made this point. "For Africans there is unity and continuity between the destiny of human persons and the destiny of the cosmos .... The victory of life in the human person is also the victory of life in the cosmos. The salvation of the human person in African theology is the salvation of the universe. In the mystery of the incarnation, Christ assumes the totality of the human and the totality of the cosmos." (Bediako, p. 102.)

> Applied to the experience of transcendence, 'vital
> participation' … then opens the way for a participation
> equally in the resources and powers of all those who are
> also brought within the community. … The divine
> presence in the community … constitutes it into a
> 'transcendent' community in which the human
> components experience and share in divine life and
> nature.[39]

When this translates into the everyday experience of "others," we
have the possibility of the introduction of the transcendent into the
mundane relationships of everyday life. It is a transcendence that requires
the presence of an "other" and therefore cannot be experienced
autonomously. Once again, this has epistemological implications. The
transcendent Other draws us out of ourselves in a continual search for
meaning and plenitude of being. Such a transcendence may be compared
with that described by Blondel. For Blondel to act, to think, to create, or to
assert oneself, is "to lose oneself, to place what is most ours … at total
risk." All acting and thinking, therefore, is associated "with self-immolation
and sacrifice" because "by acting/thinking we grope towards a synthesis
which seems 'right' to us, and yet is not originally intended by us, but only
'occurs' to us out of the future plenitude of being, and has implications we
cannot contain."[40] Such a transcendence does not seem to require the
presence of an "other." It is to be found in the very activity of (autonomous)
thinking, acting, and creating.

Open-ness and vulnerability to engage with the novel is as essential
as open-ness to the transcendent and to the Other. After Taylor describes his
experience on the lake in his "unbroken circle" chapter of *The Primal
Vision*, he recounts how before they had their meal of cooked fish on the
banks of the lake they joined hands and "intoned a Latin grace". Moments
before this they had made an offering to the god Kokola. Clearly they did
not need to understand the words that they were saying to see the necessity
of ritually enacting them, and they did not see any contradiction between
this act drawn from the Christian faith and one performed moments earlier,
drawn from African Traditional Religion. That one was entirely novel, that
is the Latin prayer, did not mean that it should be excluded. Indeed, the fact
that it existed and clearly carried with it some noumenal significance meant
that it would be advisable to include it in the unbroken circle, lest, by its
very exclusion, it might be transformed into something evil and debilitating
to life force. We have here an example of the fundamental ability of primal
systems of thought to absorb and contain elements of different or alien
systems of thought. For the circle of meaning and life to remain unbroken,

---

[39] Bediako, p. 103.

[40] In J. Milbank, *Theology and Social Theory: Beyond Secular Reason*
(Oxford: Blackwell, 1995), p. 214.

as it must, nothing must be left outside it. This is at the heart of the African propensity for syncretism.

Such open-ness to the novel or the different has defined the capacity of Africans "to borrow, re-work and integrate alien ideas (and) has given ... traditional cosmologies such tremendous durability in the face of the immense changes that the 20th century has brought to the African scene."[41] This accommodative style of African epistemologies, says Horton, contrasts with the adversarial style of scientific theory where the way in which change of belief is stimulated is not by novel experience but by rival theory. Bediako offers the suggestion that a fundamentally different kind of epistemology is at work here. An African epistemology, he says, lends itself to "a unified and organic view of the knowledge of truth (avoiding) the destructive dichotomies in the epistemology (of) the European Enlightenment." Moreover when this open-ness to the novel takes place in the context of the open-ness to immanent transcendence, "the real encounter with alternative viewpoints and interpretations of reality takes place not in words alone, but in the realm of the spirit and in the things of the spirit."[42] In other words the novel, the different, the Other, like everything else in the primal universe, is infused with spiritual significance.[43]

---

[41] Horton in K. Appiah, *In My Father's House – Africa in the Philosophy of Culture* (Oxford: Oxford University Press, 1992), p. 127.

[42] Bediako, p. 104.

[43] The issue of open-ness to the novel also raises the issue of credulity versus scepticism in the search for truth. The latter is traditionally seen as characteristic of the modern critical method as much as the former is seen to be characteristic of traditional thinking. Much work, however, has been done on the issue of the ostensibly uncritical nature of traditional thought. It must be emphasized, firstly, that the term "traditional" should not be used synonymously with the term "primal." However it is commonly held that in those societies that hold to a primal worldview knowledge is passed down according to unchanging traditions. Hallen and Sodipo have dedicated much of their research to debunking this impression. In their *Knowledge, Belief, and Witchcraft*, they attempt to show that while belief and knowledge are identified in the Western paradigm they are clearly distinguished in the African societies that they have studied. Before something can become known it must first of all be believed. When we are told that something is true we accept it on the basis of the "charity principle." This does not yet mean that we know it is true. Second hand truth – that is truth accepted simply on the basis of the authority of the person who is asserting it – needs to be passed through a fairly rigorous process of testing before we can say that we know it is true. Hallen and Sodipo's argument is that there is far more rigorous testing of this nature in traditional societies than there is in Western societies where most things are taken as true if important people with white coats say that they are true. (See B. Hallen and J. Sodipo, *Knowledge, Belief, and Witchcraft – Analytic*

BELIEF IN A PERSONAL UNIVERSE

The acceptance of a personal universe is probably the most controversial aspect of primal thought and yet also the most significant. At its crudest, a personalized universe is one swarming with entities that have a multitude of functions, both malevolent and benevolent, with respect to human community. At its most appealing, there is the environmental concern of a personalized universe infused with spirits that give personality to objects in such a way that makes it possible for them to have some kind of relationship with human beings. So "any object of the natural environment may enter into a totemic spiritual relationship with human beings or become tutelary and guardian spirits whilst the environment itself is used realistically and unsentimentally but with profound respect and reverence without exploitation."[44]

Both of these possibilities, according to Horton, miss the point. A personal universe, he says, is a theoretical construct developed to help explain, predict, and control the world as experienced and understood by its inhabitants. It does, in other words, precisely what theoretical constructs do in the modern scientific context. The difference is that, for one, the world is understood animately and, for the other, it is understood inanimately. Reality, Horton argues, is never experienced simply at common sense level, neither in primal nor in modern societies. Theories are constructed at various levels of abstraction and complexity to explain what we experience at the common sense level.[45] Horton argues, for example, that "concepts such as 'molecules', 'atoms', 'electron', and 'wave' are the result of a process in which relevant features of certain prototype phenomena have been abstracted from the irrelevant features" within the realm of sense experience. In the same, way traditional thought, he says, "draws upon people and their social relations as raw material of its theoretical models (that is the spiritual world it constructs) and makes use of many dimensions of human life and neglects others."[46] The fact that in some African cultures there are extremely complex spirit worlds testifies to the complex and nuanced way that the world is experienced, analysed and understood. Horton proposes the fascinating theory that in societies which are in a constant state of flux and change and where order, regularity, predictability

---

Experiments in African Philosophy (Stanford, CA: Stanford University Press, 1997).

[44] Turner in Bediako, p. 94.

[45] J. Polkinghorne argues, indeed, that in quantum field theory the theories we construct to explain phenomena are dependent on the questions we ask about those phenomena. Thus a "wave-like" answer concerning the nature of light will be given to a "wave-like" question and a "particle-like" answer will be given to a "particle-like" question. See his *Quarks, Chaos and Christianity: Questions to Science and Religion* (London: Triangle, 1994), p. 16.

[46] Horton, p. 216.

and simplicity are absent (i.e., modern societies), there is a tendency to look to the world of inanimate things where these qualities are readily seen (i.e., science) and in societies characterized by order, regularity, predictability, etc. (i.e., traditional) the unseen or "theoretical" world becomes animated.

Appiah, while recognizing the plausibility of Horton's thesis, believes it to be fundamentally flawed.[47] By imposing a modern interpretation (that is, personal universe = theoretical construct) on a pre-modern world, he has failed to recognize that such a pre-modern world has its own pre-modern theories of explanation, and these are teleological or functional in nature. Things (like spirits) are there, in other words, for a purpose. For example, they meet needs. They are not there simply as explanations (in the descriptive sense) of what is happening. They explain *why* it is happening. Appiah maintains that the positivist philosophy of science that Horton espouses seeks to eradicate functional explanation or reduce it to other sorts of explanation because it reeks of teleology. The implication is that Horton, for all his considerable scientific and philosophical acumen applied in the area of modern science and traditional thought over a considerable number of years, has yet failed to give any real credibility to the frame of reference that pre-moderns themselves are using. This does not mean that he gives no credibility at all to primal understandings of reality. Indeed, his work seems to be dedicated to the task of giving it credibility, but strictly in terms of the norms and canons of modern scientific theory. And here his teacher is clearly Durkheim, whom he quotes and praises extensively and who believed that primal thought was the precursor to scientific or "advanced" thought.

A far better explanation of a personal universe is to be found in the epistemology of Jung and Macmurray described above. The notion that all knowledge, including scientific knowledge, is anthropomorphic to some degree or another means that apprehending reality in personalistic terms is potentially ever present. Indeed, it is the objectifying of reality that becomes alien to human thought, not the personification of reality.[48] "Our knowledge," says Macmurray, "is anthropomorphic in the sense that whatever characteristics we attribute to the Other must be included within the full characterization of ourselves":

> The concept of a 'person' is inclusive of the concept of 'an organism', as the concept of 'an organism' is inclusive of that of a 'material body'. The included concepts can be derived from the concepts of 'a person' by abstractions; by excluding from attention those characters which belong to the higher category alone. The empirical ground for these

---

[47] Horton in Appiah, p. 123.

[48] Perhaps the crassest form of Western anthropomorphism is to be found in discourse around the stock market which becomes an entity more capricious and totalitarian than any being conceived of in a pre-modern world.

distinctions is found in practical experience. We cannot deal with organisms successfully in the same way that we can with material objects, or with persons. The form of their resistance – in opposition or in support – necessitates a difference in our own behaviour.[49]

The difference between using this hypothesis instead of Horton's in explaining a personal universe is the implication that *all* human thought, including scientific thought, is anthropomorphic. In other words, Macmurray eschews objectivity as being fundamentally wrongheaded. Horton clearly does not. The importance of the difference is not merely academic. Macmurray is at pains to point out that seeing things as objects and seeing things as persons makes a fundamental difference to our *behaviour*. In Buberian terms, once again, the personalized universe means we apprehend it as "thou"; the objective universe means we apprehend it as "it." Such a difference in understanding must make an enormous difference in the way we treat it. So Turner's assertion that a personalized universe means a universe that needs to be treated with profound respect and reverence without exploitation may not be wishful thinking and undue romanticization after all.

EQUATING THE POST-MODERN AND THE PRIMAL: SOME FINAL COMMENTS

This paper has attempted to argue that the primal worldview, as representative of all civilizations and cultures, including that of the Egyptians, Aztecs, and San, before they were either destroyed, colonized, or transformed by modernity, is at odds with a kind of science known as "modern" or "Newtonian" but resonates in various ways with what has been called the "new" science, or the science of Einstein and the science of quantum physics. The question will be asked how serious such an equation is.

Three positions have been suggested in answer to this question, and these have been hinted at above. The first is that the primal worldview can be compared in no way whatsoever with the scientific worldview, the second is that the primal worldview opened the way for modern scientific thinking, and the third is that the primal worldview resonates positively with a post-modern scientific worldview. The first option is connected with the idea that objectivity is impossible within a personalized and/or sacral universe. The second option is the one aspired to by Durkheim and Horton and is based on the belief that the ability to recognize an order of events "outside the direct grasp of the senses" and at the same time to grasp causal connections and unities of process which common sense could never have dreamed of, means that "we can find the vital germ of the most elaborate

---

[49] Macmurray, p. 117. Emphasis mine,

sciences in the first stirrings of the most primitive religions."[50] The third option has been the one pursued in this essay, that is, there are clear resonances between the primal worldview and post-modern science, philosophy and theology. The fact that we are in a position now to consider such options is characteristic, Lyotard would probably argue, of our post-modern condition.[51] All of these conditions – the pre-modern, modern, and post-modern – are matters of history. We cannot dispute the fact that the idea of a sacral or personalized universe collapsed with the advent of modern science. But neither can we dispute the fact that the universe as understood by modern science has been seriously challenged with respect to notions of objectivity and predictability. The search was on for an alternative universe defined more by mythos as opposed to logos once the modern paradigm began to feel the strain. This has led, on the one hand, to a somewhat wistful longing for the primal past and, on the other, to a renewed interest in alternative knowledge systems that reflect the worldview that it espoused. Associated with the first (i.e., wistful longing) is what Horton argues is the belief that these systems:

> may provide us with a clue to the nature of our lost heritage – a heritage supposedly destroyed by the advance of science [or] the belief that only through the study of

---

[50] Horton, p. 72. It may be appropriate to follow Durkheim's own reasoning here.

"For to explain is to attach things to each other and to establish relations between them which make them appear as functions of each other and as vibrating sympathetically according to an internal law founded in their nature. But sensations, which see nothing except from the outside, could never make them disclose these relations and internal bonds; the intellect alone can create the notion of them. When I learn that A regularly precedes B, my knowledge is increased by a new fact; but my intelligence is not at all satisfied with a statement which does not show its reason. I commence to understand only if it possible for me to conceive B in such a way that makes it appear to me as something that is not foreign to A, and united to A by some relationship of kinship. The great service that religions have rendered to thought is that they have constructed a first representation of what these relations of kinship between things may be. .... Today as formerly, to explain is to show how one thing participates in one of several others. It has been said that the participations of this sort implied by the mythologies violate the principle of contradiction and that they are by that opposed to those implied by scientific explanations. ... Is not the statement that man is a kangaroo or the sun a bird, equal to identifying the two with each other. But our manner of thought is not different when we say of heat that it is a movement, or of light that it is a vibration, we forcibly identify contraries. .... Thus between the logic of religious thought and the logic of scientific thought there is no abyss."

[51] See J.F. Lyotard, *The Postmodern Condition: A Report on Knowledge* (Manchester: Manchester University Press, 1984).

pre-scientific thought-systems can we get a clear view of the nature of science. Only if we have some idea of what it was like to live in a world into which the scientific outlook has not yet intruded, can we be at all certain as to what are the distinctive features of this outlook and what are simply universals of human thought.[52]

Associated with the second (i.e., interest in alternative knowledge systems) is the argument that, while Western science has become epistemologically and politically correct over the past two or three centuries, its correctness, both epistemologically and practically, is now under question and the renewed interest in the indigenous paradigm will lead to new struggles, conflicts, and synergies when they interface.[53] The fact that such struggles and synergies now exist means that the potential finally exists for serious dialogue between these worldviews.

That the primal worldview now evokes fascination and interest is not just to do with the yearning for a lost and romanticized past. This essay has tried to argue that the resonances between the primal worldview and the worldview suggested by post-modern science, philosophy, and theology are real enough and that, if it was Einstein, Whitehead, and Hartshorne and not Descartes, Newton, and Kant who paved the way for the scientific revolution, the rush to objectify the universe and cleanse it of all *anima* may not have been so frenetic! But this does not mean that accepting the validity of the primal worldview necessitates the acceptance of a world of spirits, witches, sacrifices and magic. This essay has attempted to demonstrate that there is much more to this worldview than these things. It appeals to us in many different ways, not least of which are its holism, spirituality, and inclusiveness – traits that were expunged from human experience when spirits, magic, and the numinous were expunged from the cosmos. More than this, it gives space for an epistemology that has also been long lost from Western civilization – an epistemology that nurtures faith, encourages story, believes in revelation, and allows for flexibility and adaptation.

CONCLUSION

The discussion around worldviews is not about dispensing with one in favour of another. History has delivered to us worldviews that we have to live with. But post-modernism does present us with the possibility of comparison and, indeed, some possibility of choice. In essence, the choices that are presented to us at the interface of the primal and the post-modern are to do with posture, with attitude, with behaviour. It means asking ourselves again the question: How should we approach the universe?

---

[52] Horton, *Patterns of Thought in Africa and the West*, p. 63.

[53] See Rip, quoted by Mouton in his unpublished submission to the NRF entitled *Beyond Knowledge Dichotomies*, p. 4.

Should we approach it with the self-confidence of those who entered the modern stage, certain of their ability to understand, predict and control reality, or should we enter it as those who recognize their own vulnerability, who are listening to what it has to say, and who are open to the divine? And if this is the posture not only of the truly religious but also of the truly scientific, then it would be advisable to pay attention to what the primal worldview has to teach us.

School of Theology
University of KwaZulu-Natal
South Africa

CHAPTER XXXIII

KNOWLEDGE, WISDOM AND A 'SOPHIALOGICAL' EPISTEMOLOGY

CAFER S. YARAN

Both knowledge and wisdom have many definitions, and it is difficult to give a widely accepted definition of either. Nevertheless, generally speaking, we can say that knowledge is 'an intellectual product of the mental activity of human beings, concerning mainly the true description of the related objects or states of affairs,' and that wisdom is 'an intellectual, emotional, volitional and spiritual characteristic of human beings in relation not only to true knowledge of objects, but also to true knowledge of values, virtuous action, and the self.'

People usually think that they know what knowledge is or what is meant by it; but the concept of wisdom is more controversial. According to the *Encyclopedia of Religion and Ethics:*

> Wisdom may be defined as the direct, practical insight into the meaning and purpose of things that comes to shrewd, penetrating, and observant minds, from their own experience of life, and their daily commerce with the world. It is the fruit not so much of speculation as of native sagacity and wit. Consequently, while philosophy appeals only to the intellectual élites, wisdom appeals to all who are interested in life and have understanding enough to appreciate a word of truth well spoken.[1]

According to Ibn Sina, one of the greatest Muslim philosophers, "Wisdom (*hikma*) is the passage of the soul of man to the perfection possible for him within the two bounds of science and action." It includes, on the one hand, justice and, on the other, the perfecting of the reasoning soul, in as much as it comprises the theoretical and practical intelligibles.[2] It is understood, therefore, that although they are closely related to each other, knowledge is more theoretical and intellectual, whereas wisdom is more practical and experiential.

Knowledge has been a branch of philosophy called epistemology since the seventeenth century. Epistemology deals with such issues as the

---

[1] A. R. Gordon, "Wisdom," *The Encyclopedia of Religion and Ethics*, James Hastings (ed.), Vol. XII, (Edinburgh: T&T. Clark, 1921), p. 742.

[2] A. M. Goichon, *"Hikma," The Encyclopedia of Islam*, New Edition, B. Lewis (ed.), Vol. III, (Leiden: E.J. Brill, London: Luzac & Co., 1979), p. 377.

nature and derivation of knowledge, the scope of knowledge, and the reliability of claims to knowledge. In short, "Epistemology is concerned with the foundations of science"[3] or knowledge in a scientific and systematic manner. But, unfortunately, wisdom has not been as fortunate as knowledge in being the subject of an independent discipline of philosophy where it is researched, discussed and developed by scholars in a systematic and permanent manner. Thus, it is time to develop a science, philosophy, or theory of wisdom, and to give it a proper name, as has been done for epistemology and other philosophical or scientific disciplines: we propose "Sophialogy" (sophia-logy). Sophialogy has perennial insights for the enduring problems of epistemology and ethics. We will tentatively try to determine the basic characteristics of a sophialogical epistemology, and propose that such an approach can solve many problems or crises in contemporary epistemology better than current dichotomic alternatives (such as foundationalism and anti-foundationalism, or objectivism and relativism) can.

THE DIALOGUE OF KNOWLEDGE AND WISDOM IN ANCIENT AND MEDIEVAL TIMES

Knowledge and Wisdom in Abrahamic Religions and Ancient Philosophy

When we look at the relationship between knowledge and wisdom from a historical perspective, we see that they are concepts that are part of a complementary and productive dialogue. There are many verses in the Bible and the Qur'an concerning knowledge and wisdom, and some of them speak of the two together. We have the following, for example: "To the man who pleases him, God gives wisdom, knowledge and happiness ..." (Ecclesiastes 2:26); "Christ, in whom are hidden all the treasures of wisdom and knowledge" (Colossians 2:3); "... We gave him [Joseph] wisdom and knowledge, thus We reward the doers of good ..." (Qur'an 12: 22). These examples show that knowledge and wisdom are neither identical nor unconnected concepts. They emphasize both the relationship between each other and their relationship with virtue, happiness, and eschatological reward.

Wisdom is a common intellectual concept and a cardinal moral virtue in all the major religions and philosophical systems. According to the Qur'an, the goodness of a human being is closely connected with the degree of wisdom he or she has: "He granteth wisdom to whom He pleaseth; And he to whom wisdom is granted receiveth indeed a benefit overflowing; But none will receive admonition but men of understanding" (Qur'an 2:269). In the Bible, "Wisdom excels folly as light excels darkness" (Eccl 2:13). In Christian sacred texts, people who lack wisdom are advised to ask it of

---

[3] W.V. Quine, "Epistemology Naturalized," in *Ontological Relativity and Other Essays* (New York: Columbia University Press, 1969), p. 69.

God: "If any of you is lacking in wisdom, ask God, who gives to all generously and ungrudgingly, and it will be given you" (Jas 1:5). There is no need to say that in Eastern religions, too, wisdom is regarded as extremely important. It is even difficult to distinguish Indian wisdom from philosophy, and philosophy in turn from religion; each shares in the character of the others.[4] It is also known that various moral qualities singled out by the classical writers are reduced by Confucius to the five cardinal virtues, and one of them is wisdom.[5] Therefore, wisdom is an intellectual value and an experiential virtue for all the major religions of the world.

There is a close relationship between knowledge and wisdom in Greek classical philosophy, too. As is well known, the etymological meaning of the word of 'philosophy' is 'love of wisdom.' Socrates conceives the love of wisdom as the pursuit of self-knowledge. As Donald Verene writes, Socrates

> locates the intersection of things human and divine in the task of self-knowledge. His dedication to self-knowledge as the subject of philosophy is achieved through an act of memory. In declaring that life is to be examined, Socrates remembers what is already stated on the Temple of Apollo at Delphi, attributed to the Seven Sages: *gnothi seauton*, 'know thyself.' The second famous inscription – *meden agan*, 'nothing too much' – indicates that self-knowledge requires proportion or harmony, more specifically *sophrosyne*."[6]

Plato built up his majestic system of ethical idealism, with its four cardinal virtues – wisdom, courage, temperance, and justice. Of these, wisdom is the highest phase of virtue, for it inspires and regulates the whole inner life. A distinction vaguely apprehended by Plato was sharply drawn by Aristotle. Practical wisdom, prudence, or good sense deals with matters of ordinary human interest; speculative wisdom, which is wisdom *par excellence*, deals with the first principles of things. The former enables a man to apply the right rule to every line of activity, whether professional, civic, or strictly moral; the latter leads, by a union of science and intuitive apprehension, to the knowledge of those things which are most precious in their nature.[7] The productive dialogue of knowledge and wisdom continued

---

[4] Kurt Rudolph, "Wisdom," *The Encyclopedia of Religion*, Mircea Eliade (ed.), Vol. 15 (New York: Macmillan Publishing Company; London: Collier Macmillan Publishers, 1987), p. 399.

[5] Gordon, "Wisdom," p. 744.

[6] Donald Phillip Verene, *Philosophy and the Return to Self-Knowledge* (New Haven and London: Yale University Press, 1997), p. 204.

[7] Gordon, "Wisdom," p. 745.

with the later Hellenistic philosophers, Neo-Platonists, and early Christian thinkers.

Knowledge and Wisdom in Medieval Times, Particularly in Islam

According to a widespread conviction among the Muslims, "there have been many expositions on the nature of knowledge in Islam more than in any other religion, culture and civilization, and this is due to the preeminent position and paramount role accorded to *al-'ilm* by God in the Holy Qur'an."[8] Islam is

> essentially and fundamentally a religion of moderation; its epistemology is neither exclusively rationalist, nor empiricist, nor intuitionist. It employs all the sources of knowledge – reason, sense-experience and intuition – to arrive at the knowledge of truth, and integrates the relative truth supplied by them with the absolute truth revealed by God to the Prophet Muhammad (SAWS).[9]

In Islam and the civilization which it created, "there was a veritable celebration of knowledge all of whose forms were, in one way or another, related to the sacred extending in a hierarchy from an 'empirical' and rational mode of knowing to that highest form of knowledge (*al-ma'rifah* or *'irfan*) ..."[10] In other words, Islamic epistemology "is an integrated whole of rationalism, empiricism and intuitionism, under the overriding authority of the knowledge revealed by God to the Prophet (SAWS)."[11] In Islam, reason and experience are "valid channels by which knowledge is attained – knowledge, that is, at the rational and empirical level of normal experience. We maintain that there is another level; but even at this other, spiritual level, reason and experience are still valid, only they are of a transcendental order."[12] In order to attain a true and comprehensive knowledge "we must integrate the findings of reason, sense-perception, intuition and revelation into a well-knit whole. Light from only one direction does not and cannot illumine the whole of reality in all its manifestations, temporal and spiritual."[13] Indeed, the Qur'an regards both *anfus* (subjective, experiential,

---

[8] Syed Muhammed Naquib al-Attas, *Islam, Secularism and the Philosophy of the Future* (London, New York: Mansell Publishing Limited, 1985), p. 136.

[9] B. H. Siddiqui, "Knowledge: An Islamic Perspective," (http://www.crvp.org/book/Series02/IIA-3/chapter_x.htm) (09.07.2003), p. 6.

[10] Seyyed Hossein Nasr, *Knowledge and Sacred* (New York: Crossroad, 1981), p. 12.

[11] Siddiqui, "Knowledge: An Islamic Perspective," p. 5.

[12] al-Attas, *Islam, Secularism and the Philosophy of the Future*, p. 155.

[13] Siddiqui, "Knowledge: An Islamic Perspective," p. 5.

transcendental knowledge) and *afaq* (objective, empirical, scientific knowledge) as the veritable sources of human knowledge.[14]

In addition, certainty or truth in Islamic epistemology is not a matter of either absoluteness, as in the case of extreme foundationalism, or almost-nothingness, as in the case of extreme relativism and nihilism; rather, there are at least three levels of certainty.

> The knowledge obtained through the discursive movement of thought is certain only epistemically (*ilm al-yaqin*) [102:5]. It does satisfy the mind of its certitude, but possesses theoretical certainty at best, as opposed to what the Qur'an calls the certainty of sight (*ain al-yaqin*) [102:7] characteristic of personal observation. The highest degree of certitude belongs to the knowledge revealed by God to the prophets which the Qur'an calls truth of assured certainty (*haqq al-yaqin*) [69:51].[15]

However highly knowledge is regarded in the Qur'an, it

> seldom speaks of *kitab* (knowledge) alone, but pairs this with *hikmah* (wisdom) [Qur'an, 1:129; 3:164]. The book gives us knowledge of the true objective of the creation of man. Wisdom makes us realise the rationale, value and importance of this knowledge for ordering our life, individual and collective, in accordance with it. This consists in reflecting on what we already know, and implies extention in depth, in internalising knowledge, rather than in extending the frontiers of knowledge.[16]

In the Islamic perspective,

> every wisdom is at the same time knowledge, but every knowledge is not wisdom. This gives knowledge an edge over wisdom, but it is wisdom, not mere knowledge, which has sole value in the eyes of God. 'Whosoever is given wisdom, is given abundant good,' [2:269] says the Qur'an.[17]

For most of the medieval Muslim philosophers, too, wisdom has been related both to knowledge and philosophy as well as to religion and morality. For example,

---

[14] Qur'an, 41: 53; 51:21.

[15] Siddiqui, "Knowledge: An Islamic Perspective," p. 6.

[16] Siddiqui, "Knowledge: An Islamic Perspective," p. 4.

[17] Siddiqui, "Knowledge: An Islamic Perspective," p. 4.

Ibn Rushd tried to substantiate a cultural vision of wisdom so that it could be acceptable both in the tradition of Islam (religion), and in the tradition of logic (philosophy), thereby removing a possible contradiction between faith and proof (reason). He aspired to consider the rational scope of Islamic culture as a necessary condition of ideal moderation. He regarded this as a method of overcoming sectarianism and dogmatism, lies and defects, and establishing a rich unity of truth and virtuousness. ... [For him] this was an historical-cultural form of mastering the various attempts and possibilities of the synthesis of reason and wisdom, development of rational wisdom and wise rationalism, which, in turn, were nothing else but the wholeness of the moral spirit or monism.[18]

BREAKING OFF THE DIALOGUE OF KNOWLEDGE AND WISDOM IN MODERN TIMES

The dialogue of knowledge and wisdom has broken off in modern times in both the Western world and the Islamic world. But their preferences have been different; one has preferred knowledge and neglected wisdom, and the other has done the reverse.

Breaking off in the Western World for the Sake of Knowledge: Rationalism, Empiricism, and Positivism

In the words of Donald Verene, as modern Western philosophy has developed since Descartes,

the connection of philosophy to mortality and its accompanying concern with self-knowledge have been set aside. Philosophy as the love of wisdom that considers the true to be the whole has been replaced by the pursuit of method and the truth of the part. The Renaissance humanists' attempt to discover the connections among wisdom, eloquence, and prudence has been given up. In regard to the Socratic tradition of self-knowledge and the humanist tradition of seeking to form thought and human

---

[18] Maitham al-Janabi, "Islamic Culture as Search of a Golden Mean," in *Values in Islamic Culture and the Experience of History*, Nur Kirabaev and Yuriy Pochta (eds.) (Washington, DC: The Council for Research in Values and Philosophy, 2002), pp. 252-253.

action as 'wisdom speaking,' philosophy has lost its way.[19]

The spirit of modern philosophy is extremely rationalistic in the sense that it makes human reason the highest authority in the pursuit of knowledge, and naturalistic in that it seeks to explain the inner and outer nature without supernatural presuppositions. Siddiqui notes:

> Religious humanism is replaced by a humanism of the scientific sort which puts human interests above everything else, making man the source of all knowledge – the knowledge of what is materially useful, as well as of what is morally good.[20]

For the ancients, the philosophical search was identified with the pursuit of the Good, the True and the Beautiful. In contrast, according to Brenda Almond, modern philosophy, especially in

> the twentieth century[,] has tended to prefer more modest and more prosaic goals: … It has been more at home in the area of knowledge than in the area of ethics and, as a result, its command of technology has found more and more deeply corrupt applications in both war and peace. Perhaps worse, where it does give lip-service to ethics, it is to an ethics divorced from moral sensitivity.... [In this case] it has to be admitted that contemporary Western philosophy has very little to offer in the way of reflection or insight in relation to either practical or philosophic wisdom. Instead it tends to be constrained in a narrow professionalism that detaches itself deliberately from the world.[21]

At the end, knowledge without wisdom has made modern men spiritually homeless, alien to themselves, and has challenged humanity and the earth with many global, cultural, ethical and environmental crises. Rationalist and positivist epistemologies – accompanied by an atheist and naturalist ontology and by relativist and nihilist ethics – exhibit more knowledge, but probably less wisdom, more power but less virtue, and more pleasure but less peace to the modern world.

---

[19] Verene, *Philosophy and the Return to Self-Knowledge*, p. ix.

[20] Siddiqui, "Knowledge: An Islamic Perspective," p. 7.

[21] Brenda Almond, "What's the Meaning of All This?," (http://www.philosophynow.demon.co.uk/almond.htm), (24.01.2003), pp. 1-3.

Breaking off in the Islamic World for the Sake of Wisdom: Mysticism, Fideism, and Dogmatism

Islam played the dominant role in the shaping of world history from the time of its advent onwards for at least a thousand years. The Western counter-attack came gradually, beginning with the scientific revolution in Western Europe in the thirteenth century, and then with the gradual growth in subsequent centuries in military and economic power. The geographical expansion of Western Europe eastward and westward, and the establishment of its trading posts in the Indian Ocean in the sixteenth century, caused grave economic repercussions in the Muslim world. Together with these external factors, certain internal elements "had made possible the Western colonization of a significant part of that world from the 17th century onwards till our own times."[22]

In seventeenth century, the contemporary philosopher of Descartes (1596-1650) in Islamic World was Mulla Sadra (1571-1640) and he chose, in contrast to Descartes, to address wisdom rather than knowledge. One of his major philosophical works is "Transcendental Wisdom," better known as "The Four Journeys" (*al-Asfar al-Arba'ah*). He distinguishes between two categories of ancient Greek philosophers. The first category starts with Thales and ends with Socrates and Plato, the second starts with Pythagoras, who received wisdom from Solomon and from Egyptian priests. Among the "pillars of wisdom," he mentions Empedocles, Pythagoras, Socrates, Plato and Aristotle. All the above-mentioned Greek "pillars of wisdom" are said by al-Shirazi to have received the "light of wisdom" from the "beacon of Prophethood."[23] After the time of Mulla Sadra, dialogue and the balance of knowledge and wisdom did not continue in the Islamic world as well as it had. The spirit of the last few centuries in the Islamic world has been a mainly mystical rather than rationalistic or balanced one, and many people have seen practical wisdom as enough for living a good life. As Iqbal said:

> The more genuine schools of Sufism have, no doubt, done good work in shaping and directing the evolution of religious experience in Islam; but their latter-day representatives, owing to their ignorance of the modern mind, have become absolutely incapable of receiving any fresh inspiration from modern thought and experience.[24]

In the end, wisdom without knowledge has made the Muslim man and woman materially homeless, scientifically and technologically

---

[22] al-Attas, *Islam, Secularism and the Philosophy of the Future*, p. 98.
[23] Majid Fakhry, *A Short Introduction to Islamic Philosophy, Theology and Mysticism* (Oxford: Oneworld, 1998), pp. 115-16.
[24] Mohammad Iqbal, *The Reconstruction of Religious Thought in Islam* (Lahore: Muhammad Ashraf, 1986), p. v.

backwards, and culturally fragile. Mystical and practical wisdom followed by an idealist ontology and universalist ethics brought to the Muslim world more wisdom but less knowledge, more virtue but less power, and more internal peace but less international prestige.

CONTEMPORARY NEED FOR A "SOPHIALOGICAL" EPISTEMOLOGY

Contemporary Epistemological Crises and Hopeless Dichotomic Proposals

Neither the Western nor the Islamic world, which engaged in the dialogue of the accompanying and complementary concepts of knowledge and wisdom for three centuries, could have escaped from the various crises, arriving at a more ideal situation. Muslim intellectuals (i.e., the modernists and some others) became aware of the crisis in their world about 100 to 150 years ago; Western intellectuals (the postmodernists and some others) became aware of their crisis about 50 to 100 years ago. But, in our view, these searches for a solution do not provide much hope; it is too simple for each to reject the past approach completely and to adopt the other extreme of the dichotomy. For most of the postmodernists (and their Western or Muslim followers), such concepts as foundation, knowledge, reason, rationality, reality, truth, objectivity, science, universal values and virtues, and so on, are taboo and reactionary concepts; everything is relative and "anything goes."

> Many prominent philosophers of this century may better be described as anti-philosophers because of their tendency to see philosophical problems merely as linguistic muddles and because of their conviction that the human mind is incapable of actually knowing anything; nihilists like Richard Rorty even says that 'the best hope for philosophy is not to practice Philosophy' and that we must 'drop the idea ... that Truth is 'out there' waiting for human beings to arrive at it.'[25]

There are many contemporary Muslim intellectuals repeating these ideas in the Islamic world. As just one example, one can mention the last sentence of a paper by a Turkish philosopher, delivered at a symposium on Knowledge and Value in the year 2002: "The source of values is 'natural'

---

[25] Roy Abraham Varghese, "Introduction: A Return to Universal Experience," in *Great Thinkers on Great Questions*, ed. R. A. Varghese (Oxford: Oneworld, 1998), p. 1.

languages in the last analysis; and Heidegger and Derrida are right: there is nothing outside language."[26]

For most modernists, too, such concepts as wisdom, heart, spirituality, goodness, subjectivity, belief, faith, traditional values and virtues are almost taboo and reactionary concepts; everything is dependent on science and reason, and nothing is allowed to go except with their permission. As just one example of this sort of idea defended in the symposium mentioned above, one can mention another Turkish philosopher's last words quoted from a poem written in 1911:

The empty belief will sink to the bottom of the earth, will become extinct,
By the ability of reason, the great sorcerer, I believed.
One day technology will make that black soil golden
Everything will become through the power of science ... I believed.[27]

These two alternative proposals seem to be the simple projection of what Brenda Almond describes in general:

---

[26] Hüsamettin Arslan, "Bilgi, Naturalism ve Değerler," *Bilgi ve Değer: Muğla Üniversitesi Felsefe Bölümü Sempozyum Bildirileri*, ed. Şahabettin Yalçın (Ankara: Vadi Yayınları, 2002), p. 100. See, for the evaluation and reasonable criticisms of this sort of philosophical ideas, Tran Van Doan, *Reason, Rationality and Reasonableness* (Washington, DC: The Council for Research in Values and Philosophy, 2001), chapters II and III. According to Doan, for example, "The fact is that language is limited, and sometimes, cannot express all human acts, especially human aesthetic life. It is not true that the world is limited by language, but rather, the reverse, i.e. language is limited by the world." (p. 110). In addition, Heidegger's "insistence on eternal return of reason, in the sense of Nietzsche's, analogous to the return to the original, authentic Being, seems to be sheer rhetoric. It lacks concreteness and thus it is of little help in the context of a real, functional society." (p. 8).

[27] Bedia Akarsu, "Değişen Dünyada Bilim ve Değerler," *Bilgi ve Değer: Muğla Üniversitesi Felsefe Bölümü Sempozyum Bildirileri*, ed. Şahabettin Yalçın (Ankara: Vadi Yayınları, 2002), p. 29. See, for the summary of the evaluations and criticisms of this sort of ideas in contemporary philosophy, Doan, *Reason, Rationality and Reasonableness*, chapter I. See also, Richard J. Berstein, *Beyond Objectivism and Relativism: Science, Hermeneutics, and Praxis* (Philadelphia: University of Pennsylvania Press, 1983), Part One and Part Two; Derek Stanesby, *Science, Reason and Religion* (London: Croom Helm, 1985), Part I; Nicholas Maxwell, *From Knowledge to Wisdom: A Revolution in the Aims and Methods of Science* (Oxford: Basil Blackwell, 1984), Ch. 2 and ch. 3; Jonathan Dancy, *Introduction to Contemporary Epistemology* (Oxford: Basil Blackwell, 1985), Part II.

Professional and academic philosophy has become identified at the end of the twentieth century with a choice in the area of knowledge, between irrationalism and empty logic-chopping, and in the area of morality, between moral nihilism and a shallow utilitarianism.[28]

Indeed, in our view, she has rightly says that,

Against these prevailing trends, it is only possible to repeat that the true mission of philosophy is, after all, the pursuit of wisdom – an understanding which is in keeping with the initial and etymological meaning of the word.[29]

Thus there seems to be an urgent need for a new or renewed type of epistemology.

Towards a "Sophialogical" Epistemology

A better way of addressing the epistemological crises seems to be in the recovery of the dialogue of knowledge and wisdom. First of all, wisdom should be an independent branch of philosophy ("Sophialogy"), and so should be studied in detail everywhere permanently and systematically. As part of this proposal, one can speak of "sophialogical epistemology" (particularly in the context of the Western philosophy) and "epistemological sophialogy" (particularly in the context of the Islamic philosophy and mysticism). We will deal just with the former here briefly.

"Sophialogical epistemology" may be described in general as an epistemological approach that looks at the philosophical problems concerning knowledge from the perspective of wisdom. Although there may be different versions of wisdom in different cultures and civilisations, there is a global and perennial essence common throughout the well-known traditions of philosophy and religion all over the world. We will try to determine tentatively some of the basic characteristics of this approach starting from philosophical wisdom in the ancient philosophy, particularly from the etymological analysis of the word "philosophy," and the two

---

[28] Almond, "What's the Meaning of All This?," p. 2. In the area of religion, too, there seems to be a similar dichotomy. Science, particularly when championed by the logical positivism of philosophers such as A. J. Ayer, has often appeared to be the enemy of religion. It is, therefore, perhaps hardly surprising that some should willingly embrace postmodernism as a way of rescuing religion from the overbearing claims of science. "This is, however, a terrible mistake." Roger Trigg, *Rationality and Religion: Does Faith Need Reason?* (Oxford: Blackwell, 1998), p. 2.

[29] Almond, "What's the Meaning of All This?," p. 2.

statements on the Temple at Delphi, which are well known among the philosophers since the time of Socrates.

"Philio-sophia" is the Knowledge between Foundationalism and Anti-Foundationalism, Objectivism and Relativism. Against the prevailing contemporary trends such as absolutist, objectivist foundationalism and irrationalist, subjectivist anti-foundationalism, "the true mission of philosophy is, after all, the pursuit of wisdom – an understanding which is in keeping with the initial and etymological meaning of the word."[30] The Pythagorian story about the choice of the word as philio-sophia and not as only sophia is very illuminating for the solution of the foundationalism debate (*bu kısım için sosyal bilimler felsefesine bak, kavramları kontrol et*). Human beings are neither God, who has absolutely pure knowledge and who can perform absolutely good actions, nor animals which are completely dependent on their instinct and environment. The conscious and deliberate choice of the word 'philosophy' shows rightly that philosophical inquiry of a wise human being should be neither after objective certainty and absolute truth, as in the case of major trends of modern philosophy, nor aimed at submission to and condemnation of the subjective uncertainty and historico-cultural limitations, as in the case of some trends of postmodern philosophy. The word 'philosophy' is very wisely chosen, and the story behind it is illuminating for contemporary epistemological debates and dichotomic crises.

Despite the fact that nihilism afflicts much of modern philosophy, it must be said that not all present-day philosophers, scientists and theologians "have turned their backs on reality, rationality and truth."[31] This does not mean that they turned back to the eighteenth and nineteenth centuries' exclusivist rationalism and positivism, either. There is always a third way – a wiser or sophialogical way – to accept.

Colin Gunton, for example, has drawn our attention to the contemporary epistemological dilemma mentioned above. On the one hand is modernity's longing for foundationalism, the titanic quest for universal and certain knowledge – in Gunton's terminology, the search for the One. On the other hand is post-modernity's form of the assertion of anti-foundationalism, the dissolution of knowledge into private and particular points of view expressed through fideistic assertion or the playing of an idiosyncratic language game – in Gunton's terminology, the role of the Many. Today, the former does not convince, and the latter does not satisfy. Gunton seeks a middle way. "The quest must therefore be for non-foundationalist foundations: to find the moments of truth in both of the

---

[30] Almond, "What's the Meaning of All This?," p. 2.
[31] Varghese, "Introduction: A Return to Universal Experience," p. 2.

contentions, namely that particularity and universality each have their place in a reasoned approach to the truth."[32]

Alvin Plantinga seems to have similar ideas. In his view, too, there are three approaches in this matter. First, is that of the classical foundationalists. For them, life without sure and secure foundations is frightening and unnerving; hence Descartes's fateful effort to find a sure and solid footing for the beliefs with which he found himself. Hence also Kant's similar effort to find an irrefragable foundation for science. Second, is that of the postmodernists. They

> nearly all reject classical foundationalism; in this they concur with most Christian thinkers and most contemporary philosophers. Momentously enough, however, many postmodernists apparently believe that the demise of classical foundationalism implies something far more startling: that there is no such thing as truth at all. No way things really are.[33]

In this case, "the thing to do," for postmodernists,

> is dispense with the search for truth and retreat into projects of some other sort: self-creation and self-redefinition as with Nietzsche and Heidegger, or Rortian irony, or perhaps playful mockery, as with Derrida. So taken [according to Plantinga], postmodernism is a kind of failure of epistemic nerve.[34]

There is a third approach between them. Such thinkers as Pascal, Kierkegaard, and Kuyper

> recognize that there aren't any certain foundations of the sort Descartes sought – or, if there are, they are exceedingly slim, and there is no way to transfer their certainty to our important non-foundational beliefs about material objects, the past, other persons, and the like. This is a stance that requires a certain epistemic hardihood: there is, indeed, such a thing as truth; the stakes are, indeed, very high (it matters greatly whether you believe

---

[32]   Colin Gunton. *The One, the Three and the Many* (Cambridge: Cambridge University Press, 1993), esp. Chap. 5; quoted from John Polkinghorne, *Belief in God in an Age of Science* (New Haven and London: Yale University Press, 1998), p. 123.

[33] Alvin Plantinga, *Warranted Christian Belief* (New York, Oxford: Oxford University Press, 2000), p. 436.

[34] Plantinga, *Warranted Christian Belief*, p. 437.

the truth); but there is no way to be sure that you have the truth. ... This is life under uncertainty, life under epistemic risk and fallibility. ... That is simply the human condition...[35]

Scientist theologian John Polkinghorne is another example. According to him,

the success of the apparently objectified account of science should not tempt us to commit the Enlightenment error of rejecting the subjective as a source of real knowledge. Our thoughts far exceed an impersonal evaluation of logical entailment. Kurt Gödel has taught us that even pure mathematics involves an act of intellectual daring, as we commit ourselves to a belief in the unprovable consistency of the axiomatic system under consideration. The Cartesian programme of seeking to found knowledge on the basis of clear and certain ideas has proved to be an unattainable ideal.[36]

But this conviction does not cause him to pass into the extreme edge of the opposite pole. He says rightly and wisely:

I do not think that this realisation of the necessary precariousness involved in human theorising, condemns us to a post-modernist belief in the personal or communal construction of a variety of views from which we are free to make our a la carte selection. There is a middle way between certainty and relativism, which corresponds to the critical adherence to rationally motivated belief, held with conviction but open to the possibility of correction.[37]

"Know Thyself": Knowledge Oriented to Self-Development, Ethics and Action. As we saw above, Socrates conceives the love of wisdom as the pursuit of self knowledge. He locates the intersection of things, human and divine, in the task of self-knowledge. His dedication to self-knowledge as the subject of philosophy is achieved through an act of memory. Recall the quotation from Verene, cited above:

---

[35] Plantinga, *Warranted Christian Belief*, pp. 436-37. Cf. Richard Swinburne, "Relativism," in *Great thinkers on Great Questions*, R. A. Varghese (ed.) (Oxford: Oneworld, 1998), pp. 23-25.

[36] John Polkinghorne, *Belief in God in an Age of Science* (New Haven and London: Yale University Press, 1998), p. 15.

[37] Polkinghorne, *Belief in God in an Age of Science*, p. 15; (italics are mine).

In declaring that life is to be examined, Socrates remembers what is already stated on the Temple of Apollo at Delphi, attributed to the Seven Sages: *gnothi seauton*, 'know thyself.' The second famous inscription – *meden agan*, 'nothing too much' – indicates that self-knowledge requires proportion or harmony, more specifically *sophrosyne*"[38]

In terms of this concept of philosophy and epistemology, the central concern of almost all kinds of knowledge should be ultimately self-knowledge, self-development and self-realization.

Brenda Almond writes:

But, of course, we do still continue on the whole to teach our students to be critical rather than trying to encourage them to be wise; to perform moral gymnastics rather than to take seriously the search for a meaningful life. All the same, being wise may well mean looking to the past and being willing to learn from it, rather than parroting dubious refutations of philosophers' arguments. For in the end, it is only by learning to transcend the narrow limitations of one's own epoch – both to look backwards and to think forwards – that there can be any hope of gaining some sense of what we like to call 'the meaning of life.'[39]

For philosophy to achieve its rightful place as a guide to life, "it must reexamine the relation between word and action that is present in the classical and humanist conception of prudence."[40] There is a prudential sense of wisdom (*phronesis*) that is crucial to moral goodness and that connects knowledge to action. Indeed,

the opposition between theory and practice – the opposition between knowledge and action – has been denied and overcome by Socrates, raising it in a synthesis to a new level. Socrates seems to reject the opposition; for him all knowing is doing.[41]

And as such,

knowledge is directed toward an ordered reality – ours and

---

[38] Verene, *Philosophy and the Return to Self-Knowledge*, p. 204.

[39] Almond, "What's the Meaning of All This?," pp. 3-4.

[40] Verene, *Philosophy and the Return to Self-Knowledge*, p. xiii.

[41] Verene, *Philosophy and the Return to Self-Knowledge*, p. 23.

that of the entire globe – the central questions are not merely epistemological, but ontological and ethical, namely, what is the global whole in which we exist, and how can we act in relation to other peoples and cultures in ways that promote a collaborative realization of global community in our times?[42]

Knowledge of the self or subjective knowledge should also be considered as a source and criterion of knowledge; and the development of the self (and of the human condition in general) should be considered among the main aims of getting knowledge. There should be a close relationship between all kinds of knowledge and human discourse and action, and knowledge should have the quality of being a guide to life and of finding a meaning in life.

"Nothing Too Much": Knowledge Originated from Various Complementary Sources. "Sophialogical" epistemology requires not being extremist and exclusivist with respect to one source or one criterion of knowledge; by contrast, it requires a pluralistic, holistic, and complementary or integrative perspective regarding all the epistemological problems. It usually requires a middle way between the opposing poles or extreme edges. This point of view is valid and useful in solving several problems in contemporary epistemology, such as the problems of empiricism, rationalism and mysticism, objectivity and subjectivity, foundationalism and anti-foundationalism, universalism and particularism, certainty and relativism, and so on.

Unfortunately, philosophy as the love of wisdom that considers the true to be the whole has been replaced in the modern period by the pursuit of method and the truth of the part.[43] In the words of S. H. Nasr:

> The unifying vision which related knowledge to love and faith, religion to science, and theology to all the departments of intellectual concern is finally completely lost, leaving a world of compartmentalization where there is no wholeness because holiness has ceased to be of central concern, or is at best reduced to sentimentality.[44]

But, as he pointed out,

---

[42] George F. McLean, "Globalization as Diversity in Unity," in *Philosophical Challenges and Opportunities of Globalization*, Volume II, ed. O. Blanchette, T. Imamichi, G. F. McLean (Washington, D.C., The Council for Research in Values and Philosophy, 2001), p. 456.

[43] Verene, Philosophy and the Return to Self-Knowledge, p. ix.

[44] Nasr, *Knowledge and the Sacred*, p. 48.

in such a world those with spiritual and intellectual perspicacity sought, outside of the confines of this ambience, to rediscover their traditional roots and the total functioning of the intelligence which would once again bestow upon knowledge its sacramental function and enable men to reintegrate their lives upon the basis of this unifying principle, which is inseparable from both love and faith.[45]

that

John Polkinghorne rightly defends the similar ideas when he says

as a passionate believer in the ultimate integrity and unity of all knowledge, I wish to extend my realist stance beyond science to encompass, among many other fields of inquiry theological reflection on our encounter with the divine.[46]

Consequently, a sophialogical epistemology does not see sense experience, reason and intuition, or empiricism, rationalism and mysticism, or science, philosophy and religion, as mutually exclusive and conflicting sources of knowledge; by contrast, it regards them as mutually supportive and complementary sources.

Several results may follow: first, the recovery of the old productive and constructive dialogue of knowledge and wisdom; second, making the pursuit of wisdom an independent branch of philosophy known as "sophialogy"; finally, adopting the approach of a "sophialogical" epistemology that can contribute to the solution of our personal, social and global problems, no matter we live – in the West or East, North or South. There is no need to waste more time on the alternative and exclusivist extremes of modern and postmodern epistemological dichotomies such as objectivism, relativism, and the rest. Knowledge left uncomplemented by wise action is insufficient to prevent or lessen the sufferings of human beings and to promote their self-knowledge and self-realisation. In the same way, mere "practical" wisdom or simple free action not originating from or supported by firm knowledge is not secure and sound enough for the same purposes. We should try to develop a "sophialogical" epistemology which has a global and perennial foundation in all the great cultures and civilisations of the world. Only in such a case will the two beautiful hopes come together: tomorrow there will be fewer things we don't know, and tomorrow there will be less evil we cannot prevent.

---

[45] Nasr, *Knowledge and the Sacred*, p. 48.
[46] Polkinghorne, *Belief in God in an Age of Science*, p. 110.

448   Cafer S. Yaran

University of Istanbul
Faculty of Theology
Istanbul, Turkey

CHAPTER XXXIV

WITOLD GOMBROWICZ AND HAROLD GARFINKEL: OR, ABOUT AN ATTEMPT TO EXPOSE SOME MYSTIFICATION

DARIUSZ DOBRZANSKI

INTRODUCTION

Witold Gombrowicz was the kind of writer who, as a matter of principle, wrote about Witold Gombrowicz. All his writings have an autobiographical character. Their philosophical goal was to trigger the process of objectivisation of individual reality. The perusal of the *Diaries*, which constitute my principal source material, clearly reveals such an intention. Gombrowicz's writing about Gombrowicz was not simply a spontaneous artistic provocation, a marketing ploy, or an indication of pathological megalomania, but in fact a calculated attempt – an experiment – aimed at reaching for the hidden reality constituted by the self-consciousness of a writer.

The fundamental issue around which the problems taken up in the present paper revolve boils down to the question of whether the recognition of the ambiguous status of the methods of inquiry employed by a practitioner of sociology, on the one hand, and those of a writer, on the other, leads to the conclusion that the principles governing the process of constructing the self-consciousness are similar in the cases of a practitioner of sociology and of a writer. I will leave this question unanswered. I will focus mainly on the reconstruction of the problem of the method, which has induced me to pose such a question.

WITOLD GOMBROWICZ, OR "I MAY KNOW SOMETHING BUT NOT TOO MUCH"

In his *Diaries*, Gombrowicz admits on many occasions that the realisation of what he has written descended on him only *post hoc*, through acts of rationalisation, when he began to interpret the result of his actions – the text – and its meanings. A similar conclusion, although drawn in another field (that of a social researcher) was formulated by Harold Garfinkel. Garfinkel pointed out that the research practice of sociologists is accompanied by an interpretative process of constructing the self-consciousness of research. It includes the component of the so-called *post hoc rationality*, which is essential, yet concealed by researchers.

In his *Diaries*, in addition to using first-person narration, Gombrowicz introduces the "second voice" – that of a commentator, biographer and critic of his own writings. This procedure allowed Gombrowicz to talk about himself "through someone else," from a certain distance. He wrote:

> Great style has its own master of ceremonies, as well as exponent and commentator. And thus the division into voices was substantiated by the very structure of the style and based firmly on reality. But besides that – what enrichment to be able to talk about myself in the first and third person at the same time! After all, the one who speaks about himself,"I", must of necessity leave so much unsaid, so much falsified; the one who refers to himself as " he" and tries to describe himself from the outside also uses only part of the truth. Thus the *alternating* between "I" and "Gombrowicz" could lead (gradually, as this practice was perfected and made more profound) to interesting results.[1]

This "second voice," often ironic (in fact auto-ironic) with respect to the lyrical "I" of the diaries, operates in conformity with the principle it has developed – that the "I" should devise for itself a role of its own and that the writer who cannot write about himself is incomplete. As an attempt to reach for the reality constituted by the self-consciousness of the writer, the *Diaries* are simultaneously an exposition of the method of acquisition of such self-consciousness. The realisation of the necessity of applying a *method* in creating a work of literature, which is inherent in the *Diaries*, may be surprising. After all, it was Gombrowicz himself who professed that writing is a "matter of physiology, not of consciousness" and that the meanings of the text are born independently of the intentions of the writer. It is science, not art, which is the field where a method is consciously applied.

In contrast to the task of researchers or philosophers, whom Gombrowicz often derides, the duty of artists is the defence of their own creativity against unambiguity. Artists are in their own element when immersed in ambiguity or immaturity of the form, whereas the destiny of science is syllogism. Gombrowicz holds that the contemporary concept of science is based on the pursuit of the principle of imitation which is proper for all actions based on collective or herd instinct. On the other hand, radical idealism is the principle of art. Science is the language of rationalised *inter-human* wisdom, which goes against the very nature of an individual mind. Gombrowicz holds that the rule "the more wisely, the

---

[1] Witold Gombrowicz, *Dziennik (1957 – 1961)* (Instytut Literacki Paryż, 1982), p. 135.

more stupidly" dominates contemporary science, and the method of the contemporary humanities abides in his opinion by this rule:

> Finally, I will mention the obvious stupidity of the methods, which are handicapped by the same internal contradiction I have referred to. The more strict the methods of the Western humanistic *episteme* are, the more nebulous is their subject: the more scientific, the less their subject lends itself to scientific formulation. The departments of humanities at universities abound in heavy, academic nonsense. *Delenda est Cartago*! Let us get rid of it![2]

Witold Gombrowicz was a philosopher. He did not formulate a theory or a philosophical system, yet he systematically engaged in reflections on the fundamentals of social reality and the nature of the social order. This fact, in my opinion, gives grounds for classifying Gombrowicz's reflections – on form, the inter-human church, the nature of the "I – the Other" relation, and the social sources of knowledge – as the issues liable to be taken up by social philosophy.

To be sure, Gombrowicz's judgements on science, quoted above, cannot be interpreted as the celebration of the idea of scientificity. And yet, in my opinion, notwithstanding the criticism that the writer of the *Diaries* expresses about the idea of method, he himself employed a method similar to the one which is present in the research practice of sociology. Ethnomethodology calls this method *documentary interpretation*, and the *post hoc rationalisation* of the meanings of the investigated subject is characteristic of it. According to ethnomethodologists, such rationalisation has become the actual practice in research, accompanying also the process of constructing the self-consciousness of the researcher.[3] I will present here

---

[2] Gombrowicz, *Dziennik (1961 – 1966)* (Instytut Literacki Paryż, 1982), p. 208.

[3] Ethnomethodology is the study of the "ethno–methods", that is, the folk or lay methods, which people (including researchers) use to make sense of what others do, and, particularly, what they say. All of us apply methods of making sense in our interaction with others, which we normally employ without having to give any conscious attention to them. We can make sense only of what is said in conversation by means of knowledge of the social context that does not appear in the words themselves. Derived from phenomenological sociology (mainly from Alfred Schutz, and introduced by Harold Garfinkel in his book *Studies in Ethnomethodology* of 1967), ethnomethodology aims to guide research into social practices as experienced by participants. A major objective of the method is to interpret the rules that underlie everyday activity and thus constitute part of the normative basis of a given social order. Research from this perspective generally focuses on mundane social activities—e.g., jurors deliberating on defendants' culpability, or coroners judging causes of death.

the basic concepts of ethnomethodological reflection about the method of social sciences which are involved in the concept of the so-called documentary interpretation and the post hoc rationalisation connected with it.

HAROLD GARFINKEL, OR "EVERYONE IS A SOCIOLOGIST"

Everyday life as *the subject-matter of reality* is a meaningful reality, being constructed as it is by our knowledge, basic expectations and interpretative procedures. The "irremediable" occasionality of the meaning of phenomena of everyday (social) life is the fundamental assumption of ethnomethodology about the nature of such phenomena. Ethnomethodologists expanded the scope of the occasionality of meanings: the whole stock of common-sense and scientific knowledge are now included with terms, statements and actions.

Following Karl Mannheim in adopting the theoretical assumptions of the method of documentary interpretation, Harold Garfinkel focused in his research on the question of *exposing* the use of this method in the empirical research of sociology. Documentary interpretation is a procedure of formulating the meaning of the phenomenon or the fact being investigated as a document, as a manifestation of "the pattern which is behind it". The pattern which is present – although imperceptible – in everyday conversations is derived by the participants of everyday and scientific conversations not only from the experience of their individual lives, but also from the stock of knowledge which is universally known and accessible. The prospective-retrospective rationalisation of interpreted meanings is a characteristic feature of the documentary method. There are many situations in sociological investigation where the researchers are forced to assign a certain status to a phenomenon (e.g., action) being observed only by means of relating this phenomenon to *their own biography and their own perspective*. The examined problem is viewed through the time horizon of both retrospection and prospection. In order to reasonably decide what they are currently observing, the practitioners of sociology must wait to see how the events will develop, because only with the benefit of hindsight will they be able to know what they have seen. It is during the process of waiting for future events that they learn – acquire knowledge – about what they have observed previously. Because of the time limits on observation of their objects of research (e.g., the observation cannot possibly last indefinitely), the researchers have to choose between alternative interpretations. Garfinkel points to the fact that this does not involve a choice between clearly defined and specified alternatives, and that the knowledge accompanying the choice is not the full knowledge relating

---

The investigator then attempts to reconstruct an underlying set of rules (methods) and *ad hoc* procedures that may be taken as having guided the observed activity.

to the complete paradigm of the goals and means as well as relations between them, which have been set. In the course of their research, sociologists cannot possibly know what they are doing in the strong sense of the term "knowledge."

The method of documentary interpretation has a reflexive character. Not only is the meaning of the emerging phenomenon additionally determined in terms of the pattern behind it, but it is also the pattern itself, and is additionally determined in terms of the interpreted phenomenon. The post hoc rationality (rationalisation) is characteristic of the above-mentioned method of interpretation.

The sociologist embarking on an inquiry into everyday reality (i.e., whose meaning is occasional), must choose one out of many research strategies – e.g., theory, hypothesis underlying his research, and method. According to ethnomethodologists, in the course of their research, sociologists find themselves in the *situation of the common-sense choice,* the characteristic feature of which is the incompleteness of knowledge. In actual research practice, it is only after obtaining the result of the research, that the researchers make an effort to impart the character of actions, based on deliberate decision, to their theoretical choices. One can say, thus, that in the practice of research, in the situation of the common-sense choice, the *result* of research precedes the theoretical *decisions,* which in turn ensures that the procedures of research are not rational actions. In the practice of research, the aim of the adopted strategy is made more precise by the successive steps which constitute a research situation. It is only in the course of manipulating the actual situation that the essence of the matter of the future state of affairs becomes clear. Therefore, it is the rule rather than the exception that, only at the end of their work, do researchers actually realise the problem they have investigated and the actual strategies they have adopted.

The correctness – i.e., the compatibility of the obtained description of the investigated reality with the pattern (e.g., scientific theory) – is a derivative of the work of the researcher and of the contingent situation. In practice, acting in the situation of common-sense choice, the researchers apply the rule which was described by Garfinkel in the following way:

> One has to cope somehow with the risk of unfavourable results. After all the actions taken by the researcher will be subject to the appraisal of other researchers and must be validated. One has to prove their congruence with the result which should have been expected according to the criterion of reasonable appraisal, and the whole process must take place in the conditions determined by the rules

of social activity proper for this professional group and by the respect for these rules.[4]

According to ethnomethodologists, rational knowledge and rational choice – postulated as they are in social theories as the fundamental elements constituting the consciousness of the researcher – are absent in the practice of sociological research. On the other hand, they accompany scientific theorising. The conduct of a social researcher, who rationalises the result of the research and the theoretical elements of the chosen research strategy, reminds the writer of the acquisition of self-consciousness in terms of the applied method – the process, as described by Gombrowicz in his *Diaries*:

> Enter the realm of dreams. Then start to write any story whatsoever which comes to your mind and write 20 pages. *Then* read. On these 20 pages you will find perhaps one scene, some individual sentences, some metaphor which seem exciting. *So write everything once again*, trying to take these exciting words as the groundwork – and write without taking the reality into account, aiming only to satisfy the needs of your imagination. *While producing the second draft* your imagination will follow some definite course... Write 20 more pages [...] *later write everything once again.* By doing so you will hardly notice when a series of key scenes is created [...] and everything will begin to take shape under your fingers through the power of its own logic; the scenes, the characters, the terms, the scenery will demand its completion and what you have already created will dictate you the rest.[5]

Prevalent in the research practice of a sociologist is a process which (in the quoted excerpt from the *Diary*) Gombrowicz dubbed *alternating between the "I"* (the participant of everyday life) *and the "I"* (the sociologist-researcher) – i.e., between one's own biography and the vantage point of the participant of everyday life, on the one hand, and paradigmatic, scientific knowledge on the other.

In the opinion of ethnomethdologists, the essence of the social reality is to be found neither in the occasionality of its meaning, nor in its ambiguity, nor (for Gombrowicz) in its antinomy, which has its source in the antinomous structure of the human nature:

---

[4] Harold Garfinkel, *Studies in Ethnomethodology* (Englewood Cliffs, NJ: Prentice-Hall, Inc., 1967), p. 100.
[5] Gombrowicz, *Dziennik (1957 – 1961)*, p. 115.

However, the most important, serious and unsolvable dispute is the one which is carried on within us by our two most fundamental drives: the one which craves for the form, shape and definition, and the other which defends itself against the shape and does not want the form. Humankind is made in such a way that it must constantly define itself and evade its own definitions.[6]

CONCLUSION

Through the results of its empirical inquiry into the self-consciousness of social researchers, Ethnomethodology reveals that the latter did not manage to find unambiguous answers to the question that gives that activity a scientific character. The rules, theories, and scientific textbooks which were used by researchers did not determine the status of the activities undertaken. Moreover, such rules, theories, and the like, were semantically ambiguous and occasional in character. This fact forced the researchers to undertake the (unconscious) effort of interpretation, the objective of which was to rid the phenomenon under investigation of its ambiguity. The procedure of interpretation determined the possibility of further explanation of an investigated event and of formulating a positive corollary. The application of norms and rules by the practitioners of sociology, which was determined by the strategy adopted, was nevertheless accompanied by the constant recourse to the common-sense methods of interpretation. In their research practice, the social researchers were motivated by some added factors – often neglected or concealed – which had a real though frequently imperceptible or deliberately belittled impact on the course of their research. Ethnomethodologists listed such circumstances as the fact that the researchers were in a way "compelled" by their social status to engage in research; their actions had to be completed within specified time and at a specific pace and be co-ordinated with the actions of other researchers. The explanations about the course of the process of decision-making in research omitted all sorts of negligence and transgressions. The researchers, as H. Garfinkel wrote, were definitely reluctant to admit that they learned to make research decisions only *post hoc*, during seminar discussions, when the result of the research was already "obvious." In their comments, the researchers underscored that they had known from the beginning what could be expected in the course of their research. When during the interview their attention was brought to the differences between their idealised explanations and their actual practice, the researchers became impatient and in most cases declined further interviewing.

A similar attitude of unmasking the scientific praxis can be found in Gombrowicz's *Diaries*:

---

[6] Gombrowicz, *Dziennik (1957 – 1961)*, p. 122.

What is happening today to the intellect and the intellectuals is simply a scandal – and a mystification, one of the greatest in history. This intellect had been engaged in "demystifying" for so long that it became an instrument of monstrous mendacity. Wisdom and truth have long ceased to be the prime concern of intellectuals – they have been replaced by a simple concern that others do not learn that they do not know. The intellectuals, ostensibly bursting with ideas of which they are actually ignorant, hedge as much as they can in order not to get caught. What are the precautions they take? They formulate their thoughts cunningly so that they are not caught by their word. They avoid venturing outside the field which they have more or less mastered. They use the terms in an off-hand manner, as if these were perfectly known to everyone, but in fact in order not to expose their own ignorance [...]. There has emerged a special art of quoting and savouring names.[7]

Institute of Philosophy
Adam Mickiewicz University
Poznan, Poland

---

[7] Gombrowicz, *Dziennik (1961 – 1966)*, p. 52.

CHAPTER XXXV

AVICENNA'S METHOD FOR TRANSLATING GREEK PHILOSOPHICAL TERMS INTO PERSIAN

MOSTAFA YOUNESIE

Avicenna, as a philosopher who is primarily concerned with mind and reason, does not ignore language, for, as a rule, *logos* contains both mind and language. But his attention to and interactions with other philosophies, works, and texts (or pseudo-texts), written in his own and foreign languages, makes this point more powerful. In other words, Avicenna thinks about language in the context of his own philosophy and logic/*mantiq*. By reflecting on logos as both reason and speech, he does not limit himself to the first moment – that is, speech or *nutq*. But, more importantly, he directly and indirectly interacts with the "other" philosophies and philosophical traditions. We can say that he has a "reading" of "other" philosophies and traditions – a reading that more or less is a conversational hermeneutic construction of the meaning of words and terms with regard to the related text of a philosopher – as well as his own context. As Dmitri Gutas writes, "It is, in effect, a record of the way in which Avicenna received, disagreed with, modified, integrated, and communicated philosophical knowledge ... "[1]

Avicenna's own philosophy and his approach toward other philosophies, therefore, stimulate our interest in examining his method (as an issue that can be discussed today) in order to better understand and translate these philosophies and traditions. In this paper, we will focus only on the Greek philosophy and its philosophical terms and expressions.

But there is another important event that makes our attention to Avicenna's philosophy more acute and justified. In comparing Avicenna (428-370 AH [980-1037 CE]) with his contemporaries, like the Iranian philosopher Al-Beruni (440-362 AH [973-1048 CE]), we see that Avicenna uses similar terms to translate Greek words.[2] We can say that thinkers after him, such as Naser Khosrow, Al-Ghazali, and Afzal al-ddin Kashani[3] have been influenced by Avicenna in their translations of Greek philosophical terms into Persian, though there are some differences. But we can say that Avicenna translates methodically and intentionally while having certain cultural causes in mind. There is little known about those who came before

---

[1] Dimitri Gutas, *Avicenna and the Aristotelian Tradition* (Leiden: E.J. Brill, 1988), p. 5.

[2] Sina, *Festschrift*, Vol. 2 (Tehran, 1334), p. 347.

[3] Op. cit., Vol. 2, pp. 368- 379.

him, and at best I can only make speculations. Therefore, in this paper, I limit my discussion to Avicenna.

It seems justified to say that from his Persian translated terms we can derive and deduce an intentionally methodical and cultural horizon and perspective: Avicenna did not see his work as limited to his discipline. Broadly speaking, he is a so-called "cultural revivalist" and not merely a translator. In other words, Avicenna, by transmitting and translating Greek terms into Persian, performs an action/praxis that is philosophizing in a distinct cultural way, for he sees Greek terminology as a cultural text and thinks about language and its words as a cultural phenomenon. Therefore, his action is a kind of cultural philosophizing.[4] Thus, when (with attention to the above mentioned points) we compare Avicenna's equivalents, either generally or in a case-by-case manner, with the translations of other philosophers contemporaneous with or succeeding him, we do not see merely formal differences, but we also see an infrastructure that is not necessarily limited in and chained to the language and translation, for these translated terms are manifestations of the cultural basis.

If the cultural transmission and translation of the Greek terms in the field of philosophy is a manifestation of a broader and distinct infrastructure, the quality or method (or logic, according to classical and medieval language) of the linkage between these two sides can be stated as a problem – for us as well as Avicenna. It seems possible to understand this method by moving from the whole to the particulars, or vice versa. Holistic movement means looking at only the related basis, and in accordance with this we discover the method for proposing and creating corresponding Persian terms; in contrast, the incremental movement involves a systematic collecting and connecting of the related Persian terms, from which we discern Avicenna's method and infrastructure. Each one of these alternatives has its positive and negative aspects. The holistic option keeps us free of difficult analyses and efforts, but at the same time imposes a special and permanent stereotype that, on the whole, encourages us to relax too comfortably in one-sidedness. But though the incremental option can be biased, corrupted, and one-dimensional, it can also be more reliable and is open to testing. Therefore a composite or synthetic alternative may be more appropriate. We can begin with a vague (neither too clear nor too dark) and holistic infrastructure and then, through continuous reference to different and diverse translated Persian terms, make some accommodation and mediation between the primary and the Persian terms.

Usually a discussion of method addresses two things: Avicenna's own method(s), and the method of the researcher. If Avicenna had no method(s) of his own, the researcher would have a relatively free option for choosing the appropriate method for the related subject matter. But this is not the case; Avicenna has his own method(s), and it therefore seems proper that the chosen methods of this paper take Avicenna's method(s) into

---

[4] Gutas, p. 216.

consideration.[5] With this perspective, we shall pay attention to the internal logic of Avicenna's ideas and accept the active and living – not the passive and dead – presence of the author. Further, there must be interconnections between the researcher's method and Avicenna's. In this way, the two distinct identities may be safely preserved.

Earlier we pointed to the special quality of Avicenna's reading of Greek philosophy and now, with this background, it seems justified that we speak of his method(s). But what does this really mean? Avicenna transmits and translates the Greek terms in accordance with his reading(s) of Greek philosophy, though he is not a mere translator. At the same time there is a kind of continuity and permanence in this task. In other words, if in the overall context of his reading(s) Avicenna transfers and translates Greek philosophical terms in a constant and stable way, it is reasonable that we speak of his method(s) in doing so. The reading(s) and method(s) have connections with each other; the transmitted and translated philosophical terms have meanings with different shadings and connotations – this is a very important point. Accordingly, Avicenna's perspective has a basic, though not a wholly semantic dimension. In the context of his different reading(s), Avicenna pays attention both to the real meanings of the Greek terms and their connotations, and this gives a kind of stability, complexity, contextuality and interrelation between form and content to the transmitted and translated terms. Therefore, Avicenna's approach is based on the Aristotelian dualistic model of form and matter; every word has two dimensions, and the translator (here, Avicenna) is free with regard to the form of the word, but about the matter or meaning he is not. In other words, the transferred and translated Persian terms in the field of philosophy lie between two worlds – the world of meaning and the world of different connotations – because he sees language as a culturally imbued construct. Or, more generally, it seems that we can say that Avicenna, like other mediaeval philosophers, sees translation as a movement across hermeneutics and rhetoric[6]; that is, he wants to understand the meaning of the word and, at the same time, convince his audience and readers about this meaning.

After attending to Avicenna's method, it is now time for elaborating, developing and proposing the method of this paper, which is itself primarily concerned with method. In order to better understand the method of this paper, it would best to mention the special situation of the researcher. The researcher is distanced from and has differences with Avicenna and his works in terms of language, time period, society, culture, being a reader (and not the author), and exploring Avicenna's own relationship with Greek philosophy. This matrix and complex of distances and differences results in a multi-layered and opaque horizon. But in the

---

[5] Gutas, pp. 298-299.

[6] Rita Copeland, *Rhetoric, Hermeneutics, and Translation in the Middle Ages* (Cambridge: Cambridge University Press, 1991).

context of considering the methodical identities of both the researcher and the author, this situation is inevitable, predictable and yet also acceptable.

In accordance with the situation of the researcher and the special kind of reading given by Avicenna of the related Greek philosophical terms, it seems appropriate that we choose an interpretative method. This method is not explanatory, for the opacity and ambiguity that result from difference and diversity do not let us adequately pinpoint and find out causes and effects in a mechanical and linear way. Also, it is not hermeneutical for, in this opaque and indeterminate horizon, we cannot search directly and immediately for the root and the primary foundation. Therefore, the method of this paper is schematic, and it glosses rather than explains.

Now, by applying the above-mentioned method to the related problem, we can gradually approach the idea or proposition of a particular conception or notion. Here we have a suggestion and starting point that is an association of empirical and justified notions; this serves as a kind of criterion against which the correctness and coherence of our arguments will be tested.[7] In other words, we are in a special relation with Avicenna that is analogous to being faced with black and white images, and for this reason we have a particular conception – a conception that is more classically inspired.

It is clear that, in some cases, there are reasons for a concrete and objective describing and understanding of the constructed Persian (not Arabic-Persian) equivalents of the transferred and translated Greek terms. But there are some occasions when we cannot be completely sure and certain about with respect to the concreteness and objectiveness of the reasons. In these cases it seems appropriate that we propose justified reasons that common sense can accept. Therefore, we come to face with some black or white situations. These situations are not unfruitful and useless, but rather provide a background and context that is useful for the main purpose of this paper. Our main idea with regard to the subject matter, then, is a network of empirical facts and justified notions. The black and white images are the result of this situation. But it seems that this is the natural and justified relation between Avicenna and the Greek terms in the field of philosophy, his knowledge about the Greek language, and the differences among the Greek, Persian and Arabic languages, as well as the Greek resources available at his time, etc.

Yet Avicenna's supposed cultural mission makes the whole matter more complicated, and takes it beyond the boundaries of language and translation. It even seems better that his position about the Persian language can be understood in the context of this supposed cultural mission or duty. It means that if, in contrast to many philosophers, Avicenna believes in the capacity and ability of the Persian language to express abstract and logical ideas, and he does not think that these drawbacks or defects of the Persian

---

[7] F. E. Peters, *Greek Philosophical Terms: A Historical Lexicon* (New York: New York University Press, 1967), p. 93.

language are eternal and unsolvable obstacles, then this is a particular, culture-bound position.

But this matter is not merely limited to the Greek language, for Avicenna applies his idea to the Arabic language as well. It seems that, in regard to the Arabic philosophical terms that are translated from their Greek equivalents, he uses a broad approach in translating them into Persian. In doing so, he transforms and appropriates the accustomed meaning of the Persian words for philosophical language; for example, for the simple Greek *psyche*, in Arabic we have *nafs*, but he uses the Persion *ravan* or *Jan*. For the Greek *soma* he uses the Persian *tan* in place of the Arabic-Persian *jism*. For supposedly compound and derived Greek words, too, he uses a combination of Persian or Persian and Arabic words. An example of the first case is the Greek word *gignoskein*, for which he uses two Persian words, perception *andar* + *yaft* in place of the Arabic word *edrak*; as an example of the second case, we have the use of *elm* (Arabic) + *tarazoo* (Persian) for the Greek word *logike*.[8] We have to say also that, in some cases, he introduces no word in place of the Arabic equivalent of the Greek term; for example, he accepts and uses the Arabic word *mumkin* as the equivalent of *to endechomenon allos echein*.

By examining these and the other Persian equivalents of the Greek words and terms, it becomes clear for us that, as a philosopher with a special attitude towards the Persian language as a whole and to the Greek terms as cultural entities, Avicenna pays both direct and indirect attention to the root meaning of the Greek word as its matter, and then expresses this content with his particular style as the form of this matter. This is his philosophy of translation. In other words, Avicenna's practice and method or logic, in its intent to find Persian equivalents for Greek philosophical terms, is positive attention to the capacity and ability of the Persian language to provide and accommodate abstract and subjective thinking; this consists of the practical accommodating of the root meaning of the Greek terms (reflecting the classical perception about etymology and its use for finding the true and correct sense of the word) in an appropriate and suitable Persian form.

The above-cited etymological view can be seen in four respects.

First, Avicenna is a philosopher and this raises the disciplinary status of Avicenna's contributions: we are faced with a philosophical perspective among other possible perspectives such as linguistic, epistolary, logical, and so on. Moreover, we expect to see transferred and translated terms that are suitable for and specific to the field of philosophy; they are part of the special jargon of philosophy and not common words. Although Avicenna pays attention to the ordinary words and terms of the common people and does not neglect them, he does not limit himself to this sphere. It is interesting to draw attention to both of these features by talking about the

---

[8] Ibn Sina, *Danesh Nameh A'lai (Theology)*, Mohammed Mo'in (ed.) (1334), pp. 354-359.

term *hasti* as Avicenna's equivalent for the term '*to on he on.*' In comparison with the Arabic-Persian terms, *hasti* as a purely Persian term is more abstract, in the sense of being the most determinable concept in its meaning. It is therefore more suitable for the sphere of philosophical thinking and reasoning. We might also consider his Persian equivalent *maya* for the Greek *hyle*, which originally means "wood".[9]

Second, his participation in and engagement with the Greek terms is not direct and immediate but indirect and mediated – his native language is not Greek, and his acquaintance with it is not direct, but mediated through interpreters. Therefore, if there are differences between his and our conception of the meaning of the roots of the Greek words, it is natural – although some may say that, because he is nearer than we are, his understanding is more accurate.

Third, we have the category of etymology in its classical (and not contemporary) context and connotation as the true sense of a word with Plato's *Cratylus* as its culmination.[10] Although we need not exaggerate this matter, we can grasp and discover from a comparison of the Persian terms and words with the related roots of the Greek words a kind of relation that exists between them, and this notion is not an isolated fact or accident, but a reflection of a perspective and idea. Discussion about etymology (as the true sense of a word) is a very profound and pervasive idea in the contemporary debate day on the relations among language, thought and things. In other words, it seems that Avicenna speculates about the role and function of the etymon in the showing-of and the guiding towards a proper or improper relation among things, thought and language. This point is true in regard to both simple and compound roots. For the simple root we can mention the following:

- The root of the Greek word *oligo* is *leig*, which means 'few' and 'little' and Avicenna renders it into *andakih.*
- The root of the Greek word *polo* is *pel*, which means 'much' and 'many' and Avicenna renders it into *bishih.*[11]
- The root of the Greek word *mathematikos* is from *math*, which means 'to learn' and Avicenna renders it into the Persian *farhang*, which has the same meaning as its Greek equivalent.

Avicenna tries to use a compound Persian equivalent for Greek words whose root is a compound, thereby reflecting the compoundness of the root of the original word in its Persian equivalents. For example,

---

[9] Parviz Morewedge, *The Metaphysics of Avicenna* (London: Routledge and Kegan Paul, 1973), p. 173, 60, 308.

[10] Peters, pp. 144-145.

[11] Soheil M. Afnan, *A Philosophical Lexicon in Persian, Arabic, English, French, Pahlavi, Greek and Latin* (Tehran, 1363), pp. 15, 35.

- The root of the word *dialysis* is *dialuein*, which is a compound root: *dia*, apart + *luein*, to loosen. We can see that Avicenna reflects this point in his Persian equivalents: baz – burdan.
- The root of the Greek word *noesis* is *noein*. Now it seems that the root of the mentioned Greek term is *nous* as a simple root, and means 'reason' and 'intellect,' but Avicenna's Persian equivalent shows that the root of this Greek term is compound, therefore he renders it into *andar – rasidan*. But as we have said, this difference between him and us is natural, because we can say that our relations with the original texts are indirect and have different motivations.
- The Greek compound word *suntetos* is composed of *sun*, to place or to put + *tetos*, together, and Avicenna renders it in a compound Persian word such as *gird* + *amadan*.[12]

But the fourth and last part of our analysis of Avicenna's etymological views is about his special style (as the combination of distinctive features of a praxis). This style does not mean a kind of isolation, idiosyncrasy or privateness, but only points to a combination of features that make Avicenna's praxis particular and distinct, and in contradistinction with other authors in regard to transferring and translating Greek terms of the field of philosophy. In other words, It seems that, with respect to his orientation and perspective in regard to Persian culture and language, he tries to make manifest this point in a proper way through his style, which is a combination of different features. The most important ones are as follows:

- Avicenna accepts (limited) interchangeable features in the field of grammar. It means that Avicenna sees the possibility for a kind of limited grammatical interchangeability between the Greek and Persian terms as two branches of the Indo-European language group. For example, he employs verbal forms as nouns, such as *katarsis*, which he renders as *palayesh*; *dunamia* becomes *tawanesh*. Furthermore, he uses active agency in place of passive agency, such as we see in *to kinoun* which he renders as the Persian *junbandeh*; *dektikon* he translates as *pazirandeh*.[13]
- Avicenna sometimes proposes two or more Persian equivalents for one Greek term. If the root of the Greek term is such that a single root cannot reflect its meaning, or if the root has some related meanings, it seems that Avicenna, in accordance with his justification or logic, uses a number of interconnected Persian equivalents. Among the benefits of this feature we may mention that it allows the recognition of the diversity and different aspects of a word, his attentiveness to the logic of different Persian equivalents for one Greek word, and the provision of an open space of

---

[12] Morewedge, p. 51.

[13] Afnan, *Philosophical Terminology in Arabic and Persian* (Leiden: Brill, 1964), p. 67.

thinking for the reader(s). For example, for the word *meta* + *physics*, Avicenna proposes two Persian equivalents from different perspectives, both of which are correct: *ilm-I-barin* and *ilm-I-pishin*. In accordance with the different meanings of the prefix *meta* in classical Greek language, it seems proper to speak of metaphysics as *ilm-I-barin* or as a universal and general truth, and of *ilm-I-pishin* as a fact that had to take shape, though it did not.[14] He also proposes *vaqeya* and *haqiqa* for the Greek word *aletheia*, for it seems that this Greek word can mean both reality and truth.[15]

  - Avicenna uses Pahlawi forms for some Greek philosophical terms. For example, he renders the word *pneuma* into *jan* and the word *genesis* into *bavishn*.[16] He translates the Greek word *anatetos* into *akhshij* as a Pahlawi equivalent.

  - Avicenna proposes equivalent Persian words in a contrastive and comparative way in place of the Arabic or Arabic–Persian words. For example, the Persian word *chandi* is used in contrast to the Arabic-Persian word *kammiya* for the Greek word *poson*, which means 'quantity.' The Persian word *chigunagi* is used in contrast to the Arabic-Persian word *kaifiya* for the Greek word *poion*, which means 'quality.' The Persian word *dasht* is used in contrast to the Arabic-Persian word *mulk* for the Greek word *echein*, which means 'possession.' The Persian word *nisbat* is used in contrast to the Arabic word *idafa* for the Greek word *pros ti*, which means 'relation.' The Persian word *gauhar* (probably from *gaw* meaning 'to grow') is used in contrast to the Arabic-Persian word *jauhar* for the Greek word *ousia*. The Persian word *kujai* is used in contrast to the Arabic word *aina* for the Greek word *pou*, which means 'place.' The Persian word *kaii* is used in contrast to the Arabic word *mata* for the Greek word *pote*, which means 'time.' The Persian word *nahad* is used in contrast to the Arabic-Persian word *wad* for the Greek word *keisthai*, which means 'posture.' The Persian word *kunish* is used in contrast to the Arabic word *an yafal* for the Greek word *poien*, which means 'action'. The Persian word *bakunidan* is used in contrast to the Arabic word *an yanfail* for the Greek word *paschein*, which means 'passion.'[17]

  We can see, then, that Avicenna's method for translating Greek philosophical terms into Persian shows not only great care, but also exhibits a thoughtful approach – if not a philosophy of translation – to representing the meaning of philosophical terms to a wide audience.

Tarbiat Modares University
Tehran, Iran

---

[14] Ibn Sina, *Danesh Nameh A'lai*, p. 3.
[15] Morewedge, p. 300.
[16] Ibn Sina, *Danesh Nameh A'lai*, p. 47.
[17] Morewedge, p. 187.

CHAPTER XXXVI

IN QUEST OF QUALITY OF LIFE: CREATIVITY AND CULTURE

DEBIKA SAHA

From the dawn of civilization, culture has shaped the course of history. Culture pursues creativity and creativity implies freedom. In fact, creativity is a subset of a larger setting of culture and even goes beyond age; it is a great way to connect people in a globalized world. Now, what is culture? The term can be defined in various ways. One way of defining this term is the following: Culture consists of cultivation of faculties and powers pertaining to reason, ethics and aesthetics in light of the pursuit of the values of Truth, Beauty and Goodness. Culture also consists of infusing the influences of this pursuit into physical and vital impulses, so as to refine them and to transmit the resulting experiences through various modes of expression, including those of poetry, music dance, film, art and craft. The height of a culture is to be judged by the depth and height that are reached in terms of an ascending process of harmonization and, in that process, the development of the quest of spiritual inspiration and revelation and their manifestation in various domains of life. Therefore, every developed culture inspires methodologies of transmission of accumulated normative lessons of culture to succeeding generations, and this process of transmission is greatly secured by a process of education which, in turn, discovers and implements a more and more ripened system of acceleration of progress. Among the various modes of creative expressions, the present paper selects only two, *viz.*, handicraft and films, and tries to show that in search of a quality of life, these issues (i.e. creativity of handicrafts and cultural fusion in films) play a very decisive role in bridging the gap between different cultures. Likewise, these issues are important for the search for quality of life.

We talk of our different social problems and expect culture to take a back seat as if it were not a basic necessity. But in a country like India with its great cultural heritage, different cultural forms can be used as a tool for development of the larger common mass to interact in a globalized world. To say that the country is not so rich, and that culture must be treated as a luxury, is like requesting someone to stop breathing because the air is polluted. There is no doubt that a nation's economic progress is intrinsically dependent on the cultural awakening and pride of its people.

Culture, then is both a study and pursuit. It is not merely the development of 'literary culture', but of all sides of our humanity. Nor is it an activity concerning individuals alone, or some part or section of society; it is and must be essentially general. The question now arises as to how we should use culture in its full capacity so that it can enhance the well being of society and equip individuals to interact in a globalized world. To explain this point we will take, first, the handicraft industry of our country as an example.

India is a country with various cultures, and the creative impulse of the people can be observed in different arts and crafts. This craft industry can be viewed not merely as a repository of man's material culture or as an appendix of our civilization's aesthetic standards, but also as a basic human necessity and as something vital to our survival that is both for our physical and mental well-being – as, for example, the handicrafts of Rajasthan or the cultural centers of different states. Now, it is almost customary to set up a 'Shilpagram' in every state. This 'Shilpagram' is simply the craft village industry of that particular state. Here one can display his or her own creative work which helps to enhance the creative impulse of individuals and, at the same time, to sell the products in order to earn one's livelihood. It is true that the contemporary explosion of information and increasing spread of sophisticated information technology have changed the present life styles of people. One may question whether it is possible to keep pace with this advanced world.

How can the artists and artisans be helped in their journey to rediscover their creative place in society? Notwithstanding the fact that new ideas and new ways of working lead us to modernize, there is a way not to neglect the tradition but rather to develop it through a dialogue between the maker and the consumer. This will facilitate the introduction of new designs, for example, without alienating the traditional craftsman or impairing marketing and management.

There is a need to evolve a whole range of new prototypes that could explore and demonstrate the vast range of handicraft skills available throughout India. Of course, one has to take great care in the introduction of new ideas and patterns. In this way the creative spirit of the artist can be employed to bring harmony and unity to other parts of the world. And this process will equip artists with the ability to interact in the globalized world in a better way. Here we are viewing creativity and culture not from a cosmetic, but from a basic dimension – the needs of the artist as a person. It is not the handicraft industry alone, but other art forms like film as well which can play an important role as a mediator between varying cultures. Films have a universal appeal to viewers, and it is through this medium that one can, though he or she may have roots in one part of the world, be part of a larger plan – that is, a universal pattern. Film can foster universal brotherhood, and intercultural communication and learning can be achieved through it.

However different we may be, there are certain basic similarities in human behaviour all over the world such as expressions of joy and sorrow, love and hate, etc. At the same time, it is also true that films can exhibit local variations which can sometimes present a true message – but that a foreigner who is not well acquainted with these variations may not get the message that the film wants to convey. But this distinctiveness of different cultures does not stand as a barrier in the true sense of the term. Moreover, the hurdles of communication in films are less in comparison to other art forms like literature. In literature, one has to capture the sense of the language. For example, there are certain typical words in the writings of Rabindranath Tagore, translations of which need much care. Even if one tries to be exact, it happens that there remains the difficulty of conveying the nuances through translation. The above fact is applicable to any creative writer, irrespective of society. But in films, even if one does not know the particular language, one can be informed by gestures and actions. After all, we are all human beings, and this sense of oneness brings people together. Due to the technological revolution, the world is now a global village. There may be difficulties in inter-cultural communication but this does not mean that cross-cultural comprehension is impossible. Through film, it is possible to take note of the importance of one's cultural background without denying what there is to learn from other places. Such openness should be maintained, and this leads to a more dynamic and adaptable world, rather than to a closed one.

In India, there are some directors who, through their cultural openness, tell us something about possible communicability across cultural boundaries. Here we may take the works of Satyajit Ray. His eagerness to adapt different cultural events is clear from his depiction of characters in films. The famous movie "Pather Panchali" is a striking example of the above fact. While making this film, he himself confessed that he was directly influenced by Vittorio De Sica's "Bicycle Thieves." He says that he had seen "Bicycle Thieves" within three days of arriving in London and further comments, "I knew immediately that if I ever made 'Pather Panchali' – and the idea had been at the fact of my mind for some time – I would make it in the same way using natural locations and unknown actors."[1] And Amartya Sen comments that "Pather Panchali" is a quintessentially Indian film, both in subject matter and in the style of presentation – and yet a major inspiration for the film's organization came directly from an Italian Film. The Italian influence did not make "Pather Panchali" anything other than an Indian film – it simply helped it to become a great Indian film.[2]

In fact, all these forms of culture, though rooted in human praxis, are more pervasive in their scope. The role of mixed heritage in the history of science and culture cannot be denied. That the Indo-European family of languages has played a big role can hardly be disputed. Most of the cultural, material and intellectual production is mixed or composite in character. Amartya Sen illustrates this point beautifully: "Given the cultural and

---

[1] Satyajit Ray, *Our Films, Their Films*, 3rd ed. (Bombay: Disha Book/Orient Longman, 1993), p. 9.

[2] Amartya Sen, *Our Culture, Their Culture* [Satyajit Ray Memorial Lecture] (West Bengal Film Centre, 1999), p. 17.

intellectual interconnections, the question of what is 'Western' and what is 'Eastern' (or Indian) is often hard to decide, and the issue can be discussed only in more dialectical terms. The diagnosis of a thought as 'Purely Western' or 'Purely Indian' can be very illusory."[3]

In conclusion, it may be pointed out that the difficulties of communication across cultures are there, but this recognition should not create such a barrier that our place becomes a closed island. Culture signifies "a way of life" in which human beings think, create, believe and behave, according to their own will.[4] In fact, it is in our heterogeneity and in our openness that our pride, not our disgrace, lies. Here lies the true meaning of the quest of quality of life.

Barasat College
University of Calcutta
West Bengal, India

---

[3] *Ibid*, p. 20.

[4] Partha Chatterjee, *The Nation and Its Fragments* (Princeton: Princeton University Press, 1993).

CHAPTER XXXVII

MAHATMA GANDHI'S *WELTANSCHAUUNG* AND FUTURE GENERATIONS

GEETA MEHTA

I.E. Hulme writes that "A *Weltanschauung* should be the highest possible exaltation of the life and culture of [a] period. ... A *Weltanschauung* can only spring from the highest possible development of personality."[1] According to this definition, any comprehensive philosophy may be called a *Weltanschauung* or "world view," provided its theoretical component has practical bearing. R.R. Diwakar clarifies the relation between theory and practice:

> Philosophy without an ethical code of conduct based on the truth arrived at, is an intellectual exercise with, perhaps, the pleasure of logic added on. It is only barren theory producing no effect in life and offering no help to the progress and evolution of life and humanity.[2]

LIFE IS AN INTEGRATED WHOLE

Gandhi's *Weltanschauung* can be linked up with future generations because he was a thinker far ahead of his time and many modern economists and environmentalists accept this. He was not a philosophical system builder, but he was a synoptic, consistent and integrated thinker, with a definite world-view, representing an amazing unity of thought and action. Gandhi viewed life in its totality, as an integrated and indivisible whole, and every aspect and part of it he understood as vitally significant in the constitution of the whole. This holistic approach makes Gandhi's world-view unique and relevant in the search for alternative paradigms.

Gandhi was not simply a *Satyagrahi* – i.e., a practitioner of nonviolent resistance – experimenting with Nonviolence and Truth, but, further, he was a multifaceted genius who wrote, spoke and dealt with various worldly problems such as full employment, cooperative farming, nutrition and health, communal harmony, the value of education, raising the status of women, equality of human beings, the environment, etc. Gandhi's

---

[1] T.E. Hulme, *Speculations* (London: Routledge & Kegan Paul, 1936), p. 30.

[2] R.R. Diwakar, *Gandhi a practical Philosopher* (Bombay: Bharatiya Vidya Bhavan, 1965) p .17.

social philosophy is becoming more and more relevant in the establishment of new peaceful world order.

INDIVIDUAL AND SOCIETY

Gandhi viewed the individual as an integral part of society and hence found no ground for accepting any dichotomy between individual and social interests and goals. The distinctions among individuals point to the many-sidedness of reality and its not unbridgeable differences. According to Gandhi, true self-interest is that which sustains society and enables self-expression and development of all individual members of society; as all individuals are interrelated and interdependent, one man's welfare is intrinsically interconnected with the welfare of others as well. That was why Gandhi insisted on *Sarvodaya*, the welfare and all-round development of *all*, and rejected the utilitarian theory of the greatest good of the greatest number.

The process of self-transformation leading to self-realization must take place in this world, in our social milieu. Self-transformation and social transformation were not separate or disconnected processes for Gandhi. Hence, he used to observe fasts in order to engage social problems.

SARVODAYA: ITS COMPREHENSIVENESS

Gandhi's vision of Sarvodaya – meaning, 'universal uplift' or 'progress of all' – is based on the spiritual perception of the oneness of existence. It suggests the evolutionary all-sided development of all human beings without any distinction between them. It presupposes a social order that would provide equal opportunity for all to develop all dimensions of their personality. This would further imply the establishment of socio-economic-political and education structures that would facilitate the development and expression of the latent potentialities of the individuals.

SOCIAL ORDER

Gandhi visualized a new social order, which would be egalitarian, classless and caste-less, guaranteeing the flowering of the human personality. He perceived that the law operating at the sub-human level was the force of gravitation, while at the level of human societies it was the law of nonviolence or love.[3] If we look at the evolution of human society, argued Gandhi, we find that humanity has been steadily and slowly progressing towards *Ahimsa* or nonviolence. The world is held together by bonds of love. Nonviolence in the sense of creative and active love must become the basis of the socio-economic-political and cultural structures of society. Gandhi visualizes a nonviolent economic, political and social

---

[3] See *Harijan, an English Weekly* (Feb. 11, 1939), p. 8.

structure in his worldview, which is the only way for future generations, if future generations want to survive.

NONVIOLENT ECONOMIC STRUCTURE

Gandhi did not recognize the separation of economics from ethics, and what he wanted to achieve in the economic field was the ethical ordering of the economic life of society. He wanted to reinstate the human element and the value factor into economics and, thereby, achieve the integration of moral sentiments and the science of economics: "True economics stands for social justice, it promotes the good of all equally, including the weakest, and is indispensable for a decent life."[4]

Gandhi strips the illusion from those who conceive of modernity and progress in terms of a high standard of living measured by conspicuous consumption, instead defining true civilization thus: "Civilization, in the real sense of the term, consists not in the multiplication but in the deliberate and voluntary reduction of wants."[5] He considered poverty to be materially harmful and morally degrading. "Earth has enough to satisfy everyone's legitimate needs but not anyone's greed."[6] Given the finite nature of earth's resources, any attempt to continue artificially multiplying human wants is doomed to failure. Thus, the limitation of wants becomes a *sine qua non* for sustaining the earth's Eco-system.

Gandhi wants to substitute mass production with production by the masses. He advocated decentralization as a remedy for the evils of industrialism. The need for a decentralized order has been emphasized by eminent economists and thinkers such as Gunner Myrdal, E.F. Schumacher, Wilfred Wellock, Bertrand Russell, Aldous Huxley, and Herbert Marcuse. Decentralization has also been included in the manifestos of such groups belonging to the New Age movement as the German Greens.

Gandhi did not accept the concept of ownership as such, whether it be private or state. He considered both as equally exploitative and hence inconsistent with Nonviolence. In tune with the basic tenets of non-possession and non-stealing, Gandhi formulated the theory of Trusteeship in order to save society from rampant capitalism and bureaucratic socialism. Gandhi's economic ideas are perfectly consistent with his metaphysical and ethical propositions. The end sought in a nonviolent economic order is happiness combined with full mental, moral and spiritual growth.

POLITICAL STRUCTURE

Gandhi says, "My politics and all other activities of mine are

---

[4] *Harijan* (Oct. 9, 1937), p. 292.
[5] M.K. Gandhi, *Hind Swaraj* (Ahmedabad: Navjivan Publishing House, 1962), p. 45.
[6] *Harijan* (March 31, 1946), p. 63.

derived from my Religion."[7] He believed that the only way of identifying oneself with God's creation was through active love, and active love for Gandhi was nothing but dedicated and selfless service of humanity and the rest of creation. "I felt compelled to come into the political field because I found that I could not do even social work without touching politics."[8] Gandhi adds:

> Politics bereft of religion is absolute dirt, ever to be shunned. Politics concerns nations, and that which concerns the welfare of nations must be one of the concerns of a man who is religiously inclined, in other words a seeker after God and truth. ... Therefore, in politics also, we have to establish the kingdom of heaven.[9]

By the progressive unfolding of the power of Nonviolence in all human transactions, the need for a violence-based state can be eliminated. This according to Gandhi was a state of pure and enlightened anarchy, and it was realizable to the extent that Nonviolence was realizable.

NATIONALISM AND INTERNATIONALISM

For Gandhi, there is no contradiction between Nationalism and Internationalism. They are complementary. He observed: "It is impossible for one to be internationalist without being a nationalist. Internationalism is possible only when nationalism becomes a fact, i.e. when people belonging to different countries have organized themselves and are able to act as one. It is not nationalism that is evil; it is the narrowness, selfishness, and exclusiveness, which is the bane of modern nations, which is evil."[10] He also once said, "The golden way is to be friends with the world and to regard the whole human family as one." The application of nonviolence in international relations calls for sacrifice and martyrdom if need be.

The *Sarvodaya* approach to life and its problems is holistic, integrates the individual into the communitarian milieu, and harmonizes the material aspirations and goals with the Spiritual, thereby insuring the evolutionary and all-sided development of all sentient beings.

PANACEA FOR THE PRESENT DAY CRISIS

The paradox of the modernization praxis has added a new dimension to the crisis we confront today and calls for a fresh look at its valuational aspect. Only a nonviolent, non-exploitative environmental

---

[7] *Harijan* (March 2, 1934), p. 23.
[8] *Harijan* (Oct. 6, 1946), p. 341.
[9] *Young India, an English Weekly* (June 18, 1925), p. 214.
[10] *Young India* (June 18, 1925), p. 211.

Gandhian world order can meet the challenge. The world is groaning under the impact of advancement of science and technology and the possibilities it has opened up. In the age of rapid industrialization, urbanization, and the telecommunications revolution, the individual is lost sight of and alienated and is subordinated to economic values. The Gandhian strategy of development would offer the possibility of a comprehensive and permanent solution to the modern dilemma and build up a qualitatively better social order. A better quality of life would depend upon the extent and degree of harmony future generations are able to secure between the ecosystem, the personality system, and socio-cultural systems. Harmony, which is the foundation of the Gandhian model, is to be attained and maintained by social actions of individuals and groups based on intricate relationships and an aptitude developed from a commitment to values of peace and nonviolence. Such development will give rise to the evolution of a better, livable world – an interdependent, enlightened, and peaceful world. The values of peace and development should emanate ultimately from the individual. The development of the individual self would take place first, and should proceed to the Village, the Nation, and the World. The value-oriented Gandhian model of sustainable development is perhaps the only alternative available for devising strategies for the survival of humankind. As early as 1903 he had said, "All of us have to live in the present life merely as a preparation for a future, far more certain and far more real."[11] Gandhi has showed how to live truthfully and nonviolently in the present, a way of life that would lead humanity into a future worth living.

Arnold Toynbee has rightly observed that:

> At this supremely dangerous moment in human history, the only way of salvation for mankind is the Indian way. The Emperor Ashoka's and Mahatma Gandhi's principles of nonviolence and Sri Ramakrishana's testimony to the harmony of Religions: here we have an attitude and spirit that can make it possible for the human race to grow together into a single family … and in the atomic age this is the only alternative to escape from destroying ourselves."[12]

RECONSTRUCTING THE FUTURE

The Gandhian or *Sarvodaya* social order will be characterized by a personality structure oriented around individual reformation, a cultural structure oriented around values of nonviolence, and a social structure oriented around altruism. The ecosystem of a Gandhian model would be

---

[11] *Indian Opinion, an English Weekly* (August 20, 1903).

[12] Arnold Toynbee, *One World and India* (Calcutta: Orient Longmans Pvt. Ltd., 1960), p. 54.

based on the ecological values of harmony between four major components, namely population, organization, energy and technology. Harmony will be established through a decentralized, handicraft-based, community-oriented production system, which will promote the value of dignity of labour and, particularly, of bread labour, thus giving an opportunity for individuals to be in direct contact with nature and the environment. A Gandhian social reconstruction programme is not only production-oriented but is holistic and multi-dimensional. The all-comprehensive Gandhian approach would emphasize the need to protect the environment and maintain its purity and cleanliness and avoid biological and all other kinds of pollution.

In a nonviolent world, relationships between man and man, and between man and nature would be peaceful, accommodative and harmonious. Nonviolence avoids a verticality of relations and stands for the horizontal and equal relationships of (what Gandhi regarded as) "oceanic circles" of villages. Satyagraha is an innovative technique of conflict resolution with unlimited potentialities for building a peaceful society.

Gandhi's thoughts and deeds have relevance today, and will for centuries to come, for they contain universal recommendations transcending time, place and other differences. Gandhi's ideas concerning the relationship of means and ends, his concept of truth and nonviolence, freedom, social injustice, basic education, self-reliance, the dignity of labour, the equality of all religions, *Satyagraha*, trusteeship and, above all, his theory of social reconstruction based on the *Sarvodaya* ideal, will continue to be relevant. Satisfying the basic needs of all, acceptance of voluntary poverty, "to be" rather than "to have," strict adherence to values, respect for human rights, removal of racial and sex differentiation and, above all, creation of a non-violent peaceful society in which disputes can be resolved in a nonviolent fashion – all these constitute the ideal society of Gandhi's dreams. It appears a utopia, but is a relevant, feasible fact that coincides with new ideas that are slowly showing their relevance in the contemporary world.

If wiser future generations adopt the Gandhian approach in international relations, the billions and trillions of dollars spent on armaments and war preparations shall become available for the reconstruction of humanity and the building up of a qualitatively better world social order.

Ananthacharya Indological Research Institute
Mumbai, India

CHAPTER XXXVIII

PHENOMENOLOGY IN SCIENCE AND LITERATURE

MAMUKA G. DOLIDZE

INTRODUCTION

The problem under discussion refers to the phenomenological way of thinking in various fields of human activity. The phenomenological conception of quantum theory, resulting from the analogy between Husserl's phenomenology and Bohr's interpretation of quantum theory, is used as a basic conception here. We certainly realize that the hypotheses and results of our investigation go beyond Bohr's interpretation, but at the same time, they are a logical extension of Bohr's position with respect to the field of existential phenomenology. By extending Bohr's interpretation through the complementarity principle, we link "orthodox" quantum theory with the theories of stream of consciousness and polyphony in contemporary fiction. The basis of such an analogy is the fact that both areas (i.e., the atomic world and artistic reality) use the same phenomenological method of object construction.

By treating the following assertions on the basis of existential phenomenology, we attempt to reveal how consciousness, as a stream of existence, acts in both the physical and artistic areas. All this reflects modern scientific thinking and the art of fiction; it highlights an important feature of contemporary thinking: the appearance of polyphonic forms in the existential unity of human consciousness.

THE EXPANSION OF BOHR'S INTERPRETATION OF QUANTUM THEORY

Bohr's principle of complementarity expresses not only a new situation in quantum physics, but the essence of contemporary thinking in science. One feature of this way of thinking is the rejection of the common basis of cognition, which is responsible for the grounding of consciousness in terms of "the truth." Thus, complementarity acquires a meaning with regard to independent and self-existent layers of consciousness which are mutually exclusive and imply non-existence beyond themselves. According to the principle of complementarity, in spite of the denial of the common world, we have a meaning of existence which comprehends mutually exclusive parts of the mind. Therefore, it is advisable to regard them as mutually complementary. We do not mean the existence of things surrounding us. Complementarity is a regular principle of subjective being, which is a process of the acquisition of meaning. This process creates existential meaning within the perspective of infinity.

By asserting that complementarity introduces the meaning of subjective being in the quantum area, we also confirm the integrity of atomic experiments (i.e., the interaction between microparticles and measurement instruments). This is not a reflection of the interaction between the classical and the quantum object, but rather between the subject and object, or strictly speaking, between subjective and objective being. Otherwise, the uncontrolled character of the interaction would be impossible to explain. Only the assumption of a subject-object interaction allows for explanation.

The subject can control this interaction, as it can objectify itself, but this act of objectification cannot exhaust it. There is always a certain extent of subjectivity which ensures objectification. At the classical level, this subjective component is beyond the picture of physical reality, but in the quantum area this is an inner component of atomic action and the picture of reality. Therefore, the interaction between particles and the instruments has an uncontrolled nature.

We obtain an important result from this: in contrast to classical physics, subjective existence is an inner part of quantum reality. (We mean the picture of reality, but the denial of the basic world beyond quantum descriptions opens a possibility of identifying the picture of reality with the reality itself by stating that the act of description, as an ontological act, reveals – and thus creates – the different aspects of quantum reality). But, according to our suggestion, subjective being is an ontological act of the acquisition of meaning, and no more than that. Therefore, the measurement and classical language of atomic events, by means of which the theory gains physical meaning, are not the components of knowledge (as was the case in classical physics), but the components of physical reality itself.

Bohr realized these difficulties. He understood that, despite the non-existence of the individual subject in the quantum area, atomic measurement is more than a mere action between classical and quantum objects, an interaction which cannot explain its integrity. In contrast to physical being, Bohr assumed a new form of existence in the atomic world, which introduced the necessity of classical terms, inequity of indeterminacy and the principle of complementarity. We call it subjective being – the being of consciousness.

Another feature of subjective being is an aspiration for independence and self-existing statement. In our opinion, this is expressed through the indeterminate and individual conduct of atomic particles; they are undetermined as much as they are founded by subjective existence. Therefore, quantum probability, in contrast to classical quantity, is a peculiarity of reality due to its irreducible nature. Quantum probability is bounded by the inequity of indeterminacy. Moreover, statistically, it excludes any probable error, exactly maintaining its internal equality (as determined by Schrödinger) of probable meanings. This peculiarity of quantum probability contradicts the general classical concept of probability. For that reason, basing their approaches on quantum probability and using the theory, physicists could successfully solve physical problems and consider the quantum dualism and indeterminacy as non-physical – indeed, as metaphysical – problems. But their approach was not justified. The wave-particle dualism is, first of all, a physical problem; but the examination of wave and particles as mutually exclusive aspects is a classical abstraction, which is far from atomic reality. A mutually exclusive relationship means that a particle is measured absolutely and precisely, and is located in a certain point; consequently, a wave spreads infinitely, and the information on its location cannot be available. But such a state of affairs cannot exist in the quantum reality, because the precision of measurement is limited. In the quantum reality, the wave and the particle do not in fact exclude each other, but they can coexist, unless their exact values are lost. In short, instead of precise parameters of wave-particles, we have probability quantities.

In contrast to the classical case, the quantum probability (i.e., the statistical exclusion of probable error) makes a statistical theory complete and fully predictable; the non-exclusive, actual correspondence and the simultaneous preservation of wave-particle dualism require a fuller and deeper explanation. Our explanatory model is the following: the wave-corpuscular atomic dualism echoes the total dualism of existence – the dualism between spirit and matter, physical being and spiritual reality, subjective and objective being. A great miracle of life and existence is the fact that, in spite of a mutually exclusive dualism between matter and spirit – i.e., the nonexistence of a logical bridge between them – our consciousness as a living entity is permanently transformed from spirit into matter and vice versa. It keeps the exclusive aspects of existence together, even though this is logically impossible. How can this happen? This question has no answer. Since life is miraculous, we should not search for solutions, but instead accept the dualism containing integrated reality. Existence is an indivisible result of the interaction between mutually exclusive sides: subjective and objective being. This is plainly revealed in the atomic field. The quanto-physical reality is an integral result of the interaction between subjective and objective being, and wave-particle dualism is an unsolved phenomenon, just as the miraculous, exclusive integrity between matter and spirit is. By eliminating the dualism we destroy life in the atomic world. The principle of complementarity, on the contrary, helps us to maintain the dualism and relate it to the real wave-particle wholeness, just as living consciousness keeps the physical and mental aspects of existence together despite their difference.

Wave-particle dualism and irreducible quantum probability cannot prevent physicists from finding successful solutions to various physical problems; this shows that there are some interconnecting wave-corpuscular sides of the atomic world which maintain this dualism. Therefore, we can use the principle of complementarity with regard to the above dualism, and state that the wave-particle dualism is an individual case of dualism between matter and spirit.

A PHENOMENOLOGICAL CONCEPTION OF QUANTUM THEORY

The interpretation of quantum reality as a result of subject-object action creates an opportunity to connect quantum theory with Edmund Husserl's phenomenology. Husserl aspired to discover the basis of existence. He thought that the way of traditional philosophy was wrong, for it used the concept of causality. Causality implies an infinite chain of reasons and results and, thus, is useless as a substance. Another way of determining existence is to search for its meaning. Phenomenology investigates the factors creating the meaning of existence. These factors exist in an ontological depth of intelligence. It is in this way, Husserl emphasized, that consciousness forms reality.

Husserl criticized the natural position of science, which unreservedly assumed the existence of reality. He remarked that abstention from the assertion of existence is a way to reveal its meaning. Such an abstention is not the same as a doubt or denial of the existence of reality. The two last statements imply an understanding of the meaning of existence. The goal of phenomenological abstention is to throw light on just this meaning. The phenomenological method brackets this assertion, retaining it conditionally. Husserl's requirement is to break the chain linking consciousness and the external world, for being as an absolute and self-existing essence exists not *outside* consciousness, but in the depth of its ontological level.

Thus, searching for the absolute source, Husserl turned his mind from the relationship of the external world to the absolute clarity of consciousness. Such a difficult task requires a definite method, the method of so-called "phenomenological reduction." According to this method, the first step in the purification of consciousness from alien elements is to remove the orientation towards external things. Thus, consciousness gets rid of the actual world, and the content of consciousness acquires a conditional nature, unrelated to reality, beyond the issue of objective substantiation. This is called "putting consciousness in brackets." It is remarkable that the nonexistence of the relationship between consciousness and existence is a way to reveal the meaning of existence and to present consciousness as the constructor of reality.

The situation is the same with quantum theory. Because of the integrity of actions, there is a prohibition to represent the atomic object beyond classical conditions of its measurement and cognition. These conditions do not apply to the subject as an individual. Nevertheless, they are not a mere system of objects, surrounding the atomic world. They acquire a meaning of cognitive conditions. The latter play a part of consciousness, which attaches physical meaning to quantum objects and thus forms the atomic reality. Husserl turns his attention to clear consciousness, substantiating being through the existence of consciousness.

Perceiving classical instruments as conditions for quantum cognition, Bohr substantiated the atomic being using these conditions – i.e., through subjective existence. Bohr brings classical terms into the quantum area which, at the same time, limits their use. In short, his non-classical description is composed of classical elements. It means that he breaks the link between classical terms and classical reality, taking the classical picture in brackets.

Let us compare this method of substantiation with the first step of the phenomenological reduction. According to Husserl, while taking the actual givenness of being in brackets, we consider it as content of consciousness and raise the issue of the conditions of its emergence. This means that we consider it not as the only reliable picture of the world, but as one out of many probable pictures, which appear in other conditions. Thus, each reflection of being is surrounded by various pictures, as a possible reflection of the same object in other cognitive conditions. Husserl denotes this as "unrevealing the horizon of possibilities." Here, he implies that possibilities are not an outcome of the actual picture, but precede it. Therefore, "The science about pure possibilities precedes the science about the reality and makes the latter possible as a science."[1]

We see here the resemblance with the quantum situation: the classical experimental picture of the atom is the empirical givenness of quantum reality. Quantum theory, as a microstate theory, is a theory of possibilities, but not of reality. The theory is not a result of generalization of atomic experiment uncovered through the classical discourse. Therefore, the latter – in particular, the continuity of classical terms – contradicts quantum theory. Quantum theory, the theory about quantum possibilities, precedes the classical description of quantum reality and substantiates it, but there is no agreement between them; the formalism of quantum theory and the classical picture of atomic reality are mutually exclusive as well as complementary descriptive forms of the atomic world.

Hence, as in the case of phenomenology, Bohr considers the actual quantum picture as a probable picture, which is surrounded by pure quantum possibilities, arising in different experimental conditions. The above is reflected in the following inequity of uncertainty: Opening the horizon of possibilities, Husserl intends to reveal some stable and constant value which is maintained through all these changes. He considers every actual state of mind as probable, putting it in brackets. Passing from one kind of possibility to another, he gradually gets free from actual givenness and tackles the pure form of it, which is nothing more than the experience of pure self as a form of absolute being (for this subjective component is present in all cases). Thus, according to Husserl, the fundamental being, which constructs the world, is a subjective being which is given through the

---

[1] E. Husserl, *Erfahrung und Urteil*, Bd. 1 (Prague, 1939), s. 106.

experience of pure self – the invariant value of various possible pictures of reality.

To continue our analogy with quantum physics, it should be noted that, while passing from one picture to another (in particular, we have in mind the wave-particle pictures of atomic world), everything changes – for, according to quantum theory, there is no common ground underneath. Nevertheless, there is an unchangeable point, maintaining itself through mutually exclusive states – the integrity of quantum experiment, based on the indivisible measurement process (i.e., on the interaction between a measurement tool and the quantum object). This interaction keeps its uncontrollable integrity throughout quantum states. It is remarkable that tool-object integrity is a result of quantum theory – the theory about pure quantum possibilities – while, on the other hand, it is a result of Bohr's principle (Bohr insists on the classical description of measurement tools).

Consequently, we have a classical picture of atomic measurement on the one hand and, on the other, pure quantum possibilities expressed through the quantum theory. The actual atomic state somewhat agrees with probabilistic quantum theory, even though, using the mutually exclusive languages, there is no functional dependence between them. This situation bears a strong resemblance to phenomenology, which implies that the classical picture of the atomic experiment is open to the horizon of quantum possibilities. Therefore, it is not surprising that we obtain an indivisible (tool-object) system thanks to the phenomenological approach to the quantum area.

The integrity of quantum experiment, as an unchangeable point maintained throughout quantum states is comparable with a phenomenological invariant. As shown above, the invariant is pure self – the subjective point revealing itself through various states of mind. Such self exists only as an orientedness towards or on the object. The orientedness means that pure self has the idea of object and, simultaneously, some relationship with this idea. The self is readiness to fulfill the idea – and, hence, it is more than an idea; it can be considered as a possibility and motion towards the fulfillment of an idea. Such a definition agrees with the thesis that the source of being (subjective point) is the act of attaching meaning.

Let us trace the link between the phenomenological self and the integrity of tool-object interaction in the quantum area. Our analogy leads to a subjective understanding of this interaction. Otherwise, it would neither correspond to the phenomenological self, nor play an invariant part in quantum states. The integrity of the tool-object system reveals itself in the process of quantum measurement. Hence, it is a system that attaches physical meaning to a quantum object. Given its resemblance to the phenomenological self, we can consider this system as a subjective being, creating the meaning of quantum reality.

But despite the resemblance there is a difference: Husserl distinguishes the pure self as an internal component of experience, whereas the quantum invariant is an external integrity of the tool-object interaction. Phenomenology makes it possible to bring into correspondence these inner and external aspects of cognition. When considering the pure self, a phenomenologist supposes that the existential basis of consciousness lies beyond its psychological level. Therefore, he first emphasizes the self as an experience of being and then as an experience of self. The self has a phenomenological value as an inner expression of absolute existence, for this component of cognition has a quality of being present always and everywhere.

Phenomenological analysis shows that the sense of self-being is given through the perception of the actual world. I perceive the world, and through phenomenological analysis I realize that my self participates in the construction of the given world. Here we do not try to find out whether the self really creates the picture of the world or not; we only assert that the creation of the meaning of existence is a way to reveal the self as a motion of being. When creating the meaning of something, I experience my own existence. Hence, my existence expresses itself through the pure self, which constructs the meaning of my existence. The identity of self-consciousness and existence is possible if consciousness presents itself as an act of attaching meaning.

Thus, there is a constant entity, pure self, which is the act of attaching meaning. Totally comprising the subject's self, it presents itself as a dynamic form of self-existence as an indivisible act that cannot be cognized, for there is no subject beyond this that differentiates and cognizes such an integral act. The similarity to quantum physics is obvious here: although tool-object integrity presents an external fact, it corresponds with the internal self – both are subjective beings. When creating a physical meaning of quantum particles, the tool-object action plays the part of self-existence in relation to the atomic world.

Just like in the case of phenomenology, we encounter an indivisible and noncognizible act of the attachment of meaning expressed through an uncontrollable integrity of quantum measurement. Niels Bohr wrote that it was senseless to speak about the atomic object without referring to the act of measurement (the latter is an indispensable and existential component of the former). The above shows that, in the quantum area, the concept of physical value is replaced by a symbol of integral action; this action, together with quantum theory, acts as consciousness, transforming the formal structure of quantum state into the elements of physical reality.

As we intend to extend our analogy from quantum phenomenology to the art of fiction, it becomes clear that the quantum situation is comparable with Joyce's stream of consciousness, for the writer shows miraculous unity of formal and objective-realistic layers of consciousness. Therefore, Robert Humphrey remarks:

> I should like at least to suggest one important achievement
> of Joyce's in 'Ulysses' which is central to his whole

purpose and which is greatly dependent on stream of consciousness techniques. This is the marvelous degree of objectivity which he achieves. Joyce, more than any other novelist, gains what Joseph Warren Beach terms 'dramatic immediacy.'[2]

We see that Joyce achieves objectivity through stream of consciousness, which has a formal nature. In a similar way, Niels Bohr achieves the objectivity of quantum particles (giving them a physical meaning) through the integrity of quantum measurement, which acts as consciousness and stems from formal quantum theory. Later, we will go back to the similarity between quantum theory and fiction, but before that we would like to define the principles of quantum phenomenology once again:

1a. Criticizing the natural position of science (i.e., the unreserved assumption of the world's existence), Husserl brings up an issue of the limits and conditions of the correspondence between scientific description and the world.

1b. Considering the quantum theory through the inequity of uncertainty, Bohr brings up an issue of the limits and conditions of correspondence between a picture of physical reality and the atomic world.

2a. Husserl considers the picture of the world as a phenomenon of consciousness without its relation to objective reality; i.e., to use phenomenological language, he puts the picture in brackets.

2b. Bohr considers the wave-particle pictures of the atomic world as phenomena in themselves, for he implies the existence of non-objective reality beyond them. Thus, he puts the wave-particle picture in brackets.

3a. According to Husserl, every actual picture of the world, as a phenomenon of consciousness, is surrounded by various pictures which are possible in other cognitive conditions. This means that the phenomenon is opened to a horizon of possibilities.

3b. According to Bohr, the actual picture of the atomic world is surrounded by possible pictures, which arise in other conditions of measurement. Quantum theory anticipates these possible states. The latter create a horizon of possibilities, preceding the actual quantum picture.

4a. Passing from one phenomenon to another, through the various possibilities, Husserl gradually frees himself from the phenomenon's content and reaches a stable and invariant component – the pure self, as a ground for the construction of the picture of the world.

4b. Passing from wave to particle pictures, through the mutually-exclusive atomic states, we distinguish a stable and invariant component – the integrity of tool-object's action as a ground for the construction of the picture of the atomic world.

---

[2] R. Humphrey, *Stream of Consciousness in the Modern Novel* (Los Angeles: University of California Press, 1962), p.15.

5a. We assert that pure self in its existential dimension is an act of the attachment of meaning. The latter is an indivisible and undifferentiated act, since it exists as subject-object wholeness, and there is no subject beyond this as a basis determining the act. Thus, the pure self, as mind-orientedness towards the object, exists as an undifferentiated act of the attachment of meaning.

5b. We assert that quantum measurement is an act of attaching physical meaning to quantum particles. This is an uncontrollable and undifferentiated act, for it presents the subject-object wholeness and there is no subject beyond this as a basis determining the act. Consequently, non-determinism and uncertainty in the quantum area have a principle.

As we see, the methodological structure of "orthodox" quantum theory resembles the phenomenological method used by Husserl. Moreover, we think that Bohr unconsciously used the phenomenological method when interpreting quantum theory. Used in various fields of human activity, phenomenology presents a strong basis for contemporary thinking and shows that consciousness, as a motion of existence (as an act of attachment of meaning) is the factor giving form to objective reality.

QUANTUM PHENOMENOLOGY AND POLYPHONY IN FICTION

Husserl's phenomenology has greatly influenced different spheres of contemporary thinking. This new viewpoint established the polyphonic style of thinking in philosophy, science, and art. Our objective is to investigate such a way of thinking, particularly in literary works. However, it is advisable to use several components of Bohr's conception of quantum theory besides the phenomenological method for, despite the crucial difference, the same effects of the phenomenological approach have occurred in both the above-mentioned spheres. Thus, the aim of our investigation is to use a phenomenological approach and Bohr's quantum conception to explain the polyphonic style of literary works. Besides Joyce and Proust, we consider Dostoevsky's novels and intend to research William Faulkner's works. These great writers, in our opinion, developed polyphonic prose in modern literature.

We assert that the occurrence of analogy between Bohr's conception and the "polyphonic style" in literature was not coincidental, for this analogy had a philosophical ground; i.e., both areas use the same phenomenological approach: one deals with the construction of the object of science, and other with the creation of an artistic form. The phenomenological approach shows that the reflection of the premise of mind anticipates the reflection of objects and events of the cognizable world. The premise of mind includes the possibility of knowledge, i.e., the possibility of correspondence between external things and the nature of thinking. According to it, a physical object should be considered as integral to the conditions of cognition, which determine the possibility of such a correspondence. Therefore, a physical object, taken in this integrity, is unique since it is determined by irreversibly changing consciousness.

Bohr's understanding of quantum theory meets this phenomenological requirement. The famous scholar emphasized an indivisible coexistence of subject and object when speaking about the impossibility of considering the atomic object apart from its measurement conditions. Consequently, we observe the subject's penetration into the quantum area, as it is distinct from classical physics. Therefore, the description of the atomic world disintegrates into two independent (wave-particle) parts; we obtain polyphonic pictures of physical events instead of a single, integrated form. When moving from one picture to the other, subjective conditions irreversibly change without having a common integrating ground. The subject takes part in the construction of the quantum object, not as a transparent, immaterial mirror, reflecting the atomic world, but as a special form of existence which gives quantum particles physical meaning. The subject's consciousness is regarded as a vital essence, but not as an absolute, all-powerful mind – the determining basis of classical physics.

Now, let us trace a link between the construction of the physical picture and forms of fiction. When the author substitutes the scientific subject, two different forms of the subject-object relation arise. If a literary work presupposes the author as an omnipotent subject, it means that the author controls and fully determines his work, solving every conflict within it. Here the author acts as a narrator who knows everything about the story, and tells the facts as if they had happened in reality. Therefore, such an impartial author is beyond the story and his work acquires an objective form of reflection of the actual events. We denote such literary works "single base forms." The subject-object relation resembles the picture of classical physics, where physical objects and interactions are given in the objective form of being, as if they were independent from the subjective conditions determining the physical objects. These conditions are considered beyond the physical picture.

Unlike classical physics, the quantum picture is constructed according to the phenomenological method. That is why the mind participates as a subjective existence here. We have, instead of a physical object, the concept of quantum phenomenon, which is an indivisible result of the subject-object interaction. If a writer is in a position to apply the phenomenological method to fiction, a situation similar to that in the quantum sphere arises. The phenomenological approach considers a literary work as a phenomenon, which implies that the process of its creation is in itself. This work involves the author's stream of consciousness. The author, neither personally, nor objectively, but through a subjective process of creation, penetrates into the story, and the works loses its strictly objective form. The author does not intend to present facts as if they have really taken place. All this results in the impression that a real stream of the author's consciousness runs through his creation, causing the deletion of borders between the characters and the author.

Thus, once entering his creation, the author destroys its objective form and the work acquires the conditional nature of invention. Strictly speaking, the story shows itself in an undetermined area, lying between the forms of reality and invention, for no act of objectification takes place with regard to the external world or in the inner world of the author. On the whole, the subject's penetration implies a loss of certainty and clarity concerning the objective content of a fiction. Absurdity and uncertainty become features of artistic reality as it is in the case with quantum reality. Absurdity reflects not a chaotic state of the external world, but the uncertainty of our consciousness. Thus, the subject's penetration disassembles the single-base form of fiction into mutually independent parts of which exhibit the polyphonic structure of creation where the author's single consistent position is never revealed. The creator neglects the verisimilitude of the story, or, using phenomenological language, takes its objectivity in brackets, and a literary work, instead of reflecting the "real facts," shows itself as a phenomenon of consciousness in its existential dimension.

Before considering individual writers, we would like to explain once more how we understand the author's penetration into his novel. As for prose, a phenomenologist should raise the issue of correspondence between reality and invention. When bringing up the correspondence issue, he, at the same time, puts forth questions about the limits of such a relationship and assumes the possibility of non-correspondence between art and reality beyond these limits. Finally, the phenomenologist evaluates creative work as being independent of the external world.

But such an evaluation is somewhat dangerous. While freeing itself from the external reality, the work of fiction may find itself in a field of the author's psycho-emotional gravity. The existence of creative work as an independent phenomenon indicates its "non-inclination," – it is inclined neither towards the external objects nor towards the author's subjective world. Therefore, the writer has created the area of uncertainty and unclarity within his story to maintain the middle, independent position of his work between the external world and the psychological subject. This concept refers to subject-object phenomenological integrity, for, due to the uncertainty, there is no distinct border between the subject and the object, between the author and the object of his imagination. This is what an author's subtle penetration into the fiction implies.

Now, to illustrate our conception, consider Dostoevsky's novels (*The Devils*, first of all). The writer creates the impression that he knows no more about his story than the characters do. The author's voice is one of the voices among others. Denying the omnipotent author, absorbing him as one of the voices, the work seems to be "hanging in the air". Therefore, the dispute among the voices is endless; it may be interrupted, but not completed, for there is no common position to resolve the conflicts. This fact shapes the polyphonic structure of such novels, and these literary works acquire the character of an independent artistic phenomenon.

The same effect of author's penetration can be found in Joyce's prose. There is no distinct border among the characters in *Ulysses*. One character sometimes speaks as another, the voice of whom intermixes with the voices of the others and so on. It seems that Joyce has adopted a phenomenological approach. The stream of the author's consciousness seems to penetrate his work. Because of this penetration, the writer manages to move in a subtle way from one character to another, and by doing so he gives his works a conditional nature of invention.

The subject's penetration into the story was a main principle used by Marcel Proust. The author, for him, is a sequence of mutually independent selves. Memory cannot reach the past, for it (i.e., the past) existed with the unique, irreversible self, which is lost forever. Because of the loss of self, we cannot reproduce past events. We are only able to give the meaning of the past to our present *state*. Thus, the writer does not imply that there is a common ground of consciousness beyond the novel, which determines a mutually independent and irreducible nature of selves.

Further development of this hypothesis would benefit from intensive research into William Faulkner's works, as the polyphonic style seems to be the main principle of his creative activity. We focus on the following question: how is the polyphonic style connected with the stream-of-consciousness in Faulkner's novels (*As I Lay Dying* and *The Sound and the Fury*)? Our analysis shows that both the polyphonic style and stream-of-consciousness are based on *one and the same* ground, i.e. the non-existence of an absolute, omnipotent author and the author's penetration into the novel. As a result, the writer creates a work which seems to move and develop spontaneously and independently of the author. Despite the difference between Joyce and Faulkner (the first used stream-of-consciousness as a formal structure, whereas the latter achieved the effect of verisimilitude of consciousness), both considered stream-of-consciousness as a primary and independent phenomenon of being in itself. Instead of stating determining roles of external reality, Faulkner assumed the existence of a correlation between the world and consciousness. Such an understanding implies dualism, which eventually results in polyphony since consciousness and the external world are represented as mutually independent parts of being.

Had stream-of-consciousness been based on the external world, no polyphony would have existed. Only the assumption of the independence of stream-of-consciousness from the external world makes it possible to explain the polyphonic style of Faulkner's prose. Stream-of-consciousness acquires the features of external being, since the writer aspires to comprehend consciousness not on the reflective level, but through its ontological ground, as a stream of being. Faulkner's stream-of-consciousness is a stream of being in itself, which implies a correlation between consciousness and the external world.

Finally, let us make explicit and clear the analogy between "orthodox" quantum theory and the polyphony of modern fiction:

1a. The picture of classical physics appeals to the external position of the omniscient subject; classical concepts are determined though the level of absolute knowledge. Therefore, as there is a common ground of determination, classical physics presents monologue-like, completely determined pictures. This picture excludes the subject and has an objective form of description, as if classical events were independent of the subject.

1b. The single-based form of fiction appeals to the external position of the omniscient author. The author creates a common ground of determination and thus resolves every conflict within the story. Artistic reality has an objective form of expression, as if artistic events were independent from the author and took place objectively. Here the author acts as a narrator who retells the story as if it happened in reality.

2a. The picture of quantum physics destroys the external position of the "omniscient" subject. The subject, as a special form of existence, as a stream-of-consciousness, penetrates into the picture of quantum reality, and destroys the objective, singular base of the expression of physical events. Introducing the polyphonic forms (wave-particle dualism), the subject creates an area of uncertainty, the area of subject-object indivisible wholeness, where no distinct border between subject and object appears.

2b. The polyphony of modern fiction destroys the external position of the "omniscient" author. The author, as a special form of existence, as a stream-of-consciousness, penetrates into the story, which loses its objective form of the expression of artistic events. To maintain the middle position between the external world and the author's psychological sphere, the author creates an area of uncertainty within the story, where no distinct border between the hero and author exists.

Thus, the analogy between quantum theory and the polyphony of fiction is not coincidental, for it has a philosophical ground: both areas use the same phenomenological method. One deals with the construction of the object of science and the other with the creation of artistic form.

As we see, in modern science as well as in modern literature, similar forms of polyphonic thinking exist, which reject the "omniscient" subject as a common ground of determination and are based on the phenomenological principle of subject-object integrity.

Institute of Philosophy
Georgian Academy of sciences
Tbilisi, Georgia

ON H.-G. GADAMER'S *TRUTH AND METHOD*: THE HERMENEUTICS OF INTERPERSONAL COMMUNICATION

IRINA BOLDONOVA

In this paper, I suggest several theoretical points concerning the hermeneutics of interpersonal communication, based on my reading and analysis of Hans-Georg Gadamer's philosophical hermeneutics. I apply the hermeneutical categories of Gadamer's theory of understanding to research in interpersonal communication. Traditionally interpretive research focuses on Gadamer's ideas taken from more than one book, but here I would like to concentrate on the theoretical and practical value of his main work, *Truth and Method*. There are a great number of contemporary inquiries into the field of interpersonal communication, including the study of communication theory in American thought.

Among the large number of theories based on hermeneutics and applied to the analysis of interpersonal communication, those of S. Deetz are of particular interest.[1] Deetz criticizes the general tendency in the study of interpersonal communication to privilege psychological orientation. Interpersonal communication studies should reflect specific characteristics of oral discourse, such as the physical presence of partners and their ability to engage in argument. Oral interaction allows partners the chance to express themselves and to reveal the modality of meaning. According to Deetz, Gadamer does not describe the advantages of oral interpersonal communication, which are absent in all the other forms of communication. Deetz expresses the important idea that understanding interpersonal interaction provides an understanding of interpretation – in all its forms.

T.M. Seebohm distinguishes understanding, misunderstanding and non-understanding in oral and written discourse.[2] Written discourse has its own specific structure; contemporary hermeneutics shows the difference between oral and written communication, given the different ways in which understanding is reached. At the center of K.W. White's inquiry is a concentration on the problem of interpersonal understanding.[3] By offering

---

[1] See S. Deetz, "Hermeneutics and Communication," *Interpersonal Communication: Essays in Phenomenology and Hermeneutics*, J.J. Pilotta (ed.) (Washington, DC: University Press of America, 1982).

[2] See T. M. Seebohm, "Phenomenology of Writing" in *Interpersonal Communication: Essays in Phenomenology and Hermeneutics*.

[3] See K. W. White, "Hans-Georg Gadamer's Philosophy of Language: A Constitutive-Dialogue Approach to Interpersonal Understanding," *Interpretive*

to address Gadamer's theory, he illustrates how particular constructs of Gadamer's work can provide a means for articulating the process of human understanding.

In order to understand Gadamer's contribution to the study of interpersonal understanding, one must realize that understanding is communicative. In his paper, White describes the categories and elements of Gadamer's conversational framework. Gadamer's personal approach is developed through the concept of play, the structure of question and answer, the concept of prejudice, 'historically effected' consciousness, the centrality of the subject matter, and the fusion of horizons. White suggests Gadamerian postulates of interpersonal understanding as relevant to this research. According to White, a conversation is a primary event of human understanding: he regards interpersonal understanding as a dialogical, dialectical, and transformational process.

The object of philosophical hermeneutics is no longer a text, as it has traditionally been in the history of its development. The sphere of research is now extended to structures of society and social relationships. The structures are mainly based on communication processes. Very often interpersonal dialogue, as a means for establishing personal contacts and trustworthy relations, plays an important role in society. If interlocutors in a certain conversation use a hermeneutical model, they could reach much more understanding. Hermeneutics provides attentive readers and skillful interlocutors with a method for revealing the experience of consciousness in communication.

The hermeneutic approach concentrates mostly on perception – i.e., on the receiver and the feedback he receives. Another focus of attention is the process of interaction itself, where exchange of meaning, social cognition, realization of purpose, and interpretation take place. Gadamer, in *Truth and Method*, analyzes fundamental conditions of understanding, and concentrates on the process of understanding between the author of a text and an interpreter. Taking into account the difference between oral interpersonal communication and textual interpersonal communication, we can find specific theoretical postulates for applying them in the study of oral interpersonal communication. In the process of a conversation, each person represents his self and his social and communicative role. There, those holding the conversation can express self-actualization as a mode of being within the process of a dialogue. The concept of play is closely connected with self-presentation – in other words, with a person's subjective view of himself and his observations of his image and identity. The self depends on the responses of the partner so that the self can be corrected; it cannot, however, overcome the shape of an individual's personality. The category of self-presentation is important at the beginning

---

Approaches to Interpersonal Communication, K. Carter and M. Presnell (eds.) (Albany, NY: State University of New York Press, 1994).

of a conversation, when the interlocutors express their social roles and their practical skills of performative competence.

If both of the partners have intentions to exchange messages and they want to play, they develop the conversation – until they wish to do something else. Gadamer describes it in the following way: "The structure of play absorbs the player into itself, and thus frees him from the burden of taking the initiative, which constitutes the actual strain of existence."[4] An interlocutor is involved in the game of communication; he moves from self-presentation to a further condition, only when the spirit of the game (its unique atmosphere) exists. Instead of there being interlocutors, there is only what they are playing and saying – the conversation as it is, without interlocutors. The conversation goes on and on because the partners obey the rules of the game. The concept of play helps one to visualize the very being of a communicative activity in the form of interpersonal interaction. As Gadamer says, "Play fulfills its purpose only if the player loses himself in the play."[5]

Self-actualization should, then, lead to self-disclosure, which presupposes the ability to reveal the inner motives, the likes and dislikes, and the deepest streams of the soul. If the self of a partner in dialogue really changes, it means that he is genuinely involved in the hermeneutical dialogue and has acquired the rules of hermeneutical activity and hermeneutical consciousness. From that moment, this interlocutor looks at himself and analyzes his self-concept and the way of understanding of his partner, taking into account the point-of-view of the other person. Opinion about another person appears in Gadamer's book under the term "A Thou"; an understanding of this sort is still a form of self-relatedness. It reveals the idea of the constant struggle for mutual recognition, and the complete domination of one person by the other.

As an opposed concept to "A Thou" in Gadamer's work, there is the experience of historically effected consciousness, which realizes knowledge about otherness. An interlocutor with a hermeneutical consciousness faces certain questions: "How does each person view this dialogue?" "What explanations do the participants provide to evaluate their own and each other's involvement and opinion?" "What does each participant do to understand the other(s) better?" Social cognition takes place, and a person classifies his partner and forms expectations based on his previous interactions with other members of the same social group. Experienced analysis is an important part of communication.

Gadamer's hermeneutics describes the whole system of categories generally related to the concept of historically effected consciousness. Whoever participates in the dialogue is absorbed by a tradition. Our perception of a partner is under the influence of past experience,

---

[4] H-G. Gadamer, *Truth and Method* (New York: Continuum, 2nd ed. 1989), p. 105.
[5] Gadamer, *Truth and Method*, p. 102.

background knowledge – and, particularly, historical and cultural tradition. These factors affect the way a conversation starts, goes on, and comes to a result. Gadamer presents a theory of hermeneutic experience and begins with the fore-structure of understanding. A person who is involved in a communicative process and possesses a hermeneutic consciousness tries to analyze fore-meanings, and false and true prejudices – 'prejudice' is used here in the sense of 'pre-judgement.' Gadamer writes:

> Long before we understand ourselves through the process of self-examination, we understand ourselves in a self-evident way in the family, society, and state in which we live. The focus of subjectivity is a distorting mirror. The self-awareness of the individual is only a flickering in the closed circuits of historical life. That is why the prejudices of the individual, far more than his judgments, constitute the historical reality of his being.[6]

The agreement concerning the subject matter refers the interlocutors to the process of anticipation of the whole. The concept of the hermeneutic circle provides the explanation of the circular movement of understanding, which runs from the parts of the conversation to the whole conversation, and back. In *Truth and Method*, the interlocutor calls the expectation of meaning a fore-conception of completeness; this solves the problem of the contradiction between something unknown and the familiar. "The task of hermeneutics is to clarify this miracle of understanding, which is not a mysterious communion of souls, but sharing in a common meaning."[7] The fore-conception of completeness anticipates our understanding. As far as interpersonal communication in the oral form is concerned, all the conditions of communication should be taken into consideration. These include voice, loudness, non-verbal signals, and so on. Moreover, every generation has to understand a transmitted text in its own way, and an interpreter understands the text better than the author himself. In oral interpersonal communication, a transmitted text (message) can be understood immediately, and there can be a response without the mediation of a historical distance. The true meaning of a written text is never finished – even at the point at which it might be analyzed – and temporal distance helps distinguish false prejudices from positive ones.

The one great horizon is a single historical horizon; it envelopes heritage and tradition. Thus, we place ourselves in the interlocutor's position when we wish to evaluate the other person. The concept of horizon gives us the opportunity to go beyond our false prejudices and our subjective points of view, and to look at the situation from another angle.

---

[6] Gadamer, *Truth and Method*, pp. 276-277.
[7] Gadamer, *Truth and Method*, p. 292.

Gadamer emphasizes thus: "When a question arises it breaks open the being of the object, as it were."[8] This is how a conversation starts, and interlocutors become involved in it. Nobody knows how the conversation will go on, nobody can plan the exact scheme of the future dialogue and determine the details and possible directions. It is like an event which has its own spirit, bringing the conversational partners to the very depth of it.

Gadamer emphasizes the priority of the question to all knowledge. In interpersonal communication, the answer of the receiver contains another possible question. And the answer is also knowledge. A particular lack of knowledge leads to a particular question. When an idea occurs in somebody's mind, it produces a certain question and a message. The concept of the question is closely connected with the skill of verbal competence, because questions can be asked rightly or wrongly. The ability to formulate a question that will "open-up being" means one must be devoted to hermeneutical experience and be responsible for the perspectives and results of the conversation.

A good question is often a good starting point. Not all questions can be used as a way to start a conversation. The best conversational question is always open-ended, making contacts and activating the mind. Interesting questions make the interlocutor think of something in detail and express it in more than two or three sentences. A good conversation goes on successively from one set of questions and answers to another, from one topic to another. Each new question contains yet another question. To conduct a real dialogue means that knowledge should be shared and the purpose should be reached. "What characterizes a dialogue, in contrast with the rigid form of statements that demand to be set down in writing, is precisely this: answer, giving and taking, talking at cross purposes and seeing with respect to the written tradition, is the task of hermeneutics."[9] Gadamer analyzes conversation through dialectically working out the common meaning. Taken separately, statements do not give the possibility of developing the unity of a dialogue. The attitude of both partners to the subject matter and their desire to share the meaning provides the inner logic of the conversation. The concept of the question can be considered as a primary ground of the phenomenon of communication.

In hermeneutics, language is considered not as a tool, but as a universal medium in which understanding occurs. "The whole process is verbal."[10] Gadamer writes about the main function of language: to get to know the unknown. Language is an important medium for getting information and for message exchange. It allows us to interpret the information we receive from our interlocutors. Language is self-reflexive and it fulfills a meta-communicative function. This means that language gives us the possibility of expressing our attitudes towards what we had

---

[8] Gadamer, *Truth and Method*, p. 356
[9] Gadamer, *Truth and Method*, p. 368.
[10] Gadamer, *Truth and Method*, p. 383.

learned; through language an attentive interlocutor can understand himself, the world around him, and the spiritual traditions of humanity.

There are differences between the language of a written text and the language of interpersonal oral communication. The hierarchy is *word – sentence – speech* act in interpersonal communication, and here language is colloquial. In everyday speech, phrases are short and very often incomplete or reduced. We can speak of a chain (*written text – interpretation – understanding*), as analyzed in traditional hermeneutics; applying its principles to the study of oral discourse, we could speak of *verbal expressions (speech acts) – interpretation (if there is any) – understanding – feedback*. Gadamer writes:

> Certainly, in relation to language, writing seems a secondary phenomenon. The sign language of writing refers to the actual language of speech. But that language is capable of being written is by no means incidental to its nature. Rather, this capacity for being written down is based on the fact that speech itself shares in the pure ideality of the meaning that communicates itself in it. In writing the meaning of what is spoken exists purely for itself, completely detached from all emotional elements of expression and communication. A text is not to be understood as an expression of life with respect to what it says. Writing is the abstract ideality of language.[11]

In oral speech, language expresses meaning, it speaks itself and, in speaking, a person can use voice quality, intonation, loudness or non-verbal signals for revealing the idea. Meaning is not repeated (except in some occasional cases), but is shaped in real sounds, words that are alive, facial expressions, different tones of voice, etc. Meaning is produced in a special context under particular circumstances.

There are two possible directions in what is said: the infinity of what is actually said, and the infinity of what is not said. Speech is always full of equivocations, hints, and pauses. The context hides what has not been said, but gives prompts for understanding. Here another problem is bound to arise: the problem of interpretation.

In a situation when two people come together – when they are in direct face-to-face contact – the way interpretation is realized differs from the way in which Gadamer applies it to literary texts. The first aspect of this problem is the fact that, in direct interpersonal communication, interpretation may or may not exist; interlocutors can absolutely understand each other. If they realize the importance of verbal and interpretive competence, they do not need the special participation of an interpreter.

---

[11] Gadamer, *Truth and Method*, p. 392.

The second aspect of the same problem is seen when someone who repeats his statement, changes the meaning of what is said; this can be considered as a type of personal interpretation. Gadamer sees it as "an element of speculative reflection" or "still the purest reproduction of meaning."[12] In this case, the interlocutor tries to interpret his own words, to make it easier for his partner to understand the meaning. Poetic words and words with additional special connotations require a special attitude: if there are any in the speech, the hermeneutical experience takes place. Interlocutors should be prepared to listen to each other with great care and interest. Direct answers and questions, the active participation of interlocutors, and immediate feedback make the movement of the conversation possible. 'Intentionality of the partners' refers to the desire to speak in the proper way and to follow the logic of questioning and answering; this develops the ongoing process. A word's own physical being exists only in order to disappear in what is said.

The third aspect of the interpretation problem occurs when people speak different languages. In such a case, they need an interpreter for translation, and this interpreter is at the same time a mediator. Gadamer writes:

> Every conversation obviously presupposes that the two speakers speak the same language. Only when two people can make themselves understood through language by talking together can the problem of understanding and agreement even be raised. Having to depend on an interpreter's translation is an extreme case that doubles the hermeneutical process, namely the conversation: there is one conversation between the interpreter and the other, and a second between the interpreter and oneself.[13]

A hermeneutic problem is connected with the problem of proper and adequate translation from one language to another, revealing the proper sense, and thus making meaning accessible.

Traditionally, interpretation involves something written, but in interpersonal communication interpretation exists in oral form. In written communication, texts don't speak themselves; words and sentences do not express ideas unless a reader or an interpreter starts reading. The interpreter is the mediator through whose help texts speak to an audience. Understanding in interpersonal communication requires a complete involvement in a common subject matter. When a conversation is being translated by an interpreter, he should have a consciousness of hermeneutics and participate in the creation of meaning.

---

[12] Gadamer, *Truth and Method*, p. 465.
[13] Gadamer, *Truth and Method*, p. 385.

Communication and understanding are realized when the interlocutors achieve "commonality." Gadamer calls this phenomenon a "fusion of horizons," and describes this type of conversation as "hermeneutic conversation." The shared meaning is applied to the present situation. Another concept from Gadamer's hermeneutics can also serve in the study of interpersonal communication; this is "application." Application is connected with feedback in the form of verbal expressions or actions as a result of understanding. In interpersonal communication, interlocutors must have proper listening skills, interpretive competence, and the ability to give immediate feedback.

The hermeneutical experience adds some more responsibilities, according to which interlocutors reach a shared meaning.

These issues concerning the meaning of what is said and understood is apparent in our everyday practice. Interpretation is the result of message production, understanding is the achievement of interpretation, and application is the goal of understanding. Understanding is applying something universal to a particular situation, so if the knowledge taken as a result of communication is not applied, communication does not reach its goal. The activity of communication can be regarded as a realization of application. Application involves both partners, because it comes from their fusion of horizons and understanding.

There are different levels of knowledge perception within the concept of application. The initial level of application is the response itself as the direct reaction to the question. Feedback helps to regulate the message we send to one another. Then, the next level of application is the practical realization of the perceived knowledge: actions, a changed attitude, successful companionship, love, friendship, sympathy, shared feelings, and so on. There is yet another level of application where the problem of social applicability appears, and it is closely connected with social perception, social relationships, social environment and – what is most important – significance and sense of social activity. Important here is that meaning is not applied mechanically; it depends on social rules, regulations, people's intentions, and so on. But this is the theme of another research project.

Oral interpersonal communication differs from that of written textual communication. Traditionally, philosophical hermeneutics considered literary texts as its objects of primary reference. Hermeneutics originated first as a theory of understanding written texts. In the twentieth century, the field of hermeneutics was extended so that the discourse of our everyday speech became one of the successful spheres of the study.

Each interaction in the form of hermeneutic conversation makes another contribution to the improvement of human relationships. A hermeneutical approach emphasizes the creativity of both interlocutors-interpreters, and enhances the significance of verbal and interpretive competence. Hermeneutics not only treats interpersonal communication as a two-way, face-to-face interaction and exchange of meanings, but also provides an ontological status to the phenomenon of human communication as mankind's main activity.

The George Washington University
and
Department of Social Technologies
East-Siberian State Technological University
Ulan-Ude, Russia.

CHAPTER XL

CONTEMPORARY HERMENEUTICS AND INGARDEN'S AESTHETICS AS METHODOLOGICAL SUPPORTS FOR DIALOGUE AND COMMUNICATION

ZBIGNIEW WENDLAND

INGARDEN'S AND GADAMER'S CONTRIBUTIONS TO DIALOGUE AMONG PEOPLES AND CULTURES

The problem of dialogue and communication among peoples as individuals, social groups, nations, generations, and (in particular) cultures and civilizations, has become in contemporary times so important that philosophers, and all humanists, ought to pursue this issue wherever possible. Good allies in resolving this problem may be found in some contemporary philosophical currents like, for example, phenomenology, hermeneutics and postmodernism. The purpose of this article is to introduce and discuss two arguments for strengthening the need for dialogue and communication; these come from two currents of contemporary philosophy, namely, the hermeneutics developed by Hans-Georg Gadamer during approximately half of the twentieth century, and the phenomenological aesthetics created by the Polish philosopher Roman Ingarden. The concept of the aesthetic object and other views of Ingarden concerning aesthetic and artistic values or aesthetic experience can be regarded as a substantial contribution from philosophy to the main topic of this volume: "The Dialogue of Cultural Traditions: A Global Perspective." The same can be said about hermeneutic notions like understanding and interpretation, the concept of fusion of horizons, and other essential notions and concepts of contemporary hermeneutics, which are rightly called philosophical or post-phenomenological. Both orientations discussed in this paper have common roots in phenomenology, and both include some substantial similarities in approaches to their objects of interest and to their methods of argumentation.

Ingarden came to his opinions in the 1920s, after the period of his study under Husserl and during the time of further closed cooperation with him, while Gadamer developed his hermeneutics and confirmed its significance later under the long-lasting influence of Heidegger's fundamental ontology.

The orientations of Gadamer and Ingarden are complementary, and together they provide many theoretical concepts and methodological procedures; these can constitute essential supports for dialogue and communication by working out many detailed ideas for something that could be regarded as a philosophical methodology of dialogue and communication. The philosophical heritage of Ingarden has especially valuable potential for the dialogue and communication among, or across, cultures, while the main principles of hermeneutics can be fruitfully applied to dialogue and communication in a broader sense.

THE IMPORTANCE OF PHILOSOPHICAL HERMENEUTICS

Hermeneutics has a long history of its own, dating back to antiquity, but today it is most readily regarded, in accordance with the description of Paul Ricoeur as a "shoot on the tree of phenomenology" – despite the considerable contribution made to hermeneutics by philosophers who lived prior to the twentieth century and independently of thinkers who did not belong to the phenomenological tradition. Contemporary thinkers who are regarded as representatives of this philosophical orientation acknowledge that all reality resembles a written text, which requires that its meaning and truth be understood and interpreted as such. This is precisely what hermeneutics tries to do, by basing itself on the premise that the meaning or truth of every object is never given directly, nor do meaning and truth impose themselves with irrefutable obviousness. Capturing them calls for complicated, and time-consuming efforts of a cognitive-interpretative nature.

The initial assumption of hermeneutics is that it is impossible to grasp the meaning and truth of a text, speech, work of art, or reality itself in a way that does not involve a connection with some sort of subject. This assumption can be seen as the Kantian perspective adopted by hermeneutics; however it should be noted here that, in hermeneutic thinking, there are no traces of the Kantian and Husserlian transcendental subject. In any case, the cognitive or interpretative subject in hermeneutics always consists of individuals existing in a certain historical period, in a given cultural environment, and possessing some amount of fore-knowledge, prejudgments, anticipations as well as prejudices, superstitions, practical interests and existential problems. All this constitutes a sort of inescapable encumbrance, and thus the burdened subject of cognition or interpretation tries to become acquainted with its object, aiming to discover its truth or to determine its meaning.

Before Gadamer, Heidegger described the problem of understanding in reference to individuals who live in given historical and cultural conditions. He regarded this problem as one of the most important philosophical questions, which he presented in *Sein und Zeit* in the form of the analysis of Dasein. Heidegger believed that philosophical reflection should not be concerned with Being, but with the "being of Being," and the understanding of 'Being's being' is something which characterizes human existence in the most essential manner. Moreover, the "being of Being" is always an open question, a constant 'becoming,' and it is always the result of the human's active participation. When we speak about Heidegger's view, a key statement is the recognition that "man is the shepherd of Being" – that man permits "Being to be" and that the "being of Being" is the only object of his concern (i.e., he grants Being meaning and direction, grasps its truth, simultaneously helping its truth to take place). And when Heidegger proclaimed that the most essential ontological determinant of man's being was understanding of Being in general ("existence is only possible upon the basis of understanding of Being"[1]), then all this means that Heidegger's analytic of Dasein does pass over at certain moments into hermeneutics – something which was successfully continued by Gadamer.

The important elements which form the conditions for a hermeneutic understanding of written texts, works of art, or reality as a whole, include such components as means of expression, concepts, words, linguistic structures and rules of thought and speech, which possesses their own indelible significance, and their own permanent functions (thanks to which understanding and interpretation of objects are in an essential manner predetermined). Subsequently, the linguistic means make possible the expression of the obtained knowledge in a verbal display, because understanding and interpretation through verbal expression are the main tasks of hermeneutics. The outcome of all hermeneutical activities is a situation to which the contemporary hermeneutics draws attention – by claiming that truth and meaning, which are the targets of cognition and understanding, are achieved through historical process. We see an infinite number of revelations, many superimposed acts of cognition, fusions of different horizons, and assorted acts of understanding and linguistic interpretations. Thanks to an infinite input of collective effort, truth and meaning are realized in the course of inter-personal and inter-cultural communication.

The above position, contained in works of representatives of hermeneutics, is intended to legitimize the critique of cognitive absolutism and traditional objectivism (i.e., metaphysical stands which claim to recognize an absolute truth, historically invariable and in no way conditioned). One could reduce this interpretation to several statements, such as: Peoples of each epoch, or peoples of each culture, are the possessors of their own truths; Truth as a whole is always open and incomplete; No one can claim that his reasons are universally right, etc. This situation was summed up by Gadamer who in one of his studies expressed the laconic view that "statements which were simply true could not exist."[2] One of the reasons for this conclusion is that the truth of any particular statement always depends on the truthfulness of our holistic vision of the world in accordance with Hegel's dictum, "Das Ganze ist das

---

[1] M. Heidegger, *Kant a problem metafizyki* [*Kant and the Problem of Metaphysics*], Polish Edition, (Warszawa, 1989), p. 253.

[2] H. G. Gadamer, *Cóż to jest prawda?* [*What is Truth?*], in *Rozum, słowo, dzieje* [*Reason, Word, History*], Polish Edition (Warszawa, 1989), p. 253.

Wahre"[3] ("the whole is the truth"), and the idea that the truth of the whole
is a historical process, ongoing according to the principle of incessant
fusions of eternally new and different horizons. In other words, the truth of
the whole goes on successively and through many differently determined
points of view. Gadamer proclaimed the view that truths and
understandings of the reality come to light in the course of inter-human
communication, which has a linguistically, temporally, and historically
determined character. Men – who belong to different historic epochs and
different cultural formations and have different individual experiences,
needs, fancies, etc. – are involved in an ongoing dialogue of different
opinions, and points of view which, according to the very foundations of
hermeneutics, always have the character of prejudgments. Through
dialogue, dispute, and confrontation on the ground of manifold and
temporal views (which leads to understanding and interpretation of objects),
we get knowledge containing meaning and truth, which is at any given time
available to the participants of the dialogue. But this knowledge, accepted at
a moment, has only a temporal and non-ultimate character. Every bit of
knowledge is of something earlier, or is a kind of later fore-knowledge. It
can be replaced in the future.

THE HERMENEUTICAL CIRCLE

The dialectics of knowledge and fore-knowledge is something that
has much to do with the notion of the hermeneutical circle introduced by
Heidegger and further substantiated by Gadamer. The latter wrote: "Only
that which is laden with anticipations can be understood; we would never
understand anything we had to understand, if we were to stare at this as at
something non-understandable."[4] The hermeneutical circle – a circular
movement of understanding – always runs from an initial project of fore-
understanding to its revision, resulting in a more and more exact penetration
into the meaning and truth of any object. This process can repeat itself until
it becomes fixed as an ultimate truth of any phenomenon. Every
understanding and interpretation comes from initial notions (entrances and
approaches); in other words, there is some kind of fore-understanding of the
truth, which then passes into notions or understanding more adequate to an
object.

The graphic picture and the very essence of the movement of
understanding are circular; understanding repeatedly turns from the
interpreter to object. In his *opus vitae*, Gadamer presented the dialectics of
subjectivity and objectivity of the hermeneutic circle by means of the
example of fixing a meaning (understanding) of written text. We read:

---

[3] G. W. F. Hegel, *Fenomenologia ducha* [*Phenomenology of Spirit*],
Polish Edition, Vol. I (Warszawa, 1963), p. 28.
[4] Gadamer, *Rozum, słowo, dzieje* [*Reason, Word, History*], Polish Edition,
op. cit., p. 79.

He who wants to understand will not be able to do so through his initial opinion, as though it were fortuitously set above the problem; on the contrary, with stubborn consistency he may try to hear the tone of the text – until this tone is distinctly heard and destroys the apparent understanding. He who wants to understand any text is indeed ready to accept what the text has to tell him. That is why the hermeneutically educated consciousness must already, from above, be sensitive to the otherness of the text. Such sensibility, however, supposes neither material 'neutrality' nor, moreover, self-liquidation, but it contains the conscious adoption of own initial opinions and anticipations. It is necessary to be already inside one's own previousness so that a text may present itself in its own otherness, thereby allowing for the possibility that it gain material truth with respect to ('towards') one's initial opinion.[5]

The above cited statement shows the way from the preliminary subjective proposals of understanding to understandings which are more objective. To put it another way, as it was maintained earlier in the tradition of hermeneutics, we now see the way from the present to the past, and to the new present, which soon becomes a new past. Traditional representatives of hermeneutics developed the principles of hermeneutic understanding and interpretation in reference to the objects which came to us – who live in the present – from the past, e g., past writings, past laws, historic events, etc. Nowadays we can learn from Gadamer's approach to hermeneutics that the hermeneutic methodology can be applied to understanding and interpretation of all possible objects (the whole of reality), and not only of written documents, historic events, and objects existing in the past. This opinion is of great importance for theoreticians of dialogue and communication who want to see hermeneutic principles of understanding and interpretation as the philosophical methodology of dialogue and communication.

THE FUSION OF HORIZONS

Besides the hermeneutical circle, another very important component of Gadamer's hermeneutics (which, in the highest degree, gives contemporary hermeneutics the role of the philosophical methodology of dialogue and communication) is the notion and procedure or method (principle) of the fusion of horizons. A very distinctive element of contemporary hermeneutics is that it does *not* interpret the understanding as

---

[5] Gadamer, *Prawda i metoda* [*Truth and Method*], Polish Edition (Kraków, 1993), p. 259.

the restoration of the past (e.g., a once-established meaning or discovered truth). In this regard, an essential change of assumptions took place in present hermeneutics in contrast with the former hermeneutics (i.e., the hermeneutics of the nineteenth century). In so-called romantic hermeneutics, whose main representatives were Schleiermacher and Schlegel – and likewise within views announced by representatives of historical hermeneutics, e.g., by Ranke and Droysen – there was an obligatory stereotype that hermeneutics had an essential assumption that understanding consisted in a reconstruction of the original meaning or interpretation of texts or events; this included the reconstruction of psychological or historic contexts which were once worked out, interpreted, and understood. Such a conception of hermeneutics was tied to the idea that an interpreter was transported into the past, thereby overcoming the temporal distance between the present and the past; this was understood to take place through the simple exclusion of the present and of all lapse of time. The understanding had an exclusively reconstructive – not a constructive – character. Every chance of understanding and interpreting a past text or a historic event depended upon reaching the truth that had been discovered or the meaning that had been assigned; neither present nor future would have an influence on it.

In post-phenomenological hermeneutics, the relation between the past and the present looks quite different, as does the significance of the lapse of time for the process of understanding. According to representatives of contemporary hermeneutics, the art of understanding and interpretation cannot be described correctly by saying that it consists in the skill of transmission into foreign horizons that which necessarily belong to the past. This dissimilarity comes from the extremely strong emphasis (e.g. by Heidegger and Gadamer) on historicalness ('temporalization') of human existence, which leads to the recognition of the hermeneutical productiveness of the temporal distance. The temporal distance is no longer anything which must be overcome by jumping into the past. Contemporary hermeneutics acknowledges that the temporal distance belongs to creative circumstances of understanding. The temporal distance is the distance between two horizons: on one hand, the horizon of the past (of an object itself) in the frame of which something happened (e.g., when the historic event took place), and, on the other hand, the horizon of the present (of an interpreter) when any attempt of understanding and interpreting an object or event is undertaken. One of the most important features of contemporary hermeneutics is the point of view that every successful attempt at understanding and interpretation is undertaken, and – on the methodological level – should be undertaken, in accordance with the principle of the fusion of horizons.

The representatives of historical hermeneutics, including Dilthey in the twentieth century, accentuated the importance of two temporal horizons. We who are nowadays looking for effective methods of dialogue and communication could regard the principle of the fusion of horizons as more broadly applicable than that compared with historical hermeneutics; we could talk here about the fusion of many horizons (not two only), and move beyond exclusively temporal horizons, looking also at horizons which are determined by many simultaneously existing peoples or cultures.

Looking for an effective methodology of dialogue and communication, we can learn many useful concepts from the contemporary representatives of hermeneutics. The concept of the fusion of horizons, especially as worked out by Gadamer, is without a doubt one of the most valuable. From this concept one should draw a primary conclusion that, in order to understand or know any objective truth, many different horizons are needed, including those which have already emerged and those which will be emerging through future peoples, civilizations, cultures, nations, generations, individuals and so on. The many different horizons are indispensable and if we have them at our disposal, they constitute very fruitful conditions for the process of right understanding and the discovery of objective truth. Heidegger was of the opinion that "things like staying hidden" and that they should be uncovered by "use of force." Knowing the truth (*aletheia*) means, for Heidegger, seeing things in their 'non-secretiveness' ("non-concealedness") or bringing them to light from their "concealment."[6] Openness and non-secretiveness has its own "temporality" and "historicality." The process of knowing or understanding moves forward through dialogue and communication among peoples, civilizations, cultures and so on. It is in no case anything – as Hegel remarked – like a gunshot. The truth about the world comes to light little by little in the course of inter-human communication. The process of knowing and understanding in hermeneutical experience – realization through the fusion of different horizons – always means climbing to a higher generality, one which overcomes peculiarities of earlier existing horizons. As Gadamer wrote, "The process culminates always in a single interpretative horizon at a higher level, into which we step, and which steps together with us. During this march horizons change constantly."[7]

The argumentation concerning the fusion of horizons leads to some very important conclusions in relation to history as a science. From the perspective of contemporary hermeneutics one can say this about the science of history: it should be written continually anew, which means it must be written again and again, because in our interpretations of historical events we are constantly determined by our present. The meaning and any estimation of some concrete historic event is never constant, unique and binding for all times. The understanding and interpretation of that which did happen in a given place and at a given time are always variable and relative to the interpreter's context. Contrary to what the representatives of the 19th century school maintained, it is *not* true that historians always seek to answer the question of "how it really was" (see Leopold Ranke: "wie es

---

[6] Gadamer, *Rozum, słowo, dzieje* [*Reason, Word, History*], p. 38.
[7] Gadamer, *Prawda i metoda*, op. cit., pp. 288-289.

eigentlich gewesen sei").[8] Representatives of the present hermeneutics are of the opinion that to understand the past means to hear what it had to tell us as a truth, which would be our truth and not the truth of the past. There can never exist a single 'proper' interpretation of an event, nor can it exist as historically true in only one way. The historicity of events consists in many, constantly new acts of understanding and interpretation. Every understanding and interpretation is a product of the hermeneutical situation to which it belongs.

UNDERSTANDING, LANGUAGE AND COMMUNITY

The next important component of contemporary hermeneutics is the use of language in understanding and interpretation, which by necessity binds people's communities together. Every fusion of horizons in the above discussed broad meaning of the concept, and every act of hermeneutic understanding and interpretation involves some use of language in the forms of words, linguistic structures, discourse, conversation, speech, talk, etc. Understanding leads to interpretation, and interpretation is possible only in notions and, at the end, in words. Lingualness ('linguicity') is in general the essence of hermeneutic experience. We can read in *Truth and Method*: "The interpretative notion and language... is recognized as an inner moment of the structure of understanding and hence the problem of language, from its accidental and marginal position, passes over into the center of the philosophy."[9] Gadamer and Heidegger accentuated the inner connection between understanding and notions, which for Heidegger was further underpinned by his conviction that there had to be some kind of unity within notions and words, on the one hand, and beings in themselves on the other.[10]

A very important contribution to the theme of dialogue and communication is made when we learn from hermeneutics that every use of language leads to the creation of some kind of community, because when someone speaks or talks, he always speaks or talks to or with somebody else. Speaking or talking as such does not belong to the sphere of individuality, but to the sphere of community. Gadamer writes: "He who speaks with a language which is comprehensible to nobody does not speak

---

[8] L. Ranke, *Geschichte der romanischen und germanischen Völker von 1494 bis 1514, in Sämtliche Werke* (Leipzig, 1885), p. 8.

[9] Gadamer, *Prawda i metoda*, op. cit., p. 291.

[10] Many philosophers before Heidegger (e.g. Plato, Nicholas of Cusa, Descartes, Leibniz) did not regard notions and words as created signs, but rather, first of all, as mirrors (mimesis) of beings. Z. Wendland, "Zagadnienie czasu i rola języka w doświadczeniu hermeneutycznym" ["The Problem of Time and the Role of Language in the Hermeneutical Experience"] in *Edukacja Filozoficzna* [*Philosophical Education*], 32 (2001): 128-134.;

at all."[11] The reality of language consists in intellectually unifying me with you, me with other peoples. Language realizes itself in speaking and talking, connecting peoples with each other. Every incident of speech or talk creates some common language in which the co-partners come to some agreement, not forcing one standpoint onto the other. Agreement does not grow out of a monologue, but rather out of the transformation of co-partners into a kind of community in which nobody remains who he was at the beginning. In successful talking, co-partners are surrendered to the truth of things; they are connected through the bonds of a growing community. Gadamer emphasizes a very astounding feature of language: when I talk to someone, I need not confine myself to the conclusion that neither of us is fully right; I can watch how the truth comes gradually into light from what each of us has to say.[12] The nearer a talk or a conversation comes to the hermeneutical ideal, the less its course depends upon participants. In other words, a talk or a conversation never depends on how it is led by its participants; rather, one is involved in a talk or in a conversation in which no one has knowledge from above of what will come from the talk. Every talk or every conversation has its own spirit (inner logic) and leads to the discovering of its own truth which comes into existence. Moreover, every talk, conversation, and dialogue exhibits an inner infinity and substantive lack of an end. The course of linguistic events can in any moment be interrupted, as when the participants wish to come to a conclusion. Enough has been said, but the interruption is never ultimate, because the linguistic event could, at any free moment, be undertaken again and anew.[13]

All the issues heretofore connecting understanding, the hermeneutical circle, the fusion of horizons, and the use of language indicate how many useful and creative ideas one can obtain from contemporary philosophical hermeneutics which, we have seen, can be applied in the methodology of dialogue and communication. The phenomenological aesthetics of Ingarden are similarly rich in suggestions for our theme.

PHENOMENOLOGICAL AESTHETICS OF INGARDEN

Roman Ingarden (1893-1970) was Husserl's student and, later, one of the most outstanding Polish philosophers, recognized in many philosophical centers as an authority whose source was first of all, though not exclusively, the extraordinarily fruitful use of the phenomenological method in the sphere of aesthetics and theory of art. Ingarden was the founder of the phenomenological center in Krakow (at the Jagiellonian University), which continues to have a productive existence.

---

[11] Gadamer, *Rozum, słowo, dzieje*, op. cit., p. 59.
[12] Gadamer, *Rozum, słowo, dzieje*, op. cit., p. 51.
[13] Gadamer, *Rozum, słowo, dzieje*, op. cit., p. 60.

The phenomenological aesthetics of Ingarden was determined by the development of general Husserlian phenomenology and, in particular, by the application of the phenomenological method to the creation of many strong phenomenological bases in different concrete branches of science. Ingarden's aim became the creation of a single possible phenomenological ontology that would work for aesthetics and the theory of art. This phenomenological aesthetics and art-theory had to provide truth-knowledge about the very essences (*eidoi*) of aesthetic and artistic objects such as works of art, aesthetic experience, aesthetic subject matter, aesthetic value, and so on. The first major work of Ingarden was *Das literarische Kunstwerk*[14] (*On the Literary Artwork*) published in German in 1931; the second was *Der Streit um die Existenz der Welt*[15] (*The Dispute About the Existence of the World*), published in both Polish and German after the Second World War.

Ingarden acknowledged as indisputable that works of art are objects which owe their existence and properties to the elaboration of them in acts of consciousness. Works of art have an intentional character in the Husserlian sense, which means that every work of art was born in the consciousness of its creator as a certain 'something', on which the consciousness was directed in the act of artistic creation. From the point of view of general phenomenology, every consciousness was always a consciousness 'of something', and Husserl called this 'something' the 'intentional object'.

Ingarden's own contribution to phenomenology was the recognition that, although works of art, emerging as intentional objects, came into being in acts of creative consciousness, they existed beyond these acts and their creators in that they were built in a material substratum. Ingarden attended to the question of how printed sheets, painted canvases, worked plates of marble, and so on, became works of art: he answers that the causes were the intentions of the creators as transmitted to those material things, which were given shape and certain meanings. These were later "decoded" in many intentional acts of perception on the part of the receivers of the works of art.

Some of the Polish philosopher's writings might be understood as a considerable weakening of Husserl's absolutism and idealism. In discussions with his mentor Husserl, Ingarden expressed his own point of view on the issue of ontological and epistemological realism in a way that differed considerably from Husserl's attitude of transcendental idealism. For Husserl, the only kind of knowing subject, which played the most important role in cognitive relations, was the transcendental ego, which discovered in

---

[14] R. Ingarden, *Das literarische Kunstwerk. Eine Untersuchung aus dem Grenzgebiet der Ontologie, Logik und Literaturwissenschaft*, German Edition (Halle 1931).

[15] Ingarden, *Der Streit um die Existenz der Welt*, German Edition, Bd. 1 (Tübingen, 1964), Bd. 2 (Tübingen, 1965).

itself the so-called intentional objects. Contrary to this point of view, in Ingarden's opinion, was that sensible data originated from existing things as the real ground of every process of knowledge. On the basis of these data the transcendental consciousness passes through acts of eidetic intuition into the indirect watching of the very essences of things (*Wesenschau*). But even in the cases of objects which seemed to be in principle creations of consciousness (like an imagined hero of a literary novel, somebody's painted picture, or a scientific theory discovered by a researcher), all objects of this kind (creations of arts or of sciences) were not interpreted by Ingarden as exclusively creations of pure consciousness. The Polish philosopher considered these kinds of objects as 'derivatively' intentional (i.e., they had the sources and the causes of their being in acts of consciousness), but the necessary foundation for the existence and the basis for the inter-subjective identity of those objects was always specific physical beings such as physical books, pictured canvases, creations of technique, and so on.

The very achievement of Ingarden in matters of truth and meaning, which could be compared with the achievements of representatives of twentieth century hermeneutics like Heidegger and Gadamer, was his interpretation of the work of art as a creation by its author, though not limited to any defined end as expressed through its intended (deliberate) schematic; rather, it has no ultimate concretization. The significance of Ingarden's conception consists in the fact that many authors of works of art left 'empty' places in their artifacts: these schemata cause allow the life of a work of art to persist, and these gaps and schemata rely on perpetual, ever-new concretizations undertaken by new receivers. Thus every receiver of a work of art is simultaneously its co-creator, and there are always many possible new concretizations. A work of art constantly provokes its receivers to discover new meanings in it and to create new interpretations. A great work of art speaks to people of different times and to men shaped in and by different cultures; it offers many meanings and tells them many truths. Ingarden underlined that the work of literature after release (i.e., publishing) leads its own life; it lives in the experiences of receivers as long as its vocabulary retains the same sounds which it possessed in the moment of its arising, and (especially) as long as its words and sentences are comprehensible to future generations. The same is valid for other spheres of art which likewise live in the many concretizations of their receivers.

And so in the case of Ingarden's phenomenology of aesthetics, the existing work of art causes its permanent transformation into many aesthetic objects, and this status, as in the case of hermeneutical understanding and interpretation, involves peoples and cultures in continual dialogue and communication.

University of Life Sciences
Warsaw, Poland

PART IV

GLOBAL HORIZONS

CHAPTER XLI

NATIONAL AND ETHNIC CULTURES IN A GLOBALIZING WORLD

LEON DYCZEWSKI

GLOBALIZATION AND CULTURAL IDENTITY

The processes of globalization are most advanced in the areas of technology, economics,[1] and politics.[2] Indeed, many observers stress the fact that globalization creates communities of welfare and of security. But it is clear that the processes of globalization cannot be based on economics and politics alone. People must be related by more than a common market and political treaties. They must develop cultural bonds. Having a common culture connects people in a profound way. According to Jean Monnet, one of the architects of today's European Union, this is far more important than uniting countries, which is the task of political globalization. It is culture that contributes most to the economic development of particular countries as well as of the world. Likewise, culture has a decisive role in establishing peaceful co-operation between countries and individuals.[3]

A number of questions arise in connection with these statements: Has a global culture of Europe yet been formed? If so, what is it? What are its main characteristics? Does globalization of culture encourage or discourage forming a collective identity? Does progressing globalization bring about an annihilation of ethnic and national cultures? Will a global

---

[1] See U. Beck, *Was ist Globalisierung? Irrtümer des Globalismus, Antworten auf Globalisierung* (Frankfurt am Main: Suhrkamp, 1997) and U. Beck (ed.) *Politik der Globalisierung* (Frankfurt am Main: Suhrkamp, 1998); H. Berg (ed.), *Globalisierung der Wirtschaft: Ursachen – Formen – Konsequenzen.* Schriften des Vereins für Sozialpolitik NF 263 (Berlin: 1999); W. von Bülow et al., *Globalisierung und Wirtschaftspolitik* (Magdeburg: Metropolis Verlag, 1999); J. Frankel, "Globalization of the Economy," NBER Working Paper 7858 (Cambridge, MA: 2000); World Bank, *Economic Prospects and the Developing Countries 2002* (Washington, D.C.: World Bank, 2002).

[2] See Beck, *Was ist Globalisierung?* and *Politik der Globalisierung.* See also K. Hübner, *Der Globalisierungskomplex. Grenzenlose Ökonomie – grenzenlose Politik?* (Berlin: Edition Sigma, Rainer Bohn Verlag, 1998); W.H. Reinicke, *Global Public Policy. Governing without Government?* (Washington, DC: Brookings Institution Press, 1998).

[3] C.f. B. Axford, *The Global System Economics, Politics and Culture* (Cambridge: Polity, 1998).

village ultimately emerge, where everybody will think, dress and have fun in the same or similar ways?

Doubtless, a global European and worldwide culture is being formed.[4] Broadening the market, breaking down political borders, forming a common system of education and of law, and a rapid development of the media are conducive to this process. Media, like veins taking blood to various parts of an organism, spread certain values, ideas, patterns of behaviour, objects, and ways of thinking and of reacting throughout the world with exceptional speed. Also, the flow of information through the media makes it easier for people to see their options, and to shift their domiciles from one place to another.

The globalization of culture implies a relativization of values, norms and social memory. It implies uniformization, trivialization and commercialization of culture. It makes culture changeable and detaches it from the lived environment and from the human person. Global culture, which many people define as consumer culture or as "McDonaldization,"[5] "Cocacolization,"[6] or "McWorld",[7] does not make the personalities of the individuals who live within it more profound. They become empty inside and lonely; they expect only satisfaction of their worldly needs, surrendering to ever-changing fashions. These phenomena are perfectly illustrated by the following description of a middle-aged woman, an employee of a multinational trading company, who speaks five languages fluently and has three addresses in three cities quite distant from each other:

> She is continuously travelling, moving from one place to another, always 'between'... She travels alone and not as a member of a community, although she is always surrounded by people similar to her... The culture she participates in is not the culture of any place: it is the culture of time. It is the culture of the absolute present. Let's follow her in one of her ever-repeated voyages – from Singapore to Hong Kong, London, Stockholm, New Hampshire, Tokyo or Prague. In each of these cities she stays in the 'same' Hilton Hotel, at noon she eats the 'same' tuna sandwich, and if she feels like it, she will go

---

[4] See B. Wagner (ed.), *Kulturelle Globalisierung. Zwischen Weltkultur und Kultureller Fragmentierung* (Essen: Klartext, 2001).

[5] G. Ritzer, *Die McDonaldisierung der Gesellschaft (Originaltitel: The McDonaldisation of Society)* (Frankfurt am Main: Fischer, 1995).

[6] Zdravko Milnar, "Individuation and Globalization: The Transformation of Territorial Social Organization," in his *Globalization and Territorial Identities* (Aldershot: Avebury, 1992), pp. 15-34. at p. 21.

[7] B. Barber, *Coca-Cola und Heilige Krieg: wie Kapitalismus und Fundamentalismus Demokratie und Freiheit abschaffen (Originaltitel: Jihad vs. McWorld)* (Bern: Scherz, 1996).

to a Chinese restaurant in Paris or to a French one in Hong Kong. She will use a similar fax, telephone, computer, she will see similar films, discuss similar questions with similar people.

To the above description Agnes Heller adds:

"Even foreign universities are not foreign. After a lecture we can expect the same questions in Singapore, Tokyo, Paris or Manchester. These universities are not strange places; and they are not home either.[8]

Such a vision of the future is terrifying for many researchers – and also for politicians. If the processes of globalization proceed in such forms and at such a pace, before two or three generations pass the world will become boring and its only diversity will be a difference in where one lives. Hence researchers and politicians alike demand the existence of a variety of cultures in the world. They suggest that every region, every nation, and every ethnic group should cultivate its own cultural heritage and create its own culture. In letting go of globalization, then, Europe must be both united and varied. It must unite people living in their local cultures. According to this view, globalization should help to unite Europe, but at the same time preserve the different cultures, maintaining their richness and their inner dynamism of development. Justification of these two directions is based on the following premises:

a. Globalization makes the world uniform and at the same time pluralistic. It becomes pluralistic because, by facilitating communication among nations and ethnic groups, it shows their different values, cultural products and psycho-social states. Without globalization, the world would not know much about numerous ethnic groups and nations. It is precisely owing to globalization that even small local cultures are made known to the general public. They become more conspicuous and, one could say, universal.

b. Globalization significantly loosens the strong relationship between nation and state which has existed up to now; this process is taking place in most contemporary European states. In the conception of a united Europe, regions and ethnic groups are more strongly stressed than countries and nations. Europe is increasingly perceived as a union of regions, or, putting it in a different way, a federation of small homelands, and not of states. It becomes apparent that an ethnic group or a nation may exist even if it does not form a state. Sovereignty is based on culture and the legislation of the European Union.

---

[8] Z. Bauman, "Glokalizacja, czyli komu globalizacja, a komu lokalizacja (Glocalization, or who gets globalization, and who gets localization)," *Studia Socjologiczne* 3 (1997), p. 65.

c. Globalization brings centres closer to the peripheries, and vice versa. This is done first of all thanks to the development of the electronic media, tourism and emigration. The electronic media facilitate communication among, and promote familiarity with different ethnic and national groups. Tourism and immigration deepen this familiarity through direct contact. Nation-states that have been homogenous up to now have become multicultural as result of immigration. Germany is a good example here; in December 1999 of its 82.1 million inhabitants, 7.3 million people held foreign citizenship – i.e., 8.9% of the total population.[9]

d. Globalization loosens the relationship between individuals and their environment and introduces individuals into a wider world.

Globalization also has many hidden dangers, especially for the weak. This is because, in the globalization process, strong nations and countries dominate by means of their political conceptions, their products and services, and their cultures. The products and services of rich countries flood the markets of poor countries. And economic domination is soon followed by cultural domination. In recent years, English has passed from markets and economic transactions to universities and scientific conferences. In the modern world it is becoming the *lingua franca*. American pop culture clearly dominates television, film and the internet; thus, American values, norms and behaviour patterns are becoming omnipresent. Experts from the West are swarming the Eastern countries, and most of them do not even go out of the luxury hotels in the capital cities: hence, for example, their popular Polish name, "the Marriott brigades." They teach people in Poland how to do business, how to win elections in a democratic society, how to do research, how to command the army, and even how to spy – everything, according to the patterns of Western culture. Their 'instructions' go so far as to dictate what Poles should wear and how they should eat.[10] These experts who control the globalization process in Poland are aiming at wiping out the characteristics of Polish culture. They want to form a citizen society in Poland that would not have any specific cultural characteristics.

However, if someone believes that the process of globalization is going to erase nations, ethnic groups or local communities, he is making a mistake. The more the globalization process is intensified, becomes universal and includes more domains, the stronger the tendencies become in great and small nations to maintain their own identity; defence mechanisms reflecting a group's sense of cultural identity are quickly triggered.

---

[9] *Statistisches Jahrbuch 2001* (Wiesbaden: Statistisches Bundesamt, 2002), pp. 58, 65.

[10] M. Buchowski, "Tożsamość Europejczyków: jedność i podziały (Europeans' Identity: Unity and Divisions)" in *Dylematy tożsamości europejskich pod koniec drugiego tysiąclecia (Dilemmas of European Identities at the End of the Second Millennium)*, eds. J. Mucha and W. Olszewski (Toruń: 1997), pp. 69-70.

Admittedly, while this is relatively easy for strong and great nations, weaker and smaller nations or ethnic groups have to make serious efforts to maintain their cultural identity and develop it. Still, they gain from this process by the fact that particular members of the group realise their cultural identity more fully. Globalization leads some people towards cosmopolitanism, and some towards a more conscious cultural identity.[11]

VARIETY OF CULTURES AS A FACTOR IN INDIVIDUAL DEVELOPMENT

Many empirical studies support the statement that the multiplicity of cultures is an expression of human creativity and is humanity's great wealth. If not for that variety, the world would be monotonous and boring. If we went by train from Madrid to Vladivostok, and during this long journey heard the same language, the same music, saw the same houses and gardens, ate identical foods prepared in the same way, and saw people wearing the same clothes, our knowledge and our experiences would not be enriched, our imagination would not be excited, and the journey itself would drag on and would be terribly tiring. We already have an inkling of this when we look at modern residential areas built in the same manner, when we do our shopping in super-markets arranged in the same way, when in modern big cities we walk along the same kind of commercial-entertainment route from the railway station to the centre of the city. In these places, and in other ones similar to them, we soon feel bored and conclude that everything looks the same, follows the established pattern, and is trivial and trashy; there is nothing to see and nothing to buy, although there is a lot of everything.

We do not want to accept a uniformity of cultures, and we like cultural variety because it is in this variety that the potential of human nature as well as creativity of particular peoples and whole communities is manifested. Learning about different cultures and experiencing them are important factors in the development of our personality. This helps us to realise and experience our cultural identity, to evaluate it, and to be united with it still more closely.

By coming into contact with groups that are culturally different, individuals are made to learn different values, norms, behaviour patterns, objects, and then to continuously make choices. This encourages several things: learning to live together with different people and forming the attitude of tolerance for "the others" or "the different"; forming the ability to join various elements into new wholes and to keep order in variety; shaping the ability to oppose uniform tastes and to surpass mediocrity. Ultimately individuals become more creative.

---

[11] See J. Friedman, *Cultural Identity and Global Process* (London, Thousand Oaks, New Delhi: SAGE Publications, 1994).

In coming into contact with other cultures, individuals have a good chance to build their personhood. Encountering various values, different ways of perceiving reality, different customs and products, they continuously learn, evaluate and choose something new – in this way, attaining a peculiar kind of independence from the environment they live in. Also, with respect to the social-cultural groups they belong to, they remain to a large degree autonomous. No group owns them completely, and they are not just an element of the group; they remain free members of the group and may stay in it or leave it. They are externally independent and internally free. It can be said, then, that the multiplicity of cultures is an important factor in the development of both an individual's cognitive and volitive properties, which favours strengthening and experiencing his or her autonomy; at the same time, this gives them a chance to consciously deepen their own cultural identity and personal dignity.

Seeing the various advantages of the multiplicity of cultures to the personality development of members of social-cultural groups and, in this way, acknowledging its great value, one cannot treat this multiplicity as an absolute or autotelic value. With respect to individuals and society, it always remains an instrumental value (i.e., it should be cultivated and conditions should be created for its development), but its final aim should be the development of the whole society and all its members, as well as of the groups that exist in it. However, it should not be apotheosised and not all social life should be submitted to it. In a particular society, it either exists or does not and, according to this fact, legislation and internal policies should be created.

MULTIPLICITY OF CULTURES AS A FACTOR IN CULTURAL DEVELOPMENT OF PARTICULAR SOCIETIES

Multiplicity of cultures is an important factor in the development of the social culture (in the broadest sense of 'social') of particular societies. This is clearly seen when a society, for political reasons, is separated from other cultures, or its contacts with other cultures are drastically limited or selectively regulated. In as little as one generation, lack of contact with other cultures results in slowing down the pace of development of a society's culture. China is a perfect example of this process. Chinese culture, one of the oldest and richest cultures in the world, lost the dynamism of its development when, after establishing the People's Republic of China in 1949, it was radically cut off from other cultures. After World War II, societies of Central Europe experienced a similar process – although the situation was much softer than in the case of China – when, within two generations, the Hungarian, Polish, Slovakian, and Czech Christian cultures were forced to join the newly-formed Soviet culture; at the same time, these cultures were separated from the cultures of Western societies. Today the situation is completely reversed; we are witnessing societies of Central Europe voluntarily turning to the West. This too is disadvantageous for the cultures of these societies; Western and Eastern cultures should intersect, as they have done historically.

The culture of any society, when it is left to itself or remains in contact with one type of culture only, loses dynamism and versatility in its development. The versatile development of any society requires contacts with many cultures because no culture develops purely autonomously. Having analysed this phenomenon with respect to the example of American (and other) cultures, Ralph Linton thinks that, "At present there is no culture which owes more than 10% of all its elements to the inventions made by members of its own society."[12] Thus, much of the culture that we call our own has borrowed from other cultures, transforming and adopting them as our own cultural centre.

We need not embark upon a discussion of the correctness of Linton's estimates, for it remains an undeniable fact that many elements of cultures, generally considered as one's "own," come from other cultures. Every society oscillates between two tendencies: keeping together and doing everything after its own fashion, on the one hand, and following others, on the other. These two tendencies have to be kept in balance, in a proportional dynamism. If the first tendency dominates too heavily, the society loses the dynamism of its development; if the latter dominates, the native culture grows weaker.

The uniting of Europe cannot be a process of levelling cultural differences. Unity does not mean uniformity. If this were to happen, Europe would become a dull and boring assemblage of some 800 million people who think in an identical way, have the same aims, live the same lives and, what is worse, would be permeated by "Americanism" or "Japanism" as conveyed through satellite television. A multiplicity of cultures is appropriate to Europe's culture, and to the federal character of the future Europe.

The unity of Europe postulates the acceptance by all Europeans of the same fundamental values, norms, and ideas, and a common vision of the future, which is manifested in enacting common law and creating a common currency and a common educational system; beyond this, it assumes there will be a variety of situations and forms of its realisation. It also assumes the existence of different ways and means of satisfying fundamental needs, laws, beliefs, customs, events, experiences, impressions and desires. Moreover, ever-larger groups of people come to Europe with completely different cultures. In the united Europe, the multiplicity of cultures is a sign of spiritual wealth and is a lasting factor in the development of particular cultures as well as that of the European.

At the same time, the federal system at which Europe aims assumes the existence of various nations and states with their own cultures.

---

[12] R. Linton, "Dyfuzja [Diffusion]" in *Elementy teorii socjologicznych. Materiały do dziejów współczesnej socjologii zachodniej*, ed. and selected by W. Derczyński, A. Jasińska-Kania, J. Szacki (Warszawa: 1975).

These nations and states have the right to further shape their cultures, as the cultures secure their cohesion, identity, lasting existence and development. Without culture, they would be like grains of sand, not tied to anything, and which could be taken from one place to another without any real change in them. This cannot be done to members of a nation, however, without risking disintegration.

The 'Nation' is an especially important group that creates culture. The connection between culture and nation was strongly stressed by the World Conference on Cultural Policies in Mexico; a nation may show its existence in the world only by its culture.[13]

The history of many nations proves that they survived only thanks to their culture, even though they did not have their own states, and were severely oppressed or decimated or even exterminated by foreign powers. Jews, the Irish, Poles, Serbs, and Croats are examples here. Culture is the foundation of the existence and expression of the nation. The right of every nation and of every ethnic group to have its own culture is the same fundamental right as an individual's right to live and develop. This is why sovereignty of culture should be guaranteed to every ethnic group and to every nation, as it is in culture that their members express their perceptions of themselves and the world, their experiences and talents, strivings and aspirations, and also their inner bonds.

Thus, it is in the individual, social, national, and international interest that a variety of cultures should exist, both on the international scale and within the same state community.

MULTIPLICITY OF CULTURES ON AN INTER-STATE SCALE

Stressing the sovereignty of culture of every ethnic group and of every nation in Europe is not a manifestation of separatism or nationalism, but shows an understanding of the essence of cultural wealth, because "all cultures form part of the common heritage of mankind."[14] Everything should be done so that no culture loses its heritage. In order to make sure that sovereignty and development are guaranteed, many principles should be adhered to. Here are some of them:

a. We must reject the division of cultures into superior and inferior, developed and undeveloped, rich and poor. In the consciousness of many Europeans, the valuation of cultures and dividing them into developed and un- or underdeveloped, into noble or good and less noble and less good (or even bad) ones is thoroughly established. Over long ages, some nations considered themselves creators and carriers of the high culture. This is the base on which prejudices and stereotypes have been born which,

---

[13] See the *World Conference on Cultural Policies*, UNESCO (Mexico: 1982). http://portal.unesco.org/culture/en/files/12762/11295421661mexico_en.pdf/mexico_en.pdf

[14] *World Conference on Cultural Policies*, article 4.

groundlessly, extol some cultures and belittle others, or even destroy them, robbing them of their most valuable works. For example, Poland experienced this as a result of many wars, and especially during World War II. Polish culture was deliberately destroyed, and its more valuable works were stolen and taken away from Poland. After the end of World War II, in the so-called American zone, forty thousand boxes with works of Polish culture that had been stolen by Germans were found. Even today many Polish works of culture are in German museums and repositories as well as in the territories of the former Soviet Union.

In relation to other cultures, an attitude of respect and positive openness is necessary. It helps to notice common elements as well as elements that are valuable in other cultures; this facilitates contacts, exchange, and co-operation.

b. One should love one's own culture and maintain a sense of its importance – though not to the point of megalomania. Man has a need to belong to small cultural communities in which immediate contacts are possible and everything is familiar and understandable. Individuals belong to these communities most often because they were born and live in them; however, it is important for them to accept these communities and, moreover, these communities should be ones of their own choice. This happens when individuals acquaint themselves with elements of their culture, grow accustomed to them, understand their symbolic meaning and their role in the history of the nation, hand their culture down to the next generation, and supplement it with a new interpretation and new products.

c. Dialogue with other cultures should be maintained. Knowledge of and love towards one's own culture does not isolate a person from other cultures; on the contrary, it makes contact with them easier and more creative. It is also the case that the more creative one's culture is, the more consciously one's partners develop their own cultural heritage.

Dialogue with people who are culturally different has a double result for one's own national culture. First, it helps one to better realise one's own differences and cultural values. Second, it is a factor in the development of cultures. "The cultural identity of a people is renewed and enriched through contact with the traditions and values of others. Culture is dialogue, the exchange of ideas and experience and the appreciation of other values and traditions; it withers and dies in isolation."[15]

d. Exchange and mutual creating – instead of domination, absorption and polarisation – should be practiced. The European Union appears now as a cartel of the richest countries, which condescendingly let some, but not all, poorer countries sit at their table – and even this they do only gradually. They flood the poorer countries with their products, changing them into markets for their wealth and thus undercutting these countries' own production.

---

[15] *World Conference on Cultural Policies*, article 4.

European experience in the cultural field is similar. Nations with strong economies are convinced that their cultures are rich, have an exceptional value, and encourage poor nations to avail themselves of them. They advertise them so strongly and in so many ways that poor nations often use them uncritically, neglecting their own culture, which gets weak and finally dies. This was said as early as 1980, in the report of the International Commission for the Study of Communication Problems, under Irish Nobel laureate Sean MacBride's direction and presented at the 21st General Conference of the UNESCO in Belgrade. According to this report, many old African cultures have been superseded by those of rich countries.[16] The danger of "missionaries" of culture is present, always and everywhere. It is still worse if the "mission" is carried out for money. Consumer culture impairs many nations' own creativity to an appalling extent.

There is also a danger of polarisation of cultures or of a cultural melting pot in the uniting of Europe. It would be worse if the French, German or American "acid" dominated in this melting pot, and dissolved or polarised other cultures. It is good if the contacts among cultures occur as a common and creative exchange based on partnership and common creativity, and dominate over the elements already produced by particular cultures. Hence, for the dialogue of cultures, it is more important, e.g., to organise common French-Austrian or Polish-German workshops whose results are common works of art, than to put on an exhibition of Austrian art in France or of Polish art in Germany.

e. Institutionalisation of mutual contacts ought to be observed. Exchange and co-operation in the field of culture needs unhampered contact as well as institutionalisation. This is easier now than it was in the past. Also, many institutions that have a European character have been established. An instance of this was the meeting in Cracow (25 May – 7 June 1991), which was organised by the Conference for European Security and Co-operation, during which 34 countries unanimously accepted the so-called Charter of Krakow. The Charter is a political declaration of the will to co-operate in preserving cultural heritage. It makes exchange of information obligatory and defines areas of special care in the field of culture.

MULTIPLICITY OF CULTURES USING THE SCALE OF 'ONE COUNTRY'

Even if we come to agree on the value of the multiplicity of cultures on the international scale, questions and doubts on the scale of

---

[16] "International Commission for the Study of Communication Problems: Final Report (Provisional Version)." Paris 1979. A final, full version of the report was published as a book entitled *Many Voices, One World* (London: 1980).

one's own country may still arise. In our own countries, we tend to see one culture only. But the reality of Europe is different. Of the 345 million people making up the European Community in 1994, about 50 million spoke minority (i.e., non-state) languages.[17] And if we take into consideration European countries that do not belong to the European Union today, we see an even more complex mosaic; in Central-Eastern Europe, there are more ethnic groups that do not live in their own states than there are in Western Europe.

For social life, and the more so for the state, it has never been – nor is it now – a meaningless question as to what cultural groups live within it and which of them dominate. It has always been asked whether all groups should be allowed to develop freely, or whether assimilation should be the ultimate aim. Those who exercise power display two extremely different tendencies. One results from considering cultural differentiation to be an obstacle to forming a strong state; hence, the activity of various cultural groups is decidedly to be limited, and one cultural group is supported in order to shape the whole of social and state life on the base of it. This is the mono-cultural model. The other tendency is to foster the existence and further development of many cultural groups. This is the model of a multicultural society. Internal policies of states oscillate towards the one or the other model.

The mono-cultural model in a modern state is theoretically rejected, but it occurs in practice. Hence it is worth making a few general remarks about it. The mono-cultural model is based on ontological, epistemological, axiological, cultural and praxiological monism – on the fear that what is different constitutes a danger. This model suits practical personalities who want to achieve their aim quickly. They assume that uniformity in everything, including culture, strengthens efficiency of action. This was well expressed in the motto of Communist organisations: strength is in unity. Eventually, there was neither unity nor strength. I would like to express a reservation here regarding this model: it is not characteristic of totalitarian states only. In different variants it also occurs in democratic countries. For example, its peculiar variants can be seen in the United States' internal policies up to the 1980s and in the German Federal Republic up till today.

In the United States, the 'minority cultural groups' policy was, for many years, based on the conception of the so-called melting pot. It meant that all the cultures were to be mixed, to lose their characteristic features and, after melting, form a new American culture. Putting this conception in effect has been given up. Today, in the internal policies of the United

---

[17] J. Smolicz, "Naród, państwo i mniejszości etniczne z perspektywy europejsko-muzułmańskiej (Nation, state and ethnic minorities from a European-Muslim perspective)" in *Komunikacja międzykulturowa. Zbliżenie i impresje*. Ed. A. Kapciak, L. Korporowicz, A. Tyszka. (Warszawa: Instytut Kultury, 1995), p. 153.

States, the multicultural model dominates. Variety of cultures has been recognised as a peculiar beauty of the American society. Cultural groups have been granted freedom in cultivating their own culture on American soil. It has been accepted that there can be Polish, Czech, Spanish, German or Serb Americans. The United States has followed in Australia's and Canada's footsteps. These two countries had accepted the multicultural model earlier. Canada accepted it in 1971 as a response by Prime Minister Pierre Elliot Trudeau and his government to the so-called Quebec problem: that province had displayed strong separatist tendencies, desiring to establish an independent state on the grounds of cultural dissimilarity from the English majority inhabiting much of the rest of the country.

The German Federal Republic, in turn, still maintains the position that it should be a mono-cultural country. The freedom that is given to ethnic-cultural groups is only supposed to subdue conflicts that could arise because of the differences, disturbing the functioning of the state. It is better to make concessions; however, the ultimate aim is a complete integration of minority groups into German society until they completely lose their cultures. A non-German does not have a good chance of taking a higher social or state position. His lasting ties with the country of his origin are an obstacle.

In modern Europe, Sweden introduced the multicultural model first, in 1975, and Denmark followed. This model of culture appeals to those who perceive and recognise that there are many problems in social reality, and who accept the right of individuals and social groups to preserve their own distinct character and autonomy. The multicultural model appeals to those who have far-reaching visions of development and who seek to form unity out of multiplicity. As characteristic features of a multiplicity of cultures within a country, the following can be mentioned:

a. Different cultural groups live together, having the same rights; they complement one another and stimulate one another to develop. In everyday life, individuals, belonging to one cultural group, also participate in other groups' culture. They generally form their basic personality in the cultural group in which they were born and brought up, but they enrich it with the culture of other groups they come into contact with. In such a situation, none of the cultural groups is doomed to annihilation – to being assimilated into the general culture of the society.

b. The culture of the society that develops on the basis of the multicultural model has a relatively open character toward other cultures and, in other respects, a relatively closed one. This is accompanied by a relatively great interest in other cultures, usually chosen ones, and accepting various elements from them relatively easily. This, however, does not mean that it cannot be closed to a certain degree to a definite culture as a whole or to some elements of it. This closedness is caused by an anxiety about the identity of the culture or by a disinclination towards strangeness. The openness of one's own culture to others is also expressed by the fact that the ones who create their own group culture can express its contents and form in a way that can be understood by members of other cultural groups.

c. The cultural policy of a multicultural state exhibits patronage, not simply supervision and administration. State authorities accepting the multicultural model do not identify themselves with any particular cultural group, in the sense of choosing it to be the national, obligatory or privileged one. They do not ignore or disregard any of them. They act as a mediator between different cultural groups. The state supports all valuable forms of creativity; it also allows any other patrons (individuals or groups) to act. It takes many patrons for the culture of the whole society to flourish, to be varied in its contents and forms, and to develop. It is a most human and normal thing that a patron generally supports the kind of creativity that suits him, that he likes, and that he would like to propagate.

d. Culture is not to be treated as an instrument. Ruling groups should not treat culture as a tool for propagating their own ideology, and the more so for strengthening their power or the power of their party. If this claim is not satisfied, the phenomenon of 'selling their services by authors' occurs. This involves the erosion of their [the ruling groups'] authority in the society, and a resulting decrease in their influence.

The forming of a multicultural model in society is dependent on the following circumstances: a) multi-ethnicity of the state, b) the variety of religious groups, and c) a non-absolutist type of authority.[18] How does it

---

[18] Poland is an example of such a multicultural state. In Polish history, the multicultural model decidedly predominates over the model of a cultural monolith, although in some periods the latter was clearly preferred in the state's internal policies. This multicultural model was made up of: a) the multi-ethnicity of the Polish state; b) a variety of religious groups; and c) a non-absolutist type of authority, in the form of an elective monarchy, which provided opportunities to formulate personal rights and numerous political liberties, making it possible to organise various political parties.

In one state, then, Poles, Lithuanians, Ukrainians, Ruthenians, Germans, Jews, Armenians, Tartars, and Karaites lived together in relative peace and solidarity for many centuries. The variety of ethnic and cultural groups sometimes led to tensions, but culturally this enriched the whole of society. Until World War II, Poland belonged to what was one of the most ethnically, religiously and culturally differentiated countries of Europe. The census of 1931, with respect to the language spoken, revealed that within the Polish state (whose population was then 31,915,800), a total of 21,993,400 (68.9%) spoke Polish, 3,222,000 (10.1%), Ukrainian, 2,732,600 (8.6%), Jewish-Hebrew, 1,219,600 (3.8%), Ruthenian, 989,900 (3.1%), Byelorussian, 741,000, German, 138,700 (0.4%), Russian, and 878,600 (2.8%), other languages (or they did not specify the language) (See *Mały Rocznik Statystyczny* [*Little Year-Book*] (Warszawa: GUS, 1939), pp. 24-25). After World War II, Polish society became nearly mono-national. Ethnical-cultural minorities constitute only about 3-4 percent of the total population now. In spite of this, the multicultural attitude that has established traditions in Poland is still deeply rooted in the

happen that different ethnical-cultural groups can make up a common social and state system?

The basis for the formation of an overall cultural system in a given state society is its members' acceptance of a definite group of values, ideas, norms, behaviour patterns, cultural products, historical events and hero-figures important for that society – that is, by all the cultural groups. Having a common history and experiencing common vicissitudes occurs here. Hence, unity is given to the cultural system not by the political authorities but through a consensus among the existing cultural groups.

Recognition – consensus – of superior values, ultimate aims and principles of co-operation, and events and cultural products, connected by different cultural groups, becomes the basis for establishing institutional frames of culture and for the formation of common centres that will co-ordinate and plan cultural development. The multicultural model that functions in this way does not rule out planning and co-ordinating cultural activity, but it opposes the domination of one cultural group over others, and prevents the struggle for exerting exclusive influence on other cultural groups. It assumes the existence of many cultural centres and their co-operation, and not competition. The overall society's culture is developed in co-operation amongst different cultural groups and numerous cultural centres.

In a multicultural situation, a society is not divided into various parts, but is a varied whole – a rich unity in multiplicity – and, hence, is a multi-factor environment where its members can develop.

CONCLUSION

The problem of keeping and developing one's cultural identity and connecting it to a wide culture is not a novelty for small societies and weak states. It emerged quite clearly during periods of occupation or partition. For example, it is not a new problem for the Irish, Hungarians, Poles, or Slovaks. For Poles it emerged quite clearly during the period when Poland was partitioned. Poles, living on their own land, were citizens of foreign states or had to emigrate to other countries. It was then that the Polish elite already held the view that, in the world of culture, it is necessary to merge what is local with what is European and universal. This attitude was expressed by the poet and political leader Adam Mickiewicz when he characterised Joachim Lelewel, writer and politician, in the following couplet:

---

consciousness of Poles. (See L. Dyczewski (ed.), *Values in the Polish Cultural Tradition* (Washington, The Council for Research in Values and Philosophy, 2002), pp. 17-18).

And so, wherever you turn, you will always show
That you come from the Niemen bank, that you're a Pole,
inhabitant of Europe.

And Lelewel himself advised the Polish Parliament in 1831 to be able to "associate the past and the future, to join what is Polish with the tendency of the age,"[19] that is, Polish national culture with the culture of Europe and of the world. This advice is still relevant for Poles.[20]

Pan-European culture is like a modern commercial district in a large city. There is everything for everybody here: supermarkets and small shops, churches, theatres and cinemas, museums with masterpieces of art and shop windows with trashy art, professional musicians playing classical music and amateur groups introducing the music of their circles. Styles and languages are mixed. This provides the conditions for a peculiar system of interpersonal communication. It is open and intelligible for everybody.

National culture is like a private flat with windows looking out onto this public world. Here, there is something homely, familiar, unique, intimate and warm to be found.

A modern European needs both these worlds: the street and the home. European culture and national culture are the two lungs of individual culture. Breathing with these two lungs, and creating both of these cultures, allow for the formation of creative, open and individual personalities. According to Ernest Gellner, Bronisław Malinowski is an example of such a personality; he "constitutes a peculiar mixture of cultural nationalism, political internationalism and political antinationalism."[21] The more people of this kind there are, the greater harmony will exist between the all-European and national systems of communication, the more certain peace will be in Europe, and the more familiar and open, colourful and creative life in it will be.

Institute of Sociology
Catholic University of Lublin
Lublin, Poland

---

[19] J. Jedlicki, "Narodowość a cywilizacja [Nationality and Civilisation]" in *Uniwersalizm i swoistość kultury polskiej.* Ed. J. Kłoczowski. Vol. 2 (Lublin 1990).

[20] See Dyczewski, *Values in the Polish Cultural Tradition.*

[21] E. Gellner, *Europa i co z tego wynika* [*Europe and what results from this*] (Warsaw: 1990), p. 353.

Chapter XLII

THE *WEICHENG* (FORTRESS BESIEGED) OF MODERNIZATION AND ITS TRANSCENDENCE: ON THE VALUES OF CONSTRUCTIVE POSTMODERNISM

OUYANG KANG

INTRODUCTION

Modernity attracted more attention as a hot topic in China 10 years ago than it does now. However, since China is still in the process of modernization, the question about how to recognize and understand modernity and how to construct Chinese modernization remains an important problem. Today, China is facing the challenges of globalization and the WTO; insofar as it is also facing an encounter with postmodernism, this problem becomes more urgent. It is therefore important to probe the problem of Chinese modernization based on the background of globalization and postmodernism.

There is a special background for the encounter of Chinese intellectuals with postmodernism – the common attention to modernization. But each person investigating the relation has his or her own social foundation, research angle, and key in researching modernization. Western scholars live in an advanced modern society, consume the benefits of modernization, find the serious social problems caused by it, reflect and critique modernization and modernity, and even try to destroy and deconstruct it. Chinese scholars live in a country that is still looking for 'modernization.' They especially feel the attraction of modernization because of China's backward state with respect to productive and other forces. They have a strong desire to increase the speed and the level of modernization in China. At the same time, they are surprised to find that modernization and modernity have been strongly criticized by the most developed countries. They have, therefore, come to pay close attention to this situation and to postmodernism. Actually, when we note the debate about the relationship between China and the West, among the groups known as the pre-modern, modern and post-modern, as well as modernism, anti-modern and post-postmodern, we find a general phenomenon that acts as a kind of *Weicheng* or "Fortress besieged." It is important to look beyond this *Weicheng* to the Chinese people themselves. We will therefore find some enlightenment in and from "constructive postmodernism."

"WEI CHENG" AND THE 'WEICHENG' OF MODERNIZATION

Wei Cheng is a well-known novel written by the famous Chinese writer Qian Zhongshu.[1] It is a story about some young Chinese intellectuals who have just finished their studies abroad and have come back from France. Through several of the characters, with a focus on Fang Hongjian, the book gives a careful and vivid description of their work, their daily life and their love stories. The author has two very famous metaphors for marriage. One metaphor is borrowed from English: "Marriage is like a golden birdcage." Those who are outside want to get into the birdcage, while those who are inside want to escape from the birdcage.

Another metaphor drawn from the French tradition is also used: "Le mariage est comme une forteresse assiégée; ceux qui sont dehors veulent y entrer, et ceux qui sont dedans veulent en sortir." Indiana University Press published the English translation of *Wei Cheng* as *Fortress Besieged* in 1979. On the title page of the book, there is a paragraph in both English and French which explains the title: "Marriage is like a fortress besieged: those who are outside want to get in, and those who are inside want to get out."

Modernization as *Weicheng* reflects a comparison between the attitudes towards modernization in different countries. On the one hand, China and almost all developing countries are trying their best to increase the speed and the level of their own modernization. They take modernization as their ideal goal and direction. On the other hand, modernization has become the subject of critique and deconstruction by postmodernism and other theoretical approaches. They strongly criticize modernization and modernity as the root of all evil in today's world. They announce the coming of a postmodern time and postmodern cultures. After 9/11 in New York, in reply to my letter of sympathy, an American scholar said, "The event is not an attack on New York and on American people, but an attack on modernization, capitalism, and the globalization led by capitalism."

The intense debate about modernization has come as a surprise. Whatever attitude or approach one has to modernization, whether one of agreement or disagreement, constructive or deconstructive, it is important to have a comprehensive understanding and analysis of it.

THE DOUBLE VALUE OF MODERNIZATION

On my view, the deepest reasons for the *Weicheng* of modernization are the multiple and non-neutral value characteristics of modernization. In fact, almost all the core value elements of modernization are both positive and negative. Modernism and postmodernism are different

---

[1] Qian Zhongshu, *Fortress Besieged*, tr. Jeanne Kelly and Nathan K. Mao (New York: New Directions, 2004).

reflections of the different values. What are the core values of modernization? We can list at least six.

First, it is a process of rationalization, with a capitalist outlook and culture. The original idea of modernization can be traced to the Renaissance in Italy. Its main purpose was to fight against the rule of medieval religion and to propagandize capitalism, praising human nature and human reason.

Second, it is a process of industrial revolution and industrialization, based on natural science and technology. Industrialization is the most important foundation of modernization.

Third, it is a process of commercial revolution and marketing. Modern industry required a national and international commercial market. Continental exploration gave the chance to set up an international market. The market became one of the most important elements in social development.

Fourth, it is a process of urban revolution and urbanization. The development of industry needs 'free' labor and seeks to employ peasants from the countryside. More and more people live in the city and prompt the rapid development of urbanization. Big cities become political, economic and cultural centers in social and national life.

Fifth, it is a process of political revolution and democratization. The capitalist economy required an appropriate political system to protect itself. Democracy became the political requirement of modernization. Democratization is a key element of modernization.

Sixth, it is a process of legal revolution and legalization. The democratic political system needs the protection of a sympathetic legal system. The constitutional system became the most important social system for a modern society.

There might be many other values inherent in modernization. However, the above six are the main elements in Western modernization. All of them have two sides to their value and functions. If we cannot control them rationally, they may bring about negative consequences. For example, over-rationalization may restrict human non-rational aspects and lead to a one-dimensional development of the human being; unlimited industrialization may aggravate the ecological crisis and lack of resources; too much marketing may lead to the development of a philistine society; unlimited urbanization may give rise to complex social problems; unlimited democracy may lead to anarchism; the incomplete law system may reduce the efficiency of government. These problems are the actual foundation of Western postmodernism.

THE VALUES OF CONSTRUCTIVE POSTMODERNISM

Up until now, we have heard primarily about deconstructive postmodernism. We respect these schools for their critical attitude and deconstructive work on contemporary Western society and Western modernization. However, we still feel confused: what can we do and what should we do after deconstruction and destruction? We cannot get any positive opinions or suggestions. For the Chinese in particular, there is a much stronger need for construction and creative work than for deconstruction. Because of this, we have had to keep our distance from postmodernism for a long time. Now, however, we have come to know of "constructive postmodernism." We find that we can learn something from this form of postmodernism.

There are some common features between constructive and deconstructive postmodernism. According to John Cobb, for example, both forms deconstruct the substantial self that has been so central to modern thought. Both reject the reductionist mechanism of modern science. Both oppose as futile and dangerous the effort to find a starting point for thought that is itself beyond question, what is often called "foundationalism." Both deny that there is any empirical experience that is not already informed by interpretation. Both reject the claim of reason to discover an a priori starting point or ground. Both are critical of Euro-centrism, nationalism, hierarchy, patriarchy, current forms of globalization, and all forms of imperialism.

However, there are several important differences between these two postmodernisms. According to Cobb, there are six primary points of divergence.[2]

(1) Whereas deconstructive postmodernism presupposes the Kantian critique, Whitehead understood himself to be providing an alternative to Kant. Kant's critique has intensified the radical separation of the human sphere from the natural one – a movement initiated by Descartes – and, because of Kant's influence, most deconstructive postmodernism attends almost entirely to the human sphere. Whitehead's alternative overcomes this dualism and intimately interrelates the human and the natural worlds. As a result, constructive postmodernism participates in the effort to reformulate the sciences in ways that are radically distinct from deconstructive postmodernism.

(2) Constructive and deconstructive postmodernists share with most contemporary philosophers a recognition of the great importance of language. However, constructive postmodernists do not agree with the widely-held view that language is self-contained and lacks any reference beyond itself. In contrast to the Kantian tradition, we hold that there is a real world which impinges on us and informs our experience. Much of our language refers to this real world of other people, animals, and objects. What we say is, of course, deeply shaped by our own histories and the language we use, but it is also affected by the impact of the other upon us.

---

[2] Please see my interview: "Constructive Postmodernism and Globalization—an interview with Professor John B. Cobb," [Chinese version] *World Philosophy*, vol. 3 (2002).

The ecological crisis, for example, was real before we expressed it in language. Of course, as many philosophers now rightly emphasize, every verbal formulation about this crisis is profoundly shaped by the history of the use of the language, and the language that we use to describe what is happening will shape our response. But language also points to natural events that genuinely threaten the future of humanity, and it does so in more and less adequate and accurate ways. It is important to seek more adequate and accurate descriptions.

(3) Whereas deconstructive postmodernism opposes every effort to take an overview as hegemonic, Whitehead offers an overview that we believe is not hegemonic. Whitehead agrees that such an overview is nothing more than what Plato called "a likely story," but he believed – rightly, we think – that it is better to counter the unlikely stories by which most people live with one that is likely. In short, whereas deconstructive postmodernists would have us live without any generalized view of our cosmic or historical situation, Whiteheadians seek the best account we can find, agreeing that this is subject to constant correction and that we should take precautions because of the danger of dealing unfairly with those who have had a radically different life experience.

(4) The divergence identified in (3) is closely related to different views of the role of "reason" in modernity. Deconstructive postmodernists suppose that modernity was characterized by excessive confidence in reason and that postmodernity should abjure such confidence. This image is encouraged by the fact that the early Enlightenment is often called "The Age of Reason." But the appeal to reason was in fact an appeal to a rather simple form that eschewed speculation and stayed close to common sense and what worked in physics. Whitehead argued that the movement from the Middle Ages to modernity was away from confidence in reason, towards an emphasis on experience and practice. Kant advanced this movement through his analysis of the limits of theoretical reason and his emphasis on practical reason. Subsequent modern thinkers have gone still further in delimiting the role of reason. From this perspective, the deconstructive postmodernists are carrying the modern tradition to its logical conclusion rather than turning against it, as they suppose. Whiteheadians, on the other hand, affirm the speculative use of reason. We should develop hypotheses and test them. We believe that the likely story we seek should be as rational as possible. Consistency and coherence are extremely important considerations, although, of course, until the applicability of ideas and the adequacy to the whole of the evidence have been established, ideas should not be accepted.

(5) Although Whiteheadians agree with deconstructive postmodernists that the various efforts of modern philosophy to achieve certainty by progressively limiting the claims of philosophy have failed, they do not draw extreme relativistic conclusions. We believe that there are inescapable elements in human experience, and that ways of thinking that make sense of these are better than those that deny them. For example, we

think that no one can really believe that subjective human experience is disconnected from the body. Our experience of the body is too emphatic and too inescapable for us to be able to act except in terms of that belief. Of course, many people have accepted philosophical doctrines that imply this extreme dualism, but we think that this is a weakness in those philosophies. We believe that holding to beliefs that one cannot act on in practice is harmful. Similarly, people cannot really believe that they are simply automatons operating according to mechanistic physical laws. At the very least, they cannot act as if they believed this. We think that a philosophy that corresponds to the beliefs presupposed in our actions is better than one that does not. We think this is an advantage of constructive postmodern thought in comparison with both modern philosophies and deconstructive postmodern ones.

(6) Deconstructive postmodernists tend to celebrate forms of life that modernity has undermined. They call this "local knowledge." They tend to treat modernity as a whole, with its efforts to impose universal principles, as negative. Whiteheadian postmodernists see strengths and weaknesses in both the pre-modern and the modern. We appreciate the more holistic character of much pre-modern thinking and deplore the dualism of the mental and the physical that Descartes and Kant imposed on the modern Western mind. On the other hand, we think that most pre-modern societies failed to give sufficient encouragement to individual independence of mind and action, and we appreciate the modern effort to celebrate the rights of individuals simply because they are human. Although we see many connections between the understanding of reality offered by Whitehead and the modes of thought and life of traditional societies, we believe the world needs a new vision of reality that draws on many sources but does not simply repeat or continue any one of them. We emphasize dialogue among members of various traditional, modernist, and postmodernist groups as a promising step toward a new, more inclusive worldview. Such a worldview will remain provisional, because human beings will never arrive at the inclusive truth. But it can provide far better guidance for life than what is now governing our thought.

CONCLUSION: A CHINESE PERSPECTIVE ON THE TRANSCENDENCE OF THE 'WEICHENG' OF MODERNIZATION

What may we say in conclusion?

First, we should critically reflect on our views about modernization and eliminate any misunderstandings in order to master its whole and real meaning in a complete way. Second, we should analyse our own direction and the place of modernization as set against the background of economic globalization. Third, we should learn from traditional Chinese culture and philosophy and draw on their insights in order to retain our national character. And fourth, we should be very attentive to any problems arising in the process of our modernization. We should learn from the experience of the Western world and avoid its mistakes.

Insitute of Philosophy
Huazhong University of Science and Technology
Wuhan, Hubei, P. R. China

CHAPTER XLIII

THE FALLACY OF GLOBAL PEACE WITHOUT CONFLICT

MILOSLAV BEDNAR

The concept of human rights originated from the concept of natural law. The original cultural context of human and civil rights, therefore, became global. Since the rise of Marxism, it has been challenged by a view of human rights which separates them from their original roots in natural law. Developments in the Czech tradition of political philosophy, marked by the founder of Charter 77, Jan Patočka, renewed the original concept of human rights based on natural law. Current world view paradigms show, especially since 1989, a clear ideological preponderance of various and interconnected neo-Marxist ideologies of human rights and globalization. This crucial characteristic of some of the present mainstream intellectual ideologies proves that peace on the basis of natural law and the respect of human rights is not without the risk of conflict. Both global and local unity, in regard to uniformity and diversity in issues of tradition, seem to provide a source of perennial global conflict in terms of Heraclitus's invisible harmony.

The concept of Natural Law as an absolutely binding ground legitimizing the creation of laws of the people, by the people, and for the people, represents a remarkable achievement of so-called Western civilization in general as well as of ancient Greek philosophy in particular. Strictly speaking, the phenomenon and concept of Natural Law create the very foundation of political philosophy as such.

In my view, the phenomenon of the Law of Nature provides a limitation to and a preservation of the order of being. More precisely, the order of being is the order of the phenomenon of appearing as such. What follows from this origin is simply being as such, which makes any particular being possible. In this ontological way, the Law of Nature provides the crucial phenomenon of Openness, which, auspiciously, allows for differentiation and, thus, elucidation by determining the distinction of the phenomenon in the lifeworld. By the same token, the phenomenon of the Law of Nature is the only phenomenon which reveals to human beings our origins in time and its order, and, thus, the very origin of the meaning of the universe and life, and the substance of truth. Thus, care of this law is the utmost natural obligation of humanity.

This fundamental context of the phenomenon of the Law of Nature has an obvious religious and ethical corollary and has universal human significance. The original European (i.e., Greek) tradition of Heraclitus[1] and Sophocles[2] presents a concept of human law depending on the divine law, but one that, as in Aristotle's account of 'just by nature,' bridges the gap between divine immutability and human mutability, and always applies to every specific human condition.[3] It does not mean, however, that the Aristotelian who is naturally just (*fysei dikaion*) does not hold the same in every case – i.e., quite independently from human preference.[4] In other words, natural justice is applied by people in regards to specific situations, and in respect to specific human conditions.[5]

In Thomas Aquinas, the Law of Nature belongs to the divine, not to human law. This crucially hierarchical relationship takes place *via* human participation in the divine law through the light of natural reason (*lumen rationis*) by means of which the divine light (*impressio luminis divini*) is active in us.[6] That is why and how the Law of Nature creates the ground and prime norm of all human legislation and law. The discovery of the Law of Nature, respecting the Natural Right, is explained by Aquinas explicitly by analogy with philosophical cognition. This implies that the Natural Law bears upon its rational application as the systemic philosophical insight on the differentiating systemic rationality of scientific cognition.[7]

On the basis of Aristotelian Natural Law conceived in terms of Christianity, Aquinas infers, for example, that the government becomes unjust if it despises the common good of community, and seeks instead the private good of the sovereign.[8] From this follows the natural right of the community to resist a tyrannical will. For if there is a right for a community to institute the king, the same community can (by virtue of the same right) depose him or tame his power if he abuses it in a tyrannical manner.[9]

The modern formulation of natural (i.e. civil, in comparison with so-called human) rights in John Locke, obviously belongs to the above-mentioned classical tradition and to the typically European or Western culture of natural rights, in contradistinction to the concept of the Law of Nature in Hugo Grotius and his followers (e.g., Jean Jacques Burlamaqui, Samuel Pufendorf, and Emerich de Vattel).

According to John Locke, every human being is born

---

[1] See Heraclitus, *Fragment B*, 114
[2] See Sophocles, *Antigone*, ll. 450-470
[3] Aristotle, *Nichomachean Ethics*, 1134b-1135a.
[4] Aristotle, *Nichomachean Ethics*, 1134b.
[5] Aristotle, *Nichomachean Ethics*, 1134b-1135a.
[6] Aquinas, *Summa Theologiae*, I-II, q. 91, a. 2.
[7] Aquinas, *Summa Theologiae* I-II, q. 91, a. 3.
[8] Aquinas, *De regno ad regem Cypri* in *Opera Omnia*, Book 42 (Rome: San Thomaso, 1979), p. 756.
[9] Aquinas, *De regno ad regem Cypri*, p. 770.

... with a title to perfect freedom, and an uncontrolled enjoyment of all the rights and privileges of the law of nature, equally with any other man or number of men in the world, has by nature a power not only to preserve his property, that is his life, liberty and estate, but to judge of and punish the breaches of that law in others as he is persuaded the offence deserves ... within the bounds of the law of nature, without asking leave, or depending upon the will of any other man.[10]

This state of liberty is not a state of licence. It is governed by a law of nature, which obliges everyone and which is detectable by natural human reason.[11] By virtue of a social contract, individuals transfer their equality, freedom and the executive power that follow from the law of nature, in respect to natural right, to the legislative power. Having been constituted in this way, the legislative power of the body politic or commonwealth is authorized to dispose of those rights and liberties for the benefit of the whole of the people (who are now citizens) in order to improve the preservation of their lives, freedom and property.[12] Yet this supreme legislative power has only a fiduciary power to act for certain ends; there still remains in the people a supreme power to remove or alter the legislature when they find the legislature acting contrary to the trust reposed in it. For all power given with trust in the attainment of an end is limited by that end, and "whenever that end is manifestly neglected or opposed the trust must necessarily be forfeited, and the power devolve into the hands of those that gave it, who may place it anew where they shall think best for their safety and security."[13] Analogous to this is Locke's evaluation of a body politic, where "a long train of abuses, prevarications, and artifices, all tending the same way, make the design visible to the people," which contradicts the ends of that delegated power, and so leads them to "rouse themselves, and endeavor to put the rule into such hands which may secure to them the end for which government was at first erected."[14]

Thus, it should be clear that in Locke – the genuine founding father of the modern concept of human rights – the key element is the original, ancient, and Christian concept of the unequivocally hierarchical relationship between natural rights and the Law of Nature. This concept makes it possible to define and limit natural human rights on the basis of Law of Nature, which is the only criterion of human rights and liberties. It was precisely this philosophically-grounded Lockean concept of natural law and right which provided the explicit legitimacy for the founding of American

---

[10] See John Locke, *The Second Treatise of Government*, sect. 87.

[11] Locke, *The Second Treatise of Government*, sect. 6.

[12] Locke, *The Second Treatise of Government*, sect. 89.

[13] Locke, *The Second Treatise of Government*, sect. 149; cf. sect. 226.

[14] Locke, *The Second Treatise of Government*, sect. 225.

republican democracy in the Declaration of Independence in 1776. This American achievement marked the first overseas step in the subsequent development, whereby the original philosophical context of human and civil rights became global.

At least from the time of the rise of Marxism, the world has been evidently and more or less explicitly facing a challenge, which consists in the existence of two theoretical foundations for human rights: one is traditional, the other is non-traditional. More specifically, this key issue of our times consists in the fact that, besides the mentioned Lockean modern concept of natural right (inferred from the classically conceived Law of Nature), there is another concept of human rights that is being applied nowadays in obvious contradistinction to the former. This other, competing concept of human rights is founded on an entirely different account of justice. It sees liberty as an expression of an absolutely independent willing of the self, in principle not burdened with any given community bounds and identities, let alone the traditional concept of the Law of Nature. This sort of liberal position is marked by a huge increase in demands for human rights where there is no structuring, or hierarchical distinction in value between elementary (i.e. natural) human rights and particular rights, which are putatively inferred from the former.

Moreover, such a pseudo-inference occurs in the form of highly vague, undefined, and loose accounts, permitting such formulations as the right to personal integrity (contradicting rights to unlimited information on the one hand and to privacy on the other hand), the right to protection from economic exploitation, the right to protection from a damaging social development, and so on. Moreover, Article 52 in the original version of the Charter of Fundamental Rights of the European Union allows the limitation of all the rights of this Charter when it is in the interest (sic!) of the European Union (E.U.).[15]

Since the rise of Marxism, this has become the typical – indeed, prevailing – challenge posed to human rights, which has become more or less explicitly (and, in fact, ideologically) separated from their original roots in natural law. A proof exemplifying this is seen as follows: many of those often partly-substantiated economic and social rights, such as the social right to equipment in work, social and financial safety, and collective rights of particular human groups are, nevertheless, understood as equivalent to the obviously basic rights to life, freedom and property. As a result, the very substance of the ancient, Christian – and also modern Lockean – concept of justice (i.e., of natural law and right) is gradually being clouded, blurred and finally eliminated. This is a highly sinister process that favours ethical relativism. This ultimately equates positive right (which is by far the bulk of conspicuously extensive lists of human rights) with natural right.

---

[15] See, for example, the Charter of Fundamental Rights of the European Union (Brussels, 2000); see http://ue.eu.int/df/default.asp?lang=en, passim.

This ideological "human-right-ism" cancels out the basic distinction, as well as the structuring and hierarchical relationship, between positive and natural right. It is therefore necessary for political philosophy to criticize cogently the very foundation and legitimacy of today's conspicuously non-structured plurality of human rights.

What seems to be particularly absent in our contemporary – and systematically mistaken – pseudo-concept of natural and positive law is the demonstrable priority of moral choice as the explicit or implicit basis of meaningful human co-existence. This priority of moral choice in natural right surpasses the current untenable partitioning of the concept of the human being as, on the one hand, an almost mechanical system of impersonal rationality, and, on the other hand, a personal, ethically-proven will. Along the lines of the priority of moral choice in natural right, the standard of human rights would be to conceive human rights on the basis of a new synthesis of individuals, community, and philosophical and moral tradition – of a tradition that hearkens back to Platonic care of one's soul and of the institution of a constitutionally democratic state. A concept of human rights and justice based on such a ground would be rooted in, and reflect the inseparability of, both the moral and public spheres of human existence and, consequently, in the hierarchical values which are the basis of the original understanding of the Law of Nature.

It was the development of the Czech tradition of political philosophy in the 1970s, marked by its philosophical 'Founding Father' Jan Patočka, that renewed the original natural law concept of human rights. Patočka's concept of political philosophy seems to provide appropriate insights that allows human rights to meet such a demand.

First of all, Patočka offered a philosophically-founded reconstitution of the natural unity of human freedom and responsibility. This was the proper meaning of Patočka's (as he put it) "fundamental human notion of truth."[16] For Patočka, it is always up to human decision making, whether we disperse into and lose ourselves in the particular, or find and realize ourselves in our own nature in relation to Being, the universe and life. There is a possibility for a radical turn in life with respect to the relationship to others and, consequently, to human community. Once a life recognizes its finality, the purpose of such a self-appropriation consists in self-dedication. In this way, Patočka framed the phenomenon of sociality which grows out of a radical shaking of a putatively unshakable movement that consists in providing, supplying and self-prolonging attitudes and activities of human life and, by the same token, makes human beings alien to each other.

This is the very core of Patočka's philosophical revival of the phenomenon of the Law of Nature. For Patočka, it is absolutely impossible that the functioning of any society, even one that is technically well-

---

[16] See Jan Patočka, *Heretical Essays in the Philosophy of History* (Chicago and La Salle, IL: Open Court, 1996), pp. 29, 33.

equipped, not be conditioned by a shared moral basis of inner conviction. That phenomenon is not really a matter of opportunism, circumstances and expected advantages. Rather, generally speaking, the purpose of morality is not to guarantee the functioning of society, but is simply given by the sheer humanity of human beings. In Patočka's words: "It is not man who, according to his own needs, wishes and tendencies, arbitrarily defines what morality is, but morality itself defines man."[17] This is why Patočka could define anew the obligatory character of politics along the lines of his revived concept of natural law – and he does so as follows:

> The idea of human rights is nothing other than the conviction that even states, even society as a whole, are subject to the sovereignty of moral sentiment: that they recognize something unconditional that is higher than they are, something that is binding even on them, sacred, inviolable, and that in their power to establish and maintain a rule of law they seek to express this recognition.
>
> This conviction is present in individuals as well, as the ground for living up to their obligations in private life, at work, and in public. The only genuine guarantee that humans will act not only out of greed or fear, but freely, willingly, responsibly, lies in this conviction.[18]

Patoka's account of natural law, central to reflection on natural rights, entails conclusively and decisively the fact that the very existence of man, society and the just state depend entirely on a non-instrumental natural right that is founded on the basis of an ancient and Christian natural law. Patočka's political philosophy succeeds in defining exactly, and providing a comprehensive grasp of, the proper origin and relationship of natural law, natural right and justice. The core of that renewed conception is the recognition of the verifiable validity of the unconditional and uniting purpose of both private and public spheres of human life. Thus, in Patočka, the phenomenon of natural law regained a central position in the investigation of justice in political philosophy. The answer to the problem of how to understand the public good, once regained (thanks to Patočka), could have a correlative real attainability, validity and lasting non-relativistic definition.

Current world view paradigms show, especially after 1989, a clear ideological preponderance of various and interconnected neo-Marxist ideologies of human rights and globalization. Under this title belong

---

[17] Jan Patočka, "O povinnosti bránit se proti bezpráví" in *Charta 77* 1977-1989 (Prague, 1990), p. 31.

[18] Jan Patočka, *Philosophy and Selected Writings*, ed. Erazim Kohák (Chicago, IL: University of Chicago Press, 1989), p. 341.

The Fallacy of Global Peace Without Conflict

multiculturalism, various strands of post-Rawlsian liberalism, leftist communitarianism, neo-feminism (in terms of the bulk of present gender studies), many ecologist and other versions of so-called anti-globalism, anti-consumerism, and so on. On the one hand, these (in principle) neo-Marxist ideologies of justice present various forms of ethical relativism and a neutralism of positive right (equipped with varieties of large numbers of human rights, which are, as mentioned above, obviously mingled with and ultimately mistaken for basic natural rights). On the other hand, the neo-Marxist foundation of these present mainstream ideologies reveals itself in their underlying ideological concepts of perennial antagonistic struggle between suppressed majorities and oppressing villainous minorities which allegedly manipulate and exploit them systematically as far as possible. In summary, the decisive – by origin, obviously Marxist – basis of present mainstream intellectual ideologies proves and confirms a much more general fact: peace on the basis of natural law and in regard to human rights, is *not* at all free of conflict. What is more, the bloody turn of global history that began on September 11, 2001 demonstrated plainly that, and how, the current neo-Marxist opinion leaders and their visions actually concur with the global network of terrorist zealots. Both would like to finish off the existing democratic civilization and uproot its philosophical and religious foundations. This reminds us of the deep insight of Thomas Garruigue Masaryk, that the real basis of all current political and economic issues and conflicts is ethical and religious – and, let me add, 'philosophical,' in the proper sense of this word. The American President, Calvin Coolidge, grasped in the same way the stamina of American democracy, now under attack: "Our Government rests upon religion. It is from that source that we derive our reverence for truth and justice, for equality and liberty. Unless the people believe in these principles, they cannot believe in our Government."[19] This is why the American Republican Senator James M. Inhofe could recently say:

> Make no mistake about it. This war is first and foremost a spiritual war. It is not a political war. It has never been a political war. It is not about politics. It is a spiritual war. It has its roots in spiritual conflict. It is a war to be fought to destroy the very fabric of our society and the very things for which we stand... It is not just simple greed that motivated these people to kill. This war has been launched against the United States of America. It is a spiritual

---

[19] See Coolidge's speech at the unveiling of the equestrian statue of Bishop Francis Asbury, 15 October 1924. Available at the site of The Calvin Coolidge Memorial Foundation, http://www.calvin-coolidge.org/html/at_the_ unveiling_of_the_equest.html

attack... It is not just the selfish ambitions of an egoistical leader.[20]

To elucidate the enduring basis of the present situation of the issues of global and local unity, of uniformity and diversity, of conflicts amongst traditions, and of interests and ideas from a spiritual point of view, perhaps we could turn to an insight of Heraclitus again. This would be his little-understood comment concerning the preponderance of invisible harmony over the visible.[21] It seems that a philosophical and broadly academic reflection along those thoughtful Heraclitean lines results in the conclusion that there can be a consistent creative response to the two present mainstream varieties of neo-Marxism and the antidemocratic sects of Islam – i.e., through the philosophical recuperation and revival of the crucial phenomenon of natural law. Such a profound change in the mainstream academic direction will lead us to a proper ground to create a common basis of mutual, in-depth understanding for a real, meaningful dialogue with so-called 'other' cultural environments and civilizations.

Institute of Philosophy
Academy of Sciences of the Czech Republic
Czech Republic

---

[20] See "America's Stake in Israel's War on Terrorism," Senate Floor Statement by U.S. Senator James M. Inhofe (Republican-Oklahoma), December 4, 2001 at http://www.dunamai.com/articles/Israel/absolute_victory.htm

[21] Heraclitus, *Fragment 54.*

CHAPTER XLIV

IN SEARCH OF 'IDENTITY': THE FLUID BOUNDARIES BETWEEN THE 'RIGHT TO DIFFERENCE' AND 'ENTRENCHMENT IN DIFFERENCE'

PANAGIOTIS NOUTSOS

The prefacing of the title of this paper with the phrase 'in search of' is not the result of some 'postmodern' evasion or opposition to 'normalities' and the 'longues durées' phenomena of today's societies, in whatever form their schematisation is codified. It is simply an intensification in the process of delineation of the 'identities' and, in a related manner, the expression of the 'flux' inherent between the 'right' to and the 'entrenchment' in difference. Clearly, the views which I shall now attempt to document will not be derived from the familiar theory and research of Microsociology ('individual identity – social identity,' according to the distinction made by Erving Goffman). Moreover, I shall not overlook the fact that the neo-liberalism of recent decades has also disgorged itself into sociological research, in which the theory of the 'construct' of 'identities' presupposes, for example, the pronouncement of Margaret Thatcher that "there is no such thing as society, just individuals and their families."[1]

SOCIAL CONSCIOUSNESS

Social consciousness, as a coherence of 'identity' and 'otherness,' could, with respect to the present matter, have 'localism' as its field of emergence and formation: that is, the whole of a small geopolitical unit, rich in definitions and relations. In this interpretative enterprise, the 'whole' projects its particularity in relation to the 'centre' under discussion, and constitutes its individuality through a composite complex of coefficients and factors, the relations between which transcend their individual proponents. This is not, of course, a matter of isolating the 'local' in any spirit of a 'provincial' approach, explicit or otherwise, but rather of the verification of both the 'narrow' and the 'broad' horizon on which it appears. Consequently, 'endogenous' and 'exogenous' terms operate in its formation and, *a fortiori*, the historicity of its manifestations is obvious. If the ultimate unit of analysis of 'localism' is 'needs' (with their self-evident ranking) and the ways in which they are satisfied, the interpretative

---

[1] See David McCrone, *The Sociology of Nationalism: Tomorrow's Ancestors* (London and New York: Routledge, 1998), p. 33.

framework for their formulation and understanding is transposed from political economy (which, obviously, is not ignored) to the field of 'Moral Economy' (to use E.P. Thompson's term), in which the content of the rules and of the reciprocal obligations is determined by custom. Moreover, the 'microphysics' of power is suggested – that is, the way in which the everyday routine of the subjects is regulated as specific communicative action on the basis of local conditions of their social integration.

With the interest centring on the ways in which the '*Weltgeschichte*' emerges – in any event, it was not always there – one might attempt to clarify what channels today link the 'local,' the 'nation state' and 'globalisation,' extending the field of analysis of agoraphobic practice to the bounds of the planet. Time – as in 'working time' and 'free time' – measures the cycles of needs of the same market in a unified manner from the point of view of its subjects, which (by different routes, of course) take steps to acquire values of use in satisfying these needs. Such a perspective renders predictable the demand that 'free individuality' should presuppose the 'overall development of individuals' and the elevation of 'social productiveness' into 'social value.'[2] The increasing denseness of the field of international relations, as concerns these differing routes, does not suggest only the establishment of a single-dimensional network of diffusion of agoraphobic practice in a universe of social and political exclusion; it also suggests an abstract universality as an alibi. The various 'we's' who throng the banks of the multifarious routes have emancipatory behaviour as the shared crossroads of their 'identities,' with a view to achieving 'locality-individuality' without the walls of agoraphobic practice, which no longer knows any frontiers.

In our time, 'locality' is subjected – in spite of surface appearances – to most of the pressures which the 'nation state' undergoes from the conduits of 'globalisation,' that is, from the internationalised mechanisms of production of, first and foremost, symbolic goods. From this starting-point, it is possible to discern a need for the emergence of a cultural 'nationality' movement, imbued with a spirit of active understanding of differences in order to lay claim to the right of self-sufficiency of cultural minorities. However, the neutralising of the innate cultural 'populism,' which contrasts the chthonic 'us' with the alien 'others' and fosters the practice of xenophobia and racism, would be a *sine qua non* for the effectiveness of such a movement.

---

[2] See Karl Marx, *Outlines of the Critique of Political Economy* [*Grundrisse der Kritik der Politischen Ökonomie*], tr. Martin Nicolaus (Harmondsworth, Middlesex: Penguin Books Ltd., 1973), p. 158: "Free individuality, based on the universal development of individuals and on their subordination of their communal, social productivity as their social wealth, is the third stage."

TRADITION

'Localism' as a form of social consciousness develops together with what is apprehended as 'tradition.' More precisely, how does 'minor' tradition (as the expression of a 'folklore') interweave with the 'major' tradition (as a creation of a cultural 'élite')? More particularly: through what resistances is this done? Is the bipolarity of 'survival – revival' confirmed, and to what degree? Are we speaking of 'relics' of earlier cultural forms or of 'archaisms' which are resistant to historical time and its *longue durée*? How are the 'fabrics of meanings' which the framework of values of a past (or merely different) social formation bequeaths us endowed with significance in each instance? All these questions on occasion take on the form of an acute dilemma, which can be condensed into the formulation: is 'tradition' inherited, or is in learnt? As to the first point of the dilemma, Wittgenstein pronounces, "Tradition is not something a man can learn; not a thread he can pick up when he feels like it, any more than a man can choose his own ancestors. Someone lacking a tradition who would like to have one is like a man unhappily in love"[3] On the other hand, those who continue in the 'historical empiricism' of the anthropologist Franz Boas define 'culture' as "the experienced totality of the socially acquired behaviour of a group", and consequently observe that "knowledge of this behaviour is handed on from generation to generation by example and practice."[4]

If 'tradition' permeates the complex of factors which makes up the subject, that is, his/her social 'identity,' this means that we have an institutionalising of socialisation, but within a given community of practices and symbolic goods. 'Forms of life' are externalised as a criterion for self-recognition by the subjects by familiarisation with and experience of knowledge, symbols, messages, classifications and relations which have 'otherness' as a limit of reference. Thus, 'tradition' is an on-going 'apprenticeship' and at the same time individual participation in the collective memory which is reproduced through the everyday practices of the 'social whole' with 'orality' as a central – but not sole – pivot of their meanings.

A 'social totality' further apportioned refers us, *inter alia*, to the fluctuating relations between a 'learned' tradition (which covers the territory in a hegemonic fashion) and a 'folk' tradition (which suggests different 'localisms' in the process of its emergence). Does the establishment and expansion of the former shrink and marginalise the latter? If the marginalisation of the forms of 'folk culture' is a fact, this is brought about by the birth and domination of the 'nation state.' It is the

---

[3] L. Wittgenstein, *Culture & Value*, G.H. von Wright and Heikki Nyman (ed.), Peter Winch (tr.) (Oxford: Blackwell Publishing, 1980), p. 76e.

[4] See Franz Boas, *Race, Language and Culture* (New York: Macmillan, 1948), See also Skouteri-Didaskalou (1995), p. 29.

side-effect of an amalgam of factors which function independently and cumulatively, and, in any event, not in the sense of the positivistic offsetting of 'supra-historical constant entities.'

Of course, local communities in Greece, for example, have been, during the post-War period, consistently losing their self-sufficient existence because of successive admixtures of 'learned' and 'folk' 'tradition,' the rate of industrialisation, the attraction of the cities, agricultural migration, and civil war. In recent decades, the spread of the mass media and, above all, television (which has penetrated most homes and coffee-shops in the countryside), has given shape to new codes of behaviour, has reinforced stereotypes and has determined attitudes with consumable symbolic goods produced within the context of consumer capitalism. In any event, the manner of organisation of private space, in which the everyday routine of the subjects is more 'organically' involved with the 'orality' of their practice, depends upon the 'national' television instruction-book, which is developing into a mechanism of cultural hegemony which is a law unto itself. If the printed word demanded a readiness for abstraction which was realisable within the framework of the 'learned' tradition, the 'culture of the image' wins over with less resistance the local agents of the 'minor' tradition.

ENTRENCHMENT IN DIFFERENCE

A recent variation – and one coming, moreover, from the '*Grécistes*' – of this 'entrenchment in difference' provides evidence of the manner of the 'legitimation' of racism by the reasoning of the 'right to difference.'[5] This is occurring now, when racist political parties or parties susceptible to racist demagoguery become active in the European Union, when stricter measures of control over would-be immigrants are voted, and when practices involving flexibility in the supply of labour are becoming easier, leading to seasonal and unhealthy employment which bring about the cheap reproduction of working people and encourage discrimination on racial criteria. Racism, then, as a relation between parties lacking equality of status in the same society transforms 'otherness,' or merely 'difference,' into hostility by the firm establishment of 'prejudices' and 'xenophobia,' which entails an unwavering hostility to those coming from alien parts. Of course, *praejudicia* – that is, that which comes before any reasoned judgement and any institution of law – flows from and is channelled through the 'hot' and 'cold' of the same tap: 'from above,' as features of the dominant ideology or as an active sub-section of it, by the side-effects of intellectuals of unimpeachable respectability, and 'from below,' within the framework of pressing everyday needs of survival and co-existence. In recent decades, following general opposition to the brutality of the Nazis,

---

[5] Michael Torigian, "The Philosophical Foundations of the French New Right," *Telos*, (1999): 6 - 42.

and in spite of stillborn attempts to absolve the Holocaust of guilt and to repress it, racism directed from above has undergone a certain transformation: it has relegated to second place (or ignored) 'race,' giving prominence to the cultural differences of national or ethnic groups which, instead of being regarded as a creation of history, are treated as their 'second nature': differences in language, customs, religion, which have served as the 'springboard' for the racialisation of the 'right to difference.' The 'right' of protection, in a complex of 'aggressive alertness,' of 'our' 'identity' as French, Spanish, and so on, is put before all else. Racism filtered from below has institutional underpinnings, and involves the whole of the discrimination, which is to be found at work, in housing, in education, in health care, and so on. There is, in other words, an underlying, established complex of social inequalities and concomitant oppression, in the process of marginalisation of social groups, that is, in the difficulty of their access to the labour market and, related to this, to the public goods that the perception of modern societies attaches to the dignity of the citizen.

RIGHTS OF CULTURAL MINORITIES

Undoubtedly, the policy of safeguarding the right of 'difference' is underpinned by noteworthy reasoning and, concomitantly, has a strategy, deserving of respect, of the new movements in society which in the last decades of the twentieth century promoted it as a transcendence of the 'class identity' in which the labour movement has persisted. However, the crucial question is whether the 'policy of difference' favours or disarms the success of an alternative practice: whether, that is, self-restriction within the framework of 'difference' contributes to the shaping of a reality, existent and 'iconic,' which provides new stimuli for the handling of 'difference' as 'cultural pluralism.' One might at this point wonder, together with the ancient sage who was accustomed to 'displace civilisation,' how we are to carry our humble barrel to all points of the planet (and not only there), pointing out the need for the planning and emergence of an 'anti-society,' a wedge in the back of surrounding society. At the opposite extreme from an attitude which has been termed 'cultural absolutism,'[6] there is no cultivation of the ideological equipment of a single-dimensional globalised discourse which turns towards uniformity and the derivation of a lowest common factor imposed by internationalised 'intellectual technology' and related directing mechanisms. These two forms of apprehension of today's reality have a complementary function, and over against them they have, as a common antithesis, an approach consisting of the specific highlighting of differences, without the slide into the expediencies of a naive hegemonism in the delineation of cultural phenomena. Over and beyond the rhetoric of 'identity,' of the microcosms and the megacosms, the rights of cultural

---

[6] See Rhoda E. Howard, "Cultural Absolutism and the Nostalgia for Community," *Human Rights Quarterly* 15, no.2 (1993): 315-338.

minorities, and, first and foremost, of cultural creativity itself, are stated and claimed. The latter, moreover, is not apprehended as a channel for the conveying of related 'goods' which precludes improvisation, active apprehension and diffusion, and a variety of forms of 'syncretism' or 'hybrid' contextualisations.

CONCLUSION

By way of conclusion: the issue of 'homotopia' cannot be detached from the issue of 'heterotopia'. Moreover, at the present time, because of the way in which the frontier between the economy and politics is treated, the risk of 'localisms' does not presuppose enclosure in a 'part,' a fact which constitutes one more form of legitimisation of the 'whole' and of the concomitant homogenisation which it attempts to impose. This is because often, to paraphrase Lenin's diagnosis, the 'part' does not suffer from the 'whole,' but from the inadequate diffusion of the latter to its individual parts. If, then, both the 'part' and the 'whole' have two faces, like the god of the Roman marketplace, it would be useful for us to prevent the right to 'difference' from declining into a practice of 'entrenchment,' which would serve the purposes of those who are opposed to 'localisms'; at the same time, it would be useful for us to realise that the 'megacosm' is not the prisoner of an economic and cultural hegemony, but involves the right of humanity to conceive of and realise a different society. To carry forward Lenin's thought, it seems that in the friction between the 'microcosms' and 'megacosms,' politics again takes precedence over the economy. Such an 'alphabet' of practice presupposes a realisation that the 'historical design' for the genesis of capitalism in Western Europe, which was indeed a 'part' with intentions of becoming the 'whole,' cannot be apprehended as a "philosophical and historical theory on general evolution" which "inevitably all peoples will pass through."[7] Finally, undertaken by a social consciousness with its feet on the ground, such a risk of the 'partial' on the open horizons of the planet has as its starting-point the certainty that "World history would have a very mystical character if there were no room in it for chance,"[8] which would sum up the possibility of the speeding up or slowing down of a 'localism' in relation to the 'general tendency' towards the unfolding of the 'whole.'

University of Ioannina
Ioannina, Greece

---

[7] Karl Marx, Letter from Marx to Editor of the Otyecestvenniye Zapisky [Notes on the Fatherland] (Nov. 1877) in *Marx and Engels Correspondence* (New York: International Publishers, 1968), p. 111.

[8] Marx, cited in Jacques Le Goff, *History and Memory*, tr. Steven Rendall and Elizabeth Claman (New York: Columbia University Press, 1992), p. 125.

CHAPTER XLV

THE NATIONAL IDEA OF KAZAKHSTAN

ABDUMALIK NYSANBAYEV

The most difficult decade in the development of a sovereign Kazakhstan has passed in a deep breath, in one moment. There is not even a word of a transitional period anymore, due to the significant economic progress. The growth of a middle class – which is a basic factor for economic stability – is continuing; it is also remarkable that a change is being made from an image of the Republic as a source of raw materials, to that of a country with innovative technologies and the development and implementation of advanced telecommunications. Kazakhstan is gaining a reputation in the international arena as an initiator of various forums, such as the Congress of World and Traditional Religions recently held in Astana, and forthcoming congresses of scientific and educational leaders, where representatives of many peoples, parties, cultures and denominations have been focused on a highly promising productive dialogue. The young republic reveals high levels of creative potential and an enviable passion, setting the tempo at many international gatherings. Recently, the Russian leader V. V. Putin agreed that Kazakhstan was a leader in the signing of the quadripartite agreement on economic and cultural integration in Yalta, creating a new page in the history of the post-Soviet states. Kazaks are not likely to leave their native republic anymore without understanding their future and the future of their children in a manner that is influenced by the country's new opportunities. It is not certain, but it is probable that every child born in the near future will receive a good amount of money in Kazakhstan, so as to start life with few doubts and full of confidence. The wealth of our country can support these sorts of expectations. Those who left the country in search of a better life are coming back to their native land where, in accordance with our President's words, the door is always open for them.

One could refer to statistics in order to present reliable data and tables as evidence of this, but the facts speak for themselves even without arithmetical indications. Even though this is the case, we should not and must not let success cause us to be overconfident, leaving complicated issues unsolved. Indeed, there are some challenges. Kazakhstan is witnessing an increasing polarization of society, for example. While the middle class is in the process of forming the foundation of society, there is an increasing division of wealth. It is sometimes heard that nowhere but here are there such a great number of big expensive vehicles; nowhere is wealth exhibited so impudently and ostentatiously; there are gorgeous and expensive houses in the suburbs, casinos, expensive restaurants, entertainment centers and disco clubs.

It is considered improper and inappropriate to demonstrate one's wealth in Europe, where a different image of wealth and success exists. The level of a nation's wealth is shown by material possessions and bank accounts in underdeveloped countries, but in developed ones other factors exist: education, prestige of profession, and the general level of culture. Kazakhstan is not far from this.

What might alarm many people in seeing this increasing this polarization, is the lack of a unifying inspiring idea for all ethnic groups, classes and strata, that would fuse them spiritually and morally into one nation and one people. The question is whether it is possible to develop such an idea at all: how to unite 130 ethnic groups; how to come to an agreement with the owners of very expensive houses, on the one hand, and inhabitants of simple multi-flat houses, on the other – and, even worse, with those people living in shelters.

There are many questions to be asked here. Must we return to the notorious former ideological system in order to form a national idea? What is ideology, and what functions does it have? Is it possible to create one united state when there is no single ideology – where there can be an ideological pluralism?

In the abstract, each and every ideology can be rejected – but what does this mean? If it means that the position advocated here is an historical type of Marxism or totalitarianism, then this 'ideology' was rejected a long time ago. Ideology can certainly be understood in different ways. It can be perverted, it can be an illusion or a mere system of ideas where reality is distorted in order to approve and legalize the interests of specific social groups. Such an ideology is an effective method in the manipulation of the masses. A good example is the communist ideology, a totalitarian system that does not allow any different trend of thought or action, spreading the stereotypes and dogmas of Marxism and Leninism at the level of governmental politics.

Yet there is another aspect of ideology: namely, a system of ideas, whereby the society is guided by being consolidated around a single program, stratagem, or paradigm. The existence of society here is neither a simple empirical reality, nor purely ideal. A society can certainly be a real one, not as a sum or aggregate of individuals or ethnic groups, but as a primary and authentic reality.

This discussion leads us to deal with the dialectics of real and ideal, real and duty. Threads of the ideal are sewn into the cloth of daily life. This ideal is not a consequence of tendencies of the real, but it can be produced by the power of a human being's spirit aimed at completing a breakthrough and projecting from the future to the present. The ideal is both accessible and not; it can and cannot be achieved, but the life of a human being becomes one-dimensional, uni-planar, senseless, and flattened in time and space without it.

Ideology can be understood as the totality of such semantic ideas, program of change, and spiritual development. *Logos* as the second component of definition is the law, the universal, the highest word. If one considers ideology from this point of view, then undoubtedly it is necessary to us, since society senses a lack of spirituality, humaneness, love, and compassion. Steady tendencies toward consumption, over-consumption, and luxury are outlined. Young people flaunt their lack of spirituality, believing that everything can be purchased – from a degree in education to the benevolence of a chosen one. Mass media exhibit actions unprecedented in their history, asserting the cult of violence, cruelty, and sexual perversion – inculcating a habit of not valuing the life of a person and, moreover, not valuing human dignity. It is now old-fashioned even to mention honor and conscience, for these are obsolete words; they have no place for those seeking success and big business deals. Ideology, as the study of spiritual, moral, and truly humanistic values in the social sphere, is as necessary as the air; otherwise it is possible to choke.

Having an ideology that unites the people of Kazakhstan is essential in preserving national and cultural identity, particularly when confronted by the threat of loss of identity as a cultural and state unit through the process of globalization. The basic features of the contemporary epoch are market, financial, and technological integration, unifying ways of life so that they reflect a single world civic community and world democracy.

At present, there is much written and discussed about the globalization by scientists, politicians, sociologists, and philosophers. They tend to speak about two types of globalization: the first one has been achieved in reality precisely as Westernization or Americanization. One super-power takes over all the positions in the Internet empire, becoming increasingly richer by connecting the idea of peace with its own standards of life and its global view. This world culture does not have a memory. It is converted into goods among goods, and is subordinated to the criteria of the market.

The second type of globalization is represented not only at the level of hypotheses and theories, but is also actively supported by the practical efforts of a new social movement of anti-globalists. From the theoretical point of view, the globalization that concentrates on the scientific and technical achievements of the whole of humanity is to be used for the good of all people, easing the terrestrial burden experienced by each and every individual. This "other globalization" does not spread standards or unify; it does not suppress national uniqueness; on the contrary, it encourages difference and dissimilarity, considering their existence as a condition of its own realization.

This "other globalization" is not only in our thoughts and dreams. Active measures have been undertaken in order to give globalization this very nature. If it concerns language, then English has become the language of the Internet, business, education and science, but it does not have the function of a language for interpersonal communication. In the USA, Spanish is the second language by its significance. The cultural identity of

France and the French language is being defended successfully. Much is done in Kazakhstan to develop and promote the Kazakh language in every sphere of state activity. Concerning the anti-globalists, this movement is very contradictory in terms of its social and political credo. The concept of anti-globalization is not yet fully thought out. Some anti-globalists speak against globalization by taking such extremist actions as the destruction of McDonalds. They attempt to cancel summits of "the big eight." The social composition of such anti-globalists varies a lot – including those defending freedom of commerce, those intending to protect their religious values, but also those who do not have clear ideological orientations at all.

However, there is another wing of the anti-globalists: scientists, owners, politicians and prominent people of culture who are oriented toward the idea of "another globalization," and who have united into related groups in order to act on the basis of the law, avoiding extremist practices. Such international non-governmental organizations include 'the alliance for solidarity and peace,' which works against the negative tendencies of globalization and is financed by the Mayer fund. This is a force capable of changing the course of events and influencing the objective process of globalization.

We agree that we need the system of ideas that makes it possible to be united and to rally together even more closely in order to preserve national and cultural identity. The basic boundary of the forthcoming transformations is that of worldwide pressure, which carries with itself a unification and destruction of everything not under its command and is not likely to accept dictated standards, such as those of national, traditional, and rebellious states. The outlook here is not very optimistic. The fate of national states is set, let us dare to say, 'on the map'. There are no boundaries on the flow of information. The traditional form of existence of the nation exhibits itself when the state comes into conflict with the tendency toward the dissolution of state borders. The ideology of communicative transparency is formed; the social place of an individual is allotted through a focus and tangle of communications. "Globalization includes the loss of political authority and influence on the national states' level, which seemed to be the ideal tools of territorial and political organization during the last three centuries."[1]   Power is passed to transnational corporations, and territory loses its previous meaning.

This frightening tendency still has to be grasped theoretically in many respects. Evidently, globalization opens a new era of universal history, forming a united, mutually agreed upon, and interconnected world. This unity should take into account the differences and the unique experiences of national cultures. Fear of globalization comes from an

---

[1] *Globalizatsia i Postsovetskoye Obschestvo* [*Globalization and Post-soviet Society*] (Moscow 2001), p. 31.

antiquated model of relationships between a universal and particular, where the former absorbs and assimilates differences. A different logical structure is assumed in "another globalization." This model is thought out in postmodern concepts, in terms such as "constellation" and "rhizome." 'Constellation' is an astronomical term indicating dual stellar motion around the axis and a movable center. The Universal is created by the attraction of special moments, and the more brightly individuality is expressed, the steadier is the Universal. "Rhizome" is a botanical term indicating a plant (such as the 'lily of the valley') which has many roots, but which preserves a unity. These metaphors express the idea of "nonviolent synthesis," and a unity that encourages differences. A similar type of relation can be the basis of "another globalization."

It is useful to note the remarkable statements of N. Berdyaev when he reminds us that a universal brotherhood assumes the individuality of every brother: "Nationality is an individual existence; out of this an existence of humanity is impossible. It is in the very depths of life, and a nationality is a value created by history."[2] This thought becomes a key one in works of the Eurasians, insisting that precisely a variety – a mosaic structure – of cultures ensures stability, creating the possibility of a plastic existence and allowing for the survival of the human being. L. Gumilev refers to a general theory of systems: only systems with a structure complicated enough and having a significant number of elements can be steady and viable. On the contrary, simplified systems do not have this advantage. On this view, rational globalization should be structured, avoid chaos, and appeal to local traditional cultures in order to be steady.

It is possible not to be afraid of globalization, and it is necessary to learn to live under the conditions of expanding communication in the economic, cultural, and even biographical spheres while, at the same time, retaining something for oneself and preserving and developing national culture, self-consciousness, values, and interests. The most important tasks here can be solved with the help of a system of ideas, values, and semantic aspects – that is, an ideology.

Turning to the most important issue: What national interests shall come to the fore in Kazakhstan within the next five years? What is the typology of national interests? How is it possible to formulate a national idea through an ideology – through the meaning of idea, as it is seen to be? What is the meaning of a national idea in a poly-ethnic, poly-cultural society? The category of "nation" is discussed from different points of view in contemporary science, leading to many interpretations and contradictions. There is a steady trend of the identification of this concept with "fellow-citizenship," which assumes the negation of the ethnic content of the "nation" and the inclusion of social and economic parameters alone.

---

[2] N. Berdyaev, *Sudba Rosiyi* [*The Fate of Russia*] (Moscow, 1990), p.19.

(In this respect, we can ask whether the American nation belongs to one *socium* and state.)

First of all, nation should be considered in terms of ethnic context as the most developed integral form of *ethnos*. There are other terms such as 'fellow-citizenship' and 'people,' used in order to express socio-economic and civil unity. As for the latter, in Kazakhstan there is only one nation, and the Kazakhs live on the historical, native land. All other remaining ethnic groups are in diaspora, and have their own historical native land. Discussion now addresses the unity of the Kazakh nation and the diaspora in the formation of citizenship in Kazakhstan. "The key objective of the Ethno-politics of Kazakhstan is the development of one united people of Kazakhstan in the country as a political and cultural community of citizens belonging to different ethnic groups. A similar understanding of Kazakhstani people as a qualitatively new form of self-identification differs radically from Stalin's definition of nation, the well-known features of which do not characterize a nation actually but an *ethnos* or ethno-nation."[3]

It is clear at present that the national idea indicates that the Kazakh idea is aimed at the integration, consolidation, and unity of all ethnic groups into a single one, into a fellow-citizenship, into the people of Kazakhstan. The Kazakh idea reaches the more encompassing status of the 'Kazakhstani' idea, revealing and achieving this potential of integration. This issue does not involve a 'domination' of the Kazakh nation, underlining its advantages and privileges. All ethnic groups, religions, confessions and cultures have equal rights and abilities according to the Constitution of the Republic of Kazakhstan, creating a democratic, lawful and secular state. The Kazakhs have one privilege affecting the fate of their native republic and the future of other cultures: responsibility for themselves and other ethnic groups. The demographic situation is substantially different in Kazakhstan nowadays. According to statistical data, the Republic is 51% Kazakh, 17% Turk, and 30% Slovenian. Although there are about 130 ethnic groups in the country, the Kazakhs and the Russians are the major ones, and the size of other ethnicities is small. The Kazakhs from Mongolia, Turkey, China, Russia, Iran and other countries continue to come back to the country, increasing the numbers of their *ethnos*. All this offers new possibilities for the Kazakh nation to solve global issues. "The development of the Kazakh people does not mean the dissolution and disappearance of the original Kazakh *ethnos*. On the contrary, the Kazakh *ethnos* as numerically the largest in the republic and

---

[3] A. N. Nysanbayev, R. K. Kadyrzhanov, *Institut Prezidentstva v Novyh Nezavisimyh Gosudarstvah* [*Institute of Presidency of the Newly Independent States*] (Almaty, 2001), p.140.

politically dominating it, should become the nucleus and frame around which the people of Kazakhstan are to be consolidated."[4]

How is a Kazakh national idea able to become 'Kazakhstani,' thus uniting all ethnic groups into a single one? Over the centuries, the Kazakh people have been inspired by the idea of the native earth, "Atameken," when dreaming about independence. This dream of the Kazakhs came true with national sovereignty in the 1990s. The Kazakh idea, national pride, dignity and national spirit were personified in the image of an independent national state, which asserts the principles of democracy and freedom in the international arena. The Kazakh idea as an ideal of independence is close and dear to all remaining ethnicities which belong to Kazakhstan with all their heart and soul – these people were warmed by its caressing sun, and by its kind-heartedness, sincere friendliness, culture of tolerance and the openness of the Kazakhs. In the face of advancing globalization, the national idea continues to inspire, focusing on strengthening national independence, sovereignty, preserving the originality and the unique culture of the Kazakhs in the dialogue with cultures of other ethnic groups in the framework of a unitary state.

Kazakh traditional culture contains an essential consolidating potential. The basis of this culture is unity through interpersonal communication; having kin and family is the first and unconditional vital value. In the family, one is presented not only by this or that *hypostasis*, but by the entire essence, the full weight of his or her vital and human manifestations. Two features of existence – orientation to nature and adherence to the memory of one's ancestors – represent the humanity and flexibility of this social institution. That is why the family and kin enter into the socio-political structures at different levels. Discussion is not focused on a restoration of archaic consciousness, but the use of the priceless experience of interpersonal communication, increasing the ability for mutual understanding, support and collaboration – qualities and features that are necessary for realization of the Kazakh idea as the Kazakhstani one.

Kazakh culture contains rich spiritual and moral potential. Nevertheless, it is necessary to exert efforts in order to discover it. For this purpose a large-scale state program, "Cultural Heritage," has been launched, aiming at the mastery of various layers of culture in every field: philosophy, literature, music, art, and science. In philosophy, for example, twenty volumes of the series "The Philosophical Heritage of the Kazakh People from the Ancient Times to the Present" will be soon issued in Russian. Also, it is planned to publish thirty volumes of a "World Philosophical Heritage" series, including fragments from the works of the greatest thinkers of the East and West, together with scientific commentary in Kazakh.

---

[4] Ibid. p.141.

If we say that the Kazakh national idea as the basis of national ideology is a challenge to preserving and consolidating national culture, independence, and sovereignty under conditions of globalization, then the question is as follows: what is strictly Kazakh here, if all other peoples and states advance a thesis of independence as the dominant center of their ideologies? The content of the Kazakh national idea should be concretized and clarified. What is the uniqueness of the Kazakhs? What is their national pride or the spirit of the nation?

The greatest son, poet, prophet, and thinker of the Kazakh land, Abay, helps us to answer to these questions. He penetrated the future with his gaze. He was the one who knew how to express the spirit of nation, to formulate its imperatives, and to see the value of its semantics. Abay revealed to the world something important and substantial, so that Heidegger, without even not knowing him personally, heard his cherished word and responded to his appeal: to become a herdsman, a neighbor, a keeper of existence, to recreate an integral relation of "a man and world," to forego the principle of supremacy above nature which did not let things, "little things," declare their inner essence.

Compared to the Western tradition and its special type of rationality, which develops the intellect or mind or reason exclusively, Abay emphasizes the substantial unity of mind and heart, giving preference to impulses of soul. "A wise man is the one in whom the feelings of love and justice prevail; he is a man of wisdom and a man of science."[5] Science, mind, and knowledge have to appear before the strictest judge – the heart, justice, and the moral. Shakarim says about a conscientious mind: "A human's eyes can be shut, but the eye of a soul – never."[6]

"Another globalization" assumes conscientiousness and rests on spiritual and moral priorities and general human values. The national idea as a state of independence, including the "conscientious mind," accepts the primacy of the heart and soul and, at the same time, focuses on the mind, the development of sciences, and information technologies. It seems that the "conscientious mind" is not likely to manage stronger pressures like competition and the standards of the world market, where the priorities are only 'success' and 'benefit.' However, humanity realizes already the importance of a spiritual renaissance, understanding that the meaning of human history is spiritual self-development and renovation, and regaining the lost values of love, mutual understanding and compassion. In the context of forming planetary consciousness, the "conscientious mind" of Shakarim is a principle that is very significant.

The national idea is able to provide a way of joining all the ethnic groups of Kazakhstan into a united citizenship. The inspiring idea for Americans is 'success,' the possibility of moving up the social ladder. The

---

[5] Abay, *Kniga Slov* [*A Book of Words*] (Alma-Ata, 1993), p. 90.
[6] Shakarim, *Zapiski Zabytogo* [*Notes of the Forgotten*] (Almaty, 1993), p. 119.

leading idea for the Kazakhs and other ethnic groups of the Republic is one of independence, which includes the "conscientious mind" of Abay and Shakarim. But does it expand reality – to a reality where one can meet this "conscientious mind" in the pursuit of profit, shady and dishonorable transactions, and the forgeries and bribes that abound? Let us keep in mind that the idea is an area of the ideal; it is not about what a person is and his or her moral character, but about what one should be in order to be a good human being. Since a human being is worthy of the highest and must be filled with pride for one's actions and deeds, one longs for the purity of the ideal, and desires not to remain always on the culpable Earth.

The Kazakh national idea is close to and intelligible to the Russians, where the problems of morals, conscience, and sense have always been paramount for and significant to the nation. That is where the comprehensive relationship of the Kazakhs and the Russians lies. The two grew up on common Eurasian land. Impressive analogies with the spirit of the Turkish people are revealed here. Great Russian ritual songs are comprised in a five-tone scale – a feature also of Turkish tribes. The style of the Russian fairy tale is strictly analogous with Turkish folklore. "The connection of Russians with 'Turanians' is not only ethnographically but also anthropologically sustained, since, undoubtedly, besides Slovenian, there are streams of both Ugro-Finnish and Turkish blood in Russian veins. Unconditionally, there is contact with the 'Turanian East' in the nature of the Russian people."[7]

Dialogue under contemporary conditions is a priority for solving conflicts and contradictions: this is a method through which the contemporary world can aim at agreement and mutual understanding. Recently, dialogue has been appealed to very often; nevertheless, it is important not only to proclaim and to declare the value of dialogue, but also to enter into it, actually realizing its different types and levels. A dialogue can be an illusion – a set of monologues, while positions remain external according to the relation between those involved. Dialogue can be a monologue, a point of view thrust into conversation. There is also a type of a dialogue when the opinion of an opponent is taken into consideration, but it does not influence one's point of view. Finally, a dialogue that is deep and existential – when an overall field of conversation is formed and new content arises – this dialogue leads to change in personal points of view, since to understand means to go beyond the limits, to change.

Such a comprehensive dialogue is a method with which the Kazakh national idea could come to be the common Kazakh ideal, integrating all ethnic groups into one united people, capable of not only preserving its cultural identity in the process of globalization, but also becoming the important structuring factor of its realization. Only national ideology can

---

[7] N. S. Trubetskoi, *Istoria. Kultura. Yazyk.* [*History. Culture. Language*] (Moscow, 1995), p. 126.

facilitate an entry into the world community with a feeling of national pride, and consciousness of importance.

Out of the six thousand languages existing in the world, four thousand are dying. This means that diverse pictures of life are fading, and that humanity is losing and dissipating its wealth. We should preserve our excellent language, with its rich and surprising culture, unique as it is, and as the only voice of its kind, with the intonation of the "*kuy*" of Kurmangazy, famous all over the world. Complaints of a Turkish professor at the XXI World Congress of Philosophy held in Istanbul are here pertinent: "I am dissolved in English. English made me a prisoner estranged from my roots. I feel like a pathetic marginal. The age-old senses of native culture attract me."

Thus, a component part and a key idea of national ideology can take Shakarim's portrait of the "conscientious mind" as a nucleus, as a living soul of an entire national world-view, which includes the integral system of ideas such as following: the priority of intellectual values, humanism, patriotism, democracy, tolerance, the combination of liberal values and the values of traditional culture, the development of the Kazakh national culture and its language, the orientation to the newest Western technologies connected with Kazakh spirit, and the development of the middle class as a guarantor of state stability.

Ideology also includes national interests, which determine the policy of the state for the next five to seven years. These include economic development and the awareness of the culture of the Kazakh nation; these also include the renaissance of villages and the rural areas, since the nucleus of the Kazakhstan people should be strong and healthy. National interests involve the development of specific social programs, aimed at supporting the material and spiritual development of the Kazakhs.

The system of ideas and interests is subject to being structured according to the principle of dialogue. The basic direction of national ideology is intended to move from force and cruelty to dialogue and agreement. This ideology will contribute to strengthening national independence, safety, and the civil and cultural identity of Kazakhstan; it will help the country not only to withstand the pressures of developing globalization, but also to preserve its national image as it develops itself under the sign of "another globalization."

What can keep us strong in the face of the threat of standardization and unification? Something unique that demonstrates this experience and that shows itself as a model of culture and social structure to the world. Kazakhstan has all that it needs to represent these values to the world. At a time when tensions increase, terrorist acts are being committed, and the blood of innocent people is being shed; when one superpower thrusts its will and ideology on the world, the greatest hope lies in mutual understanding and agreement amongst many ethnic groups and faiths, as represented to the world by the coexistence found in an independent sovereign Kazakhstan.

It has been considered 'worldly wisdom' since ancient times that power and force can be stopped only by power and force, although the men of authentic wisdom have asserted the opposite: "Hatred cannot be stopped by hatred; it can be stopped only by love." Kazakhstan proves a simple but great truth to the world. It is possible to live in agreement, without conflict. It is possible to resolve contradictions in the course of a dialogue, and it is possible to attain unity, preserving differences and cultural and confessional uniqueness. It is true that power has to be opposed to power, but there is good power, and an instance of such a good power is the power of a national spirit.

Institute of Philosophy and Political Science
Ministry of Education of the Republic of Kazakhstan
National Academy of Sciences of the Republic of Kazakhstan
Almaty, Kazakhstan

CHAPTER XLVI

GLOBAL HORIZON: DIALOGUE VERSUS HEGEMONY, AND CO-OPERATION AGAINST CONFLICT

RASHID HASSAN

INTRODUCTION

Aristotle said that philosophy begins with wonder: wonder about the human race and the universe that surrounds it. This notion of wonder is still a major feature of contemporary philosophy. Dialogue was conceived as a means of discovering and understanding more about other peoples' philosophical views and observations. Through dialogue, discussion, argument, and counter-argument, new thoughts have been developed which have produced new theories, and these theories, in turn, have led to new discoveries.

But dialogue can only be genuine and universal when the voices of other peoples and cultures are heard and, further, accommodated. Hegemony is born when a particular philosophical view or culture forcefully claims to be dominant and ignores or marginalises other philosophical views and cultures. Co-operation and harmony among peoples and nations can be securely established only when other philosophical discourses are given the respect and the attention they deserve; hegemony only brings about rejection and conflict.

From the outset we must bear in mind that hegemony and conflict are not only associated with people of different cultures and philosophical outlooks, but also emerge from people of the same culture or living in the same geographical space. Hegemony and lack of respect of other peoples' views and problems often develops into oppression, resulting in major conflict. In some parts of Africa, that is exactly what happened.

In Somalia in the 1970s and 1980s, a system of military governance with an authoritarian rule arose, and it waged a war of genocide against part of its nation (Somaliland) where, according to human rights organizations, more than 50,000 people were killed or displaced. Another case is Rwanda, where more than one million people of the Tutsi tribe, which constituted a major part of the country's population, were killed by their own government.

Co-operation among cultures and nations is possible and must be the ultimate goal for all peoples; the world is not a place for the clashes of civilizations or cultures as described by Samuel Huntington.[1] This-co-operation among nations and cultures is achievable only when respect and appreciation are given to all cultures and human thoughts.

The nineteenth-century faith in human progress was tempered – and nearly undermined – by the tragic experience of two world wars, and by the grim realisation that dehumanization and authoritarian rule can follow in the wake of technological progress. Immediately after the Second World War and the defeat of fascism, there was optimism, and the widespread opinion was that such horrific experiences could never happen again. But as time passed, we witnessed a series of major conflicts and wars, such as the Vietnam War, the Algerian War of Independence, the Palestine-Israel War, and more recently the wars in Rwanda, Afghanistan and Iraq. The obvious failure of dialogue in these cases has been a clear indication of how the universal mind has been incapable of emerging from its dark side and of solving differences through dialogue, before these differences reach a confrontational stage.

GLOBALISATION

Today's globalisation, which has been the focus of debate in recent years, is unlike the previous globalisation, which hinged on the expansions of empires and colonialisation. Contemporary globalisation has been more centred on culture. Many social theorists view globalisation differently. It is an ongoing trend whereby the world has, in many respects, become one without social boundaries, and this trend has been accelerating. This globalisation includes the internationalising of production, a new international division of labour, new migratory movements from South to North, a new competitive environment that accelerates these processes and the internationalising of the state, and the making of nation states into mere agencies of the globalising world.

The capitalist world-economy now dominates the global social context that conditions, measures, and determines all other aspects of social life: namely, politics and cultures. The process of globalisation has drawn attention to the debate of the relationship between state and society.

According to William Garrett and Roland Robertson,

> The processes of globalization entail more than simply the maturation of modern thought-forms and structures, however. The present circumstance presupposes, or so we shall argue, that the world is rapidly coming to be apprehended as 'one place,' that is, as a totality wherein discrete selves, nation-states, and even civilization traditions have their respective niches, each interconnected

---

[1] See S. P. Huntington, *The Clash of Civilizations and Remaking of the World Order* (London: Touchstone Books, 1996).

by complex, reticular relationships of belligerence and beneficence, competition and compromise, discordance and détente.[2]

The discourse of globalization refers – at least on the theoretical level – to a global village where harmony among nations and cultures prevails and hence minimises people's attachments to their particular worldviews. The introduction of modern communications such as e-mails and the internet has brought such a result closer. But while inhabitants of parts of this so-called global village still face hunger, acute health problems and insecurity, inhabitants of other parts of the global village are tremendously rich, with advanced facilities in every aspect of life. This is a challenge to philosophers and social theorists. The question is whether we can envisage a World Order better than the one we have at the moment.

African Renaissance Centre for Social Science Research, Media and Development (ARECSMED)
Hargeisa, Somaliland

---

[2] R. Robertson and W. E. Garrett (eds.), *Religion and Global Order: Religion and the Political Order*, Vol. IV (New York: Paragon House Publishers, 1991).

CHAPTER XLVII

COUNTER-HEGEMONY AND SAGE PHİLOSOPHY

DANIEL SMITH

INTRODUCTION

In this paper, I would like to suggest that something like a globalized sage philosophy project is a necessary condition for the development of effective counter-hegemonic philosophical theories and practices in the twenty-first century. The paper is based on the belief that such a counter-hegemonic philosophical intervention could play an important role in facilitating the emergence of the kind of inter-cultural and intra-cultural dialogues with which the papers in this volume, "The Dialogue of Cultural Traditions: A Global Perspective," are generally concerned. In turn, such dialogues are, in my opinion, a necessary condition for a relative democratization of human development in the twenty-first century.

However, the thesis of this paper is a modest one. Philosophy is not going to 'save the world.' Today, philosophers as such are rarely, if ever, as effective as Socrates was in really making a difference in their societies – let alone human development in general. My hypothesis is not that effective philosophical theory and practice are sufficient conditions for the democratization of our economic, political, and cultural development.[1] More, indeed, much more must be done that goes beyond the immediate concerns of philosophy as such, if the course of human development in the twenty-first century is to be fundamentally changed. The net effect of philosophy, as a professional discipline of academic studies and research, could, in general, be to reinforce the current hegemony under which we are

---

[1] 'Our' in this sentence means just that—the six, going on seven, billion of us. While such universalizing discursive gatherings have been subjected to a good deal of postmodern critique, I believe that globalization will force us to increasingly invoke such identifications. I also *hear* such an invocation in the very title of the conference of which these papers are a part: "a global perspective." I have argued elsewhere that, while we need to continue to deconstruct false or obsolete claims to universality and identity, at the same time we must not shy away from reconstructing and creating new foundations for universal identifications. See D. Smith, "Work, Commodity Fetishism, Ideology, and_Globalization," *The Global Economy and the National State*, International Conference, Ho Chi Minh National Political Academy, Hanoi, January 2003.

struggling.[2] In this paper I will develop some reasons for accepting the general claim that a philosophic return to what in the West is best represented by the image of Socrates, via the development of a globalized "Sage Philosophy Project," is a necessary condition for Philosophy in general to contribute to a global movement that is struggling to steer the course of globalization in a less cruel, more compassionate, and emancipatory direction based in the interests of the vast majority of humanity.[3]

Sage Philosophy was a project developed by the Kenyan philosopher, Henry Odera Oruka, in order to counter the hegemony of an image of Africa as devoid of any indigenous philosophic traditions. Concerning the question of philosophy's role in history and in relation to globalization and hegemony, it is important to recall and reflect on the fact that Hume, Kant, and Hegel all agreed that Africans (along with the Asiatics and the indigenous peoples of the Americas), were basically an inferior subspecies of humanity and devoid of any rational development prior to the coming of Europeans.[4] This 'enlightened' image of Africans, projected by the major Western philosophers of the 18th and 19th centuries, was part of a 'scientific' confirmation of the racist imagery that justified the slave trade – which lasted for over 300 years – and colonialism, and is arguably still functioning, perhaps on a more unconscious level, to justify

---

[2] I will not argue whether or not there is an established hegemony effectively determining the course of human development in relation to the economic and geo-political interests of a tiny minority of the human population, and that the consequences of the policies established under this hegemony are devastating for the vast majority of the human population and the future of the earth and humanity as a whole. In both the conferences sponsored by the Council for Research in Values and Philosophy (entitled, "The Dialogue of Cultural Traditions: A Global Perspective") and the *XXI World Congress of Philosophy* (on the theme of "Philosophy Facing World Problems"), the overwhelming majority of participants (it was perhaps as close to consensual as one could imagine on such an absolutely crucial question), agreed that though globalization is inevitable, in its current form it is being dominated by the 'interests' of a tiny minority of the human population with devastating consequences for human development.

[3] I am still inclined to say 'the real spiritual and material interest of humanity as a whole,' but at this point I will limit myself to 'the vast majority of humanity.' In other words, it seems to me that the masters of globalization must be suffering from an acute, historically constituted form of alienation from their true nature as human beings, and are pursuing ultimately self-destructive policies.

[4] See E. C. Eze, E.C. (ed.), "Introduction" to *Postcolonial African Philosophy* (Oxford: Blackwell Publishers, 1997).

the global distribution of wealth and the overt political and economic superiority of 'developed' countries over the 'developing' countries.[5]

It was primarily in order to debunk this racist imagery that Henry Odera Oruka initiated the African Sage Philosophy Project. In his project, professional philosophers ventured beyond the walls of their universities and conducted interviews with persons recognized to be sources of wisdom in their local traditional communities. One objective of Oruka's project was to document a form of African philosophy that had developed relatively independently of European influences, thus disproving "the well-known claim that 'real philosophical thought' had no place in traditional Africa ... [and that] philosophy in modern Africa is due wholly to the introduction of Western thought and culture to Africa."[6]

The motivations and objective of the original African project were complex and changed over the course of its development.[7] In relation to a twenty-first century globalized project, it is important to recognize that the primary objective would not be to prove the existence of a philosophical tradition and practice independent of academic and other institutions that are effectively embedded in the very structures of hegemony which we are attempting to challenge. Rather the primary objective would be to facilitate the emergence of alternative visions of humanity's future and help to develop effective strategies for realizing such visions. One aspect of realizing this objective would entail challenging the regimes of truth within which we, as professional philosophers, find ourselves, by introducing the popular and philosophic wisdom of indigenous communities (which has developed relatively independently of professional academia) into academic researches and debates.[8]

---

[5] Following the most recent round of WTO negotiations held in Cancun, Mexico in September 2003, 21(+) countries—representing the vast majority of the human population—'walked out' in protest to the European Union's and the United States' refusal to recognize the legitimate grievances of the 'developing' world concerning the subsidization of agriculture in the 'developed' world and other obvious injustices in the current world economic order. The response of United States Trade Representative, Robert Zoellick, to the negotiations was to lament that 'some representatives' to the negotiations were more interested in using 'inflammatory rhetoric' and 'pontification' rather than engaging in 'responsible negotiation.'

[6] H.O Oruka, "Sage Philosophy: The Basic Questions and Methodology" in *Sagacious Reasoning*, eds. Anke Graness and Kai Kresse (Nairobi: East African Educational Publishers, 1999), p. 62.

[7] F. Ochieng'-Odhiambo, "The Evolution of Sagacity: the Three Stages of Oruka's Philosophy," *Philosophia Africana*, 5.1 (2002): 19-32. See also G. Presbey, *Response to F. Odieng'-Odhiambo's Analysis of the Philosophy of H. Odera Oruka*, XXI World Congress of Philosophy, 2003, forthcoming.

[8] By 'indigenous' I do not necessarily mean geographically 'native' in the strict sense, but, more generally, groupings of people who are rooted in a

In order to introduce the general orientation of what a global counter-hegemonic sage philosophy project might entail, and clarify the specifically philosophical nature of the proposed project, I would like to briefly bring together the thoughts of a number of African and Western philosophers. The purpose of this juxtaposition is to critically reflect, from multiple perspectives, on the role of reason in traditional, modern and/or postmodern human development.

SAGE PHILOSOPHY AND HABERMAS'S THEORY OF COMMUNICATIVE ACTION

From the perspective of Jürgen Habermas, it is precisely the breakdown of an originary, unexamined core of fundamental beliefs and values, and the resulting expansion of the power of reason in human development, that led from 'tradition' to 'modernity.' In *The Philosophical Discourse of Modernity*, Habermas refers to what he calls a "communicative thawing," in which "the authority of tradition," is increasingly subjected to public discussion and critique.[9] This breakdown ushers in increasingly reflective communicative processes which at least implicitly acknowledge a set of values that point towards a progressive rationalization of human life and society. Habermas acknowledges that such processes can be, and, in fact, obviously are being, distorted and manipulated by political and economic interests which, in effect, are exercising a hegemonic hold on human development at this moment of our history. However, for Habermas, the progressive values of modern reason in human history, though violated, are inevitably acknowledged in the very distorted and manipulative practices necessary to maintain and expand the established hegemony.

For example, the use of overwhelming military force by one country to change the government of another relatively defenseless country must be justified through the assertion of a set of claims that would constitute valid reasons for others, such as the international community, to agree to, or at least allow, the intervention based on the honorable intentions of the invading country. This is new; this is 'modern'!

Presumably, before the development of 'modernity,' countries just did what they wanted and what they thought they had the power to do. Habermas argues that in the communicative processes of modern development, the values of trying to say what one believes to be true, reciprocally appealing to the rational nature of others, and being honest

---

shared local identity and *way of being*, e.g., 'indigenous communities' can be found in the barrios of East Los Angeles and the townships of Johannesburg.

[9] Qtd. in D. C. Hoy, & T. McCarthy, *Critical Theory* (Oxford & Cambridge: Blackwell, 1994), p. 46. Please note that the textual resources in English available to me in my current situation in Xibei (Northwest) University, Xi'an, P.R. China are somewhat limited.

about one's true intentions are implicitly acknowledged in modern communicative actions. A human being cannot successfully lie, manipulate or deceive without at least appearing to be telling the truth, respecting the other, and honestly revealing their true intentions.

So, in relation to the modern emergence of reason as the foundation of human development and as opposed to modernity's 'postmodern' and postcolonial critics, such as M. Foucault, J. Derrida, R. Rorty, L. Outlaw, T. Serequeberhan, and E. C. Eze et. al., Habermas still sees this historical process as holding out the traditional modern European promise of the 'Enlightenment.' Says Habermas:

> The more the worldview that furnishes the cultural stock of knowledge is decentered, the less the need for understanding is covered in advance by an interpreted Lifeworld immune from critique, and the more this need has to be met by the interpretive accomplishments of the participants themselves, that is, by way of risky (because rationally motivated) agreement, the more frequently we can expect rational action orientations.[10]

In other words, according to Habermas, as more and more people begin to question and reflect on aspects of their world that were previously taken for granted – in other words, as important 'realities' of a people's Lifeworld begin to emerge as 'beliefs' and 'values' which, as such, can be subjected to critical reflection and collective examination through dialogue – then the possibility of more rational ways of living begin to emerge.

This notion of "communicative thawing" in the transition from 'traditional' to 'modern' societies is central to Habermas's defense of modernity. In fact, this conception is based in what, to many, are some important Eurocentric weaknesses of his work, which are directly relevant to understanding what a globalized sage philosophy might entail. I will address these concerns below. For now, I want to clarify the meaning and significance of this "communicative thawing" and "the interpretive accomplishments of the participants themselves," by focusing on a critical distinction which Thomas McCarthy has developed based on Habermas's theory.

Thomas McCarthy, in a book he coauthored with David Hoy entitled *Critical Theory*, makes some of the practical implications of Habermas's work quite clear, and does so in a way that directly relates to a similar distinction made by Oruka in his Sage Philosophy Project. Says McCarthy:

---

[10] J. Habermas, *Theory of Communicative Action* (Boston: Beacon Press, 1984), p. 70.

I shall use accountability to designate an agent's capacity to engage in practical reasoning of the sorts required for everyday interaction, that is, roughly speaking, her ability to offer (typically conventional) accounts of her behaviour and to assess other's accounts of theirs (usually by reference to conventional standards). Accountability in this sense is a minimum requirement for rational agency. I will use autonomy to designate an agent's capacity to engage in critical reflective discourse concerning the justifiability of established or proposed norms and beliefs. Autonomy in this sense is central to the stronger sort of rational agency that Kant referred to as *Mündigkeit*, the capacity to think for oneself.[11]

In brief, I think this distinction could be extremely helpful in enabling us to reflect on what it means to truly think for ourselves, free from any hegemonic forces within which we might be living. True, there seems to be a bit of the isolated Cartesian cogito haunting such distinctions, as it also haunts Oruka's distinction – this too will be discussed below. However, it seems to me, such a distinction provides a good starting point, as long as we keep in mind the ghosts which might be haunting it. To approach it from a more traditional Western philosophical perspective, the distinction brings into focus the role of philosophy in challenging both individuals and society as a whole – whether it is 4th century B.C. Athenian society or societies subjected to the forces of globalization in the twenty-first century – and in recognizing the dangers of an "unexamined life" and the need to critically reflect on what is authoritatively established independent of reasoned inquiry, taken for granted, or even is just part of the 'reality' within which we find ourselves (e.g., some people are born to be 'masters' and others to be 'slaves,' warfare in human life is inevitable, etc.).

In relation to Sage Philosophy, it would seem that it is either a sign of the hegemony of Western philosophy or the universality of such distinctions that Oruka makes an extremely similar point in the development of his project.[12] As Oruka's Sage Philosophy Project developed, over the course of some 20 odd years (1974 – circa 1995), he

---

[11] T. McCarthy and D. Hoy, *Critical Theory* (London: Blackwell, 1994), p.44.

[12] On this question see: W. J. Ndaba, "Oruka's Sage Philosophy: Individualistic vs. Communal Philosophy" in A.P.J. Roux and P.H. Coetzee (eds.), *Beyond the Question of African Philosophy: A selection of papers presented at the International Colloquia, UNISA, 1994-1996* (Pretoria, South Africa: University of South Africa Press, 1996). Referred to in G. Presbey, *Response to F. Odieng'-Odhiambo's Analysis of the Philosophy of H. Odera Oruka*, XXI World Congress of Philosophy, 2003.

came to draw an important distinction between "folk" sages and "philosophic" sages. A folk sage, "though well informed and educative, fails to go beyond the celebrated folk-wisdom" of his community, whereas a philosophic sage is capable of making "an independent critical assessment of what the people [of his or her community] take for granted."[13]

In his Sage Philosophy Project, while valuing "folk sages" and what McCarthy would call rational "accountability," Oruka is most concerned to find "philosophic sages" and document those who have achieved a level of what McCarthy calls "autonomy" in relation to their community.

Before further exploring the question of 'autonomy' and the 'philosophic' as opposed to 'folk' sages, I should probably provide a quick summary of the methodology of Sage Philosophy, according to Oruka himself. In his book, *Sage Philosophy*, published in 1991, Oruka discusses the methodology that the professional philosopher employs in the quest for, or love of, African wisdom,[14] as Oruka conceives it fifteen years after he first began to envision the project. To begin with, there is the hypothesis that wisdom can be found in every community or human society. By searching within relatively traditional African communities for people known for their knowledge and ability to be helpful in the resolution of basic human problems, the professional philosopher is, hopefully, led to potential subjects. In outlining Sage methodology in 1991, Oruka emphasized that the search is not just for someone able to articulate "the unexamined beliefs of a community as a whole," but rather, "for persons capable of giving the philosophic explanation for such beliefs and the practices that arise from them."[15] He even goes so far as to say that:

> It is important not to lose sight of our most important objective: that is to get persons (wise persons) who can offer an Archimedes stand for understanding and explaining the cultural or belief system of a given people."[16]

As the relationship develops between the sage and the professional philosopher, specific statements or propositions that seem to express some

---

[13] H. O. Oruka, "Sage Philosophy, " p. 61.

[14] As my own contribution to the infamous definitional crisis plaguing African Philosophy and Philosophy in general, let me suggest my own resolution of such difficulties: if philosophy is "the love of wisdom," then *African* Philosophy is the love of *African* wisdom.

[15] H. O. Oruka, *Sage Philosophy,* (Nairobi: ACTS Press, 1991), p. 59.

[16] H. O. Oruka, *Sage Philosophy*, p. 60. This would appear to be an indication of Oruka's appeal to an abstract, ahistorical, transcendental subjectivity which, in recent years, has been the focus of a good deal of philosophical critique.

fundamental truth or wisdom become the subject of critical reflection. The sage is asked to justify such statements. Presumable, a philosophic sage will be able to offer some rational response to such requests for justification.

According to Oruka, however, this does not yet bring the two into the most developed level of Sage Philosophy. It is only when one of the conversants is provoked by the counterarguments of the other to further develop his or her original position that the realm of "sagacious didactics" is entered into.[17]

SUBJECTIVE BREAKS AND SAGACIOUS INTELLECTUALS

From Oruka's description of the methodology of Sage Philosophy, it is clear that a globalized project would be oriented towards seeking out and engaging the wisdom of peoples via their "sages " who have been marginalized and/or ignored by the hegemonic institutions of 'modern,' 'developed' and 'developing' societies. Based on this understanding, one working hypothesis of the project might be that the wisdom of a majority of the human population is currently suffering from such a marginalization and/or 'ignore-ance.' Thus, the purpose of such a project would be to expand the pool of human wisdom we have at our disposal in order to face world problems and to challenge the hegemony of those limited perspectives and interests that seem to be the source of many of these problems.

However, as mentioned above, in our concern for counter-hegemonic methodologies and a globalized sage philosophy project, questions regarding 'autonomy' and the relation between the individual thinker and her or his community inevitably arise. I will not attempt to definitively answer such questions in this paper. In fact, in my opinion, these are precisely the kind of questions that a professional philosopher cannot effectively resolve within the confines of academia. While both feminist and African philosophers such as Lorraine Code, W.J. Ndaba, Segun Gbadegesin, and Sandra Harding have done some excellent work in clarifying what such questions entail,[18] I would suggest that these questions can only be effectively discussed and understood as part of a counter-

---

[17] H. O. Oruka, *Sage Philosophy*, p. 63.

[18] Lorraine Code, "Epistemology," in *A Companion to Feminist Philosophy*, eds. Jaggar, Alison M. and Iris Marion Young (Malden, MA: Blackwell, 2000), pp. 173-184; W. J. Ndaba, "Oruka's Sage Philosophy: Individualistic vs. Communal Philosophy," in A.P.J. Roux and P.H. Coetzee (eds.), *Beyond the Question of African Philosophy: A selection of papers presented at the International Colloquia, UNISA, 1994-1996.* (Pretoria, South Africa: University of South Africa Press, 1996); Segun Gbadegesin, *African Philosophy: Traditional Yoruba Philosophy and Contemporary African Realities* (New York: Peter Lang, 1991); Sandra Harding, *The Science Question in Feminism* (Ithaca: Cornell University Press, 1986), pp. 165-90.

hegemonic philosophical intervention and strategy, and thus, in the course of the development of the proposed project; in other words, only as professional philosophers begin to philosophically engage local 'sages' in a diversity of relatively marginalized and/or ignored indigenous communities, will we begin to truly understand the nature of these kinds of questions.

So, instead of trying to resolve these questions, I would like to use them to focus on what might be involved in Habermas's concept of "communicative thawing," and to explore how Antonio Gramsci's understanding of "formation of intellectuals" could help us understand the nature of what a globalized sage philosophy project might entail. Clearly, in relation to Habermas's and Oruka's conceptual schemes, a "philosophic sage," in distinction from a "folk sage," would be a manifestation of a relative "thawing" within the Lifeworld of the community. However, without grounding such theoretical notions as a "communicative thawing" in concrete historical events, I am concerned that we run the risk of proposing an idealist abstraction based in 'historical' events of the mind, independent of human beings' struggle to produce and reproduce their lives on a day to day basis. Sages, and intellectuals such as philosophers for that matter, are living human beings who are materially dependent on society. So their sagacity, whether 'folk' or 'philosophic,' cannot be understood independently of the conditions of their actual lives as men and women.

Therefore, in terms of counter-hegemony and a globalized Sage Philosophy project, I would suggest that Habermas's "communicative thawing" might be effectively reconceptualized and placed within the framework of a more radical and self conscious, yet to some degree historically-conditioned "subjective break." "Subjective break" is a central element in Earnest Wamba-dia-Wamba's development of his understanding of "emancipatory politics".[19]

According to Wamba, such a "break" is based in the subjective realization that "the state of affairs in the world does not have to remain so because it is so."[20] Quoting Mao, who in turn is quoting Lenin, Wamba insists that "emancipatory politics," or what we might refer to as effective counter-hegemonic strategies, emerge with a "'consciousness of antagonism with the existing overall socio-political order'"[21] This "consciousness of antagonism" is not determined by one's material conditions, but is a human expression of the absolutely intolerable and materially unsustainable contradictions within which the individual and a people find themselves at particular moments of their development.

---

[19] E. Wamba, "Democracy, Multipartyism and Emancipative Politics in Africa: The Case of Zaire" *African Development* 28.4 (1993), p. 96.

[20] E. Wamba, "Democracy, Multipartyism and Emancipative Politics in Africa: The Case of Zaire," p. 95.

[21] E. Wamba, "Democracy, Multipartyism and Emancipative Politics in Africa: The Case of Zaire," p. 96.

The suggestion here is not that the so-called 'philosophic' nature of the sages should be understood as based in Wamba's radical "subjective break" – far from it. I have two points in mind. My first concern is that Habermas's "communicative thawing" and "autonomy" should not be understood in an abstract, ahistorical manner, but must be understood as fundamentally rooted in the historical development of a people. My second concern, in relation to counter-hegemony, is that we should hypothesize, or be open to, a whole spectrum of relative autonomy, ranging from an apparent lack of any autonomous or critically reflective thinking, to a radical break with the overall socio-political order within which we find ourselves.

Indeed, in a globalized Sage Philosophy project, it would be important not to let the distinction between "folk sages" and "philosophic sages" lead us into the same errors that, according to Wamba-dia-Wamba, many radical Africanists, including pan-Africanists, Marxist Leninists, and self-reliant socialists are committed. Says Wamba in 1986,

> 'Radical Africanisms' fundamentally remain outside the concrete class consciousness of the African masses: their starting point is never what actually African masses think, but what they must think... [and] Academic philosophy, functioning in a terrain closely haunted by cultural imperialism, spends most of its energy celebrating the master-thinkers of the West defending the so-called modern (advanced) forms of philosophizing... Academic philosophers denigrate the concrete thinking – seen as folklore – of the masses of the African people.[22]

As was emphasized in the beginning of this paper, Oruka's Sage Philosophy Project was explicitly developed to counter the hegemony of the racist image of Africans that justified slavery and colonialism, and today 'explains' Africa's underdevelopment. However, in both the African project and the proposed globalized project, there is a need to remain extremely wary of introducing distinctions into the methodology that, if not carefully attended to, might serve to reinforce the very hegemony we are seeking to challenge.

This brings me to a second point regarding the relation between the individual thinker (philosopher or sage) and the community. Just as we could use Wamba's notion of the "subjective break" to develop a more determinative and historical understanding of Habermas's "communicative thawing," we can use Antonio Gramsci's analysis of the "formation of intellectuals" to better understand Oruka's "sages" as expressions of the historical changes taking place within the community from which the sage

---

[22] E. Wamba-dia-Wamba, "Africanism in Crisis" *Philosophy and Social Action* 12.2 (1986), p. 27.

emerges. In Gramsci's *Prison Notebooks*, written in the 1920s and '30s while he was incarcerated by the Mussolini regime, there is a section, "The Intellectuals," which opens with the question, "Are intellectuals an autonomous and independent social group, or does every social group have its own particular specialized category of intellectuals?"[23] While it is true that by "social group" Gramsci is basically referring to the existence of distinct classes within a given society, I think we can use his analysis to better understand philosophers and sages in relation to the substantive inter-cultural and intra-cultural dialogues, with which we are concerned.

According to Gramsci there are generally two kinds of intellectuals: "traditional intellectuals," who put themselves forward as autonomous and independent of any social group, and "organic intellectuals," who self-consciously recognize themselves as rooted in the interests and perspective of either an historically constituted dominant group or the interests and perspectives of an emerging group seeking to challenge the established hegemony of the dominant group.[24] Furthermore it is important to understand that, according to Gramsci, the so-called 'traditional' intellectual in effect serves the interests of the established dominant group.

In order to use these distinctions to better understand indigenous sages and professional philosophers in a Sage Philosophy project, it is important to recognize that for Gramsci every human being,

> carries on some form of intellectual activity, that is, he [or she] is a 'philosopher,' an artist, a man [or woman] of taste, he [or she] participates in a particular conception of the world, has a conscious line of moral conduct, and therefore contributes to sustain a conception of the world or to modify it, that is to bring into being new modes of thought.[25]

What distinguishes an intellectual as such from other members of society is that their work is the "critical elaboration of the intellectual activity that exists in everyone at a certain degree of development."[26]

As Gramsci admits, "the problem [of intellectuals] is a complex one."[27] However, I think we can draw a few conclusions or at least put forth a few hypotheses concerning the relation between sages, professional philosophers, and their communities, based on his analysis. Insofar as

---

[23] A. Gramsci, "Intellectuals," in Richard Kearney and Mara Rainwater (eds.) *The Continental Philosophy Reader* (London & New York: Routledge, 1996), p. 184.

[24] A. Gramsci, p.186.

[25] A. Gramsci, p. 187.

[26] A. Gramsci, p. 187.

[27] A. Gramsci, p. 184.

everyone is to some degree intellectually engaged in living their lives as self-conscious human beings, and insofar as those who function as 'intellectuals' are in some way 'critically elaborating' the intellectual activity of some community or sector of society (otherwise they would not achieve any recognition as intellectuals, sages, or philosophers), then the question becomes: what is the social or communal base of philosophy as it is functioning today, and what kind of social or communal basis would we be searching for in a globalized sage philosophy project?

In the opening paragraph of this paper, I mentioned that philosophy, today, does not seem to achieve the kind of popular resonance in social development achieved by Socrates. At this point I would hypothesize that this is due to an effective self enclosure, based on the assumption, whether explicitly or implicitly indicated in our actual professional activities, that we are upholding some kind of 'tradition' independent and autonomous of any particular social or historical grouping. This effective self-enclosure makes it extremely hard for non-philosophers to hear anything of themselves in the work of professional philosophers. Neither the leaders (masters) of the dominant forces of globalization, nor the masses of humanity struggling in all their diversity to find ways to live with dignity and self respect as human beings, find their own intellectual activity being 'critically elaborated' in the journals of professional philosophy. This is one reason I am suggesting that something like a globalized Sage Philosophy project is a necessary condition for the development of effective counter-hegemonic philosophical theories and practices.

However, a move from a self-image, whether implicit or explicit, of 'traditional' intellectuals to the recognition of our 'organic' function is not enough. As I quoted Gramsci above, every human being, in their intellectual activity, "contributes to sustain a conception of the world or to modify it, that is, to bring into being new modes of thought."[28] Organic intellectuals can function in order to 'critically elaborate' the established and hegemonic conceptions of the world and modes of thought, or they can 'critically elaborate' and bring into being new conceptions of the world and modes of thought.[29]

It should not be romantically assumed that sages are somehow necessarily counter-hegemonic, and the counter-hegemonic nature of professional philosophers must be assessed according to their organic connectedness and successful elaboration of new and emerging conceptions of the world developing within the intellectual activity of the marginalized and/or ignored majority. This is not to suggest that a global project should

---

[28] A. Gramsci, p. 184.

[29] In a forthcoming paper, I will elaborate on the ontological implications of such a project in terms of a new understanding of truth and human development that I think is indicated in the debates between Gadamer, Habermas, and Foucualt, broadly speaking.

shun those who are effectively reinforcing the established hegemony. Rather the point is that all participants in such a project would commit themselves to exploring such questions as rigorously and systematically as possible, based on mutual respect and the shared goal of expanding the pool of human wisdom available for addressing the global problems with which we are all confronted.

TRADITION AND MODERNITY VS. HEGEMONY AND COUNTER-HEGEMONY

The emergence of the importance of this opposition or distinction between the old hegemonically maintained ways of being, and new, emergent, and presumably progressive ways of being, raises a question to which I alluded earlier. Before concluding, I want to return to what I referred to as a central weakness of Habermas's position in relation to his distinction between 'traditional' and 'modern' societies.

In the penultimate chapter of his book, *Tradition and Modernity*, Kwame Gyekye, reflects on H. B. Acton's definition of tradition as "a belief or practice transmitted from one generation to another and accepted as authoritative, or deferred to, without argument."[30] According to such a definition, it is clear that tradition would seem to fall within Habermas's realm of accountability and Oruka's notion of folk sagacity; thus, a traditional society would be one devoid of the autonomous philosophic exercise of sagacious reason. However, Gyekye challenges this concept of tradition, and insists that traditional values and practices are not just 'passed on' or 'transmitted,' but more importantly they are cultural products that have been accepted and preserved by successive generations. Says Gyekye:

> The forebears of 'the previous generations' do not 'transmit' their cultural creations as such; what they do, rather, is to place them at the disposal of subsequent generations. But the subsequent generations may, on normative or other rational grounds, either accept, refine, and preserve them or spurn, depreciate and, then abandon them.[31]

If Gyekye is right then Habermas's conception of 'traditional' society is, as Emmanuel Eze and others have argued, still mired in the

---

[30] K. Gyekye, *Tradition and Modernity* (Oxford: Oxford University Press, 1997), p. 219.
[31] K. Gyekye, p. 221.

paradigm of an invented Eurocentric idea of Africa described so well by V.Y. Mudimbe.[32]

This reconceptualization of how we understand 'traditional' values and practices as a critical appropriation of Habermas's distinction between "accountability" and "autonomy," and Oruka's distinction between "folk" and "philosophic" sages, bring into focus the role of reason in human development and the potential for a more philosophically informed approach to dealing with global problems in the context of hegemonically determined processes of globalization.

The question is not whether some belief, or value, or perhaps worldview as a whole, is 'traditional' or 'modern.' The relevant questions are whether it can sustain itself when subjected to critical examination from multiple perspectives and whether it is essentially hegemonic or counter-hegeomonic: two questions which, I would hypothesize, are, in fact, one and the same.

CONCLUSION

It is important to recognize that the proposed project would be a mutually counter-hegemonic process among all the participants in such a project. It is not a question of an academically trained philosopher suffering under the yoke of institutionalized hegemonies seeking out potentially 'enlightened' sages. Nor is it the opposite. Neither is it the purpose of the project to uncover some authentic perspective untainted by the hegemony we are trying to challenge, as Oruka himself sometimes characterized his project in Africa. The thrust of the project would be realized through establishing ongoing processes of philosophical engagement beyond the university, outside of the profession, on the current margins of the hegemonic center of human development. Through such systematic and rigorous efforts beyond the university, as professional philosophers, we would seek to institutionalize processes within the university and other research centers capable of challenging the hegemonic regimes of truth within which we are enmeshed.

We should keep in mind that the goal here is not just philosophical prowess but effective counter-hegemonic insights and strategies in relation to the nature of human development and globalization. Thus, to be effective, a whole network of institutionalized relations would need to be developed between various centers of research, universities, development agencies of the United Nations, NGOs, governments, etc.

I do not expect this one brief paper to result in the establishment of such a project. However I am heartened by the legacy of Professor Oruka. Over the course of 20 years, from the time Oruka first articulated the need

---

[32] C. E. Eze (ed.), *Postcolonial African Philosophy* (Cambridge & Oxford: Blackwell, 1997); V. Y. Mudimbe, *The Invention of Africa* (Bloomington & Indianapolis: Indiana Univesity Press, 1988).

to recognize the "philosophic sagacity" of traditional African thinkers in 1974, through the publication of his book, *Sage Philosophy* in 1990, until his untimely and somewhat suspect death in 1996, Oruka continued to develop his project. He successfully solicited funding from various sources, including the Institute of African Studies (University of Nairobi), U.S.A.I.D. and I.D.R.C., and throughout his life he continued to address practical and concrete issues such as family planning and the relation between local traditional beliefs and values concerning death and the modern legal system of the Kenyan state.[33]

Finally, in closing, I would like to briefly mention an epistemological question concerning globalization, hegemony, and a truly counter-hegemonic globalized Sage Philosophy project. I would expect that, as the project developed, an implicit epistemological position would need to be critically elaborated and become a central concern of the process. Perhaps I can briefly indicate its nature by referring to the development of liberation theology in Latin America.

In his work, Ignacio Ellacuria suggested that 'the poor' constitute a special and privileged "lugar teologico" for understanding the reality of Latin America, and what for Father Ellacuria was the historical and dialectical nature of Divine Love and the Christian promise of salvation as manifested in Jesus's redemptive sacrifice. This becomes clear, suggested Ellacuria, when we realize: first, that wealth creates poverty, and second, that 'the poor' constitute "the immense majority of humanity ... the actuality and the universality of our problem."[34]

Today, we must examine to what degree and how it is that in the production of such enormous wealth, and given such enormous technological capacity for satisfying the basic needs of humanity, the current social and economic structures of globalization are creating new forms of dehumanizing and crippling poverty. For a globalized Sage Philosophy project, liberation theology might suggest a kind liberation epistemology. One working hypothesis might be that the promise of reason in history – and/or the positive promise of globalization – can be epistemologically brought into reflective and reflexive focus only from the perspective of those whose lives express the unrealized and dialectical nature of that promise in human history. As intellectuals from a diversity of cultures I believe we all carry within us ideals such as Compassion, *Ren*, Justice, *Ubuntu*, Democracy, Islam, Communion, etc., that weigh heavily on our souls in our daily work. As Ellacuria expressed it, "those who do not struggle against the negation of [our highest ideals], do not struggle for

---

[33] See among other works: Graness, A., and Kresse, K. (eds), *Sagacious Reasoning*, East African Educational Publishers, Nairobi, '99. and G.. Presbey, *Response to F. Odieng'-Odhiambo's Analysis of the Philosophy of H. Odera Oruka*, XXI World Congress of Philosophy, 2003, forthcoming.

[34] I. Ellacruia, *Iglesia de Los Pobres* (circa 1987), p.160.

communion [their historical realization]; those who do not effectively combat it [the negation], do not really desire the truth of communion."[35]

In this introductory paper I can only suggest some of the reasons why I believe that a globalized Sage Philosophy project is not merely a good idea in relation to the challenge to develop counter-hegemonic intellectual practices within globalization; I believe that something like this project is a necessary condition for effective counter-hegemonic theories and practices in philosophy.

Wuhan University
Wuhan, P.R. China

---

[35] I. Ellacruia, p. 161.

CHAPTER XLVIII

GLOBALIZATION OR THE "ENGLISHIZING" OF THE WORLD

O. FARUK AKYOL

My point of departure for explaining what I am going to say about globalisation is the issue of language. My argument in these remarks is that it is essential that cultural traditions protect and use their native tongues. By doing this, we also have to try to develop them in order to explain ourselves much better to each other. As has often been said, globalisation is a kind of process, and it seems plausible that, at the very end of this process, human beings are going to end up sharing the same Idea and the same Value. Having only one Idea and one Value will undoubtedly lead to a very unproductive environment. For that reason, we can claim that globalisation is *not* going to make the world culturally and spiritually richer.

I would like to illustrate this point by giving some very concrete examples from the country in which I have spent my 38 years. Turkey is a rapidly developing country. As in similar countries, people here are trying to obtain more comfortable living conditions, e.g., money! One very dominant prejudice held by people on the street relates to the main tool of communication. This tool is called "English." In other words, it is widely held that English is a little magic key with which everybody can easily open all the doors.

In Turkey, people are practically dying to get a good command of English. In many private schools, education is in English. In these schools, students are forced to express their opinions and thoughts in English only. The strange thing is that students are also forced to speak English outside of schools. English is omnipresent and omnipotent in Turkey. In business, in education, on TV, in the cinema, even at home, people are trying to think in English in order to do something or to prove themselves to others.

Our environment, our world is constituted historically by our own mother tongues. Only through the help of our mother tongues can we create our world and can it have meaning. Accordingly, it is of great importance for us to think in/with our own language, i.e., that through which we can "find ourselves" accurately and precisely. Our mother tongue also gives us a vital opportunity by which we can discover our inner qualities and become familiar with them. The mother tongue is a kind of binding system with which we see ourselves in the mirror that is called the world. For all these reasons, our mother tongue is an important part of our lives without which we would lack a determinate position on the earth. Our feelings, emotions, judgments, reactions are also influenced by our mother tongue.

Unfortunately, in Turkey (as in many other countries) we have already lost our mother tongue. English has been very dominant around the globe, and people see it as an immortal "*paradeigma*." We might accept or deny the reality described above, but with English our concepts have already lost their wings and therefore the ability to fly. They are in a very vulnerable position now because of this attack of "a foreign language" on our own languages and cultures.

I ask you to consider this: "I need to know English!" People are terrified about this issue: Not being able to speak English is, for many, a catastrophe. No matter how many other languages you can speak, if you do not or cannot speak English, you can easily be labeled as ignorant of the facts of the world since the only way of understanding them is to have English. There seems to be no other way.

In the meetings at which I presented an earlier version of this paper, I heard the term "dialogue" countless times. This leads to the very basic question about having a dialogue. As I understand the term, dialogue means a kind of "talk" between two sides. It emerges right between "I" and "You"; namely, dialogue is actually "we." If you would like to engage in a dialogue, it means that you "automatically" accept the other as an agent. As it is understood, this agent must be active in every sense of the term. So the agents of both sides of the dialogue can and must show their identities and characteristics. However – and there is a big "however" here – how am I to talk about "dialogue" and "globalisation" when the communication tool for the process of globalisation is English, particularly since English is strongly forcing people to all their modes and ways of thinking. Having "dialogue" in any genuine sense has disappeared. Dialogue has disappeared because "the other" has disappeared.

I usually check every book that I come across written by native English speakers. They usually write their books in order to know or understand different thoughts, habits, cultures, etc. The very interesting thing is that these writers generally do not have the habit of using the source language when writing on, for example, "Chinese Philosophy" or "African Philosophy." If you look in the "Bibliography," you find no texts in the Chinese or African language. What kind of dialogue is this? "Some part" of the world just innocently wants to know about the other part of the world, and we, the non-native English speakers, are torn to pieces for expressing ourselves in English. Of course, by ignoring the great difficulties surrounding translation – i.e., fragmentations, expressive defectiveness, and so on – we try to say something about our cultures, in English. When we do this, consciously or unconsciously, we lose the strength in expression, thinking, and judging that we have in our mother tongues, since we have to adapt everything we have in our mental sphere into English – and of course not only into the English language, but also reflecting the mentality which rests on the shoulders of language. Accordingly, we do not live on or with our own language, but rather in a perpetual translation process. English just puts our lives onto the track of interminable translation. And for that reason, as I mentioned above, our lives become something which is increasingly intangible. Our lives become very slippery, and, unaccustomed to this kind of slipperiness, we find that we cannot hold on to anything. We exhaust our very foundations – *hypokeimenon.*

In noting this kind of habit, many stories emerge. Let me share one of them with you. In the United States, many students are interested in Continental philosophy – for example, German Philosophy. But if you do not know German, nobody would blame you. It's found to be a very innocent lack. For example, if one must study Kant's philosophy, we find in the United States an English translation of Kant's First *Kritik* by N. Kemp Smith. Believe it or not, it is said in America that this translation is even more perfect than its original. This is a perfect excuse for not being able to read German, is it not?

In conclusion, I would like to say that there is no real dialogue around here. It is an illusion. Nice, relaxing, but also frightening. Globalisation is mostly a kind of "Englishing." "The rest of the World" is suffering from an Anglo-(Techno)-Toxic Shock, if not altogether in a semi-conscious state, and trying to understand what is happening to it. In order to make our world more habitable, therefore, we need to try to understand each other more correctly, without having any nationalist prejudices. Nevertheless, we also need to free ourselves from the process of "Englishization."

Istanbul University
Istanbul, Turkey

CHAPTER XLIX

THE PROBLEM OF DEHUMANIZATION OF CULTURAL MEANING IN THE AGE OF GLOBALISM

BURHANETTIN TATAR

The Spanish philosopher J. Ortega y Gasset criticizes modern artistic thought for paving the way to the dehumanization of art. In his view, modern art keeps itself busy with pure ideas and concepts by focusing on merely observed reality, instead of relating itself to the human condition as a lived experience. Said differently, modern art focuses on instruments themselves by disregarding its goal, which is the human being in the world. Accordingly, a modern work of art is a thing of no consequence. Since it gains its place and legitimacy in its isolation from daily forms of life, it is only a subject of pure pleasure.

From Ortega's critique of modern art it follows that a modern work of art creates a unique paradigmatic case which is satisfied by its own existence; namely, the universal and particular establish a unique creation which is both instrument and goal at one and the same time. Since it does not allow for re-production of itself toward an external goal, it remains as a single case in its changeless, imaginary space. It is clear that Ortega's critique is not restricted to modern art since what he calls the "dehumanization of art" stems basically from the reification of the instruments, typical of Enlightenment and modern thought. We can see a similar line of critique of instrumentalism in Max Horkheimer and T. W. Adorno's *Dialectic of Enlightenment*. What they call "instrumental reason" is nothing but a dehumanization of reason. Human reason goes nowhere by occupying and satisfying itself merely with instruments. It is dehumanized since it is captivated by positivistic understanding, which makes a fetish of the instruments it creates.

Heidegger in *Being and Time* and Gadamer in *Truth and Method* developed an outstanding critique of instrumental thinking on the basis of fundamental ontology. In their eyes, modern thought became too subjectivistic by turning away from the question of Being and satisfying itself merely with the instruments which it creates. The self-satisfaction of modern consciousness with instrumental reasoning is the way of the legitimization of modern thought. This self-governing and self-legitimizing movement of modern consciousness deprives itself of a real point from which it could see its poverty and shortcomings. Heidegger observes this uncritical position of modern consciousness as the main characteristic of 'humanism.' In other words, the humanism of the modern age is a process of dehumanization of human consciousness simply because it aims at suppressing the finite and historical being of Dasein under the guidance of a false image of a transcendental self.

At this point, it becomes clear that there is a common point between the critique of modern art by Ortega y Gasset, the critique of instrumental reason by Horkheimer and Adorno, and the critique of modern humanistic (subjectivistic) consciousness by Heidegger and Gadamer: in modern art, in instrumental reason, and in modern subjectivistic consciousness, the difference between universal and particular, goal and instrument, consciousness and self-reflection, being and consciousness is dissolved within the false image of self-sufficient (complete) meaning. Interestingly, the plurality of self-sufficient (complete) meanings in the modern age gave rise to a new movement called post-modernism.

Whether postmodernism is a continuation of modernism or not is a topic that goes beyond the limit of our present interest. However, we should remark that, just as the Greeks of ancient times created the image of Zeus so that the plurality of self-sufficient Olympic gods can be united under a supreme power, so modern age created a new conception of globalization as an antidote for the irremediable plurality of postmodernism. The conception of globalism renders in itself the two poles of modernist and postmodernist thought as uniting and differentiating movements. From one viewpoint, it designates the unification of global culture within the image of the global village. In this sense, global culture appears to have the characteristics of one-dimensional culture under the guidance of American globalism. From another viewpoint, it signifies the free space opened to the self-representation of different local or regional cultures. What was before restricted within the limits of its natural and national region now finds an opportunity to express itself via its own conceptions.

Accordingly, globalism appears as a process of uniting global culture by differentiating regional (local, national) cultures from each other. Obviously the question is still open as to whether the movement of differentiation of regional cultures under the unity of global culture will provide those local cultures with a real freedom (liberation) to stand on their own feet. What is at stake here is the possibility of creating a false image of self-expression of regional cultures under the protection of the unity of global culture. What, indeed, does the word "self-expression" mean? Is it a free space where the unity of meaning (truth) of a regional culture shines? Or is it a medium for self-understanding of a regional culture within its conceptions? Or is it a playground for different regional cultures to satisfy themselves by playing their own games?

The problem of the false image of self-expression arises when self-expression is taken as a completion of self-understanding. Whoever understands (and satisfies) himself within his own expression becomes a victim of the false image of self-expression. This is because he restricts the dynamics of his being and his understanding to the expressions which exist on their basis. With reference to Ortega's conception of pure art, it can be said that, in the case of creating the false image of self-expression, each regional culture will appear like a pure work of art. Accordingly, the danger in self-expression as the completion of self-understanding is the identification of instrument with the goal. This implies the isolation of a regional culture within its limited possibility of expression.

If our analysis of the problem of the false image of self-expression has meaning and significance, then we should direct our attention to the relationship between meaning and expression with reference to the problem of globalism, so that the idea of the dialogue of different cultures gains a more authentic motivation. In modern philosophy, the problem of the relationship between meaning and expression has taken different and often opposite routes. For intentionalist philosophers, expression is like an empty shell, which is to be filled by the re-discovery of the intention of the author. For critical philosophers, expression functions mostly as a mask hiding the economic power interests of humans. Accordingly, meaning is not mostly within or before, but behind the expression. For hermeneutical and phenomenological philosophers, expression discloses merely some aspects of meaning in the historical tradition of interpretation. Here, expression can be identified as an expression on the basis of its previous interpretations. There is no empty shell-like expression to be filled.

Within these major trends of modern philosophy, intentionalism takes the unity of meaning and expression as an indication for self-sufficient (complete) meaning, namely, self-understanding. However, this realistic view of the unity of meaning and expression leads paradoxically to a sort of idealism by assuming that the interpreter can enact the intention of the author with respect to the author's expression. Within the limits of our present concern, it implies that a regional cultural meaning can be understood by other cultures without engaging them with its truth-claim. In other words, self-expression of a regional culture already marks the limits of the meaning of this culture. Hence, self-expression is also self-restriction.

Now we should raise the following question: does intentionalist philosophy disclose a real basis for the mutual understanding of different cultures? If self-expression is also a self-restriction, how can one culture understand other cultures by bridging the shell-like boundaries of their meaning? More importantly, if a living culture can exist as long as it has the power of continual change and movement, this shows that the self-understanding of this culture is in fact in continual change or revision. In other words, the meaning of expression gains new moments, motivations and aspects in each concretization of cultural movement. With respect to this dynamic self-understanding, how can other cultures enact the meaning of this self-expression? It seems to me that intentionalist philosophy reduces the self-expression of a culture to a mere instrument for knowledge. In other words, the basic relation between different cultures is reduced to an epistemological level. This is what we want to call "dehumanization of cultural meaning." With this expression, we mean that while the epistemological level exists on the basis of humane relation between the cultures, it is turned into an object for observing other cultures. Accordingly, the epistemological relation takes over the humane relation.

As to critical philosophy, it takes the self-expression of a culture as a mask that hides the power-relation beneath the surface – meaning that it is hidden even from the members of this culture. Under the guidance of the psychoanalytic method of discovering the unconscious, it aims at providing a culture with a critical viewpoint so that it can reflect on its real materialistic conditions with full awareness. Obviously, critical philosophy has an immense value through its goal of discovering the difference between higher and lower levels of meaning in a culture; however, it reduces all human relations to a mere economical and social power-relation. For critical philosophy, cultural meaning is essentially dehumanized meaning. What appears as a humane relation at the higher level is really an instrument for the continual existence of the lower level of economic power relations. As long as full critical awareness of the lower level functions as a liberating movement in a culture, real humane relations may be expected to come into existence. Nevertheless, in the final stage, critical philosophy takes the cultural meaning as a mere object of observation simply because the question of the meaning of real humane relations goes beyond the interest of critical philosophy. Critical philosophy is essentially a negative philosophy. This essentially has always had a risk of reducing the higher level meaning of a culture to the lower level and of preventing a culture from reaching towards other cultures in its own expression. It has always had to wait for another linguistic device created by the ones who have critical transcendental awareness. Said differently, a culture always depends on a different form of language, which is believed to be free from all types of power relation. Who, how, and what can guarantee (and justify) the idealistic belief in a critical form of language? Doesn't this idealistic belief of critical philosophy lead us to a dehumanized meaning of a cultural language?

At this point, we may wonder if a hermeneutical-phenomenological philosophy of culture can provide us with a concept of humane relation as the basis of cultural dialogue. Since it is an ever-developing philosophy, we can set a task for it to disclose the basis of the problem of dehumanization of cultural meaning in the age of globalism. This seems to be the most urgent problem, since globalism has always a risk of dissolving regional cultures into the unity of a global culture. Present cultural relations seem to take place according to an anthropomorphic image of world powers: in this image, America represents the mental dimension; Europe represents the heart dimension, while the so-called third-world cultures represent the dimension of the feet. If this image has any metaphorical sense, it is that the cultural relations take place within a vertical understanding. By the term "vertical understanding," we refer to the two poles of understanding: higher and lower. In vertical understanding, the higher meaning represents the truth of the age and has a right to guide the lower meaning within its paradigm. We can see the culmination of vertical understanding in Hegel's

Phenomenology of Spirit. According to Hegel, when consciousness reaches a higher level in its dialectical movement of thesis, antithesis and synthesis, it realizes with certainty the untruth of a lower level beneath itself. The Hegelian system is a philosophical monument of globalism, since it dissolves all differences at the highest level of consciousness – i.e., so-called Absolute Spirit.

It seems to me that Hegel's conception of Absolute Spirit discloses how human meaning is dehumanized when difference is dissolved within absolute identity. With respect to this Hegelian background, a hermeneutical-phenomenological philosophy of culture is expected to yield a dialectical conception of humane relation between different cultures, which never dissolves the finite self-understandings and self-expressions within the highest level of meaning. In other words, a hermeneutical philosophy of culture is expected to guide its conceptions on a horizontal level, so that each culture sees other cultures at the similar level, yet at and from different points. Accordingly, the problem of meaning and expression must be considered continually, so that a hermeneutical philosophy of culture prevents itself from leading to dehumanization of cultural meaning and vertical understanding of it.

Faculty of Theology
Ondokuz Mayis University
Samsun, Turkey

CHAPTER L

DIMINISHING TRADITION, CONTINUING TRANSITION: THE STATE OF SERBIA

JELENA DJURIC

As an area of significant territorial, religious, ethnic, national and ideological diversity, the Balkans are a region of many small cultures, but also a meeting point of civilizations. The Ottoman Turks, who ruled it for 500 years,[1] called it 'Rumelia' – a name recalling the early history of the area as a territory of the Roman Empire. For Europeans, it was 'European Turkey' until the mid-nineteenth century, when the term 'Balkan' began to circulate.

Balkan cultures north of Greece have long been excluded from being considered as having a European identity (either Roman Catholic, Protestant, or Modern European). This attitude towards the Balkans still holds. According to the Collins English Dictionary (1994), 'to balkanize' means to divide (a territory) into small warring states. In her book *Imagining the Balkans,*[2] Maria Todorova notes that the term Balkanism reflects the Western reduction of the idea of the Balkans to stereotypes oscillating between opposites in relation to an alternation of political interests and power. Describing the Balkans as an integral part of "the first Europe," Traian Stoianovich, the author of *Balkan Worlds, The First and The Last Europe,*[3] emphasizes the risk of its current isolation from European identity. This exclusion – the author argues – is a sign that the European structure is based on money and power rather than on culture, which could lead to the cultural collapse of Europe as such.

The structure of traditional Balkan cultures was connected with the wholeness of the cosmos, organized with subsequent strata of biology, technology, society, economy and culture. In general, a look into history reveals that, before the economic structure is stabilized, human culture, as the most delicate of all relational systems, is not feasible. This pattern is the very story of the Balkans. The lack of economic stability (and, being in the

---

[1] From mid-fidteenth to the last decades of the nineteenth century, the Balkans lay within the boundaries of the Ottoman Empire. During that long period the Balkans was cut off from the rest of Europe, and thus the history of its peoples unfolded very differently from that of other European countries.

[2] Maria Todorova, *Imagining the Balkans* (Oxford and New York: Oxford University Press, 1997).

[3] Traian Stoianovich, *Balkan Worlds, The First and The Last Europe* (Armonk, New York: M.E. Sharpe, 1994).

middle, Serbia is at the centre of the Balkans) has been crucial to the decline of individual potential in the region. This is manifest especially in the lack of a philosophical heritage in Serbia. One should simply remember philosophers' observations about the necessity of leisure time for philosophy. While building the system of knowledge (and until the eighteenth century all sciences were incorporated in philosophy) was a trend among scholars in wealthy Western Europe, Serbia had half a millennium of slavery, followed by a series of devastating wars waged for the independence of the nation. That is why the most characteristic intellectual creation in Serbia during that period was 'folk heroic epic poetry.'

One kind of poetical philosophy, 'folk wisdom inventions' (= *'narodne umotvorine'*), was influential during the Middle Ages. Much later, after a collection of these texts was published in the nineteenth century, this *oeuvre* of traditional Serbian 'national literature' became an inspiration to European intellectuals, such as Goethe. Writers in nineteenth-century Serbia provide evidence that a humanistic culture had developed. However, their works hardly conform to the spirit of rational discourse.[4] It is possible, indeed, to reconstruct, from their texts, the rational concepts that they had presupposed.[5] Yet, if we take the main philosophical tradition (such as the philosophies of Aristotle, Plato, and early modern thinkers: Descartes, Spinoza, and Locke) as a paradigm[6], the Serbian cultural heritage is deficient in philosophy. If there are some philosophers, they are not particularly original.[7] Even if we consider another kind of poetical philosophy – one which has not prevailed in the West – Serbian history is still very limited in its number of philosophers.[8]

---

[4] Thus, for example, P.P. Niegosh offers authentic wisdom of life exclusively through his metaphorical poems 'Forest Garland' ('Gorski vjenac'), and 'Light of the Microcosm' ('Luca Mikrokozma').

[5] When, for example, we read Vojislav Ilic's poem 'Istina' ('The Truth': "... go your own way / but know yourself / to know the truth..."), an epistemological and methodological approach is presumed, even if colored with psychological impressions of the world. Suffering is the predominant atmosphere in the opus of recent Serbian poetry which is undeniably reflective.

[6] According to the account given by Jorge J. E. Gracia, *Philosophy and its History* (Albany: State University of New York Press, 1992)

[7] Typical is the Neo-Kantian Branislav Petronijevic

[8] If we take one such example from the work of the Serbian bishop Nikolai, it should be stressed that this work is devoted mainly to the quest for the Serbian Orthodox faith and identity, rather than to searching for fundamental ontological and epistemological insights aimed at discovering reality. This work also defies customary categorizations, since at the empirical level it is highly critical and strict in the sense of ethical requirements. On the other hand, as it starts a discussion of the absolute (such as in "The Science of Law – Nomology"), it glorifies the almightiness of God who is in command of everything including natural laws. Like other mystical and philosophical

The Balkans were obviously predisposed to a different type of mental creation – very distant from strictly rational and systematic discourse. This is perhaps a minor disgrace for those Balkan cultures that have experienced a rather tumultuous history, especially from a contemporary perspective. After Kant, the bifurcation of philosophy into two different kinds led to a denial of any possibility of their mutual communication.[9] This has led to the notorious situation of contemporary philosophy, since the schools of thought have gone so far apart as to become anti-philosophical and dogmatic, undermining the possibility of intercommunication. Thus, philosophy has run the risk of becoming ideology, resolving differences with various kinds of political 'arguments.' Hence, in our age, concrete conscious thinking (as presented in anthropology or ecology) has become more suited to the difficult questions faced by humankind and, thus, more 'philosophical' than academic philosophy itself. These thinkers have brought an awareness of the values in the different cultural responses to environmental challenges.[10] The recognition of different cultural traditions grows with the idea of the freedom to choose values and a corresponding way of life, either individually or collectively. The purpose here is to accomplish a departure from the dominant model of totalizing globalization, which is generally presented as the only option allowed to people.

The pressure of economic globalization is so great that nowadays the Balkans are capable neither of coping with urgent ecological needs nor of achieving balance between freedom and social justice. Serbia's actual poverty and powerlessness, intensified by continuous 'transitions' (e.g. the post-communist change, and the recent conflicts and wars), inhibit an active response to what is nowadays really important – a transition to the new age of cyber technology. Without this transition, other transitions (such as the ones of 'democracy' and 'market economy') are likely to be futile, at least from the internal perspective. As merely a periphery of dominant geopolitical powers, the Balkans suffer from the ongoing turbulence of their conflicting interests. Throughout history, geopolitical relations have resulted in huge oscillations in stereotypes about the Balkans, as Maria

---

approaches, here the belief in God transcends rational knowledge: it has to be experienced in order to be understood and therefore requires a personal attitude, understandable only by the ones who share similar experiences.

[9] Poetic philosophy has had a long history from Pythagoras through Plotinus, Tertullian, Eckhart and other thinkers who believed in coming to know ultimate reality through personal mystical experience. The opposite path in the philosophical tradition has gone through positivism and analytical philosophy, ending in antagonizing and the severing of any communication with the metaphysicians.

[10] Thus, some of the ways of technologically inferior cultures, such as the Bushman and Eskimos, appear superior from the point of view of human adaptation to the environment.

Todorova has pointed out. These oscillations bring further turmoil to Balkan identity and to its development.

The current post-Cold War transition to a new global stage of human relations involves reshaping ancient as well as modern identities. This global transition coincides with the central region of the Balkans – Serbia – as a challenge to the new rising global integration. Let us explore this issue. Prospects for the global integration of different cultural traditions are a hot issue of our times. The purpose is to create a potential global society in regard to actual economic and technological processes of globalization. The fact of the matter is that the relations among the various parts of the world are becoming stronger than ever before; still, globalization might be seen as largely polarized. On one side, we observe 'globalization from above,' as a primarily economic integration of societies. This 'globalization from above' is connected with international domination and the hypostatization of a single world economic system. Its ideal is the Western neo-liberal tradition, in relation to which all marginal traditions serve as barriers to global integration depending on the possible harmonization of their values. On the other side, there is support for a complementary 'globalization from below.' The latter presumes the possibility of integration of societies while, at the same time, preserving their distinct traditional identities.

However, if we look at the 'reduction' of traditional identities to their cultural dimension (as in the second, 'globalization from below' approach), it is obvious that the two approaches are opposed only on the surface. At a deeper level, the power relations are not altered. The second approach does not search for the integrity of traditions with their respective cultures or with their political and economic spheres. It is already too late for that; the process of globalization has already gone too far. Thus, the complementarity of these two concepts of globalization relates only to the notion of tradition in the narrower sense of a culture.

Yet, there is a difference between these approaches. It lies in their relation to values. The 'globalization from above' approach is primarily concerned with material, instrumental values, that is, concrete values related to the use of power. Unlike the 'globalization from below' approach, it is indifferent to the existence of subtle values and shades of universality.

The issue of a possible universalization of values, or a non-reducible relativity, is an actual theoretical concern. It is the origin of different standpoints focusing on contrasting evaluations of traditions. We should investigate these standpoints in regard to their relation to the question: Are all traditions equally valuable? From the standpoint of universalism, the purpose of this question has been to construct a value-hierarchy of traditions, with the dominant values in a superior position. The resistance to this concept of universalization has increased with postmodern deconstruction and the relativization of values. However, from the viewpoint of value-relativity, the issue of the equal evaluation of traditions has mainly had a practical purpose; it is theoretically pointless because decisions in values cannot be comparative but rather inhere in the context of each tradition. Hence, the relativization of values denies the possibility of establishing an intercultural hierarchy and domination imposed from the position of power.

Another view of universalization is possible, though. This view does not understand universalization as the reduction of manifest differences to a generalized, empty essence – a common denominator. Rather it sees this essence as presented in various forms – as a matrix, pattern or structure – through common values and universal meaning. From this latter meaning of universalization, a value approach to the global integration of world societies may be deduced. It assumes a broad respect for values that might be recognized as common or universal. These universal values for global linkage and the integration of humanity have the potential to include various particular cultural manifestations, individual as well as collective.

For this concept of global integration, which includes mutual differences, the centralization of power is the main problem. Concerning subtle values, this power uses not bare physical force, but the power of manipulation through social consciousness.[11] Understanding the importance of collective human consciousness for the future of a global human society requires efforts to transform the structures and relations influencing it. In a time of global transition, it is necessary to reconsider the roles of cultural traditions in relation to contemporary global change. This reconsideration should enable a humanization of the idea of 'progress.' We need a progress that will allow people, apart from all rationalistic and nationalistic dichotomies, to express their identities, instead of uniformizing or impersonalizing themselves. In nature, the importance of a diversity of natural kinds is quite clear. In human cultures, diversity is important for the development of an ecology of global human society.

After the modern 'myth of progress' has been criticized and an awareness of dead-ends in civilization has occurred, it is nevertheless still possible to retain the concept of progress. In our time, it should be sought in

---

[11] Durkheim pointed out the conditioning of the social consciousness, by defining collective representation as something which is not a social or metaphysical obligation, but rather a kind of moral or intellectual obligation. Mary Douglas has recently reminded us of this point in her book *How Institutions Think* (first published in 1986 by Syracuse University Press; Serbian translation: 2001), in which she pointed out the appropriateness and applicability of Durkheim's teaching on the social roots of individual thinking for contemporary society. She supplements this teaching by Ludwig Fleck's theory of cognition as the socially most influenced human activity.

From the perspective of an ordered society, it is understandable that institutions have attributed this power to conditioned social consciousness, as Douglas has done. However, from the perspective of a destroyed society, as in Serbia, this power is transferred to authorities with strong media support.

human interests outside those spheres of political and economic power that are conducive to confrontation. But even if it is possible to find deep wisdom in universal human experience, a common language that makes dialogue possible, as well as mutual understanding among different cultural identities and traditions, there still remains the problem of how to implement this progress. For now, we can see this as a basis for the improvement of local and global structures which could permit the opening of and interconnection among cultural identities and traditions. However, before we can do that, it is important to go all the way with this global transition and its transformation of identities. This is particularly so in the case of societies that have experienced the annihilation of their earlier environments after the fall of the Berlin Wall – that serves as a symbolic end of the Cold War and the polarization of the world.

We have strong examples of this transition in the former Yugoslavia as a whole, and in Serb society[12] in particular. An effort to think consistently about Serb society today is not very easy. Apart from the fact that the term 'tradition' is frequently mentioned in the media, it seems that Serb society is left without practically any deep-rooted Tradition[13] that is 'alive' – i.e., not just in books or in the vanishing memories of our great-grandmothers, but rather in the everyday activities of the people. While it is possible to argue that the influence of Tradition is not sufficiently noticeable to me as a member of the culture lacking the necessary distance, arguments can still be adduced as to the virtual disappearance of an effective Serb tradition nowadays. Before we consider this issue, let us close the more general account.

From the thesis that Serb society was left without any evidently traditional values animating its beliefs and ways of life and which are incompatible with values of global civilization, it is possible to derive the

---

[12] English translation usually uses the term 'Serbian' to refer to its ethnic attributes or language (i.e., 'Serbian language'). On the other hand, in the Serbian language, there is the adjective *srbijanski* (Serbian), denoting "belonging to the country of Serbia." Thus *srbijanski* does not connote a reference to the national/ethnic tradition of the Serbs, or to their language as such. The adjective *srpski* (= 'Serb'), on the other hand, combines an ethnic and state reference. So it would be more adequate to say in English the 'Serb' (language) instead of the 'Serbian' (language). However, the concept of 'Serb society' (i.e. its connotation in Serb language) that is dealt with here, is a challenging notion, because it refers differently to Serbs in and out of Serbia, as well as to the citizens of Serbia themselves. It would refer all the more to the overall population, if Serbia defines its distinctiveness more clearly. In the Serb language, the notion of a 'Serbian society' was neither usual nor appropriate until now, because it excluded a substantial part of the national corpus which was united until recently.

[13] Tradition with capital letter 'T' should indicate a fundamental kind of cultural heritage which is continually transferred by the means of customs and oral history from generation to generation.

idea that the Serb tradition cannot be a barrier to global integration. However, observing everyday life in Serbia, it seems that lack of tradition as such could in fact be an obstacle for hypothetical global integration. Tradition as such presumes a certain order of values, which can then be changed, renewed, improved, harmonized, and integrated. Without Tradition, a society is left with no established values, and probably without any values whatsoever. Devoid of an order of value, a society inevitably finds itself in a critical condition – in an identity crisis. Societies do not necessarily get out of such crises, let alone get out of them in an improved condition. Crises may recur until a complete disintegration of the actual society takes place. Something like this is happening in Serbian society. Its frequent transformations and continual transitions to opposing societal systems have produced a crisis of identity for as long as its tradition has diminished; its identity has, paradoxically, become a transition.

The possibility that transition becomes the tradition seems paradoxical. From the context of rational discourse, a transition (meaning 'a passing') always involves a change to something else, to something different, rupturing with a previous tradition or at least with some of its aspects. Probably, such an idea could not even emerge if the questioning of the rationalistic dichotomies of modernity had not already led to doubt. But, after this insight, we can no longer be unaware of the dynamic nature of reality and the failure to conform to any rigid categorization. Besides, a cumulative historical change of things and relations over time causes conceptual changes. Understanding these changes makes it possible that some seemingly known things and relations no longer appear contradictory, because their inner logic and meaning are recognized.

Real changes initiate conceptual changes, and vice versa. These changes of meaning, understanding, and relations are such that is not possible to determine conclusively what is prior to what, and to what extent. Regardless of whether the present changes in conceptions and values reflect changes in society, or whether changes in society reflect the former, they obviously announce the emergence of a new age which could lead to the global integration of humankind. As we have seen, this possibility presupposes the recognition of universal values, and the idea of universality also triggers a review of various obsolete meanings. A reconsideration of these preceding meanings should enable ideas to take an appropriate position in contemporary times.

Distancing themselves from earlier traditional values, modern processes based themselves on the values of bourgeois revolutions: liberty, equality and brotherhood. Have recent historical events really devalued these ideals of freedom, equality and brotherhood? This might seem likely if we think that ideas have worth only if they are being realized in practice. However, the opposite claim is equally likely, i.e., that universal values should not be rejected, even if not practiced today, since such values (as those of democracy and human rights) contain "primordial" values which were common to both the bourgeois and communist revolutions. The endurance of these values is enabled by the power of their universality. Having in mind that the modern époque, whose dawn was announced by these values, has now announced the arrival of a global world, we can consider these values as part of the tradition of a future global society.

To ask whether universal values exist shows that much is dependent on our choices and beliefs. But if this is so, then it is more reasonable to choose an approach which has the anthropological advantage of stimulating human progress. Therefore, we believe that, if they are universal, values cannot be overcome, even though wrong ways of application (and finally, their abuse) may and should be overcome. Their misuse is frequently a consequence of misinterpretation.[14]

It is possible, then, to accept that universal values exist even if we rarely see them. If everyday reality loses sight of them, this does not mean they are just illusions to be abandoned. Even if actual experience does not show their existence, it is still worse for people to live without them. The only question is to what extent those living in such societies are responsible for this state of affairs, because humans are, more or less, always responsible for their situations. Let us, for example, pose this as the question of the responsibility of Serbs for their destiny. Unlike the dangerous potential of the notion of 'collective culpability,' the meaning of

---

[14] Thus, for instance, the idea of freedom cannot be properly applied in all spheres of human activities. From the anthroposophical perspective, it primarily belongs to the spiritual sphere. Here, it indicates a freedom of choice, thought and expression, which are considered to be basic human rights even today. In the sphere of law, however, it is not a basic value because it is limited by the laws. When this idea of freedom is accepted with no limitations in the sphere of economy, it leads to the supremacy of the stronger and to less humane social relations.

Similarly, the idea of equality primarily belongs to the legal sphere. Its application in the economic domain has proven to be wrong. We have a recent historical experience of the socialist economy, in which its application led to egalitarianism and consequent problems. In the spiritual sphere, the idea of equality regularly leads to the terror of single-mindedness.

It seems that the idea of brotherhood has experienced the greatest historical devaluation. Yet, this is not a proof that it does not represent a universal value. Although it is generally abandoned in its literal meaning, it is still present in the indispensable concepts of *humanity, solidarity,* and *altruism.* But, it is hard indeed to make it an institution, and it is not a regular practice anyway; in the sphere of law, it is not necessary and, in spirituality, it is presumed. The main area in which this value should be applied is the economic one. Not everyone is equally able to acquire material wealth, but everyone has the basic vital needs that have to be satisfied. Therefore, it is necessary to share it in a brotherly way with others if they are deprived due to the accidental circumstances. That is why universality of basic vital needs makes the value of 'brotherhood' universal.

responsibility is not so blame-centred, though many hold that leading an inauthentic life is much worse than blaming. Some modest consolation can be found, however, in certain historical streams converging in the thesis of the end of the Serb Tradition.

It is well known that a half century of the dominance of atheistic ideology brought a complete change to the earlier Serb tradition. Its place was occupied by a new 'communist tradition' of 'proletarian' principles and values. The belief that, among all the ex-Yugoslav nations, this was especially the case with the Serbs, lies in the specific circumstances of its history and culture. Its position on the borders of the Balkans worked together with the isolation of its Christian Orthodox Church. The deterioration of the Church's influence started in the Middle Ages under Ottoman rule. After a short break in the nineteenth century, it was continued in the first Kingdom of Yugoslavia, for political reasons of organizing the population belonging to different religions and for reasons of responding to the Western influences of modernization and industrialization, thus subordinating tradition based on spirituality to one trusting in science and material progress. This spirit of modernity, opposed to previous traditions, was the origin of modern European concepts of value.

The Communist government accomplished the modernizing spirit of the times through eradicating all traces of the local bourgeoisie and through transforming the former 'land of the peasants' into the 'land of the proletarians.' Compared with European countries that have not gone through communism, where previous traditions were gradually integrated into modernity, the rapid abandonment of the Serb tradition was profound. The transformation of some folk practices via the new forms of social content – as was the case with the myth of the enemy or with heroic myths – represent a continuation of the folk tradition in the level of usefulness in communist propaganda. We should also bear in mind that the cited myths were not exclusive to the Serb tradition, and often embodied archetypes reflecting the universal inheritance of humankind.

Under communist ideology several generations grew to maturity. For them, Marxism, Leninism, antifascist resistance and socialist self-government became a 'tradition.' Then came the even more suspicious concept of a 'return to the Serb tradition,' constructed and imposed during the period of post-communism and the dismantling of the SFR Yugoslavia. Indeed, the misuse of the proclaimed ideology and its values in everyday communist reality stimulated a need for values that were imagined to exist in the forms of the prohibited ancient Tradition. Actually, the proclaimed 'return to Tradition' was prevented largely because of the obsolete structure of the Church, which long ago lost the touch with the spirit of the times, and has been manipulated by politics and the media for the sake of homogenization and identification of a continuous people. Under the stream of social and mental pathology, intensified with the pressures of global transition, spirituality remained discouraged.

The previous regime resorted to abuses of power in order to condition social consciousness. By means of the mass media, neo-myths of the Serb 'tradition' were constructed. Other sources were historical fragments, the symbolism of St Sava, and the vague 'greater Serbia' projections of the SANU (Serbian Academy of Sciences and Arts) Memorandum. However, outside of the media, the living Serb tradition no longer existed. It began to vanish with the suppression of its ancient identity, because it was considered to be a hindrance to modern times. Communism required another identity and imposed another tradition and, when its system of values had almost become tradition, the new post-communist turnover happened, and this again initiated inevitable social chaos. From a humanistic point of view, the acceptable communist ideology of brotherhood and social justice, although challenged by the forbidding of traditional practices, national feelings and disappointing egalitarianism, was now replaced by the opposite ideology of the social Darwinist principles of the market as the basic value of a globalizing transition – which resulted in dangerous scarcity and new social segmentation. Milosevic's regime, isolated by the international community, managed to survive for such a long period because of the spurious conservation of the socialist tradition. Behind the scene, social property was being devalued and, through corruption, transferred into the hands of domestic private owners. Privatization is an integral part of the transitional changes of 'globalization from above,' and it has been continued after the change of government. The difference is only in the fact that the society now is 'open,' so that foreign capital arrives to heal the broken remnants of national companies. At the same time, no one seems to have noticed the sudden termination of the tradition of designating capitalist imperialism as the 'greatest enemy' of the 'transitory period' towards 'social liberation' in communism. In this way, Serbian society has remained a society in transition, only this time it is moving back to capitalism, whose power has managed to grow beyond the nation-state, increasingly assuming a global dimension.

Serbia and its society will have to adapt like the others did. In a time of the overall stimulation of the dynamic preservation of cultural heritage, who cares about the hardships of a society in permanent transition in preserving its own tradition? The idea that transition as such, regardless of its direction, may become tradition, is actually ironic, because there is only a slight theoretical chance that a society becomes so dynamic and flexible that no transition may deeply disturb it any longer. In concrete reality, again, continuous sudden turnovers of social values constantly take place; these hinder all the advantages of a continuous development of society and causes confusion in people's minds. As the most conspicuous continuity of all of the transitions of the Serbian society, there remains the negative continuity of people's alienation from the 'institutions of the system.' This gloomy bureaucratic heritage has influenced all of the apolitical individuals, who now actually comprise a majority of the population. Their apathy towards social involvement reflects the long-term hardships caused by brutal authorities who used to destroy generic values, bending and abusing them to their own ends. As a consequence of that practice, in spite of a variety of 'non-governmental organizations,' conferences, and editorials on 'civil society,' people have remained mostly alienated. They are still not able to make 'horizontal networks' to improve their daily environment. This very remoteness from being able to immediately connect oneself, keeps social values intact and hypostatizes them into the sphere of ideals, whose contact with reality becomes marginal. This creates the opportunity – on the part of those who assume power – to once again hide tyranny behind the newest ideal of 'democracy.'

What follows from the foregoing is that, of all the actual meanings of the surviving traditions of Serbian society, the negative ones are the more conspicuous, be it the abuse in conditioning social consciousness by politicizing nationalism, or the lack of tradition in the sense of the lack of civil behavior or respect for the law. The positive elements of tradition, besides the collective cultural heritage and its influence, are certainly present in homes, familial heritage and customs, and in friendly socializing. The fact that the vital elements of tradition are so personal may be pointing to the role of individuals in preserving, transferring and creating tradition. After all, one's choice of the aspects of tradition that one adopts determines what is going to be transferred to one's descendents. However, even more influential agents of tradition represent the creative contribution of individuals. Because of that, tradition, especially in the cultural sphere, is defined by creative personalities, poets and thinkers who contribute to the evolution of society. Their importance is almost (traditionally, so to say) neglected in Serbian society. However, in spite of this, the Serb tradition will always be represented by authors such as Dositej, Vuk, Zmaj, Dučić, Kostić and other creative personalities who incorporated elements of universal human experience into their works.

Even simple individuals may significantly improve daily social life by discovering the values that bring universality into the specific requirements of the present time. The appearance of a 'critical mass' of such individuals in a society facing the task of reclaiming its authenticity might enable the modeling of such a dynamic identity, organized around universal values, which is capable of surviving in the situation of the global 'transition.'

Therefore, the reconstruction of institutions as important elements of an integrating tradition of society should draw the support of the individuals who can contribute to its progress – first and foremost to its internal progress, but also to external integration. This is so because, without an internally integrated dynamic identity, it is impossible to take part in a wider intercultural integration; what remains is only a terrifying pressure of 'integrism' at all levels. These distinctions between integration and 'integrism,' tradition and traditionalism, universality and universalism, and other positive and negative notions characterize the opposition generating the current historical situation. It is in everybody's interest to resolve these dilemmas before globalization outruns human control.

Institute for Philosophy and Social Theory
Belgrade, Serbia

HUMAN DEVELOPMENT AND HUMAN RESOURCES DEVELOPMENT: THE PEOPLE'S ATTITUDE TOWARDS DEMOCRACY AND THE MARKET, ACCORDING TO THE WORLD VALUE SURVEY[1]

PHAM MINH HAC and PHAM THANH NGHI

The 1945 Constitution ushered in the era of the Democratic Republic of Vietnam. The approved Constitution created the legal foundation for the implementation of democracy. Apart from the institutional and legal framework, however, economic and cultural development serves as the most important condition for the sustained implementation of democracy. Thanks to economic development, particularly since the introduction of the "*Doi Moi*" (renovation) policy in 1986 with the transformation into a socialist-oriented market economy, the people have been able to have greater access to education and information; above all, they have become more aware of their civil rights, and there is now a greater need for the people to participate in political and social activities. Economic development also leads to cultural change, which includes a substantive democratic character in people's lives, creates confidence in one another, and enhances altruism and values of self-expression. There are guarantees for the people's participation in the policy-making process.

The implementation of the Party's renovation policy over the past few years has truly reinforced democracy. However, the violation of people's rights as true 'masters' is still a problem in many places. The Communist Party of Vietnam's Politburo Instruction No. 30-CT/TW, dated February 18, 1998, on building and carrying out regulations on democracy at the grassroots level clearly stipulates: "Expanding socialist democracy and bringing into full play the right of people as masters, are the objectives and also the driving force to ensure the success of the revolution and the cause of renovation." Expanded democracy will increase people's participation in the management and control of the State, and overcome the State apparatus' degradation and bureaucracy. Social democratization was added to the goal of the whole society in 2001; we now have "wealthy people, a strong country, and an equitable, democratic and civilised society."[2] The Government of the Socialist Republic of Vietnam has issued

---

[1] See *Human Studies Magazine*, Vols. 1, 2, and 3.
[2] Resolution of the Ninth Congress of the Communist Party of Vietnam.

3 decrees (No. 29-1998, No. 71-1998, and No. 7-1999) promulgating regulations on democracy in communes, precincts; administrative bodies, and state-owned enterprises following the standards of a modern democracy which are the contestation of power, the participation of the people, and the accountability of the powerful.[3] When people take part in the democratic process, their awareness, viewpoints, attitudes and especially their value systems, value scales and value orientations change. It is necessary and useful to conduct research into these developments. In the long run, democracy cannot be simply achieved by institutional changes or by management by authoritative bodies; its existence depends a great deal on values and the confidence of ordinary citizens in the content of democracy. Democracy and the market are essential to contemporary culture.

This paper aims at presenting a comparative analysis of the Vietnamese people's attitudes towards democracy and the mechanism of the market economy, in comparison with those of people from East Asia (China and Japan), North America (the U.S and Canada) and some parts of Africa and South America. The illustrations in this paper are taken from data released in the World Value Survey conducted in Vietnam and statistics collected from similar surveys in other countries in the world in 2001.

THE ATTITUDE OF THE PEOPLE TOWARDS DEMOCRACY

In Vietnam, surveys are rarely conducted on people's attitudes towards political and social activities, but the results of the World Value Survey in 2001 shows that people have very high confidence in democratic values. People give full support to social democratisation, namely, the inclusion of "democracy" in the goals of the country. As many as 62.6% of the interviewees expressed high satisfaction and 33.9% showed moderate satisfaction; in other words, as many as 96.5% said they were satisfied with the goal of democracy.

Referring to the democratic political system, many were doubtful of the efficiency of economic activities, the determination of the government, and the strength of the social order. Nevertheless, people indicated that they were fairly confident in the efficiency of democratic systems. With regards to the efficiency of the economic system, only 14.3% of the respondents agreed that there exists a weakness in the economy in a democratic regime.

---

[3] UNDP Human Development Report (2002), p. 58.

Chart 1. The attitude towards the economy's performance in democratic systems

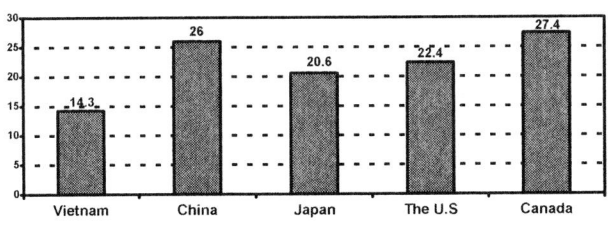

Agree that the economy in democratic systems is poorly managed

The proportion of people responding to the survey in China, Japan, the U.S and Canada who agreed with the idea that the economy in democratic systems is poorly managed was a little higher than that in Vietnam (Chart 1). This means that the Vietnamese people evaluate the market economy more optimistically than those from other countries do.

Chart 2. The attitude towards the lack of determination of democratic systems

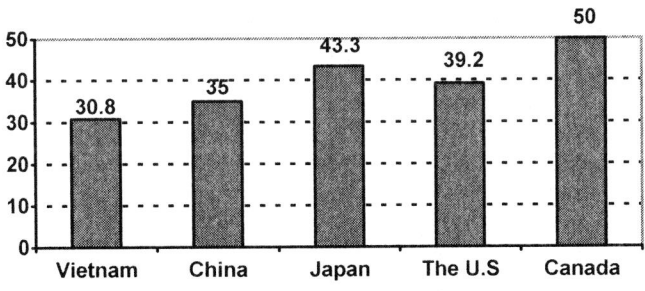

Agree that democratic systems lack determination

The Vietnamese people also have a quite optimistic assessment of the determination of democratic systems. Only 30.8% of the interviewees agreed that democratic systems lack determination in resolving social problems. Meanwhile, the proportion in East Asian countries (China and Japan) was much higher than that recorded in Vietnam. In Canada, as many as 50% agreed that democratic systems are not decisive in resolving social problems (Chart 2).

When commenting on social order in democratic countries, only one quarter of the respondents in Vietnam agreed that there are problems concerning order in democratic systems. This proportion of agreement was higher than that recorded in China, Japan and the U.S., but lower than that in Canada (Chart 3).

Chart 3. The attitude towards order in democratic systems

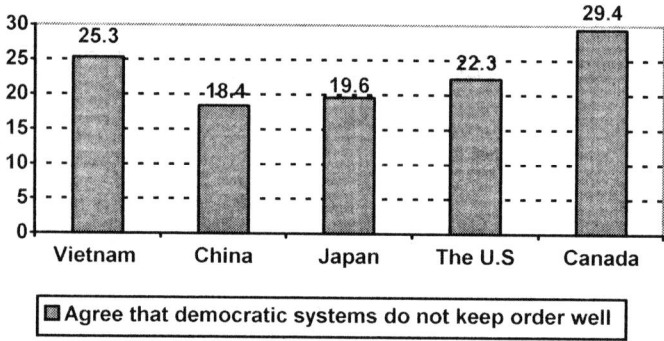

When making a general assessment about the active nature of a democratic mechanism, most of the respondents in Vietnam (72.2%) considered that democracy is the best form of government (Chart 4). The proportion of those agreeing with this idea was much higher than that in China, Japan, the U.S., Canada and Argentina. The beliefs of people and the realities of life may differ. Argentina is currently (i.e., in 2003) in a serious crisis, though this country is managed by a democratic government and the people formerly placed absolute confidence in the democratic system of the country. In Nigeria, the confidence in a democratic system is especially low compared to that in other countries, with merely 53.2% of the respondents saying that the democratic system has problems but is still a good form of governance.

Chart 4. The attitude towards the best form of government

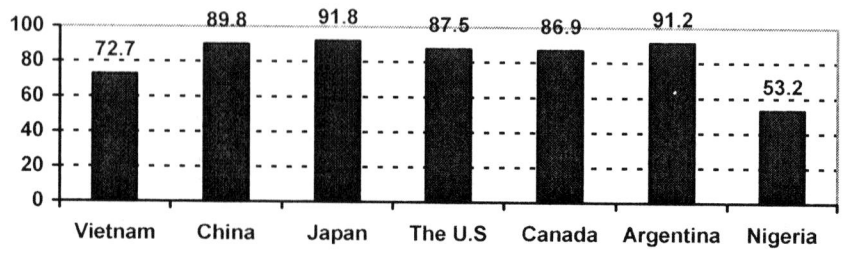

When making general comments on the role of the democratic political system, people in different countries have different attitudes. The interviewees in Vietnam highly valued the democratic political system. 58.9% of them said the democratic political system was very good and 36.6% said the system was rather good, while only 4.5% thought the system operated poorly or very poorly. Thus, in Vietnam, 95.5% of the respondents considered that the democratic political system in Vietnam played an active role.

Chart 5. The attitude towards the democratic political system

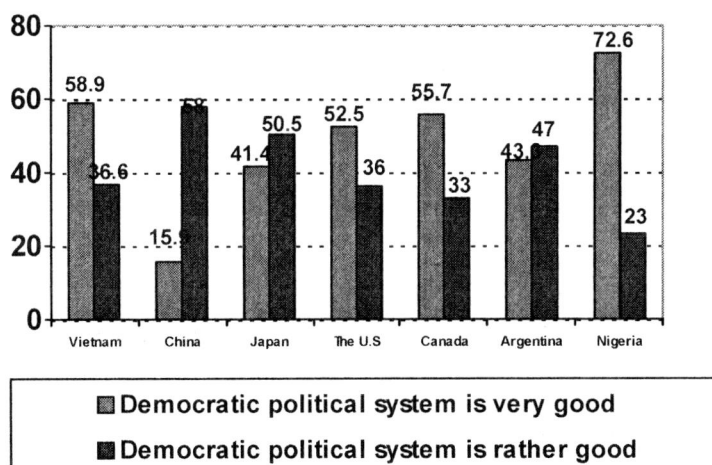

People in China valued the democratic political system a bit less, with only 73.3% of the respondents saying that the democratic political system was very good or rather good. People from Japan, the United States, Canada and Argentina highly valued the democratic political system. The democratic political system was very highly valued particularly in Nigeria (Chart 5).

Regarding the *respect* for individual human rights as an *indicator* of human rights, respondents in Vietnam said that individual human rights are much respected in their society. According to four levels (i.e., much respect for individual human rights, some respect, little respect, and no respect at all), with the exception of Argentina, where most of the respondents believed that individual human rights were not much respected or not respected at all, a majority of the respondents in Vietnam, China, Japan, the U.S., Canada and Nigeria chose "a lot of respect" and "some respect" (Chart 6).

Chart 6. The level of respect for individual human rights (% of the respondents)

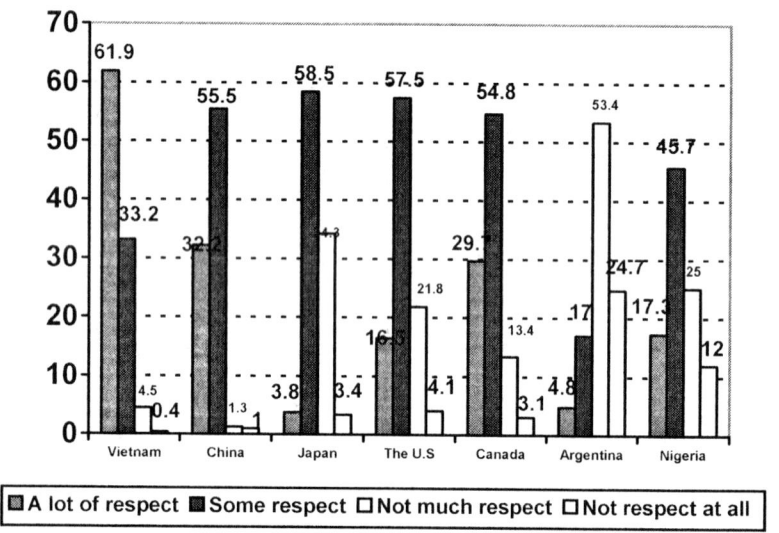

As seen from Chart 6, most respondents in Vietnam admitted that individual human rights are highly respected, while a high proportion of people in China, Japan, the U.S., Canada and Nigeria said individual human rights received moderate respect. This indicates that people in Vietnam believe their individual human rights are clearly guaranteed under the current political regime.

In order to implement the right to freedom and democracy, a society must have a democratic mechanism, respect its citizens' opinions so that everyone has the right to express his or her opinions, and the government must listen to these opinions. However, the right to democracy is not always fully used, as not everyone is aware of his or her civil rights. It depends a great deal on the awareness, attitude and responsibility towards realizing their civil rights. Culture also exerts a great impact on the implementation of civil rights in democratic systems.

When asked if they unconditionally obeyed instructions from their superiors at work, were persuaded before they obeyed, or it depended on the particular situation, a large proportion (46.2%) of Vietnamese interviewees said that they unconditionally obeyed, 40% of them thought that they should be first persuaded before they obeyed, and only 13.8% said their decision depended on the particular situation. In the United States and Canada, the number of respondents choosing immediate obedience is the highest. The difference in the mass attitude of these countries shows that instructions are highly observed in the U.S., Canada, Nigeria and Vietnam.

Meanwhile, a high proportion of people in China want to understand before obeying instructions (Chart 7).

Chart 7. The attitude towards instructions in the workplace

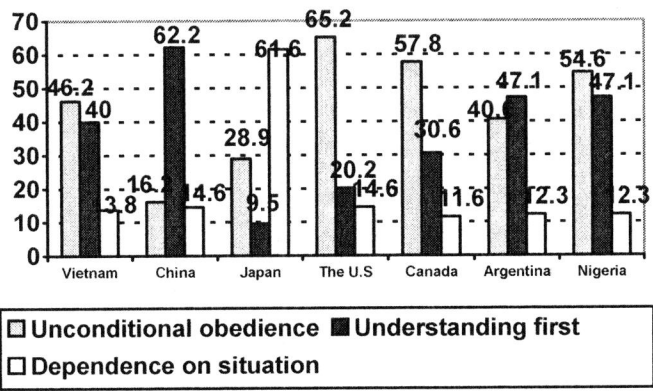

When taking into account prioritized objectives in national development, besides the goal of economic development (which was especially highly valued by Vietnamese respondents), the aim of "seeing that people have more say about the management of the country and community" was equally ranked with other aims of "making the country and the homeland beautiful" and "ensuring that the armed forces of the country are strong." In China, the aim of "seeing that people have more say" was listed at the bottom while "strengthening national defence and security" was ranked right behind the goal of economic development. In Japan, the U.S., Canada and Argentina, the aim of "having more say" was listed right after the goal of economic development (Chart 8). The difference in the attitudes of the people in these countries, compared with those of the people in Vietnam and China, is that the people in Japan, the U.S., Canada and Argentina highly valued the goal of increasing the participation of the people in social management. Thus, people in Vietnam and China have not highly valued the participation of the people in the management of the country and community as those in the above-mentioned countries have.

Chart 8. Assessment of national goals

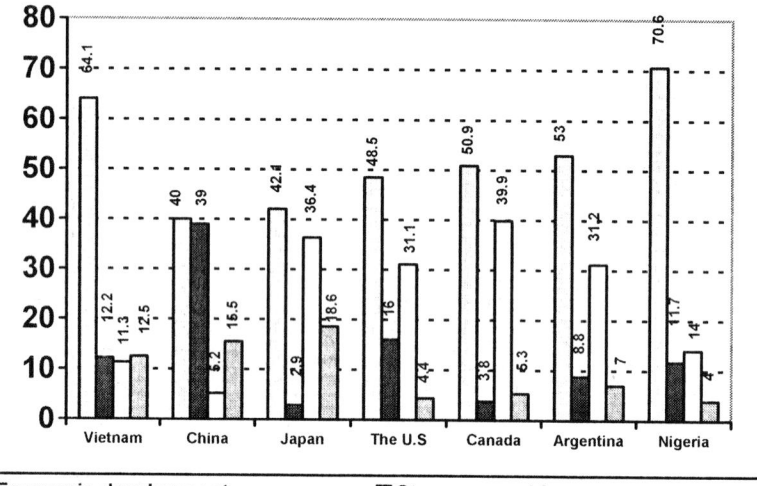

THE ATTITUDE OF PEOPLE TOWARDS THE MARKET

For more than a decade, along with opening up to the world, Vietnam has been carrying out economic reforms directed at market mechanisms. On the one hand, this has taken the country out of crisis and generated a new impetus for development, and, on the other hand, it has widened the gap between the rich and the poor and created increasingly severe social problems. There exist two trends of attitudes, i.e., one advocates more thorough market development and the other the maintenance of State-centralised control over the economy. The trend of strengthening the market mechanism has grown stronger and stronger, which is reflected by attitudes of not only managers and academics, but also the people.

Since the market mechanism has not existed in society for long, although the interviewees in Vietnam and China give rather firm support to private ownership, this trend still looks more fragile than that in Japan, the U.S and Canada (Chart 9).

Chart 9. Attitude towards private ownership

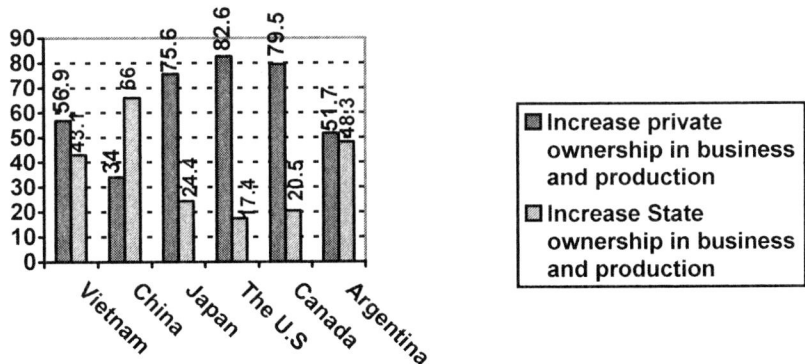

The views on income are also distinctly polarised. Most of the respondents in Vietnam believed that there should be more of a difference in income to provide labourers with incentive. It should be noted that respondents in Vietnam, China and Japan wished for more difference in income while the respondents in the U.S., Canada and Argentina wanted less difference in income; particularly those in Argentina desired more equal income among everyone (Chart 10).

Chart 10. Attitude towards the difference in income

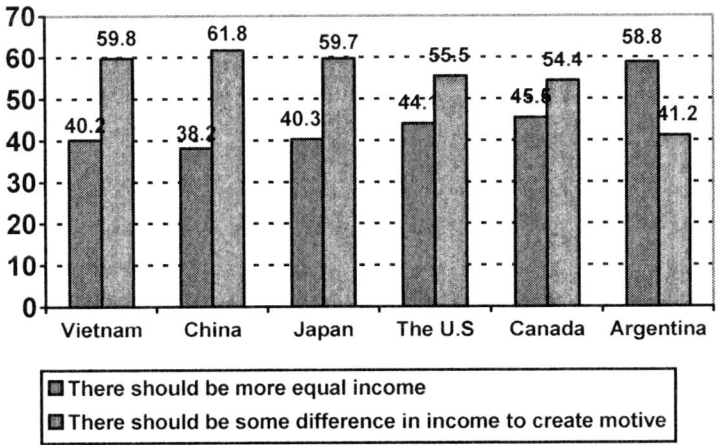

One of the characteristics of the market mechanism is free competition. The state may intervene to create a healthy competitive environment, eliminate monopolies, and establish equality among different economic sectors. The attitude of the public towards this issue may be different when its economic interests are vested in different economic sectors. The results yielded by the survey show that people in Vietnam supported free competition and thought that competition was good (75.4%). However, this proportion is still lower than that in China and those countries with age-old market economies with the exception of Argentina (Chart 11).

Chart 11. Attitude towards competition

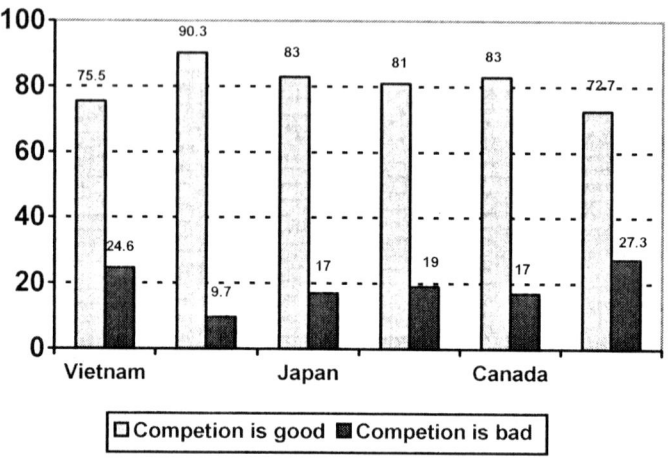

In sum, during the renovation process, we see differing ideas about the degree to which the market is transformed, and many people believe that it is necessary to reconsider such issues as 'equitization,' the abolition of State protection for state-run enterprises, further reduced intervention by the government into business, etc. The results of the public opinion survey indicate that, in general, people support the social democratisation, wish for a speedier transition to a market economy, and highly value the role of healthy competition. The issue of distribution of the fruit of labour, according to them, will be more equal if some difference in income is created to increase motivation for individual efforts. The people also show their confidence and support for the government during the renovation process. As many as 76.8% of the interviewees expressed a strong belief, and 21.1% of them indicated moderate confidence, in the government, and only 2.1% of them showed doubt. This attitude towards the government manifests the confidence in the lines set forth by the Communist Party of Vietnam and the management of the State during the transition to a market mechanism and the implementation of democracy in Vietnam.

Institute for Human Studies
Hanoi, Vietnam

CHAPTER LII

ASSESSMENT OF DEMOCRACY AND HUMAN RIGHTS IN VIETNAM: THE VALUE SURVEY

PHAM MINH HAC and PHAM THANH NGHI

Since 1991, the State-level scientific and technological programme KX-07 (entitled "The human is the objective and motive force for socio-economic development") has started to survey value in terms of value systems, value scales, value measures, and value orientations. In 2000-2001, the National Centre for the Social Sciences and Humanities Institute for Human Studies took part in the World Value Survey (WVS) which has been carried out in 96 countries and territories under identical forms and calculation methods. Some initial results were announced by Vietnamese and US researchers at the International Meeting on World Value Survey held in South Africa in October 2001 and published in the American *International Journal of Comparative Sociology* and Vietnam's *Human Studies Magazine*.

On the basis of this data, this article focuses on the issues of democracy and human rights in Vietnam, which are among key global issues like peace and environment, and which attract the interests of readers. The people have enjoyed democracy and human rights in Vietnam since 1945, but more specifically throughout the country only after April 30, 1975, when the country was reunified and power was won by the people. Democracy and human rights are closely related with liberating the nation from the semi-feudal colonial system, and from the domination of old and neo-colonialism. Opening the Independence Declaration on September 2, 1945, President Ho Chi Minh quoted from the Declaration of Independence of the United States of America in 1776: "All men are created equal, that they are endowed by their Creator with certain unalienable rights, that among these are Life, Liberty, and the pursuit of Happiness." The Constitution of the Democratic Republic of Vietnam in 1946 is called a democratic constitution for national independence, freedom and happiness.

Vietnam started the cause of "renovation" in 1986. The amended Constitution in this period (1992) stated the following: "In the Socialist Republic of Vietnam, political, civilian, economic, cultural and social human rights are respected." (Article 50) This has created a legal basis for the implementation of democracy. The Communist Party of Vietnam's Central Committee's Politburo Instruction No 30-CT/TW, on February 18, 1998, on the building and implementation of democratic regulations at the grassroots level clearly stipulates: "Expanding socialist democracy and bringing into full play the mastery of the people are the objectives and the motive force to ensure the success of the revolution and the cause of renovation." The government of the Socialist Republic of Vietnam has promulgated three decrees (Decree No 29 in 1998; Decree No 71 in 1998 and Decree No 7 in 1999) on the Democratic Regulations to be carried out in communes, precincts, public agencies, State-owned businesses, under the standards of a modern democratic society, which are the competitiveness of power, the participation of the people, and the responsibility of those in power, according to UNDP Human Development Report 2002.

Everyone agrees that democracy and human rights are not just achieved by changes in institutions or in the management of authoritative bodies. Economic development is the most important condition for the implementation of democracy and human rights. Here, I mention one basic human right, which is the right to live in a politically stable society. According to statistics provided by the General Statistics Office in 2002, during the past ten years the practical living standards of the people have increased, on average, two to three times. The UNDP Human Development Report 2003 also recognises that Vietnam has made outstanding progress in poverty reduction, human development and quality of life in the past decade. Vietnam's human development indicator (HDI) remains at 0.688, ranking 109th out of 175 countries. With regard to education development indicators, in the feudal colonial system, only 5% of the population knew how to read and write. Now the figure is 94%. This is one of the most important rights of the people. With regards to poverty indicators, Vietnam's poverty rate has been reduced sharply from over 70% in the mid-1980s to around 29% in 2002, ranking 39th out of 94 countries. Vietnam's gender development indicator (GDI) was 0.687, ranking 89th out of 144 countries and it is also the country with the best GDI in the region (the rate of women National Assembly deputies is 27.3%, the highest in the region).

These indicators show that Vietnam's policy on economic development along with its care for settlement of social issues – particularly social equality with culture and human rights – are goals that help to achieve a genuinely democratic policy. The above-mentioned results are due to many factors, of which the most important is the decision to shift to a socialist oriented market economy. Another factor is the promulgation of policies that liberate the potential of the people and of the community, and which deal more reasonably with the interests of citizens and the community, and the rights and obligations of citizens living under the jurisdiction of a State of the people, by the people and for the people. These are the basic conditions of a society with a genuine democratic political regime.

Thus, the World Value Survey 2001 shows that the people of Vietnam place their belief in democratic values. The people strongly support the social democratisation which is shown in their support to put "democracy" into Vietnam's national goals: a prosperous people, a strong country, a just, democratic and civilised society (defined in the Resolution of the ninth National Party Congress, in 2001). As many as 96.5% of the interviewees said they were satisfied with the country's democratic goals. Their own experience has given them that belief, which is further supported by Vietnam's emphasis on culture and civilisation, and on the spiritual foundation of community-family-village-country, in a spirit of democracy and unity, among different ethnic groups to co-exist, build and defend the country.

This provides a foundation for an analysis and comparison of the attitudes of the people of Vietnam concerning democracy with those of people in eastern Asia (China, Japan) and North America (the United States, Canada). The illustrations are taken from data released in the World Value Survey carried out in Vietnam and the same surveys in the above-said countries in 2001.

1. The attitude towards democratic political institutions: Concerning the value of democratic political institutions, people in different countries have different attitudes. Interviewees in Vietnam highly value the democratic political system: as many as 68.9% of them said that the democratic political system was very good and 36.6% of them said that the system was rather good. Thus, in Vietnam, a total of 95.5% of the respondents considered that the democratic political system had an important role. The figure in Japan was 91.9%; Canada, 88.7%; the United States, 88.5% and China, 73.3%. For generations now (especially during the past half century), it has been the close unity and combined efforts to promote the survival of each person, family, and ethnic group in a united and independent Vietnam, that has awakened the Vietnamese people's sense of human rights and, in reality, allowed the country to implement human rights associated with a democratic political system. Of course, people still want the democratic political system to be better. For example, as many as 30.1% of the interviewees said that they wanted the democratic political system to be more decisive (this figure in China was 35%; the United States, 39.2%; Japan, 43.3%; and Canada, 50%).

We might take another example: when asked about the objectives in national development that should be given top priority, Vietnamese respondents considered the most important goal of the country to be the development of "a high level of economic growth," while the aim of "seeing that people have more say about how things are done at their jobs and in their communities" was ranked equally with other aims – of "trying to make our cities and countryside more beautiful" and "making sure the country has strong defence forces." In China, the goal of "trying to make our cities and countryside more beautiful" was listed at the bottom, while "making sure the country has strong defence forces" was ranked right behind the goal of "a high level of economic growth." In Japan, the United States and Canada, the goal of "seeing that people have more say about how things are done at their jobs and in their communities" was listed after the goal of "a high level of economic growth." The difference in the attitudes of people in these countries compared with people in Vietnam and China is that the people in Japan, the US and Canada highly valued the goal of increasing the participation of the people in social management. Thus, the people in Vietnam and China have not highly valued the participation of the people in the work of national and community management as in the three above-mentioned countries. Nevertheless, in general, in every country today, especially in those countries that the people have high educational standards, people wish to take part in the work of national management. Social democratisation has become a global issue, be it in the United States or Vietnam.

2. *The respect for individual human rights:* Speaking about the respect for individual rights as an indicator of human rights, many respondents in Vietnam said that their individual rights are much respected. According to four levels: "A lot of respect for individual human rights," "Some respect," "Not much respect," and "No respect at all ," most of the respondents in Vietnam, China, Japan, the United States and Canada chose "A lot of respect" and "Some respect." (Table 1)

Table 1: The rate of respect for individual human rights (% of the respondents)

Levels Countries	A lot of respect	Some respect	Not much respect	No respect at all	Total
Vietnam	61.9	33.2	4.5	0.4	100
China	32.2	55.5	11.3	1.0	100
Japan	3.8	58.5	34.3	3.4	100
The US	16.5	57.5	21.8	4.2	100
Canada	29.7	54.8	13.4	2.1	100

Thus, as many as 95.1% of the respondents in Vietnam recognised that their individual rights are respected. Of course, rights go along with responsibilities. Those who violate the law must be punished. Only then can national sovereignty, political stability and social security be ensured.

3. *Rights to freedom of religious belief:* Whoever comes to Vietnam recognises that this is a country maintained by law and that rights to freedom of religious belief are respected, as defined in Article 70 of the Constitution of 1992. In Vietnam, there are about 20 million religious

followers (accounting for 25% of the population), but almost 100% of the population keeps the tradition of worshipping their ancestors which is also considered as a religion. The WVS questionnaire listed the values of God, religion, work, family, friends, and entertainment and asked respondents to indicate which one is the most important. The results show that the value of "family" tops with 82.11%; followed by "work," 56.8%; "friends," 21.8%; "religion," 10% and "entertainment," 7.4%. These figures are honest illustrations of how freedom of religious belief is respected in Vietnam. Those who take unfair advantages of religious belief to violate the law will be punished, and the people support that punishment as only then they can be able to live in peace.

The above-mentioned data was collected and analysed according to a scientific method which is being widely used around the world, ensuring a high reliability and accuracy, and reflecting, in an objective manner, the reality of the before-mentioned issue. After considering these results, scientists have confirmed that they were in conformity with the reality which has been changing in a positive way during the years of renovation in Vietnam. These results also show that socio-economic development in Vietnam has received strong support from domestic and foreign public opinion. Vietnamese society is becoming more and more democratic, and human rights are better protected.

These results, then, support our view of the importance of promoting an active dialogue on human rights and particularly on freedoms of religion and rights related to labour, the environment, science, technology and other issues. This will provide a significant basis for future political, economic, and cultural relations.[1]

Institute for Human Studies
Hanoi, Vietnam

---

[1] We wrote this article at a time when the US House of Representatives had recently adopted the Amendment to the Foreign Relations Authorisation Act for the 2004-2005 fiscal year, which included some groundless provisions relating to Vietnam. These 'additions' received strong protests from many US politicians, diplomats, businessmen, charities and religious organisations, along with an expression of hope that US political circles would have a scientific and objective basis for future equal co-operation and mutual benefit and that they would reject any action threatening the development of Vietnamese-US relations (the latter have resulted from great efforts on both sides in recent years).

CHAPTER LIII

DEMOCRACY AND THE ROLE OF PHILOSOPHY IN THE PROCESS OF DEMOCRATIZATION IN CONTEMPORARY VIETNAM

PHAM VAN DUC

INTRODUCTION

In recent decades, democracy has attracted much attention from scholars. During the Cold War era, many bourgeois scholars and Western political activists constantly criticized the lack of democracy in former socialistic nations. In their view, real socialist regimes committed "the political and intellectual error of the twentieth century."[1] They interpreted Western capitalist society as an ideal democratic model for all nations worldwide to follow.

Undeniably, the lack of democracy was among the most decisive causes leading to the collapse of the socialist bloc in the former Soviet Union and Eastern Europe. This serious and protracted lack had a far-reaching effect, restraining man's creative potential and producing social stagnation. According to various documents published at the end of the twentieth century, phenomena such as dogmatism, repression and the cult of personality had existed popularly for a long time, before ending in the late 1980s. In the former Soviet Union, for example, under Stalin's regime the dogmatism and cult of the individual leader had been accompanied by coercion and the imposition of viewpoints known in the West as 'ideological terror.' The official ideology had served as an "iron wall" with which people had to comply unconditionally: there was absolutely no room for opposition or criticism, either internally or externally. This lack of democracy was converted into a mechanism in which "one person can direct for all, and the masses are only obedient tools." In reality, there existed many serious injustices caused by the lack of democracy; according to unofficial statistics, by the year 1989 about 300 people from intellectual circles had been exiled, many of whom had not deserved such severe treatment.[2]

---

[1] Z. Bredinski *That bai lon - Su ra doi va cai chet cua Chu nghia Cong san trong the ky XX*, Vien thong tin Khoa hoc Xa hoi. Ha Noi, 1992, tr.10 (In Vietnamese).

[2] Ziuganov. *12 bai hoc lich su. T/c Thong tin Cong tac Tu tuong*, so 1 (1996) (in Vietnamese).

Similar kinds of action took place in China during the time of the "Great Leap Forward" and the "Cultural Revolution." Educated people, especially intellectuals, had to be in accord with the extreme views of some Party members. Therefore, many who deserved to be treated better by their country and nation, were purged in the struggle for power, simply because they held views dissimilar to those of Party leaders. However, by the close of the 1980s, when the Cold War ended, the collapse of the socialist bloc did not make the world more democratic; on the contrary, the situation seriously deteriorated in some parts of the world. This can be seen especially in the current context of the domination of economic globalization, which had a powerful impact on almost all nations worldwide. On the one hand, economic globalization requires a democratic mechanism but, on the other hand, it is undemocratic when the entire world economy is dependent on, and manipulated by, a few great monopoly capitalist companies.[3] It is not accidental that anti-globalization movements have often arisen in developed capitalist countries. This means that even capitalist nations themselves have not yet found an effective way to cope with undemocratic phenomena. Democracy preoccupies both developed and developing countries.

DEMOCRACY IN VIETNAM

For several reasons, including being a developing nation suffering from many cruel and destructive wars, Vietnam had long not paid proper attention to the problem of democracy. However, thanks to our patriotism and spirit of solidarity, as well as the lessons learned from the experience of other nations, our country has managed to avoid many of the extreme events which took place in the former USSR and China. Even though some destructive events did occur in Vietnam, we have learned valuable lessons from our policies on Land Reform; it is fair to say that those problems caused by the absence of democracy have been worrisome, particularly as they have been rather difficult to detect. These problems are manifested in a form of dogmatism in thinking and action, resulting in restraining or killing off individual creativity. It is very dangerous when this kind of vice becomes a habit in social life: people tend to worship power without expressing their own views, and feel no responsibility for what they are doing. They are ready to speak "in full accordance with the resolution" and to be "an obedient cog in the machine."[4]

---

[3] *Philosophical Challenges and Opportunities of Globalization*, volume 1. Ed. Oliva Blanchette, Tomonobu Imamichi, George F. McLean (Washington, DC: The Council for Research in Values and Philosophy, 2001), pp. 22-31, 85-93.

[4] De tai cap Nha nuoc (KHXH.01.08). *Chu nghia xa hoi: tu ly luan den thuc tien. Nhung bai hoc kinh nghiem chu yeu* (Ha Noi, 2001), tr. 209 (In Vietnamese).

We must say that such a vice existed during wartime in Vietnam, when top priority was given to national independence and sovereignty. In such a context, it is necessary to have full compliance with the demands and orders of leaders. But from the time that the country entered the peacetime era of reconstruction and economic development, unconditional obedience and mechanical action without reflection have held back people's creative potential and obstructed development. This has been one of the greatest shortcomings of the period of the system based on administrative subsidies in our country. Vietnam started its process of comprehensive renewal in 1986. One of the outstanding achievements is the democratization of the social life, which has been as an important factor in the policy of political "renovation" (*Doi moi*). Moreover, democracy is regarded as the objective and driving force of development, in order to attain the comprehensive aim of "wealthy people, a powerful country and an equitable, democratic and civilized society." The problem is: what is real democracy, and how is it a driving force for social development?

First and foremost, we would state that democracy is a historical category, linked closely with the existence and development of human society. During the course of social development, democracy has been enriched with new content; its present conception contains various elements which cannot be found to have existed previously. But regardless of its content, democracy has always been an aspiration of humanity. The history of the existence and development of human society has been a struggle for democracy. As a social and biological being, man has certain needs in order to sustain his existence. As an individual, man requires the right to live, to pursue happiness, to move and reside freely and so on; as a member of a community, man has the right to be free and to prosper equitably with other members of the community. He has also the right to be involved directly or indirectly in issues relating to social and individual life. In the past, many thinkers and philosophers discussed man's inspiration for freedom and self-determination. The French thinker, Rousseau, for example, mentioned the idea of human freedom in the determination of one's course of action. Man can be free only when he is able to determine all the matters relating to his own life, instead of doing them under the influence of others. This is the very criterion of freedom. Rousseau also differentiated between two kinds of freedom: authentic and feigned. The former is a kind of freedom to act freely under no external influence, and the latter is a freedom to do so under the influence of other members of society, laws and social regulations.[5] Rousseau's ideas of free will were implemented later by Kant in his views on freedom in pure ethics. According to Kant, a pure moral act is an act that a man can perform for the sake of the other, without any external motivation and interest.

---

[5]Charles Taylor. *The Ethics of Authenticity* (Cambridge, Massachusetts: Harvard University Press, 1991), pp.27–28.

The problem is that man cannot live in isolation from other members of the community. Then how can he act independently of social norms and regulations? The answer here is that he cannot. Pure liberty – freedom to determine all courses of individual action without any obligations – is only an ideal. As a member of a particular community, man is bound by social obligations and laws. The less one is tied by obligations, the more freedom he enjoys. This means that man's freedom is a social creation and depends on concrete social conditions. In other words, the freedom which man enjoys has been brought about by democracy. Here democracy can be understood as a social mechanism, a form of social organization preserving human rights.

There have existed various forms of democracy throughout the history of human society. Democracy can be categorized according to its various forms: the democracy of primitive communism, feudal and bourgeois democracy, and so on.   As a form of state organization, democracy in its earliest form, i.e., that which came into being after the collapse of the primitive commune, meant power belonging to the people. Therefore, we can state that democracy preceded dictatorship and government. However, since the introduction of class-divisions in society and government organization, democracy has often belonged to a certain class and been deformed into a kind of manipulative power of certain classes or a privilege of a group or even of a leader, who have control over the freedom of the masses. The extent to which people could enjoy their rights and freedom depended on the will of the governing class. Therefore, democracy long remained just an aspiration of the common people.

Besides material needs, man also has spiritual, intellectual, and emotional interests as well as the need to assert himself, or in other words, cultural, social, and spiritual needs, which cannot be obtained without democracy. One cannot have freedom when one country is dependent on another nation. As a country suffering from various cruel wars, Vietnam is well aware of the importance of peace and freedom: freedom is a universal human value. However, the example of many nations worldwide as well as that of the period of rebuilding our country have shown that freedom could not be obtained immediately upon a country's gaining independence. Democracy is the mechanism to guarantee man's freedom.

An authentic democratic mechanism is a direct condition of bringing about freedom for the common man. In its turn, the free development of every person contributes to the promotion of individual creativity and one's sense of initiative. It is for the benefit of the whole society and each of its members if all are free to determine their courses of action as well as manifest their abilities without any arbitrary obligations or restrictions. Therefore, the individual freedom generated by democracy is the source of creativity and innovation, which, in turn, will contribute to a more progressive development of society. For its development, a society should create the best conditions for its members to develop their potential. In this case, society needs the freedom brought by democracy. So democracy is replete with forces powerfully promoting man to act and create; it is the way that democracy advances social progress.[6] However, as stated above, every society must have regulations imposed on its citizens in order to maintain order. In every society, in order to be democratically free, man has act within the limits established by the society.

In the history of philosophy, Spinoza and Hegel paid serious attention to the problem of freedom and necessity in order to find a desirable resolution. For them, freedom meant awareness of necessity, but they worked on that relation only within the framework of epistemology. However, we should not only recognize, but also act, according to that necessity. In different historical periods and various countries, there have been, in addition to common regulations, specific conventions generated according to historical, economic, and socio-political conditions, as well as the cultural traditions. In Asian countries, for example, due to their distinctive economic, political and cultural environment, the form of democracy is different from that of Western nations. Therefore it is not possible to judge it based only upon Western criteria and values, or to impose these values dogmatically.

Here the problem is how to make democracy a driving force to promote man's activities within the specific conditions of each nation. To achieve this target, in our view, democracy should be understood as social equality. Democracy is the very mechanism guaranteeing social equality under particular social conditions. Such equality should be implemented in all sectors of social life, including the economic and the socio-political. In recent years, in the course of "renovation" in Vietnam, the problems of equality and justice have been discussed extensively. Equality and justice, despite their different manifestations, are widely understood as being on the same level in some respects: i.e. in relation to duties and interests. In addition, the contents of equality and justice have also been considered in different fields. In the past, for example, the conceptions of equality and justice were implemented in the area of distribution, but nowadays they are also given new content – namely, in relation to access to opportunity. This means that equality in society is understood as how society can create equal opportunities for its citizens to be able to fully manifest their potential.

At present, we have seen many positive results due to the policy of the comprehensive democratization of social life, primarily, in the economic sector which has been promoted since the beginning of our "renovation." Democratization in the economy can serve as a premise and foundation for the implementation of democracy in other sectors of social life. Vietnam intends to build up an economic mechanism, a socialist-oriented market economy, which would give to all economic sectors and subjects equal opportunities to participate in the nation's economic development on their own initiative. A democratic mechanism aiming at

---

[6]Le Huu Tang (Chu bien). *Ve dong luc cua su phat trien kinh te - xa hoi,* (Nxb Khoa häc Xa hoi, 1997), tr. 107. (in Vietnamese).

economic equality and justice also requires genuine respect for the individual interests of people, with their creativity, energy and capital. It is a process establishing the rights and duties of people participating in production and business.

The implementation of economic equality and justice in Vietnam also aims at the creation of a favorable economic environment. In order to practice economic equality and justice, it is important for our government to issue and put into action democratic laws to protect people's economic rights. The government also should assure democratic rights in the economy, and advance policies preventing illegal economic activity and punishing severely activities causing damage to people and the government. In short, we should enhance government effectiveness in economic management through the legal system, in order to ensure equal opportunities for all citizens to participate in legal matters as well as in economic activities.[7]

The recent democratization of the economy in Vietnam has proved beneficial not only for its government, but also for each citizen. This contributes to the creation of a powerful force, encouraging all people to be active in their work because it meets the most important democratic demands of the Vietnamese people. The process of democratization in the economy has created stable premises and favorable environments for the renovation process in politics. It has also contributed to a relatively high economic growth and rescued Vietnam from the prolonged economic crisis generated during the period of the bureaucratic economic system based on administrative subsidies. Thanks to a democratically economic environment, our agriculture has been oriented toward commodity production; there is a renewed interest in the manufacture of traditional handicrafts, and these products have contributed to significant economic growth.

With the steady development of industries and handicrafts have come the economic conditions for resolving social problems. Our society has the opportunity to repay in kind all those families whose members sacrificed their lives for our nation. Many other social problems have been addressed successfully. Together with economic and social development, the spiritual life of society has been enhanced by the diverse demands for culture and information: people are increasingly interested in political and social issues both at home and abroad. The rapid development of information technology has given people more access to various sources of information, but it also requires of the common man a certain level of processing and analyzing information. The best way to promote a people's level of information is to promote their general education through educational campaigns, on the one hand, and to implement a policy of equal access to information (i.e. to provide people with reliable information on a

---

[7] *Op cit.*, p. 114.

wide range of national and international issues), on the other. This is the way to realize democracy in the field of information.

Democratization in information can advance the people's level of analyzing and processing information. With the implementation of the policy "people to know, people to discuss, people to do, people to inspect," which has brought about many positive results in recent years, the people's right to be informed has been recognized and encouraged. Thanks to this policy, the people's political activity has noticeably improved; people have actively given their own constructive opinions on various social and political issues. As a result, we have been able to mobilize the intellectual strengths and creative potentialities of our people on a wide range of issues vital to our country. So far, in recent years, the policy of the comprehensive democratization of social life in Vietnam has brought about many positive results. Democracy has been the real driving force of renovation and development in our country.

But what role can philosophy play in the promotion of the role of democracy?

THE ROLE OF PHILOSOPHY IN THE PROCESS OF DEMOCRATIZATION IN VIETNAM

As stated above, the current process of democratization in Vietnam is defined as an objective and driving force of development. Vietnamese philosophers have contributed significantly to mapping out this policy, because one of their important tasks is to research philosophical issues arising from practice and, based on this research, to suggest solutions that help the Party and the Movement in the policymaking processes. Since the beginning of our country's comprehensive renovation, the issue of how to broaden democracy has been considered as one of the contributions of scholars in the social sciences in general, and of philosophers in particular. Democracy has been officially regarded as an objective of our country's development, and listed in the documents of the Party's Congress since 2001. Based on life practice, both before and after renovation, as well as on the experiences of many nations worldwide, the acceptance of democracy as an objective of our country has been one of the great recent achievements of philosophers in Vietnam.

> Philosophical argumentation on democracy as the driving force for the development of human society in general and of our society in particular, has been very valuable. In the coming years, our philosophical circle, with the highest spirit of responsibility and ability, should contribute to the accomplishment of the objective of building an equitable,

democratic and civilized society with a wealthy people and
a powerful nation.[8]

How can we put this guideline into practice and realize this ideal?
Based on some recent surveys, we can see that the demands for democracy
vary according to different populations. For example, to the question
regarding what the local government should do to enhance the activity of its
people or what problems the people are concerned about at this moment,
among the 1500 people questionned in rural areas, only 20% of them spoke
of the need to promote democracy. However, in another survey, of 20
universal human values, some 86% of the interviewees gave priority to the
value of peace and 76.8% to the value of freedom. According to another
survey, 85% of 40 professors and doctors from major Hanoi universities
said that they wished for "a favorable political environment in which to
work."[9] So far, then, from the results of various surveys, we see that when
economic democracy has been reached, interest in democracy in its social
and spiritual dimensions increase, though it varies according to population
group and strata, such as educational level, profession, place of work, living
standards, and so on. For example, people working in the field of social
sciences are more interested in problems of democracy than are those in the
field of natural sciences. Therefore, in order to put democracy into practice,
the task of enhancing education to activate the people is of primary
importance.

In his lifetime, President Ho Chi Minh used to urge the Party and
Government to make "people enjoy and know how to use their democratic
rights." In order to implement this, we should provide people with a certain
level of education, without which people would effectively lose the rights
they deserve. With regard, then, to education in democracy, what can
philosophy do?

Research and teaching in philosophy in Vietnam has been given
much attention. At present, about 3,000 people are engaged in researching
and teaching philosophy at a wide range of universities and colleges in
Vietnam. Philosophy has become a compulsory discipline in tertiary
education. Even in the system of secondary education, philosophy has been
introduced in connection with topics dealing with nature and society.

However, there exist different understandings of philosophy, which
in turn lead to various interpretations of the role of philosophy. In Vietnam,
philosophy has been popularly defined as a form of social consciousness,
and so has been given two major functions: knowledge and evaluation.

First, as a form of social consciousness, philosophical knowledge
plays a very important role in the orientation of human activity. Cognition

---

[8] Nguyen Trong Chuan. *Mot so van de ve triet hoc - con nguoi - xa hoi*
(Nxb Khoa hoc Xa hoi: Ha Noi, 2002), tr. 27 (in Vietnamese).

[9] Le Huu Tang (Chu bien). *Ve dong luc cua su phat trien kinh te-xa hoi*
(Nxb Khoa hoc Xa hoi : Ha Noi, 1997), tr. 116-117 (in Vietnamese).

is a necessary manifestation of consciousness, but it is not the whole of consciousness, whose other contents and manifestations it does not address. Cognition is a process of acquiring something new, a process involving the discovery of new attributes and relations existing in recognized objects. It is not always linked to new reflections but, on the contrary, can function within the limit of that which is recognized and based on the existing knowledge of given society.

In reality, all sciences have the function of cognition and providing knowledge. However, philosophical knowledge, in distinction from the other concrete sciences, is a kind of general knowledge playing a methodological role in the orientation of human activity. Similarly, when dealing with the problems of democracy, philosophical knowledge helps people correctly orient their activity. In this role, philosophical knowledge is not concrete knowledge of any particular situation, but a sort of knowledge helping people to act rationally in concrete situations.

From ancient times, philosophy has meant "love of wisdom." Nevertheless, even this definition has been interpreted in various ways. Socrates, for example, identified wisdom with truth. Plato understood it as something unchangeable and universal. According to Aristotle, there were three meanings of wisdom: true knowledge, practical knowledge and practical willingness. Catholic philosophers identified wisdom with God, who is *Sapientia sapientiarum*. The philosophers of the Enlightenment considered wisdom as a feature of reason, not of God. Similarly, Chinese thinkers regarded wisdom as the Way of the Heart, the mother of all things, and so on. There has been also a wide range of opinions regarding the way to achieve wisdom. It was mathematics according to Plato; dialectics, as Aristotle, Hegel and Marx held; or intuition according to Descartes and Bergson. The emergence of various schools of thought in the twentieth century, such as positivism, phenomenology, existentialism, realism, and pragmatism, also contributed to the vast diversity of definitions of wisdom.[10] Despite these various interpretations, wisdom is recognized as the quintessence of the human. Philosophy can help one attain this wisdom.

In general, then, through education concerning democracy, philosophy helps people to act rationally. This is the first point we would note when talking about the role of philosophy in education concerning democracy.

But second, apart from exercising cognition, human beings evaluate. This is a very important activity for human existence and development, but it has been paid little attention to in the discussion of the characteristics and forms of consciousness. What is the basis on which we can define the cognitive nature of evaluation? What is the role of evaluation in the cognitive process?

---

[10]Tran Van Đoan. *Viet triet luan tap. Thuong tap* (Washington DC: The University Press of Vietnam, 2000) tr. 94-95 (in Vietnamese).

We know that during the course of practical activity, objects and phenomena of nature gradually become meaningful for human beings. These objects and phenomena have been put into service for human activities and have become valued; thus, the relation between human beings and these phenomena has become a value relation. Therefore, the functions of objects determine their values for human beings, but the values themselves are objective in nature despite being dependent on subjects. Material production is a foundation for determining the value of objects and phenomena of the natural world for man and society. The value of a thing and its value relation have a practical or pragmatic character. Objects of the natural world have long been involved in human activities, have obtained a 'second existence' (according to their functions), and have served as important tools to meet human demands and aspirations. In this way, they have become valuable for human beings. This means also that value has originated from practical human activity, and that value has been a social feature of an object. Of course, without certain natural attributes, an object is meaningless for man and cannot become something valuable. Therefore, existence in nature is a premise required to make an object valuable for human beings. It is material human activity that makes objects valuable.

Value is objective. The functions that objects possess have originated from objective processes through the activity of material production and as carried out by human beings as subjects of the activity. Here, subjective elements like intentions, interests, and emotions are instruments to understand the functions of objects in the process of production. Through participation in human activity, objects may change their forms or structure according to human purposes and plans: this brings the character of social being to objects. In other words, value is a product of the human impact on objects; value is created from objects of the natural world that meet human needs and interests. In the process of practical activity, besides the relation between man and nature, there are also interactions among human beings or social relations. In order to harmonize human behavior, people have worked out certain practices. Gradually these practices have become social and psychological habits that regulate human conduct. This serves as a foundation to evaluate human behavior.

Evaluation is a manifestation of values. In the process of evaluation, the integration between the subjective and objective emerges in the meaning of an object. Evaluation is an objective process because it is close to the evaluated object; it is the expression of the object. At the same time, evaluation is subjective because it reflects human needs and emotions, including the material, moral, aesthetic, social, political, and so on. The particular feature of evaluation expresses itself in the process leading to truth. Evaluation is an element and a driving force of cognition, which can be found only in human beings. Thanks to evaluation, human subjects can see what they have and have not done, as well as what they should continue to do. Therefore, evaluation is a foundation of human creative activity.

The two functions of philosophy, cognition and evaluation, are therefore closely linked in education for democracy. They help people not only to recognize the role of democracy in society, but also to evaluate democracy for society. On such a basis of cognition and evaluation, society can choose to adopt appropriate democratic values, eliminate other values which are not suitable for the new social conditions, and accept universal human values.

CONCLUSION

Democracy has been regarded as an objective and driving force of social development in the context of contemporary Vietnam. In this role, democracy is a mechanism that guarantees freedom and equality for human beings. Freedom has always been an aspiration of humanity and is an important condition for human creativity. Most important, with respect to equality, is the encouragement of individual dynamism and initiative. In Vietnam, philosophy plays an important role in the process of democratization of social life. This can be seen in its functions of cognition and evaluation, which help people realize how to accept democratic values, as well as to act rationally in concrete historical situations.

Institute of Philosophy
The Vietnamese Academy of Social Sciences
Hanoi, Vietnam

INDEX

THE COUNCIL FOR RESEARCH IN VALUES AND PHILOSOPHY

PURPOSE

Today there is urgent need to attend to the nature and dignity of the person, to the quality of human life, to the purpose and goal of the physical transformation of our environment, and to the relation of all this to the development of social and political life. This, in turn, requires philosophic clarification of the base upon which freedom is exercised, that is, of the values which provide stability and guidance to one's decisions.

Such studies must be able to reach deeply into one's culture and that of other parts of the world as mutually reinforcing and enriching in order to uncover the roots of the dignity of persons and of their societies. They must be able to identify the conceptual forms in terms of which modern industrial and technological developments are structured and how these impact upon human self-understanding. Above all, they must be able to bring these elements together in the creative understanding essential for setting our goals and determining our modes of interaction. In the present complex global circumstances this is a condition for growing together with trust and justice, honest dedication and mutual concern.

The Council for Studies in Values and Philosophy (RVP) unites scholars who share these concerns and are interested in the application thereto of existing capabilities in the field of philosophy and other disciplines. Its work is to identify areas in which study is needed, the intellectual resources which can be brought to bear thereupon, and the means for publication and interchange of the work from the various regions of the world. In bringing these together its goal is scientific discovery and publication which contributes to the present promotion of humankind.

In sum, our times present both the need and the opportunity for deeper and ever more progressive understanding of the person and of the foundations of social life. The development of such understanding is the goal of the RVP.

PROJECTS

A set of related research efforts is currently in process:

1. *Cultural Heritage and Contemporary Change: Philosophical Foundations for Social Life.* Focused, mutually coordinated research teams in university centers prepare volumes as part of an integrated philosophic search for self-understanding differentiated by culture and civilization. These evolve more adequate understandings of the person in society and look to the cultural heritage of each for the resources to respond to the challenges of its own specific contemporary transformation.

2. *Seminars on Culture and Contemporary Issues.* This series of 10 week crosscultural and interdisciplinary seminars is coordinated by the RVP in Washington.

3. *Joint-Colloquia* with Institutes of Philosophy of the National Academies of Science, university philosophy departments, and societies. Underway since 1976 in Eastern Europe and, since 1987, in China, these concern the person in contemporary society.

4. *Foundations of Moral Education and Character Development.* A study in values and education which unites philosophers, psychologists, social scientists and scholars in education in the elaboration of ways of enriching the moral content of education and character development. This work has been underway since 1980.

The personnel for these projects consists of established scholars willing to contribute their time and research as part of their professional commitment to life in contemporary society. For resources to implement this work the Council, as 501 C3 a non-profit organization incorporated in the District of Colombia, looks to various private foundations, public programs and enterprises.

PUBLICATIONS ON CULTURAL HERITAGE AND CONTEMPORARY CHANGE

Series I. Culture and Values
Series II. Africa
Series IIA. Islam
Series III. Asia
Series IV. W. Europe and North America
Series IVA. Central and Eastern Europe
Series V. Latin America
Series VI. Foundations of Moral Education
Series VII. Seminars on Culture and Values

CULTURAL HERITAGE AND CONTEMPORARY CHANGE

Series I. Culture and Values

I.1 *Research on Culture and Values: Intersection of Universities, Churches and Nations.* George F. McLean, ed. ISBN 0819173533 (paper); 081917352-5 (cloth).

I.2 *The Knowledge of Values: A Methodological Introduction to the Study of Values;* A. Lopez Quintas, ed. ISBN 081917419x (paper); 0819174181 (cloth).

I.3 *Reading Philosophy for the XXIst Century.* George F. McLean, ed. ISBN 0819174157 (paper); 0819174149 (cloth).

I.4 *Relations Between Cultures.* John A. Kromkowski, ed. ISBN 1565180089 (paper); 1565180097 (cloth).

I.5 *Urbanization and Values.* John A. Kromkowski, ed. ISBN 1565180100 (paper); 1565180119 (cloth).

I.6 *The Place of the Person in Social Life.* Paul Peachey and John A. Kromkowski, eds. ISBN 1565180127 (paper); 156518013-5 (cloth).

I.7 *Abrahamic Faiths, Ethnicity and Ethnic Conflicts*. Paul Peachey, George F. McLean and John A. Kromkowski, eds. ISBN 1565181042 (paper).

I.8 *Ancient Western Philosophy: The Hellenic Emergence*. George F. McLean and Patrick J. Aspell, eds. ISBN 156518100X (paper).

I.9 *Medieval Western Philosophy: The European Emergence*. Patrick J. Aspell, ed. ISBN 1565180941 (paper).

I.10 *The Ethical Implications of Unity and the Divine in Nicholas of Cusa*. David L. De Leonardis. ISBN 1565181123 (paper).

I.11 *Ethics at the Crossroads: 1.Normative Ethics and Objective Reason*. George F. McLean, ed. ISBN 1565180224 (paper).

I.12 *Ethics at the Crossroads: 2.Personalist Ethics and Human Subjectivity*. George F. McLean, ed. ISBN 1565180240 (paper).

I.13 *The Emancipative Theory of Jürgen Habermas and Metaphysics*. Robert Badillo. ISBN 1565180429 (paper); 1565180437 (cloth).

I.14 *The Deficient Cause of Moral Evil According to Thomas Aquinas*. Edward Cook. ISBN 1565180704 (paper).

I.15 *Human Love: Its Meaning and Scope, a Phenomenology of Gift and Encounter*. Alfonso Lopez Quintas. ISBN 1565180747 (paper).

I.16 *Civil Society and Social Reconstruction*. George F. McLean, ed. ISBN 1565180860 (paper).

I.17 *Ways to God, Personal and Social at the Turn of Millennia: The Iqbal Lecture, Lahore*. George F. McLean. ISBN 1565181239 (paper).

I.18 *The Role of the Sublime in Kant's Moral Metaphysics*. John R. Goodreau. ISBN 1565181247 (paper).

I.19 *Philosophical Challenges and Opportunities of Globalization*. Oliva Blanchette, Tomonobu Imamichi and George F. McLean, eds. ISBN 1565181298 (paper).

I.20 *Faith, Reason and Philosophy: Lectures at The al-Azhar, Qom, Tehran, Lahore and Beijing; Appendix: The Encyclical Letter: Fides et Ratio*. George F. McLean. ISBN 156518130 (paper).

I.21 *Religion and the Relation between Civilizations: Lectures on Cooperation between Islamic and Christian Cultures in a Global Horizon*. George F. McLean. ISBN 1565181522 (paper).

I.22 *Freedom, Cultural Traditions and Progress: Philosophy in Civil Society and Nation Building, Tashkent Lectures, 1999*. George F. McLean. ISBN 1565181514 (paper).

I.23 *Ecology of Knowledge*. Jerzy A. Wojciechowski. ISBN 1565181581 (paper).

I.24 *God and the Challenge of Evil: A Critical Examination of Some Serious Objections to the Good and Omnipotent God*. John L. Yardan. ISBN 1565181603 (paper).

I.25 *Reason, Rationality and Reasonableness, Vietnamese Philosophical Studies, I*. Tran Van Doan. ISBN 1565181662 (paper).

I.26 *The Culture of Citizenship: Inventing Postmodern Civic Culture*. Thomas Bridges. ISBN 1565181689 (paper).

I.27 *The Historicity of Understanding and the Problem of Relativism in Gadamer's Philosophical Hermeneutics*. Osman Bilen. ISBN 1565181670 (paper).

1.28 *Speaking of God*. Carlo Huber. ISBN 1565181697 (paper).

1.29 *Persons, Peoples and Cultures in a Global Age: Metaphysical Bases for Peace between Civilizations*. George F. McLean. ISBN 1565181875 (paper).

1.30 *Hermeneutics, Tradition and Contemporary Change: Lectures In Chennai/Madras, India*. George F. McLean. ISBN 1565181883 (paper).

1.31 *Husserl and Stein*. Richard Feist and William Sweet, eds. ISBN 1565181948 (paper).

1.32 *Paul Hanly Furfey's Quest for a Good Society*. Bronislaw Misztal, Francesco Villa, and Eric Sean Williams, eds. ISBN 1565182278 (paper).

1.33 *Three Theories of Society*. Paul Hanly Furfey. ISBN 9781565182288 (paper).

1.34 *Building Peace In Civil Society: An Autobiographical Report from a Believers' Church*. Paul Peachey. ISBN 9781565182325 (paper).

1.35 *Karol Wojtyla's Philosophical Legacy*. Agnes B. Curry, Nancy Mardas and George F. McLean ,eds. ISBN 9781565182479 (paper).

1.36 *Kantian Form and Phenomenological Force: Kant's Imperatives and the Directives of Contemporary Phenomenology*. Randolph C. Wheeler. ISBN 9781565182547 (paper).

1.37 *Beyond Modernity: The Recovery of Person and Community in Global Times: Lectures in China and Vietnam*. George F. McLean. ISBN 9781565182578 (paper)

1. 38 *Religion and Culture*. George F. McLean. ISBN 9781565182561 (paper).

1.39 *The Dialogue of Cultural Traditions: Global Perspective*. William Sweet, George F. McLean, Tomonobu Imamichi, Safak Ural, O. Faruk Akyol, eds. ISBN 9781565182585 (paper).

1.40 *Unity and Harmony, Compassion and Love in Global Times*. George F. McLean. ISBN 978-1565182592 (paper).

Series II. Africa

II.1 *Person and Community: Ghanaian Philosophical Studies: I.* Kwasi Wiredu and Kwame Gyeke, eds. ISBN 1565180046 (paper); 1565180054 (cloth).

II.2 *The Foundations of Social Life: Ugandan Philosophical Studies: I.* A.T. Dalfovo, ed. ISBN 1565180062 (paper); 156518007-0 (cloth).

II.3 *Identity and Change in Nigeria: Nigerian Philosophical Studies, I.* Theophilus Okere, ed. ISBN 1565180682 (paper).

II.4 *Social Reconstruction in Africa: Ugandan Philosophical studies, II.* E. Wamala, A.R. Byaruhanga, A.T. Dalfovo, J.K.Kigongo, S.A.Mwanahewa and G.Tusabe, eds. ISBN 1565181182 (paper).

II.5 *Ghana: Changing Values/Chaning Technologies: Ghanaian Philosophical Studies, II.* Helen Lauer, ed. ISBN 1565181441 (paper).

II.6 *Sameness and Difference: Problems and Potentials in South African Civil Society: South African Philosophical Studies, I.* James R.Cochrane and Bastienne Klein, eds. ISBN 1565181557 (paper).

II.7 *Protest and Engagement: Philosophy after Apartheid at an Historically Black South African University: South African Philosophical Studies, II.* Patrick Giddy, ed. ISBN 1565181638 (paper).

II.8 *Ethics, Human Rights and Development in Africa: Ugandan Philosophical Studies, III.* A.T. Dalfovo, J.K. Kigongo, J. Kisekka, G. Tusabe, E. Wamala, R. Munyonyo, A.B. Rukooko, A.B.T. Byaruhanga-akiiki, M. Mawa, eds. ISBN 1565181727 (paper).

II.9 *Beyond Cultures: Perceiving a Common Humanity: Ghanian Philosophical Studies, III.* Kwame Gyekye ISBN 156518193X (paper).

II.10 *Social and Religious Concerns of East African: A Wajibu Anthology: Kenyan Philosophical Studies, I.* Gerald J. Wanjohi and G. Wakuraya Wanjohi, eds. ISBN 1565182219 (paper).

II.11 *The Idea of an African University: The Nigerian Experience: Nigerian Philosophical Studies, II.* Joseph Kenny, ed. ISBN 978-1565182301 (paper).

II.12 *The Struggles after the Struggles: Zimbabwean Philosophical Study, I.* David Kaulemu, ed. ISBN 9781565182318 (paper).

II.13 *Indigenous and Modern Environmental Ethics: A Study of the Indigenous Oromo Environmental Ethic and Modern Issues of Environment and Development: Ethiopian Philosophical Studies, I.* Workineh Kelbessa. ISBN 978 9781565182530 (paper).

Series IIA. Islam

IIA.1 *Islam and the Political Order.* Muhammad Saïd al-Ashmawy. ISBN ISBN 156518047X (paper); 156518046-1 (cloth).

IIA.2 *Al-Ghazali Deliverance from Error and Mystical Union with the Almighty: Al-munqidh Min Al-dalil.* Critical edition of English translation with introduction by Muhammad Abulaylah and Nurshif Abdul-Rahim Rifat; Introduction and notes by George F. McLean. ISBN 1565181530 (Arabic-English edition, paper), ISBN 1565180828 (Arabic edition, paper), ISBN 156518081X (English edition, paper)

IIA.3 *Philosophy in Pakistan.* Naeem Ahmad, ed. ISBN 1565181085 (paper).

IIA.4 *The Authenticity of the Text in Hermeneutics.* Seyed Musa Dibadj. ISBN 1565181174 (paper).

IIA.5 *Interpretation and the Problem of the Intention of the Author: H.-G.Gadamer vs E.D.Hirsch.* Burhanettin Tatar. ISBN 156518121 (paper).

IIA.6 *Ways to God, Personal and Social at the Turn of Millennia: The Iqbal Lecture, Lahore.* George F. McLean. ISBN 1565181239 (paper).

IIA.7 *Faith, Reason and Philosophy: Lectures at The al-Azhar, Qom, Tehran, Lahore and Beijing; Appendix: The Encyclical Letter: Fides et Ratio.* George F. McLean. ISBN 1565181301 (paper).

IIA.8 *Islamic and Christian Cultures: Conflict or Dialogue: Bulgarian Philosophical Studies, III.* Plament Makariev, ed. ISBN 156518162X (paper).

IIA.9 *Values of Islamic Culture and the Experience of History, Russian Philosophical Studies, I.* Nur Kirabaev, Yuriy Pochta, eds. ISBN 1565181336 (paper).

IIA.10 *Christian-Islamic Preambles of Faith.* Joseph Kenny. ISBN 1565181387 (paper).

IIA.11 *The Historicity of Understanding and the Problem of Relativism in Gadamer's Philosophical Hermeneutics.* Osman Bilen. ISBN 1565181670 (paper).

IIA.12 *Religion and the Relation between Civilizations: Lectures on Cooperation between Islamic and Christian Cultures in a Global Horizon.* George F. McLean. ISBN 1565181522 (paper).

IIA.13 *Modern Western Christian Theological Understandings of Muslims since the Second Vatican Council.* Mahmut Aydin. ISBN 1565181719 (paper).

IIA.14 *Philosophy of the Muslim World; Authors and Principal Themes.* Joseph Kenny. ISBN 1565181794 (paper).

IIA.15 *Islam and Its Quest for Peace: Jihad, Justice and Education.* Mustafa Köylü. ISBN 1565181808 (paper).

IIA.16 *Islamic Thought on the Existence of God: Contributions and Contrasts with Contemporary Western Philosophy of Religion.* Cafer S. Yaran. ISBN 1565181921 (paper).

IIA.17 *Hermeneutics, Faith, and Relations between Cultures: Lectures in Qom, Iran.* George F. McLean. ISBN 1565181913 (paper).

IIA.18 *Change and Essence: Dialectical Relations between Change and Continuity in the Turkish Intellectual Tradition.* Sinasi Gunduz and Cafer S. Yaran, eds. ISBN 1565182227 (paper).

IIA. 19 *Understanding Other Religions: Al-Biruni and Gadamer's "Fusion of Horizons".* Kemal Ataman. ISBN 9781565182523 (paper).

Series III.Asia

III.1 *Man and Nature: Chinese Philosophical Studies, I.* Tang Yi-jie, Li Zhen, eds. ISBN 0819174130 (paper); 0819174122 (cloth).

III.2 *Chinese Foundations for Moral Education and Character Development: Chinese Philosophical Studies, II.* Tran van Doan, ed. ISBN 1565180321 (paper); 156518033X (cloth).

III.3 *Confucianism, Buddhism, Taoism, Christianity and Chinese Culture: Chinese Philosophical Studies, III.* Tang Yijie. ISBN 1565180348 (paper); 156518035-6 (cloth).

III.4 *Morality, Metaphysics and Chinese Culture (Metaphysics, Culture and Morality, I).* Vincent Shen and Tran van Doan, eds. ISBN 1565180275 (paper); 156518026-7 (cloth).

III.5 *Tradition, Harmony and Transcendence.* George F. McLean. ISBN 1565180313 (paper); 156518030-5 (cloth).

III.6 *Psychology, Phenomenology and Chinese Philosophy: Chinese Philosophical Studies, VI.* Vincent Shen, Richard Knowles and Tran Van Doan, eds. ISBN 1565180453 (paper); 1565180445 (cloth).

III.7 *Values in Philippine Culture and Education: Philippine Philosophical Studies, I.* Manuel B. Dy, Jr., ed. ISBN 1565180412 (paper); 156518040-2 (cloth).

III.7A *The Human Person and Society: Chinese Philosophical Studies, VIIA.* Zhu Dasheng, Jin Xiping and George F. McLean, eds. ISBN 1565180887.

III.8 *The Filipino Mind: Philippine Philosophical Studies II.* Leonardo N. Mercado. ISBN 156518064X (paper); 156518063-1 (cloth).

III.9 *Philosophy of Science and Education: Chinese Philosophical Studies IX.* Vincent Shen and Tran Van Doan, eds. ISBN 1565180763 (paper); 156518075-5 (cloth).

III.10 *Chinese Cultural Traditions and Modernization: Chinese Philosophical Studies, X.* Wang Miaoyang, Yu Xuanmeng and George F. McLean, eds. ISBN 1565180682 (paper).

III.11 *The Humanization of Technology and Chinese Culture: Chinese Philosophical Studies XI.* Tomonobu Imamichi, Wang Miaoyang and Liu Fangtong, eds. ISBN 1565181166 (paper).

III.12 *Beyond Modernization: Chinese Roots of Global Awareness: Chinese Philosophical Studies, XII.* Wang Miaoyang, Yu Xuanmeng and George F. McLean, eds. ISBN 1565180909 (paper).

III.13 *Philosophy and Modernization in China: Chinese Philosophical Studies XIII.* Liu Fangtong, Huang Songjie and George F. McLean, eds. ISBN 1565180666 (paper).

III.14 *Economic Ethics and Chinese Culture: Chinese Philosophical Studies, XIV.* Yu Xuanmeng, Lu Xiaohe, Liu Fangtong, Zhang Rulun and Georges Enderle, eds. ISBN 1565180925 (paper).

III.15 *Civil Society in a Chinese Context: Chinese Philosophical Studies XV.* Wang Miaoyang, Yu Xuanmeng and Manuel B. Dy, eds. ISBN 1565180844 (paper).

III.16 *The Bases of Values in a Time of Change: Chinese and Western: Chinese Philosophical Studies, XVI.* Kirti Bunchua, Liu Fangtong, Yu Xuanmeng, Yu Wujin, eds. ISBN 156518114X (paper).

III.17 *Dialogue between Christian Philosophy and Chinese Culture: Philosophical Perspectives for the Third Millennium: Chinese Philosophical Studies, XVII.* Paschal Ting, Marian Kao and Bernard Li, eds. ISBN 1565181735 (paper).

III.18 *The Poverty of Ideological Education: Chinese Philosophical Studies, XVIII.* Tran Van Doan. ISBN 1565181646 (paper).

III.19 *God and the Discovery of Man: Classical and Contemporary Approaches: Lectures in Wuhan, China.* George F. McLean. ISBN 1565181891 (paper).

III.20 *Cultural Impact on International Relations: Chinese Philosophical Studies, XX.* Yu Xintian, ed. ISBN 156518176X (paper).

III.21 *Cultural Factors in International Relations: Chinese Philosophical Studies, XXI.* Yu Xintian, ed. ISBN 1565182049 (paper).

III.22 *Wisdom in China and the West: Chinese Philosophical Studies, XXII.* Vincent Shen and Willard Oxtoby †. ISBN 1565182057 (paper)

III.23 *China's Contemporary Philosophical Journey: Western Philosophy and Marxism ChineseP hilosophical Studies: Chinese Philosophical Studies, XXIII.* Liu Fangtong. ISBN 1565182065 (paper).

III.24 *Shanghai : Its Urbanization and Culture: Chinese Philosophical Studies, XXIV.* Yu Xuanmeng and He Xirong, eds. ISBN 1565182073 (paper).

III.25 *Dialogue of Philosophies, Religions and Civilizations in the Era of Globalization: Chinese Philosophical Studies, XXV.* Zhao Dunhua, ed. ISBN 9781565182431 (paper).

III.26 *Rethinking Marx: Chinese Philosophical Studies, XXVI.* Zou Shipeng and Yang Xuegong, eds. ISBN 9781565182448 (paper).

III.27 *Confucian Ethics in Retrospect and Prospect: Chinese Philosophical Studies XXVII.* Vincent Shen and Kwong-loi Shun, eds. ISBN 9781565182455 (paper).

IIIB.1 *Authentic Human Destiny: The Paths of Shankara and Heidegger: Indian Philosophical Studies, I.* Vensus A. George. ISBN 1565181190 (paper).

IIIB.2 *The Experience of Being as Goal of Human Existence: The Heideggerian Approach: Indian Philosophical Studies, II.* Vensus A. George. ISBN 156518145X (paper).

IIIB.3 *Religious Dialogue as Hermeneutics: Bede Griffiths's Advaitic Approach: Indian Philosophical Studies, III.* Kuruvilla Pandikattu. ISBN 1565181395 (paper).

IIIB.4 *Self-Realization [Brahmaanubhava]: The Advaitic Perspective of Shankara: Indian Philosophical Studies, IV.* Vensus A. George. ISBN 1565181549 (paper).

IIIB.5 *Gandhi: The Meaning of Mahatma for the Millennium: Indian Philosophical Studies, V.* Kuruvilla Pandikattu, ed. ISBN 1565181565 (paper).

IIIB.6 *Civil Society in Indian Cultures: Indian Philosophical Studies, VI.* Asha Mukherjee, Sabujkali Sen (Mitra) and K. Bagchi, eds. ISBN 1565181573 (paper).

IIIB.7 *Hermeneutics, Tradition and Contemporary Change: Lectures In Chennai/Madras, India.* George F. McLean. ISBN 1565181883 (paper).

IIIB.8 *Plenitude and Participation: The Life of God in Man: Lectures in Chennai/Madras, India.* George F. McLean. ISBN 1565181999 (paper).

IIIB.9 *Sufism and Bhakti, a Comparative Study.* Md. Sirajul Islam. ISBN 1565181980 (paper).

IIIB.10 *Reasons for Hope: Its Nature, Role and Future.* Kuruvilla Pandikattu, ed. ISBN 156518 2162 (paper).

IIB.11 *Lifeworlds and Ethics: Studies in Several Keys.* Margaret Chatterjee. ISBN 9781565182332 (paper).

IIIB.12 *Paths to the Divine: Ancient and Indian.* Vensus A. George. ISBN 9781565182486. (paper).

IIB.13 *Faith, Reason, Science: Philosophical Reflections with Special Reference to Fides et Ratio.* Varghese Manimala, ed. IBSN 9781565182554 (paper).

IIIC.1 *Spiritual Values and Social Progress: Uzbekistan Philosophical Studies, I.* Said Shermukhamedov and Victoriya Levinskaya, eds. ISBN 1565181433 (paper).

IIIC.2 *Kazakhstan: Cultural Inheritance and Social Transformation: Kazakh Philosophical Studies, I.* Abdumalik Nysanbayev. ISBN 1565182022 (paper).

IIIC.3 *Social Memory and Contemporaneity: Kyrgyz Philosophical Studies, I.* Gulnara A. Bakieva. ISBN 9781565182349 (paper).

IIID.1 *Reason, Rationality and Reasonableness: Vietnamese Philosophical Studies, I.* Tran Van Doan. ISBN 1565181662 (paper).

IIID.2 *Hermeneutics for a Global Age: Lectures in Shanghai and Hanoi.* George F. McLean. ISBN 1565181905 (paper).

IIID.3 *Cultural Traditions and Contemporary Challenges in Southeast Asia.* Warayuth Sriwarakuel, Manuel B.Dy, J.Haryatmoko, Nguyen Trong Chuan, and Chhay Yiheang, eds. ISBN 1565182138 (paper).

IIID.4 *Filipino Cultural Traits: Claro R.Ceniza Lectures.* Rolando M. Gripaldo, ed. ISBN 1565182251 (paper).

IIID.5 *The History of Buddhism in Vietnam.* Chief editor: Nguyen Tai Thu; Authors: Dinh Minh Chi, Ly Kim Hoa, Ha thuc Minh, Ha Van Tan, Nguyen Tai Thu. ISBN 1565180984 (paper).

IIID.6 *Relations between Religions and Cultures in Southeast Asia.* Donny Gadis Arivia and Gahral Adian, eds. ISBN 9781565182509 (paper).

Series IV. Western Europe and North America

IV.1 *Italy in Transition: The Long Road from the First to the Second Republic: The Edmund D. Pellegrino Lectures.* Paolo Janni, ed. ISBN 1565181204 (paper).

IV.2 *Italy and the European Monetary Union: The Edmund D. Pellegrino Lectures.* Paolo Janni, ed. ISBN 156518128X (paper).

IV.3 *Italy at the Millennium: Economy, Politics, Literature and Journalism: The Edmund D. Pellegrino Lectures.* Paolo Janni, ed. ISBN 1565181581 (paper).

IV.4 *Speaking of God.* Carlo Huber. ISBN 1565181697 (paper).

IV.5 *The Essence of Italian Culture and the Challenge of a Global Age.* Paulo Janni and George F. McLean, eds. ISBB 1565181778 (paper).

IV.6 *Italic Identity in Pluralistic Contexts: Toward the Development of Intercultural Competencies.* Piero Bassetti and Paolo Janni, eds. ISBN 1565181441 (paper).

Series IVA. Central and Eastern Europe

IVA.1 *The Philosophy of Person: Solidarity and Cultural Creativity: Polish Philosophical Studies, I.* A. Tischner, J.M. Zycinski, eds. ISBN 1565180496 (paper); 156518048-8 (cloth).

IVA.2 *Public and Private Social Inventions in Modern Societies: Polish Philosophical Studies, II.* L. Dyczewski, P. Peachey, J.A. Kromkowski, eds. ISBN.paper 1565180518 (paper); 156518050X (cloth).

IVA.3 *Traditions and Present Problems of Czech Political Culture: Czechoslovak Philosophical Studies, I.* M. Bednár and M. Vejraka, eds. ISBN 1565180577 (paper); 156518056-9 (cloth).

IVA.4 *Czech Philosophy in the XXth Century: Czech Philosophical Studies, II.* Lubomír Nový and Jirí Gabriel, eds. ISBN 1565180291 (paper); 156518028-3 (cloth).

IVA.5 *Language, Values and the Slovak Nation: Slovak Philosophical Studies, I.* Tibor Pichler and Jana Gašparí-ková, eds. ISBN 1565180372 (paper); 156518036-4 (cloth).

IVA.6 *Morality and Public Life in a Time of Change: Bulgarian Philosophical Studies, I.* V. Prodanov and M. Stoyanova, eds. ISBN 1565180550 (paper); 1565180542 (cloth).

IVA.7 *Knowledge and Morality: Georgian Philosophical Studies, 1.* N.V. Chavchavadze, G. Nodia and P. Peachey, eds. ISBN 1565180534 (paper); 1565180526 (cloth).

IVA.8 *Cultural Heritage and Social Change: Lithuanian Philosophical Studies, I.* Bronius Kuzmickas and Aleksandr Dobrynin, eds. ISBN 1565180399 (paper); 1565180380 (cloth).

IVA.9 *National, Cultural and Ethnic Identities: Harmony beyond Conflict: Czech Philosophical Studies, IV.* Jaroslav Hroch, David Hollan, George F. McLean, eds. ISBN 1565181131 (paper).

IVA.10 *Models of Identities in Postcommunist Societies: Yugoslav Philosophical Studies, I.* Zagorka Golubovic and George F. McLean, eds. ISBN 1565181211 (paper).

IVA.11 *Interests and Values: The Spirit of Venture in a Time of Change: Slovak Philosophical Studies, II.* Tibor Pichler and Jana Gasparikova, eds. ISBN 1565181255 (paper).

IVA.12 *Creating Democratic Societies: Values and Norms: Bulgarian Philosophical Studies, II.* Plamen Makariev, Andrew M.Blasko and Asen Davidov, eds. ISBN 156518131X (paper).

IVA.13 *Values of Islamic Culture and the Experience of History: Russian Philosophical Studies, I.* Nur Kirabaev and Yuriy Pochta, eds. ISBN 1565181336 (paper).

IVA.14 *Values and Education in Romania Today: Romanian Philosophical Studies, I.* Marin Calin and Magdalena Dumitrana, eds. ISBN 1565181344 (paper).

IVA.15 *Between Words and Reality, Studies on the Politics of Recognition and the Changes of Regime in Contemporary Romania: Romanian Philosophical Studies, II.* Victor Neumann. ISBN 1565181611 (paper).

IVA.16 *Culture and Freedom: Romanian Philosophical Studies, III.* Marin Aiftinca, ed. ISBN 1565181360 (paper).

IVA.17 *Lithuanian Philosophy: Persons and Ideas: Lithuanian Philosophical Studies, II.* Jurate Baranova, ed. ISBN 1565181379 (paper).

IVA.18 *Human Dignity: Values and Justice: Czech Philosophical Studies, III.* Miloslav Bednar, ed. ISBN 1565181409 (paper).

IVA.19 *Values in the Polish Cultural Tradition: Polish Philosophical Studies, III.* Leon Dyczewski, ed. ISBN 1565181425 (paper).

IVA.20 *Liberalization and Transformation of Morality in Post-communist Countries: Polish Philosophical Studies, IV.* Tadeusz Buksinski. ISBN 1565181786 (paper).

IVA.21 *Islamic and Christian Cultures: Conflict or Dialogue: Bulgarian Philosophical Studies, III.* Plament Makariev, ed. ISBN 156518162X (paper).

IVA.22 *Moral, Legal and Political Values in Romanian Culture: Romanian Philosophical Studies, IV.* Mihaela Czobor-Lupp and J. Stefan Lupp, eds. ISBN 1565181700 (paper).

IVA.23 *Social Philosophy: Paradigm of Contemporary Thinking: Lithuanian Philosophical Studies, III.* Jurate Morkuniene. ISBN 1565182030 (paper).

IVA.24 *Romania: Cultural Identity and Education for Civil Society: Romanian Philosophical Studies, V.* Magdalena Dumitrana, ed. ISBN 156518209X (paper).

IVA.25 *Polish Axiology: the 20th Century and Beyond: Polish Philosophical Studies, V.* Stanislaw Jedynak, ed. ISBN 1565181417 (paper).

IVA.26 *Contemporary Philosophical Discourse in Lithuania: Lithuanian Philosophical Studies, IV.* Jurate Baranova, ed. ISBN 156518-2154 (paper).

IVA.27 *Eastern Europe and the Challenges of Globalization: Polish Philosophical Studies, VI.* Tadeusz Buksinski and Dariusz Dobrzanski, ed. ISBN 1565182189 (paper).

IVA.28 *Church, State, and Society in Eastern Europe: Hungarian Philosophical Studies, I.* Miklós Tomka. ISBN 156518226X.

IVA.29 *Politics, Ethics, and the Challenges to Democracy in 'New Independent States': Georgian Philosophical Studies, II.* Tinatin Bochorishvili, William Sweet, Daniel Ahern, eds. ISBN 9781565182240 (paper).

IVA.30 *Comparative Ethics in a Global Age: Russian Philosophical Studies II.* Marietta T. Stepanyants, eds. ISBN 978-1565182356 (paper).

IVA.31 *Identity and Values of Lithuanians: Lithuanian Philosophical Studies, V.* Aida Savicka, eds. ISBN 9781565182367 (paper).

IVA.32 *The Challenge of Our Hope: Christian Faith in Dialogue: Polish Philosophical Studies, VII.* Waclaw Hryniewicz. ISBN 9781565182370 (paper).

IVA.33 *Diversity and Dialogue: Culture and Values in the Age of Globalization: Essays in Honour of Professor George F. McLean.* Andrew Blasko and Plamen Makariev, eds. ISBN 9781565182387 (paper).

IVA. 34 *Civil Society, Pluralism and Universalism: Polish Philosophical Studies, VIII.* Eugeniusz Gorski. ISBN 9781565182417 (paper).

IVA.35 *Romanian Philosophical Culture, Globalization, and Education: Romanian Philosophical Studies VI.* Stefan Popenici and Alin Tat and, eds. ISBN 9781565182424 (paper).

IVA.36 *Political Transformation and Changing Identities in Central and Eastern Europe: Lithuanian Philosophical Studies, VI.* Andrew Blasko and Diana Janušauskienė, eds. ISBN 9781565182462 (paper).

IVA.37 *Truth and Morality: The Role of Truth in Public Life: Romanian Philosophical Studies, VII.* Wilhelm Dancă, ed. ISBN 9781565182493 (paper).

IVA.38 *Globalization and Culture: Outlines of Contemporary Social Cognition: Lithuanian Philosophical Studies, VII.* Jurate Morkuniene, ed. ISBN 9781565182516 (paper).

Series V. Latin America

V.1 *The Social Context and Values: Perspectives of the Americas.* O. Pegoraro, ed. ISBN 081917355X (paper); 0819173541 (cloth).

V.2 *Culture, Human Rights and Peace in Central America.* Raul Molina and Timothy Ready, eds. ISBN 0819173576 (paper); 0819173568 (cloth).

V.3 *El Cristianismo Aymara: Inculturacion o Culturizacion?* Luis Jolicoeur. ISBN 1565181042.

V.4 *Love as theFoundation of Moral Education and Character Development.* Luis Ugalde, Nicolas Barros and George F. McLean, eds. ISBN 1565180801.

V.5 *Human Rights, Solidarity and Subsidiarity: Essays towards a Social Ontology.* Carlos E.A. Maldonado ISBN 1565181107.

Series VI. Foundations of Moral Education

VI.1 *Philosophical Foundations for Moral Education and Character Development: Act and Agent.* G. McLean and F. Ellrod, eds. ISBN 156518001-1 (cloth) (paper); ISBN 1565180003.

VI.2 *Psychological Foundations for Moral Education and Character Development: An Integrated Theory of Moral Development.* R. Knowles, ed. ISBN 156518002X (paper); 156518003-8 (cloth).

VI.3 *Character Development in Schools and Beyond.* Kevin Ryan and Thomas Lickona, eds. ISBN 1565180593 (paper); 156518058-5 (cloth).

VI.4 *The Social Context and Values: Perspectives of the Americas.* O. Pegoraro, ed. ISBN 081917355X (paper); 0819173541 (cloth).

VI.5 *Chinese Foundations for Moral Education and Character Development.* Tran van Doan, ed. ISBN 1565180321 (paper); 156518033 (cloth).

VI.6 *Love as theFoundation of Moral Education and Character Development.* Luis Ugalde, Nicolas Barros and George F. McLean, eds. ISBN 1565180801.

Series VII. Seminars on Culture and Values

VII.1 *The Social Context and Values: Perspectives of the Americas.* O. Pegoraro, ed. ISBN 081917355X (paper); 0819173541 (cloth).

VII.2 *Culture, Human Rights and Peace in Central America.* Raul Molina and Timothy Ready, eds. ISBN 0819173576 (paper); 0819173568 (cloth).

VII.3 *Relations Between Cultures.* John A. Kromkowski, ed. ISBN 1565180089 (paper); 1565180097 (cloth).

VII.4 *Moral Imagination and Character Development: Volume I, The Imagination.* George F. McLean and John A. Kromkowski, eds. ISBN 1565181743 (paper).

VII.5 *Moral Imagination and Character Development: Volume II, Moral Imagination in Personal Formation and Character Development.* George F. McLean and Richard Knowles, eds. ISBN 1565181816 (paper).

VII.6 *Moral Imagination and Character Development: Volume III, Imagination in Religion and Social Life.* George F. McLean and John K. White, eds. ISBN 1565181824 (paper).

VII.7 *Hermeneutics and Inculturation.* George F. McLean, Antonio Gallo, Robert Magliola, eds. ISBN 1565181840 (paper).

VII.8 *Culture, Evangelization, and Dialogue.* Antonio Gallo and Robert Magliola, eds. ISBN 1565181832 (paper).

VII.9 *The Place of the Person in Social Life.* Paul Peachey and John A. Kromkowski, eds. ISBN 1565180127 (paper); 156518013-5 (cloth).

VII.10 *Urbanization and Values.* John A. Kromkowski, ed. ISBN 1565180100 (paper); 1565180119 (cloth).

VII.11 *Freedom and Choice in a Democracy, Volume I: Meanings of Freedom.* Robert Magliola and John Farrelly, eds. ISBN 1565181867 (paper).

VII.12 *Freedom and Choice in a Democracy, Volume II: The Difficult Passage to Freedom.* Robert Magliola and Richard Khuri, eds. ISBN 1565181859 (paper).

VII 13 *Cultural Identity, Pluralism and Globalization* (2 volumes). John P. Hogan, ed. ISBN 1565182170 (paper).

VII.14 *Democracy: In the Throes of Liberalism and Totalitarianism.* George F. McLean, Robert Magliola, William Fox, eds. ISBN 1565181956 (paper).

VII.15 *Democracy and Values in Global Times: With Nigeria as a Case Study.* George F. McLean, Robert Magliola, Joseph Abah, eds. ISBN 1565181956 (paper).

VII.16 *Civil Society and Social Reconstruction.* George F. McLean, ed. ISBN 1565180860 (paper).

VII.17 *Civil Society: Who Belongs?* William A.Barbieri, Robert Magliola, Rosemary Winslow, eds. ISBN 1565181972 (paper).

VII.18 *The Humanization of Social Life: Theory and Challenges.* Christopher Wheatley, Robert P. Badillo, Rose B. Calabretta, Robert Magliola, eds. ISBN 1565182006 (paper).

VII.19 *The Humanization of Social Life: Cultural Resources and Historical Responses.* Ronald S. Calinger, Robert P. Badillo, Rose B. Calabretta, Robert Magliola, eds. ISBN 1565182006 (paper).

VII.20 *Religious Inspiration for Public Life: Religion in Public Life, Volume I.* George F. McLean, John A. Kromkowski and Robert Magliola, eds. ISBN 1565182103 (paper).

VII.21 *Religion and Political Structures from Fundamentalism to Public Service: Religion in Public Life, Volume II.* John T. Ford, Robert A. Destro and Charles R. Dechert, eds. ISBN 1565182111 (paper).

VII.22 *Civil Society as Democratic Practice.* Antonio F. Perez, Semou Pathé Gueye, Yang Fenggang, eds. ISBN 1565182146 (paper).

VII.23 *Ecumenism and Nostra Aetate in the 21st Century.* George F. McLean and John P. Hogan, eds. ISBN 1565182197 (paper).

VII.24 *Multiple Paths to God: Nostra Aetate: 40 years Later.* John P. Hogan, George F. McLean & John A. Kromkowski, eds. ISBN 1565182200 (paper).

VII.25 *Globalization and Identity.* Andrew Blasko, Taras Dobko, Pham Van Duc and George Pattery, eds. ISBN 1565182200 (paper).

VII.26 *Communication across Cultures: The Hermeneutics of Cultures and Religions in a Global Age.* Chibueze C. Udeani, Veerachart Nimanong, Zou Shipeng, Mustafa Malik, eds. ISBN: 9781565182400 (paper).

The International Society for Metaphysics

ISM.1 *Person and Nature.* George F. McLean and Hugo Meynell, eds. ISBN 0819170267 (paper); 0819170259 (cloth).

ISM.2 *Person and Society.* George F. McLean and Hugo Meynell, eds. ISBN 0819169250 (paper); 0819169242 (cloth).

ISM.3 *Person and God.* George F. McLean and Hugo Meynell, eds. ISBN 0819169382 (paper); 0819169374 (cloth).

ISM.4 *The Nature of Metaphysical Knowledge.* George F. McLean and Hugo Meynell, eds. ISBN 0819169277 (paper); 0819169269 (cloth).

ISM.5 *Philosophhical Challenges and Opportunities of Globalization.* Oliva Blanchette, Tomonobu Imamichi and George F. McLean, eds. ISBN 1565181298 (paper).

The series is published and distributed by: The Council for Research in Values and Philosophy, Cardinal Station, P.O. Box 261, Washington, D.C.20064, Tel./Fax.202/319-6089; e-mail: cua-rvp@cua.edu (paper); website: http://www.crvp.org.All titles are available in paper except as noted. Prices: $17.50 (paper), otherwise specified.